Mortgage Loan Administration

William I. DeHuszar

Senior Vice President
Dovenmuehle, Inc.

Mortgage Loan Administration

Prepared under the sponsorship of the
Mortgage Bankers Association of America
Washington, D.C.

McGraw-Hill Book Company

New York   St. Louis   San Francisco   Düsseldorf   Johannesburg
Kuala Lumpur   London   Mexico   Montreal   New Delhi   Panama
Rio de Janeiro   Singapore   Sydney   Toronto

Mortgage Loan Administration

Library of Congress Cataloging in Publication Data

De Huszar, William Ivan, 1917–
   Mortgage loan administration.

   Bibliography: p.
   1. Mortgage banks--United States. I. Mortgage
Bankers Association of America. II. Title.
HG2040.5.U5D4   658'.91'33232   72-6645
ISBN 0-07-016257-3

1234567890 DODO 798765432

This book was set in Press Roman
by Allen Wayne Technical Corp.
The editor was Jack R. Crutchfield;
the designer was Allen Wayne Technical Corp.;
and the production supervisor was Alice Cohen.
The printer and binder was R. R. Donnelley & Sons Company.

Contents

Exhibits ix

Preface xiii

Part 1 Introduction

1 Concepts of Loan Administration 3
   Functions of Loan Administration 4
   Goals of Loan Administration 6
   History and Development of Loan Administration 7
   Scope of the Study 10

2 Fundamentals of Servicing 13
   Servicing Tasks 13
   Borrower-Servicer Relationship 14
   Investor-Servicer Relationship 14
   Unwritten Duties and Responsibilities 21
   Servicing Income 23

3 The Loan Administrator 27
   Duties and Responsibilities of Loan Administrator 28
   Personal Qualifications 32
   Responsibility of Senior Management 34

Part 2 Mortgage Office Operations

4 Office Management   39
   Principles   39
   Tools of Management   41
   Planning and Operations   49
   Maintenance of Property   52
   Establishment, Maintenance, and Destruction of Records   55

5 Personnel Management   65
   Scope and Responsibility   66
   Management Philosophy   66
   Personnel Policies   67
   The Personnel Manager   71
   Employment of Personnel   71
   Training and Education   74
   Employment Manual   76
   Employee Suggestion System   77

6 Financial and Fiduciary Responsibilities   79
   Accounting Activity   80
   Borrowing Funds for Lending Purposes   91
   Establishment of Bank Accounts   96
   Financial Statements   102
   Protection of Company Assets   106

7 Planning for Expansion   115
   Conversion   116
   Acquisitions   122
   Branch Office Operations   130
   Diversification into Allied Fields   131

8 Operating and Statistical Reports   133
   Operating Reports   134
   Statistical Reports   137

9 Cost Accounting   145
   General Accounting Considerations   146
   Illustration of a Cost Analysis–ABC Mortgage Company   148
   Use of Cost Data to Evaluate Mortgage Banking Operations   162

10 Internal Control   170
   Elements of Internal Control   171
   Means of Internal Control   173
   Internal Control by Areas of Activity   176
   Relationship with Independent Auditors   184
   Relationship with Investors' Auditors   187

11 Coordination through Communication 189
  Role of Communication 192
  Coordination by Written Media 193
  Coordination by Consultation 196
  Coordination by Meetings 197

12 Customer Relations 200
  How to Build Good Customer Relations 201
  How to Preserve Good Customer Relations 205

Part 3 Mortgage Loan Servicing

13 Cashier Department 211
  Organization and Staff Requirements 211
  Operating Practices 214
  Daily Functions 214
  Periodic Functions 232
  Other Periodic Functions 246

14 Mortgage Loan Accounting Department 250
  Organization of Department 251
  Establishing and Maintaining Ledger Records .. 253
  Remitting Operations 261
  Disbursing Operations 265
  Balancing Operations 268
  Customer Service Operations 283

15 Collection Department 288
  Organizaion and Staffing 289
  Principles and Practices of Collection 291
  Preventive Collection Practices 294
  Routine Collection Practices 297
  Specialized Collection Practices 302
  Considerations Relative to Termination of Loan 324
  Execution of Foreclosure Task 334
  Collection Practices—Income Property Loans ... 337
  Supervision and Control 344
  Delinquency Surveys 348

16 Insurance Department 351
  Operations and Responsibilities 353
  Insurance for Owners of Single-Family Properties—Initial Policy 356
  Insurance for Owners of Single-Family Properties—Renewals 365
  368
  371
  Other Matters 393

17 Tax Department 395
    Organization of Department 395
    Establishing Tax Records 396
    Payment of Taxes from Escrow Reserves 399
    Payment of Taxes by Mortgagors 408
    Tax Certifications 408

Appendices

Appendix A   *Bibliography of Pamphlets prepared by mortgage companies*   **411**
                and the Mortgage Bankers Association of America

Appendix B   *B-1*   *FHA and VA Servicing Agreement*   **412**
           B-2   *Model Sale and Servicing Agreement*   **415**
           B-3   *Purchase and Servicing Agreement*   **421**

Glossary   **427**

Index   **435**

Exhibits

1	Table of Organization–Loan Administration	9
2	Servicing Manual (Table of Contents)	20
3	Organization Chart–Medium-Size Firm	43
4	Organization Chart–Large-Size Firm	44
5	Organization Chart–Highly Diversified Firm	46
6	Job Description	47
7	Servicing Staff Requirements	50
8	Automatic Record Destruction Schedule	58
9	Loan Register	60
10	Company Record Retention Schedule	63
11	Borrower's Ledger Card	83
12	Diagram Establishing Loan Inventory Card	85
13	Projection of Fund Requirements	96
14	Balance Sheet	104
15	Statement of Earnings	105
16	Income and Expense Projections for Proposed Acquisitions	128
17	ABC Mortgage Company "Mortgage Loans Serviced"	138
18	Report on Delinquent FHA-VA Residential Loans	142
19	Delinquent Statistical Report	143
20	Cost Analysis–Tasks 1 and 2	153
	Costs, Task 3	160
	Task 4	160
	Loan Servicing Income and Costs, Task 5	161
	Recapitulation of Results by Account, Task 1	162

25 Sources and Uses of Revenue—Task 6   163
26 Workflow Chart—Cashier Department   215
27 First-Payment Letter   217
28 Prepunched Payment Coupon Book   220
29 Prepunched Payment Coupon Card   221
30 Payment Coupon Cards   222
31 Machine Processed Billing Notice   224
32 Cashier Card   225
33 Prepunched Payment Card   227
34 Payoff Statement   236
35 Cover Letter—Statement of Account   239
36 Statement of Account   240
37 Assignment of Policy   241
38 Assignment and Disclaimer Form   242
39 Personal Credit Information   243
40 First-Payment Letter (Assumption)   244
41 FHA Mortgage Record Change   245
42 Workflow Chart—Accounting Department   254
43 Report of Mortgage Loan Collections   259
44 Statement of Transfer of Bank Funds   264
45 Reconciliation for Mortgage Loans—April   270
46 Delivery Schedule   272
47 Trial Balance—April   273
48 Trial Balance—May   275
49 Statement of Prepayments   276
50 Reconciliation for Mortgage Loans—May   277
51 Trial Balance—June   279
52 Statement of Delinquent Accounts   280
53 Reconciliation of Mortgage Loans—June   281
54 Annual Mortgage Loan Statement   285
55 Summary of Collection Efforts   308
56 Personal Interview Report   312
57 Application for Forbearance   313
58 FHA Home Mortgage Default Notice   320
59 VA Notice of Default   321
60 VA Notice of Intention to Foreclosure   322
61 Residential Foreclosure Recommendation   327
62 FHA Notice of Default Status on Multi-Family Housing Projects   342
63 Foreclosure Check Sheet—FHA   346
64 FHA Report on Current Home Mortgage Status   349
65 Request for Mortgage Clause   357
66 Insurance Recommendations   359
67 Insurance Order   360
68 Solicitation of Renewal of Insurance   366

69 Solicitation of Renewal of Insurance   **367**
70 Explanation of Co-insurance   **370**
71 Master Card—Insurance   **375**
72 Statement of Premium Disbursement   **377**
73 Certificate of Insurance   **381**
74 Loss Draft Letter   **385**
75 Affidavit—Completion of Repairs   **386**
76 Assignment of Policy Under Purchase Agreement   **391**
77 Transmittal Letter—Insurance Policy   **392**
78 Tax Advice   **402**
79 Tax Notices   **403**
80 Analysis of Escrow Reserve Account and Payment Change Notice   **407**

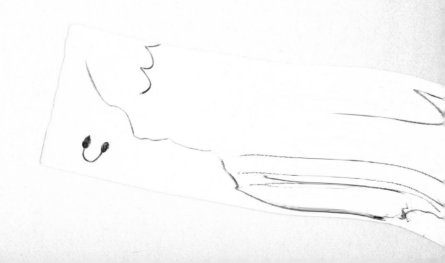

Preface

The purpose of this study is to establish and define the principles of mortgage loan administration and to describe the duties and responsibilities of the mortgage loan administrator. The scope of the study includes office management and mortgage loan servicing, the creation of those tools and the execution of those tasks which make mortgage banking profitable, and a comprehensive review of the services performed by mortgage bankers.

Mortgage Loan Administration encompasses all the functions that must be performed, including loan servicing, whether they are executed by a single individual, by one employee, or by a separate department. It charts the course of a mortgage banking entity under different conditions in different types of localities in any part of the country. It differentiates among procedures that are applicable to small- and medium-size organizations, as well as to those large firms which have attained a high degree of automation. It is of sufficient breadth in its application to accommodate operational and procedural requirements of companies exclusively engaged in financing either single-family residences or apartments, and other income properties, or both to varying degrees.

Portraying all these activities and satisfying diverse needs in a single volume is an ambitious task. Capturing and putting down in writing—as if by means of a camera—processes and ideas that are still in various stages of development is equally difficult. It involves tracing new concepts that are influenced by external as well as internal forces, for mortgage banking does not operate in a vacuum. It is often influenced and directed by outside forces—e.g., the paternalistic hand of government, the innovations brought about by the development of automation, and the changing needs of society itself. We must recognize, therefore, that a book written today cannot keep up with the application of rapid changes of technology to mortgage banking operations.

The constant influences and the elements of change have made it necessary to describe every activity of the mortgage banker involving loan servicing and office management for the third time within the last two decades. On each occasion, the volume has grown in size; each time the search for answers has reached into new areas and covered subjects not presented earlier. This is a revised edition of the earlier works only to the extent that it presents an updated version of the tasks that were described before. Fundamentally, it is a new volume, as updating required substantial changes and inclusion of tasks not found in available literature—tasks that must be performed by any modern mortgage banking firm to successfully produce and market its loan products.

In that sense, this volume is designed for management use. The author does not, however, wish to glorify the loan administrator or to aggrandize his position within a given company, but to place the man responsible for profit-making activities of the company, short of producing loans, in the spot where he belongs—on the management team. More specifically, this study's objectives are

1 To guide management on the duties and responsibilities of loan administrators and loan servicing managers.
2 To describe loan administrative procedures and loan servicing practices as they exist throughout the country.
3 To serve as a textbook for university students.

Every idea, every procedure and method of performing a certain task that is described here has been tested and used by hundreds of firms. Every recommendation for action has been screened and confirmed by experts in the respective fields. And yet it should be emphasized that nothing in this volume is unequivocally recommended for adoption. What may be a good procedure for one company may not necessarily work for another. Therefore, ideas suggested must be examined carefully, tested, and, then, if found suitable, blended into existing arrangements. Testing is often an inexpensive ticket to a better method of doing the job.

Mortgage loan administrative tasks as performed by typical mortgage banking firms are presented in two major areas of activities: office management and loan servicing. Since loan servicing complements loan production—the two constituting the business of mortgage banking—loan servicing should be considered the most important phase of loan administration. Because it is necessary to create, equip, organize, and staff an office before loans may be produced or serviced, mortgage office operations concerned with the establishment of a business entity are presented first in Chapters 4 to 12. Once the necessary facilities are properly established, organized, and staffed, the most important task—loan servicing, covered in Chapters 13 to 17—may be efficiently and profitably performed.

This volume has been prepared primarily for use by loan administrators, servicing managers, and those who aspire to the responsibilities of either position, and for students of the profession. It is addressed also to members of the management team and members of the production staff who often become so engrossed in the complexities of the acquisition and sale of mortgages that they tend to gloss over administrative responsibilities and overlook their cost-saving capabilities.

Each chapter covers a single activity or responsibility within the field of loan administration. Therefore, several practical suggestions may help readers whose interests vary depending upon their experience and knowledge of the field as well as their purpose in using this book.

1 Students who are not familiar with the mortgage business and its complexities would do well to begin with some background reading.[1]

2 Employees of mortgage banking firms performing one of the servicing or loan administrative tasks may wish to begin with the chapter applicable to their field of interest. They should, however, consult the first three chapters to maintain perspective as to the overall duties and responsibilities of loan administration.

3 Similarly, loan administrators or servicing managers may wish to review at random different and entirely unrelated loan administrative subjects for the purpose of comparison with their own operations. They would also do well to read the first three chapters.

Students and mortgage banking trainees should also study the pamphlets prepared by mortgage companies and listed in Appendix A. These pamphlets are designed to inform borrowers and employees of their respective duties and responsibilities. They deal with a range of subjects from those aimed at employees, "What Is Mortgage Banking?" (Appendix A-1), to those aimed at borrowers, "What You Should Know about Your Mortgage Loan" (Appendix A-2). Loan administrators may also adopt or use some of these pamphlets for their own purposes.

To avoid misinformation or misunderstanding, it is advisable for the newcomer in the field of mortgage loan administration to use the Glossary at the end of this volume. Certain terms, such as "investor," "principal," "mortgagee," or "lender," will be used interchangeably as long as the meaning is substantially identical. Similarly, a borrower may be called a mortgagor, customer, or client, and a mortgage banker may be defined as a correspondent, servicer, servicing agent, or servicing contractor, depending on the context of the material.

ACKNOWLEDGEMENTS

Like the former text, this volume is the work of many individuals rather than of one. It comprises the thoughts, views, and ideas of loan administrators, servicing managers, accountants, servicing personnel, and those who participated in loan administration clinic meetings as moderators, members of panels, or speakers from the floor; who

---

[1] See Miles L. Colean, *Mortgage Companies* (Englewood Cliffs, N.J.: Prentice-Hall, Inc., 1963). Saul B. Klaman, *The Postwar Residential Mortgage Market* (Princeton, N.J.: Princeton University Press, 1961), chap. 8. Robert H. Pease and Lewis O. Kerwood (eds.), *Mortgage Banking* (New York: McGraw-Hill Book Company, 1965), chap. 1.

attended classes at the School of Mortgage Banking and asked questions; and who contributed their knowledge in articles in *The Mortgage Banker.* The text also represents the merging of their ideas with those expressed by representatives of life insurance companies, commercial and savings banks, and managers of pension funds.

I find it difficult to express adequately my thanks to all those who have helped me in the preparation of this volume with their criticisms, comments, and encouragement. The list of those who have given much of their time to improving this book should appropriately be headed by members of a special editorial committee of the Mortgage Bankers Association of America consisting of James T. Hillman, Firstbank Mortgage Corporation, Seattle, Washington; Roger W. Hatch, Walker & Dunlop, Inc., Washington, D.C.; Louis P. Wolfort, First National Mortgage Corporation, New Orleans, Louisiana; Philip C. Jackson, Jr., Jackson Company, Birmingham, Alabama; and Everett C. Spelman, Western Securities Company, Denver, Colorado. Others whose contribution either to the entire text or to specific chapters has been invaluable are Frank Rees, formerly with John Hancock Mutual Life Insurance Co., Boston, Massachusetts; Leonard J. Giblin, Great Lakes Mortgage Corporation, Chicago, Illinois; John M. Costello, Percy Wilson, Mortgage & Finance Corporation, Chicago, Illinois; Donald A. Luff, Jay F. Zook, Inc., Cleveland, Ohio; L. K. Horn, Southeast Mortgage Company, Miami, Florida; Thomas E. McDonald, Peat, Marwick, Mitchell & Co., Washington, D.C.; Charles F. Steineger, Jr., Peat, Marwick, Mitchell & Co., Louisville, Kentucky; Robert Sutro, Ralph C. Sutro Co., Los Angeles, California; William B. Wood, Peat, Marwick, Mitchell & Co., Dallas, Texas; Mr. M. J. Mittenthal, M. J. Mittenthal & Co., Dallas, Texas; Harry T. McMahon, W. W. Vincent & Co., Chicago, Illinois; and H. Cecil Kilpatrick, Alston, Miller & Gaines, Washington, D.C.

The staff of the Mortgage Bankers Association of America has also been very helpful. I am especially indebted to Jack W. White for his critical comments which added greatly to the accuracy of the information and clarity of presentation; to James G. Wasson, former Director of Loan Administration, for his constructive suggestions; to Lewis O. Kerwood for his sound counsel and inspiring cooperation which led to the completion of this volume; and most importantly to Dr. Oliver H. Jones for his advice, criticism, and assistance beyond the call of duty in helping me prepare this book for publication. I am most grateful to my wife, Mary, who helped me considerably with the final draft and to Mrs. Susan Litchfield whose editorial suggestions and assistance were invaluable.

Unfortunately, there is no space here to offer individual acknowledgements to all those who have been kind enough to help me with the various problems that go into the completion of a text of this type. I hope that all those who have contributed to this book will consider my use of their suggestions an expression of my appreciation of their help and interest.

William I. De Huszar

Mortgage Loan Administration

1

Introduction

CHAPTER ONE

Concepts of Loan Administration

The modern concept of mortgage loan administration includes all activities which complement mortgage loan production and enhance its profitability. Of these activities, mortgage loan servicing is only a part. A mere bookkeeping operation in the early forties, mortgage loan administration has become today a special profession in the field of mortgage banking. By adapting the tools of management science and the computer age, it has become the hallmark of modern mortgage banking.

Today's mortgage banker originates, sells, and services mortgage loans. He risks his capital or funds borrowed from his bank to originate loans on the security of real property. He sells the mortgage loans to institutional investors, typically life insurance companies and mutual savings banks located in distant cities. Unlike his predecessor, he services the mortgage loans sold to investors, i.e., collects monthly payments of interest and principal, maintains the current status of hazard insurance and property taxes, and periodically checks the condition of the property.

Thus, mortgage banking is principally a business of producing and servicing mortgage loans. About one-fourth of the gross income of the typical mortgage banker is generated by origination fees paid by borrowers. These fees are limited by maximums set by federal agencies that ensure or guarantee mortgage loans and, of more significance, by competition among mortgage bankers and other loan originators. As a result, the cost of producing and selling a loan secured by a residential property often exceeds the gross loan origination income.

It is imperative, therefore, that the servicing fees paid by investors are not similarly eroded by the cost of administering mortgage loan accounts. About one-half of the gross income of the typical mortgage banker is generated by servicing fees. They represent a percentage of the outstanding principal balance of the mortgages serviced and are deducted by the mortgage banker from monthly remittances to investors. The essence of mortgage loan administration, therefore, is management decisions and practices that minimize origination and marketing losses and maximize servicing income.

Mortgage loan administration has its roots in mortgage servicing. Today, it encompasses the broad range of administrative functions that must be performed in a mortgage banking firm. After more than two decades, experience has proven to investors and servicers alike that administrative competence is a profit-producing tool.

Proper organization, adequate staffing, effective systems, and the use of proper equipment reduce expenditures. Administrative resourcefulness and imagination lead to the discovery of new sources of revenue. As a matter of fact, mortgage bankers have come to realize that their survival hinges upon their ingenuity in cutting costs while continuing to render service.

On a day-to-day basis, mortgage loan administration includes the execution of all tasks which supplement as well as aid loan-producing operations, the establishment and maintenance of sound operating principles, and the creation of an effective set of systems and operating tools. To all this, we can add the responsibility for administration of the company's funds as well as the funds entrusted to the company's care and custody.

FUNCTIONS OF LOAN ADMINISTRATION

Mortgage loan administration goes beyond the mere execution of administrative tasks. A successful mortgage banking operation applies the concepts of loan administration in a variety of ways.

Assists senior management   Senior management charts the company's course, sets its goals, and administers its operations. It strives for a maximum reward from existing opportunities and explores and develops new opportunities. The success of one company over another will be determined by the skills and abilities of senior management and its supporting team and how effectively they are put to work. Administrative skills take on a special significance in mortgage banking, because administration is the one area where management can take direct action to distinguish the firm from its competition. Mortgage loan administration assists senior management in the creation of opportunities, infusion of new ideas, and, in particular, the use of imagination, skill, resourcefulness, and *administrative know-how*.

Most mortgage bankers operate within the same credit markets and within the same structure of mortgage prices. Most are confronted daily with new problems and challenges that are generated by forces beyond their immediate control. For example, there may be a great demand for funds and only a limited amount of money available for lending. Interest rates on government-insured and -guaranteed loans may be fixed at unrealistic levels, adversely influencing their price and burdening builders and sellers of existing houses to the point where real estate sales are reduced. Overbuilding may take place in the area that a particular mortgage banker serves; real estate activity may be sluggish for other reasons.

The mortgage banker may also face internal problems, such as too rapid growth of the company, inroads of competition, or certain aspects of automation. Some problems seem complex, but if faced early, they can lead to easy solutions; others that may appear fairly simple on the surface may be deceptively hard to solve. All these questions, problems, and emergencies clamor for continuous attention, management concern, and, ultimately, answers and solutions.

Complements loan production The mortgage banker must produce loans and obtain customers for his mortgage loan operations. In this capacity, he must appraise the property; check the credit worthiness of the applicant and underwrite the risk; obtain commitments from his investors; and provide interim funds to enable him to complete and carry a loan package until it is ready for delivery to the permanent investor. Mortgage loan administration serves the production operations by staffing and maintaining an efficient office organization, and maintaining harmonious staff relations in producing and servicing loans.

Manages loan servicing Servicing is the source of profit during the life of a loan and, therefore, a prime reason for making loans. It is imperative, then, that servicing be performed efficiently and profitably. Efficient servicing operations can be achieved only through close supervision of all operations; the development of tools, ideas, and systems; and their implementation by skilled and trained personnel. This implies organizing operations to maintain sound cost controls, coordination, internal controls, and personnel policies. In addition, the principles of organization provided by the mortgage loan administrator make feasible the development of other profit-making activities.

Assists in diversification of company activities Mortgage loan administration's role in diversification is to use existing talents, resources, and systems profitably in the development of allied activities. These include real estate sales, insurance, home improvement lending, and property management—activities that lead to the lending of money and which are natural by-products of loan production and loan administration. Administrative know-how is as important in conducting these activities successfully as it is in loan servicing.

Enhances profitability The administrative objective is to squeeze a maximum dollar return from a nominal, and often diminishing, set of opportunities. Economy and efficiency in every operation can be attained only through control, supervision, and coordination of all operations by a single individual or authority.

This book is designed to illustrate methods of deriving additional profit by locating operating economies where profit may be increased. To achieve profit through admin istration the mortgage banker:

1 Employs modern methods of business and tools of office and personnel man- agement; trains and motivates the staff.
2 Develops effective procedures so company objectives may be more readily attained.
3 Exercises administrative supervision by channeling work to be performed to those responsible for its execution and by setting standards of performance.
4 Exercises control over all tasks to be performed by knowing exactly what jobs are to be performed and the source of each piece of information that must be obtained.
5 Coordinates all activities of the company.
6 Inspires participation in affairs of company and stimulates teamwork.
7 Performs, in an unexcelled manner, all loan servicing tasks stipulated in the mort- gage instrument in relation to each borrower and in the servicing contract as it pertains to each loan sold.

Whatever the mortgage banker does, he must act with competence and efficiency, with ease and dignity. Only in this manner can he create the image that is essential if he is to serve the public and his own interests as well.

GOALS OF LOAN ADMINISTRATION

There are two ways of increasing net income in the mortgage business—or for that matter in any business. One is to do more business; the other is to reduce the cost of doing business. Cost cutting in mortgage banking, as in any other business, is a profit- producing factor.

The primary aim of mortgage loan administration is to perform the required servic- ing tasks at as low a cost as possible without impairing the safety of funds or obstruct- ing the proper execution of the tasks involved. Also it aids in the execution of all tasks involved in the various phases of mortgage lending, processing, loan closing, and the offering and subsequent sale of loan packages to institutional investors.

Other than increasing income from fees and commissions, the only real way of raising the net income of the mortgage banker comes from increasing the efficiency of the required operations, that is, by providing maximum production with minimum expense. This is especially true of mortgage servicing since the fee for the work per- formed during the life of the loan is permanently fixed when the loan is sold, while servicing costs are subject to change. In recent years, cost reductions through mechani- zation have been under constant pressure from rising personnel costs. Clearly, the income-producing power of loan servicing can be fully realized only through savings generated by efficient operations. When mortgage loan administration does its job well, servicing is profitable; servicing income recaptures capital advanced to produce mortgage loans; profits are earned in marginal activities; and mortgage loan administration, servicing, production, and related operations are harmoniously blended.

HISTORY AND DEVELOPMENT OF LOAN ADMINISTRATION

Loan servicing began as a special field of mortgage banking during the residential building boom of the late forties. Life insurance companies, reaching across the nation for mortgage investments, sought the protection provided by Federal Housing Administration (FHA) insurance and Veterans Administration (VA) guaranty. The amortized mortgage required local representatives to make monthly collections; to remit interest and principal to the life insurance company investor; to safekeep tax and insurance deposits; and to handle an occasional delinquency. Mortgage bankers, originating FHA and VA loans purchased by life insurance companies, were the logical local representatives, so they were called upon to perform these tasks.

At first, managers of mortgage banking firms assigned the servicing function to bookkeepers. Lacking experience in an untried field, they turned to the Research Committee of the Mortgage Bankers Association of America for solutions. About this time the term *servicing* was coined and applied as a collective definition to the handling of problems that arose in this field. Loan servicing was slowly emerging as a special area of concern for the mortgage banker.

• In 1949, the first Loan Servicing Clinic was held in Chicago. The program was planned by mortgage bankers who were among the first to recognize the complexity of the problems in this field and the first to seek solutions. The opening address, "The Market Place of Ideas," was delivered by the author.

The formation of the first Mortgage Servicing Committee by the Mortgage Bankers Association of America in 1950, as a spin-off of its Research Committee, the establishment of the office of the Director of Mortgage Servicing in the same year, and the promotion of special programs designed for loan-servicing personnel helped considerably in crystallizing the duties and responsibilities investors charged to their mortgage correspondents. The recognition of problems inherent in the mortgage-lending field and the establishment of activities designed to find appropriate solutions led to the emergence of a new breed of men in the industry. Some were already working in the mortgage business as accountants, office managers, or collection personnel; others were drawn from other professions. Thus, the *servicing manager* was born.

The task confronting the men in the servicing field during the fifties was to bring order out of the chaos created by an unprecedented growth in the number of loans and in cumbersome investor requirements that necessitated extensive duplication of work. Slowly, leaders from both mortgage bankers and investors, working almost entirely within loan-servicing committees, resolved most of the conflicting requirements of investors. Standardized procedures were developed and accepted by all affected. The single-debit procedure was created, certification of payment of insurance premiums and real estate taxes was adopted, and insurance loss procedures were simplified and universally accepted. On the heels of these developments came automation, which revolutionized the handling, processing, and remitting of payments. At the present time, data processing equipment is making additional inroads in the field of loan administration, servicing, and overall management of companies.

In 1960, the Mortgage Servicing Committee embarked on a program of designing and preparing operating manuals for the use of association members. Under its sponsorship and the guidance of an editorial committee, the first manual, "Collection Department—Responsibilities and Operations," was published in 1964. This was followed by "Punched Card Data Processing for Mortgage Bankers" in 1965, "FHA-VA Foreclosure and Claim Procedures" in 1967, and "Escrow Department Procedures and Responsibilities" in 1970.

In 1962, the Mortgage Servicing Committee was renamed the Loan Administration Committee. This was not a mere change in name, but rather a recognition of the stature and qualifications of the men and women who made up these committees and headed their companies' loan administrative and servicing operations.

The evolution in servicing practices was a natural outgrowth of the mortgage banker's search for profits and the servicing manager's capacity to assimilate duties and responsibilities. Beginning with the single responsibility of loan servicing, loan administration gradually developed the broader responsibility of keeping mortgages sold to investors in good standing. Like the automobile manufacturer, the mortgage banker warrants to keep the product in good "running" condition, with the warranty codified in the servicing contract. This responsibility expanded the servicing function to the application of administrative skills to mortgage production and processing, so that today mortgage loan administration is no longer synonymous with mortgage loan servicing. It encompasses a variety of other administrative tasks, including the establishment, supervision, and control of the office.

Accordingly, a mortgage loan administrator is now manager of the mortgage loan office as well as manager of loan servicing. Whether these functions are performed by a single individual or by a department headed by the mortgage loan administrator will depend upon the size, departmentalization, and diversification of the mortgage banking company, as illustrated by the table of organization for a medium-to-large firm shown in Exhibit 1. In line with current concept of organization, only two individuals report directly to the head of the company—the man in charge of production and the man in charge of administration. The latter, the mortgage loan administrator, is responsible for managing the office, servicing, and functioning as controller. In many mortgage banking companies, all managerial tasks are performed by one or two individuals. In others, the servicing manager has broad responsibilities without covering all aspects of mortgage loan administration. Regardless of how the job is delegated, the full mortgage loan administration function must be performed in all companies.

No matter how many variations are practiced, the education and experience qualifications of loan administrators and servicing managers are not interchangeable and are not likely to be found in a single individual. Servicing managers often do become loan administrators after they gain experience. Balancing the talents of the present personnel with personnel requirements of the company is a continuing function of senior management. Although senior management of every mortgage banking company

EXHIBIT 1 ***Table of organization–loan administration***

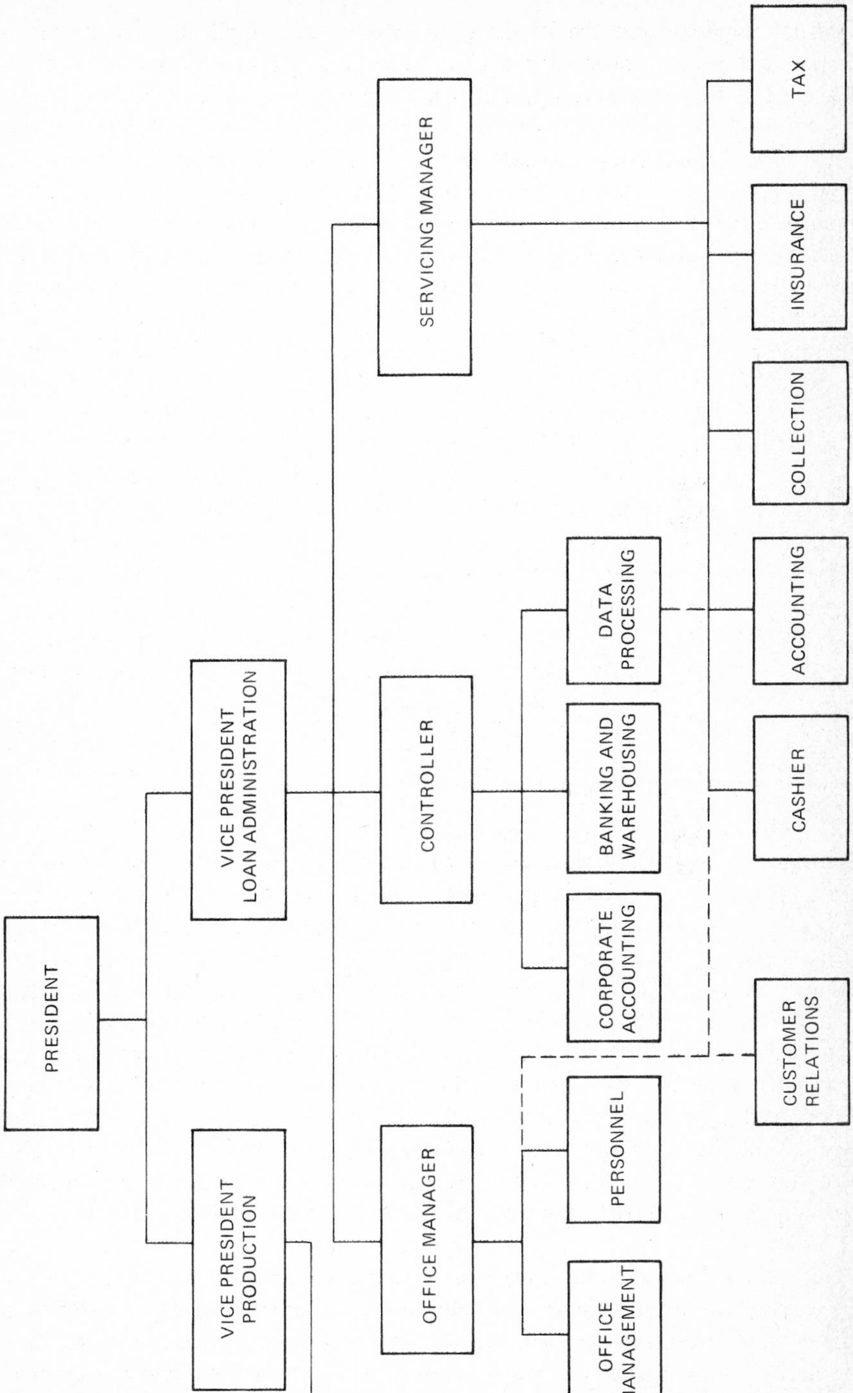

has not adopted the organizational structure shown in Exhibit 1, this chart shows the broadened scope of the loan administrator and provides a framework for this book.

SCOPE OF THE STUDY

However they are organized to do the job, both mortgage loan administrators and servicing managers, together with their respective staffs, have three distinct *masters.*

1 They serve the *investor* by performing the servicing function and discharging the servicing responsibilities in accordance with the terms of servicing contracts between investor and mortgage company. A servicing contract calls for the prompt and orderly execution of all those servicing tasks which will assure the greatest degree of safety of principal and return at the yield expected. Since mortgage bankers may service loans for as many as ten to fifty investors, there are that many investor masters to serve.

2 They serve the *borrower* by maintaining an accurate record of his payments and escrow balances, paying for and handling his property insurance policies, paying real estate taxes, and working with him to keep the loan current. Under the terms of each mortgage contract this relationship lasts throughout the life of the mortgage—as long as 30 years. The number of masters served may be several thousand depending upon the number of loans serviced.

3 They serve the *company* by establishing systems and procedures, by maintaining accurate records, by developing good office managerial tools and techniques, and by executing all the above servicing tasks properly, efficiently, and profitably.

Obviously, these services cover a wide spectrum of mortgage loan administrative operations, which are described in the following chapters:

Fundamentals of Servicing (Chapter 2)

The Loan Administrator (Chapter 3) This chapter completes the overall view. The remaining chapters deal with specific fields of mortgage banking operations assigned to mortgage loan administration.

Office Management (Chapter 4) Office management involves the day-to-day management of a mortgage banking organization. It commences with the establishment of the table of organization, work flowchart, and creation of job descriptions. It encompasses the problems of supervision and delegation, at all levels. Such duties include the establishment of an office, the creation and maintenance of records, their preservation and their eventual destruction.

Personnel Management (Chapter 5) In personnel management, the manager is responsible for the establishment and maintenance of good personnel policies and for recruitment, selection, retention, or discharging of personnel. Personnel management also involves the establishment of personnel records and training and education of employees.

Financial and Fiduciary Responsibilities (Chapter 6) The mortgage loan administrator is either entirely responsible or shares with his controller responsibility for the financial affairs of the company. This responsibility includes creation of a sound accounting system, maintenance of reliable accounting records, and presentation of reports and timely financial statements. It involves opening of company and custodial bank accounts and borrowing funds. The loan administrator or controller also preserves and protects the company's assets and resources by means of supervision, internal control, or insurance, or a combination of all three.

Planning for Expansion (Chapter 7) The mortgage loan administrator usually decides on, and recommends to management, the type of accounting equipment required and supervises its installation. He supplies and evaluates information relative to expansion through the acquisition of mortgage loan portfolios or companies.

Operating and Statistical Reports (Chapter 8) A mortgage banking firm, just as any organization that produces goods and services, maintains operating statements and statistical reports. These statements and reports, together with data included in the financial statements, provide management with information on its operations and basic data for the preparation of cost accounting information.

Cost Accounting (Chapter 9) In today's keen competition for mortgage business and mortgage servicing, operating without cost information may be disastrous. Therefore, it is essential to the operation of any mortgage banking firm to determine the cost and profitability of the various operations.

Internal Control (Chapter 10) The establishment of special systems, safeguards, and controls to eliminate procedural gaps or overlaps, and to create checkpoints for the prevention or detection of fraudulent practices, both in corporate activity and in the fiduciary role, is an important assignment of the mortgage loan administrator.

Coordination through Communication (Chapter 11) One of the most challenging opportunities in creating efficiency, and through it profits, in the mortgage banking business is the coordination of its many functions. Coordination brings information from one area of the company's activities to another where it can be used productively.

Customer Relations (Chapter 12) Good customer relations is the first step toward self-preservation and the enhancement of a good name and of good will in the communities the company serves. It is a field of activity of both the office manager and the servicing manager.

Cashier Department (Chapter 13) The cashier department is primarily responsible for the receipt and deposit of payments whether received in the mail, over the counter, or through other payment arrangements. In many organizations, the cashiers prepare payoff statements, requisition mortgage papers, and deal with the customer when the loan is paid in full.

Mortgage Loan Accounting Department (Chapter 14) The mortgage loan accounting department is primarily responsible for the recording of each payment, transmittal of principal and interest to the owner of mortgages, and the retention and custody of escrow reserve funds. The department is also responsible, when a special escrow department is not established to handle disbursement of escrowed funds, and for the analysis of escrow reserve accounts.

Collection Department (Chapter 15) The collection department is responsible for the collection of payments not made by the borrower when due. The collection staff also assists those borrowers who need temporary help in maintaining the ownership of their home.

The department is also responsible for handling foreclosures. Often the collection department becomes a *customer service department* and takes on responsibility for handling all problems affecting the borrower, and in that sense performs most services for the borrower.

Insurance Department (Chapter 16) The prime responsibility of the insurance department is to see that the real estate property is insured for fire and extended coverage hazards, at least to the extent of the amount of the mortgage. It is also necessary for this department to see that insurance premiums are paid to maintain coverage. If losses occur, it is the department's responsibility to see that the losses to the property are repaired and that bills are properly paid. It is also the responsibility of this department—unless there is a special escrow department or there are automated escrow review procedures—to see that adequate reserves are collected to pay premiums.

Tax Department (Chapter 17) Since unpaid real estate taxes and other assessments normally become prior liens on the property, which in turn can cause authorities to sell the property to satisfy unpaid taxes, it is necessary that this department either pay or cause the payment of real estate tax bills. It is usually the responsibility of the tax department to see that adequate monthly reserve deposits are collected to pay future tax bills. In some firms, this responsibility is discharged by the accounting department.

CHAPTER TWO

Fundamentals of Servicing

Servicing is performance—performance of tasks that maintain a mortgage investment in good standing. When servicing is performed effectively, the borrower meets his obligations under the terms of the mortgage and the investor receives the return expected on his investment. At the same time, the mortgage banker builds investor confidence in his ability to service mortgages, earns a profit, and maintains the good will of the community he serves.

Servicing is also responsibility—responsibility that begins when a loan is made, increases when the loan is sold to an investor, and endures as long as the loan is in force.

SERVICING TASKS

Servicing begins with the establishment of loan records in the departments responsible for the various servicing functions—cashier, accounting, collection, insurance, and taxes. Each department represents a basic task to be performed; together, guided and coordinated by the servicing manager, they comprise an effective servicing organization.

Of course, the extent of departmentalization will be influenced by the size of the firm and its servicing portfolio. Large or small, the mortgage banking firm must be prepared to perform many different servicing tasks. It receives payments by mail or over the counter, processes and reports payments received, segregates and deposits or forwards incoming payments, and maintains bookkeeping records. The mortgage company collects past-due payments and, when necessary, handles foreclosures. It retains escrow funds for future use, sets up adequate reserves, and disburses funds from such reserves. A mortgage banker also makes payments on real estate tax bills, pays hazard and FHA mortgage insurance premiums, and handles any problem relating to taxes and insurance.

As the occasion arises, it handles problems growing out of relationships among the mortgagor, the mortgagee, and government agencies—the Federal Housing Administration or the Veterans Administration. A mortgage banker also carries out other duties set out in the servicing agreement, e.g., the inspection or management of properties. This wide variety of tasks must be carried out efficiently and courteously whether they arise daily, weekly, monthly, or yearly—only once, or possibly not at all—during the life of the loan.

BORROWER-SERVICER RELATIONSHIP

The borrower-servicer relationship begins when the "first payment letter" is mailed, notifying the borrower of the date when the first payment is due. This relationship continues during the life of the loan. As a matter of fact, it can become a "cradle-to-grave" connection if the borrower finances his subsequent purchases with the same mortgage banker.

Whatever the terms of the loan, there may be hundreds of contacts with the borrower, or only a few, depending largely upon the borrower's performance. On the other hand, a borrower who makes his payments promptly, pays his tax shortages, orders his insurance policy promptly before expiration, and maintains his property in good condition requires little attention from his mortgage banker. On the other hand, bulging loan files attest to persistent problems with a borrower who has difficulties in making regular payments or must be prodded to fulfill his obligations under the terms of the mortgage. In either case, all dealings between borrowers and investors go through the mortgage banker's servicing department—the intermediary between borrower and ultimate lenders of funds.

When the loan is paid in full, the cancelled papers are forwarded to the borrower; appropriate notations are made in all records; and the files go to storage and are subsequently destroyed. Then, this particular borrower-servicer relationship has come to an end.

INVESTOR-SERVICER RELATIONSHIP

The investor-servicer relationship, ultimately codified in a servicing contract, begins with the first commitment by an investor to purchase a mortgage loan. It continues, not only for the life of that loan, but for as long as the mortgage banker sells mortgages to that investor.

The loan administrator should study the servicing contract proffered by the investor, as he is responsible for servicing the loans according to the investor's wishes. If the servicing contract does not include details on how remittances are to be handled, on reporting forms, bank accounts, and use of clearing account, for instance, these items must be spotted and worked out before loan servicing begins.

When loans are bought by an investor without a written servicing contract, the relationship between investor and servicer is established by the terms of the *commitment letter*, which specifies the terms of the purchase, the servicing arrangements, and the fees to be received for collecting payments and for attending to other servicing duties. If the commitment letter does not spell out all requirements, it implies mutual understanding regarding servicing. The terms of a commitment letter do not include provisions for cancellation of the investor-servicer relationship. Accordingly, mortgage bankers often consider a servicing arrangement based solely on the terms of a commitment letter more advantageous than one based on the terms of a servicing contract which normally provides for cancellation of servicing.

Experience shows that, notwithstanding the wording of the servicing agreement and the absence of a formal servicing manual, many investors are flexible in their requirements. They will accept changes in proposed or existing servicing arrangements as long as the servicer recommends procedures that seem reasonable and safe, generates confidence, and performs accordingly. One of the tenets of modern loan administration is that the greater the reliance on the servicer for the *complete job*, the greater will be his responsibility and his ability to perform effectively.

The Servicing Contract

The majority of mortgage loans are serviced by mortgage bankers who hold contracts which outline the duties and responsibilities for services pledged by the seller (mortgage banker) and the rights to that service acquired by the purchaser of a loan (investor). Investors often supplement their servicing contracts with servicing manuals.

Description of contract The servicing contract is a legal document that binds the servicer to the lender; it codifies the principal (owner) and correspondent (servicer) relationship; it enumerates the duties and responsibilities of each partner relative to the offering, sale, repurchase, and servicing of loans. Normally, it spells out servicing duties, responsibilities, and requirements in detail.

The servicing contract does not state *how* and *when* the various jobs are to be done. The specific method for executing each task may be elaborated in the servicing manual prepared by the investors and given to the correspondent as an operating guideline. If no manual is issued, the lender expects the servicer to perform his tasks according to prevailing practices.

The servicing agreement may be one of several types: A *general contract* is relatively short. It may cover all loans serviced by the mortgage banker or only VA and FHA loans. Details of the relationship other than those pertaining to the servicing of loans are normally not spelled out. (See Appendix B-1.) A *restrictive contract*, which is seldom used, spells out certain unusual and often restrictive clauses. For instance, a contract of this type may specifically prohibit the seller from offering loans in certain areas to other investors, at least not before offering the loans to the contracting investor. A *specific contract* usually pertains to a single loan or involves special conditions or servicing fees. It may also cover a group of loans which require special handling. A *detailed contract* enumerates the complete range of the servicer's duties and responsibilities, from the purchase of loans by investor to the termination of the contract. The Mortgage Bankers Association of America has developed a *Model Sale and Servicing Agreement* for use by mortgage bankers servicing loans for all types of investors. The association emphasizes that the agreement is a model from which an investor may establish his own agreement and is not a suggested standard form. (See Appendix B-2). Another excellent example is a *Purchase and Servicing Agreement* reproduced in Appendix B-3.

A contract is normally divided into two parts: in one part the "seller (servicer) agrees" and in the other part the "purchaser (investor) agrees," but most contract covenants apply to the servicer's obligations. In a typical contract, *the seller-servicer agrees to:* produce loans that satisfy the purchaser's requirements; deliver loans in current condition, with valid FHA insurance or VA guaranty in force, if either is involved, and without fire damage to the property, and so forth; repurchase loans, if it is determined later that there were misrepresentations or material mistakes concerning such loan; exert every effort to save the loan, through either refinancing or modification; and service the loans according to acceptable practices.

Although servicing requirements are relatively standard and normally identical, this may not always be the case. Under servicing responsibilities, *the seller-servicer agrees to:* maintain appropriate facilities and adequate and qualified staff to perform the required duties; keep complete and accurate records; pay FHA and hazard insurance premiums and taxes and make tax searches; keep insurance in force; make property inspections; notify purchaser of default and assist in foreclosure; observe FHA and VA regulations on insurance or guaranty; advise purchaser of any sale or transfer of title; arrange for audits of the company records and provide periodic certified reports of the company's financial condition; maintain fidelity bond and errors and omissions coverage.

In exchange for observance of these provisions, *the purchaser agrees to:* consider loan submissions promptly; pay for loans promptly when delivered; and pay a fee for servicing in accordance with the commitment letter applicable to each loan.

Special provisions Both seller and purchaser agree to terminate the contract by written notice only. One of the first concerns of a mortgage banker when a contract is presented to him by a new investor is to see whether it contains a favorable *termination* clause. Although he can easily satisfy most contract provisions, the stipulations about termination reflect the ultimate intention of the investor as to the position of the new servicer of his handling of loans to be purchased. The termination clause is divided into *with cause* or *without cause* parts.

The without cause part often provides for the payment of a termination fee equal to 1 percent of the outstanding principal balance of current loans being serviced. Frequently, the agreement provides that a termination fee is not required if the loans have been serviced for at least 5 to 10 years. This portion of the contract is important, since the mortgage banker expects to recover from servicing fees the loss incurred in originating a loan. Thus, the termination clause places a tangible value on the contract and gives assurance to the mortgage banker that either he will service the loans for a number of years, or he will receive a fee for the loss of income which he would otherwise have earned. Of course, the value of the privilege to service is actually greater than the stipulated 1 percent termination fee, but the fee does provide at least some degree of protection.

While this protection has become increasingly important to the mortgage banker, the stipulation has become increasingly difficult to obtain. Investors, finding themselves in a cost squeeze, often wish to consolidate their servicing portfolios in a single company in a single area where formerly they purchased loans from, and had them serviced by, more than one company. The urge to consolidate accelerates when servicers become either inactive in a field or unproductive. The stipulation that a contract is cancellable after 5- or 10-years duration without paying a termination fee does not necessarily mean that the lender will exercise his option, but it does give him the freedom to switch servicing if he is not satisfied or if it is in his interest to consolidate his servicers in a certain area.

Servicing contracts with the Federal National Mortgage Association (FNMA) have been a special case, because FNMA anticipates the resale of mortgages in its portfolio. As FNMA's operations changed, the servicer's protection from a loss of servicing for FNMA has changed from no protection at all, to a 2-year guarantee and, recently, to a pattern similar to that described above for private investors. Since March 24, 1969, FNMA will give the servicer the first opportunity to sell FNMA mortgages to private investors, thereby retaining servicing, and require buyers to retain the same servicer or to pay a fee of 0.50 percent to transfer servicing, which in turn will be paid to the existing servicer.

Many contracts contain a provision which enables the investor to terminate the contract and transfer the loans to another servicer, if the principal stockholders of the servicer—often specifically named in the contract—sell their stock or become disassociated from the company. The existence of this clause emphasizes the personal nature of the investor-servicer relationship and characterizes the personal nature of the mortgage banking business, in spite of its growth and the moderate trend toward public ownership. If the investor approves the change in ownership, a new contract may be drawn.

Some contracts require certification by the servicer's auditor that specific audit requirements have been met. Such special requirements may, of course, be burdensome and expensive to the servicer, and are not necessarily useful to the investor. Attempts are being made to reduce or eliminate such special requirements through the enlargement and refinement of audit procedures and general audit certification.

Some contracts include special requirements that a loan, or several loans, be repurchased if they go into default within a short period after their purchase. This provision is normally offered by the servicer as proof of his underwriting ability or as an inducement for the lender to purchase loans of poorer quality than he would normally consider. Such assurance by the seller-servicer minimizes the purchaser's risk in case of unforeseen collection problems early in the life of the loan. Should the requirement for repurchase arise to a significant extent, this provision can easily dissipate the capital position of the servicer.

Handling commercial, industrial, apartment, and other types of income property loans often imposes servicing responsibilities not normally involved in residential loans. In these instances, supplemental agreements are normally executed. In recent years, however, investors have tried to develop a servicing agreement which does not specify the types of loans.

Servicing contracts may be supplemented by management contracts which enable the servicer to manage the properties which the investor has acquired through foreclosure.

Evaluation and application   Before the execution of a servicing contract, each provision must be evaluated not only by the loan producer who negotiates the loans, but also by the loan administrator who will be responsible for handling the loans for decades to come. It is sound practice to have the loan administrator study the new contract first. He can determine the extent of any variation of requirements from present practice and its effect on the *cost* of servicing. It a new account is involved, he can judge the value of the new relationship. In general, sale of a loan or a block of loans should not be completed if the servicing requirements impose problems that the servicer cannot solve or that are too costly.

Once a contract is signed with a new investor who has not issued a manual, the prevailing practice today is to have the mortgage loan administrator excerpt those provisions of the contract which require special attention, which differ from requirements of other lenders or from the standard practices of his firm's departments. These excerpts, which may pertain to remittance requirements, instructions for handling insurance losses, or property inspection specifications, should then be passed on to the affected departments or discussed with them at a special meeting. Attempts should be made at the inception of the servicing relationship to detect any peculiarities of the investor's servicing requirements and to relate them to the existing servicing pattern.

It must be kept in mind that each investor will expect a perfect job, and each investor will expect priority in having his demands satisfied. If the investor finds it necessary to remind the servicer time and time again of his failure to observe certain requirements or to comply with the terms of the contract, the relationship cannot become a successful one.

(To facilitate reviewing contracts, it is strongly recommended that all servicing contracts (or copies thereof) be kept in a filing cabinet or on a bookshelf available for ready reference.)

The Servicing Manual

The servicing manual, or servicer's guide, is a reference tool normally prepared by larger investors, spelling out in detail their requirements for servicing. In effect, this manual standardizes servicing for all the investor's correspondents. It is frequently published on loose-leaf pages with a binder so that it may be updated from time to time.

The servicer's problems stem from the fact that he may be the correspondent for ten companies, each of which wants him to perform according to its particular requirements. Thus, a true testimonial of the servicer's ingenuity and competence is his ability to please each master. For this reason, he designs the routine and procedures in each area of his operations so that they may be performed specifically according to the wishes of each investor and yet be sufficiently standardized to be as economical as possible.

Many servicing manuals are simply servicing contracts in nontechnical language and narrative form. The details normally included in a servicing manual are illustrated by the table of contents of the manual of one of the largest insurance companies in Exhibit 2. The absence of a servicing manual, or of a servicing contract, does not mean that the lender has no specific servicing requirements. He usually includes them in his letter of commitment or incorporates them in a special letter of instructions.

Again, some lenders rely entirely on the *servicing skills of their correspondents,* and set no requirements for carrying out various tasks. Lenders who give a relatively free hand to their servicers are popular because the servicer can standardize his operations for a great number of investors in the most economical way without jeopardizing promptness in servicing and safety of investment and without endangering investors' economies vis-à-vis their correspondents. Standardization by the servicer, and not by the investor with many correspondents across the nation, simplifies work and eliminates or reduces costly mistakes in the offices of servicers.

Investor Rating of Servicers

Investors can help improve the quality of servicing by commenting to the management on the performance of the loan administrator or servicing manager. For example, if a job was well executed, if delinquencies were reduced, or if funds were quickly and promptly transmitted, the servicer should be complimented. On the other hand, sloppy and inaccurate reports or poor handling of delinquencies should be criticized. Of course, criticisms intended to improve performance should be made only after informal efforts have been expended to correct deficiencies.

Some investors have developed a rating system by which each person in the investor's offices with responsibility for certain functions rates each correspondent for the jobs performed. Each correspondent is identified by a code number. The results are tabulated and a list which ranks servicers by their ratings is circulated. In this way, each mortgage banker is informed of his relative standing without disclosure of his identity to other companies. An analysis of this type permits the mortgage banking firm to review its performance in relation to other companies. The firm has an opportunity to investigate possible reasons for a low rating in specific servicing areas or to appraise and commend high ratings in other activities.

Some investors have discontinued ratings of their correspondents or no longer notify them of the results. This is regrettable since the ratings, together with notification, help prevent complacency among correspondents.

EXHIBIT 2   Servicing Manual

Table of Contents

	Page
Instructions for the Sale of Residential Loans by Assignment to . . . (name of investor)	1
Form used when submitting residential applications	1
Conventional Loans	1
VA 501 loans	1
FHA 203-222 loans	2
Submission papers required on residential offerings	2
Security Instruments for Residential Loans	3
Bond or note and mortgage or deed of trust	3
Assignment	4
Title policy	4
Survey	7
VA loans	7
FHA loans	8
Certification of Purchase Price	9
Payments for Loans	10
Servicing of Loans after Payment	12
Additional Interest	13
Tax Searches	13
Prepayment Statements	14
Escrow Accumulation	15
New Owners	17
Filing Claim	17
Partial Release of Security	18
Substitution of Mortgagors—Conventional Loans	19
Substitution of Mortgagors—VA Loans	19
Substitution of Mortgagors—FHA Loans	20
Delinquent Loans and Foreclosure Cases	22
Federal Tax Liens	25
Central Mortgage and Housing Corporation and Canadian National Housing Act Service	26
Defaults	26
Foreclosures	27
Annual report	27
Foreclosed Real Estate	28
Hazard Insurance—Residential Loans	29
Hazard Insurance—Income-producing Property Loans	33
Accounting Procedure	38
Correspondence to Home Office	39

UNWRITTEN DUTIES AND RESPONSIBILITIES

The relationship between the mortgage company and investor, established through the production of loans, will endure or be strengthened only through efficient servicing. The success of the relationship hinges on mutual respect and cooperation; it requires imagination and tolerance, and calls for patience and determined effort to do the best at all times.

A servicing agreement must be regarded by both sides as the codification of a gentleman's agreement. The investor's servicing manager and the mortgage banker's servicing manager are responsible for relations between the two parties, and they must cooperate in developing smooth-running routines and a friendly atmosphere. For this reason, much depends on unwritten duties and responsibilities.

A loan administrator or servicing manager should never assume that a particular investor to whom he has sold loans and for whom he has become a servicing agent will not terminate the servicing contract or give his new commitments to a more deserving correspondent if the mortgage company fails to perform in both the spirit and the letter of the contract. The cause for termination is rarely fraudulent practice, but rather inefficient and careless performance. Mortgage company executives are not fully aware that institutional investors, deciding on one or many loans, look not only to the yield, but also to their servicing experience with the particular correspondent submitting the loans.

How Can the Servicer Improve the Relationship with His Investor?

A checklist of suggestions for successful servicing is presented below. Points that appear elementary on the surface are, in fact, fundamental. It is sometimes forgotten, for instance, that routine contacts with investors are usually impersonal. Again, in judging a mortgage company, untidy remittance reports, incomplete delinquency reports, or similarly disappointing contacts sometimes carry a weight out of proportion to the individual offense. Although compliance with some of the following suggestions depends primarily on the servicer and with others on the investor, they can also apply to both parties. In brief, the unwritten duties and responsibilities are a two-way street.

The servicing manager or loan administrator, if the company has one, or both, should follow the recommendations below:

He should strive to be prompt. Letters, if possible, should be answered on the day received. If it appears that the answer may take a week or so, the servicing manager should inform his investor that efforts are being made to secure the required information. Nothing irritates the investor more than a lapse of time and uncertainty about a matter which is important to him.

He should demonstrate that he is eager to cooperate and to work on problems that will reduce work in both offices. Cooperation can best be achieved by periodic visits to the investor's offices. Personal contact with the manager of the investor's servicing department, and also with those with whom he is corresponding, give the servicing manager a useful basis for future dealings with the investor's representatives.

He should be able to sell cost-saving ideas that will simplify certain routines. It is not enough to have a good idea; to sell the idea is often more difficult than to originate it. The remark has sometimes been made (though not so frequently in recent years) that it is "futile to make suggestions" to a particular investor. Although this may occur in isolated cases, such comment is likely to reflect the inability of the servicing manager to sell his ideas. Institutional investors have made excellent progress in recent years in streamlining procedures and eliminating duplications. It has been found that investors go along with new ideas, provided they are practical for everyone and are presented clearly.

When permitted, he should make his own decisions on matters of concern to him and the investor. If he cannot make a decision, he should offer a recommendation. The investor cannot be expected to reach conclusions on matters for which the servicing agent has presented facts and no recommendations.

He must protect the interest of the investor beyond any requirements set up in a contract. The position of the investor must be considered whenever a loan becomes a problem, whenever an insurance policy is accepted or placed, and whenever a customer relations problem arises that may involve the reputation of the investor.

He must often anticipate problems and advise the investor without any prompting if adverse economic conditions are about to affect areas where the servicer operates.

He should promptly advise his investor's servicing manager of changes in important staff assignments. Nothing is more irritating than writing to persons who have left the company's services for one reason or another, or than receiving a communication from new employees of whom one has no knowledge.

How Can the Investor Improve the Relationship with His Servicer?

The servicing manager of the investor's mortgage loan department, together with his staff, should follow the following recommendations:

He should try to reduce unnecessary requirements. Most procedures need periodic reexamination to determine whether or not they are still serving a useful purpose. Many correspondents of investors, even though they are dissatisfied with a routine, are reluctant to suggest changes. If a mortgage company becomes sufficiently annoyed or discouraged by cumbersome servicing requirements of an investor, it may offer desirable loans elsewhere.

He should try to eliminate duplication of work and records. Some investors, for instance, require their servicing agents to submit renewal insurance policies and to duplicate the job of recording such policies and of watching their expiration dates. This procedure can be readily simplified by having only the servicer perform the tasks, since this is in line with his responsibilities, and by having him certify the existence of valid policies once a year. This arrangement has become a standard operating practice in connection with policies for residential loans and, in a few instances, for income property loans.

He should realize that he usually has the last word in a dispute. He should not abuse this privilege by an arbitrary decision. If it is necessary for him to take an action which he knows will displease his servicers, he should explain his reasons fully to them.

He should have confidence in his servicers. He should give the correspondent the flexibility to which he is entitled,or, if his warnings of dissatisfaction go unheeded, he should terminate the servicing agreement. Unnecessary correspondence can be eliminated if deserving correspondents are given a greater degree of responsibility.

He should encourage expressions of opinion. Servicing managers of institutional investors should encourage the men who are in charge of servicing in the offices of their correspondents to express their views on various problems. Such an interchange of ideas can be of great value to the mortgage banking industry.

He should strive to be prompt. Tardiness in answering an inquiry may become particularly irritating if it pertains to the handling of a seriously delinquent account where promptness and decisiveness are of prime importance. He should promptly advise his servicers of changes in requirements and in the personnel handling certain problems.

SERVICING INCOME

The income of a mortgage banking firm is derived from two principal activities: production of loans (also called "origination") and loan servicing. *Production income* is derived directly from the borrowing public in the form of fees charged to the borrower when a loan is made. Under certain economic conditions, production income may also include profit or loss when loans are sold to investors. *Servicing income* is derived primarily from investors in the form of a portion of the interest collected, which is retained as compensation for the work of servicing a loan. Additional servicing income may also be obtained from borrowers in the form of late charge penalties and in fees for special services rendered.

In this volume dealing with loan administration, only those fees and charges are described which are charged and collected in connection with the act of servicing a loan. These include loan servicing fees, late charges, and special fees for transfers, substitution of mortgagors, mortgage changes, substitution of insurance policies, and replacement of NSF checks.

Servicing Fees

Each loan commitment by an investor contains a specific statement about the fee the investor shall pay for servicing the loan or specifies the *net rate* at which interest is to be remitted. The fee is usually expressed as a percentage of the outstanding principal balance, such as $\frac{1}{2}$ or 1 percent for an annual payment or as $\frac{1}{12}$ of $\frac{1}{2}$ of 1 percent for a monthly payment. The percentage is applied to the principal balance of the loan outstanding for the 30-day period preceding the date of computation, and the amount is then deducted from interest collected to determine the net remittance of interest to the investor. If, for instance, on January 1, 1971, interest is collected on a residential loan with an outstanding principal balance of $18,000, as of December 1, 1970, the interest at 7 percent amounts to $105.00 and the servicing fee of $\frac{1}{12}$ of $\frac{1}{2}$ of 1 percent of $18,000 is $7.50 for that month. Therefore, the first interest remittance to the investor will be $97.50. For each subsequent collection, the servicing fee and consequently the net interest portion of the remittance will be smaller since principal payments are applied on the loan each month.

The fee for servicing a large income property loan is usually considerably less than $\frac{1}{2}$ or 1 percent per annum, but the dollar amount is, of course, larger than it is on a residential loan. Other methods employed by investors to pay servicers, including the level payment plan, are described in Chapter 14.

The servicing fee provides the mortgage banker compensation for performing all jobs stipulated in the servicing contract. As can be seen, the fee depends on the servicing fee rate and the size of the loan. Although the amount diminishes as the loan is reduced, the work by the servicer and the cost of such work rarely decreases.

Late Charges

A late charge may be assessed against the borrower under the terms of the FHA or VA mortgage note, and in accordance with the applicable provision of FHA and VA regulations, to compensate the lender for part of the additional expense of collecting payments that are received more than 15 days past due. These late charges are retained by the servicer.

On a conventional loan, a late charge or an interest penalty may be assessed in accordance with the terms of the mortgage note if payment is not made when due. Either penalty on past-due conventional loan payments may be computed in several different ways. The resulting penalties may be nominal or substantial, depending on the size of the loan, the extent of delinquency, and the method of computation.

Investors and servicers usually establish in advance the manner in which the late charges and penalties on conventional loans are to be distributed between servicer and lender. Normally, nominal late charge penalties are retained by the servicer for additional work in collecting payments, while accrued interest penalties are paid to the investor for the loss of the use of the funds involved. In the latter instance, servicers are usually authorized by the investor to retain the same proportion of the interest penalty as the agreed-upon servicing fee rate applicable to the loan.

Special Fees

During the past two decades, mortgage bankers have imposed charges on borrowers for those services which are not called for under the terms of the mortgage. These charges are of two types: those charged for services performed upon request of borrowers and those assessed for "unnecessary work" the borrower created for the servicer. Generally speaking, these discretionary charges are imposed by the mortgage banker, not with profit in mind, but rather to reimburse him for the cost of services neither called for in the servicing agreement nor expected of him as part of the service implicit in a mortgage banker-borrower relationship. Although most investors have never openly and formally approved or disapproved the charging of fees for either of these services (since they involve the borrower-mortgage banker relationship), they have at times questioned the size of such fees.

Transfer fees   A transfer fee or a so-called "straight" assumption fee involves the sale of a property subject to the mortgage. Although the term *assumption* is frequently used, this type of transaction may or may not actually involve assumption of the indebtedness by the purchaser of the property. It involves merely the *assumption* of payments on the mortgage by the buyer of property, without release of the seller's liability under the terms of the mortgage to the Federal Housing Administration or Veterans Administration and to the holder of the mortgage.

The service, in this case, involves preparation of a pro-ration statement showing the status of the loan currently and, subsequently, upon consummation of the sale; changes in all mortgage company records; notification to the insurance carrier that the property has changed hands; and, as is often required, notification to the mortgagee of the change of ownership. The transfer fee is not assessed for preparation of the statement, since the borrower is entitled to a statement of his account, but for the work occasioned by the sale.

Fee for substitution of mortgagors   As the name implies, a substitution of mortgagors involves (1) a formal *assumption* of the debt by the purchaser, and (2) a *release* of the seller's personal liability to the Federal Housing Administration or Veterans Administration and to the holder of the mortgage. In contrast to the straight assumption, which is a two-party transaction, a substitution of mortgagors is a three- or four-party transaction, since it includes the holder of the mortgage and, except in the case of conventional loans, either the FHA or VA. Obviously, this can be achieved only if the purchaser is acceptable to the appropriate governmental agency and to the investor.

The mortgage banker's task in this instance involves services in addition to those described above under "transfer." He must take and process applications to the FHA or VA, whichever is involved, and to the holder of the mortgage; and he must draw the formal documents required to complete the transaction, and contact the title company. Many investors do not release the original mortgagor, in the hope that a new owner will arrange his own financing. Such a practice often complicates negotiations. Since a substitution of mortgagors requires considerable additional work for the mortgage banker, the fee for the "substitution of mortgagors" is normally higher than that charged for handling a transfer, i.e., a straight assumption.

Fee for mortgage changes   The mortgage banker gives service on a wide variety of special requests by borrowers, such as modifications, extensions, and partial release of the mortgaged security, modifications or substitutions of assigned leases on income property loans. All such requests require consent of the mortgage holder and, in the case of insured and guaranteed loans, of the FHA or VA. The amount of work can be as little as a short conversation with the borrower and his representatives, culminating in a formal submission to the investor, or it can involve a full appraisal, requiring a good deal of research and documentation. The fee is determined by the amount of work involved.

Fee for substitution of insurance policies   Under the terms of the servicing contract, the mortgage banker must make sure that there is proper insurance covering each mortgaged property. For this reason, he is required to accept, check, and safeguard each policy. During the term of an existing policy—which has already been accepted, processed, and carded—a mortgagor sometimes substitutes another policy. According to many mortgage bankers, their servicing responsibility does not extend to the work of such untimely and unwarranted substitutions. They often collect a substitution fee to cover the cost of the work involved if a policy is replaced at dates *other than the expiration date.*

Fee for handling replacement of NSF checks   To discourage borrowers from tendering checks on bank accounts that do not have sufficient funds to cover the check, some mortgage bankers collect a handling fee to reimburse themselves for the work involved in the handling and reprocessing of the payments after cash funds or certified checks are obtained to replace the checks returned by the bank. Any punitive effects of this charge are well justified for those mortgagors who are prone to misuse the privilege of making payments by means of checks. Both FHA and VA permit the assessment of nominal charges for this work.

CHAPTER THREE

The Loan Administrator

The loan administrator is the resident manager of a mortgage banking firm. Often second in command, he is responsible for all the varied and complex internal operations that a mortgage banker must perform. In a single afternoon, a loan administrator may be required to solve a procedural problem affecting the cashier and the collection and accounting departments; to straighten out a controversy arising from the settlement of insurance loss adjustment; to approve the hiring of a new collector; and to investigate the adverse findings of auditors representing one of his investors.

The chief executive is mainly concerned with loan production, new business development, and maintaining effective relations with investors. Because the firm's top loan producers devote their energies to the daily struggle of creating loans, they have neither the time nor the inclination to attend to administrative tasks. They tend to view overall operations only in terms of the next loan. They expect to turn over the raw materials—the approved loan applications—to personnel who are especially qualified to prepare and complete mortgage documents and to handle all related problems.

Together, the loan administrator and the loan producers form the team that determines the success or failure of the mortgage banking business. An efficient servicing operation that is profitable and that satisfies investor requirements begins with the origination of the mortgage loan. To assure maximum efficiency, the loan administrator's responsibility to the team effort must go beyond servicing and office management to assisting the chief executive and the loan producers by focusing attention on administrative problems and costs and by applying administrative know-how to the origination process. The duties and responsibilities of the loan administrator, and the general and special qualifications of individuals who occupy this position, are the subject of this chapter. In many respects, the discussion applies also to the servicing manager, since the servicing manager is responsible for part, or possibly most, of the duties and responsibilities of a loan administrator in some mortgage banking companies. For simplicity, however, references in the text are usually to the loan administrator.

DUTIES AND RESPONSIBILITIES OF LOAN ADMINISTRATOR

Some basic duties and responsibilities of a loan administrator are similar to those of administrators in other businesses. Here, attention is directed to those tasks which are particular to effective administration of a mortgage business.

To the degree that a company's organization structure permits, the loan administrator is the manager of the entire office and is responsible for the execution of all office managerial and procedural tasks. Unless there is a servicing manager reporting to him, he is also manager of all servicing activities. In this capacity, he consults with senior management on overall problems, and he discusses relevant problems with the staff. He also is the liaison officer between those engaged in producing and processing loans and those engaged in various servicing tasks.

A loan administrator is responsible for the proper functioning of the loan-producing, -processing, and -servicing facilities. In this sequence of operations, routines must be carefully established and understood. Breakdowns must be investigated promptly. The loan administrator is responsible for the establishment of workflow and the correction of errors as they occur. For instance, he knows, as few others do, that a change in the first payment date of a loan is a matter of concern to several loan-processing and -servicing areas as it requires many changes of records. He knows that failure to notify the accounting or collection departments may affect profits adversely. He also must ensure that there is no interruption in operations and that there is adequate help to perform the various functions. He should work constantly with the department heads in order to anticipate their problems and needs.

The loan administrator must exercise control either by supervision or by means of procedures established for that purpose. He also must coordinate diverse activities so that each separate action operates smoothly as part of a bigger activity. It is his business to know how one procedural change will affect the other.

In establishing and maintaining these procedures, the loan administrator must be familiar with the contents of all servicing contracts, with the foreclosure laws, and with rules and regulations affecting banking transactions.

He should not become so enmeshed in details, however, that he overlooks larger problems. He must be perceptive and free enough, if necessary, to stop and reschedule workflow or to assist in handling difficulties that arise on short notice.

Development and Training of Personnel

The loan administrator must establish and maintain an effective work force. Within this framework, basic personnel policies must be developed and maintained. Personnel policies are discussed in detail in a later chapter; a few points deserve emphasis here.

Promote from within Promotion of qualified personnel to more responsible and better-paying jobs rather than filling such jobs with new employees is not always easy to carry out, because it requires the training of two employees—the one receiving the promotion and the one hired to replace him. Nevertheless, the company benefits from such a promotion policy: employees advanced from the ranks are already familiar with company routines and are ready and willing to take on greater responsibilities.

Train for succession Successors to key personnel, at the different management levels, should be trained and ready to take over whenever necessary. This procedure should be followed whether key personnel are young or approaching retirement. And, it should be applied at all management levels. Training a successor for the loan administrator and the servicing manager is particularly important, because persons filling these positions are critical in maintaining a smooth working relationship with the company's borrowers and investors.

In this context, assistants are important personnel. One of the real tests of the success of the loan administrator or the servicing manager is the functioning of their departments when they are away from the office. Continuance of operations hinges on the entire staff, but particularly on the capabilities of the assistants and the various department heads.

One person should be selected for the job of assistant, even in companies having a servicing staff of three or four persons. He should possess as many of the qualifications described below for the loan administrator as possible. He should be thoroughly trained in all phases of the work and be kept fully informed of all proposed changes and plans so that he may constructively aid the loan administrator, the servicing manager, and the staff.

Inform department heads Department heads must be familiar to some extent with the responsibilities and duties of the loan administrator and the servicing managers. They should be able to solve most problems that arise in their departments and, if necessary, to act on behalf of their superiors. To maintain this degree of flexibility, department heads must be fully informed of all changes and plans for change which may affect the work of their departments.

Improvement in Operations

A loan administrator should never feel that operations cannot be improved. The search for better methods and procedures should be continuous, and he should encourage recommendations from all staff levels. Each recommendation should be weighed carefully. If the loan administrator finds that the recommended change will improve the system sufficiently to warrant the expense involved, the necessary changes should be made.

Recommended changes may be opposed by department heads as well as other employees. Their objections should be carefully considered, but if found invalid or simply against change itself, they should not deter management from taking action.

Some resistance to change is natural, whether the proposed alteration affects the entire system or merely a small part of an office or department. For this reason, the manager must enlist the aid and cooperation of those affected by the change in order to make it successful. In particular, a change from one method to another should be preceded or paralleled by an adroit approach to any employees who usually oppose new operating methods. Some managers who have received good suggestions from the staff have failed to carry them out because they have not discussed the suggestions with the employees concerned, nor made enough preliminary tests.

Even a change that calls for drastic reorganization of one branch of an existing system should not be dismissed as impractical. If change is advisable, the chief concern of the loan administrator is to effect a smooth change—one which does not interrupt the steady flow of work through the department or section involved and does not impair, in any respect, service to borrowers and investors.

In his search for improvements, the loan administrator should continually examine the diverse phases of mortgage banking operations. Some relate directly to his own activities; some focus on the handling of personnel; many concern procedures for fairly routine operations; and still others anticipate special problems. All these ways of making improvements are illustrated below.

Direct responsibilities of loan administrator   The loan administrator, as well as his associates, should handle important matters personally. He should answer promptly all letters which require personal attention and which deserve more than routine handling, such as those involving criticism by investors or by borrowers. This task may demand time beyond that normally available, but time used in case of urgency or emergency is usually worth the effort expended.

The loan administrator should be available at all times for consultation. For instance, he should be available when a member of the collection department reaches a stalemate with a seriously delinquent borrower, or when a dissatisfied borrower is at the cashier's window and a third person is needed to settle a dispute.

He should realize that he can make a major contribution to the profits of the company by developing new ideas applicable to both overall administration and the servicing departments. Ideas must be sought out, encouraged, and developed. Any innovations in machines and equipment, technical improvements, and efforts to streamline procedures must then be made to fit into existing arrangements.

Change for the sake of change should be avoided. Similarly, the temptation to make a change too quickly should be resisted. A drastic change or rearrangement should be preceded by a thorough investigation to see, for example, whether the alteration would constitute an improvement over the way a job has been done for 10 or 20 years.

More effective performance by the staff The loan administrator can find ways to improve operations through his handling of personnel. For instance, he should make routine operations more interesting. While considerable time and money have been spent to eliminate the monotony of menial tasks, little has been done to make the average office job more interesting.

It is important to review the duties of all employees with that point in mind. For example, the turnover in bookkeeping machine operators can be minimized by giving the operator, who may become tired of running a machine all day, responsibility for some other function in the department, if only for a few hours each day.

It is advantageous, sometimes, to rotate employees. Rotation relieves the monotony, and gives employees the opportunity to learn more than one job. From the standpoint of management, multiskilled employees are valuable assets. Job rotation is also an important consideration from the standpoint of internal control of sensitive jobs, such as those of cashiers or bookkeepers who reconcile bank accounts. (See Internal Control, Chapter 10.)

The loan administrator should also encourage employees to express opinions on established routines or contemplated changes. Those who work the closest with day-by-day details can observe possible effects of a change. It is important that management as a whole, as well as the loan administrator and servicing manager, continuously encourage employees to present pertinent suggestions for improving efficiency and to apply their experience in establishing new routines.

Review of operations In his quest for better performance, the loan administrator should review all operating procedures. One example is the procedure for controlling and reviewing incoming and outgoing mail. The review of correspondence, which is more important than is sometimes realized, can be handled by a capable assistant, but the loan administrator should review much of the nonroutine incoming mail and assign it to appropriate persons for action. In this manner he can keep informed of activities in the various departments and can detect and correct any procedural errors that may develop.

Form letters, such as first payment letters or insurance solicitations, should be reviewed from time to time. Particular attention should be given to the tone of such letters, to accuracy of facts, and even to literary expression.

Finally, he should reexamine all operations periodically. Many good administrative and servicing procedures are developed through continuous examination. It is sometimes revealing, as well as necessary, to study office procedures from a detached, critical point of view, weighing each one and deciding whether it is indispensable for the smooth functioning of office procedures. Some operations which have been unchanged for many years may be eliminated or combined with others; some should be reviewed with the "calculated risk" theory in mind—where the cost of doing a particular task is compared with the loss sustained by not doing it. A loss of $100, for instance, may compare with the expenditure of $500 to prevent the loss. Many companies, which remit gross interest to their principals and receive the investors' computation of their service fees, spend considerable time in comparing and checking the investors' statement against their own computations for errors or omissions. The application of the calculated risk theory would suggest the discontinuation of checking if, for instance, during a 3-year period only two small errors were discovered, neither of them large enough to justify the expense of checking the statements.

The nature of small improvements is such that many of them have to be initiated and used before actual cost savings show on the monthly expense statement. A good cost accounting system, however, may enable the loan administrator to show a reduction in expenses, for instance, in salaries paid or supplies purchased, probably 6 to 9 months after the change or improvement. Caution must be exercised that a simplification of routine in one department is not actually achieved merely by shifting the work to another department where the increase in expenses exceeds the cost saved in the other department.

Special operating problems   The loan administrator should anticipate operations that are not a part of his daily routine; for instance, he should devise ways of handling emergencies. The loan administrator can usually cope with emergency problems requiring shifts in personnel. He can reassign servicing personnel or transfer production personnel to servicing functions, if needed, to carry peak loads, such as the tax payment rush once or twice a year, the first-of-the-month load, or the summer vacation problems. In smaller companies such temporary arrangements are almost a necessity for successful operations.

He should anticipate in advance any problems of equipment conversion. In this age of rapid technological changes and rapid obsolescence, it is necessary to keep abreast of the development of various data processing equipment applicable to mortgage loan operations. All changes occasioned by new equipment must be well researched and well understood by all involved, and preceded by thorough indoctrination. Since most of these developments occur in the field of accounting for payments, remittances, and transfer of funds, such problems are discussed in Chapter 6, Financial and Fiduciary Responsibilities.

PERSONAL QUALIFICATIONS

Generally, the individual who can handle most of the tasks enumerated above will be a better loan administrator than one who excels in one or two ways but cannot perform many of the required duties. It is, however, the successful blending of job performance with good personal qualifications that produces the best loan administrator. Actually, before becoming a loan administrator, the individual may have had earlier experience as a servicing manager. Of course, a servicing manager must develop considerably in his post in order to be promoted to that of loan administrator.

Listing the personal qualifications of a loan administrator serves a dual purpose. It provides the executive with a checklist to consult in considering a potential candidate. It also gives a loan administrator, or a servicing manager who is interested in advancement, an opportunity to check himself against the basic requirements. Both must bear in mind, however, that it is difficult to pinpoint what elevates one man over another in a company's organization, and what really counts is a mixture of the qualifications with good judgment and tact.

Education

The loan administrator should have knowledge of accounting, though it is not necessary that he be an accomplished accountant or a Certified Public Accountant (CPA). A college degree in business is preferred, but again not necessary. A degree in the humanities or English can be just as valuable as one in business administration or economics.

He must have a basic understanding of the processing and closing activities of mortgage loan production and a thorough understanding of the workings of the Federal Housing Administration and the Veterans Administration. He should be familiar with the foreclosure laws of states in which his company operates, and have an understanding of all insurance and tax matters. This part of his education can, of course, be attained by on-the-job training as clerk or department head of the organization. In this technological age, it is also advantageous, although not essential, to grasp the complexities of the electronic computer. Most of these requirements can be met, however, by relying on an assistant with special qualifications.

Personal Traits

Courtesy and self-control are essential traits. Respect for the character, aspirations, and good intentions of fellow employees is almost sacred. A man who raises his voice to correct or reprimand has lost his right to the job he holds. *Loyalty* is elementary and self-explanatory, and must prevail among supervisors, peers, and subordinates alike. A loyal atmosphere is conducive to good performance. Good *self-management* includes proper grooming and good personal habits in relation to fellow employees as well as in personal financial matters. An individual who cannot manage his personal affairs can hardly be expected to give counsel and guidance to others. A manager must live within his income or resources; he must try to avoid debts other than, of course, a first mortgage and charge accounts. He should have no personal notes or other large debts.

An orderly mind is reflected in an orderly desk and an orderly office. Together they create good management and good public relations. *Promptness* in preparing and adhering to monthly work schedules may prevent procrastination—a disease which can immobilize the best talent. A *sense of urgency* requires the judgment to determine that the problem just presented is important, that its solution is urgent, and that it has priority over other matters.

Managerial Talent

The following abilities have a special bearing on both the handling of personnel and the performance of specific tasks.

Ability to motivate and command is a quality of leadership. The loan adminis-trator should recognize the worth of the individual employee and try to help him develop in his post. He should understand the problems and aspirations of all those who look to him for guidance and direction in the performance of their jobs. The loan administrator should be able to handle difficult situations, maintain harmony, and help others so unobtrusively that they believe they work almost without super-vision. *Ability to gain respect* can be accomplished by being fair even if an unfavorable decision is to be rendered. *Ability to get along* is midway between being aloof and overly friendly. Managers should not fraternize with employees nor should they bear the reputation of being difficult to talk to. *Ability to render justice* means that the loan administrator must have the judgment necessary to render a decision that will correct an injustice; he must be able to impress all concerned that injustice is not to be tolerated.

The loan administrator must be *resourceful and inventive* in producing creative ideas. He must be alert to new notions which often spring from unexpected sources—a magazine article, a newspaper item, and even a casual conversation. *Ability to judge and decide* involves collecting, collating, and understanding of facts; weighing of all data and alternatives; exploring ramifications; and finally choosing between the alternatives. Willingness to accept responsibility for decisions is of utmost im-portance. Since judgments must often be made without complete knowledge of all facts involved, a person's ability to judge will be accepted only if most of his decisions turn out to be right. Of course, he must be diligent in his research, because the more information he has about a given problem, the better judgment he is able to make.

Ability to maintain correct procedures is an essential characteristic of an effective loan administrator. It is often easier to correct an error or to reprimand someone for a blunder than it is to guard against repetition. Breakdown in communication and procedural errors must be noted and corrected immediately, and proper methods must be instituted to ensure against their recurrence. The loan administrator who can con-ceive a plan of action must also be able *to follow through and complete the job.* Once a project is initiated, he must be capable of finishing it.

RESPONSIBILITY OF SENIOR MANAGEMENT

Anyone with the qualifications ascribed to a loan administrator and charged with the responsibilities of that job will perform best when senior management recognizes the potentially important contribution of the loan administrator to company profits and provides achievement incentives.

First, the loan administrator should be allowed to assume full responsibility for all loan administrative operations and be elevated to a key position in the company. His title should be administrative vice president or treasurer.

Second, he should be given a definite financial incentive which could include a bonus arrangement, profit sharing, or stock options. Management usually offers such incentives to the production man, but sometimes fails to provide them for the loan administrator, not realizing his contribution to the revenue of the company through overall administrative efficiency.

Finally, the loan administrator should be recognized as part of the management team. He should participate in overall decisions affecting company policies, and management's long-range plans should be explained to him so that he can evaluate his duties within the framework of the company's objectives. He should be encouraged to participate in the affairs of both the national and the local mortgage banking associations and also in real estate and civic groups. In addition, he should be invited to meetings with representatives of the investors so that he may become familiar with investor representatives on a personal basis.

2

Mortgage Office Operations

CHAPTER FOUR

Office Management

A smooth-running, efficient office depends upon careful planning of procedures, proper selection of personnel, thoughtful execution of directives, and, most of all, continuous vigilance over the affairs of the company. The best results are usually achieved by the office manager who anticipates and solves problems in their early stages as a part of his thinking as he goes about his everyday routine. To know what to do and how to do it is much more complicated than it appears. The difficulties and involvements multiply as the staff grows, but do not necessarily diminish as employment slackens.

PRINCIPLES

To discharge office managerial tasks properly and completely, a mortgage banker and his loan administrator must recognize two basic tenets of management: first, that company objectives can be reached only through the efforts of the employees; and second, that a manager's success hinges entirely on his ability to direct and motivate personnel to work toward the company's objectives. Normally the chairman of the board or the president of the company is responsible for the attainment of company objectives and the execution of its policies as established by the board of directors. In this sense, either executive is the top policy officer. The mortgage loan administrator, then, is usually the top administrative executive, and in this capacity is in charge of the entire office and its personnel and is responsible for the smooth functioning of the office.

Actually, no clear boundaries exist between the efforts of planning in the development of the company's objectives, establishing policies, and the assumption of responsibilities for executing such plans. In mortgage banking, planning and operating officers must work in harmonious unity to achieve maximum profit from many operations.

The objective of mortgage office management is to establish and maintain the best possible office atmosphere, and to motivate, direct, coordinate, and supervise the personnel toward maximum attainment of the company's objectives.

Scope and Responsibility

Office management is a professional activity by means of which certain jobs entrusted to a company manager are performed. The term *mortgage company manager,* as used here, refers to a senior executive, the loan administrator, or more specifically, the office manager. The term office management applies both to the operations which are executed on a day-to-day basis to establish and maintain a procedural entity, and to personnel management that carries out the firm's objectives.

A mortgage banking organization is a unique operational entity. It houses, under one roof and under one direction, persons of various professions working side by side, persons who originate, finance, and then service a single intangible product—a mortgage loan. The physical product is a mortgage accompanied by a note, which is actually a set of legal documents encompassing rights of lenders and borrowers over a tangible security, which curiously enough also embodies a "lifetime" warranty of service to its owner, the mortgagee. This product represents the completion of a variety of jobs including real estate appraising, banking, underwriting, legal work, loan closing, accounting, and loan servicing. No wonder that a mortgage banking firm is a complex business entity!

Development of Office Management Function

Specialization, automation, and improved techniques in servicing have placed ever-growing demands on the mortgage banker to establish an efficient office and maintain it in smooth-running order. The office manager of a decade ago was responsible primarily for personnel, purchase of supplies, and other routine chores. Today, in contrast, the office manager also has an important responsibility for the profitability of the operations. In this sense, office management has come of age, and the office manager has acquired a professional status.

In relatively small mortgage banking firms, office management and personnel management are closely allied. As the organization grows, the two functions tend to become separated. Office management is primarily concerned with the establishment and maintenance of the physical office and the creation of procedural machinery, while personnel management is concerned with staffing this physical entity.

TOOLS OF MANAGEMENT

The tools essential to the management of an office are (1) a table of organization, or organization chart, (2) job descriptions, (3) operations guide, and (4) a procedure manual. With the aid of these tools, the manager's functions can be clearly established and defined, their interrelation spelled out, and the various requirements understood by those occupying various positions.

Many organizations, especially in the initial and somewhat formative stages of company existence, do not establish formal tables of organization or job descriptions. As the company expands and as job delegations multiply, the need develops for clarifying the company's line of command and for job descriptions that provide a better understanding of the ingredients of each task.

Table of Organization

Although all mortgage bankers perform the same basic functions and have similar operations, no two companies are completely identical in the way they operate.

An organization structure actually exists long before it is established or charted. It exists in the minds of those who run the company and those who work for it. As long as the number of people running the company and taking direction is small, no major jurisdictional problems arise. As functions broaden and as operations expand, it becomes necessary to have some understandings crystallized so that each person's perspective toward the job and his relationship to others can be officially formulated. Essentially, a table of organization or organization chart presents in visual form to both management and to those who perform the designated functions, the structure of the organization, and within it, each person's area of responsibility and authority, line of communication, and lines of promotion. An organization chart also outlines jurisdictional boundaries by picturing the chain of command and clarifying the executive relationship. It eliminates overlapping jurisdictions and illustrates the various levels of management and supervisory authority.

An organization chart that is ideal for one company may be impractical for another, not only because the individuals who comprise management have different ideas for the attainment of company objectives, but because different companies possess different resources, outlets, and objectives.

Each loan administrator should prepare an organization chart and make it available to all executives and supervisory employees. This visual presentation of relationships will facilitate understanding of the interdependence of departments and the coordination of functions. The names of those holding various positions will usually add to the effectiveness of the presentation. Posting the chart on the bulletin board, however, is not necessarily recommended.

Preparation of charts As a practical matter, there are two distinct ways to prepare a chart for any organization. One is to establish a chart based on ideal, functional relationships; the other is to base the chart on what the company is doing and then to enlarge and perfect it. The latter method involves ascertaining and defining existing relationships between people holding various positions.

Designing a chart to fit the personnel in a company may be the better way to create and perfect an organization structure, especially if the mortgage banking firm is already operating successfully. Essentially, it is more important for an organization to function properly and efficiently than to force its operations to conform to a preconceived organization chart.

Since each company prepares its first organization chart after it has been in existence for some time, the chart, of necessity, includes some peculiarities of the organization resulting from the makeup of the individuals holding specific positions. Consequently, the finalized chart carries the imprint of management's thinking about the relative importance of departments and operations as well as its existing staff.

A chart may make allowances for a "strong man." In this case, the organization structure is built around him. If he is permitted to become an "empire builder," however, the structure as well as the company is subordinated to his personal ambition and professional orientation. Alternatively, a structure built around a strong individual who serves his company well may work successfully. Its success depends upon the talents of the individual and not the structure of the organization. After his demise another must be found if the same structure is to be maintained.

Types of charts An organization chart must be elastic rather than rigid. Several types of charts which provide overall rather than specific guidance for the preparation of an ideal table of organization are shown on the ensuing pages. Some charts evolve and develop as a result of the acceptance and execution of various management philosophies rather than as a result of growth. Large companies may operate exactly like small ones. Typically, basic differences in appearance of various charts center on the position of the mortgage loan administrator, his relation to management, and his importance in the company.

Basic components of charts A mortgage banking organization usually operates in two areas—loan production and loan administration. The first term is self-explanatory and the second involves all activities other than loan production. Operations may also be charted for three operational areas—production, processing, and servicing. The chart illustrations may be applied to large, medium, or small companies. The difference in charts, and in the companies behind them, stems from the relative importance of various activities as evaluated by management.

Often the more loans an organization produces and services, the simpler its chart of operations since large organizations normally require persons of great talents who are qualified to take on considerable, wide-ranging responsibilities and to command large divisions or departments.

The chart in Exhibit 3 illustrates the organization arrangement of a typical medium-size mortgage banking firm. In this instance, the need for a loan administrator has neither arisen nor been recognized. The chart in Exhibit 4 illustrates the ideal arrangement for a typical medium- or large-size company and suggests dependence on two

EXHIBIT 3 Organization chart – medium-size firm

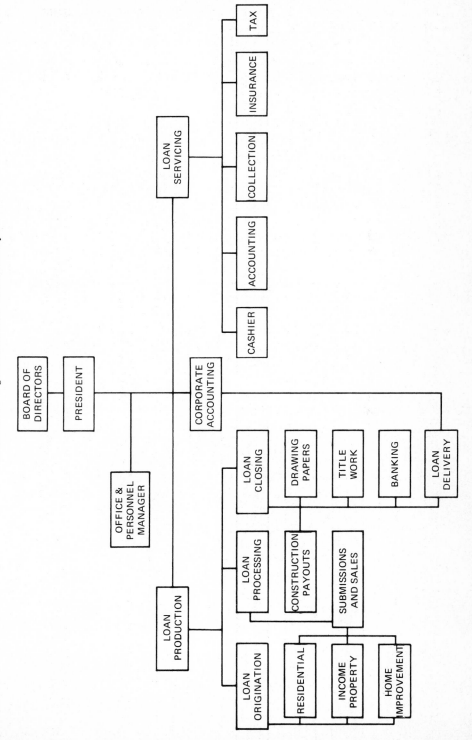

EXHIBIT 4   Organization chart – large-size firm

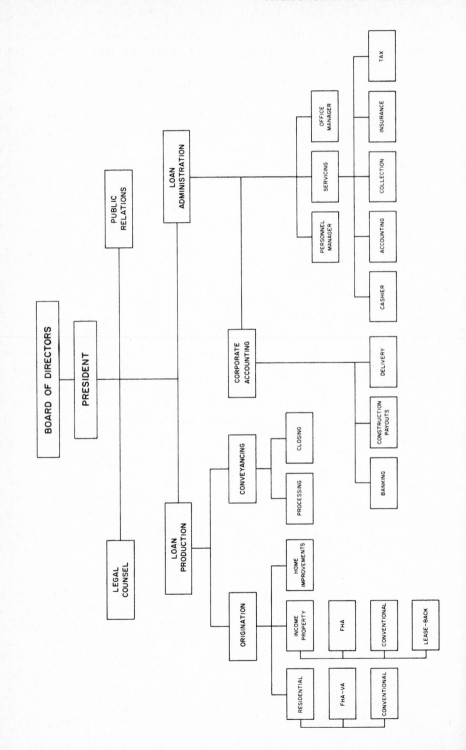

major divisions, loan production and mortgage loan administration. It should be noted here that in some companies the jobs normally classified as *loan processing* or certain phases thereof are also assigned to mortgage loan administration. The chart in Exhibit 5 illustrates a functional organization of a large, highly diversified mortgage banking entity.

Exhibits 3 and 4 illustrate different concepts of management. In sequence, Exhibits 3 and 4 also illustrate an evolution of the organization's structure; that is, they show how a chart designed for a small company expands into one for a larger company. The differences between charts, both those shown here and those in actual use, may stem either from the application of a specific mortgage banking philosophy, individual preference, or recognition by management of the relative profitability of different operations. The chart that is ideally suited to the concept of strong loan administration, and that emphasizes most effectively the beneficial consequences of good loan administration appears in Exhibit 1.

Job Descriptions

Job descriptions are vital managerial tools to supplement an organization chart. Job descriptions, however, are not normally used in smaller companies where the office manager knows the nature of each job and the qualifications required for its performance, and where the know-how of a particular job passes from person to person by word of mouth and on-the-job training. As a company grows, so does the need for job descriptions. The number and variety of jobs increase. Furthermore, less dependence can be placed on the memory and recollection of the office manager for the requirements of specific jobs and the qualifications employees need to do the job.

Purpose and use A job description enumerates the tasks a person must perform and describes his responsibility and authority. By clarifying relationships between jobs, job descriptions help management avoid overlaps or gaps in responsibilities. They may help in the detection of real or potential bottlenecks, and enable management to compare each employee's performance to the requirements of the job. New employees may be introduced to their jobs through job descriptions.

How to prepare Job descriptions may be prepared in two different ways: one, by having each person currently performing certain tasks describe his duties and responsibilities; and, the other, by describing each function without consulting employees performing such functions. While the first approach is fairly subjective and not necessarily complete, it will immediately uncover possible duplication of duties or procedural gaps. The second way is more likely to create personnel problems since a company, even if successful, rarely operates according to an ideal set of job descriptions. Whichever initial approach is used, the task of preparing job descriptions should be completed quickly.

A good job description should be brief and succinct; it should enumerate all the

EXHIBIT 5   Organization chart—highly diversified firm

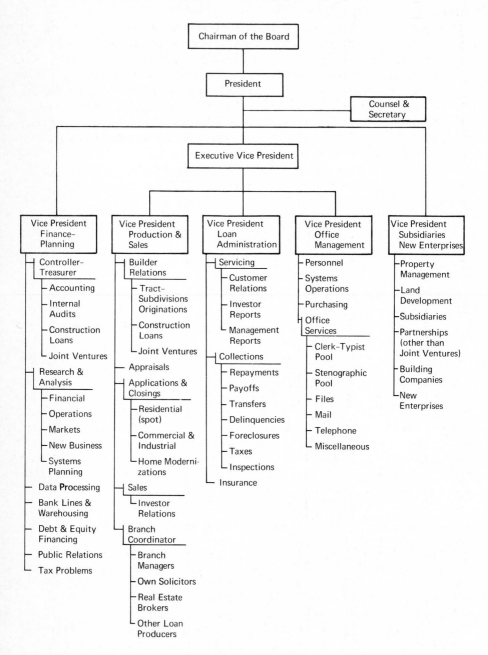

responsibilities to be covered, the functions to be performed, and the qualifications required.

In preparing job descriptions and applying them to the existing staff, it must be understood that many compromises are needed between jobs as they are described or performed and the ideal arrangement that may eventually be attained.

It would be impractical to provide a description of all jobs that mortgage bankers perform. Each mortgage banker within a large framework of standardization has his own way of setting up his operations. Local customs, laws, requirements of investors, and customers' needs demand variation in approach and performance. Then too, individuals already on a job, or those hired and/or trained by others on the job, may result in compromises in specifications and standards of performance.

The job description presented in Exhibit 6 illustrates a general approach to its preparation and the tone and the extent of details needed. A job description may include detailed instructions similar to those in an operations manual.

EXHIBIT 6   Job description

Secretary to the President

Detailed responsibilities

1 Reports directly to the president, handles all correspondence for him, appointments, and schedules.
2 Is familiar with general work of the corporation, names of customers, persons in companies the corporation deals with.
3 Makes transportation arrangements; hotel reservations, as well as reservations for customers, special meetings, and board meetings.
4 Attends meetings to take notes, when requested.
5 Keeps personal bookkeeping and correspondence of president.
6 Is available to officers and department heads for necessary contact with the president when he is out of town.
7 Maintains public relations files, publicity programs, promotional mailings.
8 Secures reports from all departments, and makes them available to the president.
9 Conducts special correspondence with banks and investors such as mailing of annual audits and financial statements.

Qualifications

1 Strong physical constitution, healthy nervous system, good outlook on life, strong outside interests.
2 Ability to work with other people in the company without friction and to aid in maintaining harmony.
3 Broad business background.
4 Ability to organize work and determine priorities.
5 Ability to work under pressure.
6 Skill in typing, shorthand, and basic understanding of the use of data processing equipment.
7 Ability to handle customers easily, with great deal of poise.
8 Discretion and tact in dealing with public.
9 Initiative to follow through on all duties without supervision.

Operations Guide

An operations guide, also called "office guide" or "manual of operations," supplements the organization chart and set of job descriptions. It presents the office as a complete operating entity rather than as a series of specific procedures. It describes what the organization does and how it does it. Often it also explains why certain jobs are performed.

The value of an operations guide in the mortgage business is fairly basic. Few financial operations are as complex as mortgage banking. Employees can work for years practically side by side without understanding the tasks performed by their closest associates. For instance, where else, other than in a mortgage banking firm, will an appraiser, an attorney, and an accountant work on the same product? In what other field does the word "service" apply equally to the areas of real estate taxes, insurance, collection of payments, and reporting to investors and borrowers? Although an operations guide is of great value to existing staff, it is of even greater value to the personnel manager who is normally hard pressed to explain the complicated nature of the mortgage business.

An operations guide differs from an employment manual which describes the company's employment policies and rules, rather than its operations. (See Appendix A-1.)

Procedure Manual

The purpose of a procedure manual is to describe in detail how a job is to be done. In contrast with a job description which describes the job to management and to the personnel officer, a procedure manual describes the job to the employee. It explains how the job must be performed on a day-to-day basis.

Three different procedure manuals may be prepared, but except for a large organization, one overall manual is usually sufficient. The three types of manuals are (1) the manager's manual, which normally includes a general work flowchart, the fundamentals of all procedures, and a schedule of reports required; (2) the supervisor's manual, which normally covers the procedures involved in various jobs under immediate supervision; and (3) the operator's manual, which includes a description of each task step by step and the details of various transactions that must be performed, together with illustrations. Form letters, or forms filled out with sample information, give invaluable aid to a new employee on the requirements of the job and on the type of routine letters the company prefers to use. The above types of manuals are almost imperative in the accounting department and in the data processing section. The continuity of operations depends greatly on the accuracy, completeness, and timing of reporting in the mortgage loan accounting department, which in turn depends greatly on whether the manuals which spell out requirements and deadlines explicitly are kept up to date.

Manuals of the above types must be prepared either by the servicing manager or the supervisor, or by persons on the respective jobs who have sufficient facility with the English language. Texts of manuals should then be reviewed carefully for accuracy and clarity of presentation.

PLANNING AND OPERATIONS

Staff Requirements

In general, the size of the office staff varies with the volume of loan production and servicing. The staff required to produce mortgage loans differs from that required to service loans. The volume of loan production may fluctuate from season to season, from year to year, or from one building cycle to another. In contrast, servicing volume either grows steadily or decreases gradually as the years pass. Exceptions occur only when acquisition of a servicing portfolio or purchase of an entire company is involved.

A pattern of stable employment is essential to ensure a sound and productive atmosphere in the office. Insecure employees do inferior work. For this reason, many mortgage bankers have found it prudent to build a base force of permanent long-term employees and to supplement this force with extra helpers often hired on a temporary or part-time basis. The latter may be shifted from one job to another as the need arises, or discharged when warranted by a serious slowdown in mortgage-lending activity. The discharge of qualified employees should always be the last step in cutting expenses to adjust for a cyclical downturn that lingers longer than expected. A constantly fluctuating office staff has detrimental effects on morale and performance, and also is very expensive.

It is not possible to establish basic standards for the number of employees required to produce mortgage loans, because production-staff requirements vary widely according to the types of loans produced, areas in which the company operates, and the types of customers served. The personnel needs of loan servicing departments, on the other hand, can be related to the number of loans serviced with reasonable accuracy. Guides for servicing-staff requirements can be estimated along the lines presented in Exhibit 7. The accuracy of any such estimate is undoubtedly influenced by the predominance of certain types and kinds of loans, the types and number of investors serviced, the degree of mechanization and the type of equipment used, and borrowers' payment habits. Although the staff projections are fairly easy for small- and medium-size firms using conventional types of accounting equipment, automation neither necessarily nor immediately stabilizes or reduces personnel requirements. This is true even when the number of loans reaches 8,000 to 10,000—the loan volume usually associated with the need for conversion from use of accounting machines to electronic data processing equipment (EDP).

Office Management—The Daily Task

The task of the office manager of a mortgage company varies considerably from office to office according to the size of the company and number of employees, the volume of new loan business produced, and the volume of loans serviced; and to the stature and ability of the loan administrator and/or the servicing manager, either of whom may perform and discharge all, or some of, the managerial functions and responsibilities of the office and related personnel activities.

EXHIBIT 7   Servicing staff requriements*

Number of loans serviced	Number of accounting machines	Number of employees needed to perform servicing efficiently		
		Type of position	Minimum number	Maximum number
With bookkeeping machines				
Approximately 2,000	1	Servicing manager		1
		Cashier	1	1
		Bookkeepers[†]	1	2
		Clerks		
		Insurance		
		Tax		1
		All other	2	
		Collector		1
		Total	4	6
4,000 to 6,000	2	Servicing manager	1	1
		Cashiers	2	2
		Bookkeepers[†]	4	6
		Collectors	1	2
		Insurance clerks	1	1
		Tax clerks	1	1
		Total	10	13
6,000 to 8,000	3	Servicing manager	1	1
		Cashiers	2	3
		Bookkeepers[†]	6	7
		Collectors	2	3
		Insurance clerks	2	2
		Tax clerks	2	2
		Total	15	18
8,000 to 10,000	4	Servicing manager	1	1
		Cashiers	3	4
		Bookkeepers[†]	7	8
		Collectors	3	4
		Insurance clerks	2	2
		Tax clerks	2	2
		Total	18	21
Data processing equipment on premises				
8,000 to 10,000	Complete data processing installation on premises	Servicing manager	1	1
		Manager, EDP	1	1
		Cashiers	2	3
		Accounting and data processing clerks	6	8
		Collectors	3	4
		Insurance clerks	2	3
		Tax clerks	2	2
		Total	17	22

EXHIBIT 7   Servicing staff requirements* (continued)

Number of loans serviced	Number of accounting machines	Number of employees needed to perform servicing efficiently		
		Type of position	Minimum number	Maximum number
		Data processing equipment on premises		
10,000 to 20,000	Complete data processing installation on premises	Servicing manager	1	1
		Manager, EDP	1	1
		Cashiers	4	5
		Accounting and data processing clerks	10	10
		Collectors	5	6
		Insurance clerks	3	4
		Tax clerks	3	3
		Total	27	30

*This tabulation is based on servicing satisfactory to both investor and borrower and represents *average* rather than exceptional situations. It is also assumed that the accounting equipment is used for other than mortgage loan accounting such as payroll, insurance and/or general ledger accounting.

†This classification usually includes the controller who handles corporate accounting; machine operators, relief operators, remittance and disbursement clerks, a supervisor (if volume warrants), and all other bookkeepers not necessarily fully occupied with mortgage loan accounting tasks.

Note: Many individuals may hold two different jobs. An attempt has been made here to identify each person with the functions performed over 50 percent of the time.

Number of departmental employees shown include departmental supervisors. Secretarial and stenographic assistance used on a pooled basis should be added unless those responsible handle their own correspondence, as is done in most small- and medium-size offices.

Collection department staff requirements depend on collection conditions—in this chart normal conditions are assumed.

Staff requirements of insurance department relate only to administration and do not include employees engaged in selling insurance.

Staff requirements may also vary according to location of the office.

File clerks, messengers, switchboard operator, and receptionist come under general staff requirements.

The two basic managerial tasks and responsibilities discussed here are (1) *the maintenance of property,* which includes planning and furnishing the office, the acquisition and care of equipment, and purchase and storage of supplies and forms; and (2) *the establishment, maintenance, and destruction of records,* which includes establishment of a filing system; creation and use of a loan register and supporting indexes; and ultimately the destruction of records and information no longer needed. The office manager's daily tasks often include the duties and responsibilities of carrying out the firm's personnel policies. These tasks are described separately in Chapter 5.

MAINTENANCE OF PROPERTY

The most important fixed asset of the company is the office in which its business is conducted. Since employees usually spend more waking time there than in their own homes, it is extremely important that the office be functional, pleasant, and attractive. To this end, the office, or "home away from home," should be well designed and, in this modern world, air-conditioned.

Establishment of Office Layout

The decision to establish a new mortgage banking office or relocate an old one is usually made only once during the tenure of most office managers. Plans for the office are normally prepared by an architect or an office designer, who takes into consideration certain peculiarities of the mortgage business. Decisions about the actual location of the office, the arrangements within such space, and the color schemes and furnishings must be made, to a great extent, by the mortgage banker and his loan administrator.

The first and most important factor in choosing a new office is the selection of the location. This involves primarily a choice between a downtown or a suburban location. A downtown location normally offers proximity to commercial banks, title companies, and FHA and VA offices. It also provides accessibility to transportation facilities for personnel and customers. A suburban location may offer proximity to borrowers and to the real estate market which the mortgage banker serves. With the upsurge of commercial lending, however, a good downtown location which provides ready access to all types of customers has become more desirable, and the trend of the sixties toward company-owned suburban offices is gradually being reversed.

If a downtown location is chosen, the next question is the location of the office *within* the building. Is it to be on the ground floor, second floor with walk-up facilities, or anywhere in the building? Such a choice, of course, is available only if a new office building is selected; otherwise, a vacant or to-be-vacated office must be accepted. In a new building, of course, many offices are usually available with different facilities and corresponding rent schedules; in an existing building, a given space is available only at a given rent. If the mortgage banker is the original tenant in, or the builder of, a new building, the plans can be made to accommodate his needs. If an old building is selected, the space must be adapted and special changes and concessions may be limited.

If a location in the suburbs is selected, the search for existing facilities suitable for mortgage banking may be more difficult. It may become necessary to construct an office building. Many of the larger mortgage bankers have resolved the problem by setting up a compact full-service office downtown with several suburban branch offices which provide only the facilities for producing and processing loans. Such an arrangement assures efficiency and flexibility in adjusting to changes in areas of operation, if necessary by opening new branches and closing others.

In weighing the pros and cons of possible solutions and in examining the functional and public relations aspects of the choice, the initial cost of construction in contrast to renting existing facilities, access to financial and other facilities, as well as other factors will have to be scrutinized in detail. Rental cost comparisons—downtown versus suburban—usually will favor a suburban location. Whichever location is chosen, the overall cost will not be greatly different. In the suburbs, where square-foot costs are lower, there will always be a tendency toward greater spaciousness, while in the downtown location, where basic costs are higher, the emphasis will be on economy of space.

Experience indicates that most companies, especially those on the move, outgrow their new and larger quarters within 3 to 5 years. It is important, therefore, for a growing organization to lease more space than is needed immediately, even if the expenditure seems extravagant at the moment. If extra space is not leased, the firm should make provision for additional space as it becomes necessary. Too often, mortgage bankers fail to lease additional space, err in their original planning, or grow unexpectedly through acquisition of servicing only to find themselves compelled to add to their facilities by relocating certain departments away from the main office. Such arrangements are likely to be costly in terms of both the extra rent and reduced efficiency. Besides, it will eventually become necessary to uproot the entire office to place it in a single location. Any relocation is costlier than carrying additional space which is not needed immediately.

Once a location is selected and leased, the interior arrangement of the office must be carefully planned. Short-sightedness in appraising space requirements for such matters as an appropriate entrance or in determining the correct number of telephone outlets may prove costly.

The specific layout of the office will depend primarily on the nature of the business. It is easier to set up an office to serve one type of customer, i.e., residential borrowers, than to establish easy access to many departments which may be vying for importance. An important consideration is the subdivision of office space into the various departments with proper access to each other and to the public. Should the various areas of activity be partitioned, or should the office be one single open space so all departments can be viewed from one end to the other? If the former seems desirable, the size and the number of private offices and conference rooms must be determined at this point.

The internal arrangement of the office—whether the partitioned or the open space variety—normally represents personal preferences. For the preservation of privacy and reduction of noise, partitioning is recommended; on the other hand, an open office, which includes a big expanse of desks with a few private offices for senior officers and private rooms for conferences and loan closings, usually creates a friendly, personalized atmosphere. Normally, the office should be designed with the entrance at the middle of a long rectangular area from which each part of the office may be easily and quickly reached. Proper arrangement also calls for locating employees who have frequent contact with the public, such as cashiers and loan officers, close to the main entrance.

Equipment, Supplies, and Forms

The office manager has the responsibility of providing the office with up-to-date equipment and related conveniences. These include a postage meter, photostating equipment, typewriters, adding machines, and maintenance and repair service. He must also provide office supplies, assist department heads with the design and content of forms, and arrange to have forms printed or mimeographed. Several of the tasks may be delegated to a full-time or part-time assistant. In that event, strict supervision must be exercised over purchases and the contracts for all office services.

It is essential that the office manager or his assistant keep abreast of the technological improvements in office equipment, by listening to the many salesmen who normally call on office managers, reading publications on office management, and regularly attending office equipment exhibits. A manager who proclaims that he does not want to see salesmen may seem to be practical, but he is not always prudent. Insistent as some salesmen may be, they do bring in new ideas which should be considered and adopted if operational savings can be achieved.

All office equipment has a normal life expectancy which is not necessarily measured by government-approved depreciation standards. While most equipment can be depreciated in 4, 6, or 10 years, many items become obsolete, unusable, or subject to continuous breakdowns in shorter periods. Similarly, machines that seem destined for the scrap heap by write-off standards provided by accounting principles may be utilized effectively for a longer period. In this area the office manager can perform a valuable, cost-saving function. Is it worthwhile to repair a particular typewriter rather than to replace it? Is a particular adding machine, which still has 5 years of remaining "life" on the books, as useful as a newly invented one, even if the acquisition cost of the latter is substantial? Equipment, like people, cannot always be measured by chronological age.

Supplies should be purchased through *purchase or work order,* or requisition forms. When the requisition is completed, it should be approved by the office manager and placed with a supplier. A system must be established which will require that a copy of the requisition form be returned with supplies listed in the invoice. For the purposes of control over purchases as well as of cost accounting, it is advisable to have department heads approve all purchases except petty items.

The office manager, or his assistant, should be responsible for storing all supplies and maintaining an inventory control. When this task is neglected, the result is the depletion of forms and other supplies at crucial times, or oversupply and waste at others. While each department head may be made responsible for the maintenance of adequate supplies and forms for his department, ordering should be done by the office manager.

ESTABLISHMENT, MAINTENANCE,
AND DESTRUCTION OF RECORDS

The efficient operation of an office can be greatly enhanced by the prompt availability of information and records when needed. This objective can be achieved only if records and files no longer needed on a daily basis are transferred from active use to storage or, if possible, destroyed immediately. According to the National Record Management Council, 40 percent of all office records may be destroyed immediately, and all but 10 percent may be destroyed after varying periods of time. Accordingly, the questions of record retention or destruction should be resolved in favor of destruction.

Except for certain legal requirements pertaining to tax and payroll records, the entire program for record maintenance and destruction depends on the judgment and common sense of management. If management feels that professional advice is needed, an attorney may be consulted or a record maintenance firm engaged.

To maintain a proper program, management must watch those who have a predilection to retain certain records long after they cease to be useful, only because they may possibly be needed to prove or justify an action taken. Management must be wary of correspondence and bits of information accumulated in files and cabinets through sheer inertia of those who feel oddly comfortable with accumulated records. While an office may survive under this type of philosophy, it cannot be run efficiently and profitably. The longer records are retained, the less likely they are to be destroyed. Yet, unnecessary records only clutter up file rooms and block the path to the records actually needed.

An aggressive record destruction program has never been so important as it is today when office space is at a premium. It can be achieved best by a carefully thought out *record-creation* plan. If there is a concentrated plan to create only essential records, if duplication of records is avoided, and if files and correspondence are constantly pruned, there will be so much less to be filed, retained, and eventually destroyed. There is a close interrelation between the creation of records and their destruction. The more orderly and systematic the former, the easier and quicker the latter can be accomplished.

A record-keeping and record destruction program for a mortgage banker should show that the mortgage business divides records into two principal parts:

1 Those that pertain to loans made and that are placed in individual loan files. Although much of the duplication of record keeping between the mortgage banker and his investor has been eliminated, particularly in accounting, insurance, and taxes, the essential data maintained by investors are often sufficient to recreate certain vital information, if needed.

2 Those records that are created in conjunction with the overall operation of the company, such as accounting and corporate records and those established in relation to the development of business in general. These include correspondence pertaining to production, processing, banking, and servicing, which are applicable to the conduct of the business in general and not to specific loans.

For Loan Files

The best receptacle for all records and information pertaining to individual loans is a *loan file*. This file contains the loan application, credit report on the borrower, the appraisal of the property, and *duplicate* copies of mortgage documents and of title and insurance policies. All correspondence for 10 to 30 years will be added to this file. Originals of insurance policies and of paid tax receipts can be placed in the loan file or retained in the respective departments. It may become a thick file if much correspondence is required, or a relatively thin file if the borrower pays promptly and creates no problems.

In the case of a substantial income property loan, it is possible to break down and separate the various types of documents within one loan file or to establish separate files for different types of documents and related correspondence. The separate sections would include, for example, mortgage documents, insurance policies and related correspondence, and construction payout records and waivers of lien.

A substantial benefit is achieved by placing *everything* in the individual loan file. If the loan is terminated, the entire file of material can be removed from the file room. After the contents of the file are reviewed by the cashier preparatory to payoff of the loan, the file is transferred into a storage room and later destroyed. The loan file may be destroyed immediately upon the termination of the loan, or from 6 months to a year thereafter. Before destroying the loan file, all records pertaining to the loan should be stamped "paid in full." Records that must be retained are listed in Exhibit 8 and discussed in detail below. Documents of value such as a survey may be retained. An unexpired insurance policy must be returned to the borrower or his attorney. Thus, a timetable for the destruction of each loan file is automatically established without the necessity of a special program or an independent decision. If files are preserved for 6 months to a year for the remote possibility that certain information may be sought by the borrower, they should be transferred from the file room to a storage room and then destroyed on a periodic schedule.

A filing system must be foolproof in the sense that individual files must be readily accessible while loans are in force and easily identifiable after the loans are paid in full. Information must be included that will establish quite quickly whether the loan is current or dead.

To create a filing system which will achieve all the objectives outlined, it is necessary to: (1) number loan files; (2) establish and maintain a loan register; (3) prepare index cards and keep information thereon up to date; (4) establish the file room; (5) provide staff; and (6) remove and destroy paid-up loan files. Much of the success of a filing system hinges on accuracy in preparing records (2) and (3), and the efficiency of file clerks who have the primary responsibility for filing the material that pertains to each file and for returning the file to the shelf or filing cabinet.

The merit of the loan file system is that it provides an automatic means by which each file is destroyed. No file can disappear in the wastebasket without its destiny being recorded on the loan register, and no file will take up valuable space in the file room after the loan is paid in full.

1 *Number Loan Files.* Numbering the file, establishing a loan register, and preparing index cards are normally functions of the department responsible for processing applications or preparing mortgage documents. These tasks are usually not performed by the servicing staff. A loan number may be assigned when the signed application is received. Since every application does not mature into a loan, however, it may not be practical to assign a number at this point, as the file may never contain more than an application. For this reason, files are often identified first by the applicant's name and are not given a number until the mortgage papers are signed. If a number has been assigned at the time of the loan application and the loan is then rejected, the numbering system would be full of gaps and the loan register bulky. For identification of types of loans, the numbering may be prefaced by F for FHA, V for VA, and so forth. Income property loans may be intermingled with residential loans or may be numbered by a separate number sequence, although a single series provides a more orderly program for numbering, indexing, and destroying all records. Also, as years pass it is easy to establish the age of a loan by knowing the series of numbers assigned to loans in a particular year.

2 *Establish and Maintain a Loan Register.* When a loan number is assigned to a loan file, the loan register sheet may also be prepared (see Exhibit 9). This sheet is invaluable for information required on a borrower or for certain legal particulars after the file has been destroyed.

To keep loan registers in current condition the cashier, or whoever is responsible for marking records, should note on the appropriate page the date when the loan was terminated and the person or firm which made the payment. This will explain at a later date why a particular file is not available, when the loan was terminated, and how payment in full was accomplished.

3 *Prepare Indexes.* After preparing the loan file jacket and completing the loan register sheet, two cards are typed. Cards 3 by 5 inches in size are adequate and convenient for this purpose. One carries the last name of the borrower and the other the street address of the property, and each is identified by the loan number just assigned. These cards are filed in two separate library-type filing cabinets, one according to the alphabetical sequence of the last name of the mortgagor, the other by the street address of the property. Each index card, therefore, contains information by which the file, the cashier card, the ledger card, and any other servicing records on a particular loan may be located.

It is not necessary to place the loan number assigned by investors on these cards since the records of the cashier and the accounting department are normally marked with this number when the loan is purchased by an investor. Correspondence from investors which may not carry the mortgage banker's loan number will show the borrower's name and address of the property. From either of these, the file number may easily be ascertained by means of the cross-index.

Care must be exercised when properties change hands or when new loans are processed for current borrowers that the alphabetical index card is updated and refiled. The borrower's name is changed if an ownership change is involved. The processing of a new loan, however, will require changing the loan number also.

EXHIBIT 8   Automatic record destruction schedule

Servicing and accounting records (excluding corporate and general ledger records) on active loans and retention thereof after payment in full

Records	Description and purpose	Reasons for keeping or destroying	Retention practice
1 Loan register (Exhibit 9)	This is a book containing loose leaf pages on each of which such data as name, address, terms of loan, legal description, title policy numbers, etc., are recorded.	A business record with no legal significance. With the aid of the cross-index the details of loans and their history may be traced.	Permanent
2 Loan file	This is a legal-size jacket containing duplicates of all loan documents (originals shipped to investor prior to sale maintained in separate jacket). All correspondence, paid tax bills, insurance policies are filed here.	When loan is paid in full, file is stripped of valuable items; these are returned to owner and receipted by him or his representative. Receipt is attached to cashier's card which is retained permanently.	Stored for approximately one year; then destroyed
3 Cashier's card (Exhibit 32)	Standard type of card; contains basic information. If payment cards are used, cashier card becomes a mere ownership information card.	Since receipt for all papers is attached to card (or series of cards), it provides a source for answering all inquiries on paid-in-full loans. (If there are no cashier's cards, receipt for papers should be attached to loan register pages.)	Permanent
4 Borrower's ledger card (Exhibit 11)	Serves as accounting card for loan closing and construction departments. Shows record of disbursement, interest adjustment, fees, and discounts. This is a record of original entry.	Contains basic information. May also be needed as reference in case of foreclosure and income tax investigation.	Permanent

EXHIBIT 8 Automatic record destruction schedule (Cont.)

Servicing and accounting records (excluding corporate and general ledger records) on active loans and retention thereof after payment in full

Records	Description and purpose	Reasons for keeping or destroying	Retention practice
5 Cross-index	Consists of two sets of 3 x 5 cards on different colored paper. Cards are filed in two sets of cabinets; one according to the street address of property, the other according to name of borrower.	Provides means of finding loan number designation	Permanent
6 Loan ledger card	This is a standard mortgage account-ing ledger record of each loan.	This provides a record of loan payment history	Approximately 10 years after termina-tion of loan

Note: Since all valuable records and information relative to each and every loan are in the loan file, the problem of record destruction is the result of *one action*, taken when the loan is paid in full. Valuables are dispatched and receipted; others held for one year. Strict adherence to the above procedures will also provide a reliable source for answering all inquiries on paid-in-full loans.

EXHIBIT 9 Loan register

BORROWER JONES, John and Mary, his wife

ADDRESS 2407 North Main Street, Arlington Heights, Illinois

LEGAL DESCRIPTION

Lot 207 in Greenbrier in the Village Green, Unit No. 5, being a Sub-
division of part of the East 1/2 of the Northwest Quarter of Section 18,
Township 42 North, Range 11, East of the Third Principal Meridian and
Resubdivision of part of Lot 11 in George Kirchoff Estate Subdivision of
part of Sections 12 and 13, Township 42 North, Range 10, East of the
Third Principal Meridian and part of Section 7 and 18, Township 42 North,
Range 11, East of the Third Principal Meridian in the Village of Arling-
ton Heights, Illinois, Wheeling Township, Cook County, Illinois.

LOAN NO. F 40272

TYPE OF LOAN FHA

FHA OR VA CASE NO 13-103021-203

TO TAKE UP LOAN NO.

DATE 3-27-71

AMOUNT $ 19,900.00

TERM 30 YEARS INTEREST RATE 7 %

PAYMENTS OF $ 110.66 INCLUDING

INTEREST PAYABLE Monthly

FIRST PAYMENT DUE 6-1-71

FINAL PAYMENT DUE 5-1-00

INVESTOR *Federal National Mortgage Association*

COMMITMENT EXPIRATION 6/30/71

COMMITMENT EXTENDED TO

DATE DELIVERED 6/22/71

TORRENS/RECORDER'S	DOCUMENT DATE	RECORDING DATE	RECORDING DATA DOCUMENT NO.	BOOK NO. VOL. NO.	PAGE NO.
MORTGAGE	3-27-71	4-7-71	1909 2955		
ASS'G'T OF MORTGAGE	7-31-71	8-5-71	19205125		
LEASE					
ASS'G'T OF LEASE					
ASS'G'T OF ASS'G'T OF LEASE					

	TITLE INSURANCE POLICIES		TORRENS CERTIFICATES		
	DATE RECEIVED	NUMBER	DATE RECEIVED	NUMBER	
				MORT. DUP.	CERT.
MORTGAGE	11-12-71	53-93-574-1			
OWNERS	11-12-71	53-93-574			

1M 2-68 MONARCH

60

Companies employing data processing equipment normally maintain and continuously update alphabetical lists of borrowers, which record opposite each name all pertinent information on the loan. This list may also be arranged by loan number or street address of property, and may contain by means of codes more information than seemed desirable when cards were typed.

4 *Establish the File Room.* A file room should be well lit, air-conditioned, and centrally located, offering easy access for all employees. Within the file room, files should be kept in filing cabinets or in a vertical file arrangement on open shelves. Although the former may provide greater fire protection, the latter arrangement is less expensive, since one-third more files may be retained in the same space on an open shelf than in filing cabinets. The disadvantage of using cabinets is that they are more expensive, and it normally takes more time to insert and remove files. Moreover, cabinets are technically not fireproof, only fire resistant.

Instead of a numerical filing system (loan files stored in numerical sequence), files may be arranged according to a *terminal digit system.* In this system, files are arranged by the last two digits of the numbers assigned to the files. One advantage of this system is that it permits complete utilization of the file space; as loans are paid in full, files are pulled throughout the system, with the result that it is seldom necessary to move the file folders backward to make room for new files. A color code in the form of a stripe, placed on ten different possible locations on the top of the file folder, is used to designate the next to the last terminal digit. By this color system, incorrect filing is quite unlikely, as a file in the wrong place can be readily spotted.

It is advisable to maintain a procedure by which a file is signed out by the individual removing it or by the file clerk. The entire filing function should be closely supervised since file clerks cannot provide good file-room service if files no longer needed are not returned promptly to the file room. The office manager has the responsibility of seeing that files are not placed in desk drawers or are not kept out of circulation by individuals retaining them in departmental file cabinets.

5 *Provide Staff.* When the number of loans exceeds 1,000, at least a part-time file clerk is needed to maintain the files. A filing system containing 5,000 to 10,000 loans usually calls for a full-time file clerk and a part-time assistant.

6 *Remove and Destroy Paid-up Loan Files.* When a loan is to be paid in full, the file is normally removed from the file room by the cashier, or whoever prepares the file for the termination of the loan. After the loan is paid in full, the file is normally placed in either a *transient* file or a storage room to await destruction. How soon the file is destroyed after the date of payoff is determined by the loan administrator or office manager. If material of value has been returned to the borrower and all records are properly marked, as suggested earlier, the remnants of the file can be destroyed immediately, but, if preferred, retained for 6 months to a year.

A record destruction schedule pertaining to the contents of paid-up loan files was established by the 1960-1961 Mortgage Servicing Committee of the Mortgage

Bankers Association of America. An abbreviated version of this report entitled "MBA's Record Retention Schedule" is listed in Appendix A-2.

For Other Records

The temporary custody and ultimate destruction of other records that are necessary for the conduct of the mortgage business, and that cannot be identified by any single loan number, are a separate task. Maintenance of sound programs must be pre-scheduled and planned, with responsibility resting on the loan administrator or office manager. The steps for establishing an effective program include an inventory of all records, analysis and classification of records, and provision of record destruction schedules.

1 *Take Inventory of All Records.* This task consists of creating a *form sample* book and establishing lists of material already accumulated by departments. In taking inventory, no material should be considered which is normally retained in the loan file.

2 *Analyze and Classify.* It is most important to analyze and classify records before establishing a schedule for destruction. Classification must be made according to the source of the material, its purpose, and its use:

   a Production records include correspondence with sponsors of projects; investors on quotas and other matters; FHA, VA, and FNMA, and all matters not readily identifiable with an individual loan.

   b Servicing records are, for the most part, created after loans are sold. They consist of cashier cards, ledger cards and tax cards, duplicate copies of remittance reports, delinquency reports, correspondence about loans and procedures, and copies of annual insurance certifications.

   c Corporate records are the foundation of the accounting and servicing system and consist of ledgers, ledger cards, bank reconciliations, cancelled checks, tax returns, reports to taxing authorities, personnel records, payroll and social security records, and time cards.

3 *Establish Record Destruction Schedules.* One of the most important aspects of record destruction is a program of elimination. How long should records be kept in active files? A suggested record retention schedule is reproduced in Exhibit 10. Although this is not a complete list, it illustrates the manner in which the classifications are made. How long should records be kept in storage before destruction? While certain records may be destroyed when taken from the active file, others may have to be moved from the office into the storage room.

   There are professional record-keeping analysts working with nationally known companies whose sole business is to advise business clients on record destruction programs. If necessary, the services of such an individual or company may be sought.

4 *To Microfilm or Not to Microfilm.* Many companies have microfilmed certain records to preserve them in case of a major disaster or of destruction resulting from enemy attack. While the first is always a possibility, the second seems

EXHIBIT 10 *Company record retention schedule*

Accounting department	To be retained
Receipts and disbursements ledger	Permanent
Cash books	Permanent
Cash journals	Permanent
Mortgage ledger cards	Permanent
Mortgage payment coupons	10 years
Disbursement tickets	10 years
Mortgage settlement sheets (daily remittances)	3 years
Bank statements	5 years
Bank deposit slips	1 year
Trial balance and work sheets	1 year

Corporate and general records

Capital stock register	Permanent
Cancelled stock certificate	Optional
Proxies and holders	2 years
Contracts and agreements	7 years
Ledgers	
General ledgers	Permanent
Cash books	Permanent
Journals	Permanent
Cancelled checks	Permanent
Corporate invoices	Permanent
Bank statements	5 years
Bank deposit slips	1 year
Fidelity bonds	3 years
Insurance records	3 years
Copies of tax records	Permanent
Records of furniture and fixtures	Permanent
Accountant and auditors reports	Permanent
Payroll records	
Payrolls and summaries	Permanent
Receipted pay checks	Permanent
Correspondence	6 years

extremely remote. It seems extravagant to invest in equipment to microfilm records just to guard against destruction.

One disadvantage of microfilming is that it usually condenses the unessentials along with the essentials in neatly packaged rolls, making too many details available for potential use and adding to the difficulties of locating the essential details. Another disadvantage is the seemingly innate tendency to microfilm even those records which can be inexpensively stored and then destroyed. The prime disadvantage is that the cost of microfilms held for periods far longer than their practical value is likely to exceed greatly the cost of storing the original documents for shorter periods of time and then destroying them.

The relative merits of microfilming as contrasted with a vigorous record destruction program can be demonstrated by comparing the cost of microfilming 10,000 documents, which are the contents of a four-drawer cabinet, with the cost of storing the same material for varying periods up to 7 years[1] (a period which coincides with the usual statute of limitations set by certain states for expiration of legal consequence relating to certain documents). To compute the cost of microfilming, the following items must be considered:

Labor for preparation of materials and filming by one employee—5 days	$ 80.00
Rent of machine @ $3.40 per day	17.00
Five rolls of film and development thereof @ $5 per roll	25.00
Total cost of filming 10,000 documents, the approximate contents of a four-drawer filing cabinet	$122.00

Cost of storing 10,000 documents in a four-drawer cabinet requiring 6 square feet for cabinet and open drawers:

Value of floor area per sq. ft.	Storage cost			
	1 year	*3 years*	*5 years*	*7 years*
$1.00	$ 6.00	$18.00	$ 30.00	$ 42.00
3.00	18.00	54.00	90.00	126.00
5.00	30.00	90.00	150.00	210.00

The taller the cabinets, the more material can be filed and retained within the same square-foot area. If the material is transferred to an eight-unit transfer file, the cost of storing for 7 years at $5 per square foot is reduced from $210 to $105.

[1]W. E. Mitchell, *Records Retention,* Ellsworth Publishing Company, 1963, pp. 57-58.

CHAPTER FIVE

Personnel Management

Three ingredients create and maintain an effective mortgage banking organization—capital, investors, and personnel. Capital, the prime ingredient, can be expressed and measured in quantitative terms; it represents the company's financial net worth and is shown in its financial statement. Investors served by the company constitute an intangible net worth of confidence that management has been able to inspire. These basic ingredients would come to very little without the productive efforts of personnel. This *unrecorded* "net worth" often bears little relationship to the measurable monetary value of the company. This is the basic reason why the actual size of a mortgage company—or, for that matter, of any company—cannot be measured by its capital alone. Without efficient, loyal personnel, successful operations cannot be maintained.

The subject of personnel management in mortgage banking can be presented only in broad outline here because of limitations of space. Likewise, the problem of management succession—the eventual replacement of owners and other key executives—can only be touched on here. This chapter will deal with general personnel philosophy and some of the day-to-day problems of personnel management.

First, a note on definitions. Although the term *management* is often used to identify the owners of the company or those responsible for its policy, its discussion here is confined to those functions of management specifically related to the management of men and women in a mortgage banking concern. The responsibility for these functions in a great number of organizations is now assumed by the loan administrator.

SCOPE AND RESPONSIBILITY

The basic responsibility of personnel management is *to recruit and maintain a stable, productive, and satisfied work force.* To accomplish this objective, the company, through its basic policies, must maintain an atmosphere conducive to performance to the top limit of each employee's ability.

Personnel management translates the philosophy of owners, stockholders, and managers into various daily acts relating to the handling of staff members. The success of management hinges not on particular personnel techniques, but on its beliefs about how to work through the efforts of others and the effectiveness with which it expresses these beliefs in its dealings with personnel. Personnel management is a continuous process involving management's attitude toward its employees and the policies by which employees are handled and treated, on both a daily and a long-range basis.

While the company's management establishes the overall personnel policies, it is the personnel manager who executes them, as well as contributes to them. His daily task consists of laying down, and executing, policies designed to establish and maintain an office force. He hires and discharges employees, imposes disciplinary actions where necessary, and undertakes training, education, and many other related functions.

MANAGEMENT PHILOSOPHY

The philosophy of management embodies its views about the worth of each employee, about his relationship to the company, and about the company's responsibility to him. Personnel management becomes, therefore, the concrete manifestation of the credo of the owners, leaders, or managers of the company about work and business; it demonstrates their principles, ideals, and opinions. The success of the company—and its degree of success over another company—depends almost solely on the attitude of the company and its personnel manager towards employees who actually spend the greatest part of the day working for the organization. This relationship hinges on mutual respect. The terms of his employment require that an employee do his best on the job; but, at the same time, he must depend on the firm for fair treatment.

Since so much in mortgage banking depends on the efforts of relatively few, teamwork is the key to the success of the organization. Teamwork, however, cannot be inspired overnight, nor induced by deferred or even immediate financial incentives alone. It can be established only through the development of mutual loyalty and cooperation, fostered by both management and employees.

Its size and occasionally its limited financial resources restrict a mortgage banking firm's ability to develop in depth in the manner of other financial institutions. Therefore, it must employ individuals with a broad range of talents, at both the supervisory and clerical levels, and be able to count on them for continuous cooperation and coordination of their productive efforts.

To ensure the continuity essential to any business operation, management in a mortgage banking organization must bring up its own successors. It must continuously build and, when necessary, replenish its manpower resources. It must attract people, develop the talents of its staff, and retain those who prove valuable.

PERSONNEL POLICIES

As a builder needs plans and specifications for building a house, the mortgage banker must have plans and specifications for building and maintaining his office staff. Faulty workmanship and poor material can wreck building and organization alike. To attract and retain above-average employees, management must make the company a good place to work. Better-than-competitive wages, short- as well as long-run incentives, and effective personnel are the usual means to this end. The day when compensation policy was played by ear—a favored method of paternalistic management—is quickly fading. In its place, a more scientific approach to the management of people has evolved.

Beyond providing adequate monetary rewards, personnel policies must be planned to answer the needs of employees for defined rules, security, opportunities for promotion, and fair treatment. Dissatisfied employees will not work efficiently, nor will they radiate the pleasantness essential to successful handling of customers and to cooperative relationships within the office.

What is difficult, however, is not the establishment and adoption of a good personnel policy, but the steady adherence to it. The company's personnel policies are usually not written; they are developed by management on a day-to-day basis and carried out by the personnel manager. Some ground rules should be written and published in an employment manual. (See Appendix A-3.) It should codify what is expected of employees in terms of attendance and good housekeeping as well as express the company's concern for the employee's welfare by listing various financial incentives, including profit sharing and provisions for vacations, hospitalization, and other insurance.

Repeated failure of the company to hold its employees signals the need for examination of personnel policies and for interviews with departing employees. Why do employees accept a job and then leave? Why did employment appear promising, wages and benefits adequate, and then suddenly unsatisfactory? Causes for turnover are many. Jobs, once interesting, may have become monotonous, or promises made by management may not have been kept. Nepotism, favoritism, poor or erratic supervision, and many other factors—obvious or barely perceptible—can cause dissatisfaction. Whatever the reason for it, turnover is an added expense, an expense for which no production is obtained. It wastes money and time, since departing employees take with them—many times to a competitor—all the training and education the company has provided.

Poor interviewing techniques, of course, can be quickly improved. But there is no quick and simple solution to the problem of holding employees, even those expertly matched to a job, if the atmosphere in the office, the spirit, the morale do not promote good performance. Employment policies, therefore, must achieve a two-pronged objective; (1) the employment of the best available talent and (2) the creation of the harmonious atmosphere needed to retain such talent.

One route to both parts of this objective, which cannot be overemphasized, lies in management's attitude toward staff. Although remuneration is important, it is not always foremost in the minds of a prospective employee. He is also concerned with his day-to-day and long-term relationship with his employer. The success of management and of the personnel manager will, therefore, depend largely on their approach to their employees as individuals, and the respect they show for their integrity and aspirations. The appropriate philosophy, though emanating from management, must permeate the supervisory staff. In whatever capacity they contribute to the company's profits, employees must also be encouraged to feel important. The company must recognize and fulfill the needs of its employees beyond financial rewards, those of recognition, a sense of belonging, and a feeling of participation in the affairs of the company.

Types of Compensation

In addition to salary, commissions, and bonus payments, a company's payroll includes such fringe benefits as paid vacations, hospitalization insurance, legally required payments to Social Security, old age benefit payments, and contributions to pension or profit-sharing plans. The payroll is usually the largest single expense for a company, normally accounting for close to 70 percent of the company's gross expenses.

Compensation of employees must be properly planned. Routine jobs must command competitive wages or better. Mortgage banking management must be especially sensitive to the needs of those with special talents, heads of departments, and employees on jobs of a nonroutine nature, such as a supervisor of the collection department, a loan closer, or an FHA loan processor. In these positions, payments must be commensurate with the unique responsibilities of decision making and risk taking. Amount of compensation—especially of bonus payments where these are applicable—should depend on the degree of authority an employee is given, how well he discharges it, and how little immediate, day-to-day supervision he requires.[1]

Various methods of compensation—direct or indirect, regular or incentive, cash or deferred payment—must be combined to attract and retain an excellent work force and to provide the greatest benefit to all employees as a group. Although certain employees are more responsible for profits than others, and should be rewarded accordingly, the success of all depends on strong teamwork. Depending on the type of incentive or job involved, differential plans of compensation for separate groups may work occasionally, but the most effective policy is the one which treats all employees on substantially an identical basis, even while it relates incentive rewards to each employee's contribution to the success of the company.

---

[1] The Research Committee of the Mortgage Bankers Association of America compiles information on executive salaries and compensation paid by its members and makes such information available to them.

An important aspect of compensation—a peculiarity of the modern business world—is to pay an employee not only for his present worth, but also for his potential as one of the leaders of the company. This technique is often the only way to retain and to develop future supervisors and department heads. Although the need to recognize future worth usually confronts management when dealing with supervisory or managerial talent, it can apply to loan producers, salesmen, or young administrators as well.

The best method of compensation is the *direct* payment of salary, commission, and bonus. As employees mature, in terms of both age and employment, they will show a greater interest in moneys to be enjoyed—and taxed—on retirement. This concern is, of course, usually felt by men and by older, single women; young women generally prefer immediate cash rewards.

Salaries In today's extremely competitive labor market in which basic skills, special talents, experience, and aptitude are equally hard to find, it is often better to pay slightly more-than-competitive salaries. Adequate replacements are not only expensive but also often well-nigh unobtainable. Furthermore, they require training, and training is costly, slows down performance, and ties down supervisors in less than fully productive activity.

Commissions A formula for additional compensation or commissions paid for producing residential or income property loans or insurance business or for selling real estate must be devised to suit the special circumstances that apply to the operation of the company and the various fields it covers. Care should be taken that a commission is paid only on business procured and consummated and that no commission is paid on "house" business. The distinction between new and old business is often very difficult to draw and must be made in advance, if possible, by senior management.

Bonuses Bonus payments are difficult to determine. The difference between a commission and a bonus is that a *commission arrangement* is usually part of the terms of employment, while a *bonus* is a *voluntary distribution of profits* by the company. In exceptionally good times, bonus payments may be made to all employees. In more normal periods, they may be paid only to those whose effective contribution to company profits can be measured by the dollar volume of business they produced. A year-end bonus may be paid to offset the wage differential that may develop between new and old employees. Bonuses may be paid for administrative excellence, for performance beyond the call of duty, and for overtime spent by supervisors which is not compensated on a month-to-month basis.

Employed properly, bonus payments are effective and flexible management tools. They can be made in good times and foregone when profits are low. They provide the flexibility to reward exceptional talent and to recognize routine clerks whose contribution to teamwork may be essential, but who would otherwise be overlooked for special reward. There is, however, one shortcoming to the practice. While bonuses normally produce continuous incentives and are discretionary distributions by management, once they appear to have become routine, those who have benefited come to expect them as a matter of course. When employees perform in accordance with the expectations of bonus payments, the real value of bonuses as incentives is seriously undermined.

Profit-sharing and pension plans Profit sharing or pensions, or a plan that combines the two by giving the employee an option to request a portion of his retirement benefits in cash each year, have several advantages. They call for specific contributions by the company; they are an unbiased distribution of profits; and they guarantee the growth of the plan and a distribution of accumulated benefits independent of the whim of management. Furthermore, profit-sharing and pension plans provide the postponement of tax payments on accumulated earnings until after retirement, when lower annual incomes reduce tax liabilities. Although profit-sharing and pension plans have become essential tools to hold valuable talent, most mortgage bankers have found that cash rewards must also be given if competing firms are not to lure away personnel with offers of higher direct compensation and promises of attractive cash bonuses.

Fringe Benefits

Most companies today supplement compensation, incentives, and pensions with fringe benefits, which have become both standard and expected by employees. These include:

Hospitalization insurance Many companies enroll all their employees in hospital and medical plans and pay all, or part of, the premium for either the employee or his dependents, or both. Major medical insurance is often arranged through a favored investor in that field.

Life insurance Group life insurance for the employee is also common. Specific plans, the amounts of insurance involved, and the extent of the company contribution vary from company to company.

Vacations Two weeks' vacation after a year's service is a standard fringe benefit. Many companies, however, offer a week's vacation after 6 months of service. As the company grows and the staff ages, vacation schedules are geared to length of service. A 3-week vacation is usual for an employee beginning with his fifteenth, or even his tenth, year of service

Use of car Some companies provide cars for their key employees. This privilege, of course, represents a considerable benefit to the employee since it can eliminate the need to use public transportation and the expense of purchasing and maintaining a car.

Lunchroom Offices employing more than twenty persons, especially those in locations with no convenient access to restaurants, offer their employees lunchrooms. These can range in elaborateness from small rooms, containing coffee or soft drink machines and a few tables and chairs for employees who bring their own lunches, to complete food service facilities.

THE PERSONNEL MANAGER

The personnel manager, a key man in any organization, exemplifies the philosophy of management, implements it, upholds it, and, if necessary defends it. In a larger sense, however, each personnel manager is a catalyst. On the one hand, he must with words and deeds carry out the policies of the management he represents; on the other hand, he must seek the best working conditions for the staff and represent them to management. If conflicts arise, he must see both points of view and search for the proper decision. Since he cannot please both sides on every occasion, his decisions must at least be respected as deliberate and fair, and not be subject to criticism as hasty or superficial.

The size of a mortgage banking organization usually determines the scope of the personnel manager's duties and responsibilities. In a small organization, the president of the company, who either is or represents management, performs all the personnel management functions. As the organization grows, managerial talent will be recruited by the head of the company, while the staff will be interviewed and hired by the office manager, loan administrator, or servicing manager. The loan administrator is usually best qualified to be personnel manager in the firm not yet requiring a full-time person. Knowing intimately the requirements of most of the jobs and generally supervising most of them directly, he is more likely than any other staff member to know the kinds of employees the company needs. His ability to assemble a qualified mortgage office team is crucial to the company's success.

A large organization, with management philosophies crystallized and personnel policies more fixed, requires a personnel manager responsible for all personnel functions except those relating to the few key executives who form the management team.

EMPLOYMENT OF PERSONNEL

Personnel selection can be described as the art of matching the individual seeking work with the position that is open. Difficult in any field, this task is even more demanding in mortgage banking, with its high degree of job specialization and diversification.

As useful as tests and accepted quantified standards of performance are, they are supplementary to the personnel manager's judgment about the applicant as the person for the job. The personality an applicant displays during an interview is a better introduction to his productive capabilities than skills which can be translated into test scores. Specific skills may be acquired when necessary, but personal shortcomings are not easily corrected in adulthood.

The good judgment and common sense of the interviewer are, therefore, more important hiring tools than tests or other objective methods. Similarly, these qualities in applicants—judgment, politeness, common sense—write a better recommendation than proof of high-level skills.

Furthermore, the lack of management depth in most mortgage banking organizations places a high premium on general, rather than specific skills for employees in most areas of operations. Nevertheless, another peculiarity of the mortgage banking business is that in areas of routine tasks, other than the most elementary operations such as typing, there is little similarity in specifications between jobs. Transfer from production to servicing, or vice versa, is very unlikely. If a transfer is contemplated or becomes necessary, however, it is easier to transfer a servicing employee, exposed to accounting and routine servicing requirements and accustomed to dealing with the public, to production activity, such as submission of loans or preparation of mortgage papers, than the other way around.

The Application Form

The qualities of personality and enthusiasm which will enable an employee to represent the company to the public and to be an effective member of the office team are more readily discovered by intelligent interviewing than by a lengthy and complicated application form. Besides not producing the essential, but intangible, information about the prospective employee, it can discourage him and compromise his trust in the company at the very point of his first contact with it. A simple job application card which requires name, address, telephone number, marital status, age, education, and other qualifications are all that is required. The applicant should also be asked to give the names and addresses of the two previous employers, and indicate the position he desires and the salary he expects.

The Interview

While the interview of the employer by the employee has become the accepted practice in some labor markets, it tends to distort the employer-employee relationship. The interviewer should promptly answer the applicant's questions about salary and fringe benefits, supply the employment manual, but otherwise hold the lead in the exchange. This often means simply letting the applicant talk, describe the jobs he has done, and explain why he left his last position. Occasionally, an applicant will talk himself out of the job faster than any test could disqualify him. In general, the interviewer should be looking for the well-rounded person, rather than one possessing specific skills alone. He should seek to identify quickly the best qualities in each applicant, and base his final decision on the presence or absence of those qualities.

The desirable combination of qualities, all or most of which are essential in one considered for more than routine work, consists of enterprise, decisiveness, energy, zeal, loyalty, and, that almost undefinable quality, a sense of urgency. The last is inherent only in a few, but it is the one that sets the best apart from the merely good.

For routine jobs, checking references is not essential. Properly interviewed, an applicant will sell or unsell himself during the first few minutes. Phone calls to former employers generally elicit a stereotyped, favorable response. If a prospective employee anticipates an unfavorable reference, he will forewarn the interviewer anyway. Letters of recommendation are seldom of value. If a less-than-contradictory reference is written, which is unlikely, it would not be offered by the applicant.

Personnel Records

The application card provides most of the information that the personnel manager and the payroll clerk initially require. As additional material accumulates on increases in pay, promotions, transfers, bonuses, vacations, and reason for resigning or dismissal, it should be meticulously recorded on a personnel record form. This record keeps management currently informed about each employee, and permits the personnel manager to provide up-to-date, accurate references when required to do so. A simple and practical means of maintaining personnel records is to file them in loose-leaf, two-ring binders in alphabetical order. As employees leave, cards can be removed from the active employment file binder and placed in an inactive file, available for any necessary further reference. Management owes departing employees as well as prospective employers the courtesy of providing accurate information.

Introduction of Employees

Trivial as it may seem, the appropriate introduction of new employees to other staff members and to the work routine is an important factor in harmonious personnel relationships. He must be given special attention on the first day on the job, as this produces the most lasting impression on the new employee. After the necessary withholding, hospitalization, and other forms have been signed, proper and unhurried introductions to his new colleagues pave the way for his acceptance as a member of the team. It is often desirable, especially in the case of a woman, to assign one of the employees of the department to keep a protective wing over a new employee for the first few days.

Intelligence or Aptitude Tests; Interview by Psychologist

If employees are obtained through reliable employment agencies and are carefully interviewed, special aptitude and intelligence tests should not be necessary. There is considerable disagreement on the desirability of special tests and interviews by psychologists for supervisory or other key positions. Most personnel managers, after a few years, develop the ability to distinguish between employable and unemployable people.

Tests often prove only that the individual possesses certain skills, not how he will apply them to the job. High scores on some form of intelligence test do not compensate for difficulty in adjusting to the work environment. Psychological tests can be useful to support conclusions reached during personal interviews, but they should serve only that purpose. The testers often describe their own reactions to a prospective employee rather than the qualifications he possesses.

Dismissal of Personnel

As a matter of policy, only the person responsible for hiring employees should be authorized to discharge them. Any employee who is discharged without an explanation should be given an opportunity to discuss the situation with management. This ensures equitable procedures and provides management with valuable insights into the effectiveness of its supervisors.

Dismissals should never be made in anger. Supervisors should not have authority to dismiss, but only the responsibility to recommend that such action be taken. It is wise to inform the employee who is to be discharged of (1) the reason for dismissal, (2) the compensation to be made through salary in lieu of notice, accumulated vacation pay, or both, (3) insurance entitlement or any other benefits accrued and to be paid, and (4) the character of the references which will be given.

Personnel Review

Management should periodically review the performance of its staff with both their supervisors and the employees themselves. At the time of employment, each employee must be informed of this practice, for it will encourage those who aspire to progress. Moreover, the review will assure management of a staff always in tune with the demands of the work.

Unfortunately, most departmental or individual personnel reviews do not take place on a regular, scheduled basis. They are often made only as emergencies and problems arise within a department, or when flare-ups occur and someone quits or has to be discharged. It is therefore advisable to review the status of personnel systematically at least once a year, not simply specifically to consider a raise or bonus, but to foster both the employee's personal growth and the company's ultimate aims.

A once-a-year salary review for the entire staff is preferable to a review of each employee's salary on the anniversary date of his employment. While such reviews require several days' conference in large organizations, the time is well spent in the interests of good personnel policies. After such a conference, the personnel manager must discuss with each employee all determinations about him, and inform him of raises or bonuses, or of their being withheld, and the reasons.

The loyalty many managements feel toward employees with long service is justified, and for the most part respected and valued by all employees, whether or not they are its beneficiaries. This feeling should, however, not deter management from transferring those employees to less demanding work if they cannot meet new requirements.

TRAINING AND EDUCATION

After hiring a capable employee, management should take a continued interest in his educational growth. This will help the ambitious employee grow and progress and be of long-run benefit to the company. The company's educational efforts consist of on-the-job training and the educational activities which mortgage banking and allied industries offer. In the early stages of employment, nothing can promote the morale of an ambitious employee more than the opportunity to attend or participate in a meeting on behalf of his company.

Training

Training means learning the rules of the job. The immediate supervisor should make the effort to explain not only the job, but the reason for each step, to each new employee. The broader the pictures presented, the sooner the employee will learn his job. Various operations manuals are also quite useful for this purpose. The importance of training new employees cannot be overemphasized. Even a capable person may fail in his new assignment if it is not properly explained, if his work is not carefully supervised at the outset, or if errors are not identified as they occur.

Although the office manager may not have the time to personally undertake the training of all new employees, he should supervise it constantly. Department heads or employees with a thorough knowledge of the requirements of the particular job are best at training.

In a medium- or large-size company, the servicing manager should train an assistant so that the smooth functioning of his department is not dependent on his continuous presence. There should always be members in each organization prepared to move up and take over jobs in an emergency. It is good practice for key persons to teach their job to the next in line in order to prevent a crisis in the event he leaves and a successor has been neither selected nor trained.

Each company should establish a program designed to acquaint new employees with the rudiments of the mortgage business. An operations guide (Appendix A-1) can serve as an outline for such orientation sessions.

An employee who sees beyond his own task, who has a grasp of the overall picture of mortgage banking, will do a better job and will make considerably faster progress than one who understands only his own particular job. Many mortgage banking firms conduct regular training sessions for new employees of a half-hour a day for as long as a week. Orientation lectures are conducted by the loan administrator, personnel manager, or department heads. Courses on new office equipment, office etiquette, and flaws in customer relations, for example, may be offered on a regular basis to all employees. In case of equipment conversion or absorption of one company by another, orientation lectures are imperative for all employees, both new and established.

Education

The ambitious employee, eager to learn, is a great asset. No opportunity should be missed to capitalize on his interest by both training and educating him. While in-house training may be restricted by lack of time, space, or qualified instructors, there are limitless outside educational opportunities in the mortgage banking field. Many trade associations, concerned with management or business in general, conduct courses of interest to supervisors and staff people. If the company is too small to conduct its own program, the personnel manager should seek out aspiring, talented employees and send them to various schools, training programs, or meetings sponsored by local mortgage banking groups, real estate groups, or the Mortgage Bankers Association of America (MBA).

School of Mortgage Banking Of the many programs sponsored by the Mortgage Bankers Association of America, the School of Mortgage Banking, in session each summer at Northwestern, Stanford, and Miami Universities, is the most fundamental and intensive. It is designed to give a broad background in mortgage banking. The school comprises three courses which encompass material ranging from the undergraduate to the postgraduate level. Each requires a full week's attendance at one of the universities, plus two interspersed home-study programs. A diploma is awarded upon successful completion. Attendance is limited to those sponsored by MBA member firms.

Loan administration conferences and clinics Normally, two clinics are held each year in different locations. These meetings are limited to loan administration and related subjects.

Other educational opportunities In many states and larger cities, local mortgage banking associations sponsor programs designed to educate either the general public or members of the local mortgage banking, real estate, or insurance fraternity. These include meetings as well as more extended courses.

EMPLOYMENT MANUAL

As the company grows both in number of employees and in the area in which it operates, need arises for the codification of rules by which it operates. To serve this purpose, an employment manual is usually prepared by the personnel manager, or where this position does not exist, by the loan administrator. It is not only a handy tool for the indoctrination of new employees, but a guide to the office manager or supervisor in administering the company's policies. It assures employees that rules are not made up to deal with particular situations, but are invoked in a fair and uniform manner. The larger the company, of course, the more elaborate the manual has to be. This is especially true if more than one official hires new employees or if the company maintains branch offices.

A good employment manual contains all the information an employee ought to know about the company. A typical booklet includes, beside a brief description of the history, table of organization, operations, and basic work rules of the company, answers to some of the questions new employees may raise during an interview. These might concern hours (daily schedule, lunchtime arrangements); salaries (payment dates, deductions); vacations; promotions and transfers; absence and sick leave provisions; and the circumstances surrounding termination of employment. It should also contain a description of all the benefits the company provides for its employees, including hospitalization and group life insurance; profit-sharing or retirement plan; and lunchroom. (See Appendix A-3.)

The employment manual may be combined with the operations guide, although each covers a distinct area. Employment manuals must be amended and reprinted as extensive revisions are made, but minor changes may be noted by handwritten amendments until the number is sufficient to warrant a new printing. Companies with less than twenty employees can mimeograph the manual; rather than present it in printed form.

EMPLOYEE SUGGESTION SYSTEM

As the size of the organization increases, the daily personal contact of the manager with his staff diminishes, the intimacy bred of daily contact among a small staff fades, and an office which ran on a comfortable, first-name basis inevitably takes on a less personal aspect. At this point, a more formal employee suggestion system may have to supplement or supplant the casual, if effective, day-to-day exchanges by which an employee could communicate his ideas for improving either his own performance or the company's overall operations. Furthermore, an incentive payment system for practical suggestions may have to take the place of the more tenuous reward of the year-end bonus or raise.

It must be emphasized that the size of the organization is not always the factor determining whether a formal suggestion system is required. Many medium- and even large-size companies can maintain a family-type atmosphere, in which ideas readily flow between staff and management. What kind of communication system a company needs usually depends on how well the personnel manager handles management-employee liaison.

The formal employee suggestion system is based on the theory that employees need an opportunity both to voice their criticism and to make suggestions for the improvement of service or operations. Its requirements are an official procedure through which views and suggestions can be channeled, and encouragement and reward can be passed on to those who submit good ideas. This, of course, can also be accomplished under an informal arrangement. The regular annual job and performance review already recommended can reduce the need for an employee suggestion system, since it affords regular opportunities to each employee to air his complaints and make his suggestions.

Those who urge the formal employee suggestion system maintain that (1) the person on the job usually knows more about it than the supervisor or manager and his valuable suggestions may be used to reduce costs, improve service, or both; and (2) the employee may be reluctant, if the manager-employee relationship is a formal one, to present his ideas, because he is not sure they will receive recognition or be used. The validity of these contentions, of course, goes back once again to the strength and depth of the relationship. If management is as anxious to please employees as employees are to satisfy management, no formal suggestion system is required.

Here are some steps to be used where a system is judged necessary: (1) establish a suggestion box; (2) appoint administrators to review suggestions; (3) create a committee to evaluate suggestions and to reward those that are good; (4) recognize and reward those who develop good ideas and give explanations to those whose ideas are not accepted so that they will be encouraged to try again; and (5) follow up to assure that ideas are put to use.

Employee suggestion systems may, of course, also be used to receive complaints and suggestions about general office policies. A simple form can be provided to elicit suggestions.

One of the dangers in adopting a formal system in organizations of less than one hundred employees, particularly in the mortgage business, arises from the special relationships that exist: a great many different jobs are so closely intertwined that a change in one cannot be accomplished without affecting the others. Another is the difficulty in attributing to a single employee a suggestion others may have had from the point of view of another department. No greater harm can be done morale than by rewarding the reporter rather than the originator of an idea. This is especially true where a supervisor takes credit for the idea of a member of his staff. Even while employees are encouraged to communicate their ideas to their superiors, and supervisors are in turn encouraged to pass them on to management, management must take special care that attribution and reward are appropriately made. A formalized suggestion system, which gives employees a direct channel to management, may best accomplish this purpose.

CHAPTER SIX

Financial and Fiduciary Responsibilities

The mortgage banker's stock in trade is credit. He marshals his own capital and funds borrowed from commercial banks to originate mortgage loans. He sells the mortgage loans to investors, replenishing his capital or repaying his bank. Accordingly, the mortgage banking business is a carousel of lending, repaying, borrowing, and lending again. As each turn of the carousel is completed, the mortgage banker also assumes the responsibility of collecting monthly payments for the owner of the permanent mortgage and accumulating reserves for payment of taxes and insurance.

Although his financial and fiduciary responsibilities are three-pronged, each transaction must be recorded on the company's books—whether it involves the company's funds, the borrowers' funds, or investors' funds. This suggests that two accounting paths should be established: one for corporate accounting, which involves responsibility for the company's funds; another for mortgage loan accounting, which involves responsibility for borrowers' and investors' funds. In actual practice, however, the boundaries cannot be precisely determined, and supervision of accounting activities is fundamentally inseparable.

This fact complicates, but clearly does not obviate, the need for proper accounting records and procedures built upon sound accounting principles. Accounting processes must produce a financial picture of the company's development and growth as well as its present condition. They must provide the information needed to assure borrowers and investors that the mortgage banker is fulfilling his fiduciary responsibilities. They must also provide the information needed to reach decisions on conversion of equipment, purchase and sale of servicing or of entire companies, and feasibility of diversification.

The accounting process begins with appropriate accounting procedures, ledgers on which lending transactions can be recorded, and controls that assure the accuracy of each transaction. It involves opening bank accounts, segregating funds while in the temporary care of the company, and organizing an orderly flow of lendable funds. The necessary accounting tasks include recording income and expense items, checking their accuracy, balancing accounts on a day-to-day basis and a month-to-month basis, auditing transactions, and preparing statements that report financial accomplishments. Finally, and perhaps most importantly, financial responsibility entails the effective use of the company's capital to maximize profits, as well as the preservation and protection of the company's assets.

Automation has increased the speed and improved the accuracy of accounting, and has eliminated circuitous routes formerly traveled to reach accounting objectives. But automation has in no way changed or eliminated the application of accounting principles to the procedure it facilitates. Since all improvements and refinements are built on the same basic accounting principles, this book emphasizes principles rather than detailed descriptions of specific accounting tasks. In this chapter, the financial and fiduciary responsibilities of the mortgage company as a whole are discussed. Those responsibilities that the company undertakes in the course of handling borrowers' and investors' funds are discussed in Chapter 14, Mortgage Loan Accounting Department.

Readers who are unfamiliar with the accounting terminology used in mortgage banking will find it helpful to consult "MBA's Suggested Chart of Accounts and Financial Statements for Mortgage Banking Companies" for technical guidance in setting up the proper accounting framework for mortgage banking transactions. (See Appendix A-4.) This chapter assumes that all, or a majority of, the recommendations made in "MBA's Chart of Accounts" have already been adopted or are being considered for adoption.

ACCOUNTING ACTIVITY

In the mortgage business, the responsibility for corporate accounting is normally under the supervision and purview of the treasurer or the controller of the company. Either of these posts may be held by, or shared with, the loan administrator. In large companies, responsibilities are divided among the treasurer, the controller, and the loan administrator. Smaller companies normally have only one person responsible for all the above jobs.

A mortgage banking firm usually chooses one of two methods of allocating accounting assignments and financial and fiduciary responsibilities. The entire financial and fiduciary task may be assigned to the loan administrator. A controller and a chief accountant, who heads the Accounting Department, may report to the loan administrator. In this case, the controller is in charge of the corporate books, and the chief accountant is responsible for the mortgage loan accounting function. Alternately, the fiscal and fiduciary responsibilities may be divided between the loan administrator, as treasurer, and the controller. In this case, the loan administrator is the policy-making accounting officer, and the controller the operating accounting officer; and the line of demarcation between corporate and mortgage loan accounting functions may not be clearly drawn.

It is important, however, to establish the respective areas of activities of the loan administrator and the controller so they cover all areas and slightly overlap most areas of accounting activity. This is especially important because the mortgage loan accounting process which involves the handling of loans purchased by investors follows the corporate accounting path, and because corporate accounting channels are often used for handling payments and their dissemination to investors. While the treasurer should be responsible for banking operations, the controller should either be involved or have a continuous working knowledge of the arrangements. Similarly, while the controller, the chief accountant, and the manager of data processing, if there is one, should be up-to-date on the accounting requirements of investors, the treasurer should also know the broad outlines of these procedures.

The duties and responsibilities of the company accounting officer, whether the loan administrator, treasurer, or controller, include:

1 Establishment of accounting systems
2 Establishment of loan accounting records
3 Establishment of lines of bank credit
4 Establishment of various bank accounts
5 Preparation of monthly financial statements, operating reports, and other accounting by-products, such as statistical and cost accounting information
6 Establishment of check-signing authority
7 Protection of company assets by means of internal control procedures, audits by outside firms, hazard and fidelity insurance, and "errors and omissions" protection
8 Deliberations and assistance concerning financial and accounting matters dealing with conversions, acquisitions, and mergers
9 Supervision of mortgage loan accounting

Establishment of Accounting Systems

A mortgage banking organization normally seeks to establish systems, records, and procedures in conformity with accepted practices, such as methods and systems created by fellow mortgage bankers and generally endorsed by the Mortgage Bankers Association of America. Most mortgage banking firms tend to orient their record-keeping systems toward the requirements of their principal investors. This does not mean that each mortgage banker merely copies its fellow bankers' systems and records. Rather it means that there are usually so few variations in the procedures followed that fundamentally all the different accounting systems employed to process and account for payments could be easily merged into one.

The demand for depositing funds promptly and for simultaneous segregation of funds not belonging to the mortgage banker has tested the inventiveness of mortgage banking firms. Today, the task is accomplished with simplicity, especially when data processing equipment is used to process payment cards.

The adoption of standards has, of course, simplified many of the accounting chores. In mortgage banking today, investors receive almost identical reports. Auditors review financial statements, which are based essentially on almost identical accounting systems. Only the various approaches to handling and processing borrowers' payments have not become uniform, as is explained in Chapter 13, Cashier Department.

It is essential to reemphasize here that in the operations of a mortgage banking entity there are two intertwined, and often overlapping, accounting paths—corporate accounting and mortgage loan accounting—and that while loans are placed on the books under a corporate accounting system, as soon as they are disbursed and paid for by investors, the same loan records are removed from the corporate accounting records and are placed into the mortgage loan accounting workstream. The accounting machinery, therefore, will always consist of these parallel records, with switching from one track to another when a loan is sold to an investor.

To illustrate the workings of these two systems and their interrelation, it is necessary first to establish basic accounting records for loans.

Establishment of Loan Accounting Records

Actually, the mortgage banker does not have a merchantable mortgage—even though the mortgage papers are signed and recorded—until the funds are disbursed. Before the proceeds of a loan are disbursed or simultaneously with such disbursement, a mortgage loan ledger record must be established on which information on the loan itself, in terms of a credit for the loan amount and subsequently the disbursements and other entries, may be recorded. In this manner, "merchandise" is being produced and placed in the inventory.

On the following pages, the placement of a residential loan on the books of a company is described in detail. The various entries leading to the establishment and subsequent closing of such records on the company's books are also explained. The description follows a fairly elementary approach in order to acquaint each reader with the mechanics of posting loan disbursements and with the reason for each entry and each mortgage accounting term. This demonstration of mortgage accounting principles should develop an understanding of basic mortgage accounting systems and records.

At the time, or just before, a loan is disbursed, two accounting ledger cards must be prepared. One may be called *loan disbursement* or *borrower's ledger card,* and the other *loan inventory card.* On the borrower's ledger card, only the payout transactions are recorded. (See Exhibit 11.) On the loan inventory card, which provides a record of some of the offsetting entries to the loan disbursement card, the loan as an inventory item is recorded and established. The loan inventory card is part of the company's loan inventory records; it represents a mortgage loan and as such is included among the assets of the company in the asset side of the balance sheet. The loan inventory

EXHIBIT 11 Borrower's ledger card

BORROWER JONES, ADAM & CECILIA	**ADDRESS OF PROPERTY** 317 MAIN STREET
	SUN CITY, ILLINOIS

SHEET NO. 1   **LOAN NO.** GI 69715

FIRST PAYMENT DATE December 1, 1968

AMOUNT OF LOAN $ 15,000.00

PERMANENT INTEREST RATE   6   %

FINAL INSPECTION PROCESSED   **TAKE UP #**

CONSTRUCTION INTEREST RATE   %

FINAL STATEMENT SENT

Service Fee: 1% - Discount: 4%

DESCRIPTION	DATE	REF.	DEBIT	CREDIT	BALANCE	PROOF FACTOR
FIRST MORTGAGE LOAN JONES GI 69715	10/16/68	69715		15,000.00	15,000.00	
1% ORIGINATION FEE	10/16/68	3715	150.00		14,850.00	
4% DISCOUNT	10/16/68	6716	600.00		14,250.00	
RELIABLE FIRE & MARINE HOMEOWNERS 10/15/68 - 10/15/69	10/16/68	313	45.00		14,205.00	
ACCURATE TITLE AND TRUST COMPANY TITLE POLICY	10/16/68	417	73.00		14,132.00	
TRANSFER - REAL ESTATE TAX RESERVE 2 MONTHS	10/16/68	tr6	60.00		14,072.00	
TRANSFER - HAZARD INSURANCE RESERVE 2 MONTHS	10/16/68	tr6	7.50		14,064.50	
INTEREST 10/15/68 - 11/1/68	10/16/68	13720	35.93		14,028.57	
DUE FROM PURCHASER - JONES	10/16/68	c789		906.93	14,935.50	
PROCEEDS OF LOAN DUE SELLER	10/16/68	ck3399	14,935.50		.00	

ABC MORTGAGE COMPANY

83

card will become the loan ledger card on which monthly repayments of principal and interest will eventually be recorded.

After the completion of the disbursements, the borrower's ledger card strikes a zero balance and may be filed. When the first payment on the loan is received, the loan inventory ledger card becomes a "repayment" card on which monthly payments are recorded. When the loan is sold to an investor, this card is removed from loan inventory and placed with the cards for other loans owned by that investor.

Since the loan disbursement process is actually initiated and completed during the "loan-closing" transaction, all entries that appear on the borrower's ledger card usually correspond to the items which appear on the loan-closing statement. The preparation of the closing statement is normally the function of the loan-closing staff of the mortgage banker or of an employee of a title company who either disburses the loan or directs the loan to be disbursed. One statement prepared for the benefit of the borrower shows what he owes and the other prepared for the seller shows what he will receive. The statement normally also accounts for the closing expenses, the various fees, and charges and escrow reserves required in connection with the loan.

Establishment of Loan Inventory Card, Recording of Loan Disbursements, and Recording of Sale of Loan to Investor

To place loans on the books, and subsequently record the sale of these loans to investors, two separate transactions must be performed. These are identified on the diagram (Exhibit 12) as *Transaction I* and *Transaction II*. The diagram is designed to provide the reader with a step-by-step description of the bookkeeping entries involved.

The basic accounting information may be obtained from the mortgage documents, from the loan application, or from a specially prepared information sheet which has been identified by a loan number and on which the terms of the mortgage and the fees and discounts to be collected, if any, have been clearly stated.

To avoid errors, the loan administrator should make certain, if, during the preparation of mortgage papers, changes in terms, fees, or dates are agreed upon, that these are corrected on the loan application or information sheet, whichever is used to set up accounting records. Differing information on interest rate or dates of first payment would adversely affect the loan-closing transaction, and might also result in loss of revenue or create an overcharge.

Information on the required monthly payments and escrow payment requirements need not be made available to the bookkeeper maintaining the borrower's ledger cards. This information must, however, be conveyed to the cashiers and those in the mortgage loan accounting department who will be responsible for servicing the loan.

Data which do not affect the accounting transactions of setting up the loan but which are necessary for understanding the illustrated accounting transaction include: the purchase price of the property, which in this case was $16,000, and an earnest money deposit of $1,000 which was made by the purchaser. This latter sum, of course,

EXHIBIT 12 Diagram establishing loan inventory card

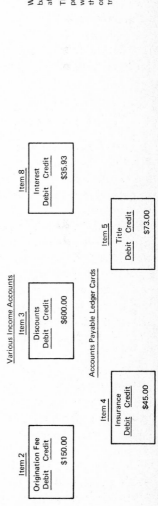

TRANSACTION I

Recording loan disbursement and establishing Loan Inventory Card

Jones (G1 69715)
Borrower's Ledger Card (Exhibit 11)

	Debit	Credit
Item 1		$15,000.00
Item 2	$150.00	
Item 3	600.00	
Item 4	45.00	
Item 5	73.00	
Item 6	60.00	
Item 7	7.50	
Item 8	35.93	
Item 9		906.93
Item 10	14,935.50	
	$15,906.93	$15,906.93

Loan Inventory Card

JONES   G1 69715

Payment	Principal	Interest	Reserves
	$ 15,000.00		$67.50

Payment due 12/1

TRANSACTION II

Recording sale of loan to investor

Loan Ledger Card

JONES   G1 69715

Payment	Principal	Interest	Reserves
$14.94	$15,000.00	$75.00	$ 67.50
	14,985.06	$33.75	101.25

formerly "loan inventory card"

Various Income Accounts

Item 3

Discounts
Debit   Credit
$600.00

Item 8

Interest
Debit   Credit
$35.93

Accounts Payable Ledger Cards

Item 2

Origination Fee
Debit   Credit
$150.00

Item 4

Insurance
Debit   Credit
$45.00

Item 5

Title
Debit   Credit
$73.00

When the investor pays for a loan, it pays the unpaid principal balance, namely $15,000.00, before Dec. 1, and $14,985.06 after Dec. 1 as illustrated above.

The purchase price is credited to loan inventory and the appropriate card (Jones loan) removed from the inventory and placed with cards representing loans already owned by the investor. At the same time escrow reserves held in the ABC custodial account ($67.50 before Dec. 1, or $101.25 after that date) are transferred by check to the investor's custodial reserve account.

85

is accounted for in the loan-closing statement, but is not reflected on the borrower's ledger card.

Transaction I involves setting up a loan on the corporate accounting ledger; Transaction II entails recording receipt of payment for a loan from an investor. As a consequence of this latter entry, the loan inventory card is transferred to mortgage loan accounting. Hereafter, all payments collected on the loan are recorded on the loan ledger card and all payments (less servicing fees) are sent to the purchaser of the mortgage. At the same time, all custodial funds held in company custodial accounts are transferred to the investor's segregated escrow reserve account

Transaction I: recording a loan on the company's accounting ledger   To set up the loan records for "Loan GI67915—Jones," certain entries must be made. Each entry, whether representing cash received, checks issued, or journal entries and the respective offsetting entries, if any, is described and illustrated on a borrower's ledger card (Exhibit 11), which shows each transaction, as well as on Exhibit 12 which shows the offsetting entries on various general ledger and income account cards after each entry is made. The ten numbers correspond with those on the exhibits.

	Debit	Credit
Item 1: First mortgage loan (GI 69715)		$15,000

This item represents the face amount of the loan Jones agreed to repay. By crediting the borrower's ledger card, Jones in essence is given $15,000 to spend for the purchase of a home.

The offsetting entry is a debit on a GI loan inventory card, which then becomes part of an inventory of GI loans. As soon as a check is issued, the loan becomes the mortgage banker's asset. In other industries, this item would be equivalent to "goods in process" or "goods held for sale."

	Debit	Credit
Item 2: One percent origination fee	$150	

This item represents the fee the mortgage banker charges the borrower for his services in making the loan. It can be either deducted from the loan proceeds as shown on Exhibits 11 and 12 or collected separately. Charges for making loans to be insured by FHA or to be guaranteed by VA are regulated by the respective agencies; the maximum origination fee is presently 1 percent for residential home mortgages and $2\frac{1}{2}$ percent for construction loans. The offsetting entry is a credit to the income ledger account (see Exhibit 12 under Transaction I).

There are several practices as to when the origination fee, which is collected at the time the loan is closed, disbursed, and entered on the income account, is taken into profit on the company books. The prevailing practice is to consider the origination fee earned when the mortgage loan is disbursed; some hold that it should not be considered earned until the loan is delivered and paid for by the investor, on the theory that the mortgage banker's job is not completed until the loan has been sold and is being serviced. In the meantime, the origination fee is usually carried in an *unearned service fee* or *deferred income account,* and when the loan is sold, a discount gain or loss is also recorded for each individual loan involved.

Similarly, some mortgage bankers maintain that a service fee on a construction loan is not earned until all the funds are disbursed. Many take only that portion of the service fee into income which relates to the dollar amount disbursed. If $50,000 of a $100,000 commercial loan is disbursed, one-half of a 2 percent fee would be considered earned with one-half held in the unearned commission account. This becomes a sound practice particularly in the case of a large construction loan with construction disbursements stretching out over a long period of time.

	Debit	*Credit*
Item 3: Four percent discount		$600

FHA and VA loans are subject to maximum ceilings on the contract interest rate, which are established by the federal agencies. When the contract rate is less than the yield available to investors in other investment markets, the mortgage loan must be sold at a discount. Roughly calculated, a two-point discount increases the yield by $\frac{1}{4}$ of 1 percent.

In this example, the investor's yield requirement is slightly more than 6 percent. The ceiling was fixed at 6 percent, and the cost of servicing was $\frac{1}{2}$ of 1 percent. A discount of 4 percent had to be charged to provide a 6.02 percent yield to the investor, or the mortgage was originated and sold at a price of 96 percent of its face value. Thus, the discount is a reduction in the price of the mortgage, calculated to adjust the yield earned by investors.

The use of discount does not usually apply to conventional loans, since a conventional mortgage will be granted at an interest rate which prevails when the loan is made. Exceptions occur in periods when market yields exceed interest rate ceilings fixed by state laws. According to FHA and VA regulations the discount cannot be paid by the borrower. It must be paid by the seller or broker, or both. In the case of construction loans, the discount must be paid by the builder. Due to the vagaries of the money market, discounts often can be as high as 10 to 12 points in certain areas and on certain types and kinds of loans. Favorable money conditions, however, would require the investor to pay in excess of $1 for each dollar of loan amount. Payment in excess of par is called a *premium*.

The 4 percent discount of $600 in connection with the Jones loan is credited to the discount account to be held aside as a credit to be applied against the inventory item of $15,000. Actually, for the valuation of the mortgage banker's loan inventory at the end of his fiscal year, each discount item is charged against the inventory. Thus, the Jones loan would only be shown as an asset of $14,400. It is important to remember, however, that Jones will repay a $15,000 mortgage.

If a loan is sold at a discount other than at which it was made, a profit is realized or a loss is sustained. If a loan of $15,000 placed on the books at a 4 percent discount, i.e., $600, can subsequently only be sold at a 5 percent discount, i.e., $750, a loss of $150 is sustained. Conversely, if the same loan is sold at 3 percent as a result of a price betterment in the mortgage market, a $150 profit is realized.

To reflect a mortgage banker's financial position properly at the end of the company's fiscal year, it is necessary to revalue mortgage loan inventories for financial statement purposes at market prices rather than at cost. Principal payments made on the loan before its sale to an investor, depending on the size of the discount, may create further nominal losses or nominal gains depending on the direction of the market.

	Debit	*Credit*
Item 4: Homeowner's policy		$45

This item represents the first year's premium on a 3-year homeowner's policy which covers the Jones' property. In this instance, the mortgage banker was successful in selling an insurance policy to the prospective mortgagor. The offsetting entry is a credit to an accounts payable ledger card bearing the name of the insurance company which wrote the policy. The check in payment of the premium for this policy, together with payment for other policies, will then be charged against this accounts payable account. Insurance regulatory agencies of certain states require that funds held to pay a premium be deposited into a *premium trust account* pending payment of bills to agency or company.

If the prospective borrower had purchased his policy elsewhere, he would be asked to present such policy at closing, providing, of course, that the policy was approved by the insurance department or by the loan closer as to the issuing insurance company, adequacy of coverage, and the mortgage clause. In this instance, a receipt would have to be exhibited that insurance was paid for. The existence of insurance coverage is imperative; without such coverage, loan proceeds would never be disbursed.

	Debit	*Credit*
Item 5: Title charges		$73

Charges paid to a title company for preliminary title work and title insurance policy can be recorded by debiting the borrower's ledger card and by crediting the title company's account, or by drawing a check and charging it to the borrower's ledger card and sending it directly to the title company. If a journal entry is used, i.e., if the amount of the bill is charged to the borrower's ledger and then credited to the title company's account, many similar bills may be posted in one operation, each charged to a different borrower's account. The title company is then paid from this account by means of one single check.

	Debit	*Credit*
Item 6: Transfer; real estate tax reserves		
2 months		$60

Government-insured and government-guaranteed loans require, and conventional loans may stipulate, that monthly deposits be made by the borrower to the lender to accumulate sufficient funds to pay real estate tax bills when due. In the community in which the Jones' loan was made, the tax payments are due on October 1 of each year, and since the first payment of the loan, which includes requirements for tax deposits, is December 1, it is necessary to collect at closing tax reserves for the 2 months. Based on an anticipated tax bill of $360, the escrow deposit for taxes for October and November, or $60, was collected.

Debit   *Credit*

Item 7: Transfer; hazard insurance reserve

    2 months $7.50

Government-insured and government-guaranteed loans require, and conventional loans may stipulate, that monthly deposits be made by the borrower to lender to accumulate sufficient funds to pay hazard insurance premiums when they become due. Since the second year's premium on the policy the borrower purchased will become due October 15, 1969, and the monthly payments which call for an insurance reserve deposit of $3.75 ($45 dividend by 12) commence on December 1, 1968, it is necessary to set aside $7.50 for October and November from the proceeds of the loan to accumulate sufficient funds to pay the premium before October 1, 1969. The total deposits transferred to the escrow account will then amount to $67.50, which represents 2 months' tax reserves and 2 months' insurance reserves.

Debit   *Credit*

Item 8: Interest $35.93

Although practices as to charges of interest at the time of loan disbursement differ, it is recommended that for consistency's sake all charges and allowances be related to the date of first payment; remember always that a mortgage note specifies that interest is charged for a 30-day period preceding the due date of the principal payment. In this case, the first payment is due December 1, which covers interest for the period November 1 to December 1. Since funds were disbursed on October 15, a charge for 15 days' interest is in order. If funds had been disbursed on November 5, for instance, the borrower would have had to be given a 5 days' interest credit.

Debit   *Credit*

Item 9: Due from purchaser $906.93

This item is the borrower's additional cash investment in his home at the time of closing. It represents the difference between the sales price of the house less the amount of the mortgage and the *earnest money* deposited with the real estate broker. This sum includes a deduction for the origination fee, and normally reflects proration of tax bills and insurance premiums. This item is collected at closing and is given to the cashier for deposit. It subsequently is posted to the borrower's ledger card.

Debit   *Credit*

Item 10: Proceeds due to seller $14,935.50

This sum represents the proceeds of the loan, the amount due the seller. In this case, it represents the sale price of the home less the seller's share of the expenses including the discount. It is fully accounted for, and explained in, a *loan-closing statement.* The sum is disbursed in the form of a check and is charged against the borrower's ledger card.

Transaction II: recording sale of loan to investor After the completion of the loan transaction, the processing for insurance by FHA or guaranty by VA, as applicable, and the assignment of the mortgage documents to the investor, the loan package is delivered to the investor for payment. The time lapse between closing and delivery is usually 30 to 45 days. Investors normally pay for loans within 10 to 15 days if the documents are in order.

When the investor pays the outstanding principal of a loan, the loan is removed from the loan inventory account, and the individual inventory card representing a specific loan is transferred into the mortgage loan accounting card tray (see Exhibit 12). The entries relative to discounts and interest involving the sale of the loan to the investor have no bearing on the principal balance of the loan; they are merely credits or debits to the discount or interest accounts, respectively.

Investors, when purchasing a loan, normally deduct the discount. The discount is based on the unpaid balance of the loan, which is reduced by monthly payments made after closing, but before the time of purchase.

If the investor makes the purchase before the first payment is received, the investor will pay $15,000 for the loan and will deduct a $600 discount. Upon recording the purchase, the reserves on hand totaling $67.50, which were transferred from the borrower's ledger to the mortgage banker's custodial account, are now transferred to that purchasing investor's escrow reserve account.

If the purchase of the loan by the investor occurs after Jones makes the first payment on the loan, the loan balance will be reduced from $15,000 to $14,985.06. The 4 percent discount will be $599.40 instead of $600. Similarly, the receipt of first payment, which includes $30 for tax reserves and $3.75 for hazard insurance reserves, has bearing on the reserve account and results in a transfer of a total of $101.25 ($67.50 + $30 + $3.75) to the investor's escrow reserve account, rather than merely $67.50.

It has to be borne in mind that upon receipt of the investor's check, the VA loan inventory must be credited with $15,000, or $14,985.06, and the discount account charged with $600, or $599.40, respectively. In the latter case, additional income of 60 cents will be earned by the mortgage banker.

Investors normally pay accrued interest at the rate at which the loan was sold to them, i.e., contract rate less the servicing fee, from the first of the month preceding purchase to the date of payment. Thus, no adjustment of interest will become necessary when the borrower remits and the servicer forwards that payment to which the investor has become entitled. It is at this time that the mortgage banker receiver his first full month's servicing fee.

If the investor does not pay interest from the first of the month preceding the purchase of the loan, the first interest remittance to the investor must be adjusted, since the borrower pays a full month's interest while the investor earns his interest only from the date of purchase. To avoid this confusion, accrued interest is normally paid by all investors. This procedure, compiled with the adjustment of interest charges and credits at closing, makes the posting and processing of payments uniform and avoids errors and adjustments.

All salient information—i.e., the name of investor, date of purchase, and the servicing fees agreed on—must immediately be recorded on the ledger card. It is also imperative to place on the ledger card the loan number the investor assigned to a particular loan, since investors, when writing to their correspondents concerning a loan, will refer to this loan number only. They also require that all loans be identified by this number when payments are reported.

The results of the transaction, as described on the preceding pages, are reflected in the mortgage company's balance sheet, as well as in its statement of income and expenses for the year in which the transaction takes place.

BORROWING FUNDS FOR LENDING PURPOSES

General Considerations

Principles If a mortgage banker were to employ only his own capital to conduct his mortgage business, he could produce only a few loans at a time. He would always be obliged to wait for payment by his investors for mortgages delivered to them before he would have funds for the next loan. To do more business and turnover his own funds more often, mortgage bankers normally employ only a portion of their own funds when originating loans, and borrow the balance from commercial banks. Their relationships with commercial bankers and, consequently, their methods of borrowing vary according to local banking customs. However, the ability of some mortgage bankers to develop bank lines beyond their local areas has tended to generate national lending patterns.

Mortgage bankers either borrow the entire mortgage amount, or a maximum of 75 to 90 percent of the face value of the loans involved, but never more than the discounted value of the mortgage. The amount borrowed, and the interest rate charged, vary according to the type and nature of the collateral and the financial strength of the mortgage banker.

Actually, there are a variety of ways a mortgage banker can secure credit from his bank. A commercial bank will lend to mortgage bankers on the basis of an investor's firm commitment. This assures the bank of the temporary nature of the loan; the bank knows that before the expiration of the investor's commitment the loan will be repaid. A commercial bank will also lend on the security of mortgages without a firm commitment, i.e., unsold loans. Borrowing on unsold loans enables a mortgage banker who has a substantial net worth and line of credit to build up a considerable inventory of residential loans and to hold the loans for sale at a later date, hopefully, at more advantageous prices. If, however, the mortgage banker's estimate of the direction of the mortgage market is incorrect, he must quickly liquidate his inventory to minimize losses and pay off his loan to the bank. Companies maintaining an inventory of unsold loans are, of course, also in a position to take advantage of occasional demands of investors for immediate delivery of loans. Having a substantial inventory position can be a risky business, but offers considerable rewards. Commercial banks may charge a higher rate of interest to mortgage bankers on inventory than on loans with prior commitments. Bank loans used to carry mortgages, sold or unsold, are sometimes referred to as *warehousing*.

In addition, mortgage bankers with strong financial statements and good track records with their banks can often borrow on an unsecured basis. Unsecured loans are granted on the general credit of the mortgage banker without any reference to a particular loan. Interest rates for loans of this type usually exceed those for bank loans involving loans secured by investors' commitments. At various times, mortgage bankers with excellent credit ratings have also borrowed on subordinated, long-term notes from their own investors at somewhat higher rates than the prevailing commercial bank rates.

If a construction loan is involved, the entire loan is pledged, but borrowings are made as specified stages of construction are completed and the total amount borrowed does not exceed 75 to 90 percent of the sums actually disbursed. Construction loans are sometimes referred to as *interim financing.*

Conventional income property and FHA multifamily loans may also be assigned to a bank during the period of construction. The mortgage banker performs all the mortgage banking functions while the bank provides the funds.

Since, on the average, it takes 60 to 90 days to disburse a residential single-family mortgage loan and for the investor to pay for it, the mortgage banker who borrows on a 10 percent margin will need a net worth of about $300,000 to produce a volume of approximately $1 million of residential mortgages each month. Since construction loans tie up funds for 6 to 18 months, this type of financing on a 10 percent margin requires a considerably larger net worth to produce the same volume of mortgage loans. In either case, if the banks require a larger margin, or it takes longer to turn over the inventory, either the mortgage banker's activities will be curtailed or he must increase his capital.

Planning   For the day-to-day operation of a mortgage company, the chief operating officer must know the company's cash position and its obligations to the banks before each day's activities begin. He must have information on scheduled payouts and contemplated deliveries of loans, and he must be aware of funds that the company is about to receive, so that all available funds may be immediately employed in lending operations. No mortgage banker can afford to have idle funds in his bank account.

This day-to-day planning must take anticipated, as well as certain, transactions into account, such as outstanding commitments not yet accepted by borrowers. Similarly, any delays in completion of projects or title complications, which set back the opening or delivery of loans, or any delays in payment for loans by investors must also be considered. All this information must then be coordinated to chart the outflow and inflow of funds properly. Only through a constant evaluation of all this information can proper plans be made for necessary arrangements to have funds available for the contemplated lending or construction payout transactions.

Since the need to borrow funds arises as a result of disbursement of loan proceeds either in one lump sum or in many checks if construction is involved, the issuance and release of checks must coincide with the borrowing of funds, often on the very same collateral on which the funds involved were disbursed. The only exception is the rare situation when the mortgage banker has extra cash in the bank which he wishes to employ in the consummation of a loan transaction.

Cost of borrowing The interest rate at which a mortgage company can borrow is usually related to the prime rate and is determined by the commercial banker. The *prime rate* is the interest rate the bank charges customers of the highest credit standing. Some commercial banks lend to mortgage bankers at the prime rate; others charge rates slightly above the prime rate. The criteria that determine the interest rate include the size of the company's capital in relation to its volume of business, the company's performance record, size of loan portfolio and related escrow balances, and the size of the loan involved. The amount of paperwork attributed by the bank to a particular lending transaction also has some bearing on rates. The rate accorded to a loan request of $100,000 involving one loan may be lower than on a similar loan request with a pledge of five to ten sets of mortgage papers.

Line of credit Commercial bank credit is essential to mortgage banking. The small, new mortgage company borrows from the bank as funds are needed, never knowing when its banker will turn down a request for credit. The volume of business it can do and its ability to plan its own lending operations are at the mercy of the banker and market forces that influence its decisions.

As the mortgage banker grows, he develops financial strength, specifically net worth, and a track record for moving mortgage loans on schedule and meeting his obligations to the bank on schedule. He needs to know what the limits of his bank borrowing are so he can plan the scale of his operation effectively. To do this, he negotiates with his bank or banker for *line of credit*, the amount of money the bank is willing to lend him. It carries an interest charge related to the prime rate. Both the amount and cost of the line are fixed until renegotiated at the initiation of either party. Even so, the line of credit is not a static measure. It changes with demands upon mortgage bankers, the vagaries of the money market, and general economic conditions, but is always related to the performance record and financial strength of the mortgage banker. Thus, an important factor in the bank's decision to establish a line of credit is the bank customer's ability to keep some funds on deposit continuously in the bank. These deposits may be company funds or those of a custodial nature.

Commercial banks normally require compensating balances equal to 10 to 15 percent of the line of credit granted. But again, the requirements for maintaining compensating balances vary by local practice and the degree of credit ease or restraint imposed on commercial banks by the Federal Reserve. Some banks insist upon a certain minimum deposit amount at all times, some may vary the amount required, and others may not require such deposits at all.

The maximum outstanding debt any national bank may carry for a single customer equals 10 percent of the bank's capital and surplus. The maximum loan any state-chartered bank may lend to any single customer in some states is 15 percent; in other states, the amount conforms to the national bank limitation. This maximum affects only the largest mortgage bankers.

Authority to borrow Technically, the borrowing relationship that a mortgage banker arranges with his commercial banker is confirmed by a resolution of the company's board of directors which authorizes its officers to borrow funds at a particular bank. The same type of resolution is used to establish a bank account. A certified copy of the resolution is sent to the bank either incorporating, or accompanied by, a certification to the bank showing the officers as elected, with their respective titles, at the last meeting of the board of directors. The resolution authorizes certain officers, who are designated by title rather than by name, to borrow funds from the company's commercial bank, as well as to deposit and withdraw company funds. The arrangements and authorizations for the pledging and withdrawal of loan collateral or the exchange of loan documents in connection with loans pledged may also be certified in this type of a resolution form. Individuals authorized to perform these banking functions are not necessarily those authorized to borrow or sign checks.

Borrowing Activity

Procedures followed to obtain bank credit vary by state and by bank as well as by the mortgage banker's financial standing. Although some mortgage bankers are permitted to borrow on a plain note with a "general pledge" agreement, others are required to pledge all or a majority of the mortgage documents as collateral for a loan. The *borrowing activity* technically consists of three distinct steps: pledging of loan documents to obtain loan, delivery of loan package to investor, and purchase of loan by investor and repayment of bank loan.

Pledging of mortgage documents to obtain loan   For a mortgage banker to borrow, it is normally necessary to pledge the following documents:

1 Mortgage note
2 Mortgage or deed of trust
3 Title report
4 FHA or VA commitment, if applicable
5 Investor's commitment, if applicable
6 Insurance policy
7 Assignment of lease, applicable to income property loans when mortgagor leases the premises to another party

Under certain circumstances, the bank will permit the execution of an "agreement to pledge" form to be substituted for one of the documents if any one of them, such as a title policy or assignment of lease, is momentarily not available. The *agreement to pledge* is what its name implies: the mortgage banker agrees to send to the bank the applicable document when available. The mortgage note must be pledged under all circumstances, and the mortgage note must be endorsed on its reverse side by a corporate officer. The loan documents are accompanied by a note for the loan amount agreed upon by the bank and the mortgage banker—for instance, 90 percent of face value of the mortgage or mortgages pledged.

If a construction loan is involved, the prevailing practice is to pledge the loan documents as described above and then borrow by means of a note signed by the mortgage banker for each disbursement made to the mortgagor. Funds so borrowed may then be credited to the company's general bank account or to company construction pay-out account, if a construction loan is involved, against which various checks for work completed are drawn. The borrowing may not amount to more than 90 percent of disbursements, if a 10 percent margin was agreed on. In both instances, the mortgage banker is expected to provide the 10 percent margin from his own resources.

Delivery of loan package to investor This step may be accomplished in one of two ways: by instructing the bank to deliver the mortgage documents to the investor for payment of the loan to the bank, or by withdrawing the documents from the bank on a "trust receipt" and then delivering them to an investor for payment.

Purchase of loan by investor and repayment of bank loan This step can be accomplished in two different ways, depending on which of the above methods is used to deliver the loan package to an investor. If the bank delivered the mortgage, the investor will send its check to the bank. Upon receipt of such payment, if for instance borrowing was at a 10 percent margin, the bank credits the mortgage banker's account at the bank, pays itself for the loan, and leaves the remaining funds in the mortgage banker's account. Simultaneously, the bank notifies the mortgage banker of the purchase of loan by the investor, whereupon servicing begins. If the mortgage banker withdraws the mortgage papers on trust receipt and delivers them to the investor, the investor sends his check to the mortgage banker who, in turn, must immediately pay the bank.

Under either arrangement, if out-of-town investors and large sums are involved, it is necessary to request the use of federal funds, i.e., checks drawn upon a federal reserve in order to obtain immediate credit for the funds deposited in the mortgage banker's account. If this procedure is not followed, the bank will charge interest on its loan until it collects the monies from the bank on which such funds were drawn—with the mortgage banker losing interest for one day or more.

Projection of Fund Requirements

Mortgage lenders must carefully forecast the need for, and the use of, their available line of credit. This is particularly true when such lending involves income property construction loans since the completion of a project, and consequently the use of funds for one single project, may extend for 12 to 18 months. The optimum availability of funds at any one time must be carefully estimated and then revised as circumstances involving the completion of projects change.

This can be done by correlating the following information: number and dollar amount of loans scheduled to be disbursed for which bank credit will be required; scheduled disbursement dates of loans; anticipated completion dates of loans where construction loans are involved; and investor commitment expiration dates, i.e., completion dates when a building under construction must be completed so that the mortgage can be perfected and delivered. One of the best ways to plan the use of funds effectively is to chart the projected use and the availability of bank credit. (See Exhibit 13.)

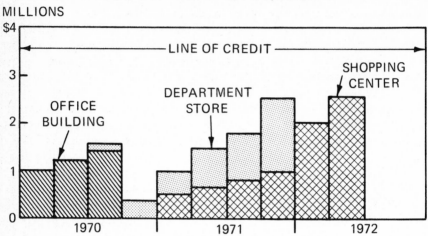

EXHIBIT 13   *Projection of fund requirements*

ESTABLISHMENT OF BANK ACCOUNTS

To maintain the custody and safety of all types of funds, mortgage bankers must maintain a great number and variety of bank accounts. The officer in charge of the financial affairs of the company has the responsibility of seeing that funds received by the company are credited to the appropriate ledgers and deposited in the proper bank accounts promptly. This responsibility also applies to the receipt of funds of a custodial or trust nature—earnest money deposits, standby fees, or tax and insurance deposits—which must always be deposited directly to one of the segregated or custodial accounts established for that purpose.

Bank accounts may be divided into two basic types: *corporate accounts* maintained for the safekeeping of funds which belong to the company or which the company has borrowed; and *segregated or custodial accounts* which the mortgage banker is obliged to maintain for the safekeeping of funds which belong to others, but which he holds for specific periods and purposes. A mortgage company usually has a variety of bank accounts of these two basic types.

Corporate Accounts

The general account is normally the principal account of the company. It contains only owned or borrowed funds, and it is normally used to clear all receipts in the conduct of all company activities. It cannot be used for the clearing or safekeeping of funds which the company acknowledges and receives in the capacity of an agent. Income to the company is deposited to this account and expense items are normally drawn against this account.

Loan disbursement, borrowers', and construction accounts, as well as the general account, may be used for disbursing of loan proceeds. It is best, however, to establish a separate account for the conduct of each type of lending activity. The account title is a matter of personal or company preference. All loan proceeds are disbursed from this type of account and so is the check charged against the borrower's ledger card. Distinction may be made in the use of accounts depending on the type of transaction involved. Separate accounts may be used for "one-payout" loans and for construction loans.

Payroll account, despite the fact that it represents company funds, is used primarily to pay company staff. A monthly or semimonthly deposit represents total funds due employees. Withholding taxes and other deductions are usually paid or deposited in a specified account at the bank with checks drawn against company funds. The account is practically self-balancing in that monies deposited represent only net payroll checks and, therefore, the account normally clears promptly. This account is usually in a bank whose location is most convenient and accessible to the employees of the company.

Segregated Accounts

Many segregated or custodial accounts involve fine lines of distinction, all of which must be carefully observed. The essential purpose of a segregated account, whether called a *trust, custodial,* or *escrow* account, with the bank specifically acknowledging such designation, is to confirm that the monies do not belong to the depositor and to preclude any possibility that the bank or other creditors may impound or use funds deposited by the mortgage banker as an offset against unsatisfied debts. Because of the trust, or fiduciary, relationship which is implied, the account cannot earn any interest for the depositor. It is not unusual for a mortgage banker servicing in excess of $100 million to have over fifty different custodial bank accounts, which must be reconciled monthly.

Segregated corporate accounts may serve one of the following purposes:

1 *Deposit account:* All deposits made by builders and sponsors to secure commitments, "good faith deposits" and "standby fee deposits" to be held during completion of a loan transaction or to be submitted to the prospective investor must at all times be cleared through, or maintained in, this type of account.
2 *Construction reserve account:* Funds set aside by the mortgage banker for the completion of a project are to be held in such account. Often disputed funds by owners, builders, or contractors may be retained in such an account pending settlement.
3 *Real estate account:* Deposits to secure acceptance of an offer, or any other funds involving a pending real estate transaction, must be carried in a special account. In many states, the laws governing real estate transactions require that such funds be deposited in segregated accounts. Even if such a law does not exist, it is best to keep a purchaser's deposit in a custodial-type account.

4 *Premium trust fund account:* Insurance commissioners in many states require that insurance premiums collected on behalf of an insurance company or an agency thereof be deposited in a segregated account pending payment of premium.

Segregated servicing accounts   There are several types of segregated accounts used in connection with mortgage loan accounting.

1 *A clearing account* is normally used to *clear* all monthly payments made to the company on mortgages owned by its investors. All mortgage loan payments are normally deposited in this account daily. Funds from this account are transferred within 24 hours either into a custodial account of one of the investors or are sent to the investor by check. Although some investors are reluctant to permit the use of clearing accounts, preferring that monthly payments tendered to the mortgage banker on their behalf be deposited immediately in an account bearing their name, they will permit the use of a clearing account which speeds up the processing of collections without impairing the safety of funds.

2 *A custodial disbursement account* is used to simplify the disbursing of funds from various custodial accounts when all funds are directed to one payee. For instance, if a tax collector is to be paid 100 tax bills from twenty different investors' accounts, the funds are first cleared into the custodial disbursement account from which only one check, accompanied by one statement, is issued to the tax collector.

3 *A custodial (escrow) account* holds monthly reserve deposits, deposited by borrowers in connection with loans owned by the mortgage banker. This may be the same clearing account through which borrowers' monthly payments are cleared. If this custodial account is also used as a clearing account, the residue of funds at the end of the month represent reserves on loans owned by the mortgage banker or by those investors who do not require the maintenance of a custodial account bearing their respective name.

Segregated investor accounts   These are designed to safekeep deposits of reserves for taxes and insurance premiums by investors. Checks for payment of tax bills and insurance premiums are drawn on this account which bears the investor's name by the mortgage banker. The establishment of this custodial account is usually discussed with an investor at the time the servicing contract is executed, unless the establishment of such account is a specific requirement of the servicing contract. Although occasionally some investors ask that a part of the funds be sent to them, most investors recognize the necessity for mortgage bankers to maintain these accounts in the community in which the funds are generated.

Replacement reserve collections in connection with FHA multifamily loans, primarily because of the size of deposits, but more importantly because of the permanent nature of such funds, are usually transmitted for safekeeping to the holders of respective mortgages. These funds are often invested for the benefit of the mortgagors.

Opening Bank Accounts

Once the mortgage company has decided that an account is to be established for a specific purpose, selected a bank, and, obtained the investor's approval of the bank if a custodial account is involved, the financial officer can begin the steps necessary to open the account. The bank selected must be a member of the Federal Deposit Insurance Corporation. An appropriate title must be selected and corporate resolutions passed authorizing the opening of such an account. The resolution is then sent to the bank accompanied by instructions for the printing of checks and other particulars on handling the account, such as mailing statements. Technically, an account is not opened until the initial deposit is made. If reserves collected for FHA loans and other loans are to be commingled in a single custodial account, permission for commingling must be obtained from the FHA by a letter requesting approval to commingle and setting forth the terms of the banking arrangements.

Corporate resolutions If company accounts are involved, corporate resolution forms may establish authority to borrow funds from the bank as well as authorize certain officers to sign checks on a specifically named account. If a custodial account is involved, a special resolution must be passed and certified to the bank. This resolution would then specifically authorize the opening of a specifically designated custodial account with the corporate officers signing on the account. Occasionally, the check-signers also include officers of the investor institution.

Suggested account titles The title of a bank account should clearly identify its purpose. Although there are no special requirements for the title of an account when company funds are involved, it is necessary to identify clearly the custodial nature of the account when monies held for investors and borrowers are involved. Recommended are the following designations:

ABC Mortgage Company
In Trust for Eastern Insurance Co.
and Various Mortgagors

or

ABC Mortgage Company
Custodial Account, FHA-VA Loans

Commingling of escrow reserves *Commingling* means depositing in a single account all escrow funds collected in connection with FHA-insured, VA-guaranteed, and conventional loans owned by a single investor, regardless of the number of borrowers. Commingling escrow reserves reduces considerably the number of bank accounts in use by mortgage bankers.

Permission for such commingling must be obtained from FHA in accordance with the requirements set forth in FHA's directive of September 12, 1956. A letter by a CPA firm written in compliance with FHA requirements should accompany the company's financial statement and describe the preventive measures that have been taken to satisfy the assistant secretary-commissioner. This letter is required in addition to a comment in the "Notes to Financial Statement," which is a part of the company's audit statement to the effect that commingling was approved by FHA. (See Exhibits 1-A and 1-B included in Appendix A-6.)

FDIC coverage   The Federal Deposit Insurance Corporation was created by the Banking Act of 1933 to protect depositors against loss in case of bank failures. To insure deposits, FDIC assesses its members in proportion to their eligible deposits for such insurance. Each depositor's account is, at this writing, insured up to $20,000. To understand the full benefit of such coverage, it must be realized that the $20,000 is intended to cover each depositor's (mortgagor's) escrow deposit rather than the total in a custodial account. Full protection is available, according to FDIC ". . . if the name and interest of an owner of any portion of a specifically designated custodial deposit are disclosed on the records of the person in whose name the deposit is maintained and such records are maintained in good faith and in the regular course of business, each owner will be recognized for insurance purposes to the same extent as if his name and interest were disclosed on the records of the bank."

Although there have been many conflicting interpretations of how an overdraft created in the account of any one of the mortgagor's accounts could invalidate the entire protection or reduce protection to only a total of $20,000 instead of $20,000 for each identifiable account, the test ruling by the FDIC, issued in February 1966, dispels all doubts and eliminates all uncertainties in this respect. It states: ". . . even though the interest in escrow funds on one or more mortgagors in a custodial account has been overdrawn so that the interests of other owners of such escrow funds have been invaded, the insurance coverage on the remaining funds in the account is not terminated. On the contrary, each such reduced interest of the various mortgagors will continue to be separately insured up to $20,000. However, although we continue to insure the reduced interests of the various mortgagors, we do not pass upon the propriety of a custodian using custodial funds belonging to various owners for the purpose of meeting the obligations of others. It is suggested that the servicing agent could avoid overdrafts by depositing his own funds in the custodial account to absorb deficiencies in various mortgagors' interests."

Establishment of Check-Signing Authority

When the correctness of the funds to be disbursed is ascertained, checks should be drawn, approved, and signed with a minimum of red tape. Centralization of check issuing and signing requires involved controls and thereby reduces the speed with which checks may be made available. Accordingly, decentralization is recommended, making various department heads responsible for issuance of checks, but not necessarily for obtaining signatures. While efficiency and the desire to serve call for prompt availability of funds, on one hand, sound business practices and internal control, on the other, demand caution and deliberation. Checks should be authorized by the person who is familiar with the purpose as well as the validity of the disbursement. Checks representing payment of tax bills, insurance premiums, or company expenditures should not be signed unless they are accompanied by either vouchers or the respective bills. The practice of exhibiting the bills should be maintained even if the check-signer occasionally signs checks without scrutinizing the bills.

If a check requisition form is being used at time of disbursement, one signature will usually suffice to validate a check. If the person requiring the check is the one who orders its issuance, it is best to have a two-signature check, the first authorizing issuance of the check before it is presented for signature to an authorized check-signer whose name is on file with the bank.

To serve customers well, a company may be inclined to appoint a large number of check-signers so that someone is at all times available to sign checks. The fewer the number of check-signers, however, the better. Check-signing machines, providing facsimile signatures, upon proper authorization of checks by those requiring them, work out quite satisfactorily only if the number of accounts and type of checks are nominal.

The responsibility for the correctness of a check—not its technical perfection as far as typing and perforation of checks is concerned—rests with the person who orders the issuance of the check rather than with the person who signs it. The latter actually must rely on an employee familiar with the transaction and entrusted to handle it. To assure prompt availability of signed checks, it is best to establish a *check issuing, authorizing, and signing procedure,* which should establish guiding principles to be enforced in writing checks. It should spell out the requirements for cancellation of checks and for issuance of stop payment orders; outline the caution that must be exercised by accounting clerks in reissuing checks which were reported lost; describe procedures for mailing refunds; and control issuance of refund checks for funds received by checks that have not yet been paid by the bank on which they were drawn. In no case should the individual responsible for corporate accounting records or for balancing and reconciling bank accounts be authorized to sign company checks.

Auditors examining operations of a mortgage banking firm often suggest that checks require two, rather than one, signatures. Although this is a practical solution that establishes sound controls, it is often difficult to carry out in mortgage banking firms of small or medium size. One signature normally suffices, provided the requirements leading to the issuance of checks are clearly established and enforced. For instance, the person needing a check should not be authorized to write one; he should be required to write out a requisition form for the check showing thereon the payee, the account on which it is to be drawn, and the purpose of the check. The check should then be drawn in the accounting department and signed by an authorized check-signer. As long as three people are involved in the issuance of a check, even though only the last one (whose signature is filed with the bank) signs it, the company's procedure is sound.

FINANCIAL STATEMENTS

Financial reports portray a firm's accomplishments and future potential. They are compiled monthly for management and annually for stockholders and the public. The annual report is reviewed and certified by a public accounting firm and is sent to investors, to stockholders, and, if filing is required, to states in which the company is licensed to do business. The Federal Housing Administration requires submission of annual audit reports 60 days after the close of the fiscal year. Illustrated annual reports which include a summary of the company's activities, accomplishments, and future prospects as well as pictures of properties the company has financed are an excellent means of building public relations.

Monthly Statements

The monthly financial statements—the balance sheet and statement of income and expense—report the company's present financial position and the results of the month's activities. They are valuable management tools, providing information on the firm's various activities as well as its overall operations, accomplishments, and pending problems.

The controller's monthly reports must be part of the top operating officer's decision-making tools. They should also be circulated to the management team and department heads who are responsible both for income and for authorizations for expenditures.

To provide perspective so vital to analysis by management, financial reports should provide for comparison of the current month with the comparable month a year ago. Cumulative comparison, e.g., the first five months of a year and the first five months of the preceding year, facilitates analysis by reducing the influence of seasonal and irregular factors. The financial reports are also essential sources of information in preparing budgets, and determining whether budgeted targets are being met.

The value of any financial report to management is directly related to its timeliness. It is imperative, therefore, that monthly statements be presented to management *no later than the tenth day of the month after the close of any month.*

The timely and accurate completion of reports can, of course, be considerably improved by using tools and observance of basic requirements, which are:

Chart of accounts The uniform chart of accounts prepared and recommended for adoption by all mortgage bankers by the Mortgage Bankers Association of America not only is an aid to the individual firm's controller, but provides a basis for comparing the firm's financial accomplishments with industry averages. The chart groups income and expense items by their logical classification and blends them into the appropriate places on the mortgage banker's books. The grouping is further systematized by coding items of income by sources, expenditures by the nature of expenditure and their classification by production, administration, or general overhead.

Printing (or preduplicating) of forms Forms on which monthly figures can be entered easily eliminate the necessity of copying of repetitious information each month and facilitate consistency in the preparation of the reports.

Closing dates These should be established to assure prompt reporting. Every reasonable effort should be made to meet specific closing dates established for bookkeepers responsible for balancing ledgers and for the controller.

Although strict adherence to accounting principles would not allow the dissemination of monthly results until all bank accounts and all ledgers are balanced and the books are properly closed, modern management techniques often permit the presentation of reports before every small discrepancy is reconciled. This does not suggest laxity; it recognizes the importance of reporting results promptly. Of course, it remains incumbent on the controller to see that all small inaccuracies or errors be located and adjusted and that the books be properly balanced and closed before the next report becomes due.

Annual Statements

A statement of the firm's financial condition is prepared annually by a certified public accounting firm. The annual audit report typically consists of an audit certification, a balance sheet (Exhibit 14), and a statement of earnings (Exhibit 15). When necessary, the auditor will explain unusual items in the notes appended to the financial statement. The monthly report, described above, should contain many additional subclassifications and greater details. The forms illustrated in the accompanying exhibits draw upon MBA's Suggested Chart of Accounts and Financial Statements for Mortgage Banking Companies and suggest some additional breakdown. (See Appendix A-4.)

Special Problems

When analyzing the financial statement of a mortgage banking firm, it must be borne in mind that in the mortgage business, profit is not fully realized concurrently with the consummation of the mortgage loan transaction. In the residential loan business, the 1 percent fee collected from the borrower may be considered earnings when the loan transaction is consummated. Alternately, it may be set aside to supplement the profit or offset the loss on the sale of the loan to an investor. Decisions on these points can certainly alter the financial results reported by the company. For management purposes, a distinction should be made between fees taken into income when received and fees that are taken into income as they are earned. From the standpoint of federal income taxes, of course, constructive receipt of fees constitutes income regardless of how the item is handled on the company's books.

In case of a construction loan, a fee may be deducted in its entirety from the proceeds of the loan, but taken into income in proportion to funds disbursed. The item "unearned commission and discounts" usually represents those fees which the company deducted from the proceeds of a loan, but does not consider earned as of the close of the year. This type of arrangement is one of the many effective methods

EXHIBIT 14 **Balance sheet**

ABC MORTGAGE COMPANY

233 Maple Street
Chicago, Illinois 60190
December 31, 1970 and 1969

Thousands of dollars

Assets	1970	1969
Current assets		
Cash	$ 193	$ 140
Marketable securities, at cost	52	30
Accounts and notes receivable	156	150
First mortgages (note 1)	3,884	2,910
Home improvement loans	123	110
Total current assets	$4,408	$3,340
Noncurrent assets		
Investments in limited real estate partnerships, at cost	$ 427	$ 372
Office equipment and leasehold improvements, at cost (less accumulated depreciation— 1970, $20,000— 1969, $18,000)	30	27
Prepaid expenses	4	4
Total noncurrent assets	$ 461	$ 403
Total assets	$4,869	$3,743

Liabilities	1970	1969
Current liabilities		
Notes payable to banks (note 1)	$3,262	$2,190
Accounts payable and other liabilities	355	317
Federal income taxes payable	60	47
	$3,677	$2,554
Long-term debt		
Note payable to insurance company— due 1972 (installment due within year included in current liabilities)	$ 415	$ 460
Stockholders' equity		
Common stock (authorized 100,000 shares of $10 par value; issued and outstanding, 25,200 shares)	$ 252	$ 252
Retained earnings	525	477
	$ 777	$ 729
Total liabilities	$4,869	$3,743

Notes to financial statements

1 First mortgage of $3,884,000 and $2,910,000 were pledged as collateral on notes payable of $3,262,000 and $2,190,000 at December 31, 1970 and 1969, respectively. On December 31, 1970, the company had investors' firm commitments to purchase all the loans in its inventory except $187,000 in residential loans. Of these, only five loans amounting to $97,600 are without investors' commitments as of the date of this report. All loans are shown at cost which is not in excess of market.

2 The company's portfolio of mortgages serviced, including those held for sale, aggregated approximately $119,000,000 at December 31, 1970 and $107,850,000 at December 31, 1969. In connection therewith, the company held escrow and agency funds amounting to $1,890,008 and $1,217,000 at December 31, 1970 and December 31, 1969, respectively, which were segregated in special bank accounts and excluded from the company's assets and liabilities.

3 The company has received permission from the Federal Housing Administration and investors to commingle escrow funds collected on FHA loans with other escrow funds, and these funds have been commingled in respective segregated accounts.

4 The Treasury Department is currently examining the company's federal income tax return for the year ended December 31, 1967. In the opinion of management, this examination will not result in any material additional assessment.

EXHIBIT 15 *Statement of earnings*

ABC MORTGAGE COMPANY
233 Maple Street
Chicago, Illinois 60190

For the years ended December 31, 1970 and 1969
Thousands of dollars

	1970	*1969*
Income:		
Loan administration	$ 270	$ 240
Loan origination	230	195
Interest on loans, net	50	42
Commissions:		
Insurance	40	36
Real estate	50	55
Other	28	35
Total income	$ 668	$ 603
Expenses:		
Personnel	$ 376	$ 348
Occupancy	38	35
Equipment rental	20	18
Office supplies and expenses	35	36
Travel and entertainment	12	13
Automobile	10	10
Advertising	12	11
Loan processing	7	9
Other	38	32
Total expenses	$ 548	$ 512
Earnings before federal taxes on income	$ 120	$ 91
Provision for federal taxes on income	60	47
Net earnings	$ 60	$ 44
Retained earnings:		
Balance at beginning of year	477	445
	$ 537	$ 489
Less:		
Cash dividends paid (50 ¢ per share in 1970 & 1969)	$ 12	$ 12
Balance at end of year	$ 525	$ 477

employed in the mortgage business to relate expenditures to income earned. If a commission on a loan is recorded as income in the second half of a fiscal year, even if all the work was not performed, and all expenses of the work are shown in the first half of the succeeding fiscal year, considerable distortions will occur. This situation may also distort results within a fiscal year by making the first half appear to be profitable and the second half unprofitable.

Notwithstanding a practice which is still in existence, it is not proper accounting practice to show company escrow funds and those retained in various investor custodial accounts in the balance sheet; they should be mentioned in the "notes to financial statements."

A peculiarity of the mortgage banking business is that the size of the mortgage company is often measured by the volume of loans it services rather than its net worth. This emphasis stems from the notion that the volume of business produced and added to the servicing portfolio is a more important growth factor than the accumulation of capital for conducting future business. While the former involves responsibilities which can produce income but do not necessarily yield a profit, the latter represents retained earnings and the stockholders' investment. For this reason, investors and commercial bankers financing mortgage banking firms have placed consistent demands on them to increase the firms' net worth. Nevertheless, the amount of servicing volume is an important indicator of the company's potential earnings. It is not only customary, therefore, but necessary to include information on the servicing volume and the amount of business produced in the annual report or in the "notes to financial statements."

PROTECTION OF COMPANY ASSETS

The company's physical assets and financial resources must be protected through administrative measures that minimize exposure to the hazards of fire, theft, and negligence. Its physical assets, such as office furniture and equipment, may be destroyed by fire or stolen. Its financial assets may be stolen or lost through forgery or embezzlement. Its financial resources are also subject to loss through the company's liability for the negligence of its employees, whether driving company-owned cars or failing to protect the interests of investors when originating and servicing mortgages.

The exposure of company assets may be protected through audits, internal control, or insurance. When the exposure is balanced against the cost of protection, the company may take the calculated business risk of self-insurance against specific risks. If the cost of protection for a 3- or 5-year period, for instance, approximates the potential loss, it may be worthwhile for the company to be self-insured. No insurance protection would be purchased, and if a loss is sustained, the accumulated savings would be adequate to cover the loss. A good example of self-insurance involves the decision not to provide collision insurance for company-owned vehicles. This may be done because any single loss is limited to the value of the automobile, which is not likely to upset the financial equilibrium of the company. If the company owns more than one car, the laws of probability would still favor management's deciding on self-insurance so far as collision insurance is concerned.

Audits and Internal Control

Protection of the company's assets begins with the closely related functions of audit and internal control. Neither frequent audits nor close supervision of each employee can completely prevent dishonest practices once they are contrived in the mind of a potential perpetrator. Together, they can only reduce the opportunities for fraudulent acts.

The most thorough auditing firm is limited by the number of visits to the company's offices, whether on a scheduled or a surprise basis. Auditors must rely on management for assistance in performing their tasks. Thus, the loan administrator must implement internal controls, developed in cooperation with the auditors. At the same time, he must know intimately the people who work in the firm and their habits.

Employment of certified public accountants Auditors should not be employed solely to prepare and certify the annual financial statement and issue a clean bill of health at the close of the fiscal year. They should conduct an around-the-clock review of operations, which include surprise visits made without notifying anyone in the organization. They should report all their findings to the chairman of the board of directors or the operating head of the company, especially if they are concerned or suspicious of any breakdown in controls.

The employment of a good audit firm, and even monthly visits by them, will provide no panacea to the problems that can arise when poor practices or inadequate supervision is tolerated. Auditors can only suggest good procedures, recommend solutions to problems, and counsel their clients. They cannot discover all the errors committed throughout the year, primarily because they cannot spend enough time with their clients.

Auditors should help plan and implement accounting changes. They should be consulted as problems arise and called in any time suspicions are aroused. Loan administrators should work hand in hand with auditors in the conduct of the company operation. Outsiders, such as auditors, can do little to insure safety of assets that cannot be done better and less expensively by management through vigilance, enforcement of various operating procedures, or "quality control" of the staff. Lax supervision helps a potential embezzler or thief. Employees, of course, should not be made uneasy by suspicion or by overly protective attitudes. They should be made aware, however, that procedures once adopted to protect the assets of the company are to be followed, and if a breakdown in such procedures is noticed, employees will be called upon to explain the reason for their failure to follow certain established routines.

Each company has special internal operating arrangements of its own. Nevertheless, members of the management team—high-ranking officers, treasurers, and loan administrators—should be subject to the same audit and internal control as are all other employees of the company. This suggestion is not only a part of fair play, but is supported by experiences of those insuring companies which have suffered greater dollar losses as a result of defalcations and embezzlements by high-ranking officials rather than the typically smaller abscondments by employees at clerical levels.

Recommendations are sometimes made to rotate audit firms in order to obtain fresh views on operating practices and habits. This is a decision management must make; however, the rotation of auditors can be an expensive procedure since each new audit staff will require considerable time to become thoroughly familiar with company operations, yet audit results will not necessarily be improved.

Single audit program   Single audit is a sound operating principle. One audit firm employed by the mortgage banker performs an audit in accordance with accepted audit practices and the specific requirements of all the investors for whom a particular mortgage banker services. Ideally, the single audit eliminates the necessity of each investor sending his audit team to check his servicer.

The National Association of Mutual Savings Banks approved the use of a single audit for their members, but most life insurance company investors feel that those who accept a single audit report from their correspondents relinquish certain safeguards. They feel that the auditor employed by the company cannot be truly objective toward the firm that is paying its bill, even though their professional status would assure fundamentally correct statements.

For the single audit to succeed, it must be adopted by all, or at least a majority, of any servicer's investors, since many of the jobs to be performed require a more thorough checking of facts than would otherwise be required. If, for instance, single audit is adopted by only five of a mortgage banker's fifty investors, it would be extremely burdensome and expensive to comply with item six of MBA's Single Audit Program, which prescribes that the auditor confirm with each mortgagee "the total of the trial balances, number of loans, statements of arrears and prepayments and mortgage documents held pending satisfaction on loans under foreclosure, as of the date of the last cut-off or trial balances for each mortgagee." The auditor must also check collection procedures and report positive confirmations with mortgagors of all mortgages in excess of $100,000 and 10 percent of all mortgages serviced, with special emphasis on delinquent and prepaid loans. Corresponding with fifty investors to satisfy five is an expensive procedure.

If, however, these confirmations are not effected, a valid single audit certification cannot be issued to the five companies willing to accept such certification. Once exceptions are noted on the certification indicating that certain jobs were not done, single audit collapses. Therefore, single audit must be adopted by all or most of the investors to create the benefits for which it was designed.

A word of caution must be introduced here. While the mortgage industry advocates stronger controls and supervision, on the one hand, single audit, on the other, provides the opposite, by offering fewer surprise audits than occurred with the successive visits of a larger number of different auditors.

A "Loan Administration News Letter" dated January 21, 1966, prepared by the Mortgage Bankers Association of America, clearly outlined the methods to be employed for the adoption of a single audit program. This newsletter stated:

> ... the program simply documents the definition and the generally accepted auditing standards and procedures required for an effective single audit program in our industry. When accepted by an institutional investor, it eliminates the need for detailed field audit procedures by its staff and the need for a special examination by independent accounting firms or others specializing in this area.

It is now the responsibility of each individual company management to arrange for the adoption of the MBA approved program by its investors.

Any Mortgage Banker that desires to adopt single audit should indicate this fact to his investor. If the investor approves, he would then:

1 Notify his CPA of his intent to adopt the program
2 With respect to future audits, notify his CPA that the investor will be supplied these data:
   a A balance sheet as of the end of the fiscal year
   b A statement of earnings and retained earnings as of the end of the fiscal year
   c The amount of the servicer's blanket bond and errors and omissions policy, with the names of such issuing companies and the dates to which premiums are paid
   d The special CPA's certification as called for by the single audit program

It would be desirable to adopt the MBA Chart of Accounts and Financial Statement format, but this is not mandatory under the program.

Installation and maintenance of internal control Internal control is both a network of procedural checkpoints and a conscientious act of checking compliance with established operating procedures. Since internal control is the least expensive method of protecting company assets, requiring extensive discussion, it will be thoroughly examined in Chapter 10.

Insurance

Mortgage banking is exposed to a greater variety of risks than those affecting other types of financial institutions. Of these risks are those affecting physical assets whose values can be appraised with a fair degree of accuracy, and the liabilities arising from negligent and nefarious acts of employees, which also can be estimated with reasonable accuracy.

The amount and type of insurance to be purchased is a management decision. It involves careful examination of risks and evaluation of potential losses in relation to the company's capital, as well as a comparison of the costs of insurance that may be purchased with the dangers of having no insurance or being underinsured. No management, however, should be in want of insurance solely because it has not considered the matter. A review of a few costly examples is often sufficient to illustrate the serious consequences of unprotected exposures. Underinsurance may be due to careless evaluation of risks or to a determined effort to keep insurance costs at a minimum. In the latter case, management must be apprised of the additional risks it takes by not protecting its activities or its assets to the full amount of the risk involved and protection available.

Care should also be taken to avoid overinsurance or duplication of coverage. Both are wasteful. Therefore, no protection should be added or coverage increased without careful examination of the policy which may already cover the exposure in question, or without reevaluating the potential top limit of exposure. It is, generally speaking, prudent to review all company insurance policies thoroughly at least once a year.

While the determination of risks involving company assets and their coverage by insurance is at the sole discretion of the mortgage banker, protection against risk from embezzlement, theft, and other fraudulent practices, as well as acts of negligence in providing insurance protection and paying taxes, is also the concern of the investor whose funds are most likely to be involved. For that reason, most servicing contracts stipulate that fidelity bonds and errors and omissions insurance should be provided by the mortgage banker. Both the coverage and the insuring company must be satisfactory to the investor. Investors usually require a copy of the policy and also often require that an endorsement be added to the policy requiring that the insurer not terminate insurance without giving the mortgagee, by registered mail, a 15-days' notice of termination. As an additional precaution, investors normally purchase blanket excess coverage of their own for that exposure which exceeds the protection afforded by their respective correspondents' fidelity bond and errors and omissions insurance.

Recommended insurance coverages The loan administrator must evaluate the insurance coverage carefully, ascertaining what the policy *does and does not cover*. The types of policies to be considered are:

1 Fire and extended coverage for office buildings which may be owned or rented. Insurance should be for full replacement cost value. This policy should include rent insurance to provide for rental payment if fire damage makes the office unusable.

2 Fire and extended coverage on all contents of the building or office, including valuable papers.

3 Extra expense insurance. This protection pays for the extra expense of maintaining operations should fire destroy or damage the company's offices.

4 Comprehensive general and automobile liability coverage for fairly high limits. This policy is normally of the "audit type," affording protection for a wide variety of exposures. Liability protection may also be obtained on properties acquired by the company through foreclosure. This protection includes coverage for all types of liabilities and reimbursement for medical payments arising, for instance, from operating company cars. It should also include protection for vehicles owned by others while on company business and when they collide with uninsured motorists.

5　Fidelity coverage of all acts of employees, including audit expense. Fidelity coverage includes losses caused by dishonest, fraudulent, or criminal acts of an employee, e.g., forgery, whether acting alone or in collusion with others. Coverage applies to both property of the company and that for which the company is liable. The bond should be based on a discovery rather than a sustained basis, which should eliminate controversies relative to policy dates. On a *discovery* basis, claims are paid for losses discovered during the term of the policy regardless of when the loss occurred. The amount of protection depends on the coverage in effect on the day the loss was discovered and not when the loss was actually sustained.

6　Burglary and theft coverage.

7　Standard workmen's compensation and employees liability protection.

8　Errors and omissions insurance. The principal purpose of this coverage is to provide the mortgage banking firm with protection for its legal liability for failing or neglecting either to write or to procure insurance policies protecting properties for which it services loans. The policy also covers errors in the policy itself which remain undetected and which would cause the insuring company to deny payment of losses.

What are some of the errors and omissions? There may be an error in the name or in the description of the property which may prompt the insurance company to refuse to settle a loss; or the mortgage banker may have failed to pay the premium for a policy from insurance reserves, which then resulted in the cancellation of the policy, leaving the property uninsured. Errors and omissions protection, however, does not extend to errors in establishing the proper amount of insurance required to protect a given property. That is an error in judgment.

The criteria for the amount of errors and omissions protection a mortgage banker should maintain have never been formally established. In practice, the amount of the coverage normally equals the amount of the fidelity bond. The amount of recommended errors and omissions coverage, however, should be related to the degree of dependence the investor places on the mortgage banker for protecting mortgaged properties by insurance. Since investors often delegate the entire task of handling insurance to their correspondents, including that on income property loans, the amount of errors and omissions coverage, of necessity, must exceed the limits of the fidelity bond coverage. If errors and omissions is part of a blanket fidelity policy, which may be for a nominal amount, the additional potential exposure must be protected by excess coverage. This policy or endorsement to primary coverage offers protection only after a claim on the basic policy has been exhausted.

The mortgage banking firms which service income property loans either in substantial volume or in large denominations should be particularly concerned with the adequacy of their errors and omissions coverage, especially if, as is frequently the case, the investors charge them with the full responsibility for maintaining adequate insurance protection. Many investors purchase errors and omissions insurance adequate to protect their interest in the event there is no adequate insurance or in case the mortgage banker did not purchase adequate errors and omissions protection.

It must be remembered, however, that an excess policy purchased by the investor may often contain a subrogation clause under which the carrier is entitled to recovery if it paid a loss and if it can prove that the correspondent was negligent in handling his responsibility relative to insurance policies. If the insurance carrier can then obtain a judgment against the negligent servicer, such judgment, if enforced, can impair the mortgage banker's financial position. Therefore, the mortgage bankers who are handling the full responsibility for insurance should carefully ascertain their exposures and set up their errors and omissions policy accordingly. Furthermore, they should make sure that their investors do not have policies with right of subrogation against them. Under any circumstance, great caution should be exercised in handling insurance and in properly determining adequate errors and omissions protection.

When a mortgage banker writes insurance on properties in connection with which he no longer services the mortgage or never did, he must also purchase an "insurance agent's and broker's" errors and omissions policy or have such a policy attached in the form of an endorsement to the Mortgage Bankers Blanket Bond. The errors and omissions coverage included in the Mortgage Bankers Blanket Bond applies only to those insurance activities which he performs in the capacity of a mortgage banker, and not as an agent or broker of an insurance company, although he may be one at the same time.

Although in standard errors and omissions insurance contracts *homeowners insurance* or its equivalent is defined as "any package policies consisting of insurance on real and personal property and personal liability insurance," this statement is included in the contract to define what a homeowners policy is, rather than what an errors and omissions contract covers. It is, therefore, incumbent on each mortgage banker to ask the company which provides the errors and omissions protection to explicitly advise him in writing whether the errors and omissions provision of the contract includes every coverage (liability, burglary, etc.) in a homeowner's package policy or only the failure to provide fire and extended coverage.

If the mortgage banker is also engaged in real estate activity, a special real estate errors and omissions bond must be obtained. This policy will protect the company for any claim made by the purchaser or seller of real estate on liabilities arising from the representations made and handling of an offer to sell real estate.

Mortgage Bankers Blanket Bond   Most of the coverages enumerated above, which a mortgage banker must provide for its own protection, are included in a Mortgage Bankers Blanket Bond. This bond was developed by the underwriters at Lloyd's of London, with the aid of the members and staff of the Mortgage Bankers Association of America. The policy is based on a *package* concept, which includes all major coverages a mortgage banker is required to have in the proper conduct of his business.

Insurance is now available on an *all-risk* basis to financial institutions which includes protection against loss due to: nonexistence of insurance or inadequate insurance on mortgaged property damaged by fire, extended coverage, homeowners or other perils which the mortgagor is required to purchase, or on foreclosed property; and all risks and perils (flood, earthquake, wave wash, collapse) on mortgaged property, but excluding those perils which the mortgagor is required to purchase. These perils are normally not included in the errors and omissions policies or errors and omissions provisions of mortgage bankers blanket bonds. All-risk insurance is difficult to obtain in today's insurance markets.

Required amount of fidelity bond coverage In addition to the mortgage banking firm's view on the correct amount of fidelity insurance it should carry, the wishes of its investors must be taken into account. The National Association of Mutual Savings Banks has taken the only positive and official stand in the field by establishing standard requirements for their mortgage servicers. Their formula judges all mortgage bankers with a single criterion: the volume of servicing. Admittedly this is a standard which can be readily established, but it is not a true indicator of the company's ability to discharge its obligation, to protect its own funds and those of its investors, or to cover any losses from its capital in excess of the fidelity coverage if such coverage is subsequently found inadequate.

The original formula was established in 1959 by the Committee on Insurance of the National Association of Mutual Savings Banks. The Insurance Committee of the Mortgage Bankers Association of America, which studied the proposed formula, agreed to accept the schedule providing it was "followed merely as a guide; and if it were subject to modifications on a case basis depending on such conditions as the financial strength of the loan correspondent, the extent of the correspondent's internal control, the size and number of employees in the correspondent's office, or by the overall risk involved conditioned upon the type of loans made." The compromise was subsequently accepted by the National Association of Mutual Savings Banks, which then advised its members as follows:

The Board of Governors of the Mortgage Bankers Association, upon recommendation of the Insurance Committee of the MBA accepted the schedule in principle if it is followed by a guide and if consideration is given to certain factors such as:

1 Financial strength of servicer,
2 Type of internal controls; periodic audits, and
3 Types of loans serviced and extent escrows may or may not be retained or collected.

The Committee on Insurance of the National Association of Mutual Savings Banks wishes to stress that the accompanying schedule is intended for use as a reference and guide in determining adequacy of the fidelity coverage carried by mortgage servicing contractors. It will not necessarily apply to every situation and, therefore, should be flexible in its interpretation.

The amount of the required fidelity bond coverage was reviewed by both associations in 1970 and the limits reduced—taking into consideration the very same financial strength criteria that was used in 1959. Both schedules appear below.

The determination of the amount of fidelity coverage is essentially a management decision, a decision which should be reviewed from time to time. The amount of coverage should frequently be more, but never less, than the amount indicated by the new formula.

Schedule of fidelity bond coverage

Total servicing portfolio	Based on 1959 formula	Based on new formula
$ 25,000,000	$ 180,000	$ 100,000
50,000,000	280,000	200,000
75,000,000	380,000	250,000
100,000,000	480,000	300,000
150,000,000	680,000	375,000
200,000,000	880,000	450,000
300,000,000	1,280,000	600,000
400,000,000	1,680,000	750,000
500,000,000	2,080,000	900,000
600,000,000	2,480,000	1,025,000
700,000,000	2,880,000	1,150,000
800,000,000	3,280,000	1,275,000
900,000,000	3,680,000	1,400,000
1,000,000,000	4,080,000	1,525,000
2,000,000,000	8,080,000	2,525,000

1959 formula

The following formula is applied to the total servicing portfolio:

2 percent of the first $2,000,000
1 percent of the next $8,000,000
0.4 percent of the volume serviced in excess of
$10,000,000

New formula

The following formula is applied to the total servicing portfolio:

0.4 percent of the first $50,000,000
0.2 percent of the next $50,000,000
0.15 percent of the next $400,000,000
0.125 percent of the next $500,000,000
0.1 percent of the volume over $1,000,000,000

CHAPTER SEVEN

Planning for Expansion

During the course of the existence of each mortgage banking firm, decisions must be made on a variety of matters that affect the future of the company. From time to time as the volume of loans produced and serviced expands, it may become necessary to make careful analyses of whether the firm's data processing equipment can carry the additional load and whether the firm's operations must be converted to more advanced equipment. Decisions may also be required on the advisability of increasing servicing by outright purchase of portfolios or other mortgage companies, of opening or closing branch offices, and of diversifying operations into related areas.

The loan administrator contributes to the decision-making process by providing the facts needed. He must research, assemble, evaluate, and present information on the relative merits of acquisition versus origination, branching versus a single-office operation, or diversifying in another area. This analysis inevitably involves determining the cost of servicing the added volume with present equipment or with more advanced equipment. The facts he presents may encourage management to expand through an acquisition or lead to a termination of negotiations. If the decision is made to expand, the administrative skill of the loan administrator and his staff will determine how successfully the added servicing portfolio can be assimilated and, if necessary, an equipment conversion carried out.

Of course, the ability to make proper recommendations is largely contingent on the availability of cost information on all activities. Without knowing the present cost of servicing, and the value of a servicing portfolio to the company, the merits of an acquisition can hardly be estimated. It is essential, therefore, that management maintain cost information on its loan production and loan servicing activities.

CONVERSION

Conversion, in the context of this chapter, applies generally to a change in accounting procedure or a change in the accounting equipment used. Conversion also means an upgrading of systems, since it is usually prompted by growth. While conversion generally applies to mortgage loan accounting, it also involves the employment of data processing equipment in every phase of the company's operations.

Conversion is typically part of the growth process of a mortgage banking firm. When management begins to face difficulties in handling an increasing volume of entries by hand and typewriters within a given time, it is time to consider installing conventional accounting equipment for recording bookkeeping transactions. Frequently, the next step involves the use of service bureaus employing data processing equipment, which is tantamount to farming out most accounting chores. The use of a service bureau frequently introduces most mortgage bankers to data processing equipment and its products. The next step, then, is the installation on the premises of data processing machines of one variety or another. A rather new development is an arrangement whereby loans of several mortgage banking firms are pooled in order to use one centralized data processing office. Such an arrangement assures that the equipment's capabilities are fully utilized and that the rising rental costs may be proportionately divided among those utilizing a complete installation.

The loan administrator must be generally familiar with the conditions that warrant conversion and the growth signs that indicate when action must be taken. He must also be aware of the dangers of premature action. To convert sooner than necessity dictates can be costlier to the company than if conversion were never attempted.

Regardless of the size of the company or the sophistication of its accounting procedures, plans to convert begin with the loan administrator. His first duty is to investigate the various means through which an existing accounting machinery can be geared, substituted, upgraded, or converted for doing the same task—namely, handling the accounting of a growing number of loans and reporting payments faster and less expensively. From these initial inquiries and probings which usually pertain solely to the servicing field may develop the search for total conversion, namely, installation and use of data processing equipment for every phase of the loan production, processing, servicing, and accounting activities.

Each growing firm passes through several or all of the following four stages of conversion: Stage I—conversion from manual operations to accounting machines; Stage II—use of service bureaus; Stage III—conversion to data processing equipment used on the premises; and Stage IV—sharing data processing equipment by several mortgage bankers.

Stage I—Conversion from Manual Operations

Every growing mortgage banking company should begin considering the installation of a bookkeeping machine when its loan volume exceeds 500, even if this means a substantial investment. An accounting machine of any make enables a trained machine operator to process from 2,000 to 3,000 payments a month. The number of loans that can actually be handled, of course, depends largely on the competence of the operator and on the details of entries made. Moreover, the longer such purchase—or for that matter, any type of conversion—is delayed, and the larger the servicing volume becomes, the more difficult and expensive it will be to effect conversion of records.

Several makes of machines now being used record essentially the same data and operate on the same basic principles. Some have special features, however, and a number of machines should be investigated before making a purchase. Some machines are designed to produce a great number of automatic totals, some of which are needed for remittance and journal reports. Some machines provide the operator maximum visibility when posting, while others do not permit the operator to see the postings until completed. The latter requires a more skilled operator. In some machines, a special "proof system" may be built in to assure the operator of accurate postings at all times. Considerations of timing, cost, and method of conversion are essential.

When? Mechanical bookkeeping becomes more effective and more economical than manual operations when the number of loans serviced reaches 1,000, especially if rapid growth in volume can be anticipated. Before making a decision on conversion, the mortgage company must also evaluate its growth potentials, the economic and social conditions that affect mortgage business trends, and overall future expectations, as indicated by general business conditions.

Generally, reports produced by bookkeeping machines which provide the required information, are acceptable to investors today. Although most investors will consent to remittance report forms prepared as a by-product of mechanical posting operations, it is imperative that when a changeover is seriously considered, the mortgage company obtain the approval of its investors on the type of reports the selected machine would produce.

Why? Accounting machines have several advantages over manual operations. Mechanical bookkeeping operations reduce the workload by performing three functions in one operation. They produce entries on individual ledger cards, post on the daily collection journal, and prepare remittance reports. Mechanical operations improve service to investors through faster operations. Payments can be processed faster, not only because the mechanical operators perform three jobs at one time, but also because the posting operations are performed more rapidly. Since most machines are fully automatic, they help the mortgage loan accounting department to keep up to date in reporting collections. They also provide greater accuracy and reliability by mechanically totaling all columns and automatically proving the correctness of totals, as well as distributing the monies to the various accounts. These computations definitely decrease the possibility of errors not only on the ledger cards, but also on the remittance reports, and thus assure the investors of accuracy and reliability. Under a manual system, the records are not uniform in appearance because of varying and sometimes illegible handwriting. The general form of the records and adherence to details depends wholly on the personality of the bookkeeper; mechanical records establish uniformity and neatness.

Cost   An accounting machine costs between $4,000 and $6,000, an investment which may be depreciated in 8 to 10 years. Used equipment may be available at greatly reduced prices. Of course, the cost of other accessories must be considered. New ledger cards must be printed and fire-resistant cabinets purchased to house them. Then there is a certain amount of waste, since out-dated supplies have to be discarded. It is also necessary to hire or train operators for the bookkeeping machine. In this connection, the average salary of machine operators is higher than that of bookkeeping clerks, and the demand for machine operators is far greater than the supply.

How?   If conversion appears advisable, other steps should also be taken to assure satisfactory performance. All mortgage servicing operations, but particularly those in the cashier and accounting departments, should be reviewed and a decision made about what should be saved and what should be scrapped when mechanical operations are started. Once operating procedures are mechanized, other changes and improvements should also be considered and planned, even though some of them cannot be effected immediately. When a ledger card is considered for adoption or drafted, at least two or three extra columns should be included in the form to take care of any special requirements of various lenders. Any other form that has been successfully used by others may safely be adopted, with any necessary changes.

Several mortgage companies using mechanical equipment should be contacted and their advice sought concerning the use of the equipment, their experience with it, and the details of their procedure. Members of the company undertaking conversion should also make arrangements to visit other companies to observe the mechanical operation and investigate its possibilities as applied to the needs of their own servicing procedure. It is also important that the accounting machine salesman fully understand the company's servicing requirements. Before deciding on the machine, the servicing manager should ascertain whether or not the particular machine considered will really fit the needs of the company.

Since it is easier to learn how to operate a bookkeeping machine than to master the intricacies of the numerous special requirements of a mortgage accounting procedure, it is advisable to select a suitable employee in the organization and teach her how to operate the accounting machine. If a new employee is hired to handle the new equipment, posting operations may be retarded because she would have to learn the peculiarities of posting requirements and understand mortgage accounting as well. All bookkeeping machine companies employ instructors whom they send out in the field to teach how to operate the machine. It is wise to train a substitute, at the same time, who can take over the machine during the regular operator's vacation and absences.

Stage II—Service Bureau

A *service bureau* is a company owning or leasing data processing equipment from one or several manufacturers and engaged in the business of performing various data processing tasks on a charge per item basis. It can provide an excellent and reasonably priced accounting service to its users because it can utilize its equipment, facilities, and trained staff to the fullest, and can perform this highly specialized service at a reasonable cost. Many mortgage bankers employ a service bureau for their mortgage loan accounting chores before they are either large enough or experienced enough, or both, to undertake the installation of data processing equipment on their own premises.

A mortgage banker's major concern in selecting a service bureau is the assurance that the service bureau *understands* mortgage accounting. The presence or absence of this single criterion is likely to determine whether service bureau arrangements succeed or fail.

The employment of a service bureau can actually serve one of two distinct purposes. It can provide a permanent solution, in that the bureau will perform all mortgage loan accounting or insurance accounting chores, or it can constitute simply a transitional stage between the use of conventional accounting machines and the installation of data processing equipment on the company's own premises. It is recommended, if servicing volume is increasing, that the employment of a service bureau be considered primarily as an educational and a transitional arrangement rather than as a permanent solution for accounting arrangements.

Specifically, the use of a service bureau gives the mortgage banker an opportunity to become acquainted with the benefits and uses of data processing equipment and thus paves the way toward purchasing or leasing equipment for use on company premises. It speeds up many of the mortgage loan accounting and servicing chores, and reduces personnel requirements and investment in accounting equipment.

Service bureau arrangements, however, may have disadvantages which must be carefully considered. Notwithstanding assurances, the service bureau may perform the work at its own convenience rather than in conformity with specified prearranged time requirements. Failure to conform to time specifications is never deliberate; it is usually caused by breakdown of machines without sufficient back-up equipment, by shortage of personnel, or by unusual or unexpected demands of other customers. Another problem, that is, the risk of loss of records in transit or on service bureau premises, is considerable. Arrangements for pickup and delivery service are often difficult to maintain or to time properly, detracting further from the benefits of a service bureau arrangement. The greater the distance between the location of a service bureau and the mortgage banker's offices, the greater the inconvenience and the exposure to risk of loss of records and information. As a service bureau is used more and more, the mortgage banker will become dependent on it for an increasing amount of information. As a result, budgeted expenditures for the service will increase considerably.

Stage III—Conversion to Data Processing Equipment

Conversion was the subject of an MBA Research Committee report "Advisability and Problems of Full or Partial Conversion to Punched Card Accounting" in 1956. It summarized for the first time what had already taken place in mortgage banking firms involving the use of data processing equipment and how conversion should be handled. A more recent publication on this subject by MBA was its manual, "Punched Card Data Processing for Mortgage Bankers" published in 1965 (Appendix A-8). This volume is an enlargement of the first publication; it provides an up-to-date guide to basic card-punch equipment employed by mortgage banking firms.

While conversion to conventional accounting equipment, with a machine added if the loan volume increased, usually involved an investment of $4,000 to $6,000, which was depreciated in 8 to 10 years, the monthly expenditures for the rental or the depreciation cost of owning a data processing installation are constant and considerable. In exchange for this expenditure, data processing equipment not only satisfies the accounting needs for which conventional machines are used, but it also opens the gate to limitless applications in mortgage loan production, accounting, servicing, and information for management use. The only barrier is cost, and it is between need and cost that appropriate compromises must be sought and found.

Because of the nature of the equipment and its high cost, no decision for conversion should ever be attempted without senior management of the company participating in the evaluation of the facts and in the ultimate decision making. Conversions that meet all technical specifications occasionally fail because planning does not have management backing and the cost of conversion and maintenance of equipment exceeds what the company can afford to pay.

Before designing and installing data processing equipment, the company's entire operations must first be carefully studied. This study must lead to the establishment of a system on every phase of the production, processing, accounting, and servicing operations. The study group should include the loan administrator, the treasurer, the controller, and the heads of departments whose loan production, loan-processing, accounting, or insurance chores may be considered for automation. This study group should be assisted by a data processing specialist whose assignment is developing and preparing a report on the feasibility of the conversion. The specialist can be a company employee or an outside consultant, although the former is preferred.

A major point to consider at the outset of an inquiry into conversion is that there should be sufficient justification for a "feasibility study," since rarely have plans for conversion been abandoned once such studies have begun. A *feasibility report* is usually prepared (1) by defining company operations and analyzing the systems; (2) by canvassing the various manufacturers for available equipment, checking equipment performance by current users, and verifying advantages of purchase versus leasing, and (3) by planning the installation and the housing of such a system. Once completed, the feasibility report should include what work is being done currently, the cost of such work, how the job can be performed by data processing equipment, the cost of operations if data processing equipment is used and the conversion costs, advantages and disadvantages of conversion, and recommendations to management.

As a result of the above approach, written material is developed on company operations, probably for the first time. This is doubly important when conversion is effected, since one of the prerequisites of successful installation and successful data processing operations is a written program for every operation of the company. The above approach should be used regardless of the size of the contemplated installation and the number of loans serviced, and irrespective of whether conversion is contemplated for mortgage loan accounting and servicing operations only or for all company operations.

From the initial stage of the feasibility study to the completion of a conversion program, the mortgage banker will need outside help. Assistance is available either from representatives of equipment manufacturers or from professional data processing consultants. In deciding whose services to obtain, familiarity with mortgage banking operations should be the first qualification of any manufacturer's representative or any outside consultant. Between the two there is a difference in the services each can render. A manufacturer's representative does not charge for his own and his company's consulting services, but must try to sell his own wares. A consultant's help may be unbiased, but charges for his services may also be considerable. In the long run, however, it is less costly to obtain an independent appraisal of the potential success of a contemplated installation than to err and pay the price of an unsuccessful experiment.

Check-list of things to do and things not to do:

Review and document existing operations. This review should serve as an occasion to simplify and streamline all accounting and servicing procedures.

Consider conversion a long-range program. Conversion plans should be an overall solution to all accounting and recordkeeping operations even if initiated because of increasing loan volume.

Plan to reduce cost per unit. Guard against the conversion fever which may satisfy only the desire to acquire a status symbol.

Retain overall control. If management, or the loan administrator, does not keep close rein on the data processing manager and operations, it may find that mortgage banking operations are being adapted to fit preconceived data processing systems.

Maximize the use of data processing equipment. Generally, data processing is used in connection with production, accounting, and loan servicing activities, but it also is used in connection with other tasks, such as writing of checks, reconciliation of bank accounts, addressing and mailing of advertising material, and preparation of payroll checks.

Resist overautomation. Make sure that only those operations are considered for conversion which lend themselves readily to data processing requirements. Many technicians in the field have the mistaken notion that the availability of data processing equipment precludes the possible use of bookkeeping machines or even handwritten entries to handle certain transactions less expensively and still efficiently. Most mortgage bankers who have data processing equipment and service less than 10,000 loans normally have excess equipment capacity. Unless they can utilize the equipment in other related operations, such as insurance and home improvement lending, the cost of data processing is more expensive than if the jobs were performed by means of several conventional accounting machines.

Avoid producing unessential reports. Make sure that management is not carried away with the beauty of reports which the machines may produce, the cost of which exceeds their value.

Realize that investors do not expect their correspondents to be automated. They accept all types of reports as long as they are accurate, monies are promptly deposited, and reports arrive on time in their offices. As a matter of fact, many investors are so highly automated today that they often prepare the mortgage bankers' single debit reports and ask that only exceptions be reported to them.[1]

Learn by experience of others. Do not ignore the unfavorable as well as the favorable conversions or cost experiences of other mortgage banking firms. It is advisable to inspect all nearby installations, study their plans and arrangements, and make comparisons.

Stage IV–Sharing Data Processing Equipment

Under this arrangement, a mortgage company which has a well-established data processing installation with excess machine and staff capacity either offers to perform accounting and servicing chores for its fellow mortgage bankers on a cost plus a percentage of profit basis or simply subleases its equipment to one or several mortgage bankers. Under the same principle, staff may be pooled for the performance of all servicing tasks whether they involve the use of data processing equipment or not. Such solution may help mortgage bankers further reduce the mounting costs of servicing loans.

ACQUISITIONS

Since the mortgage banking business is a first generation business, opportunities for acquisition arise rather frequently. Approaching retirement of principal owners, lack of adequate financial resources to meet today's operating requirements, or too rapid growth are forces that generate the sale of mortgage companies or a part of their servicing portfolios. On the other side of the transaction, mortgage bankers have often become impatient with the rate of growth emanating from within and turned to various means of stimulating growth. Some companies have sought "instant growth" by purchasing

---

[1] See "MBA's Standard Aggregate Accounting and Reporting System," published by the Mortgage Bankers Association of America (Appendix A-7).

servicing portfolios or entire companies, or by entering into allied fields of activities.

Presentation and evaluation of information upon which management can base its decision to grow by acquisition or merger are the task of the loan administrator. Since this text is on loan administration, the loan administrator's contributions are emphasized here; no attempt is made to cover completely all tax factors affecting either purchaser or seller, to suggest concern over the potential antitrust implications of contemplated acquisitions or to express opinions on the valuations of transactions since each situation creates its special problems and therefore offers diverse solutions. This is merely an introduction to the problems of buying and selling mortgage servicing portfolios or mortgage companies.

The ultimate success of the purchase of a servicing portfolio or of a mortgage company hinges on two factors: the purchase price, which is fixed before the arrangement is consummated, and the manner in which the acquired portfolio or company is integrated with existing operations. The purchase price contains several unknown tax elements which can favorably or unfavorably affect the outcome of the transaction for both purchaser and seller. The manner in which the portfolio is integrated is almost entirely within the control of the mortgage banker, since it involves handling the business acquired. The better the takeover and the assimilation are planned and executed, the more profitable the acquisition will become.

Although the loan administrator can put his knowledge at the disposal of tax consultants in evaluating and pricing the servicing portfolio and can cooperate with them in ultimately setting up the accounting details, he must first produce all the information on which the final decisions can be made.

Purchaser's Viewpoint

In considering the prospect of acquiring a mortgage banking entity, two fundamental points must be clarified to the best of the purchaser's ability. One involves the income tax aspect of the proposed purchase, the other the establishment of price. Both are intricate and involved, and no two purchases have so far been viewed in an entirely identical manner by the Internal Revenue Service. Nor has any set of absolute criteria ever been established on the valuation of servicing or of other assets of a mortgage company. Each aspect of the case contains too many variables to make any uniform evaluation possible, although consideration of the tax aspect of the purchase and setting the price are closely interrelated. Those considering purchases can always review terms of other recent transactions. Often the less complicated the transaction purports to be, the easier it will be to set the price for both servicing and assets.

The issues raised and the points made can only be applied on a general, overall, rather than a specific, sense. In this sense, the purchaser normally considers that he is buying three distinct components of the seller's company: company assets, servicing portfolio, and investor relationship.

The company's assets The company's assets include, in addition to cash and prepaid expenses, the company's inventory of loans, furniture, and fixtures. The liabilities include the notes payable against such inventory and other standard liabilities. The evaluation of company assets should start with the audit of the company by a certified public accountant. It may be necessary to inspect all properties on which loans have been made or commitments have been issued to ascertain their values. It is also necessary to check carefully the saleability of unsold loans and the discounts collected thereon. Instead of the purchaser inspecting all properties on which monies were lent and ascertaining the true value of inventory of loans, the seller may guarantee the sale of the loans and the purchaser may withhold part of the purchase price until the portfolio is liquidated.

The acquisition of a servicing portfolio In essence, the acquisition of a servicing portfolio represents the acquisition of an *income stream,* the right to service and derive the net income from servicing tasks. In considering this part of the purchase, the buyer must be certain that the price is properly set and, most importantly, that the Internal Revenue Service will allow the purchase price to be amortized. Presently, such amortization is permissible, but it has been opposed by the Internal Revenue Service in a few cases. In the past, only the length of such amortization has been questioned. The generally accepted period of amortization is 8 years.

The investor relationship Acceptance by the investor of the purchasing mortgage banker as a source of loans may be more valuable than the loans acquired for servicing. A new investor represents a new opportunity for the purchasing company to sell loans and opens up new lending territory. Establishing the best possible relationship is a crucial criterion in the acquisition since the existence or absence of new investor contracts have considerable bearing on price as well as on tax treatment. Obtaining assurances in connection with this aspect of the transaction is also often most difficult. The seller may not wish to tell his investor that he is selling and the buyer may not want to go too far for fear that a premature disclosure of his intentions may spoil the success of his negotiations.

In addition to the basic ingredients described above, there are many other intangibles that influence the worth of a company. The purchaser should seek answers to the following questions:

Are new lending areas involved?

Do quality and location of loans fit into the purchaser's present portfolio? Loans of poor quality or in poor locations will generally increase expenses, reduce opportunities for refinancing, and may cause difficulties in maintaining insurance. A volume of loans located far away from the home office premises without adequate closeby servicing facilities can also be considered an adverse factor.

What is the capacity of existing accounting equipment? Can the volume of loans to be acquired be handled by the existing equipment, or is there a need for additional equipment? Will there be an increase in rental cost of data processing equipment if such is involved? If, however, existing equipment is currently not fully utilized, to what extent will additional loans reduce per-loan servicing costs?

What is the capacity of office and personnel to absorb acquisitions? Can the portfolio to be acquired be adequately handled by existing servicing personnel? If additional staff is required, can the seller's personnel be absorbed? Is the seller's personnel compatible with existing personnel and can savings in personnel be accomplished? Does the incoming company have any employees with special or specialized talents whose services will add to the value of acquisition?

What is the value of servicing contracts? Do the servicing contracts to be assigned to purchaser contain provisions for a 1 percent cancellation fee for termination of agreement "without cause"? The Federal National Mortgage Association now permits the compensation of the seller by the purchaser, but retains the right to approve the new servicer.

What kind of reputation does the seller have in the community and with investors? Are the company and its clients compatible with those of the company acquiring it?

What is the company's capacity to finance additional business? Will escrow reserve funds to be acquired with the servicing portfolio merit additional lines of credit?

Can insurance be written? How successful was the seller with insurance? Compensation for an insurance business that is part of, or is allied to, the mortgage origination and servicing activity can be included in the offer price for the company, the servicing portfolio to which it is related, or priced as a separate entity. The cost of insurance business normally ranges from one to two and a half times the average annual net insurance commissions. Here, as in the case of servicing, the purchaser may be wise to agree to pay 50 percent of net commission income on such business for a period of three years, not to exceed a fixed price. Such arrangement automatically adjusts the transaction if the insurance business is lost after the consummation of the transaction.

What is the delinquency and foreclosure situation? Since collection expenses can dissipate much of the anticipated servicing fee income, it is imperative that the delinquency picture of the portfolio be carefully scrutinized. It is more expensive to improve a neglected portfolio or to weed out loans by means of foreclosure than to avoid purchasing it.

Seller's Viewpoint

The viewpoints of two sellers may be entirely different depending on the reasons which prompt the sales. The seller who is facing an estate problem, or the executor of an estate who wants to get out of the mortgage business, has an objective which differs from that of the seller who feels that his efforts, his staff, and his connections can be best utilized as part of a larger organization. The former type of seller seeks only a monetary return and favorable tax considerations; the latter type desires these benefits, but is also interested in a future within the company for himself and his staff.

Just as the purchaser buys three commodities, so the seller wishes to dispose of three commodities: (1) income streams derived from the future servicing of the portfolio, (2) servicing contracts with investors, and (3) a going concern or good-will value.

In contrast to the position of the purchaser who claims that he is purchasing a right to receive ordinary income in the future, the seller's position is that the servicing portfolio which is being sold is actually a property right or asset subject to capital gains treatment. When the sale of servicing contracts is considered together with good will, the capital gains treatment may be attained. Advantageous tax solutions may be worked out either through the liquidation of the selling corporation or by other acceptable means and tax methods recommended by tax consultants.

If a servicing portfolio is being sold separately, such sale does not give rise to a capital gain to the seller. To please the seller as well as the purchaser, the seller must sell the stock of the company and the purchaser must dissolve the company after the stock has been purchased.

Aside from tax considerations (for which tax consultants must be employed) there are other aspects of the transaction on which the views of the seller of an entire company would differ from those of a purchaser. Some of the considerations, of course, depend on whether the seller expects to remain in the business or intends to retire. If the seller expects to be a part of the purchaser's company, he will want to consider some of the following: Does the purchaser operate a sound mortgage banking firm? Is he considered fair and reputable? Does the firm have adequate financial resources to do its share of the business? Will investors approve of the purchaser? Are management and staff of the purchaser compatible? Is there adequate provision for management succession? Are compensations adequate and are there appropriate profit-sharing and retirement benefits for acquired employees?

Pricing of Purchase

In most instances, the pricing of an acquisition involves the allocation of a specific sum to the assets of the company and the designation of a separate sum for the servicing portfolio. The value of tangible assets of a company can be easily determined. Pricing of the loan inventory is more difficult since the appraisal of the properties, the amount of the loans, and the discounts, if any, at which they are carried have considerable influence on its value. On these items, however, ready agreements can be made between buyer and seller by asking a few simple questions. What is servicing worth? What prices have been paid? Prices for residential portfolios either by themselves or as part of the overall price consideration of a company on the average have varied from $\frac{3}{4}$ of 1 percent to $1\frac{1}{2}$ percent of the servicing volume involved, provided the majority of loans carry a servicing fee rate of $\frac{1}{2}$ of 1 percent. For residential portfolios containing loans with servicing fees of $\frac{3}{8}$ or $\frac{1}{4}$ of 1 percent, prices are scaled down proportionately. Prices have also been established at an amount equivalent to 2 years of servicing income of the loans involved.

Factors that affect the price consideration include:

Age of portfolio. The older the loan, the quicker it amortizes, and the sooner it can be paid in full. A loan with a balance of $10,000 but with 15 years remaining of a

30-year term will run off faster than a $10,000 balance that has 25 years to run. Therefore, loan amounts and average balances alone do not reveal the value of the portfolio.

Composition of servicing fees. Since totals are used to project overall servicing fee income, the source of such income must also be analyzed. Is servicing fee income earned on residential loans with large outstanding balances and serviced at $\frac{1}{2}$ of 1 percent offset by a large number of loans with small balances at $\frac{1}{4}$ of 1 percent? The composition of loans by categories and types and the relationship of unpaid balances to fees must be carefully analyzed.

Average size of loan. It is also important to ascertain the average size of loan needed to break even. This average can be determined by dividing the annual per-loan servicing cost by the annual servicing fee rate applicable to the loans involved.

The value of a specific servicing portfolio can be roughly estimated or calculated with considerable precision. An estimating procedure appears in Exhibit 16. The figures used and projected illustrate a formula that can be prepared quickly and easily. The following assumptions were made: The transaction contemplates sale of $36,000,000 portfolio consisting of 3,000 loans at a price of $360,000, which currently yields a servicing fee income of about $160,000. Servicing expenses as shown on the company books are $72,000 per year, i.e., $2 per loan per month—an accomplishment that can hardly be improved upon.

If an 8-year amortization is assumed, the proposed transaction at the illustrated price will not likely be desirable as shown in the last column (net after taxes), computed at a 48 percent rate. This type of projection can be prepared for any portfolio under consideration, with various prices and servicing costs, and with various adjustments for special factors influencing the proposed transaction. A sophisticated formula for determining the value of a servicing portfolio through computer calculations is described in an article by Irving Rose, "How Much Is Servicing Worth" in the September 1963 issue of *The Mortgage Banker.*

The price of the servicing portfolio is customarily established first, the portfolio either being the only item to be purchased or carrying the greatest weight in the purchase under consideration. Prices of other components of a company or a prospective acquisition must also be ascertained. Since contingencies, if any, must be disclosed by the seller and sought by the purchaser, it will be necessary, if purchase of the company is involved, for the purchaser to prepare, or have the seller provide, the necessary information for:

1 A pro forma balance sheet combining the assets and liabilities of both companies.
2 A pro forma income and expense statement, first combining income and expenses and then consolidating income and expense items so that the potential savings from merging a company or a servicing portfolio are clearly identified.
3 A loan inventory which provides a detailed listing of loans included in the company's balance sheet, shown by address of property, appraised value of property, loan amount and discount collected. The same information should

EXHIBIT 16 Income and expense projections for proposed acquisition

Dollar volume of portfolio: $36,000,000 worth of FHA, GI, and conventional residential loans.
Servicing fees: most loans at $\frac{1}{2}$ of 1 percent fee. Last fiscal year's servicing fee income: $160,000.

Contemplated purchase price: $360,000.

Years	Servicing income	Servicing expenses		Net before amortization	Amortization	Taxable income	Income tax	Net after taxes
1969	$160,000	3,000 loans	$ 72,000	$ 88,000	$ 45,000	$43,000	$20,640	$22,360
1970	140,000	2,600 loans	62,400	77,600	45,000	32,600	15,648	16,952
1971	120,000	2,200 loans	52,800	67,200	45,000	22,200	10,656	11,544
1972	100,000	1,800 loans	43,200	56,800	45,000	11,800	5,664	6,136
1973	80,000	1,400 loans	33,600	46,400	45,000	1,400	672	728
1974	60,000	1,000 loans	24,000	36,000	45,000	(9,000)	(4,320)	(4,680)
1975	40,000	600 loans	14,400	25,600	45,000	(19,400)	(9,312)	(10,088)
1976	20,000	200 loans	4,800	15,200	45,000	(29,800)	(14,304)	(15,496)
	$720,000		$307,200	$412,800	$360,000	$52,800	$25,344	$27,456

also be prepared for commitments—loans not yet in inventory, but for which firm commitments have been issued.

4 A pro forma personnel projection which will combine the staffs of the companies and highlight any prospective dollar savings in personnel.

5 Reports on banking and credit arrangements; employees and their compensations; all employee benefit plans including profit-sharing and retirement plans, if any, and the lease for the premises or the deed to, and arrangement for, the building.

It is important to remember, however, that the contemplated acquisition will only be profitable if the acquired company or portfolio produces a sufficient after tax return on the investment. The size of the additional income must be commensurate with the risks in prospect. These risks include changes in business and economic conditions, and the possibility that the tax plans do not work out as favorably as initially contemplated. Any such eventualities must be reflected in the price.

In recent acquisitions of entire mortgage banking firms by large publicly held companies, a pricing formula based on a price-earnings ratio has been used. In these instances, prices were primarily based on the mortgage banker's overall earnings history and future earnings prospects from loan origination and servicing at 10 to 20 times the amount of earnings, rather than on assets and servicing volume. If, for instance, a company's earnings were about $300,000 after taxes, the price ranged from $3 million to as high as $6 million.

Execution of Purchase

As stated earlier, a properly priced acquisition can yield maximum profit to the purchaser only when supported by a well-prepared plan for integration of personnel and procedures if an entire office of a company is purchased, or of the servicing portfolio if only the latter is involved. The necessary adjustment involves coordination and cooperation between personnel and the assimilation of the seller's procedures into those of the purchaser. Some of the work to achieve these objectives is done during the process of negotiations and before the transaction actually takes place. Very little can be left to the last day.

Adequate preparation for a takeover is important. Customers will expect no interruption in the promptness of service and pleasant relations they enjoyed with the seller-servicer. They do not want to be jolted by an error, oversight, negligence, or act of discourtesy.

A list of steps for providing an orderly transfer of loans or company personnel is as follows:

1 Become familiar with, and analyze the method of, handling borrowers' payments.

2 Make adequate and appropriate preparation for notification of customers of changeover and changes in servicing arrangements, if any.

3 Confirm all outstanding principal balances and escrow reserve balances with mortgagors.

4 Make appropriate plans to transfer seller's bank accounts.

5 Advise staff of acquisition well in advance and in sufficient detail to ensure cooperation and to establish good working relations with new employees. Plan to announce reasons for acquisition and benefits to be derived from it. This can be done better in a meeting than by a written memorandum to the staff or a notice on the bulletin board.

6 Create in advance new cashier, accounting, tax, and insurance records if necessary. Perhaps keep parallel records until the changeover is fully consummated.

7 Assuming that the seller's books and records were audited just prior to takeover, review all servicing contracts in detail. Also check such matters as adequacy of fidelity and errors and omissions insurance protection, accuracy of tax department records, and, in general, any records or arrangements that may involve expense or potential liability.

8 Prepare to indoctrinate employees of seller into company routine. Allow acquired personnel to continue handling those loans which they have made or serviced. This will lessen the inconvenience of the changeover as far as customers are concerned and will assure investors a continuity of proper servicing of their loans.

BRANCH OFFICE OPERATIONS

Mortgage bankers have often found that operations of branch offices help to increase the volume of loans on property in desirable residential areas. There are two types of branch offices, the "full service office" and the "suboffice." The so-called *full service branch office* is located in a city other than that in which the main office is located. This type of office is usually independent, and a company vice president normally has charge of the entire office. It performs all the origination and most of the servicing functions. It can produce and ship loans directly to the investor; in most instances, however, it sends its completed loans to the main office for centralized delivery to the investor. The only servicing function that often is not handled by a full service branch office is that of accounting, which can be handled more economically by a centrally located accounting machinery, especially if data processing equipment is used.

The *suboffice type* of branch office is used primarily to maintain loan origination facilities and contacts with builders and realtors. All work other than that of originating, and occasionally of processing loans, is then performed in the main office. Originating offices are usually located in areas near the main office, suburbs, or nearby town and localities.

Management's decisions about the type of branch office operation that is most desirable will be largely based on the needs of the communities and the company's relationship with customers rather than on any operating considerations. Once a decision is made on whether a full service branch or only a suboffice branch is desirable, its operating procedures can be quickly established to perform with maximum efficiency and minimum additional expense.

DIVERSIFICATION INTO ALLIED FIELDS

On the matter of diversification of activities, banking firms have two different operating philosophies. According to one philosophy, a mortgage banker serves his customers and investors best only if he remains a pure mortgage banker and devotes his full time to lending. Although he may diversify into the home improvement lending field or the insurance field, he remains primarily a mortgage banker. He does not round out his activities by entering the real estate or property management business. This type of mortgage banker feels that real estate brokerage and property management firms are his best source of loans, and that by competing with either of them, he cuts himself off from his best source of business.

According to the other philosophy, a mortgage banker will perform a more useful function and will operate more profitably if, through his ingenuity and resources, for instance, he can put together an entire apartment building or shopping center project— namely, arrange the purchase of land, plan its development, arrange the financing, win a management contract, and write the insurance. In addition to his normal mortgage banking responsibilities this mortgage banker becomes a partner in the enterprise, and in addition to servicing, he manages the property. In this sense, he continues to enjoy a fee for his initiative and risk taking.

Regardless of the basic distinction in philosophy of diversifying activities, mortgage bankers usually occupy a position between the two extreme poles.

The source of leads into allied activities is the customer list built up through the origination and servicing of loans, through contacts with builders, attorneys, and real estate brokers. Continuous friendly contact with a list of names offers almost unlimited opportunities for the development of real estate business, management of properties, sale of insurance of all varieties, and origination of home improvement loans. If established accounting facilities permit, accounting services for others may also be developed.

For a management decision to diversify, it usually takes a competent loan administrator to marshal information and to devise various plans by which the existing servicing and accounting facilities may be utilized for the solicitation and acquisition of other types of business. Discussion of some of the specific areas of diversification in which mortgage bankers have been successful follows.

Real estate brokerage Real estate brokerage readily leads to mortgage lending, since the house that was purchased normally must be financed. The major drawback of being in the real estate business comes from possible conflict of interest in arranging sales and in financing the same sales.

Insurance In those states in which the mortgage banker can engage in the insurance business, the development of an active "one-step" insurance department can become a source of considerable revenue and a service to the mortgage banker's customers. In addition to the sale of insurance involving the protection of the mortgagor's and mortgagee's interests, policies to cover life, accident and health, automobiles, boats, etc., may be solicited on a house-to-house basis, but preferably on a direct-mail basis.

Property management   Mortgage bankers have found it useful to have property management facilities to round out their service responsibilities to investors. Need for property management talent arises primarily if the company is extensively involved in income property lending.

The home improvement lending field[2]   This field has always been a profitable one. Many mortgage bankers have entered this field without availing themselves of FHA insurance. Although taking certain risks, they have cut their operating costs and increased the speed with which they can render service to customers.

Home improvement lending, if confined to the mortgage banker's own portfolio and generated by his own residential loan staff, is based on the philosophy that any mortgage banker's best source for home improvement lending is his own list of customers. Production and accounting machinery to make and service home improvement loans can be readily established. The mortgage banker can either provide his own funds for this type of business or can collateralize the loans with his bank as he does his residential loan business. The only lending criteria that must be observed are that lending be limited to home improvement purposes and that no borrower be granted a home improvement loan without approval of the collection department which handles the borrower's first mortgage loan.

Accounting services and rental of equipment   These activities are profitable for those mortgage companies which have achieved a high degree of accounting sophistication and have excess manpower or machine capacity. They can make their talents and equipment available on a time or cost-sharing basis.

[2] An excellent treatise on this subject may be found in the October 1970 issue of *The Mortgage Banker* by Raymond A. Jensen, entitled "Consumer Finance . . . A Profitable Service Adjunct."

CHAPTER EIGHT

Operating and Statistical Reports

As any financial institution, the mortgage banker, in addition to producing and analyzing financial statements, must produce operating and statistical reports which enable him to evaluate performance of individual operations and to manage those operations effectively. Operating and statistical reports are simply a rearrangement of the information that the financial officer develops to prepare the financial statements and cost accounting analyses—a rearrangement that permits analysis of the principal mortgage banking operations. For example, the income statement may reveal a decline in income; the operating statement on warehousing may then reveal that income is being lost by poor management of the warehousing line and inefficient use of bank credit.

Operating reports summarize results of producing loans, providing funds for lending, warehousing loans, selling loans to investors, and related activities. In essence, they provide regular information on the nature and quantity of the company's operations. Normally, these reports are originated in the departments responsible for specific functions rather than in the accounting department. In a company which employs data processing equipment, all information on operations is usually forwarded to, or is recorded by, the data processing department which prepares the reports.

Statistical reports are put together from operating reports; they enable management to evaluate the success or failure of an operation; they assist management in critically appraising the production and sales of loans, by comparison with growth targets, the level of economic activity, and the record of other mortgage lenders. Operating and statistical reports may also be developed into projections which go beyond summarizing accomplishments to project profit objectives that management

133

has under consideration. Without reports of this type and without their proper use and application, successful mortgage banking operations can hardly be maintained.

Before dealing with specific reports, some general criteria are in order. Obviously, information is only useful when it is prepared and presented as soon as possible after the close of the period it covers, or when it is needed. It must be accurate, and the essential data must be illustrated clearly and concisely. A table containing a row of figures may be as valuable as a well-conceived, but involved, report produced by machine. It is also essential that any system involving the orderly gathering and dissemination of operating and statistical reports remains flexible. If changes in format are needed to highlight certain situations, or more clearly illustrate events, such changes must be made promptly. Furthermore, reports no longer needed should be eliminated; others should be improved or expanded to correspond to changes in business requirements. Information should not be gathered and disseminated for information's sake, since meaningless and untimely reports only obscure the value of timely and informative data.

OPERATING REPORTS

Single-family Loan Production Reports

Loan production reports begin with recording each loan application in the loan inventory report and tracing its progress until it is purchased by an investor. The entire process may be maintained in a single, composite form or in individual reports. In either case, the report may be prepared daily or less often. A large, active firm will, of course, require more frequent analysis of the progress of its inventory.

If the loan producers are compensated on a commission basis or by a combination of salary and incentive bonus, and if solicitors and brokers are employed, the compilation must include the names of individual producers. In these instances, care should be exercised to see that loans are properly identified at the outset by the respective producer's name. Accurate records at this initial point can go a long way toward keeping loan producers satisfied while maintaining reliable production records.

Similarly, for proper planning of sales efforts and fund requirements, production reports must include data by location of properties, must show the timing of contemplated loan disbursements, as well as contemplated dates for delivery of the completed loan package. This is particularly significant if operations are conducted in several cities or states, and if more than one bank provides funds for mortgage lending purposes.

To keep a constant watch on the profitability of operations, some report forms contain the price of each loan when made and when sold, and the profit or loss on each loan. Thus a composite picture may be derived from which the profitability of operations, or lack of it, may be anticipated even before the financial reports of the company actually report the consummation of the transactions.

Loan inventory report The *loan inventory report* is a report of loans which were disbursed and are unsold. In essence it represents the company's investment in loans. Technically, an inventory report is similar or identical to the accounting records of the company which shows by types of loans (FHA, VA, or conventional) the inventory position of the company; it simply lists all the loans on hand by name, address of property, loan amount, interest rate, and the amount of discount at which a particular loan was made or acquired. A loan inventory report, therefore, represents a summary of loans on hand and available for sale. It should be maintained in the mortgage sale or loan-shipping department under the direct supervision of the person responsible for loan production.

Loan production and loan inventory records may be effectively combined. If a large volume of loans is produced, an up-to-date report including a summary of the previous day's transactions should be prepared each morning.

Warehousing report The *warehousing report* may combine several purposes: it can portray the entire loan production activity or can be related to loans which have been disbursed, pledged at banks, and are awaiting delivery to investors. It should distinguish loans the company made without an investor's commitment from those backed by commitments.

Commitment report There are several types of *commitment reports.* Some are designated to keep track of outstanding, but unfilled, investors' commitments, and others show loans not yet delivered against outstanding commitments. Similarly, there are commitment followup records pertaining to builder's loans showing outstanding company commitments to a builder which have or have not yet been filled. Unavailability of information on outstanding commitments can impede the company's operation and cause it to lose business. Reports of this type also show commitment expiration dates or are prepared in sequence of such dates to enable the company to keep track of expirations. If such is the case, reports must be updated daily.

Loan collateral or loan delivery report Information on loans ready to be collateralized or shipped may be incorporated into any of the earlier reports. It may also be shown in a separate *loan collateral* or *banking report.* These reports may include information on collateral available or collateral used, or loans may be listed by commitment, expiration dates, or their availability for shipping or purchase.

Report of loans purchased by investors This report is a simple listing of loans purchased by types and by investors within a particular period of time.

Income Property Loan Production Reports

Conventional loans Many of the details that go into a single-family production report also become ingredients of the income property loan production report. Because of

the size of the loan, the intricate requirements pertaining to rental or leasing requirements of most commitments, and the length of time it usually takes to construct a
project, a number of additional criteria must be built into the report form, both for
it to be informative as a report and for it to be used as a guide for following up the
processing, banking, and completion of loan package and its delivery to the investor.

In this field, loans are not normally entered on a production report until an investor's commitment has been obtained. Of course, information may be assembled on
inquiries on a "loan inquiry sheet" just to record the activity in the department.

FHA multifamily loans Information on a production report for loans of this type
may be grouped either by the sections of FHA regulations under which the loans
are processed or according to the various FHA processing stages

Other Reports

Projections Financial planning can take many forms and financial reports as described in this chapter may be used to serve many objectives. No report, however, is
as significant in planning objectives and measuring achievements as an overall projection of the company's income and expense items in terms of the specific objectives
decided upon by the company's management.

While financial reports portray results, projections measure performance from
month to month, quarter to quarter, against planned goals. For instance, origination
and servicing income can be readily projected and then measured each month as to
how, and to what extent, objectives were achieved. Similarly the expenses of such
activities may also be planned and then measured by comparing actual to projected
expenditures. Based on periodic reviews of projections, corrective measures can be
taken and performance may be judged; the cost of operation in each field may also
be established and compared with actual costs; and operations may be adjusted. Long-
range profit objectives can also be planned and the achievement of goals followed.

Projection of fund requirements This tool which is essential primarily to the production of income property loans was already discussed in Chapter 6 and illustrated in
Exhibit 13.

Cash in banks and loans payable report This report is a daily report designed to inform the officer in charge of financial planning of the cash position of the company
and its obligation to the banks from which the company borrows. It is prepared either
shortly before the close of business each day or soon after operations commence in
the morning. Once the balances at the various banks are ascertained, funds must be
either borrowed or transferred from an account which shows a credit position, particularly when on a "checks-issued" basis, an overdrawn position is indicated.

If desired, the report may also include information on the lines of credit provided
by the banks involved and on monies held in various custodial accounts. A day-to-day

relationship of the monies borrowed and the compensating balances available to the bank can thus be maintained and kept under control at all times.

STATISTICAL REPORTS

Through statistical reports which rearrange the data available in operating statements, the loan administrator can analyze specific phases of operations in order to evaluate their effectiveness, to plan expansion of business, in particular, to compete with other companies more effectively, and to keep a running report on the profitability of operations.

As the mortgage banker's area of operations becomes more extensive and his activities more diversified, other kinds of statistical information are needed to test, measure, and ascertain the profitability of each activity. For instance, for a mortgage banking firm which maintains a home office and several branch offices, a personnel report with a breakdown of staff by activities affords an opportunity to plan personnel needs as activities change, or as business conditions either surge upward or slacken. Three of the most important types of statistical reports are described below.

Volume of Loans Serviced

This compilation distributes information on the volume of servicing by type of loans and investor. It is probably the most valuable tool for forecasting loan administrative revenues of the company. It is also a basic tool for cost accounting studies.

The initial compilation is usually established by adding up the loans serviced for each investor by type of loan. Single debit reports, of course, may be the best source of data for this type of record, since they require a listing of all loans by outstanding principal balance. Once a compilation is made, it can easily be kept up to date by adding new sales to each investors' holdings and deducting amortization and pay-offs. However, it is often easier to take the balances off loan cards or to list principal trial balances for each investor by type of loans.

A summary report of the servicing volume should be prepared monthly; a more detailed analysis of changes in the portfolio need not be prepared more frequently than semi-annually or yearly. (See Exhibit 17.) The complete analysis classifies the activity in the portfolio in addition to types of loans by investor. The information may, of course, be reproduced easily by means of data processing equipment on a monthly basis.

The detailed report enables management to reevaluate its relationships with certain investors if the volume of loans for a particular investor has increased or to search for answers to problems if the volume of loans serviced for a particular investor is declining. Management should, therefore, examine these reports carefully, noting unusual reductions in volume in general or with certain investors in particular. Such reviews can be the basis for a reassessment of loan production policies.

EXHIBIT 17   ABC mortgage company—mortgage loans serviced*

Investor	FHA residential mortgages		FHA multifamily mortgages		Conventional business mortgages	
	Number	Amount	Number	Amount	Number	Amount
Saving Society	225	3,292	5	24,392		
Life Insurance Co.	537	5,538	5	2,926	17	21,518
XYZ Life Ins. Co.			2	6,395	36	25,240
Life Company	986	12,906	7	562	10	2,710
Life Assurance Co.	127	1,071			54	20,851
National Bank			2	18,675	1	69
Church Board					65	22,178
FNMA and GNMA	806	13,073				
Life Insurance Co.					43	14,273
State Investment Bd.			1	10,441		
Insurance Company	48	663			16	7,218
Life and Accident Co.					19	8,691
Savings Bank			1	6,255		
Life Insurance Co.	48	532			42	5,440
State Bank					1	2,916
Mutual Association					9	4,841
Life Insurance Co.	117	964			4	2,151
Trust & Savings Bank	20	322			13	1,693
Life Insurance Co.					26	2,921
Ins. Co. of America					14	2,861
The First Nat'l Bank	60	934	1	1,272		
Savings Bank	51	641				
Investors	6	99				
Nat'l Insurance Co.	18	108	1	69	9	1,717
Trust & Savings Bank	84	1,268			3	431
Total	3,133	41,416	25	70,991	382	147,729
ABC Mortgage Co.—to be serviced	50	698	1	15,213	12	18,522
Total serviced at June 30, 1970	3,183	42,115	26	86,204	394	166,252
Total serviced at June 30, 1969	3,077	40,705	29	84,788	420	154,471
Increase or decrease	106	1,409	(3)	1,416	(26)	11,781

*All amounts in thousands of dollars.

EXHIBIT 17   ABC mortgage company – mortgage loans serviced *

Conventional residential mortgages		GI first mortgages		Grand totals June 30, 1970		June 30, 1969		Increase or decrease	
Number	Amount	Number	Amount	Number	Amount	Number	Amount	Number	Amount
34	678	728	8,717	992	37,080	1,052	33,096	(60)	3,983
176	2,496	441	3,978	1,176	36,457	1,319	38,405	(143)	(1,947)
				38	31,636	38	32,851	0	(1,215)
96	679	677	9,347	1,176	26,206	1,958	28,529	(182)	(2,322)
4	30	312	3,009	497	24,963	527	21,772	(30)	3,190
1	32	348	4,401	352	23,178	372	23,664	(20)	(486)
				65	22,178	62	20,497	3	1,681
		143	2,345	949	15,419	587	8,735	362	6,683
				43	14,273	43	13,459	0	814
				1	10,441	1	10,554	0	(112)
139	2,141	20	251	223	10,275	238	9,808	(15)	467
				19	8,691	19	8,951	0	(159)
				1	6,255	1	6,307	0	(52)
9	74	4	50	103	6,097	106	5,302	(3)	795
54	3,001	9	125	64	6,043	67	5,941	(3)	101
				9	4,841	9	5,829	0	(988)
35	213	220	1,277	376	4,608	395	5,044	(19)	(436)
153	1,518	12	190	198	3,724	215	4,086	(17)	(362)
				26	2,921	27	3,193	(1)	(272)
1	3			15	2,864	17	2,999	(2)	(134)
2	39	27	326	90	2,573	72	2,308	18	264
		144	1,709	195	2,351	211	2,575	(16)	(223)
		146	2,046	152	2,145	160	2,235	(8)	(89)
		20	176	48	2,072	48	1,669	0	403
		20	345	107	2,046	109	1,721	(2)	324
704	10,908	3,271	38,300	7,515	309,347	7,653	299,541	(138)	9,806
		10	189	73	34,624	50	35,334	23	(710)
704	10,908	3,281	38,490	7,588	343,971				
728	11,608	3,449	43,302	7,703	334,876	7,703	334,876		
(24)	(700)	(168)	(4,812)	(115)	9,095			(115)	9,095

*All amounts in thousands of dollars.

Analysis of Loans to Be Paid in Full

This statistical compilation usually serves as a barometer of current conditions in real estate market and mortgage financing and also offers clues about competitors' mortgage lending activities. The tabulation should be obtained from notifications by borrowers of their intentions to pay their loans in full. Some pay-off notices may be regarded as warnings which call for remedial action to forestall further similar losses in an area in which one or two refinancings have occurred, particularly if it is evident that the refinancings involve one or two aggressive competitors. Others may be accepted as unavoidable or may be received by the company with a sense of relief, if the borrower was frequently delinquent or troublesome. If the borrower or his attorney does not state the reason for asking for a pay-off statement, the borrower should be contacted for this information promptly, since most investors require this information when papers are requested.

The notices should be classified according to the reasons for payment in full. Classifications should include such categories as "purchaser refinancing" or "borrower refinancing"; the latter may be broken down to show source of money by the type of institution involved, such as a bank, another mortgage banker, a savings and loan association, or an insurance company lending directly. The tabulation should also show the type of loan and the dollar amount.

The information should be prepared each month, and the total amount for the month should be compared with losses for the previous month or for the same month a year ago, or both. The information should be presented to the head of the production department each month. However, any unusual activity, such as "loan raiding," should be reported immediately.

Generally, no action can be taken when a loan is to be paid in full as the result of the borrower using his own funds or as a consequence of an all-cash sale of the property. If the borrower uses his own funds to pay off his mortgage and the balance is relatively low, the loss of the loan may be advantageous. This is true especially if the loan balance is below the servicing breakeven point, where servicing is no longer profitable.

In times of favorable mortgage market conditions, when refinancing of loans and their subsequent sale to investors is feasible, it is advisable to have the company contact all mortgagors whose mortgages have been substantially paid down, either to interest them in a larger loan or to suggest that they pay in full the small balance which makes servicing unprofitable.

Some mortgage bankers who are also in the insurance business are of the opinion that to retain a borrower as an insurance client, one must service loans below the breakeven point, while others contend that the retention of servicing is not essential to the continuation of business relationships when the insurance service is performed well.

If too many loans in a particular area are paid in full as a result of the purchaser refinancing, it is evident that the mortgage company has no established arrangements with real estate companies for mortgage financing. Under propitious circumstances, the production department can help remedy this situation by sending solicitors into the area to contact the real estate companies for an opportunity to meet competition.

An alarming situation often arises, however, when a large number of borrowers refinance with another lender. Each of the several possible reasons for such an occurrence requires careful investigation. As a practical matter, it is usually best to call the borrower immediately on the phone and to inquire as tactfully as possible why he refinanced. The answer will enable the production department to discover either a weakness in customer relations or a competitor offering better rates or higher loan amounts, or both. Once the reason for a loss is established, immediate steps should be taken to prevent similar losses. If loan raiding was accomplished by the presentation of misleading facts and figures—which can occur—the mortgage company should either send letters to all borrowers in the area where the raiding occurred or visit them in person, suggesting that they contact the company for its terms and weigh the facts carefully before applying for a new loan elsewhere.

The conclusions that may be drawn from the tabulation may be used to bring about additional business for an alert production department. The mortgage company should also make this tabulation available to those investors who, for statistical purposes or for their future loan commitment programs, are interested in receiving reports from their correspondents about competitive developments in interest rates or length of term offered by the competition.

If a notice is received to pay off a large income property loan, this information may be used immediately by an alert person in charge of income property loans to submit new business to the investor, in order to make use of funds eventually to be received by the investor.

Delinquency Report

The monthly delinquency report of a mortgage company is one of the most significant yardsticks of successful management of mortgage portfolios. Each loan administrator must know what his loan delinquencies are for the preceding month, quarter, or year. He also must know how his accomplishments compare with those of his competitors in his own area and how his results compare with those of the other correspondents of his investors. Like a golfer, for example, he must strive to improve his own results and keep his score at a minimum.

This report also enables the loan administrator to report to the FHA on the status of delinquents, or to any or all of its investors which require a report, by number of delinquents, duration of delinquency, type of loan, or reasons for the delinquencies. Delinquencies may also be broken down by subdivisions or towns in which properties involved are located or by states in which delinquencies occur.

Exhibit 18 shows a delinquency report prepared manually by a member of the collection staff for intradepartmental use. It shows delinquencies by the number of cases in the various categories (60, 90, and 120 days) and by the number of cases in foreclosure, both for FHA and VA loans and by investors. These statistics may be expanded to include a 30-day category. While the names shown on the tabulation which represent problem cases and potential foreclosure cases are meaningless for statistical

EXHIBIT 18   Report on delinquent FHA-VA residential loans
November 30, 1971

	VA loans	60	90	120	Foreclosure	FHA loans	60	90	120	Foreclosure
ABC Mortgage Co.	1,677	6	3	...	2	986	5	2	1	6
Thrifty Savings Bank	144	...	1	...	1	151	3	4	...	2
FNMA and GNMA	1,143	10	4	1	5	1,806	10	2	1	8
Investors United	146	3	3	1	...	106	2	3	1	...
Best National Bank	220	1	...	1	...	2,117	8	8	...	3
TMC Insurance Co.	441	2	...	1	3	537	3	...	1	...
XYZ Insurance Co.	728	5	2	...	2	225	2	...	1	...
Others	90	...	...	...	1	112	2	...	1	1
Totals	4,589	27	13	4	14	6,040	35	19	6	20

	Number serviced	30 days	60 days	90–120 days	Foreclosure
VA	4,589	123	27	17	14
FHA	6,040	150	35	25	20
Totals	10,629	273	62	42	34
Percentages		2.6%	0.6%	0.4%	0.3%

EXHIBIT 19 Delinquent statistical report

DATE 12/14/70   TOTAL PORTFOLIO BY BRANCH OFFICE AS OF 12/14/70   PAGE 1

BRANCH OFFICE	CODE	T O T A L S LOANS	CURRENT	PCT.	DELINQ.	PCT.	DELINQUENCY STATUS 1-30	PCT	31-60	PCT	61-90	PCT	91-120	PCT	120-UP	PCT
DETROIT	01	1398	1082	77.4%	316	22.6%	155	49.0%	67	21.2%	18	5.6%	25	7.9%	51	16.1%
ATLANTA	02	1400	1082	77.3%	318	22.7%	166	52.2%	34	10.6%	27	8.4%	8	2.5%	83	26.1%
MEMPHIS	03	3743	3161	84.5%	582	15.5%	355	60.9%	80	13.7%	25	4.2%	22	3.7%	100	17.1%
CHARLOTTE	04	2020	1631	80.8%	389	19.2%	273	70.1%	55	14.1%	16	4.1%	9	2.3%	36	9.2%
BIRMINGHAM	05	2223	1725	77.6%	498	22.4%	358	71.8%	73	14.6%	19	3.8%	10	2.0%	38	7.6%
SAN FRANCISCO	06	6280	5651	90.0%	629	10.0%	485	77.1%	83	13.1%	23	3.6%	15	2.3%	23	3.6%
SACRAMENTO	07	452	402	89.0%	50	11.0%	20	40.0%	5	10.0%	6	12.0%	1	2.0%	18	36.0%
MIAMI	08	1531	1315	85.9%	216	14.1%	143	66.2%	32	14.8%	11	5.0%	9	4.1%	21	9.7%
FORT LAUDERDALE	09	1653	1420	86.0%	233	14.0%	173	74.2%	26	11.1%	14	6.0%	6	2.5%	14	6.0%
NAPLES	10	512	411	80.3%	101	19.7%	67	66.3%	15	14.8%	6	5.9%	4	3.9%	9	8.9%
TAMPA	11	372	327	88.0%	45	12.0%	26	57.7%	9	20.0%	3	6.6%	4	8.8%	3	6.6%
JACKSONVILLE	12	556	468	84.2%	88	15.8%	59	67.0%	11	12.5%	5	5.6%	2	2.2%	11	12.5%
MACON	13	1072	898	83.8%	174	16.2%	126	72.4%	20	11.4%	10	5.7%	5	2.8%	13	7.4%
BOWLING GREEN, KY.	14	1280	1119	87.5%	161	12.5%	123	76.3%	28	17.3%	4	2.4%	2	1.2%	4	2.4%
LOUISVILLE	15	1370	1082	79.0%	288	21.0%	195	67.7%	39	13.5%	7	2.4%	11	3.8%	36	12.5%
NASHVILLE	16	149	130	87.3%	19	12.7%	12	63.1%	2	10.5%	3	15.7%	2	10.5%		.0%
CINCINNATI	17	613	520	84.9%	93	15.1%	64	68.8%	13	13.9%	3	3.2%	6	6.4%	7	7.5%
DAYTON	18	1094	854	78.1%	240	21.9%	179	74.5%	27	11.2%	12	5.0%	6	2.5%	16	6.6%
ST. LOUIS	19	147	126	85.8%	21	14.2%	11	52.3%	5	23.8%	2	9.5%	1	4.7%	2	9.5%
KANSAS CITY	20	167	128	76.7%	39	23.3%	30	76.9%	4	10.2%	1	2.5%	2	5.1%	2	5.1%
DENVER	21	350	271	77.5%	79	22.5%	50	63.2%	14	17.7%	6	7.5%	2	2.5%	7	8.8%
COLORADO SPRINGS	22	645	511	79.1%	134	20.7%	67	50.0%	26	19.4%	10	7.4%	8	5.9%	23	17.1%
PROVO	24	16	15	93.8%	1	6.2%		.0%		.0%		.0%		.0%	1	100.0%
By BRANCH OFFICE		LOANS 29043	CURRENT 24329	PCT. 83.7%	DELINQ. 4714	PCT. 16.2%	1-30 3137	PCT. 66.5%	31-60 668	PCT 14.1%	61-90 231	PCT 4.9%	91-120 160	PCT 3.3%	120-UP 518	PCT 10.9%

purposes, they are important to the supervisor of the collection department or the loan administrator who periodically reviews the progress of the collection efforts with the staff.

Many investors use their servicers' monthly delinquency reports to compile a report of delinquencies of all their correspondents and rank them in accordance with their respective collection accomplishments.

Mortgage banking firms operating nationwide or handling large portfolios have their data processing department prepare delinquency reports. A comprehensive report which shows the names of locations by code number, the number of loans served in a particular city, the number and percentage of delinquent accounts on the fourteenth day of a particular month is illustrated on Exhibit 19. Similar reports, of course, may be prepared at any given date as required by the loan administrator.

CHAPTER NINE

Cost Accounting

The earliest cost accounting analyses of the mortgage banking business were developed in the midfifties. They found that mortgage bankers lose money in producing residential loans, but make a profit in servicing them. Despite the questions raised by these studies and the continuous admonishments by industry leaders, cost accounting is still a fairly neglected endeavor. Many mortgage bankers do not yet realize that appropriate cost figures are as important in managing their businesses as an accurate appraisal of property in making a loan.

The goal of this chapter is to encourage the development of cost accounting information and the preparation of cost analyses. Its scope includes general accounting considerations and basic guidelines for cost accounting, followed by a step-by-step illustration of cost analysis procedures for a typical mortgage company that is primarily engaged in producing and servicing residential loans. The illustration also presents some of the components of the cost survey initiated in the spring of 1968 by the Research Committee of the Mortgage Bankers Association of America.

Cost accounting in the mortgage banking business is a systematic arrangement of accounting information which will facilitate analysis of the profitability of specific activities in both loan production and loan servicing. Ideally, the mortgage banker must be sure that the origination fee income equals, or is greater than, production costs and that income from the servicing fee exceeds the cost of servicing.

In addition to providing data on the cost of each mortgage operation, the results of cost accounting reach every level of the company and identify profitable and unprofitable operations. In short, cost analysis can reveal specific problems and suggest solutions that are not apparent in the firm's basic financial statements.

At first, members of the production and the servicing staffs are likely to debate the interpretation of various items. These debates should be accepted as inevitable, and in fact helpful, for they will motivate officers and department heads to keep operating costs in their departments at a minimum. With experience, the staff will become cost-conscious, exert themselves to achieve cost savings, and will look forward to checking the results in the next compilation of costs.

GENERAL ACCOUNTING CONSIDERATIONS

Frequency and Extent of Cost Accounting Reports

Since loan producing operations and the profits they produce are often seasonal and since several months may elapse between origination, closing, and sale of a loan to an investor, cost accounting records on loan production activity need not be established on a month-to-month basis. Quarterly, or even better, semi-annual, or annual compilations are sufficiently frequent to provide accurate production costs and applicable trends.

The elapsed time between origination and completion of large construction loans and origination and sale of residential loans may cause profits to be recorded in one accounting period and costs incurred in another. Consistency of charges and strict observance of allocation of costs, either to projects or the appropriate periods, is of great importance. Since servicing costs do not change from month to month, their presentation may easily be tied in with the cost accounting analysis of loan production data. Although overlaps in timing may still exist, these will not distort results sufficiently to reduce the value of cost accounting. Unusual and large items of nonrecurring nature should, of course, always be considered separately and, if necessary, eliminated from comparative cost analyses.

If the company's books are so set up that income or expense items are immediately allocated to their respective sources and areas, cost information may be established and reported each month, cost trends may be watched from month to month, and corrective action may be taken more promptly.

Preparation of Records

Cost accounting records should be prepared by the accountant in charge of the company's books, or the comptroller, in cooperation with the head of the production department, or by the loan administrator in consultation with those involved. The intricate nature of mortgage production operations and of servicing demands this teamwork. The collaboration may often be limited to brief consultations on the nature or peculiarity of specific income or expense items. For example, if the cost survey covers residential loans only, careful judgment should be exercised to eliminate or properly allocate items, such as profits from interim financing, fees from large commercial or FHA project loans, income from transactions not strictly attributable to mortgage banking operations, and all related expenses which might detract from the accuracy of the residential cost analysis.

Once the framework of cost accounting is established, departmental or functional cost accounting reports become routine. To make interpretations of the accounting data internally consistent, it is advisable for the analysis to be prepared on each occasion by the same individual. The accountant, however, must continually use judgment as well as imagination in assembling the information. Salaries and fringe benefits are the largest single element of cost and must, of course, be made available in detail or in classifications required for cost accounting.

Cost Accounting Methods

Cost accounting records may be organized in several ways: the systematic or "pure" cost accounting method, the analytic or aggregate, and a compromise or allocation of aggregated costs instead of individual items to departmental subsidiary accounts.

Systematic method Under this method, items of income and expense are coded and recorded in accordance with cost accounting requirements as transactions occur. In some cases, a single item is allocated to various accounts or departments; in other cases, items may be accumulated and a single monthly distribution made. For example, all data processing costs can be accumulated and the total charged each month or each item of expenditure may be charged to specific activities, i.e., loan production, loan servicing, or insurance. This method requires maintenance of corporate books and records in a way that provides for instantaneous allocation of items by department, activity, or branch offices. It requires the maintenance of continuous, and often elaborate, cost accounting records. Because of the details involved, this procedure may not be economical for the average company.

Analytical method Under this plan, the profit and loss statement which is incorporated in the company's year-end report is reviewed in the light of the cost accounting principles outlined on the following pages for the accounting period already terminated. In contrast to the systematic approach, preparation of the cost analysis will take a few days' work and will not require the recording of each item on a day-to-day, item-by-item basis, according to preestablished cost accounting requirements.

Since the analytical method relies on certain general cost assumptions such as the allocation of administrative and general expenses, it may not be as accurate as the systematic method. In most cases, however, the inaccuracy will not be great enough to distort the results.

ILLUSTRATION OF A COST ANALYSIS–
ABC MORTGAGE COMPANY[1]

The subsequent illustration has been designed to produce accurate figures without the necessity of establishing systematic cost accounting arrangements; they follow the principles of the analytical method rather than systematic method of cost accounting. The worksheet presented on page 153 generally follows the classifications established in any company's financial statement and is based on the sequences suggested and definitions generally outlined in the "MBA's Suggested Chart of Accounts and Financial Statements for Mortgage Companies" (Appendix A-4).

Attempts have been made to describe as many income and expense items as possible, all of which may have to be considered and included in a cost analysis. Although this illustration deals only with residential costs, headings may be changed and breakdowns may be extended to fit the study into any existing accounting framework.

Basic Assumptions

1 A cost analysis should cover a 12-month period that coincides with the company's fiscal year. Quarterly or semi-annual compilations can be made only after the completion of the first annual compilation.

2 Cost analyses of a typical mortgage banking firm should be concerned primarily with two basic functions: production and servicing. For cost accounting purposes, the servicing function begins when a loan is purchased by an investor. Accordingly, production activity is credited with the interest profit or charged with the interest loss incurred during the process of warehousing. (It should be noted here that those who normally warehouse a substantial volume of residential loans contend that loan servicing commences with the first payment on the loan, and net interest income or interest charges in excess of interest income should, therefore, be credited to servicing.)

3 The income and expense of allied activities, such as insurance, real estate, property management, and home improvement lending, must be handled separately unless the activities are negligible, in which case the items must be eliminated entirely. Since mortgage bankers who are engaged in the insurance business also normally obtain many of their insurance clients as a result of mortgage production activity, some parts of insurance commissions should, where applicable, be added to loan production income or used to offset loan production losses. This, of course, should be done only after deducting the operating costs of such insurance activity.

[1]The author was chairman of the Research Sub-Committee which in 1968 initiated a residential cost survey for members of the Mortgage Bankers Association of America. The material described and illustrated in the following pages was used as a basis for this study. Similarity between the methods used to compile information in this illustration and those employed in MBA's cost survey, therefore, is inevitable.

The principle of separation can also be applied to handling net income earned from activities in the real estate field or home improvement lending. Both activities tie in closely with, or derive their leads and customers from, residential loan production, which should get some credit.

4 Unit costs can be ascertained with a fair degree of accuracy for residential loan production. Income property loans, however, do not lend themselves to meaningful unit cost determination. Unlike residential loans, they involve wide variations in the purpose of the loan, the property securing the loan, and the size of loan. They also vary in technical and legal involvements that influence income and expense from origination and sale of loans. Thus, profitability of income property lending is measured in dollars rather than units.

5 Residential production income is represented by origination fees and discounts, whether they result in gains or losses on all loans delivered and paid for by investors. (Any price adjustment of loans in inventory, due to changes in discounts, are not taken into consideration.) Profits and losses are realized *only* when loans are actually disposed of.

6 A deliberate compromise is made to eliminate insignificant distinctions which add to the workload without contributing to the overall accuracy of the cost analysis. Since the analytical method is used in determining allocations, the apportionment of telephone expenses between production and servicing, for instance, is made by a predetermined breakdown rather than by scrutinizing each telephone bill for the source, destination, and purpose of each call.

Supplemental Information

Before the preparation of a cost analysis, the following supplemental information must be prepared and/or assembled:

1 Financial statements (balance sheet and statement of income and expenses) for the period to be examined
2 Detailed monthly records of income and expense
3 Breakdown of salary and fringe benefit expenditures by department or activity
4 Loan production records for the period
5 Information on servicing volume for the period under review

Classification

Income and expense items are classified for cost analysis purposes in a form different from that used in the financial statements. This determination is the starting point of any cost study. The principal groupings include the two basic operating activities, production and servicing, and related activities such as insurance, real estate, and home improvement lending. Two additional classifications, general and administrative expenses and eliminations, are provided for the remaining items which cannot be assigned directly to operating sources.

Loan production includes:

1 Loan origination (including appraising)
2 Sale of loans (submissions)
3 Loan processing (through VA and FHA)
4 Loan closing
5 Construction payouts
6 Warehousing and loan delivery

The processing of the loan includes items 3 to 6 and is often classified as *conveyancing*. The expense of conveyancing may be separately established and accounted for. However, since the income derived from production of loans must also cover the conveyance of loans, no separate distribution is made here.

Servicing of loans includes the functions performed by:

1 Cashier department
2 Accounting department
3 Collection department
4 Insurance department[2]
5 Tax department

Although all activities, other than production, have been attributed to the loan administration department for management purposes, only those loan administration functions which pertain to servicing are included here for cost analysis. Expenses incurred in office and personnel management and other loan administration functions are included in administrative overhead, and subsequently reallocated to production and servicing on the basis outlined below.

As far as the analysis of income and expenses of insurance activity is concerned, each company must also conform to the practices of the states within which it operates. If the mortgage banker cannot engage in the solicitation and writing of insurance, the activities of an insurance department are solely a servicing function. However, if the mortgage banker maintains an active insurance department or a separate insurance agency which fully or partly depends on the mortgage producing and servicing activities for business, the income and expense of this activity should be segregated and established separately. The net income derived from such activity should be credited to the production or servicing, or proportionately to both.

General and administrative expense General or administrative overhead expenses charged directly to a specific department are accumulated and then allocated in proportion to the number of employees engaged in the respective activities, or the square-foot area occupied by the respective departments. For instance, the cost of overall supervision or management expense is first set aside as an administrative expense, and then charged to production and servicing in proportion to the approximate number

---

[2]Companies engaged in the production of insurance business allocate here the cost of handling of insurance matters that arise in connection with the servicing of loans.

of employees engaged in these activities (or in proportion to the dollar amount of salaries paid to each group). Similarly, the cost of occupancy, which includes rent, electricity, and repairs, is allocated to production and servicing on the basis of the square-foot area provided for, and occupied by, the members of these departments.

Eliminations This classification provides for income and expense items not directly connected with the mortgage business or not to be considered for a particular cost study. Items to be eliminated may be commissions derived from occasional real estate transactions or gains on the sale of stock. In the following illustration, income property income and expenses are eliminated from the cost examination, since only residential production and servicing costs are under scrutiny.

Production during the year	Number of loans	
Residential loans	800	$ 12,000,000
Income property loans	35	18,000,000

Servicing at year end:		
Residential loans	9,000	$100,000,000
Income property loans	200	50,000,000
Capital at year end		1,500,000
Net income before taxes for year		358,000

	Number of employees
Production	18
Servicing	18
Insurance	5
Management and administrative personnel: i.e., personnel manager, office manager switchboard operator, receptionist, file clerk, messenger, etc.	9
Total	50

Office space used:	Square feet
Production	3,500
Servicing	2,500
Insurance	1,000
File room, reception room, switchboard area, storage facilities, etc.	1,000
Total	8,000

Overall Information

For the purpose of the ensuing cost compilations and analysis, certain essential data are assumed about the stature and operations of the fictional **ABC Mortgage Company.** ABC Mortgage embodies some of the characteristics of most mortgage banking firms and is used solely for illustration. Resemblance to any company's cost figures is purely coincidental. The breakdown which shows income and expenses by kinds of loans produced is only necessitated by this company's diversified activities. If the company had been engaged in residential loan production and servicing only, its cost study would be considerably simplified.

Also assumed is that the **ABC** Mortgage Company employs data processing equipment in handling residential loans and conventional bookkeeping machines in handling income property loans. For the purpose of the following illustration, the detailed analysis is limited to residential loan production and servicing. Departments where income and expense breakdowns were made, but were not analyzed in detail, include (1) income property loan production and servicing, (2) insurance department, and (3) real estate operations.

For the mortgage banker to obtain full benefit from the cost worksheets and the accompanying explanations, for the purpose either of understanding this cost analysis or of guiding the preparation of one for the reader's company, it is recommended that he follow step by step both the exhibits and the accompanying directions.

The illustrated cost analysis consists of specific tasks designed to prepare a series of exhibits. Tasks 1 and 2 prepare Exhibit 20. Task 3 prepares Exhibit 21; Tasks 4*a* and 4*b* prepare Exhibits 22 and 23; Task 5 for Exhibit 24 and Task 6 for Exhibit 25 are optional. The individual items are described for each task, and then illustrated by figures in the exhibit. Subsequently, the results are interpreted to illustrate the use of cost analysis and to support certain contentions.

Task 1

The preparation of Exhibit 20 consists of two distinct tasks. Both are illustrated on a single exhibit because the execution of Task 2 is a natural continuation of the completion of Task 1. Task 1 breaks down income and expense items that are integral parts of the company's financial statement by the departmental sources from which income was derived and the purposes for which expenses were incurred. (To clarify the explanations of items contained in Exhibit 20, two types of printing will be employed in the following text. *All references to specific figures used in Exhibit 20 which relate to ABC Mortgage Company's operating results are shown in italics.*)

Enter items on worksheet from income and expense statement as follows:

Income

Line 1: *Loan administration*

This item includes servicing fees, late charges on FHA and VA loans, participation in penalty interest and in prepayment penalties, if any. (All penalties may be shown separately.) Fees assessed for work performed in

EXHIBIT 20 Tasks 1 and 2

ABC MORTGAGE COMPANY
For year ending December 31, 1968

Line		Financial statement	Task 1 Operating departments — Production Residential	Production Income Property	Servicing Residential	Servicing Income Property	Insurance	Real estate	Elimination	Task 2 Reallocations — General and administrative expenses per employee	per square-foot area
Income											
1	Loan administration	$490,000			$408,000	$82,000					
2	Loan origination	345,000	$100,000	$245,000							
3	Interest (net)	50,000		50,000							
4	Insurance commissions	50,000					$50,000				
5	Other income	12,000		2,000	2,000			$5,000	$3,000		
6	Gross income per financial statement	$947,000	$100,000	$297,000	$410,000	$82,000	$50,000	$5,000	$3,000		
			−$397,000−		−$492,000−−						
Expenses											
7	Personnel	385,000		180,000		125,000	20,000		20,000	$26,000	$14,000
8	Occupancy	51,000		21,875		15,625	6,250			1,000	6,250
9	Equipment rental	22,000		3,000		17,000	2,000				
10	Office supplies and expenses	43,000		20,000		20,000	3,000				
11	Travel and entertainment	22,000		17,000		2,000	1,000			2,000	
12	Automobile	8,000		4,000						4,000	
13	Advertising	25,000		21,000		2,000	2,000				
14	Professional fees	22,000		15,000		5,000				2,000	
15	Loan processing	8,000		8,000							
16	Other	20,000		10,000						10,000	
17	Gross expenses	$606,000		$299,875		$186,625	$34,250		$20,000	$45,000[b]	$20,250
18	Reallocation of expense per number of employees	a(18)		a(18) 16,200		a(18) 16,200	a(5) 4,500			a(9) ($45,000)	8,100
19	Reallocation of expense per square foot of occupancy			14,175		9,450	4,725				($28,350)
20	Gross expenses after reallocation			330,250		$212,275	$43,475		$20,000		
21	Net income after elimination but before taxes	341,000		$ 66,750		$279,725	$ 6,525	$5,000	$(17,000)	00	00
22	Re-add elimination	+17,000							$+17,000	00	00
23	Net income per financial statement (before taxes)	$358,000									

a Number of employees.
b This sum is reallocated on line 18.

153

connection with "transfer of property" or "release and assumption," for instance, should be classified as loan administration income, but included under "Other income" (Line 5).

Loan administration income totaled $490,000; $408,000 was earned for servicing residential loans; and $82,000 for servicing income property loans. Late charge income is also included in this classification.

Line 2: *Loan production*

a. Origination fee

This fee is paid by the borrower for services rendered by the company in connection with a loan or for disbursing a construction loan. Fees included here are *net* fees earned, which means that if brokerage commission was paid, it has been deducted from the gross fee earned on that particular loan.

b. Discount

This item is included only if the discount collected from seller or builder is greater than the discount at which the loan was sold to an investor. A discount in excess of the discount collected is a deduction.

c. Premium

1. Fee paid by investor for a loan. Premium is occasionally collected on income property loans carrying high interest rates.

2. Finder's fees for placing a loan with an investor (primarily on a brokerage-type transaction).

The ABC Mortgage Company had a loan origination income of $345,000. There were discount "losses" on some of the residential loans and discount "gains" on others. Since discount losses were greater than gains made, they were deducted from net origination fee income. Residential origination fee income nevertheless totaled $100,000. The balance, $245,000, represented fees on income property loans, including a finder's fee of $10,000.

Line 3: *Interest*

There are two significant points to be considered in the determination and allocation of interest. First, only net interest income (or expense) is considered. Therefore, interest is actually interest earned in excess of interest paid for funds used. Under certain money market conditions, when the cost of money is greater than the fixed interest rate on government insured or guaranteed loans, net interest loss may occur. In this case, negative interest for cost accounting purposes must be shown as an expense of producing residential loans.

The second point—an optional one used purely for cost accounting purposes—is that capital funds employed in any business are entitled to a certain percentage of interest return regardless of how they are used; accordingly, in the determination of the profitability of mortgage lending operations, it may be appropriate to deduct from interest earnings, say, 6 percent of the amount of capital invested in the business, before crediting net interest earned to mortgage operations.

Total net interest income in excess of interest expense was $50,000. Since ABC Mortgage Company was able to borrow from its banks at the same rate at which interest was earned on its residential loan volume, it earned no interest on its residential loan production. The $50,000 shown represents interest collected in excess of interest payments to banks at various interest differential rates on income property construction loans in various stages of completion.

Line 4: *Insurance commissions*

This source of revenue occupies a unique position among the income items. Its treatment for cost accounting purposes depends on the extent to which the mortgage banking house, through its loan production activities, participates in writing insurance. Furthermore, cost treatment may also vary depending on whether the insurance activity is performed as a part of overall company operations or whether a separate company or division is set up for the purpose of handling insurance. In the former instance, both insurance production and the administrative duties pertaining to insurance are usually performed by the same staff. In the latter instance, there is usually a separate insurance entity for the production of insurance business and a separate one to perform the insurance servicing functions.

The ABC Mortgage Company operates an insurance department which both sells insurance and performs insurance servicing functions. For the purpose of this analysis, insurance income and expenses are analyzed in detail.

Line 5: *Other income*

This item may be attributable, and allocated, to loan production when appraisal fees are involved or segregated, e.g., when occasional real estate commissions or property management fees are involved. Transfer fees, "release and assumption" fees, or other similar fees are usually credited to, or included in, servicing.

Of the $12,000 in this classification, ABC Mortgage Company received two appraisal fees on income property loans totaling $2,000, which was credited to production income. It received three real estate commissions totaling $5,000, which was so classified. The $3,000 represented a special income item of a nonrecurring variety and was, therefore, eliminated. Transfer and other fees of $2,000 were earned, which were allocated to servicing income.

Line 6: *Gross income*

The total of all income items is taken from statement of income and expense.

Expenses

Line 7: *Personnel*

This item includes salaries, commissions, fringe benefits, payroll taxes, employment agency fees, and company contributions to a mandatory profit-sharing plan. For cost accounting purposes, bonuses which are discretionary with management are not included since these do not represent cost, but rather rewards to a few for doing a job well. All personnel expense items are allocated to the departments within which the expenses are incurred. The salaries and other employment costs of those whose responsibilities straddle departmental boundaries should be distributed on a percentage basis among the activities in which they are involved. Salaries and other employment costs of company president, chief executive officer, and loan administrator are considered management expense and placed into the category to be reallocated in proportion to the number of employees who report to them. Salaries and other personnel costs of employees primarily performing office services such as file clerk, switchboard operator, receptionist, messenger, or office boy are reallocated according to the number of employees engaged in production and servicing.

ABC Mortgage Company's total personnel expenditure is allocated directly to three operating divisions: $180,000 to production, $125,000 to servicing, and $20,000 to insurance. The $20,000 paid in bonuses to certain key people and department heads is eliminated. The expenditure of $26,000 for the salary of an officer primarily responsible for the overall supervision of the company (and employment agency fees) is placed into the "general and administrative" expenses to be reallocated to production and servicing on a per-employee basis. Expenditure of $14,000 which includes salaries of switchboard operator, receptionist, file clerk, and messenger is charged to general and administrative expenses to be allocated to production and servicing in proportion to the square-foot area being occupied by each operating entity.

Line 8: *Occupancy*

This item includes rent for premises, depreciation of furniture and equipment, fire insurance protection, real estate taxes, utilities, and maintenance. Allocation should be made in accordance with the square-foot area actually occupied by those engaged in the respective activities. The area occupied by the file room, reception room, mail room, and storage space is placed under expenses to be reallocated according to square footage of occupancy.

The $51,000 expended involved the use of an area of 8,000 square feet—approximately 3,500 feet of which was occupied by employees engaged in the production of loans, approximately 2,500 square feet by the servicing staff, and 1,000 square feet by all other office services. Expense of $1,000 is allocated for the private offices occupied by the top executives.

Line 9: *Equipment rental*

All charges for rental of data processing equipment, maintenance contracts for all other office equipment, repairs, and similar charges go under this item.

Annual rental cost of equipment is $22,000. Of this, $2,000 covers maintenance contracts for typewriters and adding machines. Since the use of typewriters and adding machines is fairly evenly divided, the amount expended is allocated on a 50-50 basis between production and servicing ($1,000 to each activity). Since data processing equipment is used primarily in mortgage loan accounting and, to a nominal extent, to assist insurance department record keeping, the cost is arbitrarily divided as follows: $16,000 to servicing, $2,000 to production, and $2,000 to insurance.

Line 10: *Office supplies and expenses*

This item includes expenditures for stationery, supplies, printing and duplicating, postage and telephone, etc. (Companies which mail coupons or notices to their borrowers or have extensive collection problems which are handled by phone calls should allocate a proportionately greater amount of these expenses to servicing.)

For the purpose of this study, let us assume that one-half of the expenses were incurred in producing loans and one-half in servicing. Expenses incurred in connection with the insurance activity are estimated.

Line 11: *Travel and entertainment*

This classification includes all travel and business promotional expense.

Since a relatively small amount was expended by the loan administrator and his staff and the manager of the insurance department for travel and entertainment, these expenses can be easily extracted from the totals and the balance allocated to production. The travel and entertainment of individuals representing management can easily be ascertained as shown here.

Line 12: *Automobile*

This item includes all expenditures (depreciation or rental charges) for automobiles, whether owned or rented, and all automobile maintenance charges.

Since ABC Mortgage Company has had no collection problems which would warrant the use of company automobiles, all automobile charges are allocated to production and management on a 50-50 basis.

Line 13: *Advertising*

This item includes both institutional and direct advertising expenditures.

Although most expenditures were for magazine and newspaper advertising related to production activities, occasionally certain mailings were made publicizing servicing facilities and insurance services. Therefore, only a nominal and estimated allocation of this expenditure is made to servicing and insurance.

Line 14: *Professional fees*

This item includes primarily legal and audit fees and other fees for services rendered.

Legal fees incurred in connection with income property loans amounted

> to $15,000. The audit bill of $7,000 was distributed by allocating $5,000 to servicing and $2,000 to overall administrative expenses, since, in addition to servicing records, the corporate books were audited.

Line 15: *Loan processing*

This item includes all expenditures incurred in loan production such as the expense of photographs, credit reports, appraisal fees, and surveys, which are not paid by borrowers.

> *These are primarily production expenditures and are so charged.*

Line 16: *Other*

All expenditures not shown above such as insurance, licenses, personal and property taxes, dues, subscriptions, contributions, and small uncollected accounts are grouped under this item.

> *These items are arbitrarily divided between production and general and administrative expenses on a 50-50 basis.*

Line 17: *Gross expenses*

All expenses *before* reallocation of general and administrative expenses go here.

Task 2

Task 2 reallocates general and administrative expenses, which were established as a result of completing Task 1, to production, servicing, insurance, or other activities on the basis of: (1) number (or respective percentage of salaries) of employees engaged in production, servicing, and insurance, or other activities; and (2) square-foot area occupied by those performing any of the above tasks.

Lines 18 and 19:

After Task 1 has been completed, the items classified under "reallocations" must be charged to their respective categories.

> *"Reallocation"* involves charging general and administrative expenses to production, servicing, and insurance either on the basis of the number of employees or by the square feet occupied by the departments.

> *Since there are fifty employees, of which eighteen are in production, eighteen in servicing, five in insurance, and nine in general office services, the sum of $45,000 (line 17) must be allocated in proportion to the total employees for the respective activities. The results of this distribution are shown on line 18. The $8,100 general office cost is subsequently reallocated on the basis of square footage.*

> *Since 3,500 of the 7,000 square feet office area (not counting administrative areas representing 1,000 square feet) is occupied by production, one-half of $28,350 (i.e., $14,175) is charged to production, $9,450 to servicing, and $4,725 to insurance. The results of this distribution are shown on line 19.*

Line 20: *Gross expense* after reallocation.

Line 21: *Net income* after reallocations and after special elimination of items not considered for cost accounting purposes, but before taxes.

Line 22: *Add eliminations*

Line 23: *Net income per financial statement*

After re-adding the items eliminated for cost accounting purposes, the total must agree with that shown in the company financial statement. All computations are always made before considering federal income taxes.

Task 3

Before developing specific cost accounting results, the production expenses for residential loans must be separated from those of income property loans. If a company has no income property loan activity, or such income is negligible, a cost analysis may be completed without the preparation of Exhibit 21. Breakdowns can be made on an item-by-item basis; they can also be made by general approximations or may be based on experience. (Both methods are employed here.) Salaries, however, must be, and can easily be, apportioned by taking actual salaries and commissions of those specifically involved in the respective activities.

In this case, space occupied by the production staff is evenly divided between those working on residential and those working on income property loans.

Tasks 4a and 4b

With all source data now available, the cost of residential loan production and of residential loan servicing can be easily ascertained. Exhibit 22 shows the cost breakdown for production of residential and income property loans. Exhibit 23 shows the cost elements in loan servicing.

As pointed out earlier, production should, theoretically, be charged for the use of the funds which constitute the company's capital, but on which it does not actually pay interest. This charge thus becomes a deduction from production income before the net cost of producing loans can be determined.

Since ABC Mortgage Company's invested capital of $1,500,000 was utilized during the year to generate $18,000,000 of income property loan business (not considering the residential business for the moment), the production income generated from such business should be reduced by whatever interest would be paid if monies borrowed had been from banks. As a matter of theory, if such a charge is not considered a part of the cost of doing business, any company employing more and more capital would *appear* to be doing business with lower and lower costs as its capital increases. Similar charges can, of course, be placed against the residential loan business to offset the return that the firm could otherwise earn on its own funds if they were not being used in making loans. However, this charge has not been included in this illustration.

EXHIBIT 21   Breakdown of production department costs—Task 3

Lines corresponding to those on exhibit 20	Residential	Income property	Total
7 Direct salaries (These may be allocated from payroll records or from special personnel tabulations and adjusted to conform to totals shown on Exhibit 20.)	$ 60,000	$120,000	$180,000
8 Occupancy	10,875	11,000	21,875
9 Equipment rental	1,500	1,500	3,000
10 Office supplies and expenses	10,000	10,000	20,000
11 Travel and entertainment	7,000	10,000	17,000
12 Automobile	2,000	2,000	4,000
13 Advertising	8,000	13,000	21,000
14 Professional fees	5,000	10,000	15,000
15 Loan processing	6,000	2,000	8,000
16 Other	5,000	5,000	10,000
18 General administrative expense including management expense	8,100	8,100	16,200
19 Reallocation of general and administrative expenses by square-foot area occupied	7,075	7,100	14,175
20 Gross expense for production	$130,550	$199,700	$330,250

EXHIBIT 22   Loan production income and costs—Task 4a

	Residential (800 loans)	Per loan	Income property (35 loans)	Per loan	Totals
Income (Line 6, Exhibit 20)	$100,000	$125.00	$297,000	$8,485.71	$397,000
Expense (Line 20, Exhibit 20)	130,550	163.19	199,700	5,705.71	330,250
Overall gain					$ 66,750
Loss on 800 residential loans	$ (30,550)	$ (38.19)			
Gain on 35 income property loans			$ 97,300	$2,780.00	$ 97,300
Overall gain					$ 66,750

EXHIBIT 23   Loan servicing income and costs[a] – Task 4b

Servicing portfolio: 9,000 residential loans totaling $100,000,000

Income

		per year	per month
Gross income (Line 6, Exhibit 20)[a]	$410,000		
Gross servicing income			
Residential loans		$45.56	$3.80

Expense (Per line 20, Exhibit 20) $212,275

Credit for income property loan servicing[b] performed by the same personnel = 10 percent of total of above cost	$ 21,228			
Servicing cost (residential loans)		$191,047	$21.23	$1.77
Net servicing income per year		$218,953		
Net servicing income per loan per year			$24.33	
Net servicing income per loan per month				$2.03
Average balance of residential loans (Based on servicing 9,000 loans totaling $100,000,000)			$11,111.00	
Breakeven point when servicing at an average of .41 percent of 1 percent[c] (This computation was made by dividing annual servicing cost per loan of $21.23 by average servicing fee rate.)	$ 5,178			

Breakeven point when servicing at 1/2 of 1 percent	$4,246
Breakeven point when servicing at 3/8 of 1 percent	$5,661
Breakeven point when servicing at 1/4 of 1 percent	$8,492

[a]For the purpose of this analysis, loan servicing income for income property loans is not examined, although the ABC Mortgage Company serviced $50,000,000 in such types of loans; however, credit is given to the servicing department for this work when computing residential loan servicing costs.
[b]The 10 percent cost is an arbitrary figure. It may be changed to suit varying circumstances.
[c]By dividing the servicing income ($410,000) by the dollar volume ($100,000,000) the average servicing fee rate can be readily determined (.41 percent). (Since late charges were included under loan administration and not under other income, the servicing fee rate is slightly higher than the composite rate at which loans were sold.)

Tasks 5 and 6

Task 5 is optional. It involves the reclassification of analyzed results by types of loans produced and by the activities that produced profit, as shown on Exhibit 24. Task 6 is also optional and is laid out in Exhibit 25. It portrays effectively the distribution of each dollar expended by the activities which produced the income and the items for which expenses were incurred. The exhibits described under Tasks 5 and 6 are actually by-products of the previous exhibits.

USE OF COST DATA TO EVALUATE
MORTGAGE BANKING OPERATIONS

Exhibits 20 to 25 clearly present all basic cost elements in the ABC Mortgage Company's operations. They show that overall loan production, when taking both residential and income property production into consideration, was profitable, but that residential loan operations, as a separate item, were conducted at a loss. Similar results will, of course, be obtained whether the analytical cost accounting method, as illustrated, or a detailed systematic method is employed. There will, of course, be differences, but these will not be significant for management decisions.

At this point the results of the cost analysis may be used for assessing and evaluating the success of the company's operations and pinpointing what is profitable and what is not, how profitable it is or to what extent one profitable activity supports an unprofitable one.

The ABC Mortgage Company has made an overall profit as shown by its certified

EXHIBIT 24   Recapitulation of results by activity—Task 5 (optional)

Results by types of loan produced			
Residential loans			
Origination fees (Exhibit 22)	$ (30,550)		
Servicing fees (Exhibit 23)	$218,953	$188,403	
Income property loans			
Origination fees (Exhibit 22)	$ 97,300		
Servicing fees	$ 60,772[a]	$158,072	$346,475
Results by activity			
Production			
Residential loans	$ (30,550)		
Income property loans	$ 97,300	$ 66,750	
Servicing			
Residential loans	$218,953		
Income property loans[a]	$ 60,772	$279,725	$346,475
Insurance			$ 6,525
Real estate			$ 5,000
Total			$358,000

[a]Income property servicing income of $82,000 (Exhibit 20) less 10 percent of total servicing expense, namely, $21,228 (Exhibit 23), totals $60,772.

EXHIBIT 25   Sources and uses of revenue – Task 6 (optional)

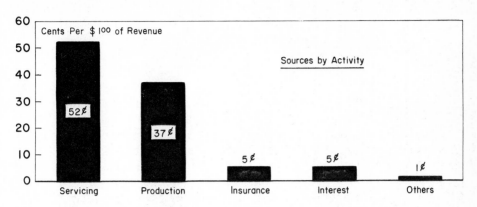

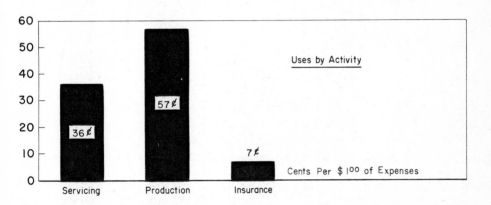

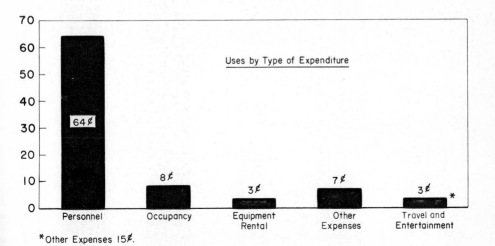

*Other Expenses 15¢.

financial statement. For the first time, however, as a result of the cost analysis, certain facts on the profitability of each operation have come to light. These were either unknown or, if they were known, were not fully developed; nor was their impact on the future of the company fully assessed or understood. The problem is: How can a business plan its operations or chart its future without knowing where it has been and in which direction it is going?

It is particularly significant that the losses in the residential loan operation have been revealed and that a "loss per loan" figure has been determined. This information can be extremely helpful in determining the profitability of operations and how such loss per loan can be offset by the income per loan derived from servicing.

The evaluation of operations, therefore, should consist of several inquiries along these lines. Such inquiries show the value of cost accounting in providing management with a guide for planning. Specifically, the following may be determined: the breakeven point in production, the breakeven point in servicing, and loan marketing based on cost.

Breakeven Point in Loan Production

A production breakeven point is a fairly recent criterion for measuring efficiency and profitability in residential mortgage loan operations. If it is assumed, for instance, that servicing produces a profit and production is a loss, both of which have been ascertained, the breakeven point in production will represent the number of years that one residential loan must be serviced to generate sufficient earnings to pay for the loss incurred in its production. While a production loss is generally determined by deducting origination income from origination expense, the latter of which often includes a discount gain or loss on the sale of the loan, net servicing income represents servicing income in excess of servicing expense.

The establishment and use of the above criteria to measure loan production profitability have led to the development of a theory called *loan marketing based on cost.* Accordingly, each mortgage banker can decide by means of formulas whether it is more advantageous to take a discount loss and make it up by means of more profitable servicing, or whether it is better to minimize production losses and take a smaller profit from servicing. The application of these formulas will be explained later.

To evaluate the production losses of the ABC Mortgage Company and find its production breakeven point, i.e., the number of years and months a loan must be serviced to offset the loss incurred in its production, certain assumptions and computations must be made.

Exhibit 22 shows that ABC Mortgage Company produced 800 loans at a loss of $38.19 per loan and that the average principal balance of these loans was $15,000 (which, for 800 loans, totals $12 million). The company also serviced a loan portfolio with average loan balances of $11,111 at a gross income of $45.56 per year, servicing at 0.41 of 1 percent (Exhibit 23). It was also established that the net servicing income on that portfolio is $24.33 per loan per year. As a result, the point at which production loss will be covered by servicing income will be reached after 1 year and 7 months of net servicing income, as shown by the following computation:

Production loss	$38.19
Net servicing income for 1 year ($24.33) and 7 months	38.54
Excess of net servicing income after 1 year and 7 months	$ .35

The above computation clearly indicates that after 1 year and 7 months of servicing, the loss of making that particular loan was eliminated and thereafter servicing will be at a profit until the company's servicing breakeven point is reached.

Of course, for the above results to be achieved, the amount of loans placed on the books during the above period must average in excess of the average loan amount serviced so that the portfolio can be maintained at its present average balance level; loans must also be placed on the books at a servicing fee at least equal to 0.41 of 1 percent. Any deviation from these basic figures—new loans either made at lower amounts or accepted for servicing at a lower servicing fee rate—will mean that additional months or years of servicing (beyond 1 year and 7 months) will be required for the company to reach a breakeven point. Put another way, a higher average loan balance is required for servicing as servicing fee rates decrease.

Mortgage companies which write insurance in connection with their mortgage lending activities can calculate their breakeven point in production by crediting the production department for the leads in acquiring insurance clients. The amount of credit, of course, must be based on a formula that relates to the success of the insurance operation. If it is assumed, for instance, that the company is successful in selling a homeowner's policy to five out of every ten borrowers, then the residential loan-producing department should actually receive recognition for its efforts in like proportion. Since the ABC Mortgage Company has a profitable insurance operation, credit for at least one year's commission should be given to the residential loan department. Thus the following computation can be made:

Per loan loss on producing 800 loans	$38.19
Assuming that 400 homeowners' policies were written (50 percent of 800) at a 25 percent commission, the first year's commission on a premium of $60 per loan equals	$ 7.50
Per loan loss on producing a loan	$30.69
Net servicing income for 1 year and 4 months	$32.45
	−30.69
Excess of net servicing income after 1 year and 4 months	$ 1.76

Now, instead of 1 year and 7 months of net servicing income, only 1 year and 4 months of net servicing profit is required to break even. Of course, if commissions for 3 years are credited to production on the assumption, for instance, that one-half the borrowers whose loans were produced in 1 year are willing to have the mortgage banker continue to write insurance, $22.50 may be deducted from the aggregate production loss, still leaving a production loss of $15.69 ($38.19 less $22.50) as measured by cost accounting. This loss can subsequently be recovered after $7\frac{3}{4}$ months of servicing ($7\frac{3}{4}$ x $2.03 = $15.73).

The foregoing computations and projections must, however, be viewed from additional angles and with additional considerations in mind. For instance, if the production and servicing results are achieved without full capacity operations in either of the areas of activity, how much more business could be produced or how many more loans could be serviced without a change in cost and, as a result, with larger profits? These factors must be closely examined, particularly when the acquisition of a loan portfolio is considered.

Breakeven Point in Servicing

The breakeven point in servicing is the point at which, after performing the servicing function, neither loss nor gain is made. Today, when servicing income is often called upon to cover production losses, the significance of the servicing breakeven point is increasing conspicuously. The level of the breakeven point indicates how successful the company is in making larger loans than its average loan balances and selling them at prices approximating its average servicing fee rate, and how successful it has been in protecting its portfolio from deterioration of various types.

The level of net servicing income is the result of three factors: (1) the outstanding principal balance of the average loan, (2) the servicing fee rates, and (3) the cost of servicing. The breakeven point may be reached by a drastic adverse action of only one, or by a moderate adverse action of two or all of the following three factors: (1) the outstanding principal balance of the average loan may be reduced to a point at which the fee produced no longer covers the cost of servicing; (2) loans may be sold at servicing fee rates which no longer produce an income to cover expenses; or (3) the cost of servicing increases. After the breakeven point is breached, profitable operations can no longer be maintained.

To make use of the illustrative cost accounting study, the management of ABC Mortgage Company must observe the following precautions:

1. It *should not make* loans in loan amounts below those which represent the company's breakeven point (see Exhibit 23) namely:

   $4,246 at $\frac{1}{2}$ of 1 percent servicing fee

   $5,661 at $\frac{3}{8}$ of 1 percent servicing fee

   $8,492 at $\frac{1}{4}$ of 1 percent servicing fee

2. It *should not agree* to make and sell loans at less than $\frac{1}{2}$ percent if the loan balances are below $4,246, and at less than $\frac{3}{8}$ percent fee if the loan balances are at or below $5,661 unless a satisfactory offsetting overall profit can be earned on the sale of the loan to the investor.

3 It *should watch* and control servicing expenses as much as possible by continuous cost controls so that such costs do not exceed $21.23 per loan per year.

However, management may have little or no control over events which may occur that may adversely affect the profitability of the operations of ABC Mortgage Company. Illustrations of such events are:

1 Increase in collection costs If, during an economic recession affecting either the entire country or the area served by ABC Mortgage Company, it becomes necessary to increase the collection staff by a collection clerk and a full-time field man, the servicing costs will increase by $15,000 per annum. This would adversely affect servicing costs and servicing income as follows:

		Per year	*Per month*
Gross residential loan servicing income	$410,000	$45.56	$3.80
Servicing expenses ($191,047 plus $15,000)	206,047	22.89	1.91
Net income	$203,953	$22.67	$1.89

The increase in collection costs, which may be offset to only a small extent by late charge income, decreases income per loan by $1.66 per year ($24.33 minus $22.67), or $0.14 per month. Although this may seem insignificant, the interplay of many other factors during adverse economic situations can quickly dissipate the profitability of operations.

2 Heavy loan payoffs If availability of funds to a competing mortgage banker or an aggressive direct lender in the area reduces the ABC Mortgage Company's ability to produce the size and quality of loans desired, the reduction of trouble-free, high-balance loans, which in most portfolios offsets the low balances of seasoned loans, can lower "average" balances.

3 Transfer of servicing by investors The adverse effects of a sudden loss of a part of a portfolio cannot be measured adequately in advance. It may upset the servicing equilibrium very easily. However, such changes must always be anticipated, and a management which has cost data at its fingertips will be able to face such a trial more readily than one that does not know the costs of its servicing and the impact of loss of servicing on its overall earnings picture.

Loan Marketing Based on Cost

Since the price of mortgage loans is negotiable within the framework of a predetermined field, the mortgage banker can sell, for instance, at a discount greater than that at which he placed the loan on the books and accept a servicing fee of $\frac{1}{2}$ of 1 percent. Conversely, he can arrange to sell the same loan at the same discount at which he acquired it and make a profit originating the loan and then service the loan at $\frac{3}{8}$ of 1 percent.

The following example illustrates the use of various marketing formulas often obscured by overall production and servicing fee income results. The examples have been simplified to show how easily various answers may be obtained.

A loan of $15,000 is placed on the books at 1 percent origination fee and a 4 percent discount. The loan may now be sold to one investor at a 5 percent discount with $\frac{1}{2}$ of 1 percent servicing fee, or to another investor at 4 percent discount with a $\frac{3}{8}$ of 1 percent servicing fee. (Often the same investor offers similar alternatives.)

Servicing at $\frac{1}{2}$ of 1 percent
Origination fee	$150.00
Discount loss	150.00
Origination fee income	$000.00
Cost of producing the loan (Exhibit 22)	$163.19
Approximate net income as a result of servicing a $15,000 loan at $\frac{1}{2}$ of 1 percent for 3 years, 1 month at annual cost of $21.23 (Exhibit 23)	$163.19 $ .00

Servicing at $\frac{3}{8}$ of 1 percent
Origination fee	$150.00
Discount loss	0.00
Origination fee income	$150.00
Cost of producing loan	$163.19
Origination loss	$ 13.19
Approximate net income as a result of servicing a $15,000 loan at of 1 percent for 5 months (Exhibit 23)	$ 13.19 $ .00

Consequently, depending on the decision about the marketing of the loan and assuming that the average life of a loan is 10 years, there are either 6 years and 11 months (first example) or 9 years and 7 months (alternate sale) of profitable servicing to anticipate. In the latter case, of course, there is an immediate origination fee income to brighten the picture; the loan servicing is actually profitable for a longer period of time, but is less profitable during such period.

The choice for the mortgage banker, therefore, may represent initial origination fee income and reduced servicing fee income during the life of the loan or a production loss and more profitable servicing. The choice is available to each mortgage banker only through the use of cost accounting.

(The best presentation of the wide range of loan marketing possibilities as far as pricing of residential loans is concerned is that by James T. Hillman, in his article

"Just How Much Do We Actually Know about Our Costs and Our Profits?" in the June 1965 issue of *The Mortgage Banker*. In this article, Mr. Hillman clearly illustrates the interrelation of income and cost "by reason of decision" in marketing a loan.)

Some Perspective on the Use of Cost Accounting

This chapter has attempted to alert the mortgage banker to the fact that his survival is contingent not so much on overall operations that appear to be yielding him a profit, as on knowing which operations are profitable and which unprofitable. To market loans advantageously for short-term profits may temporarily disguise a decaying business. To continue business over time, the mortgage banker must continue to produce and maintain a supply of loans that can be serviced at adequate long-term servicing fees which will more than absorb losses sustained at the outset. An important point here is that the production operation minimizes the initial losses.

No matter how favorable the long-run prospects appear on the basis of cost accounting, the outcome may still be contingent on two outside factors: One, that loans which were made at losses in order to profit from high servicing fees over a minimum period of 8 to 12 years are not paid in full before the period ends; and the other, that mortgage portfolios built up with investors are not transferred by those investors to other servicers.

Finally, in planning operations the mortgage banker should not limit his objectives to staying above the breakeven points in producing and servicing. He should plan a margin of profits—an excess of income over expenses—that will make it possible to weather unfavorable monetary or mortgage climates. On this, a practical consideration is that he maintain the confidence of his investors who expect their mortgage banker to carry overhead costs during unfavorable periods and to stay in business even if no loans can be produced.

CHAPTER TEN

Internal Control

Internal control is the cornerstone of strong administrative policies and procedures. An organized plan of systematic checkpoints, internal control is designed to protect the company's assets as well as the funds of borrowers and investors entrusted to its care. It is reinforced by audit and, if both fail, protected by fidelity bonds.

Internal control is a management tool for (1) preventing or discovering theft and fraudulent misapplication of funds, (2) achieving the maximum potential from every source of income, (3) exposing errors and negligence that dissipate income, and (4) assuring compliance with investors' servicing requirements. All losses due to non-compliance, negligence, lack of knowledge or training, poor supervision, disobedience, or plain carelessness cannot be protected by insurance, and herein lies internal control's exclusive contribution to mortgage bankers' sound administrative practices.

It must be emphasized that internal control is a supplement to, and not a substitute for, the work of independent auditors employed by the company, its investors, and federal agencies. Audits by outsiders are periodic, conducted primarily on a regular, and only occasionally on a surprise, basis. Internal control, however, is an intra-office activity which is conducted around the clock. Even if strict internal control and thorough audits do not eliminate all exposures to noncompliance to established procedures or to theft and fraud, they do focus attention on the financially vulnerable areas of operation.

In this chapter, internal control is reviewed from its positive aspect, by showing how it is established and by describing what it can accomplish for a mortgage banking company. Applied to mortgage banking, checkpoints are established to assure the proper use, application, and accountability of monies, and provisions are made for the constant checking and rechecking of the company's production, servicing, and accounting activities.

Internal control will also be presented from its negative side, by illustrating how the lack of internal control may harm the company. The lack of internal control, which can manifest itself in poor operating procedures, poor enforcement of good procedures, or lack of concern for compliance with investors' requirements, will, in addition to creating financial losses, create disorder in company procedures. Internal control procedures must be established and they must be enforced. They will become meaningless, if infractions, however minor, are not corrected immediately. Enforcement of corrective measures cannot be overemphasized. Although errors are usually discovered and their perpetrators admonished, too often the safeguards needed to prevent the same error from recurring are overlooked. Lack of corrective action on the part of management is often a greater crime than the error itself.

ELEMENTS OF INTERNAL CONTROL

Location of Responsibility

While internal control is generally defined as a system of controls designed to safeguard company assets, it can also be defined as an act of supervision over the propriety of steps taken in every activity of the mortgage banking firm. The complex nature of responsibilities in every field of a mortgage banker's operations makes supervisory authority an essential ingredient of good internal control. Such authority should be placed on the loan administrator, who reports directly to the president. The loan administrator, in turn, is still subject to scrutiny by the senior executive of the company.

The size of the company usually determines the possible division of duties. A mortgage banker who operates a small office, services a few hundred or a thousand loans, and employs less than a dozen employees may have sufficient and intimate knowledge of all areas of activity—corporate as well as servicing—to offset the weakness inherent in internal control of smaller companies. However, a company which has a large staff, active production facilities in the residential and income property fields, a considerable servicing portfolio, an insurance operation, and branch offices must set up a more elaborate system of controls. Branch office operations particularly emphasize the need for strict supervision and control over those activities in which a branch office may engage.

Responsibility for supervision involves authority for enforcement of internal control provisions should infractions and breakdowns occur. The authority given to loan administrators also involves the right to carry out disciplinary or corrective actions, if such become necessary. It must be emphasized again that, from the standpoint of management, an error committed by an employee is not as reprehensible as the supervisor's failure to correct it or to hold someone accountable.

In executing the control task, it is essential to recognize responsibility for maintaining controls. Those areas where plans have been made to improve existing procedures should be periodically rechecked to determine whether corrective measures were installed as recommended. One of the most frustrating experiences of auditors and corporate officers is the discovery of errors which would not have recurred had the supervisor trained the clerks in the new procedures or had the clerks heeded the advice or instructions received. Occasionally dismissal for failure to follow established procedural requirements will have greater salutary effect on the effectiveness of an organization than dismissal for any other reason.

Accounting and Administrative Controls

Within each mortgage banking entity, internal control requirements or areas of control may be *accounting* or *administrative* in nature. Accounting controls are concerned with the safeguard of assets and, therefore, the propriety of record keeping. Administrative controls are concerned with operational efficiency, adherence to policies, and compliance with requirements established by the company and its investors.

Accounting controls are designed to:

1 Prevent and detect fraud. The possibilities of fraudulent practices may be effectively reduced through controls over cash, through procedures involving issuance of checks and authorizations for signing them, and through income and expense controls.
2 Ensure accuracy. Supervision is exercised to see that accurate records are maintained and such factors as carelessness, incompetence, neglect, or poor judgment which impair effective operations are minimized or eliminated.
3 Enhance the reliability and accuracy of financial statements for the benefit of management as well as investors and the public.
4 Keep audit and bonding expenses at a minimum. Since the scope of work to be performed by either the company's own auditors or the investors' auditors is based on their evaluation of the need for such work, effective internal control will automatically encourage auditors to reduce the extent of their examinations. Moreover, a loss normally increases the cost of the next fidelity bond premium.

Administrative controls are established to:

1 Make certain that all operations are properly performed, prescribed procedures are followed, and directives are faithfully and effectively carried out.
2 Aid management in its overall planning. An effective plan of internal control makes it easier to discover shortcomings in accounting systems, loan production, loan-processing or -servicing procedures.

Other Factors in Establishing Controls

For internal control to do its most effective work, the following requirements must be created and their existence and functioning safeguarded: (1) *Functions must be clearly segregated.* This applies particularly to the closely interrelated and interdependent functions of receiving, depositing, and acknowledging payments, accounting, and collecting. It applies particularly to the handling of prepayments and payment of loans in full. (2) *A system of authorization must be created and the authorities so appointed, protected, and enforced.* This applies to controls over assets, to authorization of expenditures, and to maintenance of supervision over performance; it also necessitates establishing an authority to call to account those who ignore or break these rules. (3) *Sound operating practices must be maintained.* These must be installed primarily in the crucial income-producing area as well as in the error-prone areas in the loan-producing, -processing, and -servicing machinery. Compliance to proper practices, however, must be checked periodically because of constant change in personnel and frequent procedural changes. (4) *The employment of adequate and well-qualified personnel must be assured.*

MEANS OF INTERNAL CONTROL

A system of internal control should not be complicated nor should it interfere with the performance of the functions it intends to cover. In practice, internal control should be exercised either *indirectly through personnel* or *directly by means of overall or specific* safeguards.

Indirect Control through Personnel

Simply stated, internal control through personnel involves hiring and retaining trustworthy persons. However, as sound as it may seem on the surface, dependence exclusively on the integrity and loyalty of old-time personnel is a dangerous course. According to several recent surveys, most embezzlements have been perpetrated by employees who had considerable length of service and were generally considered reliable by management. But even if reliance on employees' trustworthiness were completely justified, it is still inadvisable because, with continuous turnover, even old-timers depart and leave procedural voids. Since all areas of activity cannot be fully reconnoitered when an employee retires, they must be covered by internal control steps which assure continuation of smooth operation. This is, of course, unnecessary if there is an adequate job description for the position. Without proper procedural safeguards which are systematically employed, weaknesses in procedures can be quickly discovered and exploited by newcomers, bringing about further deterioration in procedures among all inexperienced members of a staff.

However, internal control is not intended to instill apprehension in the employees; they should be briefed on the need for this type of surveillance and realize that through the investigation or check-up of certain activities including their own, benefits will accrue to them as well as to the company.

Generally, the greater the company's appreciation of the employee's faithful services—either in terms of good pay and/or fringe benefits—the lesser the danger of fraud and other infractions. This does not mean, of course, that well-paid employees should not be subjected to scrutiny as far as their operating practices are concerned; rather it means that there should be a definite relationship between the quality of personnel employed and the need for internal control. For instance, if the compensation of those in key positions is commensurate with the responsibilities placed on their shoulders, much of the possibility of dishonesty is automatically reduced. A review of bank embezzlements in the past few years indicates that those who defrauded the bank often handled funds without adequate supervision, and handled sums greatly in excess of the responsibility for which they were actually paid.

Adequate compensation, however, is not a panacea for all problems created by the handling of funds which must be controlled internally; it only reduces temptation from the hearts and minds of those to whom the funds are most accessible. Special care should be exercised in choosing a cashier, bookkeeper, and collector. These three, individually or in combination, have access to considerable funds and information, and exercise supervision over clerical procedures which might facilitate theft and misappropriation of funds that cannot be immediately detected. Many safeguards must be established in connection with the special duties performed in these particular positions.

In organizations where an accounting department consists of several employees, the most effective way of eliminating the likelihood of dishonest practices is to rotate the clerks so they will not necessarily post and report collections on the same account two months in succession. Although from the standpoint of effective enforcement of collection policies, for instance, it may not be advisable to switch collectors from one account or one group of accounts to another, for internal control purposes this may be occasionally desirable.

Direct Control through Safeguards

Direct controls are effected through overall and specific safeguards.

Overall safeguards are established primarily to control specific operations in more than one department of the organization.

1 Requirement to meet various "closing" and "reporting" deadlines Since the value of any information depreciates as time lapses, the efficiency of any organization is considerably enhanced by the promptness with which reports are completed and presented. Good procedural habits on the part of the treasurer and controller are necessary as good examples to employees. Management, therefore, must insist that monthly reports on corporate activity be completed and presented no later than a certain preset date, but never later than the tenth of the month. In turn, the treasurer or controller must insist that the various ledgers and books be promptly closed and balanced.

As an internal control safeguard, copies of trial balances on specific activities should be inspected and the accuracy of balancing occasionally verified. It has been found time and time again that trial balances are often hastily prepared and, because of pressures of time and other assignments subsequent to the close of the month, not balanced to the last penny. These hasty steps often create items to be adjusted later. When these adjustments are not made, accounting records may fall into a mire from which only hard work and/or considerable expense for auditors can eventually reestablish a balance. Therefore, balancing requirements should be strictly enforced by the controller, regardless of the time it may take.

Internal control steps should also be established to see that various reports and certification desired by investors monthly, quarterly, or annually are dispatched in time from various departments of the company. These reports include remittances, single debit reports, reinspection reports, and tax payment certifications.

2 Check-signing authority Outright theft and misapplication of funds can occur when checks are issued to unauthorized or fictitious individuals. The best control to prevent such a practice is a strict check-authorizing and check-signing system. A system involving requisitioning of checks is not necessarily the answer; such a procedure only slows down the process of issuing checks without preventing the actual misuse of funds.

In each department, only the person responsible for the operations involved should be authorized to requisition or issue checks. The accountant in charge of corporate books or the individual handling escrow reserve funds should not be permitted to sign checks, but they may be permitted to act as co-signers on checks requiring two signatures. Even in small organizations, checks should be issued, authorized, and signed only upon the presentation of invoices approved for payment by those who incurred the expense. Whatever safeguards are established, they should not hinder the speedy issuance of checks.

3 Budgets or income and expense controls Establishing a budget—i.e., computing the anticipated income to be derived from certain operations and predetermining the expenses involved in connection with them—provides a general, and often the most effective, means of control over income and expenses. Such control provides immediate checkpoints if certain results are or are not reached, or if certain expenditures exceed those planned. These controls, of course, cannot be made applicable to all types of operations. Furthermore, since anticipated income and expenses are in round figures, internal control in this instance does not aim to achieve accounting accuracy.

A good illustration of an effective income budget is that used by many companies for income derived from servicing fees. This budget can be readily established by maintaining an accounting record of the dollar volume of loans serviced, and applying to it either the average servicing fees or servicing fees on interest-differential groups. Companies servicing under a single debit system can use the copies of their monthly trial balances to maintain a record of the information on which the income control can then be based. At the end of the year, the actual service fee collections can be readily compared with the anticipated figures made either from month to month or on a yearly basis.

4 Supervisory control over performance   The performance of servicing tasks in all departments should be observed systematically. The loan administrator or servicing manager—without drawing too much attention to himself and thus displaying lack of confidence in the particular employee—should verify that work is performed in accordance with the requirements of both the company and the investors involved. Often the periodic review of all incoming correspondence gives a sufficiently clear picture of the propriety of actions taken. However, should repeated complaints from an investor's accounting department be merely handed to the clerk who makes the mistakes rather than to the servicing manager, the error may be corrected each time, but the prevention of its recurrence may not be guaranteed. Similarly, two or three reminders each month from investors, stating that delinquency reports have not been received promptly, should warrant a review of the collection department's procedure on this particular matter.

5 Inventory of equipment and supplies   Maintenance of an orderly storeroom and the establishment of certain supply-ordering and checking-in procedures will minimize waste and reduce the opportunity for petty thievery. Here again, internal control depends greatly on the quality of personnel.

Specific safeguards consist of either automatic, day-by-day check points or systems designed to reduce or eliminate possibilities of error, dishonesty, and fraud in a particular department of the company. Supervision of these check points and systems should be the responsibility of the loan administrator or the accounting officer in charge of the corporate books, or it should be split between the two. Safeguards may be established in the area either of corporate activity or of servicing, or may cover both. Most of the safeguards and areas in which they are to be established are covered in this chapter.

INTERNAL CONTROL BY AREAS OF ACTIVITY

Internal control arrangements and safeguards by their nature—whether they are of the accounting or the administrative variety—are presented here in their practical application to two general areas of the mortgage banking business: *corporate activity* and *servicing activity*.

Although activities in these areas may be interrelated within the organization, they are considered and presented separately in order to illustrate their intrinsic nature and relative importance. In the corporate area, the prime concern, in addition to meeting preset company standards and requirements, is the proper use and accountability of corporate funds and income derived therefrom. In the servicing area, in addition to the proper handling of trust funds, the emphasis on compliance with procedural requirements prescribed by investors in servicing contracts and servicing manuals is somewhat greater than the emphasis on monetary accuracy. Accordingly, compliance with preset standards which are intangible and normally less detectable than the loss of monies must come under continuous and close management scrutiny.

Corporate Activity

Undoubtedly, it is commonplace to state that the size of the capital used, the number of employees on the payroll, and the type of operation are factors determining the need for internal control of corporate activities. Nevertheless, this must be kept in mind. For instance, the larger the office and the sum total of funds employed, the greater the exposure to hazards that require constant surveillance and protection. A single loss in a particular area, if quickly detected, may be negligible, but if it is allowed to become repetitive, the loss may become considerable.

First, some general controls for corporate activities must be considered. A principal control comes from knowledge of the profitability of each type of operation the company undertakes. This knowledge is built up by years of experience in the business, and also from the proper use, familiarity with and understanding of, statistical and cost accounting information, other operating reports, and income and expense statements prepared by the accounting staff. Here some of the operating philosophies described in Chapter 11, "Coordination through Communication," can also be put to use.

Often the best step toward internal control is to establish procedures so that more than one person is always involved in the accounting of fees and charges, in posting ledger records or journals, and in depositing funds. The larger the number of people involved in any single monetary transaction, the less the likelihood of diversion or misappropriation of funds through collusion.

A single but axiomatic internal control requirement is that no employee other than the cashier ever be permitted to accept any money from prospective borrowers, builder clients, brokers, or borrowers, away from the office, on a collection call, or in the office. This must be a rule even if a receipt is issued. All customers with cash must always be escorted to the cashier where monies must be receipted by no one but the cashier.

Probably the most meaningful explanation of ways to establish internal controls and supervision of compliance to directives is in relation to specific items in different areas of corporate activity. Such a discussion follows, with little differentiation between major and minor items.

Origination fee and/or discount charge Setting charges for services performed and their subsequent collection and recording present considerable possibilities for errors and fraudulent practices. Since these fees are charged for services and not for goods, physical controls, such as an inventory control of goods, cannot be established. After a loan closing, therefore, it must be ascertained that the fee for making a loan charged against the borrower's ledger account conforms with the amount stated on the borrower's signed application. By means of an offsetting entry, this sum is then normally credited to the income ledger. If the fee is increased or decreased, the difference will in no way materially increase or decrease the amount of service to be rendered, but it will increase or decrease earnings for the company. Since no one, other than the person recording the transaction, knows what is to be earned on a particular transaction or what is recorded as having been earned, it is imperative that no alteration of the original charges on the application be permitted. If an additional fee is to be earned and collected, it is a good practice to indicate an additional charge on the loan application, and so record it on the ledger card.

Similarly and often more importantly, when it comes to handling discounts, the amount of discount to be collected from the seller, broker, or builder should be properly ascertained and collected in a manner identical to the recording and collection of fees for making the loan. The determination and collection of proper discount is also important because discounts are often subject to change, even in the midst of loan processing, closing, and delivery. This area is particularly vulnerable to errors during a period of loan price changes when a larger discount may be expected by the investor than that collected from the seller or vice versa. The combination of circumstances that may create or require changes in charges and discounts, and which may have to be acted on as far as corporate books are concerned is almost limitless.

If such changes do occur, it is important that they be promptly recorded, and properly authorized, by an officer of the company, and that the correctness of the respective adjusting entries be supervised by the loan administrator. It is, therefore, necessary to establish a point in the production or corporate accounting procedure where loan applications which carry the information relative to charges and discounts, or closing statements on which these charges are shown, are actually checked and compared with ledger entries. These internal control check-ups can be made for each loan transaction or on a frequent spot-check basis.

Reviewing cases of embezzlement and diversion of funds, investigators have found that this accounting area—fees charged to borrowers or discounts collected from sellers and builders—is where most of such funds have been created or built up; in other words, these were the same funds which were subsequently embezzled either by paying commissions to fictitious parties or by depositing monies to accounts other than legitimate accounts of the company.

Interest charges to borrowers are the second most vulnerable income item. A loss here may not necessarily come from nefarious practices, but rather, and more frequently, from erroneous computations of either the number of days lapsed or the interest rate to be charged. While some errors may be purely mathematical and non-repetitive in nature, others may stem from improper use of interest tables and the erroneous assumption that interest on funds loaned are to be charged on a 365-day basis and not on a 360-day basis.

The loan administrator should establish the ground rules for charging interest by adopting the following rules by which the banks charge for the monies lent: (1) charge for each day lapsed in each month, 30 days in a 30-day month and 31 days in a 31-day month (a practice not usually followed by mortgage bankers accustomed to the principle of amortization which automatically divides each year into 360 days and each month into 30); and (2) compute interest on the basis that each month is only a 30-day month and that each year consists of 360 days, and use interest tables accordingly.

However, once amortization starts, interest must be charged in accordance with the amortization schedule provided for the loan, since the mortgage documents call for predetermined monthly payments for a predetermined term. It is, therefore, advantageous to set up construction loans so that amortization of the loan coincides with the completion of the project. By establishing this practice, one of the objectives of internal controls may already be realized.

To avoid errors in charging or in allowing interest, depending on the due date of the first payment, the best practice is to adjust interest at closing to the next first of the month preceding the first payment date, so that the first payment always includes a full (unadjusted) interest payment. In this manner, all adjustments are made at closing, and none at the commencement of amortization. For instance, if funds are disbursed on October 14, on a loan on which the first payment will become due December 1, interest on the closing statement is charged to the borrower from October 14 to November 1. Conversely, if the loan is closed on the tenth of November, the borrower is allowed 9 days of interest, since in December he will be obliged to pay a full month's interest. Actually, whatever method is employed, *consistency must be observed.*

Specific procedures must also be established for the practice of changing the first payment date of the loan. Failure to follow appropriate procedures may create particular vulnerability to losses if the loan involved has already been closed; i.e., interest has been adjusted at closing to 30 days before the first payment date, since the responsibility after the closing of the loan may have already been turned over to the cashier or the collection staff. Change of records, as to first payment date, must be made simultaneously on all records, upon receipt of written instructions from the person authorized to initiate such change. Similarly the responsibility for charging additional interest or seeing that interest charges are properly made must be established and assigned in advance.

Interest charges made by banks must be carefully checked in an effort to ascertain that interest was charged properly and that loans repaid to banks were promptly credited. This is especially necessary if the mortgage banker maintains a number of accounts with similar designations or consecutive account numbers in one bank. Credit as a result of transfer of funds from another city in payment of a loan, but credited to a noninterest bearing account, can be costly if such credit is not made promptly and if an error by the bank is not spotted and promptly corrected.

Arrangements must be made and maintained with the bank for prompt notification to the mortgage banker of funds transferred to the mortgage banker's account in payment for loans sold. This will enable the mortgage banker to pay his loan to the bank promptly and reduce his interest costs.

It is advisable for the loan administrator or the chief accountant to exercise uninterrupted supervision over both the interest-charging and the interest-collecting procedure.

Pledging of collateral Since the prompt availability of funds is always of prime importance, the borrowing-lending relationships between mortgage banker and commercial banker must be perfected to smooth-running procedures. It is possible either through failure to follow prescribed routines or through deception to borrow on one loan from two different banks by using one set of papers as collateral at two banks, supplementing the missing documents with "agreements to pledge" at each bank. Of course, the banks have strict rules relative to the substitution of documents, are strict with paper requirements, and frequently audit the status of collateral. Nevertheless, it behooves the mortgage banker to supervise his borrowing activities very closely. Although the greatest number of embezzlements have not occurred in this area, it is here that the largest sums have been directed to personal use.

Collection of late charges As it will be pointed out in Chapter 15, "Collection Department," late charges on FHA and VA loans must be assessed automatically, but may be waived at the discretion of the head of the collection department if circumstances warrant such action. During the last days of the month, a collector hard-pressed to improve his collection record may accept late payments without enforcing the collection of late charges. This infraction will not only cause the company to lose income, but will also cause the deterioration of the enforcement procedures of collection and damage the effectiveness of loan servicing.

Inactive corporate accounts In the course of mortgage-lending activity, good-faith deposits are often required for various purposes from prospective clients, builders, and sponsors of projects. Monies which are set aside from the proceeds of a construction loan for disbursement at a later date may be forgotten by the owners, who subsequently pay for the completion of certain jobs themselves. These and other types of funds which may remain on deposit for varying periods of time may be easily forgotten not only by those who deposited them but also by the individuals in the company who collected them. While the sums may not be large, the number of such accounts may increase over the years and may create a pool of monies not directly overseen. It is recommended that accounts on which entries have not been made for over six months or a year be systematically reviewed for refund or other disposition.

Accounts payable All invoices which have been appropriately approved by those authorized to order services or to purchase goods should be forwarded upon receipt to the individual responsible for paying bills. This person is normally the accounts payable clerk. Title bills or insurance bills to be charged against the proceeds of loans should be processed promptly; they should not be held pending receipt of credits since unusual delays in the receipt of credits may delay processing of such bills until after the funds available for paying the particular item are disbursed and an unnecessary account receivable is created. Whenever possible, all bills incurring corporate expenses should be signed by the loan administrator, who, by the very nature of the assignment, can exercise additional controls over expenditures.

Collection of accounts receivable Debits created on the borrowers' ledger cards for insurance bills, title bills, appraisal fees, and other charges or items must be billed and collected promptly. Unpaid items for title fees, recording charges, insurance premiums —all of which were created because they were neither charged nor accounted for properly at the closing transaction—must be followed up promptly. Collecting these items must also be supervised through a periodic review of outstanding items. The longer action is delayed, the harder it will become to collect an outstanding item. Collection of small or uncollectible items should not be waived without establishing a procedure and authority to take such steps. Uncollectible items should be written off at least once a year, but preferably at the end of each quarter.

Reconciliation of bank accounts Many companies, large and small, do not maintain a definite system of reconciling bank statements of both escrow and corporate bank accounts. Good internal control can be established simply by a periodic, if not a month-by-month, rotation of reconciliation work among bookkeeping clerks. If time permits, the controller himself should occasionally reconcile one bank account to demonstrate supervision over this phase of accounting activity.

Expense accounts Establishing expense budgets by individual or by type of expense provides a basis for control over expense accounts. Once this is done, expenditures for travel, entertainment, dues, subscriptions, and automobiles must be maintained in proportion to income from corresponding corporate activities. The review of corporate expenditures is a task for the controller or loan administrator. Infractions must, however, be reported immediately to department heads or to the president of the company, depending on the individuals involved.

Servicing Activity

In servicing activity, internal control and supervision of procedural requirements should be focused on several specific areas and the following items:

Mail desk. Distribution of mail often holds the key to some of the best internal control measures.

1 *Spot checks* The loan administrator should sample incoming mail frequently to see that procedures are being followed. He should check to see that the clerk charged with the responsibility for the distribution of mail is, in fact, directing letters requesting pay-off statements to the servicing manager rather than to the

cashier and that this requirement is strictly enforced. Servicing activity at the mail desk may be easily checked from time to time by reviewing outgoing mail.

2 *Allocation of control* Cashiers or other individuals entrusted with accepting and processing payments should have no control over the opening and distribution of incoming mail. They should have no access to the mail other than to receive and handle what is given them.

3 *Routing checks* All checks containing payments of loans in full must be routed to the person, usually the cashier, responsible for accepting payments, so the checks can be deposited for the benefit of the investor or forwarded promptly. Checks from investors for the purchase of loans should be handed to the person responsible for paying the company's loan at the bank or that person should be promptly notified of such payment. Failure to correctly direct a single piece of mail may result in a loss of return on the funds by either the investor or the mortgage banker.

Cashier department

1 *Relation to bookkeeping operations* In companies which service a small number of loans, the teller is often the bookkeeper, and thus has easy access to bookkeeping records. In this instance, locked journal tape and the use of prenumbered receipts for cash payment help minimize the chance for theft.

As soon as practicable, the functions of the cashier and bookkeeper should be separated, making each responsible for only one operation, i.e., handling of cash or the maintenance of bookkeeping records. This division of duties will create the first effective means of control. Thereafter, the cashier should be required to balance on a day-to-day basis with the totals established by the bookkeeping clerk, either before or after the posting operations. In large organizations, the totals obtained by the cashier and the totals obtained by the bookkeepers should be summarized independently and balanced by the controller or accountant in charge of corporate records.

2 *Relation to deposit of funds* The deposit of funds in appropriate bank accounts is also of prime importance. Monies received in a fiduciary relationship, such as good faith deposits, stand-by fees, or deposits required in connection with FHA multifamily loans, may not be placed into a company account. They must be placed into a segregated corporate account established for monies belonging to others.

3 *Relation to collection activities*

a *Currency in envelopes* If, on occasion, a borrower makes a payment by including currency in an envelope, payment should be promptly acknowledged in writing by the loan administrator or servicing manager. This acknowledgment, however, should be accompanied by a strong warning that the company takes no responsibility for future payments in currency.

b *Past due notices* The cashier should never be charged with the responsibility of handling collections and preparing or sending out past due notices. Actually, the functions of the cashier should be separated from those of the collector in order to strengthen internal control by indirect supervision over receipts of cash.

c *Principal prepayments* Proper handling of principal prepayments is most significant—prepayment may often be substantial and may easily be used by the cashier to cover up a considerable shortage, or it may in itself constitute a single item for misappropriation of funds. Furthermore, due to the elimination of borrowers' records and the simplification of routines involving the handling of payments, detection is usually difficult, except by direct verification of principal balances by auditors or investors, which may not occur until the loan is about to be paid in full.

Notification of the borrower's intention to make prepayment should always be directed to the loan administrator, servicing manager, or the head of the collection department. As a further protection, the switchboard operator and the individual distributing the mail should be instructed to turn over all inquiries and notifications on prepayments to the collection department rather than to the cashier.

Another excellent means of effecting internal control over prepayments or the receipt and recording of escrow reserve shortage payments involves preparing and mailing from the accounting department a photocopy of the servicer's accounting ledger card or an annual mortgage loan statement (Exhibit 54) to the borrower after the end of each calendar year.

d *Collection of reserve shortages* The collection and entry of all *additional* escrow reserve deposit payments must be carefully supervised, since payments made to cover tax shortages by mortgagors, for instance, are deposited in the escrow account without the investor's knowledge and usually without a receipt to the borrower. They are not necessarily accounted for to the borrowers until either the results of subsequent escrow analysis are revealed or the loan is paid in full.

e *Cash drawer—petty cash account* The cash drawer should never include a check made payable to the company for which a corresponding receipt was not issued or an entry not made on the cash blotter, or both. Since free access to cash may be abused by the cashier if he fails to balance, or by those employees who rely on monies for temporary advances, the status of the petty cash fund should be reviewed frequently. Such a review will assure proper and accurate explanation for all petty cash items and will also guarantee the maintenance of a maximum amount available for necessary disbursements at all times.

Bookkeeping department

1 *Reconciliation of investors' bank accounts* This task should be rotated among employees. It is also advisable to check the time lag between the receipts of funds and remittances to investors. This delay or time lag in processing of funds is also reviewed by investors' auditors as it may entail the loss of interest.

2 *Handling escrow reserve funds* Checks issued in payment of tax bills and insurance premiums from the escrow reserve account often require special scrutiny.

The check authorization and signing procedure described earlier should be strictly enforced. Each refund of FHA mortgage insurance premium, for instance, should be documented by a copy of FHA Form 2344-4 if the loan has been terminated. Payment of taxes or insurance premiums should be supported by the tax or insurance bills. Checks should be signed only by an individual familiar with servicing operations. Under no circumstances should the cashier be permitted to sign these checks.

3 *Inactive escrow reserve accounts*   Inactive accounts are most often created when a loan is paid in full without the proper and formal disposition of escrow funds. Therefore, it should be a company practice—reviewed periodically by the loan administrator—to return escrow reserve funds to borrowers promptly or to allow borrowers to have escrow funds credited in reduction of the balance due on the loan. If a refund check is issued and is subsequently returned because the owner left no forwarding address, and the amount represented by the cancelled refund check is credited to the former loan account, the funds thus made available should not be left without supervision and control. If further attempts to locate the rightful owner of such funds fail, the monies should either be transferred to an "in abeyance" account pending claim by borrowers or be sent to the investor who owned the mortgage for disposition. Since these monies are especially vulnerable to misapplication and misuse, this area of accounting activity should be of prime concern for the individual responsible for internal control.

RELATIONSHIP WITH INDEPENDENT AUDITORS

The function of the independent auditor employed by the company is to supplement what the company does for itself. Therefore, the sufficiency or insufficiency of internal controls will determine the amount of time the auditor will consider necessary to spend in the company, to assure efficient operation and to allow the company to obtain maximum profit from operation. It must be emphasized, however, that auditors are concerned primarily with reporting financial results and not with administrative accuracies.

If it is assumed that there are no marked fluctuations in business activity, the size of the audit bill from year to year depends largely on the degree to which the mortgage banker keeps his financial household in order throughout the year, rather than on what the auditors actually have to do each year to complete their task and sign the audit certification. To a large measure, the size of the bill also depends on management's handling of many of the problems that normally arise before and/or after the close of the fiscal year. Management should foresee such problems before the end of the year and solve them either by itself or in cooperation with the auditors.

For completeness and accuracy of information, the auditors normally rely on the facts presented by management and on the cooperation extended by company officials. Internal control is part of a continuous program of cooperation and collaboration.

Therefore, those responsible for internal control should anticipate ways to facilitate the work of the company's auditors.

Since the company-auditor relationship is a confidential one—like consulting one's doctor—management must communicate its problems to the auditors promptly and without solicitation. Nothing destroys an auditor's confidence in a company as quickly as a controller's or treasurer's clumsy effort to withhold information. Failure to reveal potentially damaging problems must be aired and resolved sooner or later. An open discussion of all anticipated problems and possible solutions at the earliest possible moment is advisable. Even more useful is calling the auditors any time a problem arises. It is easier to consult the auditor concerning proper entry of certain transactions in the books when they first occur than to have an incorrect recording subsequently challenged by the auditor.

Curiously enough, in the maintenance of proper books and procedures, auditors employed by the company, as well as those hired by investors, often place greater reliance on the integrity of personnel than on strict observance of all operating practices. Similarly, auditors prefer to deal with the same personnel year after year rather than meet new faces on each audit occasion on either the clerical or key accounting levels. From the auditors' point of view, frequent turnovers breed the risk of fraudulent practices and doubtful procedures. Also, ingenious solutions are more often frowned upon than hailed by auditors. The audit staff prefers to find frequent elementary errors than deal with a clever accountant who can initiate shortcuts but in the process reduces or eliminates controls.

The audit of records maintained by means of data processing equipment is particularly difficult for auditors, especially since they cannot always trace information that goes into these machines. As a result, most auditors work around the machines, testing procedures and results rather than the transactions themselves.

Auditors should be apprised of the number of investors' audits made throughout the year, their scope, and the reported results of such audits. It is often advisable to suggest to the auditor that he obtain directly from the investor the results of such examination in order to fortify his audit report and eliminate duplicate testing of respective investors' bank accounts or duplicate verification of borrowers' loan balances.

Auditors should be assisted in their audit of the servicing requirements since they normally cannot be expected to know either the contents of all servicing contracts or the up-to-date requirements expressed in the latest directives. This is especially important because mortgage bankers are entrusted not only to handle monies, but also to perform ever increasing services for the investors which they no longer check or duplicate.

There are three separate time periods during which management can effectively prepare for the visits of auditors or cooperate with them, both to ease the burden of the audit chores and consequently their cost and to improve the quality of the report: (1) before the auditors arrive; (2) before the close of the fiscal year; and (3) after the close of the fiscal year.

The arrival of the auditors should not cause concern. Since the auditors' interests are identical, to a great extent, to the company's, every effort should be made to simplify the audit work. Regardless of whether the company is on a cash or accrual tax basis, an approaching fiscal year-end is an excellent opportunity to search out the skeletons in the closet and pave the way for a smooth-running audit and a clean financial statement.

It is a good idea to confer with the person in charge of the audit within the last 30 days before the end of the fiscal year. This is the time to apprise the auditor of the volume of business transacted by the company and its profit expectations. At this time, the auditors should be informed of all the problems encountered during the year that may have been solved or that may present problems in completing the audit and preparing an audit report. Also, the auditors should be told of any unusual items which may have to be treated in a manner different from other items. Such disclosures will enable the auditors to check the law and advise the mortgage banker on recording a particular item or transaction on the books as of the year-end or, if necessary, on disposing of the item or writing it off.

All changes in procedures, new accounting arrangements, new banking relations, and new investor relationships should be mentioned at this time even though most of this information is available from the company's corporate records. The auditors should be aware of the possible effects of such changes or improvements to understand the company's progress in other than monetary terms.

Some of the specific areas which should be examined before year-end, together with the steps that can be taken to improve the audit report, are

1 Review every investment to determine whether its value should be written down or reserves should be established for possible deterioration of the investment. In a good year, opportunities to sell a loan which will eventually have to be sold at a loss should not be overlooked.

2 Write off bad debts or any of the uncollectible items which, though not entirely hopeless, should be charged against good times. If such items are written off and then collected, they can still be taken into profit, maybe in a less profitable year. These items also include uncollected commissions or insurance premiums, items in litigation or debit items that were created by errors.

3 Since cash-basis taxpayers can accelerate or defer payment of deductible items to a certain extent in order to reduce or increase income in any one year, all bills must be scrutinized for prompt or postponed payment, depending on the circumstances. A similar consideration applies to the payment of charitable contributions and dues payments.

4 Capital gains and losses should be offset, if possible.

5 Considerable care should be taken, particularly before year-end, to prevent overdrafts in escrow accounts, to collect any existing overdrafts, and to retrieve corporate funds no longer needed from escrow reserve accounts.

6 Study carefully, preferably 3 months before year-end, the inventory of unsold loans. If it contains too many delinquent loans or loans at discounts not compatible with current market prices, these items should be eliminated, if possible,

to avoid adverse comments by the auditors on the value of the loan inventory.

7 All ledgers and custodial accounts should be balanced. Under the pressures of the daily volume of work, there is a tendency to postpone unpleasant tasks, such as the balancing of an inventory or ledger or custodial account, even though each month's delay only compounds the difficulty of locating and correcting an error.

8 Care should be taken to reduce to a minimum all delinquencies, particularly on loans owned by the company.

9 To facilitate the auditor's work, and thus speed the completion of the audit, efforts must be expended—through the use of overtime if necessary—to close all books and ledgers as promptly as possible. Cooperation with auditors at this time may involve expeditious preparation of those listings and statements that the auditors want to review first. Prompt balancing, of course, will do a great deal to aid the performance of the auditors. Needless to say, all closing entries or adjustments before or after audit should be properly shown on the books.

RELATIONSHIP WITH INVESTORS' AUDITORS

Audit by an investor may be performed by its own audit staff or by an independent audit organization that it hires. Although employing an audit firm may be less costly to the investor than maintaining a traveling audit staff, an audit by the latter is preferred by most mortgage bankers. This is so because investors' auditors traditionally know the mortgage field while employees of audit firms follow their own prescribed routines and, although performing a good service for their clients, cannot deepen the investor-mortgage banker relationship. Essentially, they merely represent the mortgagee and are not familiar with its policies.

Although it would be logical to expect that good internal controls manifested by servicers and observed during audit visits would be rewarded by a reduction of audit activity both in number of audits by investors and in scope and intensity, that is, unfortunately, not normally the case. Investors' audits are necessary evils that mortgage bankers must endure with good grace. Auditors are sent by investors to perform prescribed audits, not because of distrust of company operations. Therefore, investors' auditors should be assisted courteously whether they are on the investors' audit staff or from an independent public accounting firm because they have come to do a job.

Unfortunately, independent audit firms employed by an investor often send audit trainees to do a job that tests the competence of even a seasoned auditor. In spite of the hardships thus imposed on the servicer's staff, cooperation entails prompt compliance with requests for trial balances, bank statements, loan files, insurance policies, etc., including preparation of audit verification letters. In this connection, it is advisable to remind auditors to use the identifying loan numbers assigned by the mortgage company for verification of balances and not those of investors, which are unknown to mortgagors. Efforts should also be made to persuade investors' auditors to refrain from sending verification letters to those borrowers whose accounts were recently verified directly by company auditors.

CHAPTER ELEVEN

Coordination through Communication

In a symphony orchestra, each individual musician is a master of his own instrument. Alone, each musician can produce beautiful sounds by playing his instrument well. If each were to play the same piece of music at the same time without the coordinating baton of a conductor, cacophonous sounds would invade the ears of the audience.

The analogy with mortgage banking is obvious. Without the coordinating efforts of the loan administrator, without training that teaches individuals to pull together, without communications that tell them when to pull together, the best efforts of individual employees would fall short of the team effort that is essential to the maximization of profits.

Coordination is nothing more than guided cooperation that makes it possible for all members of the team to work together to achieve a common goal. It is accomplished through regular, established patterns of communication that make certain that those who need to know what others are doing do in fact know. It is a continuous process—not something that can be started today and forgotten tomorrow. It involves analyzing change and new developments by thinking through each process and activity in the overall terms of the goals of the firm rather than of the goals of a single activity. Once this is done, it is a relatively simple matter to decide who should be informed about a new development, a revised procedure, or termination of an existing activity. Knowing "who" and "what" also simplifies the decision of "how" to inform others to achieve a maximum coordination of effort.

The individual employee seeking to maximize his contribution to the firm's success by coordinating his activities with others should not be restricted to the executive suite, to the flow of information from managers to their subordinates. Subordinates must also keep their supervisors informed, let their peers know what is going on, keep other departments informed when their activities are interrelated, and, finally, help the firm communicate with the public.

Coordination is, therefore, a joint effort of all employees in the art of communication. Consider, for example, the proposed entry of the residential loan department into the home improvement lending field. This cannot be accomplished without the effective cooperation of the collection department, which becomes a part of the screening team for such credit and will be required to collect past-due home improvement loan payments. Nor can the new activity become profitable without the effective cooperation of the accounting department in developing a simple system for processing payments.

The more diverse the mortgage banker's operations, the greater the need to coordinate activities effectively. The loan administrator is a prime candidate for the responsibility of coordinating the wide span of the company's multioperation activities. He must be intimately acquainted with all the company's diverse operations. Even so, he cannot coordinate these operations effectively without the support and active cooperation of his supervisors as well as his subordinates. It is vital, therefore, that the management team train each employee to understand how the functions he performs fit into the activities of others, whether in the same department, outside the department, or even outside the firm itself. Thus, the loan administrator's responsibility is to guide as well as to communicate, and top management's responsibility is to listen as well as to order.

The quality of a communications system designed to coordinate activities of a multioperation firm is a function of leadership traits at all levels. It begins with the chief executive communicating with his lieutenants and their communicating with lower echelons. Interdepartmental coordination must be established between production and servicing and the construction and loan-closing departments. Individuals in related jobs, such as the cashier, collector, and bookkeeper, must learn to coordinate their activities. And finally, the team as a whole must coordinate its activities with investors on matters of loan submission, accounting, and servicing.

Once established in the thinking process of supervisors and department heads as well as individual employees, efforts to improve coordination generate further efforts to coordinate. Like a stone rolling downhill, coordination gathers momentum as it progresses.

The benefits of effective coordination through communication are multifaceted, flowing to the company, its borrowers, and its investors.

Benefits to the Company

The benefits accruing to the company can be illustrated by an incident which indicates what can result from the lack of coordination. Several years ago a company president, eager to sell loans, visited the head of an investor's mortgage loan department. From all appearances, the call promised a sure sale; the price was right and the yield was competitive. When the conversation turned to problems the insurance company was experiencing with the loans they bought from the mortgage banking company a few years earlier, the president of the mortgage banking company turned silent. He did not know that there had been problems, and he was not aware of the delinquency difficulties. He had not been kept informed by the loan administrator, and he had not consulted the administrator about the status of the portfolio before he left on his trip.

Company presidents or loan officers must always be up to date on what is taking place in their investors' offices. They, in turn, must keep their staff advised on what they are doing or plan to do. Presidents unfamiliar with the facts are caught by their own ignorance; a loan administrator not informing the president of company problems is equally at fault. Although the loan administrator may not have known that the call was being made, the results indicate a common breakdown in communications. In this case, no mortgages were sold. When the life insurance company later consolidated its servicing, the uninformed company president was the first to find his servicing transferred.

Benefits to the Borrower

Next to lending money, each mortgage banker wishes to create a satisfactory relationship with each of his borrowers. Therefore, every effort must be expended to keep the borrower pleased with the company and informed of what he ought to know about his loan. Communicating misleading or erroneous information will only backfire, even if such information is provided by the realtor or the builder with whom most mortgage bankers have close ties. It is always preferable, for example, to verify information about taxes which is given to the mortgagor by the realtor or builder, especially if tax bills in a new subdivision are involved. If a builder or realtor is allowed to misquote the tax bill, only the mortgage banker will suffer, since the crisis created by a bill that is higher than estimated will linger long after the builder or realtor is out of the picture.

Effective communication on insurance matters also benefits the borrower. While the mortgage banker's prime responsibility is to protect the investment of the mortgagee, he also has a responsibility to the mortgagor to maintain adequate insurance. Many companies review the entire insurance coverage even if they do not write insurance, and advise their borrowers of any inadequacy of coverage.

Benefits to the Investor

Top personnel in investors' offices, responsible for allocation of mortgage funds, often complain that the financial reports of their mortgage bankers portray only the accomplishments that can be translated into dollars and cents. They note the absence of supporting comments on the condition of the real estate market, building activity, and bank credit conditions, which are necessary to assess the true accomplishments of problems of their mortgage banking correspondents. Accordingly, keeping investors advised on current mortgage lending trends, interest rates, construction or real estate activities in areas where the mortgage company represents them is a task that mortgage bankers must perform as members in good standing of the correspondent system. The preparation of such reports and their dissemination to each chosen investor should become an important, and often joint, task of the president of the company, his loan administrator, and other key members of the management team. This information may accompany, precede, or follow the financial statement, or if the company distributes printed reports, such information may be incorporated in the report.

ROLE OF COMMUNICATION

To coordinate, one must communicate, for effective coordination demands communication that is appropriate for the occasion and to the point. Whatever the means, the communication must reach those for whom it is intended promptly and in as concise a manner as possible. For example, informing the loan solicitors in the field of a change in mortgage prices two days after the change has been made will result in considerable loss of business, and will demoralize the solicitors, who will see their counterparts obtain new business. The entry or withdrawal of an investor from the market is another piece of information that must be quickly communicated. Changes in fees to be charged or in the acquisition of new outlets looking for certain types of loans must both be promptly relayed to those involved.

Each item of information, depending on the speed with which it must be relayed, automatically determines the communication medium through which it should travel to those affected. The servicing manager knows that he cannot wait until the next staff meeting to inform the collection staff that a certain investor decided to ask for written monthly reports on all 2-month delinquents. He must write an interoffice memo on this subject promptly so that records may be developed for the eventual execution of the new task. He knows, however, that he can wait to discuss, for instance, the results of new insurance solicitation methods with the staff of the servicing department.

In carrying out his coordinating tasks, the loan administrator must fully recognize that the channels of coordination flow up as well as down. Information developed in a staff meeting must often be taken to individual employees performing a certain task; this is downstream coordination. Conversely, information developed by the staff must also be brought to a management meeting and presented in the form of either a written report or an oral report; this is upstream coordination.

Coordination, generally, may take three different forms: written media, consultations, and meetings. Any one or a combination of these methods provides the basic means for interchange of information and suggestions for action. Each method is discussed here with illustrations of types of information that may be interchanged most effectively among the departments.

COORDINATION BY WRITTEN MEDIA

Written communications take many forms. The nature of the items to be communicated and the speed with which a particular item must be relayed often determine the format. Even if a piece of news is relayed by word of mouth, it should be confirmed in writing. Otherwise details are lost or misconstrued and members of the department who were not present for the oral statement may not receive the information accurately and completely. Misinformation or misunderstanding caused by careless instructions or forgotten details can often be costly.

Reports

There is virtually no limitation on the number of times and ways that reports and information properly presented at the right times can enhance management's ability to make appropriate decisions. Reports may be prepared and circulated before a meeting, for example, so participants can consider the subject and prepare for an effective discussion. Reports may be in narrative form, may contain only statistical information, or may be a combination of both. Certain types of reports tend to become permanent fixtures of the management's coordinating efforts. They can be submitted upon request by the president on a specific subject, or they can be periodic reports on certain activities or certain results. Reports may be sent by one person to all department heads simultaneously, or one report, such as a statistical compilation, may be sent by a routing slip from one department head to another and back to the sender. Often the latter method is more effective since the initials on the routing slip assure the sender that all concerned *have read* the material.

Reports are more widely used to convey data by the servicing department than the production department. The nature of the information that the production staff usually provides to those engaged in servicing is best communicated through direct consultation. In many instances, of course, both departments issue brief intra-office memorandum to transmit information on new developments or changes. Operating and statistical reports such as those described in Chapter 8 are unique as means of coordinating activities between production and management, servicing and management, and production and servicing.

Loan officer to management Prior to the opening of a branch office, for instance, a loan officer familiar with that particular area may be asked to prepare a report describing the area, its population, and industry; evaluating its prospects for success; and estimating the amount of business that the particular area may generate. The report may be used subsequently as source material.

Servicing manager to head of production department A great variety of reports may be prepared and disseminated by the controller, the loan administrator, or the servicing manager. Some of these, such as reports on loans serviced, on loan delinquency, and the analysis of loans to be paid in full, were illustrated in Chapter 8. Here only those reports are described which suggest the coordinating value of communication.

One report, which may be prepared from time to time, consists of listing loans about to mature or which have principal balances of approximately $8,000 or less, a balance that represents the company's breakeven point in servicing. The production staff may then review these loans and offer new loans for larger amounts to those borrowers who can make productive use of the additional money, own desirable property, and have good payment records. If conditions for this activity are favorable, this report can help create a substantial amount of new business.

When refinancing is propitious, a special report should be prepared for the production department on those slow-paying borrowers who have substantial equities in their homes and whose payment problems may be solved by a larger loan to consolidate debts. In these situations however great care should be taken that new loans are made only to deserving customers who essentially have the ability and apparent willingness to meet their obligations.

A list should also be prepared periodically of the FHA loans that have a principal balance of about $500 or less and at the same time a credit in the reserve account of about $200. This should include loans which have only 2 to 5 years left before maturity. Borrowers on this list should be informed of the status of the loans and the amount held in the reserve account (most often they are not aware of this), and be reminded that they may pay the loan in full. The advantages of persuading the borrower to terminate such a loan with the payment of $300 are not exclusively those of the mortgage company, which, then, eliminates a loan which is no longer profitable to service. The borrower is also saved the inconvenience and expense of making monthly payments. Proposing ownership without a mortgage may be the most appealing approach in contacting these borrowers. Under no circumstances should the borrower be made to feel that the company wants to get rid of him now that his loan has become unprofitable.

Intra-office Memos

The difference between an intra-office memo and a report is that an intra-office memo is a directive or is instructive in nature, while a report is intended to convey factual information. While the former is written to relate certain events or requirements and is nonrecurring, the latter is prepared and disseminated on a regular basis.

Changes affecting operations which evolved in a meeting, or were decided upon by a manager of a department, or were necessitated by written directions from investors to government agencies may be best communicated to the staff by an intra-office memo. Such memos, however, should cover only those decisions and changes which cannot be countermanded. Matters whose solution may create a difference of opinion can best be relayed to the staff in a meeting. Subjects can be discussed first, such as changes in insurance solicitation methods, and then summarized and codified in an intra-office memo or in an amendment to, or a revision of, the pertinent existing job description. Intra-office memos can be written to set up new ground rules and pave the way for a meeting to discuss problems that may arise as a result of new changes. For instance, an intra-office memo, relating to an investor's new requirements on its single debit procedure cannot be questioned; subsequent to the reading of such requirements, however, any problems not fully anticipated can be discussed in a meeting.

Company Stories

Rather than encourage the dissemination of a plethora of individual reports from department heads to various members of the management team and others interested in various topics, it is often desirable to establish a clearing house for all available and useful information. Under this concept, all departmental reports are sent first to the loan administrator who culls, edits, and screens the information, and finally writes up and circulates a composite report which is then named a *company story*. The company story does not replace the flow of reports from department heads to senior management; rather it supplements and reproduces the parts of such reports that the entire office team should see and know about.

The story may include the following:

1 A summary of general business conditions affecting the mortgage business, such as mortgage interest rate changes, discount problems, market changes, and changes in bank borrowing rates.
2 A monthly report from the income property loan staff on all newly signed up business and on new prospects.
3 A report from the residential loan department on loans committed, loans sold, unused commitments, market prospects, and new investors acquired.
4 A report on the real estate activity in the area regardless of whether or not the mortgage banker is directly engaged in such activity.
5 A report on any insurance activity; sales of residential insurance, life insurance, and accident and health insurance; also a report on insurance market conditions.
6 A report on the status of delinquent loans, comparing company delinquency rates with those reported by MBA.
7 An earnings forecast by the treasurer of the company.

The report must be informal and the information must be meaningful and useful to those receiving it. Accomplishments of those engaged in one of the activities should be appropriately commended. Others who may not have had identical accomplishments will be spurred on for better results.

A company story may become the best source of a complete picture of the company's progress and problems. It enables each department head to envision his associates' problems and appreciate their contributions to profit. The insights that each member of the company gets, from realizing that others face problems equal to, or greater than, his, enhances his understanding of the workings of the entire mortgage banking firm and helps him coordinate his activities with others.

Those who receive the story, and who in turn participate in providing the material for it, should generally be the following:

Manager, residential loan activity

Manager, income property loan activity

Manager, processing activity

Legal counsel

Head of construction payout department

Manager, insurance department

Manager, real estate department

Manager, management activity

Loan administrator

House Organs

In contrast to the company story, a *house organ* is a more formal, often printed, presentation of company progress. It is typically a general picture of the company's progress or success rather than specific and statistical material. It is usually a story of who has done the job rather than what was accomplished. Office publications are often designed to improve employee relations since they are used to report special activities of employees and special events concerning them, their employment, and anniversary dates. In this sense, the house organ is also a personnel management tool. In addition, a house organ can be an educational tool informing employees of legislative and political changes affecting the business on both national and local levels.

COORDINATION BY CONSULTATION

Some information may be passed on more readily and intelligently by consultation between staff and department heads than through circulation of memoranda or occasional or periodic reports. The following illustrations show the beneficial effects of consultations.

Delinquent Loans and Pre-Foreclosure Cases

Members of the collection staff should be encouraged to consult with one of the company's lending officers on each loan which is unusually troublesome or "slow pay." Delinquencies which are serious enough to warrant eventual foreclosure action should be reviewed by a loan officer. Such consultation should include discussion of current appraisal value, sales price, sales potentialities of the property, and other factors which have a direct bearing on future negotiations with the delinquent borrower. If the company has a real estate department, its manager may be asked to take part in the consultation.

All those participating will benefit from such a discussion. The collector learns about the method employed to determine values, and the loan officer gains firsthand knowledge of collection difficulties in an area in which he may be currently trying to make loans for a builder.

Remakes of Loans to Existing Borrowers

Members of the production staff should always consult the collection department before considering a new loan for a current borrower. Information on the desirability of a borrower is not always self-evident by merely scanning the cashier card or accounting records. Often information on the efforts that had to be expended to keep the loan current or within the 15-day grace period may make the rejection of a new loan advisable. Only the collector who knows each account can properly evaluate the desirability of a former borrower or a borrower whose loan he presently handles.

Reinspection of Properties

Consultation regarding reinspection of properties is the joint responsibility of the production and servicing departments. Preferably, the appraiser who originally determined the value of the property should reinspect the property and see to what extent, if any, the premises have been improved or have deteriorated. Correspondence with the borrower whose house requires care, cleaning, and paint and who is often also delinquent or a slow payer should then be handled by the collection personnel or by the servicing manager.

COORDINATION BY MEETINGS

The most effective medium for coordination is a meeting of those charged with various responsibilities in production, processing, and servicing. All information disseminated by reports or exchanged through consultation may be discussed at such meetings. Meetings, however, should be brief and include discussion of only those problems that *need deliberation and a collective decision.*

Meetings should be called for the general purpose of considering overall policies and procedural problems or for the special purpose of discussing departmental problems. The meetings should be informal and held at a specified time each week. Monday morning, for instance, or one evening after office hours.

Participants should include the managers in charge of production, of processing, of legal staff, and of servicing, together with all supervisors and key employees. The discussion of a special problem pertaining to a certain operation may sometimes require the attendance of the members of an entire department. Participation in the affairs of the company, by attending meetings and at times helping in making decisions, can greatly increase the staff members' interest and opportunity for efficiency. It is useful in building cooperation to bring to such meetings reports on certain special activities by various department heads who do normally not participate in them. Generally, discretion in selecting those who should attend meetings must be exercised by management and respective department heads.

Before each meeting is held, a brief agenda must be prepared. By following such a timetable, participants of the meeting will give attention to all pertinent matters, and there will be less chance that proceedings will bog down in irrelevant or rambling discussions. Reports should be organized but need not be written out. Meetings should not be considered by members of the management team as bull sessions even, if after certain reports, the material presented is discussed or dissected.

Meetings can be time-wasters, especially if those attending have not prepared their reports or if the presiding senior member of the group present, who may be the president of the company, the executive vice president, or the loan administrator, does not expedite the proceedings. Reports should be short and to the point, and the meeting should be held to a minimum of time. Those who tend to be verbose should be urged to make brief reports and, if necessary, should be cut off.

General Meetings

Subjects that should usually be considered at general meetings are problems affecting all departments, arising from loans for a new investor or from a new builder or arising from changes in investors' investment policies or in FHA or VA regulations. These topics are strongly recommended for discussion, because management often fails to consider and review significant changes from any other view than that of the loan production department. Operations of many a company become inefficient because the information received by one individual is not passed on to all who are concerned. For instance, when a new investor's account is acquired, the question of a special bank account or the investor's special servicing requirements will automatically be raised and settled beforehand if the loan administrator has an opportunity to participate in the negotiations affecting his department's work. Without proper coordination, however, most of the servicing details are not considered until the loans are delivered to the investor and the actual task of servicing begins, at a point when it is often too late to simplify procedures for all parties concerned. Thus, failure to exchange information and consider all aspects of each operation by the entire staff may often result in unnecessary expense or undue embarrassment.

Special Purpose Meetings

Meetings to consider specific problems should be held weekly or even twice a week, as necessity demands. Some illustrations of special purposes follow.

Loans The loan production staff and the appraisers should meet to approve loans. It is also advisable to include the loan administrator, not only because he will be responsible for the loans after they have been made, but because he may have pertinent suggestions regarding the servicing problems of the particular type of loan under consideration. He may point out cumbersome requirements specified by a certain investor, unknown to the production staff, which may prompt the company to raise the commission for the loan, reject it, or submit it to an investor other than the one originally considered.

Servicing Meetings on servicing matters should be called by the loan administrator or the servicing manager to discuss the requirements of a new investor or changes initiated by an old one, as well as to consider general servicing problems that arise. It is often advisable for the head of the loan production department to attend such meetings. Staff reports may also be discussed in such meetings.

Collections Meetings on collection activities should be called at regular intervals, at least monthly, to discuss month-end delinquency reports. These reports include those prepared and disseminated to investors and those prepared on all loans serviced by the company. Participants should include the loan administrator, servicing manager, or both, the head of the collection department, and all collectors. During the course of the meeting those accounts which are delinquent 60 days or more should be discussed and measures to cure the delinquency considered.

Other Joint meetings arranged for the servicing staffs of two or three companies in a particular location are invariably beneficial to all concerned. Such meetings are often promoted by servicing committees of local associations, but can be initiated by two or three servicing managers. Meetings with groups of realtors or home builders can often be helpful in enlarging the scope of operations or in exploring problems of mutual interest.

CHAPTER TWELVE

Customer Relations

Good customer relations are the mortgage company's most effective advertising. A satisfied borrower will return for a larger loan or a loan on another property, or become a source of insurance business. An enthusiastic borrower will recommend the mortgage company to his friends and neighbors. People do talk about pleasant experiences just as much as they complain about discourteous treatment in their contacts with the business world. The smile of the cashier, the pleasant voice of the switchboard operator, or the helpfulness of the loan officer is a great inducement to a prospective mortgagor to do business with the company. In short, a mortgage company is primarily a service organization in which *every employee is a salesman for the company.*

The loan officer may talk to a prospective borrower once or twice, but cashiers and members of the collection, tax, and insurance departments may deal with him for 20 to 30 years. He begins the relationship by starting with the "best foot forward"; they must maintain and cultivate the relationship once it is established.

Unfortunately, many employees tend to look upon the borrower as just another loan number and treat him accordingly. Too often, they fail to realize that the terms of the borrower's mortgage are not always self-explanatory and the various rules and regulations affecting the loan may be unfamiliar to him. Thus, a large number of requests made by borrowers to servicing employees may be exasperating, but an employee who can handle such requests in a patient and understanding manner is worth many times the salary he is paid.

The following discussion deals with techniques, and comments generally on the experiences of mortgage bankers, especially of the larger and more rapidly growing firms whose progress is partly the result of effective customer relations. It is hoped that it will assist many other companies in their efforts to create and to preserve good customer relations.

HOW TO BUILD GOOD CUSTOMER RELATIONS

Good customer relations begin with management, but they cannot be built at the management level alone—they must be practiced at every level of the organization. Customer relations are complex because they are based on the harmonious relationship of each borrower with all members of the organization whom he encounters. They are important because carelessness or rudeness of a single employee may adversely affect the company's relationships with many borrowers.

To create satisfactory customer relations, the mortgage banker must first place himself in the borrower's position and ask himself what he would want most from the company with which he is dealing. Usually, he expects efficiency, fairness, friendliness, and patience. Since these qualities are developed rather than innate, they cannot be acquired by employees overnight. Management must, however, gradually establish good practices in customer relations and maintain them by (1) watching every activity of the company, (2) exercising good judgment in selecting employees, (3) placing in contact with customers only those who demonstrate their ability to handle the public, (4) being considerate toward both public and fellow employees, and (5) providing the public with information whenever an actual or prospective need arises.

Handling Personal Inquiries

Borrowers who deal with the company in person at the office or by telephone judge the company partly, at least, from first impressions. These may be created by the general appearance of the office and the desks of those the customers see first as well as by the response and attention they receive from the receptionist or the switchboard operator. A receptionist or switchboard operator who is pleasant and courteous can affect the firm's business volume as much as a good salesman. If the telephone operator is not eager to locate the party called or does not offer to put the caller in touch with someone who can take care of the inquiry, the company may lose the opportunity to make a new loan or acquire a customer. This employee must be taught to match a request for information with the individual who can handle it so that the inquiry may be answered with a minimum of time and effort. Admittedly, this is a fairly difficult task, but it must be done. There is nothing a customer dislikes more than to be switched from one person to another, or to be directed from desk to desk.

The receptionist and the switchboard operator should, therefore, know how to question each caller intelligently and courteously to determine the nature of the inquiry. A borrower may ask for the cashier when he actually needs to talk to a member of the collection staff on a delinquent payment, or he may look for the FHA department when he actually intends to pay the loan in full and has a few questions about the required notification. Persons in various servicing departments who most frequently accept outside calls should be able to answer a majority of the questions asked. If unable to help themselves, they should assume the responsibility for obtaining the information and sending it to the borrower.

The loan officer, the collection manager, or the cashier should always be cognizant of the fact that the person who telephones or who sits beside the desk has an important problem on his mind, that he needs accurate information and, most of all, that he needs help. The borrower's inquiry is important to him or he would not take the time to ask. It deserves the employee's personal and undivided attention. To do otherwise— for example, to carry on another conversation in his presence—is discourteous and poor customer relations.

Handling Complaints

All complaints, either written or oral, should receive prompt and courteous attention. It is important that errors be rectified as quickly and amicably as possible. Willingness to make an immediate correction may make the mortgagor forget the mistake, but a grudgingly made adjustment or a half-hearted apology is often worse than no reaction at all. Nor is it wise to argue with a person with a chip on his shoulder, or to fail to give his anger a chance to cool.

A large portion of the complaints come from borrowers' wives who are unfamiliar with business practices. A man should handle these complaints because a peculiar feature of feminine psychology is that an answer received from a man will be accepted far more readily than the same answer from another woman.

All specific complaints on company policy or operations or on the conduct of an employee, whether made in person, over the telephone, or in writing, should be handled by the loan administrator or one of the senior officers. This is axiomatic since three actions must be taken: (1) satisfy the customer—i.e., apologize and explain —(2) locate or pinpoint the cause, which may be a rude employee or a cumbersome requirement, and (3) either remove the offending employee from further contact with the public or improve the faulty procedure.

Complaints about an employee addressed to the company president should be answered by letter only after a thorough investigation of the facts. If the employee erred, the letter should admit that an error was committed. If the employee acted correctly and the borrower was either unreasonable or discourteous, the complaint must be answered diplomatically, pointing out clearly and courteously that the employee was right. It is often better to lose an unfair customer than a good employee. A company president or loan administrator who does not support the correct actions of his staff will have difficulties in maintaining proper morale, securing competent employees, and rendering efficient services.

Disseminating Information at Closing

The voluntary dissemination of information to the borrower on any matter concerning his home and his finances constitutes good customer relations. An enlightened, well-informed borrower is a much better customer than one who knows little about his rights or obligations under the terms of the mortgage or learns about them only when difficulties arise. A homeowner should know the basic facts about such matters as protection of his home against fire and other hazards, his real estate taxes, and the sale potential of his home. When or how he is informed of these facts is up to the discretion of each mortgage banker. A company's willingness to spend money on educational material is a rare characteristic, but it is usually appreciated by its borrowers.

Pamphlets on the mortgage loan   Of the many useful publications mortgage bankers give their customers, the most fundamental is one usually entitled "What You Should Know about Your Mortgage Loan." (See Appendix A-5.) This pamphlet condenses all the essential information that the loan-closing officer has told, or should have told, the mortgagor and his spouse at closing. It is a handy reference, aimed at making homeownership through financing with a mortgage banking firm simple and understandable. While a first-payment letter sets forth the new mortgagor's monthly payments, all other useful information in connection with homeownership and mortgage indebtedness is incorporated in the pamphlet.

The booklet includes a brief description of the various mortgage documents, with pertinent comments about their purpose; the monthly payment and its composition; the amortization schedule, with illustrations for its use and application. Most booklets describe the procedures for making prepayments or paying the loan in full and explain FHA mortgage insurance and the use of escrow deposits to pay real estate tax bills and insurance premiums.

Distribution of the booklet has improved customer relations and reduced operating expenses, because inquiries have decreased about 50 percent. However, not all booklets used today accomplish the desired results because those who prepared them have attempted to condense too much information into a few pages and have written one pamphlet to cover all types of loans. Instead, it is advisable to prepare separate booklets or a few mimeographed pages of information specifically for FHA and GI borrowers. Conventional loan borrowers do not necessarily need elaborate information and instructions, since the mortgage documents usually contain a description of all the borrower's rights and responsibilities. In this case, the salient points of the terms of the mortgage may be presented in a special letter.

Pamphlets on insurance   A booklet similar to the one on the mortgage loan may be prepared *on the type of insurance* a homeowner should have to protect his home, its contents, and his liabilities in owning them. The pamphlet may also describe all types of insurance that a homeowner should consider, as well as the type of insurance the mortgage banker may be able to procure for him. Therefore, the information pamphlet may also be good sales literature. (See Appendix A-11.)

The requirements of lenders, relative to handling insurance losses, often puzzle both borrowers and insurance agents. Nothing will do as much harm to the mortgage banker's image of efficiency as a delay in processing a loss draft because of administrative requirements that have not been explained to the borrower. For instance, the borrower may be duly apprehensive if, after the repairs have been made, the release of a loss draft—which he thought would only be held pending the completion of the repairs—is suddenly held up further because the check must first be endorsed by the holder of the mortgage.

If the mortgage banker is also in the insurance business, it is good business procedure to notify the borrower, either immediately upon his reporting a loss—or preferably in advance, by means of a release which may be repeated from time to time—exactly what the fire loss requirements are and how loss drafts have to be handled. This information may be included in the above pamphlet also.

Disseminating Information Periodically

Annual statement   As a good customer relations gesture, most mortgage banking firms inform each mortgagor, usually within 10 days after the close of the calendar year, of the amount of taxes that have been paid from the mortgagor's reserve account to the tax collector for real estate taxes and the amount of interest the mortgagor paid the company. Some annual statements also provide the borrower with an analysis of his account.

Newsletters   On the assumption that a well-informed borrower is a satisfied borrower, it is advisable from time to time to send out information on such items as how special tax assessments are created or how to save money on heating fuel. Such items may be sent out monthly, quarterly, or semi-annually. If coupon books are mailed yearly or notices monthly, the mailing of how-to information merely involves stuffing an extra sheet of paper in the envelope. This is an inexpensive medium of communication and a customer relations tool worth considerably more than its cost. Such newsletters can also contain general information on various types of insurance protection.

Property tax information   Although the various taxing authorities disseminate information to the property owners on the composition of the property tax bill and the purpose of each tax dollar, it is often advisable to inform the mortgagor how his property is assessed, how the taxes are related to the assessment, and how tax bills are paid. The procedure that must be followed to protest a tax bill is a newsworthy item when taxes are on the rise. General information on assessments and other liens should also be mailed out on appropriate occasions.

Welcome letter Simultaneously with the mortgagor's move into his home, a personalized letter may be sent by the president of the company congratulating the mortgagor on achieving his life's dream in acquiring a home. The letter should, of course, be brief and its tone fairly light. Instead of a letter, a welcome card may also be used.

Good payment record letter If the borrower maintains a good payment record, a congratulatory letter may be sent to him by the president of the company. When a large portfolio is serviced, the names of borrowers eligible for this type of recognition are easily obtained with the aid of data processing equipment.

Reinstatement of delinquent loan letter Occasionally a delinquent borrower will exert considerable effort and bring a seemingly hopeless loan into a current condition. It is good customer relations to recognize such accomplishments and, if deserved, to compliment the borrower in a special letter.

Loan completion letter A letter dispatched by the president after the loan has been paid in full from the borrower's own funds is usually very much appreciated. It is a good ending to a long-term relationship and a good customer relations builder.

Miscellaneous In states where there is a tax exemption for homestead owners (such as Florida, Indiana, Texas) or a special tax exemption for veterans (New Jersey), mortgage companies should remind such borrowers each year to file for tax exemption. Borrowers appreciate this service even if they have already filed on their own.

At certain times of the year, the company is often so deluged by inquiries concerning taxes or the status of reserve accounts that it cannot give a prompt answer. When this happens, it is advisable to notify the borrower immediately by a post card—mimeographed, if necessary—that his inquiry was received and that it will be attended to as soon as possible.

HOW TO PRESERVE GOOD CUSTOMER RELATIONS

Good customer relations, like good employee relations, can be maintained only through continuous efforts. Management cannot simply decide to improve and maintain customer relations, pass out a few overall instructions, and then sit back and watch it develop. The loan administrator or personnel manager must acquaint and repeatedly re-acquaint employees with company objectives and train them in the proper attitudes—first toward the company, and then toward its customers. Of course, the entire management must also set a good example to guide its staff. Specifically, management and its loan administrator must do the following to preserve as well as to build its most precious asset: good customer relations.

Maintain Good Employee Relations

Since people usually treat others in a manner in which they are treated, there is a close interrelation between the way management treats its employees and the way employees treat the customer. Employees who are dissatisfied with their wages or who have a grudge against their supervisors or the company for its policies or actions will not radiate the pleasantness so essential for successful dealings with customers. It is false management economy, then, to try to keep expenses down by paying low wages. Those who pay well find that one contented clerk usually works harder and does a better job than two underpaid ones. A happy employee will be eager to make customers of the company as pleased with the organization as he is himself. Similarly, it is foolhardy to expect two cashiers to perform the cashiering function which normally requires three cashiers. Cashiers who are pressed for time not only make too many errors—which then require a lot of time to find and correct—but they cannot be pleasant to borrowers. It is wiser to have excess capacity in the cashier department, which is constantly exposed to public contact, than to rush and press cashiers in their work.

Management responsibility for good employee relations includes observing and correcting the conduct of employees. Employees quite often are not aware of their own shortcomings as far as customer relations are concerned. Instead of singling out an offender and telling him that he has been impolite or curt, the approach should be to pass out memoranda on customer relations from time to time, citing instances when customer relations could have been improved. If such an approach fails, it may be necessary for the office or servicing manager to have a talk with the offender or to shift him to a job where he has no contact with the public.

Accept and Acknowledge Compliments Properly

A procedure must be developed and maintained for accepting compliments on behalf of the company as a whole or for an individual employee. All letters expressing satisfaction with the service rendered by an attentive employee or by an entire section or department should be routed to the president of the company, the senior operating officer, or the loan administrator for a prompt response.

It follows that members of the management team should use every possible means to compliment employees when they have done a good job or to name the individual or department when a compliment is received. Not only should the individual be informed of favorable observations received on his work, but his supervisor and often his fellow workers should be informed, either by circulating the complimentary letter or by placing it on the company bulletin board. Such action will elicit similar acts from others.

Maintain Good Company Image

Employees should be encouraged to participate in civic and social activities. Much of this encouragement can come from members of the management team through their own participation in various activities and events. The company officer in charge of the company's advertising and public relations programs should be constantly aware of the various activities of the employees and, whenever possible, see to it that their participation or leadership in them be reported in local publications and newspapers.

Train Employees How to Use the Telephone

Since most customers contact a mortgage banking firm by telephone, good habits and manners on the telephone are essential. The following rules—elementary as some may seem—should be strictly observed and enforced.

1 Telephone calls should be answered promptly, after one ring if possible. The recipient of the call should not just say or grunt "Hello," but he should identify himself by his name and/or his department. The identification should always be distinct, courteous, and cheerful.

2 The employee should be attentive to the problem and should attempt to be helpful. If an apology is in order for an error or delay, it is well worth saying, even if the facts are not fully ascertained and all extenuating circumstances are not disclosed.

3 Customers should not be kept waiting on the telephone too long. If the information sought is not readily available, it is best to inform the caller of this fact and offer him the choice of waiting for the answer or receiving it by letter or return call.

4 If the recipient of a call becomes aware at the outset of the conversation that he is unable to handle the inquiry, he should arrange to switch the call promptly. There is nothing more annoying than to have to restate an involved inquiry. If the company receives many toll calls, answering telephones should be assigned to those who can handle all inquiries addressed to the department. It is both expensive and annoying for the customer to call, especially if a long distance is involved, only to be told five minutes later that the particular information sought is not available or that it cannot be released over the telephone.

5 All calls should be concluded with a word of "Thanks" or by saying, "You're welcome." An employee should never replace the receiver before the customer has indicated that he has received a satisfactory answer.

Periodically Review Services to Borrowers

A good motto here is that each borrower likes to be treated as if he were the company's only customer.

Solicit comments on service Not until an irate customer is actually complaining about an employee's action or a procedure can a thorough investigation be made of the source of trouble and corrective measures finally taken. Many mortgagors who are irritated by individual discourtesies or puzzled by specific requirements do not write letters, but let the dissatisfaction build up within themselves. Therefore, it may be worthwhile to ask borrowers at random about their relationships with the company, to solicit and encourage their opinions and observations about matters that may please or annoy them. Discussions of the reported reactions in a group or at a staff meeting may serve to highlight good as well as bad points in the company's relations with its customers. Such analysis and review may be of great value in building and maintaining good customer relations.

Determine and release credit information carefully Often little thought is given to the fact that poorly evaluated and carelessly handled credit information may endanger customer relations. Although admittedly the release of credit information is a time-consuming and unprofitable task, it is necessary, and care must be exercised that the information given out be accurate and disseminated promptly.

Gear information to borrower's needs It is an old mortgage company adage that the best informed borrower is not necessarily the best borrower. This means that the relationship must be geared to the need of the borrowers: too much information may disturb some; too little will leave others disgruntled. Since it is easier to increase the flow of information than to reduce or eliminate it, it is best to keep information to the essential minimum. The loan administrator should frequently review the nature and extent of all customer services rendered.

Avoid irritating borrowers Notifications of changes in certain requirements, such as a change in the amount of monthly payment, which are apt to upset or irritate the borrower, should be carefully worded and clearly presented. For instance, information regarding a prepayment penalty, which the borrower most likely has forgotten, or a reminder that the borrower failed to give the proper notification prior to paying the loan in full must be diplomatically conveyed to the borrower. All similar situations where controversies can be anticipated should be minimized.

Customers like conveniences they have grown accustomed to and resent having to accept a less convenient arrangement, even though it is more economical for the company. Management, and particularly the loan administrator or servicing manager, often gives too little thought to how the customer will be affected by simplification of procedures. While streamlining operations may save a few hundred dollars in a certain phase of the work, it may often hurt customer relations. A brief handwritten note from the cashier, instead of a short letter, for instance, may save some time, but it may also offend the borrower. The elimination of monthly billings may cut expenses, but may also inconvenience the borrower who expects a monthly reminder that his payment is due.

Check the tone of delinquency notices and content of collection letters periodically Members of the collection staff often take pride in the forcefulness of their collection efforts and the subsequent results. However, they may overstep the boundaries of good taste to achieve their objectives. Although some frequently hit their targets with forceful demands, others scatter their shots and offend those who are victims of unfortunate circumstances. Occasionally, even printed delinquency notices or forms may be in poor taste or offensive in language and should, therefore, be frequently reviewed.

3

Mortgage Loan Servicing

In the chapters which follow, each of the five basic servicing functions of a mortgage banking organization are assigned to a separate department. Each department—cashier, mortgage loan accounting, collection, insurance, and tax—are headed by a department manager; together they are under the supervision of a servicing manager. Auxiliary servicing functions, which must be performed from time to time do not require separate departments. These miscellaneous functions which do not lend themselves to easy classification or warrant the creation of a department will be described where they seem most appropriate. These include, for instance, reinspections of properties required under the terms of the servicing contract by some lenders or the preparation of payoff and property transfer statements and the execution of attendant tasks. In this book the latter are included in the cashier department operation, but they may be assigned and treated as the function of the mortgage loan accounting department.

Some mortgage bankers are of the opinion that for the administration of escrow reserve funds involving disbursements from, and adjustment of, all reserve accounts a special escrow disbursement department is needed. In this volume, the task of disbursing reserve funds is described under the departments which perform them, namely, the insurance and tax departments, respectively. In each case where the performance of a task straddles various departmental activities, the decision where each task is to be performed must be made by the loan administrator or servicing manager, taking into consideration various factors peculiar to the company involved. Those who wish to gain merely an overall perspective of all servicing functions will do well to re-read Chapter 2, Fundamentals of Servicing, before reading the ensuing pages for specific guidance.

CHAPTER THIRTEEN

Cashier Department

There is no better place to start the presentation of servicing activities than in the cashier department. It not only occupies the space near the entrance of the mortgage banking firm, but also is the department which accepts and processes payments—the first step in the servicing process.

ORGANIZATION AND STAFF REQUIREMENTS

The duties of a cashier in a mortgage banking firm consist primarily of handling payments and depositing funds received. As the volume of loans to be serviced grows, however, this function often expands to that of a mortgage loan cashier, who assumes responsibility for many related cashier-type functions. Curiously enough, as the number of loans serviced achieve substantial proportions, the cashiers once again become mere tellers, with members of a separate unit executing most of the related tasks.

It is difficult to regard any one type of record or type of payment processing system as unequivocally the best for all companies. Company requirements vary, as do borrowers' habits and the general conditions under which a company operates. Only after a complete review of the entire cashier operation can a suitable system and appropriate records be developed. A single factor, such as the predominant type of loan, the particular make-up of borrowers, or the special requirements of investors may make one type of record or payment processing arrangement more desirable than another. Often, even within one organization, it is best to handle differently certain types of loan payments or collections for certain investors.

Operating efficiency in this department results from the effective combination of good, carefully arranged records, handy methods of payment identification, effective procedures for the deposit of payments, and the performance of personable, highly satisfactory, and well-trained employees.

Function of Cashier

The cashier performs three basic functions: (1) receives payments from mortgagors, (2) deposits funds received daily in appropriate bank accounts, and (3) transmits payment and deposit information to the mortgage loan accounting department. Although the cashier and accounting functions are clearly interdependent, *internal controls demand that the operations, responsibilities, and functions of these departments be separate and distinct.* In small organizations, the closeness of the areas in which the jobs are performed as well as the number of personnel make the separation difficult. However, management must exercise close supervision so that functional segregation remains inviolate.

Qualifications of Cashier

Cashiers must be able to handle money easily and accurately and must be generally familiar with mortgage payment requirements. They must have an aptitude for figures. Other qualifications will depend upon the size of the firm and its operating arrangements. The cashier's work area is located at the entrance of the office. As a result, he comes in direct contact with the public more often than any other servicing employee. He accepts borrowers' payments when made in person. He is often called upon to answer questions which are not related directly to his duties. Accordingly, he must be personable, courteous, and well-groomed. Although the cashier cannot be expected to answer all questions posed by borrowers, general familiarity with all phases of mortgage banking helps maintain good public relations. Small- and medium-size companies often encourage cashiers to be sufficiently familiar with servicing activities to assist borrowers and maintain a good company image. Large companies seldom find this qualification necessary for cashiers, as most payments are received by mail.

If handling of payoffs and preparation of payoff statements are the responsibility of the cashier, as is customary in many firms, the cashier must also know the payment and prepayment requirements of the company's investors, be familiar with FHA and VA regulations, and have an understanding of the basic mortgage documents. The cashier need not be familiar with these activities in firms where processing payoffs are assigned to the mortgage loan accounting department or a service department superimposed on the five basic operating departments.

In addition to receiving and depositing payments, the cashier may be assigned a number of periodic functions. These are discussed at the end of this chapter and are noted here as an additional cashier qualification.

Staffing

The number of permanent cashiers needed for the department should be based on the volume of over-the-counter payments that must be processed during the course of the day and the nature and extent of periodic functions assigned to the department. As an organization grows, the number of permanent cashiers also grows, but instead of a large number of full-fledged cashiers, only one or two qualified cashiers and several tellers are required. Tellers are primarily processors of payments who are normally assigned from other departments to help the cashiers. If the periodic functions including the preparation of payoff and proration statements are not handled by the cashiers, one fully trained cashier assisted by tellers may adequately perform the requirements of the department. (See Exhibit 7.)

It is often difficult to maintain the right number of employees in the cashier's department, even if it has a fluctuating yet predictable workload. This is understandable since 90 percent of all payments due are usually received by mail, most of which reach the mortgage banker during the last 2 and the first 10 days of the month. This concentration of the workload can be eliminated, or considerably reduced, if the "lock-box arrangement" is installed, as discussed later in this chapter.

The most common solution to a staffing problem is to have the regular cashiers handle the over-the-counter borrowers and as many of the mail payments as they can. They are then supplemented, under the supervision of either the cashier or a servicing employee, by assigning to them a number of servicing employees or available helpers to act as tellers. These part-time tellers sort and open the payment envelopes, remove the checks, and pull and match payment cards. After the checks and payment cards are balanced, they are handed to the cashier as a completed package. The cashiers add to their own finished work those processed by others, and strike a balance to complete their own daily task.

Some companies which have a considerable peak load prefer to establish special work teams to handle all mail payments during the first 10 days of the month. These teams often consist of such employees as the receptionist, extra filing personnel, and tax department employees (not at "tax time"). This temporary arrangement prevents the accumulation of unopened payment envelopes or unprocessed payments, since these work teams can be expanded or reduced as the need for them arises or can be asked to work overtime if necessary to complete the task.

The loan administrator is responsible for seeing that cashiers are not overloaded with work. Under pressure they may become irritable and create poor impressions on borrowers. Cashiers must smile when they do not feel like doing so, either because of the conduct of a particular customer or because of their own workload. Cashiers may also have difficulty in performing accurate work and balancing their cash drawers if they are required to handle too heavy a workload. The loan administrator's task is not easy, since most employees resent the idea of helping others, often feeling—at times justly—that no one helps them. He can surmount these difficulties if he picks good employees and imbues them with the proper spirit to cooperate in the execution of this peculiar, but unavoidable, servicing task.

OPERATING PRACTICES

The operating practices of the cashier department are presented in two broad groups of duties and responsibilities: those which must be performed daily and those which must be performed only when required, i.e., periodically.

The cashier's daily tasks are to accept over-the-counter cash, to handle checks and money orders which arrive by mail, to verify payments, to issue receipts when required, to make appropriate entries covering these transactions, to balance funds against entries on cashier cards or against prepunched payment cards, to prepare deposit tickets, and to be responsible for the accuracy of entries and deposits.

For the purposes of analyzing these transactions and reviewing the forms and methods used, the transactions are grouped in three basic daily functions: (1) receiving payments, (2) depositing payments, and (3) transmitting information to the mortgage loan accounting department. The most important and most time-consuming function is that of receiving payments. The workflow chart in Exhibit 26 illustrates the progress of a mortgagor's payment to the investor.

In addition to these daily functions, the cashier is called on from time to time to perform other, closely related periodic functions which include preparing statements on termination of loans and on sale of property subject to mortgage. Other periodic tasks are described under four headings: (1) billing of quarterly and semi-annual payments, (2) maintaining card indexes, (3) handling principal prepayments, (4) handling not-sufficient funds (NSF) checks. The most time-consuming periodic function is the preparation of statements.

DAILY FUNCTIONS

Receiving Payments

Receiving payments requires that borrowers' records, cash or checks, are matched with the cashier's records or payment cards. This task includes recording and acknowledgment of payments, and may involve all or any of the following: (1) acceptance of cash payments over the counter, (2) issuance of receipts for cash payments, (3) acceptance of checks and money orders which arrive by mail, (4) verification of payments and making appropriate entries (or pulling payment cards) for monies received, and (5) balancing of funds against entries on cashier cards or payment cards. The tools available to the cashier for handling payments are discussed under two headings: "borrowers' records," which help borrowers make their payments or identify them, and "cashier records," which cashiers use to record receipt of payments.

Speed and efficiency in accepting and entering payments on cashier records do not depend on the capabilities of the cashier alone, nor on the type of loans handled. They do not even depend on the effective application of use of *one single medium,* whether that be a cashier record or a borrower's record. Rather, speed and efficiency are contingent on the combination of many different factors.

EXHIBIT 26 Workflow chart – cashier department

STEPS TO BE FOLLOWED

CASHIER DEPARTMENT

I. Mortgage banker provides each borrower with *one* of the following:

    Coupon , Billing , Payment Envelope , or Loan Identification Number

    Borrower mails check to mortgage banker, using one of the above to identify payment.

II.

III. Cashier performs each of the following functions:

    A. Remove "cashier record" which is either a

        Punched Card , Receipt or Cashier Card

    B. Match "cashier record" with identification medium in Step I and with borrower's check.

    C. Total cash and checks and balance with "cashier record."

    D. Deposit checks in Clearing Account.

    E. Simultaneously transmit "cashier record" to the Mortgage Loan Accounting Department.

MORTGAGE LOAN ACCOUNTING DEPARTMENT

IV. The Mortgage Loan Accounting Department will then:

    A. Post payments to ledger records.

    B. Simultaneously prepare remittance reports and send them to investors.

    C. Transfer funds from Clearing Account to Investors' Accounts and/or mail checks.

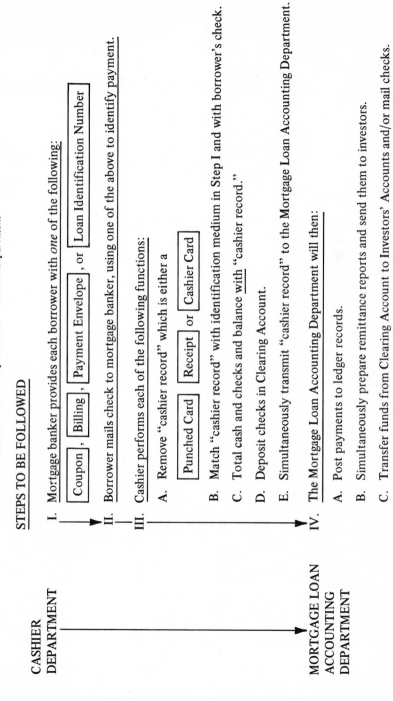

215

Mortgage bankers have found that four preliminary and precautionary steps can help considerably in promoting speed and efficiency in accepting and processing payments. These include:

1 Use of a comprehensive and clear first-payment letter (see Exhibit 27) which is dispatched by a clerk either in the collection or loan-closing departments and acquaints each borrower with the company's methods of handling payments.

2 Distribution of a booklet describing the company's servicing procedure and the borrower's rights and responsibilities. (See Appendix A-5.)

3 Rounding monthly payments upwards to the next even dollar on FHA, VA, and those conventional loans which require tax and insurance deposits. This practice may create a small cushion in the escrow reserve account to cover slight increases in taxes or insurance premiums. Neither FHA nor VA objects to this procedure.

4 Marking cashier or payment cards to indicate that for one reason or another payment is not to be accepted and processed. A card may be marked by a collector who wishes to have a payment referred to him before it is accepted; or a card may be marked to show that a statement was issued for full repayment of the loan, and, therefore, the acceptance of an additional payment should be questioned before it is processed. Often it is preferable to remove the payment card that should not be processed so the cashier inquires into the special reason or circumstance why a card is unavailable.

Under no circumstances should internal control in this department be sacrificed for the sake of expediency. For each over-the-counter cash payment which is not receipted on the duplicate copy of the notice of payment, a receipt must be issued by the cashier. Receipts should be prenumbered and prepared in duplicate, with the original given to the borrower and the duplicate retained by the cashier. The cashier must be responsible for all numbered copies of receipts, since the receipts provide an effective control on his operations. To assure proper internal control, the practice of some borrowers of placing currency in payment envelopes should be most emphatically discouraged.

Care should be exercised that all payments tendered to the cashier are actually made by owners of properties whose names are properly shown on the company's records. As it will be pointed out in Chapter 16, the mortgagor has no protection if the casualty company insuring the property is not notified of, and does not consent to, a change of ownership. Of course, the responsibility for notifying the mortgage banker of a sale can easily be placed on an uninformed or negligent real estate agent or attorney. The mortgage banker, however, must attempt to prevent sales of properties from going unnoticed, in order to reduce the mortgagee's exposure as well as to collect the fees for changing records. Accordingly, after a sale of property, the cashier or payment cards should be promptly updated as to ownership. All differences in names of property owners and those making payments should be promptly investigated: (1) to keep as accurate a check as possible on changes in ownership of properties, (2) to make certain that company records are appropriately changed, and (3) to follow up in case a sale took place without the benefit of a proration statement and the fulfillment of attendant requirements.

EXHIBIT 27　First-payment letter

ABC MORTGAGE COMPANY
233 Maple Street
Chicago, Illinois　60190

June 15, 1970

Loan No.　F44089

Dear Mr. and Mrs.

In accordance with the terms of the mortgage papers recently signed by you, the first payment on the above loan will be due on　　July 1, 1970.　Your payments are always due on the first day of each month, and we urge you to remit your payments promptly so that they may reach us on the first.

The twelve self-addressed envelopes enclosed are to be used for remittances only.　When this supply is depleted, we shall send you a new supply.　Please make all checks payable to the ABC Mortgage Company and write the loan number shown above in the upper left-hand corner of the check.　Your cancelled checks or money order stubs will serve as your receipts.

Your monthly payment is $　126.00　and this amount will be distributed as follows:

Principal and Interest	$ 88.19
Reserves: FHA Mortgage Insurance	3.15
Hazard Insurance	4.50
Real Estate Taxes	30.16

The amortization schedule enclosed indicates the breakdown of each installment between principal and interest; it also shows the outstanding principal balance after each remittance has been applied.　Since only one schedule is issued with each loan, we ask that you keep it in a safe place though handy for reference purposes.

Soon after the first of each year, we will send you an "Annual Statement" in which we will confirm to you the outstanding balance of your loan and give you the amount of interest you have paid and the real estate taxes we have paid from your reserve account.　You can use this information to prepare your income tax return.

If you have any questions regarding your mortgage loan, do not hesitate to call us.　We shall be happy to help you whenever we can.

Very truly yours,

Collection Department

Borrower's records (payment identification media)   The majority of mortgage banking firms provide their customers with a means of identifying the monthly payments that they mail to the company. The types most often provided are (1) loan number identification cards, (2) payment envelopes, (3) coupons, and (4) monthly billing of payments. There is a growing tendency, however, to eliminate these media or to simplify them. Instead of coupons or monthly billings, borrowers are merely provided with addressed (but not stamped) envelopes or supplied with a loan number. The mortgage banker relies solely on the borrowers' cooperation in identifying their checks with such numbers on each payment occasion.

Regardless of which payment identification medium is used, the loan administrator must see to it that those checks sent by mortgagors which do not show appropriate loan numbers or are not accompanied by coupons or payment notices do not accumulate in the cashier's hands. An up-to-date card index file, which provides a crossindex of loan numbers by names of borrowers and by street addresses of properties, can be used to reduce the number of unidentified checks. It is also a good practice to send the borrower a reminder to place his loan number on the check or to use coupons or billing forms regardless of which method is used to identify an account. Unless the borrower is given a receipt for each payment, the first-payment letter should adequately stress that he should retain cancelled checks and check off payments on the amortization schedule in order to keep track of his payments.

Loan number identification card   Possibly the simplest and the least expensive arrangement is for the mortgage banking firm to ask the borrower to identify each monthly remittance by his loan number. To enable the borrower to do so, mortgage bankers often provide him with a loan number identification card. Of course, an actual card need not be provided if using the loan number to identify the payment is adequately stressed in the first-payment letter. Entries on the repayment or amortization schedule corresponding to payments then supplement the cancelled checks or receipts for cash payments and constitute a continuous record of payments which provide the mortgagor with an easy means of determining the unpaid balance of his loan at any time. The use of the schedule and loan identification number is, of course, explained in the first-payment letter, and an annual statement then confirms the accuracy of the borrower's record keeping. The annual mortgage loan statement (Exhibit 54) normally shows the total interest paid, the unpaid balance of the loan, and the amount of real estate taxes disbursed from the tax reserve account during the preceding calendar year.

Payment envelopes   Providing the borrower with envelopes bearing his loan number, for mailing payments is a recent development. With the first-payment letter twelve payment envelopes are mailed to the borrower. A gummed sticker which in essence is a request form for additional envelopes is attached to the eleventh envelope. When the borrower reaches the eleventh envelope, he fills it out and mails it with his payment. The cashier then places this sticker on a large envelope to be used for mailing twelve new payment envelopes to the borrower. The flaps of all envelopes and a new sticker will be perforated with the loan identification number by an inexpensive electric perforating machine or coded by addressograph equipment. The perforated loan number is used only for identifying a remittance on which the borrower failed to place his loan number. This procedure eliminates one of the most cumbersome and time-consuming tasks the cashier is required to perform—that of identifying payments that bear neither a loan number nor a property address.

Mortgage bankers who maintain separate bank clearing accounts for FHA, VA, or conventional loans or who wish to process payments separately by types of loans may assign envelopes of different colors to different groups of loans and thus establish an automatic and visual means of sorting envelopes by contents. Different colors may also be assigned to various investors' payments if such instantaneous sorting by investors facilitates processing payments.

To enhance the use of different envelopes and to have the U.S. Post Office Department automatically sort incoming mail either by types of loans or by investors, many mortgage bankers rent two or more post office lock boxes and imprint the appropriate post office box number on the envelopes supplied to mortgagors. Different lock box numbers are assigned to different types of loans or loans for different investors. In renting lock boxes, care should be taken to obtain nonconsecutive numbers to eliminate possible sorting slip-ups in the post office. The annual rental fee for lock boxes is nominal.

Coupons There are two types of coupons in use: (1) preprinted paper coupons and (2) prepunched payment coupon cards.

1 Booklet of paper coupons   Paper coupons are usually placed in small booklets of twelve, twenty-four, or even as many as thirty-six coupons. A blank coupon, inserted before the last three coupons, is forwarded to the company to obtain a new booklet. An additional blank coupon may be included to enable the borrower to notify the company of a change of mailing address.

The upper portion of Exhibit 28 illustrates the inside cover of a coupon book, describing the use of the coupons by the borrower. The lower portion is the coupon itself, together with the stub, which, of course, remains in the book. The outside cover (not shown) carries the name and address of the borrower and as much pertinent information as can be incorporated on an addressograph plate, which is usually used to imprint the face of the book. The loan number shown as 768 on the sample is perforated on each coupon to assure proper identification of the payment. The amount of payment, $68.41, is also prepunched. Many organizations also punch a mortgage code number or bank number on the coupon to facilitate processing.

Notice the method by which the due date of the first, and of each subsequent payment date may be readily established for the borrower and for the cashier who processes the payment. If the first payment of the loan is due in April, as shown on the sample, the second coupon placed behind the first

EXHIBIT 28 Prepunched payment coupon book

READ CAREFULLY TO AVOID MISUNDERSTANDINGS

1. Monthly notices are not mailed. When making payments, detach and send one coupon with each payment. Please fill in NAME, ADDRESS, AMOUNT, and PAYMENT NUMBER on each coupon. DO NOT SEND THE ENTIRE BOOK.
2. Payments should reach this office on or before the FIRST day of EACH month. Late payments are subject to a late charge.
3. DO NOT SEND CASH BY MAIL. Payments may be made by check, bank draft, express or postal money order, and will be accepted subject to collection. No receipts will be mailed.
4. Please bring this book when making payments in person so that the stub can be receipted.
5. Notify us IMMEDIATELY of any change of address or ownership.

IMPORTANT—It is advisable to have your broker consult with us before entering into any written agreement to sell or refinance. This may save you money.

DATE PAID	PAYMENT NUMBER
CHECK NO.	

AMOUNT OF PAYMENT

$________

KEEP YOUR RECORD OF PAYMENTS BY MAIL ON THIS STUB

SEND COUPON ONLY

768 6041

PAYMENT No.________ AMOUNT $________

COVERING PROPERTY________

NAME________

Payment Is Due on the First Day of the Month Punched	JAN	FEB	MAR	APR	MAY	JUN	JUL	AUG	SEP	OCT	NOV	DEC
				●								

FILL IN AND SEND THIS COUPON WITH PAYMENT

ABC MORTGAGE COMPANY
000 South State Street
Chicago, Illinois

one shows "May" in the same position; the third coupon shows "June," and so on.

To enable the cashier to identify the payments by type of loan more readily, most companies use different colored coupons to signify FHA, VA, or conventional loans. Generally, the use of a color scheme, whether it be for coupons, billing notices, or payment envelopes, is a valuable tool in handling calls from borrowers inquiring about their prepayment privileges or presenting other problems. If they fail to remember the type of loan they have, they always know the color of their coupons or payment envelopes; thus the type of loan involved is easily identified.

2 Prepunched payment coupon cards This type of coupon (Exhibit 29) is prepared by data processing equipment and shows basically the same information as the paper coupons. However, a substantial volume of loans must be serviced—unless a service bureau facility is employed—before the system involved in preparing and disseminating the cards becomes practical and economical. Using card coupons, of course, speeds up payment handling. By means of these cards, corresponding prepunched payment cards may be pulled by a data processing machine, and incoming payment coupon cards can be turned over to the data processing department for processing. These cards are then used to prepare a list giving an appropriate total for which a deposit of an equal amount must be provided by the cashier.

Arrangements can be made with post office authorities to employ bulk mailing in order to reduce postage expenses for the annual mailing of the twelve payment coupon cards to borrowers. (See Exhibit 30.)

Monthly billing of payments If the volume of loans serviced does not exceed 1,000, payment billings can be typed. For a larger volume, monthly billings are usually prepared after the fifteenth of the month by means of data processing, addressograph, or other printing equipment in one operation on carbonized snap-out forms. The forms may be made up of three, four, or five copies and may be printed to permit mailing in window envelopes. Each copy may be in a different color to indicate its purpose. The information not desired on the borrower's copy can be blocked out. Most payment notices prepared by data processing equipment include a complete breakdown of payments and are normally printed at the rate of about a hundred notices a minute.

The payment system most frequently used entails five identical copies. The original or first copy serves as a payment notice which is sent to the borrower each

EXHIBIT 29 Prepunched payment coupon card

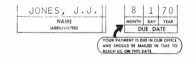

MORTGAGE PAYMENT COUPON

PROMPT PAYMENT INSURES A GOOD CREDIT STANDING

IMPORTANT

ABC MORTGAGE COMPANY
233 Maple Street
Chicago, Illinois 60190

ALWAYS MAIL THIS CARD WITH YOUR PAYMENT

WHEN PAYING BY MAIL BRING THIS CARD WITH

YOU WHEN PAYMENT IS MADE AT OUR OFFICE.

PLEASE DO NOT FOLD, SPINDLE OR MUTILATE.

EXHIBIT 30   Payment coupon cards

WHAT THE SYSTEM IS AND HOW IT WORKS...

To make it as easy and convenient as possible for you to make your monthly payments, ABC MORTGAGE Company is changing to a new loan payment system that provides electronic accuracy in the handling of your payments.

Each year you will receive 12 payment coupons, 12 reply envelopes and a detailed mortgage payment analysis showing how your money was disbursed during the past year.

Each payment coupon shows a DUE DATE, PAYMENT AMOUNT and your LOAN NUMBER. A typical payment coupon and a detailed explanation of the coupon are shown below. The payment packet in which your payment coupons come to you, provides a place for the recording of your payments. After reviewing this material, please contact us if you have any questions.

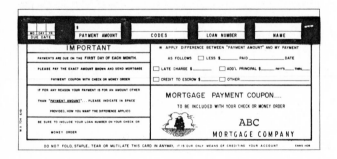

DUE DATE...

Appearing here will be the date each payment is due. Be sure you send the right payment coupon each month.

TOTAL PAYMENT...

The total amount of the payment due appears here. This amount includes principal, interest, taxes, insurance and any other monthly requirements. For a detailed breakdown of this amount, see your enclosed mortgage payment analysis sheet. When your payment is for any amount other than the "payment amount" shown on the coupon, please be sure to indicate how the difference should be applied in the space indicated at the right side of the coupon.

LOAN NUMBER...

Your loan account number will appear here on all of your payment coupons. IT IS ESSENTIAL THAT YOU WRITE THIS NUMBER ON ALL CHECKS OR MONEY ORDERS YOU SEND. Also, please include this number in any correspondence with us pertaining to your loan.

NOTICE...

In the future you will NOT receive monthly statements as you have in the past, nor will you receive any reminder about when your payment is due. To avoid late charges, it is important that you remember to make each monthly payment on or before the first of each month.

month; a second copy is held by the cashier until the payment is received, when it is used as a posting medium. A third copy is used only as a receipt for cash payments. The fourth copy is used as a past due notice, and the fifth copy may be given to the collection department as a follow-up reminder. For a small volume of loans under a similar arrangement, two payment notices are sent to the borrower, one of which he is asked to return with his payment, the other to be kept as a record of payment.

After the receipt of payments by the cashier, copies of billing notices may be used by the accounting department to remit the payment to the investors. A check, together with ten or twelve such receipts representing one day's collections, is a satisfactory means of remitting payments.

A frequently used billing form, shown in Exhibit 31, requires the borrower to detach the payment coupon from the right side of the notice, to note if exceptions thereon are required or if a principal prepayment not anticipated by the mortgage banker is made, and to send the coupon with his check. Most billings used today, however, do not have detachable portions; instead a duplicate copy of the bill is designed for remitting payment.

When mailing the billing for the current month, smaller companies may enclose a receipt for the previous payment by marking the billing form "paid." This method gives the borrower a receipt of each payment, but it is an expensive one for the mortgage company to provide and, therefore, is not recommended.

At the end of the day, copies of bills are added and matched with the funds received. These bills constitute cashier records, or are used to pull payment cards and provide information to the mortgage loan accounting department on the payments received.

Cashier records   In contrast to the variety of borrowers' records and their numerous applications, only three types of cashiers' records are in common use.

Cashier card   The cashier card which is in predominant use contains entries made in advance for each interest payment, principal payment, and the principal balance. (See Exhibit 32.) It may also show the servicing fee, unless this is computed on the basis of the aggregate interest collected or by means of data processing equipment as remittances are made.

Various methods of preparing prescheduled cashier cards are now in use. The cards may be prescheduled from the amortization schedule by data processing equipment, manually in ink, or in pencil. If ink is used, the entry to signify receipt of payment is a check mark or a lump sum entry. If pencil is used, the entry is made by pen over the distribution previously made by pencil. Amortization schedules may be pasted on the cashier's card as shown on Exhibit 32.

To identify loans by type (FHA, VA, conventional), the cards should be of the same colors already assigned to the borrower's records or envelopes. Then, if the ledger cards are also printed on stocks of corresponding colors, a definite color scheme is established which is often useful in identifying types of loans promptly.

EXHIBIT 31 *Machine processed billing notice*

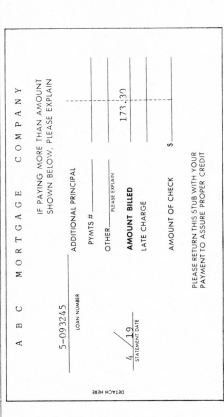

A B C M O R T G A G E C O M P A N Y
233 Maple Street, Chicago, Illinois 60190

DATE DUE MONTH	DAY	PAYMENT NUMBER	INTEREST	PRINCIPAL	FHA INS.	TAXES	PROPERTY INSURANCE	MORTGAGE LIFE AND OR A.S. INS.	LATE CHARGE	AMOUNT
5	1	106	61.82	46.05	5.43	53.00	7.00			173.30

5-093245
LOAN NUMBER

4 / 19 / 72
STATEMENT DATE

JOHN S. JONES
159 TREE TOP LANE
ANYTOWN, ILLINOIS

PAY THIS AMOUNT →   173.30

PRINCIPAL BALANCE AFTER THIS PAYMENT   14083.52

IMPORTANT
SEE REVERSE SIDE FOR FURTHER INSTRUCTIONS AND FOR EXPLANATION OF PROPERTY INSURANCE AND MORTGAGE LIFE AND/OR ACCIDENT AND SICKNESS INSURANCE.

7.5 % A N N U A L P E R C E N T A G E R A T E

ALL PAYMENTS ARE DUE ON THE FIRST DAY OF THE MONTH. A LATE CHARGE WILL ACCRUE ON ANY PAYMENT RECEIVED BY LENDER MORE THAN 15 DAYS AFTER PAYMENT DUE DATE.

PLEASE KEEP THIS STATEMENT FOR INCOME TAX PURPOSES

DETACH HERE

A B C M O R T G A G E C O M P A N Y

IF PAYING MORE THAN AMOUNT SHOWN BELOW, PLEASE EXPLAIN

5-093245
LOAN NUMBER

ADDITIONAL PRINCIPAL

PYMTS #

OTHER ____ PLEASE EXPLAIN

4 / 19
STATEMENT DATE

AMOUNT BILLED   173.30

LATE CHARGE

AMOUNT OF CHECK $

PLEASE RETURN THIS STUB WITH YOUR PAYMENT TO ASSURE PROPER CREDIT

DETACH HERE

224

EXHIBIT 32 Cashier card

1	2	3	4	5	6	7	8	9	10	11	12	13	14	15	16	17	18

CONVENTIONAL 43074

MORTGAGEE NO: 345,266

	ORIGINAL	CURRENT
INT. & PRIN. $	451.07	$
TAXES	93.93	
HAZ. INS.	20.00	
TOTAL	565.00	

NAME HARRIS, Martin and Stella, his wife

ADDRESS 624 Antietam Street, Highland Park, Illinois COOK

HOLDER XYZ LIFE INSURANCE COMPANY SOLD AT 7 3/4%

MORTGAGE $ 47,200.00 TERM 15 YRS. RATE 8 % FIRST PAYMENT DUE: 12-1-69

PAYMENTS $ 451.07 DATE: 9-23-69

Prepayment Option: See loan file

DATE PAID	TOTAL PAID	DUE	ESCROW DEPOSIT	NO.	INTEREST	PRINCIPAL	BALANCE OF LOAN
MAR 3 1971	565 -	3 - 1	113 73	16	300.37	150.70	44,904.96
APR 5 1971	565 -	4 - 1	113 73	17	299.97	151.70	44,753.26
MAY 2 1971	565 -	5 - 1	113 73	18	298.56	152.71	44,600.55
JUN 7 1971	565 -	6 - 1	113 73	19	297.34	153.73	44,446.82
				20	296.31	154.76	44,292.06
				21	295.28	155.79	44,136.27
				22	294.24	156.83	43,979.44
				23	293.20	157.87	43,821.57
				24	292.14	158.93	43,662.64
				25	291.08	159.99	43,502.65
				26	290.02	161.05	43,341.60
				27	288.94	162.13	43,179.47
				28	287.86	163.21	43,016.26
				29	286.78	164.29	42,851.97
				30	285.68	165.39	42,686.58

ABC MORTGAGE COMPANY

225

Cards should be filed in loan number sequence or by alphabetical order of borrowers' names in three different card trays or in one tray divided into three compartments. Each tray or compartment thus represents cards in different stages of collection. The first tray contains current cards on which payments are being received; the second, the delinquent cards; the third, cards on which payments have not yet come due (new loans) or those of loans that have been prepaid for one or several months. After the fifteenth of the month, the cards remaining in the first, or current tray, represent delinquent accounts which should be moved to the delinquent accounts tray. The cards, or lists prepared from them, can then be turned over to the collection department for the preparation of past due notices. If data processing equipment is used, past due notices and listing of delinquent loans are independently prepared by the mortgage loan accounting department and furnished to the collection department.

When a payment is received, total amount paid and due date are entered, and cards are stacked according to the investors owning the mortgages, if the volume of loans permits such a procedure, or kept separately to be segregated later. At the end of the day, all cards representing payment amounts are balanced with the receipts, and the cards with adding-machine tapes attached are forwarded to the mortgage loan accounting staff. For effective control, a copy of the adding-machine tape accompanying the cards should be retained by the cashier. After the posting operation, the cards are returned to the cashier and refiled.

Many companies which have a servicing portfolio in excess of 8,000 or 10,000 loans and employ data processing equipment, no longer use cashier cards for residential loans. However, they are still frequently used by the same companies for recording and processing income property loan payments.

Copy of monthly billing Whenever the monthly billing of payments system is employed and the borrower does not enclose his notice the second copy of the billing notice is pulled, matched with the check, and processed (Exhibit 31).

Prepunched payment card When a company is using data processing equipment, the cashier is provided with prepunched payment cards (see Exhibit 33) which are used for processing payments. If the volume of loans is in the 5,000 to 8,000 range, cards are hand-pulled; i.e., the cashier removes and matches payment cards with the identifying loan number appearing on the checks or with the coupons accompanying checks. If the volume of loans exceeds 8,000 and the borrowers are provided with prepunched coupon cards the cashier cards may be machine-pulled. This process speeds handling since some machines can automatically total the cards pulled and sort the cards into any desired sequence or group.

Prior to depositing funds received and transmitting payment information to the accounting department, checks and cash received must be balanced with the cashier or prepunched payment cards. Usually, matching adding-machine tapes, or adding-machine tapes and data processing runs, assures the cashier that he is in balance; this is his signal that deposit tickets can be prepared.

EXHIBIT 33   Prepunched payment card

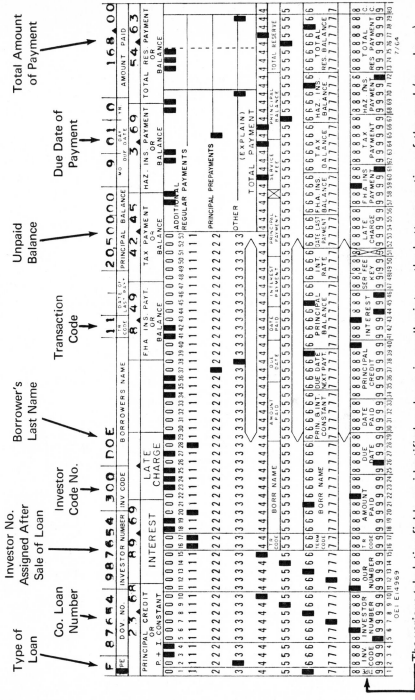

The various tabulating fields are identified as shown in small print on the bottom portion of the card (see above).

227

Advantages and disadvantages of different procedures No single arrangement assures the greatest degree of accuracy, speed, and convenience to both borrower and cashier at the most reasonable expense. The least expensive arrangement is inconvenient for the borrower and the most convenient arrangement for the borrower is expensive for the mortgage company. The loan administrator must analyze the advantages and disadvantages of each procedure and relate them to his company's special requirements. In making a decision, the loan administrator must consider three basic points: (1) To what extent can records or procedures, or both, be simplified without impairing speed and accuracy in service for both borrower and investor? (2) Which record or combination of records involves the least amount of work at the time of receipt of payment? (3) Which record is most readily accessible in the cashier department, and what does preparing such a record involve?

The loan administrator may conclude that in a favorable economic climate, particularly when dealing with well-educated borrowers, supplying the borrowers with a loan number and a number of envelopes is the most economical procedure that doesn't jeopardize the cashier's ability to identify borrowers' checks. The requirement that the loan number be placed on the check provides the mortgagor with certain assurance that his payment will be properly applied and that the cancelled check will serve as a receipt.

The advantages of a billing system will be apparent only if a great number of payments, at least 40 percent, are made in cash. Duplicate copies of bills then replace receipts for cash payments which, if prepared in longhand by the cashier, would slow down operations. Many companies feel that the regularity of monthly payment billings is good service which assures prompt payment. They also feel that if collections slow down, monthly notices will serve as constant reminders of obligations yet due. However, other companies contend that it is unnecessary to remind a person each month that a payment is due on his home since this is an obligation unlikely to be forgotten. Actually, a coupon book system does seem to have an advantage over the mortgage payment billing system in that a minimum of effort is expended by the cashier in identifying and processing payments, with no mailing expense required for monthly billings.

Each of the systems described has certain merits, and many mortgage companies have improved or simplified their methods of handling payments. It would not be prudent, however, to adopt a system, because it has worked well for another company, without studying the circumstances which made its success possible. Often the requirements of a single investor may make an arrangement which is practical for Company X impractical for Company Y.

If entirely new procedures are to be established because of close interrelations between the cashier department and the mortgage loan accounting department, it is advisable to plan operations of both departments simultaneously. Under the circumstances, the internal control aspects of the workflow should be considered more carefully than if the two systems are evolved separately.

In many companies, attempts to change from one system to another within the cashier department have bogged down, even if the conversion was badly needed, because of the monumental task of changing records and reeducating employees and borrowers. Although a decision to change cashier records can easily be reached, a changeover involving the borrowers' records must be made with the borrower's reactions in mind. To change the habits of borrowers is not easy; it requires reeducation; it requires a logical explanation because borrowers do not like to surrender any of their conveniences. The substitution of payment envelopes for a monthly billing system would certainly make the borrower feel that the company is planning to perform less service than before. Or if a borrower, who is in the habit of receiving a bill each month, is asked to mail his payment with a coupon, he may blame any delinquency that might occur on the discontinuance of the billing system.

Depositing Payments

Depositing payments involves depositing cash or checks into one or more bank accounts, and calls for (1) endorsement of checks, (2) preparation of bank deposit slips, and (3) accurate balancing of entries with deposits. The task is completed only when the total for the package of cashier's cards equals the funds being readied for deposit. A balance is normally taken at a specific cutoff time, say, between 1 and 2 P.M. This time officially terminates a day's work; all payments made over the counter or processed later in the afternoon constitute part of the next day's work. The speed of the balancing operation depends not only on the cashier's skill and the efficacy of the records, but also on the system employed in making deposits.

After balancing, checks can be readied for deposit for the next morning. To deposit *all checks* on the same day the checks are received is an unusually difficult task for the cashier under ordinary circumstances and should not be attempted. Checks for substantial amounts, however, whether involving monthly payments, payment in full of loans, or other nonrecurring items, should be deposited on the day of their receipt since investors require prompt remittance of such receipts. Deposits may be segregated by investor and deposited in as many investors' accounts as the mortgage banker services, or they may be placed into a clearing account, as explained below.

Use of investors' accounts Under this system, the cashier records (cashier cards or duplicate copies of billing notices) are segregated according to investors as payments are received, and the corresponding funds are deposited directly to the investors' bank accounts on the day of receipt or no later than the next morning.

Use of clearing account Under this system, a lump-sum deposit is made for each day's collections in a clearing account. The use of separate clearing accounts for FHA loans and non-FHA loans increases the flexibility of this arrangement and helps localize errors. Clearing accounts, if properly designated as custodial accounts, are protected by the FDIC up to $20,000 for each individual borrower's payment.

For control purposes, as soon as the totals of cash and checks received are established they must be recorded in a cashier journal either in one or two lump sums depending on whether one or two clearing accounts are used or by as many totals as there are investors for whom collections are made. After the receipt of all cashiers' records, a similar entry of totals is recorded by the mortgage loan accounting department on the completion of the posting of that day's total collections, by checking either the cashier records received or the bank deposits made by the cashier. From the standpoint of internal control, it is important that the functions of adding up checks by the cashier and of tracing deposits be separated, and that the accuracy of these totals be checked from time to time. As of the end of the month, the two totals that represent (1) deposits by the cashier and (2) postings by the mortgage loan accounting department must balance. Supervision of this activity must be exercised by the controller of the company and not by the cashier or the bookkeeper involved.

Evaluation of use of investors' accounts versus use of clearing accounts A lump-sum deposit for a day's total collections reduces the cashier's work and shifts the burden of segregating payments by investors to the mortgage loan accounting department where, especially when using data processing equipment, segregation by investors may be made in a matter of seconds or minutes. A clearing account thus relieves the cashier of much detail work during rush hours and around the first of the month. It speeds up processing of payments and strengthens internal control. The arrangement is particularly desirable if the volume of loans serviced is substantial, if there are a large number of investors, or if there are a large number of over-the-counter payments.

Most investors today permit the use of clearing accounts if the clearing account is established in a bank which is insured by FDIC, the custodial nature of the account is acknowledged by the bank, and the funds are cleared within a prescribed time. To establish the custodial nature of the account, the bank should be asked for a letter stating that the bank "waives any claim, lien, or right of set-off of any nature against such funds on deposit in this account which the bank might otherwise have or obtain against the mortgage company." The alternative, direct depositing of payments in investors' accounts, is feasible only if the company handles a relatively small volume of loans for a few investors or services for no more than one or two investors.

From the standpoint of safety and immediate availability of funds, the direct depositing of funds by the servicer into the investors' accounts is preferred by investors. Investors, however, recognize that to segregate payments by investors on a same-day basis creates an almost insurmountable burden on the servicers' cashiers. Accordingly, investors normally permit the use of the clearing account, but make permission contingent on the speedy removal (within 24 to 48 hours) of the funds from the corporations' custodial clearing account. Most servicers, particularly those using data processing equipment, establish procedures that enable them to deposit into a clearing account and then later, through the identification of bank accounts by means of pre-punched payment cards, distribute the same funds into the various investors' accounts.

Lock box arrangement The lock box plan offered as a service by commercial banks to mortgage bankers is a relatively recent development. Banks first offered this service to their commercial customers, such as mail order houses or retail oil companies, to speed up the collection of receivables and thus increase the companies' working capital while reducing their clerical workload.

The plan works fairly simply. First, it is necessary for the mortgage banking firm to rent a lock box at the local post office. The rental is inexpensive, usually around $40 per year. It is then necessary for the mortgage banker to authorize the bank to remove the contents of the box. Since the post office lock box services are open to the public on a 24-hour basis, bank clerks normally empty the contents of their lock boxes on an around-the-clock basis. Contents of the box are taken to the bank where the envelopes are opened and checks and paper coupons or prepunched coupon cards, or whatever media was provided to the borrower, are then removed. The checks are totaled and so are the payment media. The checks are then endorsed and deposited in the mortgage company's clearing account, and the payment media or a listing thereof, with a deposit ticket for the total of the day's receipts, are either delivered to, or picked up by, the mortgage company before the termination of the cashier's operations for that day.

The plan can be used *without providing the mortgagor with coupons, payment cards, or payment notices only* if the mortgage banker provides the bank with prepunched payment cards and if, in turn, the bank accepts the responsibility of pulling the applicable payment cards and of rejecting and not processing payments when the check either does not offer a loan number clue or does not match the payment card provided by the mortgage banker. The best means for the bank in rejecting or setting aside payments that should not be accepted is the use of appropriate stop payment cards. Then at the end of the day, all exceptions are turned over to the mortgage banker's cashier for handling and disposition.

The advantage of this plan to mortgage bankers servicing 10,000 or more loans is considerable, since much of the drudgery of opening envelopes and sorting and processing checks is removed from the office—a task which creates peak loads, personnel problems, and often a two-to-three day backup of unprocessed payments. Accumulation of unprocessed payments not only deprives the investor of funds, but creates additional problems for the collection department, which is anxious to receive delinquent payments. One company, which has a lock box plan, provides delinquent borrowers with special envelopes addressed directly to the collection department to speed up the receipt of such payments and to assure the collection staff that it is not collecting automatically an amount less than is required.

A lock box arrangement is not a panacea for all cashier problems. If not properly adapted, if not executed by a knowledgeable bank staff, and if such staff is not given proper instructions and tools to work with, the arrangement can create greater problems than it was designed to eliminate. Proper planning of forms and procedures for handling exceptions and scheduling is critical.

Transmitting Information to Mortgage Loan Accounting Department

This task involves transmitting all cashier cards to the accounting department. Before transmittal of such information, totals of cards and of related deposits must be in balance. Simultaneously with the depositing of monies in either the investors' accounts or the clearing account, the cashier transmits the cashier records (or payment cards) to the mortgage loan accounting department (refer again to Exhibit 26). This transfer of all information on payments received terminates the cashier's daily functions.

Processing payments to investors by the mortgage loan accounting department commences after this daily activity by the cashier is concluded. If all monies are deposited into investors' accounts, the only reports required are those which substantiate and identify deposits, in addition to recording receipts on the borrowers' ledger records. If monies are deposited into the clearing account, the funds must then be transferred into the investors' accounts or sent to investors with a remittance report that identifies payments.

PERIODIC FUNCTIONS

Preparing Statements

Preparation of statements pertaining to loans to be paid in full or to sale of mortgaged properties is included in this chapter with the proviso that they are the responsibility of the cashier department only if the cashiers are properly trained for these tasks and appropriate internal control measures are established. The size of the company, the borrower-company relationship, and the extent of supervision have considerable bearing on the success and propriety of this arrangement.

As an alternative, the mortgage loan accounting department may be responsible for preparing statements and may be asked to cooperate with the cashiers in handling terminations and assumptions. Whatever procedure is adopted, the request for statements should first be channeled to the loan administrator. When a payoff is involved, the cashier then requests the necessary papers from the investor. Whether the statements are prepared by the cashier or the mortgage loan accounting department, the cashier handles the payoff transaction with the borrower or his representative.

In cases of transfer of property involving substitution of mortgagors, the change of loan records may be initiated by the cashier and completed by him or by another member of the servicing department. Releases to be executed by investors and/or one of the governmental agencies are normally handled and processed by a staff member of the loan-processing department rather than the cashier, although the latter may initiate the entire transaction.

As a third alternative, all these functions may be performed in a special department.

Before a statement can be prepared on the status of a borrower's account, the purpose of the statement must be ascertained. This is particularly important, because the nature of the transaction determines both the type of statement that is to be issued and the steps the cashier must take. When a property is sold, two entirely different types of transactions may take place, each triggering entirely different steps in helping mortgage customers consummate their business. The first transaction involves the sale of property and the termination of the loan; the second, the purchase of the property by a new owner subject to the existing mortgage. The latter may be accomplished with or without the release of liability of the original borrower by the investor or the governmental agency involved.

When a loan termination is involved, the cashier must notify the holder of the mortgage that a notice to pay a loan in full has been received. This notification serves either as a request to the investor that it send the papers to the mortgage company or as a notification that the mortgage documents are to be prepared for shipment to the mortgage banker upon receipt of the funds involved. When a property transfer takes place and the investor is not being asked to release the seller's liability, the investor's prior approval of the new mortgagor is not required. He is notified of a change of ownership after the transaction is consummated.

Two types of transactions' statements are described here: a statement when a *termination of a loan* is anticipated, and a statement when the *sale of property subject to mortgage* is involved. In the latter instance, the original mortgage remains in effect. When a statement is issued on termination of a loan to a third party who will rely on it, there is an implied warranty of accuracy (which can be modified only by noting that "the statement is subject to the approval of the investor"). When a statement is issued to the borrower and an error is made or an item is omitted, it is still due and collectible from the borrower. Although both types of statements must be prepared carefully, the difference in responsibility implied in the issuance of a payoff statement and the liability arising from erroneous statements to the borrower must be constantly kept in mind.

ON TERMINATION OF LOANS

After it has been clearly determined that the loan is to be paid in full by the purchaser of the property or by another lending institution, and the date of such transaction has been scheduled, the following steps must be taken:

Written notice Before the preparation of any statement is started and an investor is notified of the pending termination of a loan, a written notice should be received. This notice should set forth the specific date on which the transaction is expected to be consummated, the nature of the transaction, and the source of funds. Most mortgage bankers keep track of the reasons for loan payoffs, and investors also wish to know the source of funds which terminated their investments.

It is best to avoid issuing tentative statements. If possible, issuing statements should be delayed until a definite closing date is established. This will avoid the necessity of issuing several statements, each superseding the one previously issued, which not only is confusing, but can be a source of errors and misunderstandings. This will also prevent a loan from becoming delinquent before it is paid in full. The request for a statement may be signed by the mortgagor, his attorney, a real estate firm selling the property, or the institution handling the new financing. Payoff figures should never be quoted over the telephone; if, however, some preliminary information is released about the loan, complete information should be promptly confirmed in writing.

Preparation of statement of account The statement of account issued to the borrower, his attorney, or to the institution which is to pay the loan in full should contain the following information:

1 Unpaid balance of the loan on the day the statement is issued.
2 Interest per month and per diem.
   a FHA regulations require that the mortgagee be given a full 30-day notice of a contemplated payment in full. This means that if notice is not received by the mortgage banker on the first of the month, in addition to the interest for the balance of the current month, 30 days' additional interest should be charged. For instance, if notice is received on June 3, interest should be collected to August 1. FNMA permits interest be charged to the date of final payment.
   b Under VA regulations, the mortgagor may repay his loan at any time without notice. Interest may be charged only to the date of payment in full.
   c On conventional loans, interest is often charged in accordance with the stipulation that payment be made on the due date only and that either a 30- or a 60-day notice be given. This normally means that interest is computed from the first due date of payment following the date of notice.
   d If the loan was delinquent prior to payoff, late charges should be added. However, according to FHA and VA regulations, late charges other than those on installments currently unpaid cannot be assessed and collected.
   e It is advisable to show on the statement the per diem interest due if a VA loan is involved and the amount of monthly interest charge in case FHA or conventional loan terminations are expected to be delayed.
3 Prepayment charges.
   a Under FHA regulations,[1] upon termination of loan prior to maturity, a 1 percent charge is collected, except as stated below, from the borrower and sent to FHA. This charge defrays the cost of closing out FHA's file on the loan.
      Borrowers are permitted to prepay 15 percent of the original amount of the loan annually without penalty. After the loan has been in force for 10 years, all FHA loans may be prepaid without penalty.
      If an FHA loan is refinanced by another FHA loan, no prepayment penalty need be charged. As a safety measure, however, it is best to show FHA prepayment charges on the payoff statement to the borrower even if FHA refinancing is involved, since if FHA refinancing does not materialize, any FHA prepayment penalty that is due must be collected.
      Under FHA regulations, the mortgagee is responsible for the computation and collection of an adjusted prepayment premium, as well as any mortgage insurance premium due. Prepayment premium must be remitted with a request for termination except in cases described above. The method of computation of prepayment premium charge is clearly described under Instructions on Form 2344, "Lenders Request for Termination of Home Mortgage Insurance," a copy of which must be submitted with a request for termination.
   b Under VA regulations, there are no prepayment charges.

---

[1]Effective May 1, 1972 FHA regulations were amended to eliminate the requirements for payment to FHA of an adjusted prepayment premium as well as a prepayment (termination) charge when either a home or a multi-family mortgage is paid in full.

c Each conventional loan document contains its own special prepayment requirements in the event of payment in full before maturity. Normally, a borrower
is required to pay 2 to 3 percent of the unpaid amount of a home loan prepaid within a specified number of years, 1 percent if prepaid within a subsequent number of years, and none after that period ends. Many mortgage notes
involving home loans permit the prepayment of 10 or 20 percent of the original amount of the loan each year on a noncumulative basis, so that if a loan is
paid in full, the prepayment penalty need not be charged on that part of the
amount paid that could normally have been paid that year without penalty.

On income property loans, prepayment penalty charges may start at 5
percent and drop down at a rate of $\frac{1}{2}$ of 1 percent per year. Some loans of
this type may contain no prepayment clauses. Often, when there are no provisions in the loan instrument to prepay the loan, the investor will permit
prepayment if certain unusual circumstances arise or fix a prepayment penalty
to fit the circumstances.

4 FHA mortgage insurance   At termination of a loan, the mortgage banker must
compute not only the adjusted prepayment premium, but also the prorata-earned
FHA mortgage insurance premium. Method of computation for FHA mortgage
premium on termination differs on cases which were endorsed prior to August
5, 1957, from those on or after that date. On that date, the method of FHA
mortgage insurance premium computation and collection was changed from a
prepaid basis to one on which the insurance premium is paid at the end of the
year for which it is due. Thus, refunds may be expected on loans insured before
August 5, 1957, while on loans insured after that date additional premium is due
at the time of termination. Proper preparation of Form 2344 is needed to expedite FHA's action in closing its file; the appropriate form for multifamily loans
is FHA Form 311. FHA recommends that any FHA mortgage insurance premium held in the reserve account is not to be refunded until notification is received from FHA of termination of the contract for insurance. For this reason,
it is recommended that FHA mortgage insurance premium reserves held in the
reserve account not be shown on the termination statement. They should always
be refunded by a separate check at a later date.

5 Reserves on hand   Reserves for taxes and insurance may be shown in a lump
sum or broken down into respective components. If reserves are adequate to
cover unpaid items, they should be promptly paid. Tax and insurance reserves
may be refunded by check upon termination of the loan or may, at the borrower's request, be applied to the amount required to pay the loan in full. The
practice regarding reserves on hand varies; reserves may be shown on the statement with the suggestion that they be deducted before the payment of the loan
in full. In this instance, reserves on hand are transferred by check from the
custodial account. If reserves are not deducted, a refund check made payable
to owners of the property must be issued. If reserves are deducted as shown on
Exhibit 34, care should be exercised that when payment in full is made the
reserves are credited to the proper parties.

6 Insurance and tax information.

a Taxes   The statement should show the amount of the last tax bill, when it

EXHIBIT 34   *Payoff statement*

```
WHITE COPY      ATTORNEY
BLUE COPY       BILL FILE
YELLOW COPY     MORTGAGEE
PINK COPY       —CASE FILE
```

RE: 71302   PAYOFF STATEMENT   notice dated 12-12-67

LOAN NUMBERS: 10990 _____ (73) ICM 34419 FHA   **DATES:** 3-1-68 _____
                 (JWR)   (INVESTOR)   (REQUEST)   (SETTLEMENT)

ATTORNEY: Security Title Guarantee Corp. _____   727 4456 _____
              (NAME)   (PHONE NUMBER)

              Six South Calvert _____   Baltimore, Maryland 21202
              (ADDRESS)   (CITY AND STATE)

MORTGAGOR: ROSENBERGER, George W. & Norma A. _____   666 Main Avenue _____
               (NAME)   (PROPERTY)

               _____   Baltimore, Maryland 21230
               (MAILING ADDRESS)   (CITY AND STATE)

1. OUTSTANDING LOAN BALANCE—after ___ February _____ payment. $2,439.66

2. INTEREST—Collected in arrears on all previous monthly payments.
     (a.) **FHA AND CONVENTIONAL LOANS**—due for month of February & March   21.34
     (b.) **INTEREST PENALTY**—due Noteholder in lieu of written notice of intention to prepay which is
           required at least 30 days prior to first day of month in which loan is paid per contract.   _____
     (c.) **VA LOANS**—due from _____ thru _____   _____
           (1.) Interest should be added to the Total of this Statement at the rate of $ . . . . per day
                 from _____ to the date your check is received in our office.

3. PAYOFF EXPENSE—Due ABC Mortgage for Statement Preparation, Account Clearance and other   10.00
     miscellaneous costs.   Company
     (a.) **OTHER EXPENSE** _____.   _____

4. LATE CHARGE—Due on any payment more than 15 days in arrears.   _____

5. ADJUSTED PREMIUM CHARGE—Due FHA
     (a.) In lieu of above—purchasers **NEW FHA NUMBER IS** _____ or aged 10 yrs. 10th yr.   _____

6. PREPAYMENT CHARGE—Due Noteholder per Conventional Contract.   _____

7. SERVICE FEE (Type 2)—Due Noteholder per FHA Title 203 i or b. 2 mos. @ 1.06   2.12

8. ADVANCES BY ABC Mortgage Company _____   _____

                           TOTAL CHARGES $2,473.12

9. LESS BALANCE IN EXPENSE ACCOUNT—On VA and Conventional loans only   186.64
     (a.) **BALANCE IN EXPENSE ACCOUNT ON FHA LOAN**—$ 195.08 ____ to be refunded upon
           termination of FHA Insurance and final audit. Subject to change, by reason of further receipts
           and/or disbursements. Please indicate forwarding address: 195.08
                                                                      - 8.44 due FHA
                                                                      186.64

     _____
                   (NEW ADDRESS—IF CHANGED)

➡   **TOTAL OF STATEMENT** $2,286.48

           Add ____ days interest on VA only—(per No. 2 (c.) (1.)   _____

                    REVISED STATEMENT TOTAL . . . . $_____

10. DISBURSEMENT INFORMATION
       _____ COUNTY TAXES PAID $_____ on _____ | **REMARKS:**
       Balto. ___ CITY   TAXES PAID $ 224.77 ___ on 9-67 _____ |
       HAZARD INSURANCE   PAID $ 43.00 ____ on 7-67 _____ |
       FHA INSURANCE   PAID $ 24.71 ____ on 12-67 ____ |
       GROUND RENT   PAID $ 45.00 ____ on 10-67 ____ |
       _____   PAID $_____ on _____ |
       _____ COUNTY TAXES NOT PAID—BILL ENCLOSED. |
       _____ CITY   TAXES NOT PAID—BILL ENCLOSED. |
11. THIS WILL BE COMPLETED BY ___ ABC Mortgage Company ___ **FOR** |
       STATISTICAL PURPOSES. |
       (5) **RATE**   (-0-) **PART.**   (32.90) **P & I** |
       (   ) **SALE**   (   ) **REFIN.**   (   ) **UNENCUMBERED** |
                                                                  |
       THROUGH: _____. |
12. PLEASE RETURN ONE COPY OF THIS STATEMENT WITH YOUR REMIT- |
       TANCE—STATEMENT IS VOID AFTER |
                                                                  |
              March 31, 1968 |
                 (DATE)
```
```

was paid, and the period it covered. Unpaid current taxes should also be reported.

b Insurance The statement should show the policy in force, the amount of coverage, the company which wrote the policy, the terms and expiration date and the amount of premium, and whether this premium was paid or not. If a premium currently due is unpaid, this should be paid and deducted from funds to be returned.

As a matter of precaution, it is advisable to indicate that payoff information is subject to confirmation or verification by the investor.

Prepayment notification of FHA multifamily homes must be prepared in accordance with the terms of the note and the applicable FHA regulations. Otherwise, information supplied to the owner on termination of such loans is generally identical to that given to residential owners.

Notification of investor Simultaneously with the issuance of a payoff statement, the investor must be notified of the impending payment in full of his loan. It is advisable to send the investor a copy of the statement issued to the borrower for verification. Depending on the investor, the mortgage papers either will be shipped to the mortgage banker or will be held until the loan is paid and funds have been received.

In addition to cancellation of mortgage papers and issuance of releases which follow the receipt of cash, or its equivalent in the form of a certified check, the cashier must be prepared to release the following: (1) insurance policy or policies with "released" stamped thereon, (2) all available receipted tax bills, (3) surveys, and (4) other documents of value.

When a loan is paid in full from the borrower's own funds, it is recommended that he be advised to arrange for recording the release of his mortgage at the county or city office of the recorder. In case of termination of income-property loans, many other documents may be surrendered.

Marking of files and records It is advisable to mark the loan register or an equivalent permanent record, the loan jacket, and the cashier card to show when the loan was paid in full and by whom and to note any other pertinent information that may be of use at a later date. Those companies that have done so have found such information at times of considerable value.

Since the Veterans Administration maintains a record of outstanding guaranteed loans, it must be notified by letter (one letter may accompany a list of cases) that a VA loan was paid in full and that the note bearing the guaranty by endorsement was cancelled. If the VA issued a separate loan guaranty certificate, it must be returned to the VA at this time.

Receipt of funds Funds representing final payments should always be deposited promptly and remitted to the investors by the mortgage loan accounting department. It is imperative, therefore, that close cooperation be encouraged between the cashier and the mortgage loan accounting department on the preparation of a pay-off remittance report and the transmittal of funds. The larger the payment in full, the greater the speed with which payments in full are to be handled

Review of outstanding statements   Loans scheduled for final payment should be carefully checked if payment in full is not received when scheduled. This should be done at regular intervals by the cashier, servicing manager, or collection department manager. Otherwise, required default notices to the Federal Housing Administration or the Veterans Administration may be overlooked when a legitimate delay in termination occurs or when monthly payments are not made pending the sale of the property.

Internal control   To satisfy audit and internal control requirements, a copy of each statement issued must be sent to the loan administrator or servicing manager. As a control measure these statements can then be checked against payoffs reported by the mortgage loan accounting department.

ON SALE OF PROPERTY SUBJECT TO MORTGAGE

Statements prepared for the benefit of seller and buyer when a loan is not to be paid in full are called *proration* or *loan assumption* statements. The statement providing information for substitution of mortgagor, regardless of whether a release of the seller's liability is contemplated or not, is different from that needed when a loan is paid in full. A substitution or sale subject to the existing mortgage also requires that the seller and buyer supply the mortgage company with specifically executed forms and documents that indicate substantially that title has changed hands. Based on this information, all the essential company records must be changed and the insuring company must be notified of change of ownership.

Upon issuance of a *statement of account* (Exhibits 35 and 36), which is self-explanatory, the necessary forms listed below are sent to the seller, buyer, or their respective attorneys for completion and return to the mortgage banker. In addition, a copy of the deed of conveyance and payment of a fee for changing records after the transaction is consummated are required.

1   Assignment of policy (Exhibit 37). On the basis of an executed copy of this form by both mortgagor and spouse, the insuring company will usually consent to a change of ownership. Submitting this form to the insuring company is imperative since a company's failure to consent to change of ownership makes insurance coverage invalid for the homeowner.

2   Assignment and disclaimer form (Exhibit 38). The purpose of this form is to assign the reserves held in the escrow reserve account from seller to purchaser.

3   Personal credit information (Exhibit 39). This form is not required for the consummation of the transaction, but requested by alert mortgage loan administrators who wish to obtain for the collection staff as much information on the buyer as they can.

EXHIBIT 35   Cover letter–statement of account

ABC MORTGAGE COMPANY
233 Maple Street
Chicago, Illinois   60190

RE:

For use in connection with the proposed sale of the property encumbered by the captioned mortgage, we present the enclosed statement of account.

In order to enable us to change all of our records to correspond to the change of title which is about to take place, we request that the seller execute and send to us the following documents:

1. Assignment of hazard insurance policy, in triplicate (Copies to be used for this purpose enclosed).
2. Assignment and disclaimer form, in duplicate (Copies to be used for this purpose enclosed).
3. Personal credit information form to be completed by the purchaser.
4. A copy of a dated deed of conveyance.
5. Service charge of $25.00.

In order to process this transaction efficiently, we must receive all the above items in one mailing. We accept the above items without any responsibility as to the handling of the real estate sales transaction. We also assume that the seller is aware of the fact that under the terms of the transaction completed he has not been released from the obligation under the mortgage and mortgage note. If he wishes to do so, special arrangements have to be made for this purpose.

If the new owners are not planning to live on the property, please advise us of their mailing address. If the amortization schedule originally furnished with the loan is not available, upon request we will provide the purchaser with a new one.

Yours very truly,

ABC MORTGAGE COMPANY

Cashier

Enclosures

EXHIBIT 36   Statement of account

ABC MORTGAGE COMPANY
233 Maple Street
Chicago, Illinois   60190

Re:

As of the date of issuance of this statement, monthly installments have been paid to
and including the one due _____; interest has been paid to that date;
unpaid principal is $_____, and cash on deposit for required reserves
is as follows:

For FHA insurance	$_____	Real estate taxes paid in full:
For taxes	$_____	(1st installment $_____
For hazard insurance	$_____	19___ (2d installment $_____
Total	$_____	

Hazard insurance policy _____ No._____
for $_____ Term_____ Expiring_____ Premium $_____
Annual installment premium paid to_____in the amount of $_____.

FHA mortgage insurance (due) (paid to) _____Annual premium $_____.

After payment of $_____, the installments will have been paid up to and in-
cluding the one due _____, interest will have been paid to that date,
unpaid principal will be $_____, and there will be cash on deposit for required
reserves as follows:

For FHA insurance	$_____
For taxes	$_____
For hazard insurance	$_____
Total	$_____

The installment due _____ includes interest for the preceding month
in the amount of $_____.

The required monthly payment is now composed of the following items:

Deposit for FHA insurance	$_____	
Deposit for taxes	$_____	
Deposit for hazard insurance	$_____	$_____
Interest and principal		$_____
Total		$_____

The above requirement is subject to change as the amount of future taxes and cost
of future hazard insurance will not be known until actual bills are received.

ABC MORTGAGE COMPANY

By_____
                                   Cashier

Date:

EXHIBIT 37   Assignment of policy

UNIFORM STANDARD   FORM NO. 2
                                                                (Edition Aug. '54)

ASSIGNMENT OF POLICY

The undersigned Insured under Policy No......AH8516451...

of the................................XYZ Insurance Company...
                              NAME OF INSURANCE COMPANY
hereby assigns said Policy of Insurance to........John Smith and Mary Smith.................

....
                              INSERT ADDRESS OF ASSIGNEE

                                         /s/ John Doe
                                         ....
                                                INSURED

Dated........January 1,.............19.69   /s/ Mary Doe

CONSENT TO ASSIGNMENT

The said above named Insurance Company hereby consents to the foregoing assignment of said Policy.

Issued at its........Chicago, Illinois..................................Agency.   Dated......January 1,.........................19.69
                    CITY OR TOWN   STATE
                         ABC INSURANCE AGENCY
                         By: /s/ James Johnson...Agent.

[UNIFORMITY TRADE MARK logo]   Form No. 2   (8-54)

NOTE—This blank should not be used to cover Mortgage Interest.
Agents should personally attach this form to policy.

---

4 Copy of deed of conveyance. It is a good practice to have on file a copy of the deed effecting the purchase and sale transaction. If possible, a copy of the recorded deed should be obtained.

5 Service charge. Most mortgage banking firms charge a transfer fee for handling forms and for changing records, which ranges from $25 to $35. If in addition to an assumption, a release of the seller's liability is also arranged, with both investor and governmental agency involved and the purchaser's acceptability processed by both (which often involves as much work as processing a new loan), an additional charge of $25 to $50 is usually assessed. The investors who permit substitution and release of mortgagors often require a fee for handling files and for changing records.

Upon receipt of the above forms, a member of one of the servicing departments, possibly a clerk in the collection department or the cashier, must dispatch a first-payment letter (Exhibit 40) to the new owners and state in detail the requirements of the company for payments. It must be remembered that those who assume a mortgage, particularly those who do not assume the liability, may be more careless in their payment habits than those on whose qualifications the loan was originally approved.

In addition to notifying the new borrowers, the various departments affected by the change should be informed so that the names of new owners are properly shown on all records. It is most annoying to new owner-borrowers to find that the mortgage banker has failed to change his records and continues to correspond with or send routine mailings to the borrower who moved away. Most investors, particularly life insurance mortgagees, require that they be advised immediately of names of new owners on a

EXHIBIT 38   *Assignment and disclaimer form*

The undersigned, _____

_____,

being the mortgagor in that certain mortgage dated _____,

given to _____, mortgagee,

and (recorded) (registered) in the (Recorder's) (Registrar's) Office of

_____ County, Illinois, as Document No. _____,

for value received hereby assigns and transfers unto _____

_____,

all right, title, and interest in and to all moneys deposited with or paid to
said mortgagee, its successors and assigns, in accordance with the terms and
provisions of said mortgage, and hereby disclaims all right, title, and interest
of every kind and character whatsoever in and to all moneys which may hereafter
be deposited with or paid to said mortgagee or its successors and assigns in
accordance with the terms and conditions thereof.

The undersigned hereby represents and certifies to the holders of the
above described mortgage that, as of the date hereof, there are no liens or
encumbrances against the property covered by the aforesaid mortgage junior and
inferior to said mortgage, and that said property has been or will be conveyed
to the assignees aforesaid free and clear of all liens and encumbrances except
the mortgage hereinabove described and current taxes.

The words "mortgagor" and "mortgagee," wherever used herein, shall
include the persons named herein and designated as such and their respective
successors and assigns, and all personal pronouns shall be taken to include
the singular or plural and masculine, feminine, or neuter gender, as may fit
the case.

IN WITNESS WHEREOF, the undersigned (has) (have) executed this assignment this _____ day of _____, 19___.

                                        _____

                                        _____

Title was transferred by delivery of the

deed on _____.

EXHIBIT 39   Personal credit information

ABC MORTGAGE COMPANY
233 Maple Street
Chicago, Illinois   60190

Name of seller_____

Loan no. _____

Names of purchasers_____

Property address_____

Residence address (if other than property)_____

Present home phone (if other than property)_____

Do you intend to occupy this property?_____

If so, when?_____ New home phone_____

Employer_____

Dept. head or supervisor_____

Business address_____

Business telephone_____

Length of service_____ Position_____

Salary_____ Other income_____

Age_____ Number of dependents_____

Amount of life insurance_____

Purchase price of subject property_____

Other debts:_____

_____

_____

(Signatures)

Date_____ 19_____

EXHIBIT 40   First-payment letter (assumption)

ABC MORTGAGE COMPANY
233 Maple Street
Chicago, Illinois 60190

Dear   Re: 19067

We have been informed that you have purchased the property
securing the above loan. We would like to welcome you as a
customer and advise you of a few items regarding your mortgage.

The next payment will be due on   . Payments are
always due on the first day of each month and we urge you to
remit promptly so they will reach us on that day.

Twelve self-addressed envelopes are enclosed. They are to be
used for remittances only. When this supply is depleted, we
shall send you a new one on request. Please make all checks
payable to ABC Mortgage Company and note in the upper left-hand
corner your loan number as shown above. Your cancelled checks
or money order stubs will serve as your receipts.

Your montly payment is $ and this amount will be dis-
tributed as follows:

> Principal and Interest $
> Deposit to Reserves for: FHA Mortgage Insurance
>   Real Estate Taxes
>   Hazard Insurance
>   _____
> $

The former owner of the property should have given you the amortization schedule applying to this loan. It indicates the breakdown of each installment to interest and principal as well as
the outstanding principal balance after each remittance has been
applied. If you have not yet obtained this from the previous
owner, we suggest that you contact him for this schedule will
be very useful to you.

Each year, after the first, we will send you an "Annual Statement" in which we will confirm the outstanding balance of your
loan and give you the information on the amount of interest
paid to us and the amount of real estate taxes we paid from
your reserve account. This information will be useful in
preparing your income tax return.

We are also enclosing a booklet on your mortgage, which will
be helpful to you. If you have any questions regarding your
mortgage, do not hesitate to call us.

                         Very truly yours,

                         Collection Department
Enclosures

change in ownership. If an FHA loan is involved, the FHA must be notified within 30 days after the sale on FHA Form 2080, "Mortgage Record Change" (Exhibit 41), that a sale has taken place. This notice is identical to the one that must be filled out when an FHA loan is sold; it enables FHA to change the name of the borrower on all its records and on all FHA mortgage insurance premium billings.

It is advisable for the cashier or collection clerk to follow up all statements issued where the consummation of the sale transaction is pending or is delayed, and to make sure that either the seller or the buyer make the monthly payments. Failure to follow up these pending cases may create incurable defaults.

Release of seller by FHA, VA, and mortgagee   In addition to a straight assumption, whereby the purchaser of a property merely assumes the obligation of the seller under the mortgage without the release of the former owner's liability both to the mortgagee and to the FHA or VA, a release of the former owner may be arranged. As a matter of

EXHIBIT 41   *FHA mortgage record change*

U. S. DEPARTMENT OF HOUSING AND URBAN DEVELOPMENT
FEDERAL HOUSING ADMINISTRATION

FHA FORM NO. 2080
Rev. 10/68

MORTGAGE RECORD CHANGE
(For Insured Loans Only—Not for Commitment Assignments)

TO: ASSISTANT COMMISSIONER-COMPTROLLER
U.S. DEPARTMENT OF HOUSING AND URBAN DEVELOPMENT
FEDERAL HOUSING ADMINISTRATION
ATT: RECEIPTS AND DEPOSITS SECTION
WASHINGTON, D. C. 20412

1. INDICATE TYPE OF ACTION

CHANGE OF HOLDING
MORTGAGEE OR SERVICER

[ ] Sale of Mortgage

[ ] Change of Servicing

CHANGE OF MORTGAGOR

[X] Credit of new Mortgagor not Approved by FHA

[ ] Credit of new Mortgagor Approved By FHA Under 2210 Procedure.

(Home Mortgages Only)

(IMPORTANT: Please check all applicable blocks)

INSTRUCTIONS: Submit original only to FHA within 30 days of change for home or multifamily mortgage. This notice will not be acknowledged. The panels are to be completed as follows:

Sale of Mortgage: It is the buyer's responsibility to submit this form. Panels 1, 2, 3, 5, 6, 9, 11 and 13 should be completed by the seller. Panels 7, 8, 10 and 12 should be completed by the buyer. The completion of panels 9 and 10 constitutes official signature of the mortgagees and notice to FHA that this insured loan has been sold in accordance with the provisions of the FHA regulations. Seller and buyer agree that the buyer hereby succeeds to all rights and assumes all obligations of the seller under the FHA contract of insurance. Upon receipt of this notice by the FHA, seller will be released from its obligations under the contract of insurance.

Change of Servicing: Panels 1, 2, 3, 5, 7, 10 and 12 are to be completed.

Change of Mortgagor: Panels 1, 2, 3, 4, 5, 7, 10 and 12 are to be completed. If the form is marked to indicate a new home mortgage borrower with credit approved by FHA. FHA will construe such notice as certification by the mortgagee that all requirements specified by FHA have been met. On all home mortgage assumptions if new mortgagor is an eligible serviceman attach the original executed DD 802 Certificate of Eligibility, and all copies and check this block. → [ ]

2. ORIGINAL AMOUNT OF MORTGAGE
▲$23,500.00

3. FHA CASE OR PROJECT NO.
▲ 131-123456

SECTION OF ACT CODE
▲203

4. NAME OF NEW MORTGAGOR *(Change of Mortgagor only)*
▲ Morgan, Ralph and Sheila

5. *(Month)*   *(Year)*
MATURITY DATE ➝ February   1998

6. *(Complete this panel for Projects only)*

CONSTRUCTION IS: [ ] COMPLETED   [ ] UNCOMPLETED

7. DATE OF THIS NOTICE
MO.   DAY   YEAR
▲March   5   1969

8. DATE OF PURCHASE *(Sale of Mortgage only)*
MO.   DAY   YEAR

9. SELLING MORTGAGEE *(Code No., Name, Address & ZIP Code-Use Stamp or Other Approved Device)*

10. HOLDING MORTGAGEE *(Code No., Name, Address & ZIP Code-Use Stamp or Other Approved Device)*

XYZ INSURANCE COMPANY 999
15 BROADWAY STREET
NEW YORK, NEW YORK   10310

11. NAME OF PRESENT MORTGAGOR *(Or Previous Mortgagor if Mortgagor Change)*

12. SERVICER TO WHICH FUTURE PREMIUM NOTICES SHOULD BE SENT *(Code No., Name, Address & ZIP Code-Use Stamp or Other Approved Device)*

ABC MORTGAGE COMPANY
233 Maple Street
Chicago, Illinois   60656

13. PROPERTY ADDRESS

▲ *(Do not show Military Branch for Section 222 Cases)*

HUD-Wash., D. C.   U.S. GOVERNMENT PRINTING OFFICE : 1968 O · 326-401 fact, as a service to the original borrower, such release should be encouraged since in case of default the original mortgagor, if not released, is still liable for the debt and may be brought into the foreclosure suit. If, however, he is released by FHA or VA, only the current owner is liable in the event of foreclosure.

Release arrangements are usually not handled by the cashier, but by the loan-servicing or special customers service department. Since a straight assumption of mortgage is not contingent on release of liability of seller by mortgagee or governmental agency, a proration statement that assists the purchaser and seller in consummating the transaction must be issued in any event.

It is the mortgagee's prerogative whether he wishes to release the original mortgagor from liability and accept a substitute borrower. In no event can the mortgagee prevent the property from changing hands; it can only hold the original borrower, upon whose qualification the loan was originally made, liable in the event of default by any subsequent borrower-owner. Assumption by a new borrower and release of the old borrower from liability are, therefore, contingent on the ability of the new borrower to assume the mortgage and the willingness of FHA or VA and/or the mortgagee to release the original borrower. Furthermore, release of the former owner by the mortgagee must be fortified by the execution and approval of a separate substitution agreement by the mortgagee to make the release and assumption a more meaningful and more enforceable arrangement.

Under current VA practices, VA will release the original obligor from liability to the VA if the loan involved is current, if the purchaser agrees to assume personal liability for payment of the mortgage, and if the purchaser qualifies from a credit standpoint. Most mortgagees will also release the original borrower if VA has released him; however, they are not obliged to do so.

By following a simple procedure, an FHA mortgagor-seller may obtain approval for release from liability for any deficiency judgment in the event the purchaser of the property defaults and there is a foreclosure. The approval procedure must be initiated by the mortgagee, or mortgage banker as agent for the mortgagee, by means of FHA Form 2210, "Request for Credit Approval of Substitute Mortgagor." This form serves as an application for release and provides space for FHA consent to substitution.

OTHER PERIODIC FUNCTIONS

Billing of Quarterly and Semi-annual Payments

Borrowers whose payments come due monthly need not necessarily be reminded of their obligations. However, for each payment that is due on a quarterly or semi-annual basis, the lapse of a considerable time between installments makes it necessary and advisable to bill 10 to 15 days before the due date.

Notices must be prepared and mailed on those types of loans which call for constant principal payments and reducing interest requirements, even if the borrower has a payment reduction schedule from month to month or quarter to quarter. This job can be performed ahead of schedule, during the last 15 days of the month when the cashier's workload is normally light.

Maintaining Card Indexes

One of the basic servicing records that cashiers frequently use is a cross-index file consisting of two sets of cards filed in library-type index card containers. Although initial responsibility for setting up the cards should be placed on the staff of the department which prepares the mortgage documents and establishes the loan files, responsibility for maintaining updated index cards must be assumed by the cashiers.

Care must be exercised that, as soon as an ownership change occurs, the new owner's name is typed on the index card bearing the former borrower's name. The card is then refiled in alphabetical order according to the new owner's name. The new name should also be typed under the name of the previous owner on the card filed according to property address.

Handling Principal Prepayments

From an internal control standpoint, all inquiries about prepayments on loans must first be routed to the servicing manager and only then to the mortgage loan accounting department or cashier. On conventional loans, care should be taken that an appropriate prepayment penalty is charged and collected. It is also advisable to inform FHA[2] borrowers that only 15 percent may be prepaid without penalty and that if prepayment is in excess of that amount, the penalty will be charged at the termination of the loan and not at the time of prepayment.

As far as the computation and application of prepayments are concerned, it must be remembered that before any prepayment may be applied, the next monthly installment must be collected in full and applied, and that such payments must be received prior to the month on which the interest is due. For instance, if a principal prepayment is tendered on March 25 or is intended to be made on that date, such principal prepayment cannot be applied until the monthly payment of principal and interest due April 1 is received and applied. Both the monthly payment and the prepayment may be applied simultaneously, however, before or on the first of the month.

Notwithstanding the wording of the loan note, which often states that principal prepayments can be made only in multiples of $100, borrowers should be persuaded or instructed, as a practical consideration, to consider prepayments in terms of principal payments shown on the amortization schedule. This procedure makes it unnecessary to give the borrower a new amortization schedule.

There are always borrowers who believe that they are saving interest by making a number of additional monthly payments, often as many as ten or twenty. The mortgage banker should explain to the borrower that additional full payments do not accomplish this objective, but that principal prepayments do. If the borrower has made principal prepayments on an FHA loan and later finds he is unable to make his

[2] See footnote on p. 234.

payments, FHA regulations permit partial prepayments to be applied to current payments, without prior approval from FHA. The collection personnel should know this regulation.

Handling NSF Checks

Checks which are returned by the bank because the writer of the check did not have sufficient funds in his account are known as *NSF checks*. Borrowers, regardless of their economic status, often present such checks in payment of their mortgage obligations to temporarily ease the pressure from their creditors. A check may be returned for nonsufficient funds even if all but $1 of the amount required is on deposit. (Note that all checks except cashiers or certified checks are handled by banks on the first-come, first-honored basis.)

What often happens is that the borrower deposits his paycheck to cover his remittance and his check tendered to, and deposited by, the mortgage banker reaches the borrower's bank before the bank has had a chance to collect from the bank on which the employer's check was issued. If this occurs frequently, borrowers may have to be cautioned to allow their banks at least 48 hours before drawing against the checks which they deposited. In any event, for a considerable reduction in returned checks, the bank handling the company clearing account should be instructed to process automatically each NSF check a second time.

When a check is returned by the bank, it is imperative that immediate contact be made with the borrower to secure either cash or replacement by means of a money order or a certified check. Contact may be made by the cashier, although often it is best to turn this matter over to the collector since NSF checks are likely to be presented by borrowers who are delinquent, or those who are about to become so. If the borrower can be reached immediately and he requests that his check be redeposited, the check may be either handed back to the bank messenger or redeposited at the end of the day. If the borrower cannot be reached immediately, he must be contacted by mail on the same day.

A number of companies assess a penalty charge for reprocessing checks which are returned, both to discourage the borrower's practice of issuing checks without adequate funds and to obtain reimbursement for the extra work involved. The charge may range from $2 to $7.50, or even to $10 per check. This charge is assessed in addition to the late charge, which the collection department normally assesses. Companies which do not impose an extra handling charge for NSF checks normally make late charges if, for instance, the check originally presented on June 12, presumably to avoid the late charge, is returned on June 17 and replaced thereafter.

Most companies warn each borrower after the first NSF check that should another check be returned for nonsufficient funds their privilege of paying by personal check will be withdrawn and thereafter only cash, certified check, or money order will be accepted. To make certain that on subsequent occasions a personal check is not automatically accepted from this borrower, the cashier card or the payment card must be conspicuously marked "no personal checks."

Whenever an NSF check is being held in the office for redemption, it is imperative that the cashier card or payment card be conspicuously marked so that the cashier will avoid processing the certified check or money order intended as a replacement of the earlier check as a subsequent payment.

To reimburse the bank for an NSF check, the cashier should have sufficient petty cash on hand or should be allowed to draw against a special account established for this purpose. Since NSF checks are usually temporary in nature, it seems unnecessary to reverse and void a payment that was processed on the cashier card and ask the mortgage loan accounting department to return the funds if the payment has not yet been transmitted to the investor. It also is unnecessary to request funds from investors if they have been transmitted, since usually the NSF check is replaced by cash or by a certified check by the time any of these reversing arrangements are completed. The above suggestion may require a sizable petty cash or NSF check fund; yet the procedure seems worthwhile since it considerably reduces the work on NSF checks. If a loan is to be foreclosed soon after an NSF check is accepted, funds for reimbursement of such a check may be either charged against the accumulated reserves, if adequate, or requested from the investor.

If the number of NSF checks to be handled is unusually high, it may be advisable for the cashier to maintain an NSF ledger; otherwise, checks should be held in lieu of cash and replaced as redeemed.

From an internal control standpoint, it is advisable for the cashier to prepare, at least once a week, a list of the NSF checks on hand, submitting copies of the list to the loan administrator and to members of the collection team. This list will show the items which remain unreplaced for a considerable length of time, or which recur despite vigilance of the cashiers or because of their failure to heed the instructions not to accept personal checks from certain borrowers.

CHAPTER FOURTEEN

Mortgage Loan
Accounting Department

The mortgage loan accounting department is one of the company's most important links between the borrower and the investor. It records payments received and deposited in banks by the cashier. It distributes and records the distribution of funds among investors and the custodial deposits maintained for borrowers. It is, in contrast to corporate accounting, investor oriented, directed towards meeting investor requirements for accuracy and timely performance.

Mortgage loan accounting begins where the cashier function ends. It may follow one of two different forms. If the cashier deposits daily receipts directly into investors' accounts, mortgage loan accounting need only transmit information to the investor identifying the mortgage loans involved. If the cashier deposits daily receipts into a clearing account, the mortgage loan accounting department must record the payments by posting from information received from the cashier, i.e., cashier cards to ledger cards. It must then draw checks on the clearing account to distribute principal, interest, net of the servicing fee, and remittance to investors and custodial accounts. Finally, interest and principal payments and disbursements from escrow accounts must be balanced and reconciled with the amounts deposited by the cashier. Concurrently, the fees due the mortgage banker are deducted from the monies collected for investors.

This chapter describes the various accounting functions that mortgage bankers perform within the framework of an accounting system they have built out of various systems, ideas, recommendations, and requirements.

ORGANIZATION OF DEPARTMENT

Location

In contrast to the cashier, who is conspicuously located near the entrance, the mortgage loan accounting department is usually located at the rear of the office, as it has little person-to-person contact with the public. For purposes of internal control, the cashier and the accounting department should be located as far from each other as possible or at least separated by a partition. This principle should be followed regardless of the size of the company.

Supervision and Personnel

As pointed out earlier, the accounting responsibilities of a loan administrator usually encompass both corporate and loan accounting. Plans of organization that are applicable vary depending on the size of the company, degree of automation, and type of internal control. The ideal arrangement calls for dividing responsibilities among as many people as the size of the staff permits, placing one person in charge of the general ledger and corporate accounting matters and another in charge of mortgage loan accounting. Regardless of how duties are assigned, close cooperation among the various accounting clerks is essential for efficient operations.

If the company has data processing equipment, how it is used and what management wishes determine to whom the manager of data processing reports. If the installation is relatively small and is not used in corporate accounting or the compilation of production and other statistics, it is customary for the data processing manager to report to the servicing manager. In the case of an extensive and sophisticated installation, the manager may be equivalent in rank to, or attain a rank higher than, the servicing manager. Of course, many variations in reporting arrangements are possible among the servicing manager, the comptroller, and the data processing manager. However, the lines of responsibility of these men should not be to each other, but upward to a higher rank, whether it be the loan administrator, the treasurer, or the president of the company.

Depending on the volume of loans and the equipment used, the staff includes posting and remittance clerks and general bookkeepers. The latter are responsible for balancing operations, including the preparation of single-debit reports. The number of employees required does not necessarily increase proportionately with increased loan volume, but is more likely to be contingent on the method of operations, the type and number of bookkeeping machines, or the type of data processing equipment used.

The variety of accounting methods and routines that must be followed also influences the number of employees in the department. A mortgage company that services ten investors may have ten different investor-designed procedures for servicing several thousand FHA, VA, and conventional loans. Variations in the routines may not seem marked, but their existence complicates accounting tasks. The lack of uniformity and the constant concern for exceptions that must be observed daily, weekly, or monthly create the need for competent accounting talent that can handle variations in routine and repetitive as well as occasional tasks.

In contrast to the cashier department where the volume of work fluctuates like the tide during the month, the major part of the workflow in the accounting department can be stretched over time to permit a most efficient use of staff. For instance, the volume of payments arriving at the beginning of the month may be greater than the regular staff can post and remit, but as long as funds are channeled properly into investors' accounts, posting to ledger cards and preparation of remittance reports can usually be delayed for a period of several days while the staff catches up with the workload. In the cashier department, stretching out cannot be permitted because unprocessed payments must not accumulate.

Temporary help from other departments may still be needed around the end of the month when the staff prepares trial balances and balances escrow accounts and at the close of the company's accounting year. Of course, some of the month-end, year-end, and first-of-the-month tasks may be performed through overtime without shifting personnel.

Operating Procedures

Most of the operating procedures of the mortgage loan accounting department have been developed over the past decade as a result of cost-cutting efforts by both servicer and investor, each trying to do its own accounting job more effectively and as economically as possible and each relying on the other for help in cutting costs. In some respects, it has been a tug-of-war between the investor attempting to make all his servicers conform to his requirements, and the servicer trying to streamline his workflow to accommodate all his investors through a single procedure.

The investor's continuing concern for sound operating practices is eminently justified. Since the servicer's accounting department handles thousands, even millions of dollars for investors, the more his procedures conform to those devised, approved, and often controlled by investors, the greater the security of funds handled. Much of the concern for proper procedures and practices by both investors and mortgage company management is preventive in nature; the greater the safeguards and the stronger the insistence on continuous conformance to established procedures, the less the likelihood of irregularities.

The accounting department must make specific arrangements to comply with requirements of the Federal Deposit Insurance Corporation, the Federal Housing Administration, and the Veterans Administration. To mention a few, these requirements specify that the custodial (escrow reserve) accounts not be overdrawn; that FHA mortgage insurance premiums be paid even if a loan is delinquent; and in the case of VA loans that proceeds of a fire loss draft, which are not used for the restoration of a property, be applied on the unpaid balance of the loan. All these involve the use of funds that are in the custody of the mortgage banker.

The principal operations of the mortgage loan accounting department consist of posting payments to ledger cards or their data processing equivalents, preparation of journals and remittance reports, prompt distribution and disposition of funds deposited by the cashier, and balancing and reconciliation of escrow reserve accounts and of principal and net interest payments to various applicable controls, usually by single-debit accounting.

Many operations are performed daily; others weekly, monthly, or occasionally. Operations may be performed manually, on conventional accounting machines or on data processing equipment. While manual operations require each task to be executed separately, conventional accounting or data processing equipment enables the staff to execute several tasks in a single operation. There are several types of equipment of both varieties offering different degrees of automation and work simplification.

The detailed operations of five major tasks of the mortgage loan accounting department are presented in this chapter: (1) establishing and maintaining ledger records, (2) remitting collections, (3) handling disbursements, (4) balancing (reconciling) principal and reserve accounts, and (5) performing customer service operations principally by mail. (See Exhibit 42.) Basic principles and those problems which are inherent in the establishment and maintenance of efficient operations are stressed, with references primarily to manual operations and conventional accounting equipment, and only occasionally to data processing equipment. To describe a highly sophisticated automatic operation with its short-cuts and the resulting efficiencies would not as clearly reveal the basic elements and the details which are the foundations of good accounting practices.

ESTABLISHING AND MAINTAINING LEDGER RECORDS

The two basic tasks of establishing and maintaining ledger records involve posting payments to ledger cards simultaneously with preparing journals and remittance reports. Posting calls for breaking down payments into their components: interest, principal, and escrow reserves; and recording them on respective accounting ledger cards or data processing equivalents.

Functionally, the information that identifies the payments and enables the bookkeeper to post comes from the cashier in the form of cashier or payment cards (Exhibit 32 or 33) at the time when the funds involved were deposited either into a clearing account or a custodial account bearing the investor's name. The same payments are then sent by checks or transfer instructions to investors and/or custodial accounts. Before the bookkeeper can perform this job, however, the information received from the cashier must be segregated and rearranged to meet the company's, and its investors', posting and accounting requirements.

The sorting job can be performed manually if conventional-type accounting equipment is used for posting or by a sorting machine if data processing equipment is employed; the latter can sort the cards within minutes by types of loans and/or by investors and get them ready for processing according to data processing equipment requirements. Actually, the overall cashier-accounting arrangements spell out the needs for the various sorting tasks that may be performed. If there are two separate clearing

EXHIBIT 42   Workflow chart – accounting department

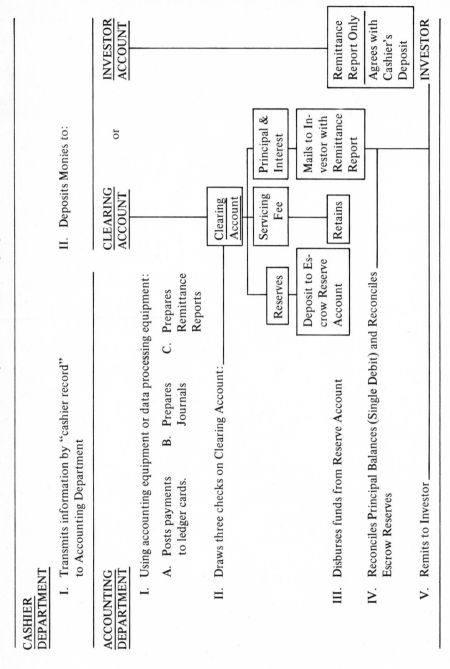

CASHIER DEPARTMENT

I. Transmits information by "cashier record" to Accounting Department

II. Deposits Monies to:

INVESTOR ACCOUNT   or   CLEARING ACCOUNT

ACCOUNTING DEPARTMENT

I. Using accounting equipment or data processing equipment:

A. Posts payments to ledger cards.

B. Prepares Journals

C. Prepares Remittance Reports

II. Draws three checks on Clearing Account:

Clearing Account

Reserves   Servicing Fee   Principal & Interest

Deposit to Escrow Reserve Account   Retains   Mails to Investor with Remittance Report

III. Disburses funds from Reserve Account

IV. Reconciles Principal Balances (Single Debit) and Reconciles Escrow Reserves

V. Remits to Investor

INVESTOR

Remittance Report Only

Agrees with Cashier's Deposit

254

accounts, one for FHA and one for VA and conventional loans, for instance, the cashier records must be sorted by investors only. If, however, there is only a single clearing account and investors wish to have FHA, VA, and conventional loans reported separately, the cards must be sorted first by type of loan and then by investor. Income property loan payments should be handled separately, since most investors have special requirements for remittances when large payments are involved.

Sorting cards is necessary only if the cashier deposited monies into one or two clearing accounts. In this instance, of course, the total of all cards after they are sorted and re-added by investor groupings must agree with the total sum deposited by the cashier. If the company is not permitted to use a clearing account, the segregation is made by the cashier as the payments are deposited into the various investors' accounts. In this instance, total postings for each investor must correspond to the various totals established and supplied by the cashier.

Those who do not use data processing equipment must further rearrange the cards by hand either in an investor loan-number sequence or in company loan-number sequence, or sort them in accordance with gross interest groups or any groups desired for purposes of accounting, single debit reporting, or servicing fee groupings.

The breakdown of the payment into its components—i.e., interest, principal, amount of servicing fee, and escrow reserve deposits—is usually provided for the bookkeeper on the duplicate copy of the mortgage payment bill or cashier card. In those cases where the bookkeeper receives a notification of receipt of a payment in one lump sum, he is obliged to obtain the breakdown of interest and principal from the amortization schedule and the breakdown of escrow reserve payments into their components, if posted individually, from the ledger card.

The distribution of the fixed monthly payment to interest and principal is made by means of the amortization schedule. The portion of the monthly payment which represents interest on the unpaid balance is first determined and then charged. The balance of the payment is then applied to principal. As the outstanding balance of the loan decreases, the interest to be charged decreases and a larger portion of the monthly payment is applied to principal.

If posting operations are performed manually or by means of conventional-type accounting machines, the amortization schedule may be kept with each ledger card or transcribed on the card itself in pencil a few months in advance. The breakdown of payments for each year may also be made available by cutting a listing of twelve payments from the amortization schedule itself and inserting it on the ledger card or pasting it on a space provided for that purpose.

The prevalent practice whenever a payment is received, unless data processing equipment is used, is to supply the bookkeeper with the appropriate cashier cards on which the breakdown of each payment is prescheduled. (See Exhibit 32.) This method accelerates the posting operations considerably.

To exercise control over each day's transactions, the bookkeeper must prove the postings for the day with the total payments received from the cashier department. If certain investor's payments are not posted every day because daily remittances are not required, they should still be accounted for daily, entered on that day's clearing sheet, and balanced against the total for the day. With this method, the search for errors at the end of the month can be minimized considerably or eliminated entirely.

Manual operations   Under manual operations, the bookkeeper must perform three separate bookkeeping functions: (1) post to the ledger card, (2) make a journal entry for each payment, and (3) type a remittance report incorporating all payments for a particular investor. If only a small number of payments must be reported, duplicate copies of the mortgage payment notices may serve as a remittance report.

An advantage of manual operation is that the company can comply readily with any investor's requirements for preparing reports since each report must be typed separately. However, this advantage is somewhat offset by a tendency for the clerk to make mistakes in transcribing the information, particularly if each form used requires the information be presented in a different sequence. To a small company, though, the workload involved in maintaining manual records is of little consequence when weighed against the cost of machine equipment and its operation.

Mechanical operations   In posting with conventional-type accounting equipment, the operator, through the use of carbons, (1) posts each payment on the ledger card and simultaneously prepares (2) a remittance report and (3) a journal sheet. After recording one payment, the bookkeeper removes the ledger card from the machine and inserts another card on which payment is to be entered. The journal sheet and remittance report which are separate copies containing identical data remain in the machine as long as payments for certain types of loans owned by the same investor are being posted. When the posting of payments for one investor has been completed, the operator clears the machine, i.e., has it automatically "cross-foot", and obtains totals for the various columns. The machine proves the accuracy of the distribution of each payment.

For the bookkeeper, the journal sheet (one of the two sheets) becomes a single-entry bookkeeping medium; it represents the payments received as well as money remitted to the investor. For the investor, the remittance report then represents an exact duplicate of its servicer's journal sheet. It also represents the postings of collections on as many individual ledger cards as the journal sheet-remittance report covered.

Data Processing Equipment[1]

By matching payment cards (see Exhibit 33) against principal balance cards, remittance reports can be prepared on data processing equipment and at the same time new principal balance cards and new payment cards can be created.

---

[1]The use of data processing equipment and the process of conversion to it is presented in great detail in MBA's manual, "Punched Card Data Processing for Mortgage Bankers," September 1965. See Appendix A-8.

Accounting Forms and Reporting Requirements

To carry out the posting operations, the mortgage loan accounting department must adopt or design appropriate ledger cards and remittance report forms. Ledger cards, remittance reports, and journal sheets, whether posted in longhand or used in an accounting machine, vary according to the desires of the mortgage company, accepted custom, or investors' requirements.

In designing bookkeeping records for manual operations, the accountant should keep in mind the possibility of future expansion. For instance, a ledger card for manual entries should be identical to that used in accounting machine operations. To standardize accounting forms, a mortgage banker who enters the servicing field, or a servicing manager who decides to improve his own forms, should study the forms used by other companies, and then select and adopt those best suited for his operations, rather than create entirely new forms.

The ledger card, the journal sheet, and the remittance report are identical in form. The main difference among those used is the internal arrangement of the columns: some show the escrow reserve funds before the principal and interest payments and others the principal and interest payments before the escrow reserve funds; some provide space for deposits of each of the three escrow reserves and others space for one lump sum. Of course, internal arrangement of the columns can be set up in any sequence desired, and should be designed to meet the basic requirements of the mortgage company's principal investors.

Though most companies no longer maintain a breakdown for the various escrow reserve funds on their ledger cards, certain advantages of such segregation should not be overlooked. Maintaining one total for three types of reserves, in case of FHA loans, often necessitates periodically computing reserves to determine whether there are enough funds for a specific purpose. If separate accumulations are maintained, reserves for each purpose are easily discerned. Often, it is less work to have an operator of a conventional-type accounting machine make individual postings twelve times a year than have the tax or insurance clerk analyze the account once or twice a year to determine the adequacy of funds on hand for a certain purpose.

When records are updated by means of data processing accounting equipment, breaking down reserves into their components creates no additional work. Punched cards contain a sufficient number of fields to easily accommodate, in addition to the basic information, all three reserve columns.

As far as the investors are concerned, the arrangement of entries often is of secondary importance if the remittance reports consistently balance and there are not too many long-hand corrections or strike-overs by the typewriter or accounting machine.

Since investors rely on their own loan numbers for identification of payments, they insist on extremely accurate reporting of these numbers. Printing incorrect loan

---

[2] Sample data processing cards for various purposes, sample historical records, and other data processing report forms may be found in IBM's publication, "Mortgage Loan Accounting."

numbers when conventional-type accounting machines are used may be avoided by incorporating a proof entry of the loan numbers in the posting operation. This can be accomplished by including the loan number, as part of an arithematical sum of proof, with the principal and interest entries and checking the accuracy of the pick-up in the proof column.

The remittance report (Exhibit 43) is another currently used accounting form which can be produced by all makes of data processing equipment. As illustrated, this report produced by using the principal balance cards and payment cards of the loans involved includes essentially all the information that is provided by conventional accounting equipment. Notice particularly the bottom portion of the remittance report which shows the totals printed for each column and especially the "total remitted." Through the use of reports of this type, remittance procedures are truly automated.

If data processing equipment is used, individual ledger cards are not maintained. Ledger cards are created from the data processing cards. The record thus produced is called the *activity report* or *historical loan record.* An activity report shows all postings to an account and differs from a ledger record only in the manner in which it is prepared. While a ledger card is a single permanent record on which each subsequent entry is entered by hand or machine posting, an activity report is the reproduction of the activity of a loan each month from appropriate and applicable principal balance, payment, and disbursement cards or other record-storing devices. The equipment always reproduces anew the information already available and adds the results of the new activity—a payment or a disbursement.

Frequency of reports The frequency with which remittance reports are prepared depends on the total volume of loans serviced and the number of loans handled for one investor. Some mortgage companies prefer to post and remit each day's collections as soon as possible, especially if a substantial number of daily payments is received for one investor. However, if the mortgage company services less than a hundred loans for an investor, it is certainly more practical to post and remit only on certain days of the month. Such an arrangement substantially reduces the number of reports to be prepared, the number of checks to be issued, and the mailings to be made. The investor's work will be reduced correspondingly.

Investors usually do not insist on daily remittance reports, provided their funds are deposited in their accounts on a day-to-day basis. Investors often are willing to ease some of the reporting burdens of their servicers by accepting weekly lump-sum deposits approximating the anticipated total monthly collections to their account and requiring that posting is to the ledger cards and detailed accounting of all funds be made once each month.

Computation of servicing fees The *servicing fee*, also called *participation* or *interest differential,* may be computed and retained from collections or may be paid by the investor to the servicer in several different ways. Basically, it is computed on the unpaid principal balance of the loan at a rate agreed upon, e.g., $\frac{1}{2}$ of 1 percent, and is retained by the mortgage banker from interest collected. Servicing fees may

EXHIBIT 43 Report of mortgage loan collections

ABC MORTGAGE COMPANY
233 Maple Street
Chicago, Illinois 60190

X Y Z LIFE INSURANCE CO   VA   050   ILL   09 30 68

MORTGAGOR	INVESTOR LOAN NUMBER	DATE PAID MO/DY	LOAN NUMBER	DATE DUE MO/DY/YY	TOTAL PAYMENT	ESCROW PAYMENT	ESCROW BALANCE	PRINCIPAL PAYMENT	PRINCIPAL BALANCE	GROSS INTEREST	PART C PAT ON OR LATE CHARGE	NET INTEREST
SHIFRIN	032841	0930	32841	100118	117.00	33.74	239.24	36.83	12,345.50	46.43	3.87	42.56
GOULD	032868	0930	32868	100118	115.00	31.74	172.24	36.69	12,382.33	46.57	3.88	42.69
LANDE	032922	0930	32922	100118	115.00	34.30	329.04	35.29	12,074.64	45.41	3.78	41.63
SCHWARTZ	032944	0930	32944	100118	121.00	36.72	369.31	36.86	12,608.65	47.42	3.95	43.47
NEWMAN	033007	0930	33007	090118	120.80	37.54	159.53	36.14	12,528.27	47.12	3.93	43.19
NEWMAN	033007	0930	33007	090118	4.80						4.80LC	
LASALLE NAT	035934	0930	35934	100118	126.00	37.60	303.20	38.27	13,329.88	50.13	4.18	45.95
STREIBEL	035936	0926	35936	100118	115.00	32.73	393.52	35.62	12,404.95	46.65	3.89	42.76
					834.60	244.37		255.70		329.73	27.48	302.25
											4.80LC	
											$ 32.28	

TOTAL REMITTED   557.95

259

actually be computed by *factors* which express the relationship of gross and net interest on each loan. This method is usually employed when a great number of loans carrying different gross and net interest rates are serviced. Factors may then be placed on the cashier card or ledger card and used to compute the servicing fee before posting of payment. For instance, if a large commerical loan carrying a gross rate of $6\frac{3}{4}$ percent is sold to an investor at $6\frac{1}{2}$ percent, the servicing fee may be computed by deducting from the interest collected $\frac{1}{4}$ of 1 percent of the unpaid balance on which interest was computed, or simply taking $\frac{1}{27}$ of the interest collected.

There are several methods used for computing and retaining servicing fees or for collecting them from the investor, contingent only on the preference of the investor and the type of operations employed by the servicer. The most commonly used methods are the following:

1 Computing the servicing fee of each individual payment. If the servicing fee is not computed in advance and is not shown on the cashier card or a duplicate of the mortgage billing notice, which is used as a posting medium, the computation must be made by the bookkeeper before posting either by computing the fee on the unpaid balance or by using the servicing fee factors. Basically, this tedious job is necessary only if a limited number of loans are serviced or if a great variety of servicing fee rates exist, as may be the case when a large number of income property loans are handled.

   If data processing equipment is employed, the servicing fee factor is permanently locked into the control card and, therefore, the appropriate servicing fee is computed automatically as the payment is processed and the remittance report is prepared.

2 Computing the servicing fee on the aggregate interest collected for groups of loans having the same gross and net interest rates. If conventional rather than data processing equipment is employed, use of this method to compute the servicing fee for a particular investor may reduce the number of computations from several hundred to possibly two or three. In this case, the computation is not made before posting, but at the time the remittance report is prepared. The computation of the servicing fee is based on the aggregate of the unpaid principal balances and is deducted in one lump sum from the total interest due the investor. Adoption of this arrangement requires the approval of the investor and grouping loans according to servicing fees.

3 Remitting gross interest collections and later receiving the servicing fees in checks. Under this arrangement, the correspondent remits gross interest and the investor computes the servicing fee and pays the correspondent. The mortgage company may receive payment for servicing after a slight delay, but this inconvenience is offset by the elimination of several computations. The investor usually prepares the servicing fee computation and reruns the remittance report on his data processing equipment; this in turn assures the investor as well as the servicer that fees have been accurately computed. The investor may either send the servicing fee on several days' collections at one time or establish an average servicing fee based

on experience, and pay the correspondent on the basis of this average, with an accounting of servicing fees once a month or once a year.

4 Computing servicing fees according to a *level-payment plan.* While the amount of the servicing fee under the previously described methods diminishes with each collection as the unpaid balance of the loan is reduced, with the level-payment plan the servicing fee remains constant throughout the life of the loan.

Under the level-payment plan, the servicer is credited in a reserve account held by the investor with the amount of servicing fee earned on the basis of the standard fee—let us say $\frac{1}{2}$ of 1 percent of unpaid balance on the reducing principal—but he can draw out of this account monthly only 25 cents for each $1,000 of the original principal balance. While the reserves for each loan increase during the early life of the loan, they are then drawn down when the amount earned according to the level-payment plan becomes greater than that which would be computed and paid on the basis of the constantly reducing principal balances. When a mortgage loan is paid in full prior to maturity, the excess accumulation is withdrawn from the reserve account and paid to the servicer.

One of the two methods may be employed to handle the month-to-month compensation of the servicer. Under one, the servicer may remit to the investor the gross fees computed on the basis of the unpaid principal balance of the loans serviced, and receive in return from the investor his compensation on the basis of the level-payment plan. The difference, if any, would then be credited or withdrawn, as the case may be, from a reserve account by the investor. Under the other, the servicer may credit to a reserve account the total servicing fees computed at the reducing balance and draw a check to himself for the fees earned. There is no need for the servicer to set up an account receivable for the deferred fees since the investor normally accounts for such accumulations.

The reserve account is always in the name of the investor with the servicer having no access to the funds in any way other than that specified by the formula. If the servicer were able to use those funds and if the funds accrued interest for him, he would incur federal income tax liability. Since the servicing fee diminishes as the loan ages, the level-payment plan provides reserves for the mortgagee from which to pay a new servicer adequate fees should the servicer originating the loans fail to perform properly or go out of business.

REMITTING OPERATIONS

Remitting operations and disbursing operations both involve distributions of funds. The mortgage banker uses the term *remit* when he forwards payments of principal and net interest to the investor. He uses the term *disburse* when he issues checks against escrow accounts for payment of certain bills or charges.

Many investors prefer to receive only one remittance a week or a month instead of daily reports of individual loan payments. Others require weekly lump-sum deposits approximating average weekly collections, with the balance accompanying the monthly single-debit report, which accounts for all payments collected.

As stated earlier, the process of remitting involves fundamentally two basic types of procedures: (1) depositing funds directly into the investor's account and (2) using a clearing account to transfer funds from servicer to investor. Except when reporting by a single-debit arrangement, remittance reports must support transactions under both procedures in order to identify payments by loan numbers and due dates.

If the cashiers deposit directly to the various investors' accounts, the remittance transaction is not performed in mortgage loan accounting, since the funds are being placed by the cashier immediately and directly into the investors' accounts. In this instance, a remittance report is required only to support the lump-sum deposit by identifying the individual payments by loan numbers and to provide a breakdown of the individual payments into their components.

Under this arrangement, the total amount of payments, which include the reserve funds and servicing fees, is deposited directly into the investors' accounts. Accordingly, the monies that should have been left with the servicer are technically in the hands of the investors, and the reserves and servicing fees must be returned to the servicer by checks either monthly or daily.

Historically, as the mortgage banking industry grew, the number of investors a servicer handled increased the work of the direct depositing, and sorting payments by investors at the cashier level became more cumbersome, unwieldy, and consequently more expensive. As a solution, the use of a *clearing account* was developed by mortgage bankers and accepted by most investors. The procedures involving a clearing account vary fairly extensively depending on investors' requirements or preference, the number of loans serviced, and the type of equipment used. Today, the use of clearing accounts is the predominant arrangement between servicer and investor since a servicer for more than one or two investors would hardly be able to segregate all payments by investors in the cashier's department, from the standpoint of both expense and time involved.

Transfer from the clearing account may be made by *issuing checks* against such account or by *bank transfer arrangements*. Whichever method is employed, the variations are considerable.

Remittance by Checks Drawn on Clearing Account

The simplest method of transmitting payments to an investor is to issue a check drawn on a clearing account for the monies due him. If only one payment is to be remitted, the breakdown of interest and principal may be typed on the check itself. Separate checks must be issued by the servicer to transfer the reserve payments to the investor's custodial account and to pay himself for servicing fee earned. If single checks are used throughout the month to remit payments, the transfer to the reserves and the payment of servicing fees may be consolidated in two separate checks at the end of the month.

When a larger number of loans is involved, a fairly standard procedure runs as follows: Based on the remittance report (see Exhibit 43), three checks are drawn on the clearing account. One check ($557.95) is drawn for principal and net interest, one is ($244.37) for escrow reserves as indicated by totals on the remittance report, and a third ($32.28) is drawn in favor of the servicer for the servicing fee and late charges. The first check is attached to the report and sent to the investor. The second check is deposited in the custodial account which bears the name of the mortgage banker "in trust" for the investor who owns the respective loans.

One popular variation on this arrangement calls for transferring principal, gross interest, and reserves from the clearing account within 24 to 48 hours into the mortgagee's custodial account. The custodial account bears the servicer's name "in trust" for the investor involved. After preparation of the remittance report, appropriate distribution is made from the custodial account for principal and net interest to the mortgagee, and for the servicing fee to the servicer. No check need be issued for reserves since the remainder as shown on the report ($244.37) actually represents the reserves.

Remittance by Bank Arrangements to
Transfer Funds from Clearing Account

To speed up and simplify the transfer of funds from the clearing account to the various investors' accounts, several mortgage bankers developed a bank transfer procedure. This procedure eliminates the necessity of issuing individual checks for each single investor because it replaces such checks by a single instruction sheet. The mortgage banker instructs the bank which maintains the clearing account to remove from the account a certain specific amount and, by means of bank transfer arrangements, to credit the accounts for which the respective deposits are intended. These transfers may be made to accounts maintained in the same bank as well as to accounts in other banks.

For transfer purposes "Statement of transfer of bank funds" (Exhibit 44), a product of data processing equipment, is used to remove all funds from the clearing account daily. (A similar procedure can be devised for a typewriter if data processing equipment is not available.) By either method, funds deposited by 2:00 P.M. on one day can be cleared through the clearing account by noon of the next day. Before appropriate forms are printed and procedures worked out, officials of the bank who will handle these transactions should approve the transfer form and agree to the procedures involved.

Technically, as soon as the funds belonging to the investors are removed from the mortgage banker's clearing account and deposited into a custodial account, the completion of processing, i.e., placing funds into the investor's hand, no longer needs to be carried out immediately. Of course, this procedure is not intended to promote tardiness in preparing reports or remitting funds to the investor; the urgency for reporting, however, has passed since the funds have already been removed from the mortgage company's account.

It is good practice to remit all payments promptly to the investor which involve substantial sums on income property loans, prepayments, and payments-in-full. This procedure is preferred even if a considerable degree of automation has been achieved.

EXHIBIT 44   Statement of transfer of bank funds

ABC MORTGAGE COMPANY
233 Maple Street
Chicago, Illinois 60190

TO: LAST NATIONAL BANK OF CHICAGO   PAGE NO. 1

DATE	ACCOUNT DESCRIPTION	ACCOUNT NUMBER	FOLIO	AMOUNT
	LAST NATIONAL BANK OF CHICAGO			
				.00−
10 16 69	ABC MORTGAGE CO. TRUSTEE FOR INS. CO AND VAR MTGRS	72 55810		658.52
10 16 69	ABC MORTGAGE CO. IN TR FOR VAR MTGRS	72 55802		1,026.00
10 16 69	ABC MORTGAGE TRUST ACCOUNT FOR XYZ LIFE INS. CO.	72 55934		3,516.78
10 16 69	ABC MORTGAGE CO. CUSTODIAL ACCOUNT	72 56205		629.20
10 16 69	ABC MORTGAGE CO. IN TRUST FOR BANK OF ANKE AND VAR MTGRS	72 56019		3,809.55
10 16 69	ABC MORTGAGE CO. FHA CUSTODIAL ACCOUNT	72 55144		2,322.87
10 16 69	ABC MORTGAGE CO. CUSTODIAL DISBURSE- MENT CLEARING ACCOUNT	72 57058		456.83

CHARGE: MORTGAGE CUSTODIAL CLEARING ACCOUNT
NO. 72 57643

	TOTAL THIS BANK	12,419.75
AND TRANSFER FUNDS FOR	SUBTOTAL	12,419.75
CREDIT AND ADVISE BY_____GRAND TOTAL		12,419.75

Authorized Signature

These payments can easily be identified at the source by the cashier for immediate remittance to an investor.

DISBURSING OPERATIONS

Disbursing operations involve requisitioning and issuing checks in payment of FHA mortgage insurance premiums, real estate tax bills, and hazard insurance premiums. They may also involve issuance of refund checks to mortgagors when excess funds are involved or when reserves on hand at the termination of loans are to be released. They may be handled either by an escrow reserve department or by the insurance or tax departments. The latter arrangement leaves only the administration of FHA mortgage insurance premiums to the accounting department. This is probably a sound approach since the payment of FHA mortgage insurance is a semi-automatic procedure.

Issuance of Checks from Escrow Reserves

Checks should be issued only when a proper check requisition form devised for that purpose is filled out. Checks should be issued by a member of the mortgage loan accounting department, whether the disbursement involves the payment of taxes, insurance, or any other special items. Only through such definite allocation of check-issuing authority can errors, such as the issuance of checks on the wrong bank account, be minimized or entirely prevented.

Before checks are issued, it must be determined whether there are adequate funds in the mortgagor's account to cover the check. The size of a company's operations and its dependence on up-to-date accounting records often make it difficult to determine the availability of funds. If through carelessness in issuing a check, overdrafts occur in an individual borrower's account, efforts must immediately be made to collect the overdraft or cover it with company funds. Auditors discovering overdrafts are disturbed less by the individual overdraft on an account than by lack of controls and plans to prevent a recurrence.

Checks should be issued only on the basis of individual original bills or of statements containing a listing of items supported by individual bills or check requisition forms. The use of the latter form is necessary if a refund is involved. Such a statement must be initiated by a member of the servicing team since the requisition usually involves either a refund in connection with the termination of the loan—at which time an error may be costly—or a refund to the borrowers of excess funds in the insurance or tax reserve accounts for which the originator of the check request must be accountable. A requisition form which should briefly identify the account involved and the purpose of the refund must be initialed (countersigned, if possible) and either retained in the mortgage loan accounting department until year-end audit or filed in the respective loan files for evidence of authority to issue the checks.

Checks representing escrow reserve disbursements can be made payable only to those designated on the respective bills, and they can be issued only for purposes stipulated under the terms of the mortgage or, if the loan is terminated, only to the legal owner of the property at the time the check is issued. This is why it is important that a change of ownership is promptly processed and records promptly changed. If the property is owned by a bank or a trust institution as trustee, any refund issued must be made payable to the bank or trust company with the appropriate trust number indicated. Checks cannot be made payable to the owner of the beneficial interest even if the mortgagor identifies himself as a beneficiary since beneficial interests within a trust can be readily transferred without any required notification to the public.

FHA mortgage insurance premium   The Federal Housing Administration requires that monthly deposits be made by the borrowers whose loans it insures to cover the expense of maintaining an insurance program and of paying losses whenever claims are made. The annual FHA mortgage insurance premiums equal $\frac{1}{2}$ of 1 percent of the average unpaid balance of the loan for a 12-month period preceding the date on which premiums become due and payable. (On loans insured before August 5, 1957, the charge covers a period of 12 months following the due date.) The premium must be paid when due whether the loan is current, prepaid, or delinquent. Even if the funds on hand are inadequate to pay the premium, the premium still must be paid since the obligation to pay is that of the lender and not the mortgagor. In this instance, the servicer should either place funds of his own into the escrow reserve account so that the bill may be paid, or request the investor provide him with such funds. In case of foreclosure claims, such an advance will be reimbursed by the FHA. Prepayment of the loan does not change the required annual premium amount from that originally scheduled.

Since the mortgagee or its servicing agent can rely on FHA to issue timely premium notices, there is no need to maintain followup records on FHA mortgage insurance due dates. Before the insurance for a certain loan account would be cancelled for nonpayment of premium, FHA would notify the mortgagee in writing. FHA does not issue a receipt for premium payments.

The conditions under which appropriate refunds of accumulated and unused FHA mortgage insurance premiums may be returned to owners of record on certain types of FHA loans are discussed in MBA's manual, "Escrow Department—Procedures and Responsibilities" (see Appendix A-6) and the "Mortgagee's Handbook," issued by the FHA.

To notify FHA of the name of the current owner of each FHA loan, the mortgage banker is obliged to notify FHA on Form 2080, entitled "Mortgage Record Change," that a change occurred so that FHA may change its records accordingly and issue the next premium billing showing the name of the new owner. This form is the same one that is used to notify FHA of a change of mortgagee and servicing agent (Exhibit 41).

Real estate taxes   According to the terms of all FHA single and multifamily loans, all VA loans, and a great number of conventional residential and commercial loans, the mortgagor is obliged to make monthly deposits to cover real estate taxes and other quasi-tax obligations. Since tax deposits are the largest of the reserve requirements and since the nonpayment of taxes may cause the placement of a lien on the property, it is imperative that tax deposit estimates be made as accurately as possible. In paying tax bills from the escrow reserve account, the mortgage banker should always expend every effort to pay the bills before their respective due date, especially if timely payments produce a discount for the owner or if late payments create a penalty. The payment of tax bills is discussed in Chapter 17.

Hazard insurance premiums Under the terms of all FHA single and multifamily loans, all VA loans and a relatively smaller number of conventional residential and commercial loans than was the case for tax deposits, the mortgagor is required to deposit a sum equivalent to one-twelfth of the annual hazard insurance premium due.

Replacement reserve funds In connection with each FHA multifamily project loan, FHA requires the establishment of a reserve fund to provide for the purchase of new equipment and replacement of other items that may deteriorate during the term of the loan. In this manner, FHA assures the proper maintenance of projects insured under its administration.

Requirement for monthly deposits commences with the first payment on the loan. Since fairly large monthly deposits are involved and disbursements for replacement usually do not occur during the first 5 years of the term of the loan, mortgagees as a practical matter require that replacement reserve funds be remitted to them. Rarely are funds for replacement reserves held by the servicer. Of course, they can never be left with the mortgagor.

Upon request from the mortgagor, however, the mortgagee may permit the investment of the funds in bonds guaranteed as to principal by the United States government—a prevailing practice—and pay the interest on the bonds to the mortgagor. However, mortgagees normally require that at least 1 year's reserves be held in cash to meet emergency disbursements. Investments may be made without FHA's prior approval.

The mortgagee or its agent is not required to act as broker in the investment of the fund or to assume any responsibility in any transaction involving purchase, sale, or replacement of bonds. Furthermore, the mortgagee at no time can relinquish custody or control of cash or of bonds. There is no requirement to adjust investments in bonds, should the value of the bonds decline, until the bonds are sold and an exact determination of values can be made. Of course, if bonds are sold for monies in excess of deposit requirements, the mortgagee may return the difference to the mortgagor.

Use of a Disbursement Clearing Account

The need for this type of disbursement clearing account—different from a clearing account—arises only when disbursing operations are automated and a large number of items are paid on a large number of different bank accounts involving a large number of investors. Instead of issuing twenty checks to one payee for taxes, for instance, funds from twenty different accounts are first transferred to a disbursement clearing account on which a single check is then drawn to the payee.

BALANCING OPERATIONS

In the process of channeling funds from borrowers to investors, all transactions must be accounted for and balanced whether they are applicable to the recording and subsequent transmittal of principal and interest payments (remittances) or to disbursing escrow reserve deposits made by mortgagors. Accounting transactions can never be considered complete until the entries are balanced against controls. When principal payments are involved, balancing primarily means bringing monthly payments received in accord with payments anticipated and reconciling these payments with pre-established controls. When escrow funds are involved, balancing means the accounting of deposits to, and disbursements from, custodial accounts by reconciling trial balance totals with bank statements.

During each day of operation, all payments processed by the cashier department must be accounted for not only by the cashier, but also by the accounting department. Monies deposited by the cashier into the clearing account must be identified by cashier cards or prepunched cards, and must be balanced by the accounting clerk against the deposit made; a corresponding deposit ticket must always be supplied by the cashier—regardless of whether posting operations are performed daily or payments to ledger cards remain unposted for a day or two. Actually, ledger cards may remain unposted so long as a remittance report, or monthly report, does not have to be prepared and submitted. Summaries of daily cash books must be balanced against accounting department journals either for the day or for at least the month. Deposits to the escrow reserve account and disbursements for various purposes therefrom must also be balanced after being posted to ledger cards.

There are two types of trial balances: one involves the unpaid principal balances of loans and the other the custodial or escrow reserve funds. The trial balance of principal balances constitutes the listing of loans that the company owns called the *inventory of loans*. It includes the loans which have not been sold to investors. The payments received represent a reduction of debt by the respective borrowers and a reduction of the mortgage banker's loan inventory. When a loan is delivered to an investor and the investor pays for the loan on the basis of the outstanding balance at the time of purchase, such loan is removed from inventory and placed with loans to be accounted for to the particular investor. Thereafter, all payments received on that loan are forwarded to the investor.

After removal of a loan from inventory, unless single-debit accounting is required, the servicer is no longer obliged to maintain controls on the loans it services. If good accounting practices are desired, however, such controls must be maintained, if for no other reason other than statistical information and better overall control.

Single-debit Accounting for Preparing and
Reconciling Principal Trial Balances

Fundamentals of method   *Single-debit accounting,* which means accounting by means of single, nonduplicated entries, is also known by other names such as *exception* *accounting,* meaning accounting by exceptions, or by *block accounting,* meaning that instead of single, individual entries, payments are actually accounted for in blocks.

Single-debit accounting is a most significant accounting innovation which is designed to simplify reporting payments from servicer to investor. It is based on the simple premise that as long as each payment must be posted to, or recorded on, the servicer's ledger card, there is no reason why such entry should also be made on an identical ledger record maintained by the investor. Thus single-debit accounting was devised to eliminate the duplicating entry or entries by posting to block controls maintained at the investors' offices. The servicer continues to maintain its ledger records, posts to them as payments are made, and then, in lieu of a remittance report (for in addition to a remittance report depending on the single-debit requirements of the investor), prepares a special single-debit reconciliation form. The investor, as suggested earlier, no longer maintains detailed records.

A single-debit report consists of a *trial balance* containing a list of unpaid balances of any number of loans, an advance and a delinquency report, and a reconciliation form. Each group contains loans of identical gross and net interest rates only. Separate groupings and controls for loans located in different states are often maintained.

Payments are controlled by means of *constants* which represent the fixed principal and interest payments for each loan. A constant equals that monthly sum of money which will fully amortize the loan—i.e., which will cover the interest and liquidate the loan and which represents the aggregate total of principal and interest payments for any number of loans. Since the interest is always computed on the unpaid balance and the principal reduction is determined by deducting interest from the constant, it does not matter whether one or one hundred loans are involved, the difference will always represent by one entry the reduction in the total unpaid balance from one month to another. The individual ledger cards representing a group of loan accounts, of course, show how such reduction affected each loan. Single-debit accounting is maintained, then, by preparing a trial balance and accounting for payments made in advance and payments not received by means of advance and delinquency reports in a reconciliation form.

At the other end, the investor places all his loans of the same gross and net interest rates in one block or group. To this block account the investor does not make individual entries, but makes one entry for the total sum of payments reported, one entry representing a group of principal payments in accordance with a reconciliation form (Exhibit 45). The amount of such entry, in addition to being accounted for in the reconciliation form, is substantiated by the difference in principal balances between the totals appearing on the trial balance at the closing of the period involved and those of the preceding one.

Single-debit accounting makes it unnecessary for the investor to maintain detailed records of the loans he owns. The investor, however, must claim ownership of the servicer's ledger cards, without which he cannot substantiate the unpaid balance of each loan.

Mechanics of single-debit accounting To illustrate the mechanics of single-debit and

EXHIBIT 45 *Reconciliation for mortgage loans – April*
ABC Mortgage Company

INVESTOR Progressive Trusteed Fund   CODE 688

TEXAS	550	050	FHA	5	2
State	Interest Rate	Servicing Fee Rate	Type	Servicer	Interest
				Control Code No.	

Cut-off Date: Mo 4 | Da 20 | Yr 67

DESCRIPTION	REMITTANCE		PRINCIPAL CONTROL			SERVICE FEE	NET REMITTED
	Interest	Principal Credit	Constant	Principal Balance	No. of Loans		
1. CONTROL TOTALS (PREVIOUS RECONCILIATION)							
2. TOTAL CASH COLLECTED							
3. CURTAILMENTS							
4. LOANS ADDED			1,185.66	200,403.74	14		
5. LOANS REMOVED			-0-	-0-	-0-		
6. TRIAL BALANCE (SUB-TOTAL PRIN. CONTROL)			1,185.66	200,403.74	14		
						FORECAST	
						INTEREST	PRINCIPAL
7. DELINQUENT INSTALLMENTS						-0-	-0-
8. PREPAID INSTALLMENTS						-0-	-0-
9. CURTAILMENTS AFTER PREPAYMENTS							
10. ADJUSTED PRINCIPAL BALANCE & NORMAL PAYMENT DUE				200,403.74		918.52	267.14
11. ADJUSTMENTS AND FORE-CASTED TOTAL CREDIT						918.52	267.14

REMARKS:

ABC Mortgage Company

(Name & Title)

270

to present the records and controls that must be established by the mortgage banker and the controls that the investor must maintain to receive and to record payments for the loans, a hypothetical investor-servicer single-debit reporting arrangement is presented here.

For purposes of illustration, it is assumed that ABC Mortgage Company, a servicer, sold on April 9, fourteen FHA loans in Z state to XYZ Insurance Company, an investor. (See Delivery Schedule, Exhibit 46). Before consummation of the transaction, the investor requested that payments be reported according to single-debit accounting and that in addition to trial balances and reports of delinquents, prepayments, and advance payments, a group control reconciliation form be submitted each month in lieu of individual remittance reports.[3] The cutoff date suggested for the report was the twentieth of each month. The investor also requested that no remittance be made until the twentieth and that a single check for the principal and net interest payment accompany the entire package of forms.

To help understand how single debit works, a sample reporting arrangement between servicer and investor is presented chronologically as reports are prepared by the servicer and entries are made on the controls by the investor.

Step 1: Mortgage Banker, April 20

On this cutoff day, it is necessary to prepare a group reconciliation form and to forecast thereon the payments that may be anticipated by the investor on May 20, assuming that each borrower makes the May 1 payment, no more and no less. The group control reconciliation form (see Exhibit 45) is then accompanied by the trial balance (Exhibit 47). Since there are no payments received between April 9, the day on which the fourteen loans were purchased by the investor, and April 20, the trial balance is identical to the delivery schedule (Exhibit 46). The twentieth is an arbitrary date but may be designated as the eighteenth or the twenty-fifth, or any date in between. The earlier the date, the greater the number of payments that must be listed as delinquent; and the later the date, the more names have to be listed on the advance or prepayment reports, since many people make

Step 1: Investor, April 20

Based on the same delivery schedule used to establish the mortgage banker's records and to prepare a group reconciliation form, the investor sets up a *single* control card and shows thereon the *aggregate unpaid balance* of fourteen FHA loans, namely, $200,403.74.

Since there were no payments between April 9 and April 20, there is nothing for the investor to record. However, based on the mortgage banker's group reconciliation form, he can set up an interest receivable for $918.52 (which represents $5\frac{1}{2}$ percent interest for 1 month on $200,403.74) and $267.14 for principal to be anticipated by May 20.

---

[3] A prepayment, which refers to a payment of principal only, must be accounted for in a different manner from an advance payment of principal and interest for one or more months.

EXHIBIT 46 Delivery schedule

MORTGAGEE CODE 2	TYPE FHA	STATE Tex.	INTEREST RATE 550	SERVICING FEE RATE 050	Delivery schedule no. 1				Page 1 of 1 page / Date of schedule 4/9/67 / No. of mortgages 14	
Mortgagee loan no.	MBA loan no.	Mortgagor	Constant payment prin. and int.	Maturity date	Unpaid principal balance after 4/1/67 installment	Price %	Discount or premium amount	Net principal	Net accrued interest on total only	Total purchase price
1	9027	Axtel, F.	$ 85.74	3/1/97	$ 15,083.47	98	$ 301.67	$ 14,781.80		
2	9028	Morgan, Samuel	101.43	12/1/89	16,026.80	98	320.54	15,706.26		
3	9029	Smith, Ralph G.	64.24	1/1/97	10,965.24	98	219.30	10,745.94		
4	9030	Jones, Bernard S.	85.85	1/1/97	14,653.54	98	293.07	14,360.47		
5	9031	Granger, Phillip	89.35	1/1/97	15,251.66	98	305.03	14,946.63		
6	9032	Beran, Joseph R.	92.27	1/1/97	15,750.08	98	315.00	15,435.08		
7	9033	Meyer, Wilbur G.	81.76	1/1/97	13,955.75	98	279.12	13,676.63		
8	9034	Pope, John R.	91.69	12/1/97	15,650.38	98	313.00	15,337.38		
9	9035	Roberts, Calvin	101.03	12/1/97	17,245.34	98	344.91	16,900.43		
10	9036	Dotson, Roger L.	90.09	12/1/97	14,234.98	98	284.70	13,950.28		
11	9037	Johnson, Alfred B.	92.27	1/1/97	15,750.08	98	315.00	15,435.08		
12	9038	Mason, Paul J.	88.18	1/1/97	15,052.29	98	301.04	14,751.25		
13	9039	Grant, Herbert O.	58.98	1/1/97	10,068.10	98	201.36	9,866.74		
14	9040	Schultz, Olen G.	62.78	1/1/97	10,716.03	98	214.32	10,501.71		
Total			$1,185.66		$200,403.74		$4,008.06	$196,395.68	$445.34	$196,841.02

EXHIBIT 47 Trial balance – April

INVESTOR: Progressive trusted fund	STATE: Texas	TYPE LOAN: FHA	INTEREST RATE: 550	PART. RATE: 050	FOR MO. ENDING: 4-20-67

Loan no.	Name	Mortgagee Loan no.	Pd. to date (Mo. Day Yr.)	Principal balance	Escrow balance	Fixed payment control
9027	Axtel, F.	27	4 1 67	$ 15,083.47	$ 146.67	$ 85.74
9028	Morgan, S.	28	4 1 67	16,026.80	154.70	101.43
9029	Smith, R. G.	29	4 1 67	10,965.24	121.44	64.24
9030	Jones, B. S.	30	4 1 67	14,653.54	130.03	85.85
9031	Granger, P.	31	4 1 67	15,251.66	134.49	89.35
9032	Beran, J. R.	32	4 1 67	15,750.08	126.16	92.27
9033	Meyer, W. G.	33	4 1 67	13,955.75	139.03	81.76
9034	Pope, J. R.	34	4 1 67	15,650.38	145.08	91.69
9035	Roberts, C.	35	4 1 67	17,245.34	171.07	101.03
9036	Dotson, R. L.	36	4 1 67	14,234.98	114.81	90.09
9037	Johnson, A. B.	37	4 1 67	15,750.08	154.74	92.27
9038	Mason, P. J.	38	4 1 67	15,052.29	124.29	88.18
9039	Grant, H. O.	39	4 1 67	10,068.10	173.07	58.98
9040	Schultz, O. G.	40	4 1 67	10,716.03	116.99	62.78
Total				$100,403.74	$2,952.57	$1,185.66

the payment for the succeeding month during the last few days of the month.

The group control reconciliation form consists of three main sections:

a *Remittance section* which controls the funds collected in the current period and which proves that the funds forwarded to the investors are correct.

b *Principal control section* which controls the constant amount—the fixed monthly payment of principal and interest for all loans in the group—and the outstanding principal balance, which is used to arrive at the amount on which interest due for the following month is calculated.

c *Forecast section* which shows on line 10 the principal and interest amounts due in the following month. By calculating interest due and deducting it from the constant, the principal repayment is the automatic result. Then, by adding and subtracting prepayments and delinquencies, the net payment is accurately established and controlled.

Step 2: Mortgage Banker, May 20

As of this day, a principal trial balance must be prepared (Exhibit 48). To support the trial balance, since one borrower paid the payment due June 1 before May 20, a report or prepayments must also be prepared (Exhibit 49). Since there were no delinquent payments, there is no need to prepare a delinquent loan report. To accompany the (1) trial balance and (2) report of prepayments, (3) a new group control reconciliation form must be prepared and submitted. (See Exhibit 50.)

The three forms, namely the group reconciliation form, the trial balance, and

Step 2: Investor, May 20

Having received a total of $1,160.48, the investor credits $280.87 to principal which brings the unpaid balance of fourteen loans to $200,122.87, as shown on line 6 for May 20, and credit to interest earned $879.61 (line 2, $967.57 less servicing fee deducted by mortgage banker). This transaction involves two simple entries, one on a group control card and one on an interest receivable ledger.

EXHIBIT 48 *Trial balance – May*

INVESTOR: *Progressive trusted fund*		STATE: *Texas*	TYPE LOAN: *FHA*			INTEREST RATE: 550	PART. RATE: 050	FOR MO. ENDING: 5-20-67
Loan no.	*Name*	*Mortgagee loan no.*	*Pd. to date*			*Principal balance*	*Escrow balance*	*Fixed payment control*
			Mo.	*Day*	*Yr.*			
9027	Axtel, F.	27	5	1	67	$ 15,066.86	$ 166.67	$ 85.74
9028	Morgan, S.	28	5	1	67	15,998.83	174.70	101.43
9029	Smith, R. G.	29	5	1	67	10,951.26	141.44	64.24
9030	Jones, B. S.	30	5	1	67	14,634.85	150.03	85.85
9031	Granger, P.	31	5	1	67	15,232.21	154.49	89.35
9032	Beran, J. R.	32	5	1	67	15,730.00	146.16	92.27
9033	Meyer, W. G.	33	5	1	67	13,937.95	159.03	81.76
9034	Pope, J. R.	34	5	1	67	15,630.42	165.08	91.69
9035	Roberts, C.	35	5	1	67	17,223.35	191.07	101.03
9036	Dotson, R. L.	36	5	1	67	14,210.13	134.81	90.09
9037	Johnson, A. B.	37	5	1	67	15,730.00	174.74	92.27
9038	Mason, P. J.	38	5	1	67	15,033.10	144.29	88.18
9039	Grant, H. O.	39	5	1	67	10,055.27	193.07	58.98
9040	Schultz, O. G.	40	6	1	67	10,688.64	156.99	62.78
Total						$100,122.87	$2,252.57	$1,185.66

EXHIBIT 49 *Statement of prepayments*

INVESTOR:	STATE:	TYPE LOAN:	INTEREST RATE:	PART. RATE:	FOR MO. ENDING:
Progressive trusteed fund	*Texas*	*FHA*	550	050	5-20-67

Loan no.	Name	Mortgagee loan no.	Due date Mo. Day Yr.	Interest	Monthly installment Principal	Total	Remarks
9040	Schultz, O. G.	40	6 1 67	$49.05	$13.73	$62.78	
Total				$49.05	$13.73	$62.78	

276

EXHIBIT 50 Reconciliation for mortgage loans – May
ABC Mortgage Company

INVESTOR Progressive Trusteed Fund CODE 688

State	Interest Rate	Servicing Fee Rate	Type	Servicer / Control Code No.		Cut-off Date
TEXAS	550	050	FHA	5	2	Mo 5 / Da 20 / Yr 67

DESCRIPTION	REMITTANCE			PRINCIPAL CONTROL		FORECAST		SERVICE FEE	NET REMITTED
	Interest	Principal Credit	Constant	Principal Balance	No. of Loans	Interest	Principal		
1. CONTROL TOTALS (PREVIOUS RECONCILIATION)	918.52	267.14	1,185.66	200,403.74	14				
2. TOTAL CASH COLLECTED	967.57	280.87		280.87				87.96	1,160.48
3. CURTAILMENTS									
4. LOANS ADDED									
5. LOANS REMOVED									
6. TRIAL BALANCE (SUB-TOTAL PRIN. CONTROL)			1,185.66	200,122.87	14				
7. DELINQUENT INSTALLMENTS									
8. PREPAID INSTALLMENTS	49.05	13.73		13.73		49.05	13.73		
9. CURTAILMENTS AFTER PREPAYMENTS									
10. ADJUSTED PRINCIPAL BALANCE & NORMAL PAYMENT DUE				200,136.60		917.29	268.37		
11. ADJUSTMENTS AND FORE-CASTED TOTAL CREDIT						868.24	254.64		

REMARKS:

ABC Mortgage Company

J. R. Noble, Vice President
(Name & Title)

277

the statement of prepayments, are then accompanied by a check for $1,160.48, which represents principal and net interest due investor.

Step 3: Mortgage Banker, June 20
This is a repetition of the steps described for the mortgage banker under Steps 1 and 2 above. He will now (a) prepare a principal trial balance (Exhibit 51); (b) prepare a report of delinquent accounts (Exhibit 52); and (c) prepare group reconciliation form (Exhibit 53). This time it was not necessary to prepare a statement of prepayments. On the group reconciliation form, after transferring totals from lines 6 and 11 of the May reconciliation form to line 1 on the June form, the principle of zero balance is used to reconcile control totals. A check in the sum of $984.27 accompanies the report.

Step 3: Investor, June 20
From the check of $984.27, the sum of $240.58 is credited to the group control card, since $14.04 represented by a payment in arrears for the Smith loan was not received. See statement of delinquent accounts for June 20. The amount $743.69 goes to interest ($818.06 less servicing fee of $74.37).

The mortgage banker during the periods of April 20 to May 20, May 20 to June 20, etc., regularly posts the payments received to the individual loan ledger cards. On April 20, May 20, and June 20, the mortgage banker remits the monies due the investor in accordance with the group reconciliation form.

If instead of fourteen loans, a much larger group is involved, say, 200 loans, the investor may require that the mortgage banker remit payments more often than monthly, e.g., amounts equivalent to a week's collection. He will also ask that as of the twentieth, when the group reconciliation form clearly indicates the total amount of principal and net interest collected, a reconciliation be made of the monies received and submitted and that the group reconciliation form be accompanied by a check representing the difference.

Of course, the larger the number of loans in a group, the greater the number of exceptions in terms of delinquent payments and prepayments that must be reported. These exceptions, in turn, involve lengthy listings and often require laborious work in terms of reconciling reports and controls. The work of preparing and submitting single-debit reports, therefore, can cause delays in mortgage bankers' offices if many groups and many investors are involved and if most of the work in completing the report is done manually.

The delinquency reports, which are prepared in triplicate, are a great advantage in controlling and reporting delinquencies. The original copy is dispatched with the single-debit reports shortly after the cutoff date, and two copies are retained by the mortgage banker. On one of the copies, the collection department is required to record the results of their collection efforts, namely, that a payment was received or

EXHIBIT 51   Trial Balance – June

INVESTOR: Progressive trusteed fund	STATE: Texas	TYPE LOAN: FHA	INTEREST RATE: 550	PART. RATE: 050	FOR MO. ENDING: 6-20-67

Loan no.	Name	Mortgagee loan no.	Pd. to date Mo.	Day	Yr.	Principal balance	Escrow balance	Fixed payment control
9027	Axtel, F.	27	6	1	67	$ 15,050.18	$ 186.67	$ 85.74
9028	Morgan, S.	28	6	1	67	15,970.73	194.70	101.43
9029	Smith, R. G.	29	5	1	67	10,951.26	141.44	64.24
9030	Jones, B. S.	30	6	1	67	14,616.08	170.03	85.85
9031	Granger, P.	31	6	1	67	15,212.67	174.49	89.35
9032	Beran, J. R.	32	6	1	67	15,709.83	166.16	92.27
9033	Meyer, W. G.	33	6	1	67	13,920.07	179.03	81.76
9034	Pope, J. R.	34	6	1	67	15,610.37	185.08	91.69
9035	Roberts, C.	35	6	1	67	17,201.26	211.07	101.03
9036	Dotson, R. L.	36	6	1	67	14,185.17	154.81	90.09
9037	Johnson, A. B.	37	6	1	67	15,709.83	194.74	92.27
9038	Mason, P. J.	38	6	1	67	15,013.82	164.29	88.18
9039	Grant, H. O.	39	6	1	67	10,042.38	213.07	58.98
9040	Schultz, O. G.	40	6	1	67	10,688.64	156.99	62.78
						$199,882.29	$2,492.57	$1,185.66

EXHIBIT 52 Statement of delinquent accounts

INVESTOR: Progressive trusteed fund	STATE: Texas	TYPE LOAN: FHA	INTEREST RATE: 550	PART. RATE: 050	FOR MO. ENDING 6-20-67

Loan no.	Name	Mortgagee loan no.	Due date Mo. Day Yr.	Monthly installment Interest	Principal	Total	Remarks
9029	Smith, R. G.	29	6 1 67	$50.20	$14.04	$64.24	
Total				$50.20	$14.04	$64.24	

EXHIBIT 53 Reconciliation of mortgage loans – June
ABC Mortgage Company

INVESTOR Progressive Trusteed Fund CODE 688

TEXAS	550	050	FHA	5	2
State	Interest Rate	Servicing Fee Rate	Type	Servicer Control Code No.	Interest Control Code No.

Cut-off Date: Mo 6 | Da 20 | Yr 67

DESCRIPTION	REMITTANCE Interest	Principal Credit	Constant	PRINCIPAL CONTROL Principal Balance	No. of Loans	SERVICE FEE	NET REMITTED	FORECAST INTEREST	PRINCIPAL
1. CONTROL TOTALS (PREVIOUS RECONCILIATION)	868.24	254.64	1,185.66	200,122.87	14	74.37	984.27		
2. TOTAL CASH COLLECTED	818.06	240.58		240.58					
3. CURTAILMENTS									
4. LOANS ADDED									
5. LOANS REMOVED									
6. TRIAL BALANCE (SUB-TOTAL PRIN. CONTROL)			1,185.66	199,882.29	14				
7. DELINQUENT INSTALLMENTS	50.20	14.04		14.04				50.20	14.04
8. PREPAID INSTALLMENTS									
9. CURTAILMENTS AFTER PREPAYMENTS									
10. ADJUSTED PRINCIPAL BALANCE & NORMAL PAYMENT DUE				199,868.25				916.06	269.60
11. ADJUSTMENTS AND FORE-CASTED TOTAL CREDIT	.02	.02–						966.26	283.64

REMARKS:

ABC Mortgage Company

L. L. Noble, Vice President

(Name & Title)

that arrangements have been made for payment. It must be remembered that the investor has no knowledge or record of which payment was or was not received between the cutoff date and the first of the month as far as delinquencies are concerned until he receives the next month's trial balance. Therefore, the second copy is dispatched to the investor on either the last day of the month or the fifth of the following month, which shows which payments *have been received.* Through these forms, no loans escape attention or report. Thus copies of single-debit delinquent reports are an effective means of keeping track of past due accounts.

Aggregate or modified single-debit accounting[4]   Aggregate accounting is a refinement of single-debit accounting in that it involves reporting only nonroutine payments to the investor and the reconciliation of cash received and remitted to a precalculated amount due. The investor, instead of the servicer, prepares the necessary reports and the loans are no longer segregated by type, interest rate, or servicing fee as in the single-debit procedure.

A listing of the loans in the portfolio in the form of a bill for a given period or billing cycle is prepared by the investor on his data processing equipment. The bill includes the details of the payments due of all types of loans regardless of repayment plan; this automatically eliminates the need for separate group controls of any sort. Separate remittance reports are required on only those loans which are paid in full, on advance payments, and on principal prepayments. The delinquent loans are indicated on a detachable copy of the list, which then becomes the remittance report. The amounts shown on the bill, the total of the delinquent payments, and separate reports representing prepayments are reconciled to the check or deposit ticket which is enclosed. For the succeeding month, the investor automatically updates all loans not marked delinquent and those loans on which a separate report was submitted, calculates the amounts due for the next billing cycle, and prepares a new bill.

Aggregate accounting arrangements can only be established by the investor who has high-speed computers which enable him to prepare a complete listing of loans each month by servicers and by interest and principal groupings without the necessity both on his own part and on the part of his servicers of segregating loans by different interest rates.

Preparation and Reconciliation of Escrow Reserve Trial Balances

The monthly task   As soon as the posting of payments to escrow reserve accounts and the checks drawn on the same account for disbursements have been completed for the month, a trial balance of escrow reserve accounts must be run. The total of this listing of individual loan ledger cards must correspond to the funds kept in a custodial bank account as represented by a bank statement. One escrow reserve trial

---

[4] See *MBA Standard Aggregate Accounting and Reporting System,* Appendix A-7.

balance must be run for each bank account the servicer has under his control. These trial balances include the servicer's own custodial account, representing reserves on loans not yet sold, reserves of those loans for which the investor did not require that a separate custodial bank account be established, as well as escrow reserve trial balances for each custodial account maintained for each investor requiring a separate account.

These trial balances must then be reconciled with the bank statements forwarded by the bank to the mortgage banker. Investors often request that copies of bank statements be forwarded directly by the bank to their audit department, presumably to spot check the amount of funds in the account and to detect any unusual activity.

It is imperative that each account be balanced each month. If there are discrepancies, they must be traced and corrected promptly. No other infraction increases year-end audit work and audit bills more than escrow reserve accounts which are out of balance.

Some companies have shifted the balancing from the first of the month, the usual date, to other dates. This arrangement relieves work congestion from other month-end requirements and first-of-the-month volume. If a date other than the first of the month is used for balancing, this alternative must be consistently maintained, and escrow trial balances must be balanced to bank statements issued on days corresponding to these arbitrary during-the-month dates. At the end of the company's fiscal year, however, escrow reserve accounts must be balanced to year-end bank balances.

Handling overdrafts An overdraft occurs when a bill is paid which exceeds the reserves which have been deposited, for FHA mortgage insurance, taxes, or insurance premiums. In reality, mortgage companies pay proper bills as long as funds are available in the borrower's escrow reserve account without regard to the purpose for which the reserves were originally accumulated. An overdraft may also occur if a bill is processed when an account is delinquent on the assumption that the payment will be received shortly and posted to the ledger card before the disbursement is recorded.

If an overdraft occurs, whoever is responsible for the adequacy of reserves should be notified and immediate steps should be taken to cover such overdraft. Strict observance of the FDIC ruling of February 1966—i.e., depositing company funds to absorb possible overdrafts—will tend to reduce the overdraft exposure.

CUSTOMER SERVICE OPERATIONS

Three types of customer service operations—preparing annual statements, answering inquiries about income tax deductibility, and responding to credit inquiries on borrowers—are classified as accounting functions, because the information used is maintained by the mortgage loan accounting department. Answering inquiries, however, about income tax should be discouraged where the response may be construed as giving tax advice.

In most companies, the preparation and dissemination of annual statements is the only function of the mortgage loan accounting department in the customers' service area. In some firms inquiries about the deductibility of items on income tax returns are answered by the mortgage loan accounting department, while other firms handle such inquiries through an employee who is sufficiently versed in such matters. Credit information on borrowers should be handled and released by the collection department staff, even if the information used is available only from mortgage loan accounting records.

Whether any information is disseminated automatically, disclosed upon request, or even volunteered varies among mortgage bankers and depends on the degree of automation and the mortgage banker's concept of the customer relations aspect of the job. Usually public relations-minded companies feel that it is their job to counsel their customers readily on any matter which is related to the mortgage and benefits their customers financially.

Annual Statements

An annual statement is distributed to inform the mortgagor of the amount of real estate taxes that have been paid out of his reserve account to the tax collector for real estate taxes and the amount of interest the mortgagor paid on his mortgage. The purpose of such disclosures is to assist the mortgagor in preparing his federal and state income tax returns, if the latter is also required. To serve the customer further, many companies use a fairly detailed report to give the borrower a complete accounting of the monies he paid and of the activity in his account. Often, disseminating such accounting information can be best accomplished by photostating a copy of the mortgagor ledger card—providing the card is designed for such specific purpose—and sending it to the borrower at the end of the year.

In whatever manner of whichever special format annual statements are prepared, care should be exercised that the information sent to home owners is sent promptly (no later than January 10) and that information is both complete and accurate. A late and inaccurate statement can do more harm to customer relations than no statement at all. The use and application of data processing equipment has made the preparation and dissemination of these annual statements a reasonably automatic chore.

Several types of annual statements are used. Exhibit 54 illustrates a simple form which under most circumstances is adequate. Some forms give the borrower an accounting of his payments to interest, principal and reserves, and a record of various disbursements.

The decision whether to use a short form or one of the more detailed forms varies according to the makeup of the mortgage banker's clientele, the availability of facilities to produce the statements, and the mortgage banker's wishes on customer relations service. The short statement unquestionably furnishes the minimum essential information. Such a statement, however, may raise the question in the borrower's mind of how the information was prepared. However, detailed statements

EXHIBIT 54 *Annual mortgage loan statement*

ANNUAL MORTGAGE LOAN STATEMENT

YEAR	TOTAL INTEREST PAID	REAL ESTATE TAX BILL PAID	PRINCIPAL BALANCE	ACCOUNT NUMBER
1967	$ 631.87	$ 612.24	$ 17,890.14	G - 36482

DEAR CUSTOMER,

    THIS STATEMENT HAS BEEN PREPARED AS OF THE CLOSE OF BUSINESS DEC. 31, FOR THE YEAR INDICATED.

    PLEASE RETAIN THIS FORM FOR YOUR RECORDS AND FOR USE IN PREPARING YOUR INCOME TAX RETURN.

    IF THE FIGURES SHOWN ON THIS STATEMENT DO NOT AGREE WITH YOUR RECORDS PLEASE CONTACT:

ACCOUNTING DEPARTMENT

MR & MRS MARY AND JOHN DOE
932 AVENUE M
ELK GROVE VLG IL 60007

ABC MORTGAGE COMPANY
233 Maple Street
Chicago, Illinois   60190

which present all entries leading to the results often elicit questions which place additional, nonproductive demands on the servicing personnel's time. The detailed annual statement form or the reproduction of an actual ledger card reflecting the entire activity in the account may be embarrassing if the statement reflects posting errors and their corrections, since such adjusted entries tend to irritate and confuse the mortgagor.

Information Regarding Income Tax Deductibility

Most mortgage banking firms inform their customers in annual statements and reference booklets of the two basic items paid in connection with home ownership when a mortgage is involved, which provide them with deductions for their federal and/or state income tax returns; namely, real estate tax payments and interest paid on the loan. In response to any inquiry on the subject beyond general points, the caller should be referred to a tax counselor, a tax attorney, or an agent of the Internal Revenue Service for advice.

A few basic general tax facts relating to deductibility of items on the federal in-income tax returns are presented here, however, primarily to inform the servicing employee of what can be done in general terms, rather than to provide him with information for the mortgagor. This information relates strictly to standard items paid by mortgagors.

An owner of a residential property in which he resides is entitled to deduct from income: (1) real estate taxes paid in the year the tax is paid (the borrower is entitled to deduct only taxes actually paid and not the amount of tax deposits made in any given year); and (2) interest actually paid on the loan. If, for instance, only eight monthly payments are made in any calendar year or the taxpayer's tax year, only 8 months' interest payments can be deducted. Conversely, if fourteen monthly payments are paid in any one calendar year, the aggregate total of fourteen interest payments may be claimed as an interest deduction.

Items paid by residential mortgagors which are *not* deductible on the federal income tax returns are

1 FHA mortgage insurance premium It is a deductible expense only if the property is rented and if the tenant pays rent to the mortgagor, who in turn makes the monthly mortgage payment. In this instance, the FHA mortgage insurance premium becomes part of the expense of renting the home.

2 Prepayment penalty This is a charge for the privilege of prepaying the loan ahead of schedule; hence, this item cannot be construed as an interest expense. Distinction must be made, however, between a prepayment penalty and the amount of interest that may be paid if the loan to be paid in full calls for a charge representing 60 days' interest (whether the loan is paid before the 60 days elapse or at the end of such period). In this instance, the charge paid as additional interest is a deductible interest item.

3 Special assessments or municipal assessments for services, such as water bills and garbage collection fees, are not tax deductible items. Interest on assessments, however, is deductible.

Credit Information on Borrowers

This is a third-party service; i.e., information is provided to someone other than the borrower about how the borrower makes monthly payments on his loan. The information is supplied either to a credit bureau which requested information on behalf of a merchant, sales organization, or other lending institution wishing to grant credit to the mortgagor for merchandise or other services, or to any of these types of organizations directly. Since ultimately the borrower also benefits from this service, it is important that credit inquiries be handled promptly and correctly. Inaccurate credit information may be injurious to the borrower's credit standing.

From an operational standpoint, handling inquiries on borrowers who have good payment records poses no problem since they normally can be answered in a routine manner by following the procedure outlined below. Inquiries relating to borrowers with less-than-good records may be given to a member of the collection staff or to the head of the department who is familiar with all problem cases.

As a matter of procedure, phone inquiries should not be honored. First, it disrupts the operations of the company since a clerk must stop whatever he is doing to accommodate the caller; and, secondly, phone answers can be easily misinterpreted, and then will be of little value, if not harmful, to the borrower. Written inquiries can be answered readily by the staff with a minimum of inconvenience at one time or another in the day.

In answering credit inquiries, it is best not to allow each clerk to make up his own definition of what constitutes an excellent, a good, or a slow account. Each loan administrator should set up a schedule for his staff for this purpose which may read as follows:

Category	*Rating*
Pays consistently no later than fifth	Excellent
Pays consistently no later than tenth	Good
Pays between eighth and fourteenth	Fair
Pays late, often beyond fifteenth	Poor

The above ratings, of course, are only suggestions; categories may be extended and ratings may be described differently than illustrated. *The important point, however, is to establish categories and ratings.* All mortgage bankers in one area should coordinate their rating schedules among themselves as well as with local credit bureaus and banks for a more meaningful exchange of this vital information.

Inquiries on borrowers who do not readily fit into any of the above categories, or requests which fall into the fourth classification and may require some explanation, should be referred to the supervisor of the collection department or to the collector handling the account of that particular delinquent borrower.

Mortgage lenders wishing not to be classified under the Fair Credit Reporting Act (15 USC 1601) as "consumer reporting agencies" must be careful that information they supply to third parties does not constitute a consumer report. An exception to the definition of "consumer report" (15 USC 1603(d)) is "any report containing information solely as to transactions or experiences between the consumer and the person making the report."

CHAPTER FIFTEEN

Collection Department

The basic purpose of the collection department is to obtain payments when due and efficiently follow those which are not made when due. As the medical profession wages war on disease, the collection department wages war on delinquency, with professional know-how as well as with compassion. The collection department employs a combination of preventive measures to head off problems before they occur, corrective measures to cure problems after they have arisen, and follow-up techniques to prevent recurrence of previously "cured" cases. Just as the medical profession must be prepared both to help cure a great range of individual illnesses and to deal with occasional medical problems of epidemic proportions, a well-managed collection department must be prepared to cope with situations caused by economic depression of local, regional, or national proportions.

In a general sense, the collection department is the heart of the servicing activity; it is handed all the problems, and hears the complaints, not only of the individual borrower's financial distress, but often that of the world at large. In this department, which has the least amount of mechanization, success depends primarily on the individual's ability to perform his job and induce delinquent mortgagors to make payments.

Many mortgage banking companies route all general inquiries relative to payments, insurance, taxes, and prepayments to this department, with the result that the collection department often acts as a clearing house for all servicing problems. Other companies distinguish between inquiries that involve servicing and problems that in one way or another have a bearing on the borrower's ability or willingness to pay. Simple inquiries may be routed to the insurance or tax departments, for instance, but a complaint involving construction, although referred to the construction department for handling, is also routed to the collection department since a dispute on such matters may lead to serious collection problems or may indicate poorer-than-expected physical security for the mortgage.

The collection department's responsibilities are to

1 *Maintain a continuous liaison between mortgagor and lender* relative to the terms of the mortgage.
2 *Enforce the terms of the mortgage* if the mortgagor is past due or delinquent in his payments.
3 *Carry out the collection policies established by:*
   a *The lender* whose loan payment is past due or delinquent.
   b *The mortgage company.*
   c *FHA or VA* which prescribe certain procedures for handling delinquencies and want every effort to be expended to avoid foreclosure.
4 *Execute all the tasks and discharge all the responsibilities relating to termination of a loan through legal means.* This activity is a highly specialized segment of the servicer's responsibility; it involves a very close cooperation with attorneys handling foreclosure cases for investors. In this area, the servicer can be very valuable to the lender.

ORGANIZATION AND STAFFING

The size of a predominantly residential collection department varies with both the number of loans serviced and the extent of the collection problems. In large organizations, the department is headed by a senior officer of the company, who has a large staff reporting to him; in others, a collection chief with long experience in the collections field heads the department and reports to the servicing manager, to the loan administrator, or often directly to the president.

It is incumbent on the management of a mortgage banking organization to supervise the entire collection activity closely. Supervision may be exercised directly by the head of the company, the loan administrator, or both. It may be best to establish a chain of command by which the supervisor of the collection department and his key collection personnel report to the loan administrator, who in turn reports to the head of the company. In this manner, individual problems are reviewed and solved at the supervisory level, and management is informed and appraised of overall results, trends, problems, and foreclosures.

Personal Qualifications of Staff

It is as difficult to define and describe all the qualities a good collection manager or a collector should possess as it is to find them in one single individual. In no other activity within the domain of loan administration is success as contingent on the personality and individuality of its supervisor and staff as in collections.

First of all, the man or woman who holds the top post must have executive as well as administrative ability and must possess keen judgment, tact, perseverance, and, most importantly, the unique ability to handle people. He or she must have above-average intelligence; must be flexible, consistent, persistent, fair, and, most of all, be able to deal with collection problems without becoming emotionally involved with them.

A good memory is a great asset. This faculty is especially useful in recalling the source of the real problems of a borrower when the follow-up record only indicates that a call was made and only shows the perfunctory excuse that was given by the borrower for his delinquency.

The difficulty in elaborating on some of the requirements for both the supervisor and his staff stems from the fact that a collector is many different individuals to many different borrowers. He must be tough and unrelenting or compassionate and helpful, and must change these characteristics on a ring of the telephone. He must lead his customer out of a financial predicament, he must guide and counsel, and he must see ahead. But because he must do all this, he must also be perceptive. He must like to deal with people and get a sense of satisfaction from doing so. He must know when to believe a story and when to doubt it; he must be able to distinguish fairly accurately a person who needs help from a phony and to treat each accordingly. The requirements of the job make it imperative that the supervisor has the compassion of an army chaplain, the toughness of a master sergeant, and the firmness of a parole officer—all in one.

In actuality, collectors are born, not made. While it is easy to learn the regulations and procedures, it is difficult to acquire the knowledge and judgment of which tool to use, when and how, and when to try a new approach after another method has failed. The important personality traits required for the job, such as innate intelligence, good disposition, and understanding people, are hardly acquirable traits. It takes finesse, adaptability, and imagination to be able to talk to different people in their own language; to converse with a professional person one minute and a blue-collar worker the next; to separate those who are truthful from those who are not; and to know when to give a delinquent borrower encouragement and when to give him no sympathy at all. No one looking from the outside can really know or understand what feat the collector has accomplished in performing his task.

Women are often more effective than men in dealing with home loan problems. Usually, women are better listeners, a qualification highly important in the home loan collection field; they hear out a man or woman, while men may be less sensitive and more likely to prejudge their customers and make up their minds on what the answer ought to be. Borrowers, especially young couples, frequently need mothers or mother substitutes, and, therefore, some of them prefer to talk to women rather than men. Persons of either sex, however, sometimes tend to be dogmatic, often judging the other person's problems by their own, and thus become prejudiced in their attitude toward problems and hardships. Some collectors are prone to become vindictive when dealing with problems of delinquents from an economic stratum above their own.

Background and Work Assignment

In addition to evaluating human problems and working out solutions, the collection chief and staff must have a thorough knowledge of VA and FHA requirements applicable to residential loans, as well as an understanding of the foreclosure laws of the states in which the company has mortgages. The collection supervisor and staff must also be familiar with the requirements of the lenders for whom they service loans. Although overall practices are fairly uniform, some of the instructions for handling delinquent loans are contained in the servicing contract or manual, or both, or in special instructions especially designed for handling these problems. Handling foreclosures may require the mortgage banker to deal with attorneys or realtors and in certain states to testify in court at the request of foreclosure counsel. At no time must the mortgage banker forget, especially when the lender's investment is involved, that although he often acts on instructions, he is still responsible for the protection of that investment if the unexpected should create the need for immediate answers or decisions. If he knows his investors well, of course—as he should—he is unlikely to make mistakes.

Loans may be assigned to the collection staff by investors, by geographical area, or by type of loan. The last arrangement is recommended. It is not a good idea to assign the accounts on the basis of 30-, 60-, or 90-day delinquency. However, it is best to devise a separation of functions after loans have reached the foreclosure stage, since from this point on the job of handling the account is no longer a mere collection task.

In large, high-volume organizations, overall collection efficiency can usually be increased by assigning one definite group of loans to one collector who can, over a period of time, become quite familiar with his accounts and then classify his delinquency problem accounts properly as temporary or chronic. Groups of loans should be assigned according to history of delinquency rather than by an equal division of the total loans serviced; i.e., in some cases a total of 1,000 loans serviced for one investor may contain a much greater delinquency history than another group of 1,000 loans. Group assignment provides a means of comparing the effectiveness of individual collectors after they have been assigned workloads of approximately the same degree of difficulty.

Depending on the volume of delinquent loans reaching foreclosure stage, consideration should be given to assigning foreclosure cases to one individual who thus can become a specialist and can become thoroughly familiar with the multitude of details involved in handling foreclosures of several types of loans. The qualifications for this task differ greatly from those for a collector—it is rare indeed to find one individual who can handle both jobs effectively.

PRINCIPLES AND PRACTICES OF COLLECTION

No other single ability of a mortgage banking organization is of greater value and significance than its ability to handle collections effectively. The concept of collections no longer means only enforcing the terms of the mortgage on a day-to-day or month-to-month basis, nor only dealing with problem cases, nor only complying with numerous and often complex governmental regulations affecting insured and guaranteed loans. Today, the process of collection encompasses the entire effort, from mailing the first courtesy reminder to terminating the borrower-lender relationship by one means or another, including foreclosure.

Thus, the loan administrator or the supervisor of the collection department no longer submits recommendations solely to investors and accepts instructions from them for the pursuit and termination of a delinquent loan. He is now entrusted with the responsibility to make the appropriate decisions and carry them out. Of course, various other arrangements exist between servicers and investors, not all of which allow complete freedom to the servicer in handling the lender's investment, but the trend is in the direction of greater freedom in decision making.

Although the execution and timing of most collection steps are clearly outlined in investors' servicing manuals and FHA and VA regulations, much of the job of handling a delinquent account, curing a default, or terminating an incurable loan is full of problems which cannot be anticipated and for which solutions cannot always be prescribed in advance. One characteristic of collection work must be noted. The amount of equity each borrower has in his property, differences in the nature of the three types of residential loans, and variations in the return of investment to the lender in different states under different foreclosure laws—all these factors determine whether borrowers in identical adverse financial predicaments receive different consideration and treatment from mortgage bankers.

Handling delinquent income property loans is a different field, where only some of the routine steps in the determination and initial pursuit of delinquency may be identical to that prescribed for handling residential loan delinquencies. Thereafter, as soon as any temporary cause such as an oversight in remitting is removed, a highly technical approach involving the use of specialized skill must be applied. Of necessity, this must frequently include consultation with the income property loan staff, appraisers, legal counsel of mortgage bankers or investors, or any or all of these.

Although servicing fees pay for handling loans whether in current or defaulted status, there is no special provision in most servicing contracts for the investor to reward the mortgage banker for the exceptional services he must often render in the foreclosure of loans. Under some servicing contracts, the shortcoming is more serious. Mortgage bankers may not receive servicing fees after foreclosure action begins, although their work does not cease. Since investors do not wish to pay attorneys' fees in excess of the VA maximum allowable fee or more than their share of the expense under FHA loans attorneys in some states are not always adequately compensated for the work they are required to perform.

Requirements for Good Practices

Good collection practices can be defined easily since they consist of only two basic components: (1) a strong collection team headed by a man or woman of executive and administrative ability and (2) an effective collection system geared at all times, in terms of both intensity and specialization, to the number and nature of existing delinquency problems.

The collection philosophy that must pervade the actions of the team must stem from strength. However, the milk of human kindness, often frowned upon in business, cannot be eliminated from the workings of lending and collecting money, even if the dictates of reason would indicate otherwise. For every decision of leniency which should not have been made, there are countless cases where patience and faith in human dignity have saved a home and a loan. The need for an occasional act of compassion is not tantamount, however, to weakness in dealing with human problems, most of which must be handled with firmness. An essentially weak and too understanding collection team can induce tardiness and encourage delinquency. Borrowers often respect a firm, but dignified hand and voice. Rudeness, of course, should never be tolerated in a member of the collection team.

It must be remembered that a good collection record cannot be achieved overnight. It is the result of planning, development of efficient techniques, good follow-up records, and a continuous review of delinquent accounts by capable first-line and supervisory collection personnel.

The importance of staffing this department with top grade talent cannot be over-emphasized. The value of the entire collection machinery becomes meaningless without a strong leader whose personality and drive must pervade the entire effort. Just as exaggerated appraisals which overstate value have been likened to time bombs that explode to bring financial distress and disaster to the holders of such mortgages, so inadequate collection efforts from the beginning of servicing responsibility can light a fuse to the soundness of the lender-servicer relationship. This is axiomatic, because poor collection work is not necessarily revealed by a single poorly handled loan, nor is it evident under a good economic climate. Occasional mistakes can often be corrected by a showdown instigated by the lender, but the creeping paralysis of a slowly decaying portfolio, induced by inefficiency in collections, has a long-range effect on the portfolio and on the mortgage banker's servicing income.

Collection Procedures

In collection activity, the mortgage banker's task encompasses two distinct yet inseparable areas: *collection* and *foreclosure*. As these two words imply, collection involves all efforts expended to prevent and cure defaults, while foreclosure includes all activities performed to terminate the loan in compliance with the regulations of the FHA and VA, if applicable, and in accordance with the laws of the state within which the property is located. Each mortgage banking firm puts the stamp of its own individuality either on the forms or in the procedures used to prevent and to cure defaults.

The collection activity itself must be viewed in several phases. First, the important steps that precede any actual collection effort are designed to prevent delinquencies—especially applicable to new borrowers and new owners. These include indoctrination of the borrower with the idea that his most important single obligation under the terms of the mortgage is prompt payment of each monthly installment. This is done by dissemination of informative literature in advance and by certain procedural steps at the first sign of slowness, which are designed to promote good payment habits.

It is only after education has failed to accomplish its objective and only after the borrower is actually late with a payment that the collection machinery must really come into action. Here, collections may proceed in low or high gear, or a variety of methods between the two, all designed to persuade, assist, or compel the borrower to make the payments which he once so readily agreed to make promptly. The tempo quickens as normal collection steps do not bring results, as the delinquent borrower becomes careless about, or seeks to avoid, making payments.

After indoctrination has failed, *routine* collection methods and devices must be applied. The routine approach is geared to the greatest number of loans which do not need individual and specialized handling. It includes mailing past due notices and the use and enforcement of late charges and interest penalties. When this approach fails to remove the delinquency, consideration must be given to a process of escalation, which employs more and more refined and specialized methods, as if the collector were to zero in on his target with each successive step.

Subsequently, a *selective* approach—the use of specialized collection tools, each presumably the appropriate one to deal with the problem—is applied. Since routine approaches can be used only before the true nature of the delinquency is ascertained, specialized approaches are used only after the source of the problem has been discovered and the nature of the delinquency established. At this point, the proper classification of delinquents becomes an important task.

This chapter deals with the various types of collection techniques and procedures and of ideas and recommendations that can help collection departments responsible for single-family residential loans, take appropriate steps in handling their routine and difficult problems. Income property loan problems will be dealt with separately though briefly, later in this chapter.

PREVENTIVE COLLECTION PRACTICES

There are two ways to combat the problems of delinquent accounts. One is to collect the payment when it is not made, which is the obvious approach; the other is to take steps to emphasize to the borrower his basic obligation—i.e., the necessity to pay on the date due.

The establishment of preventive practices rests with the loan administrator. Some steps must be initiated when the loan application is taken. At that time, the loan officer must stress the importance of paying on the first of the month. These precautionary comments must be repeated when the loan is closed or when the first-payment letter is dispatched. Often the importance of the points to be made lies not in what is done—namely, emphasizing the necessity of prompt payments, which often is automatic—but how it is done and what emphasis is placed on the necessity of paying promptly. While some suggestions may seem elementary, their value has been tested time and time again, and their adoption and use can often be considered the foundation of good collection practices.

Setting First Payment Date

In this age, when homeowners often spend their last dollar to buy a home and arrange for maximum financing, the establishment of an appropriate first-payment date may be of some significance, especially if the purchase involves a new house which requires buying many new household items. If the first-payment date was not set sufficiently far in advance and there are complications prior to closing—a condition which, in turn, creates delays—the first payment may become due immediately following closing of the loan, if not before. Therefore, if delays are anticipated so that one or two payments come due very near to, or even before, the loan closing, the mortgage payments should be extended as far as permissible to avoid overburdening the mortgagor as he begins homeownership. It is best to schedule at least 30 days between loan closing and the due date of the first payment.

Stressing Prompt Payment Habits

Care should be exercised at closing as well as later in writing that the importance of observing the due date is established and emphasized. This is particularly important in those areas where mortgage closings take place in offices other than the mortgage banker's premises, where loan closings cannot be supervised. Of course, even if the requirement for prompt payment is mentioned, the message may be forgotten by the time the new homeowners reach their property. When loan closings are performed outside the company office, it is best to have information on the necessity of paying promptly incorporated in a booklet, or in a letter of instructions, to be given mortgagors. The use of an attractive brochure is usually very helpful. (See Appendix A-5.) The necessity of paying promptly should be reemphasized in a first-payment letter, normally dispatched 15 days before the first payment is due. This letter should not mention penalties for late payment. (See Exhibit 27.)

Informing New Owners

A new owner, who assumes an existing mortgage, must be treated as a new borrower. It is a good idea to obtain credit information on him or at least to have him complete a credit information questionnaire. This questionnaire is often more reliable than credit information obtained from trade sources. A credit questionnaire should accompany the statement of account which is sent by the cashier to both seller and purchaser or to the attorney or the real estate agent who handles the sale transaction. (See Exhibit 39.) Although there is no way to enforce filling out this questionnaire, experience indicates that only a few new borrowers refuse to cooperate and that many at least submit answers to some of the particulars.

A letter welcoming the new owner should be similar to the first-payment letter if an FHA or VA loan is involved, and should be accompanied by the informative booklet.

After the transaction is completed, all cashier and collection records as well as the loan jacket should conspicuously indicate that a new owner is involved. Since new owners are not given the same underwriting scrutiny as original borrowers and, therefore, are more apt to develop into problem cases, they should be given more careful scrutiny and follow-up than the original borrowers. Some mortgage bankers invite the new owners to the office of the company to avoid any misunderstanding about which payment is next due and to discuss the loan and its terms with them in the same manner as if they were new borrowers of the company.

Follow-up of Late Payers

One of the most significant collection procedures is a reminder by phone or notice mailed to a borrower whose payments, after a good beginning, arrive later and later each month. For instance, if the first payment was made on the third, the second on the fifth, and the third on the tenth, the first occasion when a payment does not arrive within a week should immediately prompt the collector to call the borrower, to inquire why he is making his payments late, and to remind him of his contract date and of the need to mail the payment to arrive in the office on time. Although this reminder may seem superfluous, the psychological impact on the borrower at the beginning of his relationship with the mortgage banker will have long-lasting effects on the mortgage banker-borrower relationship. Mailing a personalized courtesy notice may suffice; however, a call is definitely preferable to get this initial message across.

Handling Loan Assumptions

Under FHA or VA programs, if the purchaser can qualify for FHA insurance or VA guarantee, the seller may be released from his obligation. It is often advisable to encourage sellers to ask for such a release, to free them from involvement in a fore-closure suit or from being served with a deficiency judgment, should the loan go into default at a later date. The assumptor, after the previous owner is released, becomes a better mortgage risk since he is solely accountable for the loan obligation. Some investors agree, in case of sale, to release the original debtor; others consider this a nuisance and an unnecessary expense and prefer to keep the original mortgagor accountable. The VA will release the mortgagor and the FHA will consent to the release only if the purchaser qualifies under their respective credit requirements.

It is important to keep in mind that collection efforts must begin immediately if payments are not made, even if the release of the original borrower is still in progress. These circumstances have no bearing on the responsibility that the owner of the property has to make prompt payments. Nor is a sale being in escrow acceptable as an excuse for delay.

Educating Loan Staff

As an educational practice, some mortgage bankers refer to the production staff for review loans which become collection problems within a few months. This review should be done on a selective basis to allow the production officer to investigate the predicament in which new mortgagors may find themselves. This review, it must be emphasized, is not intended to embarrass the loan officer or make him overly wary of his underwriting processes, but to make him alert to potential problems and to establish guidelines to avoid similar loans.

Coordinating Lending and Collection Activities

An established borrower should not be granted a new loan without the express approval of the collection department. This precaution must be instituted since there is a tendency to judge a loan on the basis of the loan file, which may not reveal the number of collection efforts expended to extract monthly payments. Similarly, a cursory check of the payment record may not reveal some of the borrower's intimate problems or some of the methods that may have been employed to collect over the years. Furthermore, some borrowers who made their payments poorly for years often suddenly pay promptly solely in anticipation of applying for a new loan.

ROUTINE COLLECTION PRACTICES

Collection practices follow an orderly process beginning with preventive measures and moving through routine practices to specialized procedures for dealing with problem cases. Routine collection practices are designed to reach all delinquent borrowers by the twentieth of each month. Specialized collection practices are initiated on or about the twentieth of each month to deal with the smaller number of borrowers who fail to respond to routine procedures.

Definitions

Before the routine stage of the collection process can be explained, expressions in common usage in the mortgage field must be defined as precisely as possible.

Past due payment; delinquent payment Examination of various documents, regulations, and instructions reveals little unanimity on what constitutes a "past due" loan or "delinquent" loan. Sometimes, these terms are used interchangeably. Sometimes, *past due* implies only a short period from the due date, while *delinquent* implies nonpayment for at least 30 days. For the purpose of this book, a payment that was not made on the day it was due is *past due* and a payment that is past due more than 15 days is *delinquent*. If it is past due for 30 days, the loan is in *default*.

FHA requires, and VA prefers, that residential loans be scheduled for monthly payment on the first day of each month. As a result, practice has largely been standardized by scheduling most, if not all, residential loans for first-of-month payments. In a strict sense, then, each loan payment is past due on the second of the month. If payment is made in person at the office of the mortgage company, payments made on FHA and VA loans become technically delinquent on the seventeenth. As a practical matter, payments received on the seventeenth in an envelope which is postmarked the sixteenth of the month may be considered late, but not delinquent, and may be accepted without a late charge. If the sixteenth falls on a Sunday, the grace period may be extended by a day. The decision to charge or not to charge a penalty is strictly up to the mortgage banker administering the loan. Collection procedures must be based on the observance and enforcement of two key dates, the sixteenth and the last day of the month.

Late charges and penalty interest Both FHA and VA specifically prohibit the collection of late charges by deduction from the monthly payment. However, both agencies support the servicer if he rejects payments made after the penalty date without the appropriate penalty charge, provided it is done as a collection device and not in an effort to force default and foreclosure.

1 FHA loans—late charges Subject to slight changes in wording depending on the states, FHA mortgage forms state: "Any deficiency in the amount of any such aggregate monthly payment shall, unless made good by the Mortgagor prior to the due date of the next such payment, constitutes an event of default under this mortgage. The Mortgagee may collect a 'late charge' not to exceed two cents (2¢) for each dollar ($1) for each payment more than fifteen (15) days in arrears, to cover the extra expense involved in handling delinquent payments." The charge is assessed on the aggregate amount of the monthly payment, including escrow deposits due as well as interest and principal.

2 VA loans—late charges Similar wording appears in the VA mortgage form except that the late charge is 4 percent "of any installment when paid more than fifteen (15) days after the due date." For the sake of uniformity, if the mortgage banker so wishes, he may assess only the 2 percent penalty applicable to FHA loans. Here again, the charge is on the aggregate monthly payment.

3 Conventional loans—late charge or interest penalty Most mortgage notes read as follows: "The principal of each said installment unless paid when due shall bear interest after maturity at the rate of ___ percent per annum." Penalty interest on conventional loans may be charged either on the delinquent installment only (at either the mortgage rate or at a higher rate) or, upon default, on the entire unpaid balance of the loan (at a higher rate) depending on the wording of the mortgage note. Enforcement of these provisions, of course, is optional.

To accomplish the above objective, the following type of wording in the note of conventional loans is recommended:

While any default exists in the making of any of said payments or in the performance or observance of any of the covenants or agreement of this note or of any instrument now or hereafter evidencing or securing the indebtedness evidenced hereby, the undersigned further jointly and severally promise to pay, on each date aforesaid, additional interest on the principal balance of this note then outstanding at the rate representing the difference between the aforesaid rate and ___ per centum per annum, provided that any additional interest which has accrued shall be paid at the time of and as a condition precedent to the curing of any default. Upon any such default the holder of this note may apply payments received on any amounts due hereunder or under the terms of any instrument now or hereafter evidencing or securing said indebtedness as said holder may determine and, if the holder of this note so elects, notice of election being expressly waived, the principal remaining unpaid with accrued interest shall at once become due and payable.

An effective collection tool is often created by including the following late charge provision in the conventional mortgage:

In the event the Mortgagee shall, from time to time, accept payment of any installment required on the note and under this mortgage which is more than fifteen (15) days in arrears without exacting payment of interest at the higher rate payable after maturity, Mortgagee may, in lieu of such higher rate of interest, collect a 'late charge' not to exceed one cent ($.01) for each one dollar ($1)(or $.02 if so desired) of each such delinquent installment payment to cover the extra expense involved in handling delinquent payments; provided, however, that nothing in this paragraph contained shall authorize the Mortgagee to collect or demand any payment which would result in the imposition of interest in excess of the maximum amount allowed by law.

When applied to collection of a late payment on a $150 conventional loan payment, the charge amounts to $1.50, which is actually a 24 percent annual rate on the unpaid installment. As a practical matter in computing interest penalties or late charges—both cannot be assessed—the mortgage instrument and the usury laws in effect in the state in which the property is located should be checked and carefully observed. Certain states prohibit the charge of penalty interest on a delinquent interest payment. Usury laws vary greatly and their interpretation and application to mortgage loans are involved, as are the penalties for violating the law.

Determination of Delinquent Accounts

The routine work of the collection department begins each month in a cycle, with a meticulous review of the list of delinquents, which is prepared by either:

1 The data processing department. The delinquency report lists the unpaid loan accounts as of the date of the report, the name of the borrower, the amount delinquent, and usually the investor's code number. Income property loans should be coded for specialized action.
2 The collection staff. In the absence of data processing equipment, typed lists are prepared from the unpaid cashier cards or unpaid duplicate notices that remain in the cashier department for processing payments.

These lists may be prepared between the seventh and the tenth of the month or as of the sixteenth. If the list is prepared after the sixteenth, the amount of penalty or late charge should be included to facilitate collection efforts. The tabulating department normally prepares courtesy reminders or past due notices as of these dates. In nonautomated companies, these notices must be typed by a member of the collection staff.

Mailing Routine Notices

Routine notices mailed automatically at predetermined dates remind the forgetful borrower of his obligation and notify all delinquent borrowers that the mortgage company is aware of their failure to meet their obligations. The most common practice on residential loans is to send out routine courtesy reminders on the seventh or eighth of the month and routine past due notices on the sixteenth or seventeenth. Delinquent conventional loan borrowers should be telephoned routinely on the sixteenth of the month since nonpayment is often a legitimate oversight.

Courtesy reminder   A *courtesy reminder* is a simple statement that the payment is past due. The borrower is reminded of the amount due and that the due date is the first of the month. It may state that a penalty may be assessed after the fifteenth although most courtesy notices do not mention a penalty.

In prosperous times, some companies do not mail courtesy reminders, but rely strictly on the use of past due notices mailed on the sixteenth. Companies using data processing equipment find it advantageous to have both notices prepared simultaneously on a double form; they use the courtesy reminder first and the past due notice later, if necessary. However prepared, notices, as a matter of internal control, should always be checked and disseminated by collection clerks, rather than by cashiers or accounting clerks.

The head of the collection department can make the decision in any particular month whether to mail the courtesy notices. If mailed regularly, courtesy reminders lose some of their effectiveness as borrowers become accustomed to receiving them. This is why it makes sense to eliminate a mailing from time to time, replacing the reminders with phone calls or form letters.

Past due notice   It is a common practice to follow up all residential delinquencies by mailing past due notices on the sixteenth of the month. This notice is similar to the courtesy reminder, but it does specify the amount due as a penalty for late payment and may caution the borrower to maintain his good credit rating by paying promptly.

If not prepared by the data processing department with the courtesy reminder, past due notices should be prepared by the accounting department, preferably prior to the penalty date. Notices are eliminated at the last minute if the borrower makes the payment before the deadline. This procedure is suggested so that the notices are *ready* for mailing on the sixteenth, and not a day or two later.

If there is no response to the notice mailed on the sixteenth, some firms mail a second notice or a final notice—with the designation often printed on the face of the notice. These subsequent notices seldom bring in the payment from the borrower who does not have the cash or who was compelled to route his paycheck for the payment of medical bills or other pressing obligations. Therefore, if one notice does not prompt the borrower to pay, or does not make the borrower present his problem by phone or in writing, a second routine notice is not recommended.

Some companies find it helpful to mail a form letter in lieu of the past due notice on the theory that (1) a letter gives the appearance of a personalized approach and thus deprives the delinquent borrower of the comfortable feeling that he may have when receiving machine notices, and (2) the text of the letter can be changed monthly to make it appear less routine. Some companies inject humor into their past due notice forms. This practice may occasionally be useful but is not recommended. The inability to meet a financial obligation should not be considered a humorous matter, even if failure to pay was caused simply by oversight.

All late payers, or those who occasionally or with some regularity are 30-day delinquents, must be closely watched for signs of further deterioration in their payment habits. Their names should be kept, and their payment habits recorded, on the follow-up records. A chronic delinquent should not receive the customary past due notices since he usually does not respond to them. Instead, he should be called on the phone or contacted in person until the delinquency is cleared.

Enforcement of Late Charges

While finance companies may garnishee wages or repossess the collateral to satisfy an unpaid debt, the mortgage banker's only recourse when loan payments are delinquent, short of the acceleration of the debt or foreclosure, is a nominal late charge. Choosing between the assessment of a late charge or institution of foreclosure is like choosing between an arrow and a howitzer. Of course, the collection effort strives to return the loan to a current status, turning to foreclosure only as a last resort. Effective and firm enforcement of late charges is a vital tool in preventing delinquent loans from becoming foreclosures.

Some mortgage bankers believe that the existence of the penalty should be clearly stated in the first-payment letter and in the information booklet provided new borrowers so the mortgagor will be forewarned of the consequences of his tardiness. Others believe that it is best not to mention that a late charge may be imposed, since this information in itself may lead to tardiness, in that the borrower will immediately know that it is not unusual to pay after the penalty date. Those who argue for not informing the mortgagor of the penalty date feel that the immediate jolt of a penalty is a more forceful deterrent to future tardiness than prior knowledge. Most prefer not to incorporate the late charge information in their first-payment letters. Of course, the collection of the first penalty is always waived when the borrower has not been notified in advance. Even when the borrower has been forewarned, it is good business practice to waive the penalty on the first occasion. A letter of explanation, of course, is in order under either circumstance. Technically, late charges should always be assessed automatically; many borrowers would become tardy or delinquent if it were not for the penalty. Therefore, the company's policy should always be firm and consistent.

Late charges are not made to provide additional income, but as a deterrent for delinquency. Mortgage bankers prefer not to have delinquents rather than to collect the penalty, which actually is only a token return for their efforts. Penalty may be waived at the collection supervisor's discretion if he believes that a waiver will be more effective in preventing future delinquencies. If not waived, a late charge can be collected only as an addition to the monthly payment. It is advisable to return payments received after the sixteenth if the penalty is not included, especially if the borrower has been reminded of the penalty charge and collecting the penalty has been an issue before. The payment cannot be shorted by reducing the amount to be applied to one of the reserve accounts. Some servicers accept late payments without the penalty and then ask the borrower to remit the late charge with the next monthly payment, insisting on two penalties if the successive payment is also late. It must be remembered, however, that unpaid penalties cannot be accumulated and collected when the loan is paid in full or when a claim is made for payment to FHA or VA.

A borrower who has been consistently late and who has consequently paid numerous penalties should be reminded that he could have saved, let us say, $30 to $40 during a period of a year had he been prompt during this period. Many a borrower has changed his payment habit when confronted with this information.

SPECIALIZED COLLECTION PRACTICES

The complexity of the collection job cannot be portrayed effectively unless we follow the mental processes of a collector as he faces the wide range of problems borrowers may have; as he evaluates his borrower and his problems; as he selects and then rejects and then selects a new method to reach the person to cure the problem and to find a solution for the problem posed by *that particular borrower*. In the expression *that particular borrower* lies recognition that each borrower is different from every other and that each, although he may suffer the same hardships or misfortunes as other people, reacts and responds differently to the trials of life.

To come too quickly to the decision that a property must be foreclosed because the borrower does not pay or is uncooperative is often a hasty and irresponsible conclusion made by inexperienced collectors. Avoiding foreclosure is basically the true nature of the collection job. Only after every consideration has been extended, and every avenue explored, can the property be foreclosed. However, if there is strong evidence that foreclosure is inevitable, it must be instituted without fail.

The method employed in handling a delinquent borrower is, therefore, contingent on the type of delinquency. While a temporary delinquent may be approached by routine procedures, a chronic delinquent cannot be prodded into paying by the same methods and must be handled strictly by special approaches.

To use the proper collection technique, the collector must first classify the delinquent according to the nature of the borrower and his problems. This classification should then indicate the type of approach that has to be used, since there is nothing more wasteful in collections than working on an incorrect assumption about the nature of the delinquency. Therefore, it is most important to make the proper diagnosis in order to start out *right*.

Classification of Delinquent Borrowers

Follow-up contacts and collection procedures and policies must be based first on the *attitude* of the delinquent borrower and then on the cause of the delinquency. These specifications require careful examination of the borrower's makeup and determination of the exact nature of his problem. These are not easy tasks, but must be performed to find appropriate remedies and solutions. Accordingly, during the first person-to-person contact with a borrower who has missed his payment for the first time or has been late on several occasions, or both, the collector must make every effort to *classify* the borrower as either a temporary delinquent or a chronic delinquent.

Temporary delinquent borrowers   These borrowers usually need attention in the form of automatic follow-ups. If generally cooperative and prodded constantly, they usually pay the overdue installments. Their problems may be caused by one or more of the following: brief illness of borrower or member of his family, change of jobs, strike—if settled within 30 days—temporary overstretching of budget, carelessness and forgetfulness, sale in process, or rental of property.

Chronic delinquent borrowers   These borrowers require careful and constant watching, preferably by the head of the department. Chronic delinquencies may be caused by one or more of the following: continuous illness of borrower or members of his family, unemployment, either seasonal or too frequent, strike, if it lasts beyond 30 days, marital difficulties, business set-back, long-term reduction in income, excessive spending, or default not known to both married partners.

While the different classifications are fairly arbitrary and often must be changed if new evidence is uncovered, they help in selecting different collection methods. When appraising delinquents in any of these classifications, distinction should be drawn between those who have the best intentions but are unable to pay, and those who do not have proper regard for their obligations. Some delinquencies are difficult to classify. The borrower may appear to be a temporary delinquent when he is already chronic; he may be potentially a chronic delinquent, but by a twist of fate be saved from serious problems. If an error in classification is uncovered, immediate reevaluation with resulting reclassification is recommended. Borrowers called into the armed services cannot be classified by any of the above categories; they should be handled in accordance with the provisions of the Soldiers and Sailors Civil Relief Act of 1942.

As there are various types of delinquent borrowers identified as temporary or chronic delinquents, there are various phases that must be distinguished in the development of delinquency. Each borrower first appears as a late payer, rather than as a temporary delinquent, and only later becomes a chronic one. Some delinquencies have attributes of several categories the first time; then again some may become chronic without any of the earlier symptoms. Some slip gradually from one category into the other and often suddenly appear as "cured," only to reappear later and come precipitously close to being a foreclosure case. For each case which falls into a specific category, another lingers for considerable time between categories and cannot be readily classified or cured.

For the purpose of presentation of the trials and tribulations of a collector and of his pursuit of a delinquent account, the follow-up process may be classified in one of three groups: initial person-to-person contact (Size up the delinquent and his problem), follow-up contact (Was original diagnosis correct?), showdown (Is foreclosure inevitable?).

Initial Person-to-Person Contact

At this stage, the job is to size up the delinquent borrower and his problem after routine measures have failed to cure the delinquency. When a borrower, especially one whose name appeared on the delinquency list before, does not respond to a routine reminder, no further notices should be mailed to him. It is inconceivable that he does not know that he owes the monthly payment. The collector should then contact him on the phone at his house or place of business. If these efforts do not succeed, someone should be sent to the house of the mortgagor. One of the first basic collection rules is to *keep after the delinquent until his problem is diagnosed and a collection plan, a "cure," is found.* An on-again, off-again approach may ruin the company's reputation for firm collection policies. Whatever plan or method is decided upon, it must be followed consistently.

A phone call is worth three past due notices. The expense of mailing notices or of making telephone calls is almost identical, but calls yield more satisfactory results. A phone call not only notifies the borrower of the delinquency, but often gains a response or a promise of payment. A phone call impresses the borrower with the urgency of the matter and frequently enables the collector to appraise the situation. In a few minutes, he may be able to discover what type of person he is dealing with, whether he needs help or advice or whether he takes his obligations seriously. If the borrower or his spouse is not at home, he should be called in the evening, or during the day at his place of employment. The possible annoyance of having to talk about his payments in his office or factory may prod him to be more prompt.

The phone call technique requires properly trained collectors and assignment of no more calls to each collector than can be completed promptly. The wrong kind of call may run like this:

Collector: "Mr. Jones, this is Mr. Smith of ABC Mortgage Company calling about your mortgage payment which was due on the first of this month."

Borrower: "The payment will be mailed on the twenty-ninth."

Collector: "Okay. Thank you, Mr. Jones."

They both hang up. Since collection phone calls are both diagnostic and remedial, they should not be rushed. Basically, only four questions need to be asked: "When will the payment be made?" "What will be the source of funds?" "Why wasn't payment made when due?" "What about the future?"

The key to any further collection work and to the procedures to be used depends on the classification into which the collection clerk places the borrower on the basis of his answers to intelligent questioning during this first phone contact; it also depends on the performance the borrower then makes on the promises. If the payment does not come in, further immediate collection action is indicated, which then must be made in accordance with the attitude the borrower displayed when he was first contacted.

Essentials of telephone work

1 *Timing of call* The paramount principle of good collection practice is a *prompt follow-up*. While follow-up dates may be jotted on the calendar and calls made accordingly, it is safer to maintain follow-up records. As pointed out in the section "Follow-up records," it is imperative that the collector call consistently and enforce promises persistently, since the borrower tends to follow the path of least resistance and soon finds that the easiest way to satisfy the collector is to make a promise. The collector's only real counteraction for unfulfilled promises is to call again on the day when payment was promised.

2 *Tone of call* The telephone is a sensitive piece of equipment through which the sentiments and, therefore, the attitude of the caller can be easily conveyed. Accordingly, telephone calls must be made without threatening tones and without sarcasm. Courteously worded expressions get responses in kind, while hostility over the wire meets hostility on the other end.

3 *Attitude of collector* At no time should the collection clerk apologize for having to do his job. This is why initial contact is so important; each contact creates an *impression*. There is no reason to be bashful at this point; nor is there any justification for being rude or harsh. A businesslike attitude must be maintained. A policy of strictness earns more respect than meek letters or cajoling approaches. Never should the collector imply that he is doing the job for the investor and that it is the investor who requires such promptness. Payments must be made because they are due and because the mortgagor agreed to make payments when he signed the note.

4 *Attitude of borrower* It is a good idea to point out to the borrower from time to time, in person or in writing, as well as on the phone, that it is his responsibility to contact or come to the mortgage company when he is unable to make payments. The first sign of a problem or first phone conversation that indicates a problem is the time to point out to the borrower that a discussion initiated by him of the on-coming problems will result in more lenient treatment if such troubles materialize. The borrower's attitude during such crisis is of prime importance. If he is cooperative, even in the face of his pressing problems, he should receive consideration; however, if he disregards his obligations and ignores attempts to help him, he should receive no consideration.

Evaluation A final evaluation can rarely be made following the first real person-to-person contact, especially since such a contact may not always reveal the true nature of the problem. Even the most trained eye and most attuned ear can come up with an incorrect diagnosis, not permanently, of course, but often long enough to allow the case to become hopeless or to give the delinquent borrower time enough to pull out of a long delinquency. While the collector is planning his strategy, some problems work themselves out without his help. Then again, a sudden blow such as a layoff or death in the family may jolt the mortgagor into a lethargy from which he is unable to recover.

1 *Initial diagnosis* After the initial personal contact, the collector performs his first, but often most important, function by asking himself: "What is the real problem?" "Is there hope?" "Can it be worked out?" If a serious problem exists, this is the time when a borrower's predicament should be reviewed with the supervisor to determine the next step. Often it seems best to wait—a difficult assignment for some collectors—yet patience has cured many a delinquency. The pitfalls of deciding too quickly that a borrower is in a hopeless situation and that foreclosure is the only answer must be resisted and, if possible, avoided. Foreclosure usually serves no one. It not only may leave an economic stigma on the mortgagor for life, but also is costly to the mortgage banker, the government, if involved, and the lender. Even the loss of revenue to the servicer should be given some consideration.

Judgment enters the scene in evaluating whether a repayment plan can work. There is no sense trying one, however, if at the time of such decision, the plan seems hopeless; miracles rarely happen. A plan should be established with the mortgagor if it appears to have a reasonable chance of success. If it does not work, then the ultimate decision usually must be made quickly.

2 *Sample analysis of delinquencies* This is the time to return to the classifications of causes and remedies made earlier and to establish, if possible, the various remedies available for the problems indicated, bearing in mind the necessity of reevaluating the problems of the delinquent borrower on a continuing basis. Temporary delinquents do not become chronics overnight; yet the collector's appraisal of his client must be changed when appropriate, and the proposed remedies must then be adjusted accordingly.

3 *Classification of delinquent borrowers* Classifications of delinquent borrowers by causes of delinquency and recommendations how to deal with them are summarized in Exhibit 55. After placing a delinquent borrower in any of these classifications, distinction should still be drawn between those who are victims of problems beyond their control or those who bring about their own downfall by being reckless and delinquency prone. Then again, there are those who have the best intentions and are eager and willing to cooperate, but are unable to pay.

Follow-up Contact

No evaluation is final unless proven so by success. In the course of follow-up contacts with a delinquent, new facts or changes in the borrower's circumstances may come to light that could change the course of collection plans. Each contact must be made by experienced collectors who can seek out information, understand problems and people, and apply the psychology of collections to discover the true cause of the borrower's delinquency. The borrower may conceal his problems if the collector's approach is conducted in a routine manner or is too casual or too severe. Pride often prompts people to hide the clues to their problems. A man may try to cover up his marital problems which cannot be resolved or be reluctant to talk about a relative or child whose incurable sickness may devour his income. The delinquent may be reluctant to reveal the truth, which may be embarrassing, or he may exaggerate his problems to obtain sympathetic treatment. Upon the discovery of such details, the collection effort may be changed.

When the follow-up process shows that the plan arranged to cure the default is not working—because either the analysis was faulty or the borrower will not cooperate—a new approach should be selected quickly. Subsequent follow-ups must be predicated on this decision and must be reasonable and consistent in following a predetermined plan. Never ask more in payments than the delinquent borrower can pay. Excessive demands placed on a cooperative borrower by an overzealous collection clerk often put an account into a truly hopeless category.

If the original appraisal was made without *all* the facts on hand, a personal interview report or an application for forbearance form should be prepared. (See Exhibits 56 and 57). These forms can be completed by going to the home of the borrower or by having both borrowers come to the office for an interview. These reports may be extremely useful in stating all the facts surrounding the case, if foreclosure recommendations are to be made at a later date.

The seriousness of the delinquency is not always measured by the number of months the loan is in arrears. The question more often is: "Is the borrower making an effort to make payments and does he have a reasonable chance of being able to restore the account to a current standing?" An indication might be the degree of regularity with which he sends in money even though the payments remain several months behind.

Sometimes a chronic delinquent may be classified as a *distress case*. In a *distress*

EXHIBIT 55 Summary of collection efforts

A Temporary delinquents

Cause	Findings and analysis	Recommendation
1 Brief illness of borrower or member of family or accident	Ascertain insurance coverage and availability of other help. Determine exact period of disability and cost to borrower. Be alert for exaggeration.	Exercise such patience as is reasonable, especially if borrower has had good payment record.
2 Change of jobs, unemployment of short duration (self-employed, where business is poor because of seasonal changes, normally fall into this category)	Obtain information on the following: When did employment terminate? Is layoff temporary? Is unemployment compensation available? Other source of earnings. Status of family reserves.	If change was initiated by borrower (and even if first paycheck is held back as is customary with some firms) it is worth exercising patience, especially if new job is a better paying one. Similarly, patience is to be exercised if unemployment is involuntary, providing payment record was always good. Be sure that neither reserves nor other sources of income are available.
3 Strike—if settled within 30 days	Ascertain what union will do for worker. Check family reserves.	Seldom should a strike be considered as a valid excuse for slowness. Insist on payment from union assistance funds or ask for payment from family reserves. Unions are presumed to supply strikers with necessities of life which include payment for shelter.
4 Temporary overstretching of budget	Temptation often gets the best of even a conservative soul. It is often the very same person that will correct his own fling.	Give each borrower who is delinquent for this reason one chance to make good. Emphasize priority of protecting family shelter.

Cause	Findings and analysis	Recommendations
5 Carelessness and forgetfulness	Investigate whether carelessness or forgetfulness is genuine.	Watch these accounts carefully since careless people can easily become chronic delinquents.
6 Sale of property in process	Ascertain whether there is a bona fide sale. Obtain projected closing date.	Insist that seller makes payments unless closing statement was issued and sale is imminent. Follow up promptly and follow loan closely.
7 Rental property	Ascertain terms of lease and methods of payment by tenant.	Insist on prompt payment and use every means available to force prompt remittance.

B Chronic delinquents

Cause	Findings and analysis	Recommendations
1 Continuous illness of borrower or member of his family, disability—incurable disease	If mortgagor himself is involved, check whether there is any salary continuance or group insurance plan by employer, any workmen's compensation, or any mortgage payment protection or accident and health insurance in force. Before considering recommendation, review equity position of borrower since it will have a bearing on the length of time that may be allowed for recovery and/or nonpayment. Confirm medical diagnosis with doctor.	If there is no insurance, but there is hope for recovery for the mortgagor or member of family, exercise compassion. If case is hopeless, suggest outside help or less expensive accommodations. If borrower has substantial equity, consider a work-out plan or suggest sale or rental of the property.
2 Unemployment—either seasonal or too frequent	Since unemployment compensation checks go to feed and house the family, it is necessary to assess the use of unemployment compensation, family assets savings, and to check income of other members of family.	Depending on cause of unemployment (industrywide layoff or poor worker) suggest either less expensive accommodations or sale of home while there is equity. Meanwhile, seek housing share of any unemployment allowance.

EXHIBIT 55 Summary of collection efforts (continued)

B Chronic delinquents (continued)

Cause	Findings and analysis	Recommendation
3 Strike of long duration	Place burden on union. Evaluate family assets and press for payments.	Extend indulgence only if borrower is cooperative, has substantial equity, and his payment record was satisfactory prior to the strike. Follow up closely and work out payment plans involving reserve funds of borrower. If strike is too lengthy, suggest sale or rental of property. If case is hopeless, move swiftly to force sale. Alternative: foreclosure.
4 Marital difficulties	After having listened to *both* parties, evaluate claims of reconciliation for your own satisfaction but don't try to act as a judge. If there are small children involved, consider case even more complicated. Let attorney of either or both parties get involved since only one may be concerned with property. Stress personal liability of both borrowers.	
5 Business setback	The man who is in business is one of the most difficult types of delinquencies. A lack of cooperation in midst of his other problems may accelerate his downfall. However, help and patience at the right moment may save borrower and loan.	Obtain all facts and evaluate them carefully. Exercise patience only if cooperation is forthcoming from borrower. Discourage unwarranted optimism. If situation is hopeless, press for sale of property.
6 Long-term reduction in income	A long-term reduction in income can arise in several ways; a permanent physical handicap resulting from an	The objective should be to force the borrower to face reality. While some understanding is appropriate, it should not be admitted to the

injury, loss of wife's income upon birth of a child, a permanent reduction in overtime, a return to normal earnings following a period of high windfall income. The borrower faces a difficult adjustment to a lower standard of living and may be inclined to view his present situation as more temporary than it is.

borrower. Approach the borrower with firmness, with collection on a strict pay-or-else basis. Obtain income and expense statement. The execution of an application for forbearance form under proper guidance may help force recognition of realities. If attitude is good, assist with budgeting.

7 Excessive spending

Excessive spending can be either mild or severe. For couples unsophisticated in family budgeting, excessive spending can creep up without being noticed. However, it can also be compulsive in nature, to satisfy some basic psychological need such as status, security, or recognition. An extreme case of keeping up with the Joneses usually falls into the compulsive category.

Compulsive spending cannot be cured by a collector and leniency only tends to aggravate the problem. There is no substitute for firmness in these cases, with collection on a strict pay-or-else basis. If excessive spending is a result of lack of sophistication, obtain income and expense statement and help with family budgeting. Some young couples need special counseling on priorities.

8 Default not known to *both* married partners

Frequently, the husband leaves all bill paying to his wife and disassociates himself from household responsibilities except for turning all or part of his wages over to his spouse who may be improvident or a poor planner. Plausible excuses may be given by her, with exaggerated stories of hardships. Sometimes gambling is involved. Or it may be the husband who is the guilty party. In either event, the other spouse may be ignorant of the default situation which would not otherwise exist.

Never let a default persist or be repeated without talking personally with both parties. Calling both to the office for a conference (making an evening appointment if necessary) or sending a collector to visit *both* spouses may bring speedy results. It is best not to make it too easy for them.

EXHIBIT 56 *Personal interview report*

PERSONAL INTERVIEW REPORT

Requested by __Samuel Tuttle, ABC Mortgage Co.__ Date __June 8, 1971__ Loan # __G43700__
Investor __Eastern Life Insurance Company__ Investor # __409683__ Type __G.I.__
Mortgagor(s) __William F. and Ethel Walker__
Property Address __9533 Wells Avenue, Chicago, Illinois__
Mailing Address __Same as property__
Phone Number - Home __483-2086__ Phone Number - Business __521-4039__
Mortgagor's Age __35__ Wife's Age __32__ Children's Ages __8, 6, 3__
Reinstatement Amount __$582.40__ Payments @ $ __145.60__ each, including late charge, Total $ __582.40__
Second Mortgagee __National Loan Company, 137 West Fifth Avenue, Chicago, Illinois 420-7986__
(Name, Address and Phone Number)

Property Occupied __Yes__ Owner __Yes__ Tenant _____
Name of Tenant _____
Type and Terms of Lease _____
Amount of Rent $ _____ per _____ Paid to _____
Condition of Property __Average__ Suggested Repairs __Needs painting outside__

Is property listed for sale __No__ By Owner or Realtor _____
Realtor _____
(Name, Address and Phone Number)
Sales Price $ _____ Mortgage Balance $ __14,411.18__ as of __February 1, 1971__

Mortgagor's Employer __Johnson Plumbing Company__
(Name and Address)
Position __Plumber__ Length of Employment __5 Years__ Salary $ __200.00__ per wk/mo
Wife's Employer __Interstate Insurance Company, 9528 Morris Avenue, Chicago, Illinois__
(Name and Address)
Position __Clerk__ Length of Employment __5 Years__ Salary $ __200 - $275__ per wk/mo
Other Reliable Income (Explain) __None__
Total __$1,000 per month approximately__

First Mortgage $ __140.00__ Second Mortgage $ __55.52__ Total $ __195.52__
Food $ __160.00__ Clothing $ __50.00__ Utilities $ __40.00__ Total $ __250.00__
Repairs $ __20.00__ Drug, Medical and Dental $ __25.00__ Total $ __45.00__
Other Monthly Obligations - Amounts, How Paid __Family Finance - $75 mo., Standard Adjustment Bureau -__
__$85 mo., 2nd Credit Card - $60 mo., Doctor - $15 mo., Allen Associates - $140 mo.,__
__Neighborhood Bank - $100 mo., PDQ Department Store - $45 mo.,__ Total $ __Unknown__
__Taylor's Dairy - $10 mo. - (unable to furnish any other information)__
Mortgagor's Explanation of Delinquency _____
__Each borrower blames the other for incurring bills in excess of their combined income.__
__Divorce proceedings have been started.__

Interviewer's Assessment (Sincerity, Cooperation, etc.) _____
__Neither borrower is willing to make further payments.__

The above information has been voluntarily given and is, to the best of our/my knowledge, true and correct.

William F Walker
Ethel Walker

Date: __June 8, 1971__

EXHIBIT 57   *Application for forbearance*

APPLICATION FOR FORBEARANCE

TO   ABC Mortgage Company   Date ___July 1, 1971___
    233 Maple Street
    Chicago, Illinois

We own the property located at ___489 Willow Road, Carrington, Illinois___
on which you hold or service a mortgage loan, Number __F-28476__ . The loan is in default because we have not made the following payments: __April 1, 1971, May 1, 1971, June 1, 1971, and July 1, 1971__

Realizing that it is our responsibility to put your mortgage payments ahead of other debts in order to keep our property and to honor our moral and legal obligations under this loan, we hereby apply for forbearance, promise to faithfully meet the payment schedule offered below, and to pay our future obligations promptly on each due date to the best of our ability.

1. Personal Information: Residence address (if different) ___Same___
   Name of Husband ___Steven A. Long___ Age _33_ Tel. Nos. Home _438-6039_ Business _505-6011_
   Name of Wife ___Susan A. Long___ Age _31_ Other Dependents: No. __3__ Ages _8, 6 & 2_
   Husband's Employer ___Budd Motor Company___ Position _Die Maker_ How Long _2 Yrs._
   Business Address _488 West 6th Avenue, Hometown, Iowa_ Type of Business _Motor Manufacturer_
   Wife's Employer _Conner's Restaurant_ Position _Waitress_ How Long _8 mos._
   Business Address _766 W. Walton St., Carrington, Ill._ Type of Business _Restaurant_
   If not the original signers of mortgage, we acquired the property ___Original Signers___ (approx. date)
   If not occupied by us, property is rented for $ _____ per month to __Occupied by owners__

2. Our Income: **Per Month**
   Husband's current base pay (weekly rate × $\frac{30}{7}$) . . . . $ _680.00_
   Husband's commissions or fees (dependable monthly average) . . . . $ _____
   Husband's overtime or other earnings (dependable monthly average) . . . . $ _120.00_
   Wife's current base pay (weekly rate × $\frac{30}{7}$) . . . . $ _____
   Wife's overtime, commissions, or other earnings (dependable monthly average) . . . (part time) . . . . $ _150.00_
   Our dependable average income per month from all other sources (explain) _____
   _____ $ _____
                                                  Total current monthly income $ _950.00_

3. Our outgo (show average monthly costs):   **Per Month**
   Mortgage payments: First Mortgage $ _165.00_ Other _2nd Mortgage_ $ _50.00_ Total $ _215.00_
   Taxes $ _incl_ (if not included above) Property Insurance $ _incl_ (if not included above) Total $ _____
   Food $ _160.00_ Utilities $ _40.00_ Heat $ _25.00_ Repairs $ _20.00_ Clothing $ _15.00_ Total $ _260.00_
   Medical and Dental $ _20.00_ Income Taxes $ _--_ Personal Insurance $ _20.00_ Total $ _40.00_
   Transportation (incl. auto ins.) $ _27.00_ Other salary ded. $ _____ for _____ Total $ _27.00_
   Loans: Auto (_12_ mos. to go) $ _140.00_ Furniture (_6_ mos. to go) $ _80.00_ Total $ _220.00_
          Other (_12_ mos. to go) for _Loan to consolidate bills_ Total $ _125.00_
   Other expenses (itemize): ___Doctors___ Total $ _50.00_
                                           Total expected monthly outgo $ _937.00_

4. Our other assets and debts not above listed:
   Assets and values of each_____ -- _____
   Purpose of debts and amounts owed _____ -- _____

5. Our mortgage is in default because (explain fully): __Mr. Long was out of work during April and May due to a__
   __strike. During that time he was injured in an automobile accident and was delayed in__
   __returning to work until June 24th.__
   If accident, sickness, or unemployment, we have received or will receive the following compensation or aid: _____
   __An insurance claim has been approved for $5,000.00 and will be received within 60 days.__

6. In view of the above facts, we request your temporary forbearance and offer the following payment schedule, *each payment to be made promptly:* __One payment on the First of each month beginning August 1, 1971, until the__
   __insurance money is received at which time the loan will be brought current.__

We certify that all statements herein are true and are made to induce you to grant us forbearance. We agree that any rights now or hereafter possessed by the mortgage holder shall in no way be prejudiced by accepting payments or granting forbearance. You may request our employers or others to confirm our statements.

Supplemental data should be attached if the foregoing does not supply the mortgage holder with all information which might be helpful in considering this request.

Steven A Long
Signature of Husband

Susan A. Long
Signature of Wife

case, the delinquency is caused by events beyond the borrower's control and may deserve special consideration. Unfortunately, many borrowers in the distress category turn into chronic cases because they give up fighting. The real menace is the chronic delinquent who does not respect his obligation. A distress delinquent would pay if he had the money, but the financially irresponsible borrower is the cross every collection department must bear. Only quick steps toward foreclosure will remedy this situation. Occasionally such shock treatment brings the borrower to his senses and converts him to good payment habits in the future.

While recognition is given to these many distinctions by collectors, in the end there is little difference between the decision to foreclose and the outcome of foreclosure. Court records do not show the compassion the collector exercised during the various stages of delinquency; nor is there a celebration at the investor's office when a particularly troublesome chronic borrower disappears from the books. Once it has been established that the borrower has more obligations than he can handle, that his marital problems are beyond repair, or that he is uncooperative, the pursuit must be forceful and must be followed to the end. Of course, even the distress delinquent cannot be kept on the books indefinitely without an inevitable showdown. Arrangements for forbearance, recommendation for sale of the property, or a deed in lieu of foreclosure must be made, and if those arrangements do not work, foreclosure must follow.

Promises to pay   Collectors rarely, if ever, receive payments in person from their borrowers. Rather, they communicate with borrowers in one manner or another and accept their promises to pay. When a promise is kept, the delinquent payments are received, usually by mail, and the collector is then finished with the case—at least until the next time the borrower becomes delinquent. With repeated experience with this pattern, it is easy for a collector to conclude that his most important job is to elicit a promise to pay from the borrower. In this context, a good promise is defined as one that calls for the greatest amount of money at the earliest date. Actually, nothing could be further from the truth, and every collector must eventually learn this lesson before he can become truly effective.

Mortgage loan payments ordinarily require 25 percent of the borrower's income and, for all practical purposes, a 30-year loan is "forever." These two facts make mortgage loan collections unique with respect to other types of collection work. A collector who is working to obtain such a large share of the family income cannot concentrate his attention on the act of collecting delinquent payments. If he does, he is likely to end up with little more to show for his efforts than more delinquent payments to collect next month. To be effective over the long haul, he must concentrate on diagnosis, analysis, and treatment of the underlying causes of delinquency. With this larger objective in mind, the promise to pay becomes a means to an end rather than an end in itself. This is true whether an individual promise to pay a single delinquent payment or a long-term program to clear a substantial default is considered.

If 25 percent of the borrower's income is required to *maintain* payments, then more than 25 percent is ordinarily required to bring a delinquent account back to a current status. This is an inescapable fact in most cases, and it must provide a framework for evaluating all promises and programs. The collector must require his borrower to do his best, but he should never permit the borrower to make a promise that cannot be kept. To settle for less than the borrower is able to pay is a failure in the basic collection job that lengthens the time required to bring the loan up to date.

Most causes of delinquency are variations on the single theme of poor financial management—i.e., unrealistic, inadequate, or no budgeting. To demand or accept an unrealistic promise to pay merely aggravates the problem. When a promise is accepted, the collection effort stops until the promise date. This takes the pressure off the borrower and enables him to continue to view his situation unrealistically for another several days or perhaps even weeks. When an unrealistic promise is broken, the collector is reluctant to bear down on the borrower because he didn't really expect the promise to be kept in the first place. This, in turn, encourages the borrower to think of promises as flexible rather than absolute. Moreover, one unrealistic promise that is broken tends to be replaced by another unrealistic one. All the while, valuable time is being lost that could be spent working on a solution to the underlying cause of the delinquency. Eventually, accumulated delinquencies may turn what was originally a curable case into a hopeless one.

Promises to pay should always be geared to the borrower's cash flow and his other basic expenses. This affects both amount and timing in relation to paydays. The collector must take into account installment payments on obligations other than the mortgage. If the borrower's income is not sufficient to enable him to cover all necessary expenses and all outstanding obligations, this problem should be dealt with immediately. If it is impossible to end a conversation with a workable promise to pay, the collector should not be reluctant to end it without any promise at all. He should simply instruct the borrower to explore any suggestions he may have given him and to review his situation again. The collector should then reestablish contact in a day or two and start over again.

Special collection aids and techniques In contacting the borrower to obtain payment, many different tools and ideas have been developed and used with varying degrees of success.

1 *Telegram* Quite often a telegram is the best method of eliciting a telephone call from a borrower who has been difficult to contact. The change of pace and implied urgency of a telegram may jolt a serious delinquent out of bad paying habits and induce him to pay. It may also be used as a last resort before foreclosure. A telegram must always be carefully worded since its contents are not hidden from the public. A mortgage company may be subject to a libel suit if telegrams are not worded carefully since the borrower may feel his privacy and character are being attacked if the telegram demands money or implies that he has not kept his word.

2 *Collect telegram* This practice is not recommended for general use, though it may be tried occasionally if other methods have failed. It can, of course, be used

only once on each borrower since, after the first telegram, the borrower will not pay for another.

3 *Special delivery letter* A special delivery letter is a tool of a desperate collector and may be effective especially if it is dispatched late in the evening so it is delivered in the middle of the night. This tends to arouse anger and resentment in the recipient, an approach that is risky and is usually worth taking only as a last resort. While this approach may sound a bit harsh, its impact is usually electrifying. But then, there are delinquent borrowers who respond only to this type of treatment.

4 *Letter by certified mail* Letters containing an ultimatum or returning a check because it was not in accordance with agreed repayment plans should always be sent by certified mail with return receipt requested.

5 *Visit to the mortgagor's home* After visiting the borrower in his home, seeing his home on the inside and outside, the collector can frequently work out a mutually satisfactory payment plan and make a definite recommendation to the lender for a solution. A visit to the mortgagor's home should not be made with the intention of collecting payments. Even if payment is offered, it is a good policy not to accept it. If payment is accepted, the borrower may well assume that whenever the delinquency becomes serious someone will call at his house to collect the payment. The purpose of the personal call is to uncover the cause and nature of the delinquency after other methods of contact with the borrower have failed and to inspect the whole property for possible neglect. A personal visit is also an important means of obtaining basic information required to determine whether the borrower should be given a chance to work himself out of the trouble, or whether the mortgage company should proceed with foreclosure. A borrower's failure to keep his property in good condition will influence the collector's decision very materially. A personal interview report or an application for forbearance form should always be filled out at the time of the visit. Normally, a foreclosure recommendation should not be made without the collector's seeing the property and attempting to talk things over with both mortgagors at the house.

6 *Personal interview in the office* Often it is best to insist that the delinquent mortgagors come to the office to discuss their problems. It is imperative, however, that both the husband and wife come. One without the other may prove to be a time-waster since it may be difficult to get the full story from only one spouse. The most important part of the personal interview is the opportunity it provides for analysis and diagnosis of the borrowers' problems. A personal interview or an application for forbearance report should always be filled out at the time of the interview. It is often best to work out a plan for curing the delinquency within the mortgagors' budget, and then have the arrangement written up and signed by both mortgagors. Care should be exercised, however, that the letter containing the plan bringing the loan current can in no way be construed as a recasting of loan payments or a legal extension of time to pay the obligation.

7 *Collection letter by attorney* It is often a good technique to turn an otherwise unresponsive delinquent account over to an attorney prior to foreclosure, instructing him to write to the delinquent and to add an attorney's fee to the amount already owed by the mortgagor, if such a charge is not usurious in the state in which the account is located. The significance of the letter, plus the additional charge, not only may prompt the delinquent to pay the arrears, but may also press him into better paying habits. Attorneys should not be used routinely as collection agents and a case should not be turned over to an attorney unless all other collection efforts have failed and the mortgagee intends to proceed with foreclosure if the account is not brought current immediately.

8 *Threat of acceleration or foreclosure* No threat should ever be made unless the collector knows that his company and the investor involved will go through with it in case the borrower does not heed the warning. To threaten and not to carry out the threat is poor policy.

Follow-up records If the mortgage company wants its borrowers to develop good payment habits, the company must have good collection habits. If the borrower forgets his promise to pay, the mortgage banker cannot forget that a promise was broken. Accurate records on all payment plans and strict follow-ups are essential. If the mortgage company keeps a close watch over its delinquent accounts, borrowers may become educated to make payments when due and may continue to pay on time long after the collection department has ceased to give them special attention.

Accurate and detailed records must be kept on all types of delinquent accounts. The record-keeping requirement goes beyond keeping a tab on chronic cases; it should also include those who occasionally show up on the past due list on the sixteenth of the month. Information pertaining to a payment plan arranged with the borrower cannot be kept on slips of paper on the desk or filed in the loan jacket. It must be noted in a record which can be referred to at a moment's notice and which is available to all collection employees. The information cannot be kept on the cashier cards or ledger cards either, chiefly because they are not always accessible and usually contain no space for such information.

Follow-up records must be special collection records set up and kept up to date by the person dealing with delinquencies. The follow-up card system described on the succeeding pages is widely used with highly successful results. The adoption of this type of record keeping on a visible card system kept either in a cabinet or a book unit is strongly recommended.

This card system can easily be established for any type of portfolio, whether all payments become due on the first of the month or on various dates. If the former is the case, the card records are kept in order of loan numbers; if the latter, in order of due dates. This system is used by companies servicing a few hundred loans, as well as by companies servicing several thousand loans. It may be especially useful in helping the collection department maintain a close watch on certain special loans which demand careful attention.

Each collection effort made by the collector and the response of the delinquent borrower, if any, are entered on the delinquency card. The notations on these cards automatically create a complete history of each delinquent account. This may then become a permanent record for future use. One routine notice and a few phone calls, the results of which are entered on the mortgagor's delinquency card, comprise an accurate picture of the borrower's delinquency history.

As payments are made and this information appears as a special entry on a data processing report or is obtained by checking daily collections, colored slides can be moved forward progressively on the visible portion of the card to cover up the month paid. Small colored signal cards or tabs can be used in later stages of delinquency to indicate that personal investigation has been made or that foreclosure proceedings have been instituted.

When calling the borrower, the collector establishes a definite date for payment of the delinquency and places a slip of paper in the visible celluloid margin of the card holder, indicating the date on which the payment was promised. These numbers are visible, and each day the collection clerk can tell which payment should be received. If the mortgagor's payments do not arrive on the day specified, e.g., on the twenty-third, the collector should immediately call him, inquiring about the promised payment. Such a close follow-up will impress the borrower; it will make him feel that the mortgage company is really watchful, and discourage him from making promises that he cannot keep. If the collector does not check that particular payment on the twenty-third and does not call the borrower until the twenty-sixth of the month, for instance, the borrower will know that the mortgage company is lax in its follow-up and may try to take advantage of this fact.

The collector should jot down on the follow-up records such irregularities as the borrower's habit of issuing checks which are returned from the bank for non-sufficient funds. This information should also be noted on the cashier card or should be placed on the payment card to warn the cashier not to accept any further personal checks. If the borrower calls to say that he cannot make the payment, this information should be jotted down. That the borrower called on his own volition is an important fact in the delinquency history. It indicates that the borrower cares, that he wants to work himself out of his predicament. A glance at the follow-up records will also enable the collection personnel to determine which loan requires filing a default notice with FHA or VA. When foreclosure is recommended and commenced, a separate card system should be established and maintained.

FHA-VA preliminary reporting requirements Great care should be exercised by the collection personnel to see that the reporting requirements of both FHA and VA are always promptly and accurately met. The follow-up record system if maintained as described earlier aids the staff considerably in not missing the required deadline dates.

1 Reporting requirements: FHA loans The Federal Housing Administration requires that its office having jurisdiction in the area in which the property is located be notified by the mortgagee or servicing agent (not both) on Form

2068, "Home Mortgage Default Notice," when an insured loan has three installments in default. The report may be filed before this date if circumstances
warrant that foreclosure proceedings be instituted at an earlier date—e.g., when
property is abandoned and subject to vandalism. The notice (see Exhibit 58)
is a five-part snap-out form of which the top copy provides instructions for
completion of the form, the first two of the remaining four parts (bottom copy
on Exhibit 58) serve as notices to the FHA field office, the third provides an
office copy for the mortgage banker, and the fourth is designed to be mailed
to the borrower at the mortgage banker's discretion. As indicated on the instructions, reinstatement of the loan, announcement or starting date of foreclosure, and completion of foreclosure must again be reported through this
form. Because of the brevity and simplicity of the form, however, mailing a
copy of this notice to the borrower is not as impressive as those used by the VA
(see Exhibits 59 and 60).

2 Reporting requirements: VA loans   The VA involves itself in delinquencies to a
much greater extent than the FHA, and requires two different reports before
foreclosure may commence. These provide a basis for assistance to lenders in
attempting to cure defaults. These notices are Notice of Default (26-6850)
(Exhibit 59), and Notice of Intention to Foreclosure (26-6851) (Exhibit 60).

VA requires that a Notice of Default be filed with the VA office having jurisdiction in the area in which the property is located within 45 days after a loan
has been delinquent for 60 days (105-day delinquency counting from the due date
of the earliest unpaid installment). A report may be filed earlier if circumstances,
such as abandonment of property, warrant such action. It is often advisable to report
earlier than the above deadlines so that under no circumstances is a deadline overlooked. Filing a notice ahead of schedule is also useful since before the VA gives
permission to foreclose, a representative of the VA may make contact with the
borrower in an effort to induce him to make payments. In some areas the veteran borrower is contacted at this time, while in other areas this is not done until a Notice
of Intention to Foreclose is filed. Although a personal call on the borrower from
representatives of the VA does seem like a duplication of effort, lenders have often
benefited from last-ditch efforts of the VA to save the loan. Sometimes prodding
by governmental authority is more effective than that by private lenders or their
representatives. For these reasons certain investors require, and so instruct their
servicers in their manuals, that Notice of Default be filed 75 days after the first
unpaid installment rather than the specified 105 days.

A Notice of Intention to Foreclose, which is required by VA, may be filed when
a loan has been in default continuously for three months; and it must be filed not
less than 30 days prior to commencement of foreclosure. This notice should be filed
by certified mail and, if a Notice of Default has not been filed earlier, such notice
should also be submitted.

Under unusual circumstances, e.g., if the property is vacant and subject to waste
or if the owner rents the property but does not use the rent money to make the

EXHIBIT 58   FHA home mortgage default notice

FHA FORM NO. 2068 Rev. 4/66

U. S. DEPARTMENT OF HOUSING AND URBAN DEVELOPMENT
FEDERAL HOUSING ADMINISTRATION

HOME MORTGAGE DEFAULT NOTICE

THIS NOTICE MAY BE SUBMITTED BY EITHER THE MORTGAGEE OR ITS SERVICER, BUT NOT BY BOTH.
Detach the first 2 copies and mail to FHA. Retain the third copy for your files. We recommend that the last copy be mailed to the Mortgagor at the same time; however, its use is optional.

1. Send report to the FHA office having jurisdiction on or before the date on which three installments are in default. When an installment due Sept. 1 is not paid by Oct. 1, the mortgage is in default on October 1, and if payment is not made in the meantime, a report is required by Dec. 1.

2. After the first report is filed, reports are not required unless:

   a. The account is reinstated.

   b. Six installments are delinquent in which event a report must be submitted immediately and every 60 days thereafter until the default is corrected.

   c. Foreclosure becomes imminent regardless of the number of installments delinquent.

   d. Foreclosure is started.

   e. Foreclosure is completed.

3. No report is required between the start of foreclosure and the report of completion unless in the meantime the default is cured or the foreclosure is suspended.

FHA FORM NO. 2068 Rev. 4/66

Form Approved Budget Bureau No. 63-R0734

| FHA Case No. 131-049362-203 | U.S. DEPARTMENT OF HOUSING AND URBAN DEVELOPMENT
FEDERAL HOUSING ADMINISTRATION
HOME MORTGAGE DEFAULT NOTICE | Date of this report 12-5-68 |

| Section of National Housing Act 203 | Mortgagee's Reference No. 154801 | Number of payments past due   3 |

Mortgagors
(*Last Name First*) Adams, John V. & Marilyn D.

☐ Mortgage is reinstated and current.

Property
Address   205 Nanti Street

☒ Foreclosure is imminent. ☐ Foreclosure is started.

City
State   Forest Park, Illinois

☐ Foreclosure is completed

┌─────────────────────────────┐
│   │
│   ABC Mortgage Company   │
│   233 Maple Street   │
│   Chicago, Illinois   │
│   │
└─────────────────────────────┘

MORTGAGEE'S NAME, ADDRESS AND ZIP CODE

FIELD OFFICE INSTRUCTION

PLACE OFFICE RECEIVING STAMP ON
REVERSE AND RETURN TO MORTGAGEE
IN WINDOW ENVELOPE.

EXHIBIT 59   VA notice of default

Form Approved
Budget Bureau No. 76-R130.7

VETERANS ADMINISTRATION

NOTICE OF DEFAULT

(SUBMIT ORIGINAL ONLY)

PART I - HOLDER'S NOTICE

TYPE OF LOAN (Check)	VA LOAN NUMBER	HOLDER'S LOAN NUMBER	DATE OF THIS NOTICE
[X] GUARANTEED [ ] INSURED	LH 239736	G-43700	June 15, 1968

TO: (Complete Regional Office Address)

Veterans Administration
Loan Guaranty Division
1310 West Elm St., Chicago, Illinois 60612

FROM: (Holder's name and address)
Eastern Life Insurance Company
By: ABC Mortgage Company, agent
233 Maple St., Chicago, Illinois

DESCRIPTION OF DELINQUENT LOAN

1. NAME AND ADDRESS OF ORIGINAL OBLIGOR(S)	2. NAME AND ADDRESS OF PRESENT OWNER(S)	3. PROPERTY ADDRESS
William F. & Ethel Walker 9533 Wells Avenue Chicago, Illinois	Same	9533 Wells Avenue Chicago, Illinois

4. ORIGINAL OBLIGOR'S SOCIAL SECURITY NUMBER, IF ANY	5A. DATE OF FIRST UNCURED DEFAULT	5B. INSTALLMENT PERIOD (Specify)	6. AMOUNT OF EACH INSTALLMENT	7. OTHER DEFAULT (Specify)
312-15-0761	March 1, 1968	Monthly	$140.00	None

8. INSTALLMENT PAYMENTS NOT MADE / 9. AMOUNT OF DEFAULT

	MONTH	YEAR		MONTH	YEAR		MONTH	YEAR			
	JAN		√	MAY	1968		SEP		PRINCIPAL	$	166.69
	FEB		X	JUN	1968		OCT		INTEREST		251.11
X	MAR	1968		JUL			NOV		Tax & Ins. xxxxx	$	142.20
X	APR	1968		AUG			DEC		10. OUTSTANDING LOAN BALANCE		560.00-Total

10. OUTSTANDING LOAN BALANCE $ 14,411.18

HOLDER'S LOAN SERVICING

11. CONTACT WITH OBLIGOR MADE (Check)	12. LOAN HAS BEEN EXTENDED (Check)	13. DATE OF EXTENSION (Month, day, year)
[X] BY LETTER [X] IN PERSON	[ ] YES [X] NO	

14. IS PROPERTY VACANT?	15. PROPERTY OCCUPIED BY
[ ] YES [X] NO	[X] ORIGINAL BORROWER [ ] TRANSFEREE [ ] TENANT [ ] OTHER (Specify)

16. REASON FOR DEFAULT (Check (√) appropriate reason, or specify other reason in space provided.)

DEATH OF OBLIGOR	X EXTENSIVE OBLIGATIONS	OBLIGOR ENTERED MILITARY SERVICE
ILLNESS OF OBLIGOR	IMPROPER REGARD FOR OBLIGATIONS	
X MARITAL DIFFICULTIES	UNSATISFACTORY PROPERTY OR EQUIP.	
CURTAILMENT OF INCOME	POOR MANAGEMENT	

17. FURTHER INDULGENCE IS WARRANTED:
[ ] YES [ ] NO REMARKS:

18. SUMMARY OF LOAN SERVICING FOLLOWING DEFAULT (Include results of personal contacts and names and addresses of other obligors not shown in items 1 and 2. Continue on reverse, if necessary.)

The borrowers are considering filing bankruptcy due to the number of obligations they have incurred. They are also being divorced. They have informed us that neither of them has any intention of making further payments on the mortgage and they are unable to sell the property or give title to the Veterans Administration because the title is encumbered by a large second mortgage.

OBLIGOR'S MILITARY STATUS

19. OBLIGOR IS NOW ON ACTIVE DUTY OR HAS RECEIVED NOTICE TO REPORT THEREFOR IN 90 DAYS	20. DATE OF ENTRANCE ON MILITARY DUTY	21. MILITARY RANK
[ ] YES [X] NO	22. BRANCH OF SERVICE [ ] ARMY [ ] NAVY [ ] AIR FORCE [ ] MARINE CORPS [ ] COAST GUARD [ ] U.S. PUBLIC HEALTH	

23. MAILING ADDRESS

24. NAME AND TITLE OF AUTHORIZED OFFICIAL (Print or Type)	25. SIGNATURE OF AUTHORIZED OFFICIAL
Samuel Tuttle, Collection Supervisor	*Samuel Tuttle*

VA FORM 26-6850

EXHIBIT 60   VA notice of intention to foreclose

Form Approved
Budget Bureau No. 76-R131.6

VETERANS ADMINISTRATION **NOTICE OF INTENTION TO FORECLOSE** *(Submit original only by Registered Mail)*	DATE OF THIS NOTICE June 15, 1968	LOAN NUMBER LH 239736

PART I—HOLDER'S NOTICE

TO *(Complete Regional Office address)* **Veterans Administration Regional Office, Loan Guaranty Division,** 1310 West Elm Street Chicago, Illinois 60612	DATE OF NOTICE OF DEFAULT June 15, 1968	TYPE OF LOAN *(Check)* [X] GUARANTEED [ ] INSURED
	FROM *(Holder's name and address)* Eastern Life Insurance Company By: ABC Mortgage Company, agent 233 Maple Street Chicago, Illinois	

1. OBLIGOR(S) *(Name and present or last known address)* William F. and Ethel Walker 9533 Wells Avenue Chicago, Illinois	2. LOCATION OF PROPERTY 9533 Wells Avenue Chicago, Illinois

3. DATE OF FIRST UNCURED DEFAULT March 1, 1968	4. POSSIBILITIES OF CURING DEFAULT HAVE BEEN EXHAUSTED *(If "No," explain)* [X] YES [ ] NO

5. FORECLOSURE DATA			6. UNPAID BALANCE OF LOAN, INCLUDING INTEREST	
A. PROCEEDINGS WILL BE INSTITUTED ON OR AFTER *(Date)* July 15, 1968	B. PROCEEDINGS UNDER EMERGENCY PROVISIONS OF SEC. 36.4317(A) WERE INSTITUTED ON *(Date)*	C. ESTIMATED COST OF FORECLOSURE $ --	A. DATE after 2-1-68	B. AMOUNT $14,411.18 + 251.11 int. $ 14,662.29

7. TOTAL AMOUNT OF DELINQUENCY		8. OTHER PRIOR LIENS *(If any)*	
A. PRINCIPAL	$ 166.69	A. SPECIAL ASSESSMENTS *(Include future installments)* $ None	B. PAST DUE GROUND RENTS $ None
B. INTEREST	251.11	C. DELINQUENT TAXES $ None	D. OTHER *(Specify)* $ None
C. ~~XXXXXX XXXXXXXXXX~~ Tax & Ins.	142.20	9. VOLUNTARY DEED DATA	
		A. IS DEED IN LIEU OF FORECLOSURE OBTAINABLE? [ ] YES [X] NO *(If "Yes," fill in Item B)*	B. WOULD IT BE LEGALLY FEASIBLE TO ACCEPT DEED? [ ] YES [ ] NO
D. TOTAL DELINQUENCY	$ 560.00		

10. SUMMARY OF LOAN SERVICING SINCE NOTICE OF DEFAULT WAS GIVEN
The borrowers are considering filing bankruptcy due to the number of obligations they have incurred. They are also being divorced. They have informed us that neither of them has any intention of making further payments on the mortgage and they are unable to sell the property or give title to the Veterans Administration because the title is encumbered by a large second mortgage.

11. OCCUPANCY DATA			
A. IS PROPERTY OCCUPIED? [X] YES [ ] NO	B. OCCUPANT IS *(Check)* [X] ORIGINAL BORROWER [ ] TRANSFEREE [ ] TENANT [ ] OTHER *(Specify)*		C. RENTAL RATE *(Month, year, etc.)* $ PER
	D. IF VACANT, KEYS TO PROPERTY MAY BE OBTAINED FROM:		
E. NAME OF OCCUPANT *(If other than original borrower)*	F. IF VACANT, HAVE STEPS BEEN TAKEN TO PROTECT PROPERTY? [ ] YES [ ] NO		G. DATE TO WHICH RENT IS PAID
			H. DATE LEASE EXPIRES

12. NAME AND TITLE OF AUTHORIZED OFFICIAL *(Type or print)* Samuel Tuttle, Collection Supervisor	13. SIGNATURE OF AUTHORIZED OFFICIAL *Samuel Tuttle*

VA FORM 26-6851

required mortgage payments, the servicing agent may file both notices immediately. However, no step which is not in accordance with general requirements should be taken without special permission by the local VA office.

Sending the delinquent borrower a copy of VA's Notice of Default or Notice of Intention to Foreclose, which requires a narrative description of the servicing efforts and the results of various contacts, or both, is an excellent means of jolting him to the reality of an impending disaster. A borrower normally does not like to see the recital of his unkept promises on paper, and, therefore, such prompting occasionally causes borrowers to bring their loans current. Nevertheless, VA prefers to have a Notice of Intention to Foreclose filed only when the mortgagee intends to terminate the loan. In other words, the VA prefers not to have the form used merely as a collection device.

Copies of reports also serve as a summary of the collection efforts and provide a history of the case. These may also be used to substantiate foreclosure recommendations. Investors often require that copies of reports to FHA or VA be enclosed with month-end reports to bring them up-to-date on each seriously delinquent case.

Although filing a Notice of Intention to Foreclose with the VA earlier than prescribed may bring a rejection by the VA, filing any of the reports later than prescribed by the VA does not invalidate the VA guaranty. A loss or other deterioration that may have taken place between the time the report was due and the time it was actually filed does reduce the claim to be paid by the amount of loss sustained.

It is often advisable, when a property has changed hands, to contact the original mortgagor who was not released from the liability or to send him a copy of the required notice. He may reenter the picture either to help out the current owner or to repurchase the property, or sometimes just to provide additional pressure on the borrower since the foreclosure will also be a blot on his record.

The Veterans Administration makes every effort to collect any amount it has paid to the mortgage holder in a claim under loan guaranty from all parties who are personally liable for repayment of the related VA loan, including an original veteran borrower who has sold the property securing his loan. These efforts may include legal action to enforce collection of deficiency judgment and/or withholding VA benefits for which the veteran may be, or may become, eligible in the future.

Showdown with Delinquent Borrower
(Is Foreclosure and/or Acceleration Inevitable?)

If it looks as though there is little or no hope of bringing the loan up-to-date by any method other than a drastic jolt, refusing a single or two monthly payments, when two or three installments are due, is often quite effective. The borrower's payments should be returned with a statement similar to the following: "Two payments are now necessary to bring your loan current and forestall legal action." This usually makes the borrower realize the seriousness of the situation and forces him to make a real effort to remit the overdue payments.

If everything else has failed, it is the best policy to send the mortgagor a letter by certified mail, return receipt requested, recommending that he select one of three alternatives: (1) pay up arrears within a specified short period of time, (2) refinance the loan with another lender, or (3) sell the property and obtain less expensive accommodations.

This letter should be concluded with a statement that unless the mortgagor chooses one of the three suggestions, acceleration of maturity and/or foreclosure proceedings will be instituted or recommended if the investor involved has not given the servicer authority to foreclose. The letter demanding payment or issuing an ultimatum should be signed by a person other than the one who has contacted the borrower in the past, perhaps by the loan administrator or the president of the company. The mortgage banker must be ready to carry out his threat if the borrower does not send in the requested payments.

Before considering foreclosure or acceleration, it must be remembered that a person who has an investment in his home will struggle to keep it. Therefore, it is suggested that the payment record and the loan file again be carefully scrutinized at this point. Every aspect of the loan, the borrower, and his equity must be properly reevaluated and the property reappraised before foreclosure or acceleration can be recommended.

CONSIDERATIONS RELATIVE TO TERMINATION OF LOAN[1]

The intricate nature of the foreclosure laws affecting mortgage investments in every state, as well as the rules and regulations of FHA and VA, make it quite obvious that termination of loans is not a simple task. It is also abundantly clear that proper execution of this task places a heavy burden of responsibility on the mortgage banker, which he can discharge only with a competent staff versed in the technical and legal details and requirements of governmental regulations and foreclosure laws.

To change the perspective for a moment, the difficulties of complying with the many provisions of various state foreclosure laws are multiplied many times for an investor making loans in all fifty states. This is one of the prime reasons why the mortgage banker's job is so valuable to his investors in foreclosure cases. In effect, the mortgage banker becomes a specialist for his investors in handling foreclosures.

When the loan reaches the pretermination phase, when foreclosure or its alternatives are to be weighed and considered, the mortgage banker no longer plays the dual role of trying to help the borrower and keeping his investor apprised both of his actions and of the borrower's progress toward recovery. Instead, the mortgage banker becomes advisory counsel to his investor, trying to help him recover all or most of his investment. Of course, in this process he does not foresake the delinquent borrower, but his concern for his investor now becomes greater than that for the borrower.

---

[1] Also see "FHA-VA Foreclosure and Claim Procedures," (Exhibit A-9).

Acceleration or Foreclosure Action

When the showdown with the delinquent borrower does not produce the desired results and when further delay would only postpone the inevitable, foreclosure or its alternatives must be considered. Failure to initiate foreclosure when such action is appropriate is a disservice to the investor and often to the mortgagor. Conversely, hasty foreclosure decisions can be equally harmful. They hurt the mortgagor and adversely affect the public image of both servicer and lender.

Considerations   There are several prerequisites to commencement of foreclosure. These include filing required reports, if FHA and VA loans are involved, a complete re-review of the file, inspection and reappraisal of the property, establishing its current market value, personal interview with the mortgagors and the evaluation of the possible outcome of the foreclosure action, its possible hazards, and its results in terms of cash return to the lender.

The investor's return varies in infinite variety according to the following conditions:

1   Unpaid balance of loan (including interest, tax arrears)
2   Value of property
3   Type of loan
4   Foreclosure laws of the state, specifically whether foreclosure will be under power of sale provisions where deed may pass within 60 days, judicial action with a short or a long redemption period, and whether the redemption period begins before or after sale
5   Cost and length of foreclosure and costs of property rehabilitation under conventional loans
6   Extent of reimbursement of costs by FHA or VA

Of course, it may be advantageous for the investor to acquire the property, rehabilitate it if necessary, and sell it to recover his investment. Servicers may be of great help to their investors in this respect, especially if they have a real estate or property management department.

In many instances, acceleration of maturity is a good alternative to foreclosure. It involves election by the mortgagee to call or terminate the loan by insisting that the entire debt be paid. No prior approval of either FHA or VA is required for acceleration of maturity. VA, however, is of the opinion that no loan should be accelerated until the loan has been serviced properly and it is determined that the security should be liquidated.

Recommendation to foreclose or to accelerate   Most investors entrust the handling of the entire foreclosure proceedings and filing of FHA or VA claims to those correspondents who have both expressed willingness to do the job and shown the ability to handle it. Whether the investor sends the mortgage documents to the servicer for referral to his attorney or directly to an attorney of the investor's choice, a recommendation to foreclose must be prepared. The text of the servicer's recommendation, if done properly, not only depicts the mortgagor's problems, but also reflects favorably on the servicer's ability to assemble the facts and make a proper evaluation.

Before the servicer can decide to recommend foreclosure, all basic facts must be considered and evaluated. This evaluation may be made by the loan administrator or servicing manager in consultation with the head of the collection department or by a committee which includes the loan administrator and/or servicing manager and/or head of the residential loan production department. The evaluation requires that the following facts be ascertained, checked, and taken into consideration:

1 Original sales price, down payment, and loan amount
2 Present market value of property; unpaid balance of loan and potential equity of owner
3 Condition of property on basis of latest report and cost of repairs, if conventional loan is involved
4 Payment record of borrower throughout the term of the loan
5 Financial position of delinquent
6 Attitude of borrower
7 Anticipated outcome of foreclosure as far as investor's return of investment is concerned
8 Use of special forbearance or modification of terms
9 Use of a deed in lieu of foreclosure

The residential foreclosure recommendation form (Exhibit 61), developed by the Loan Administration Committee of the Mortgage Bankers Association of America and approved by most investors as an accepted means of recommending foreclosures, contains most of the information required to substantiate the need for legal action. Copies of various forms which have been filed (FHA or VA–Notice of Default, Notice of Intention to Foreclose) normally round out the story. It is often advisable, but not absolutely essential, to write a brief letter accompanying this recommendation. A letter can generally explain what final act of the mortgagor, or what overall consideration other than what is self-evident from the completed form, prompted the final decision.

At no time should the servicer in his recommendation express any doubt about the correctness of his views, present the investor with alternatives, or ask for his evaluation and decision. *It is the servicer's job to make the foreclosure recommendation.* He is the only one who knows both the borrower and his problems and the location and property intimately; only he knows what is the best course to take. At this crucial point, vacillating collection policies and unsure recommendations do not enhance the reputation and stature of the mortgage banker.

The Nature of Foreclosure

For all practical purposes, foreclosure may be described as the acquisition of property by a mortgagee from the owner by legal means to satisfy a debt on which the required payments were not made. The manner in which this may be accomplished differs

EXHIBIT 61   *Residential foreclosure recommendation*

DATE April 4, 1971

RESIDENTIAL
FORECLOSURE RECOMMENDATION

To: Eastern Life Insurance Company
_____Investor_____

Re:
303069   13-133023-203 F31613
Investor's No. FHA/VA No. Servicer's

From: ABC Mortgage Company
_____Servicer_____

Type of Loan ( ) VA (x) FHA ( ) Conv.

First Unpaid Installment:
Due Date 12-1-67   Amount $ 135.00

233 Maple Street, Chicago, Illinois
_____Servicer's Address_____

Balance: $ 14,700.00 $ 11,748.29
_____(Original)_____(Present)
Date of Mtge. 8-7-61 Term 25yrs Rate 5¼

Mortgagor: John Windham and Mary Windham
_____Name_____

Escrow:
A. Balance on hand $ 475.02

Property Address: 239 Elm Street

B. Hazard Ins. paid to 8-31-71
   Annual Premium $ 47.00
C. Taxes & Liens next due 6-1-71 &
Mailing Address: (If other than above)   9-1-71   Amt. $ 440.30 (1969 bill)
D. MIP paid to 10-1-70
   Amount next due $ 58.32

1. Record of Payments:

   Prompt ( )   Good ( )   Fair ( )   Chronically Late (x)

2. Personal Contacts: (Number & Dates)   (If none made, reason therefor)
   6-28-69, 2-15-70, 12-2-70

3. Family's obligations other than Mortgage Contract:
   Statewide Consolidation - $2,300 balance   Standard Fuel - $230 balance
   Family Loan - $1,500 balance   Second Credit Card - $900 balance
   General Loan - $876   Doctor - $130 balance

4. Family's Income:
   (a) Main Income: Source or Employment Place Southside Finance Company
       Length of Time 5 Years   Amount per Month $ 800.00
   (b) Supplemental Income: Which Family Members None
       Source (If employment, place & amount)

   (c) Total Monthly Income Available $ 800

5. Occupancy:
   (a) Is property or any part thereof rented? No   If so:
       1. Monthly Rental $
       2. Rental Terms
       3. Name of Tenants
   (b) Is property vacant?   No   If so:
       1. Has property been secured?   Winterized?
       2. Hazard Insurance Company Notified?

6. Condition of Property:
   (a) Exterior and Grounds: Good ( )   **Average** (x)   Poor ( )
   (b) Interior: Good ( )   Average (x)   Poor ( )
   (c) Estimated Cost of Repairs for Purpose of Resale $ 200.00
   (d) Opinion of Current Market Value $ 15,500

7. Has sale been suggested? Yes
   Have reasonable sale attempts been made by owner?   No

8. Is Owner entitled to relief under Soldier's or Sailor's Relief
   Act? No

9. Default Notices: VA Default Form 4-6850 Filed
                                              (date)
                    VA Intent to Foreclose 4-6851 Filed
                                              (date)
                    FHA Default Form 2068 Filed   3-5-71
                                              (date)

10. Servicer's Reasons for Recommending Foreclosure:
    The mortgagor has been given every opportunity to work himself out of his
    financial predicament. He and his wife are habitual spenders beyond their
    joint incomes.

11. Additional Remarks:

                    ABC MORTGAGE COMPANY

               By_____
                          (Title)

327

from state to state. The difference is not only in the manner in which foreclosure is consummated, but also according to the time it takes to divest a defaulted borrower of his title to the property. Generally, there are two main types of foreclosures and a great number of variations on either type: (1) foreclosure by means of judicial proceedings and (2) foreclosure by means of a power of sale provision incorporated in the security instrument. At this writing, almost half the states employ judicial proceedings, with most of the remainder using a power of sale procedure. A few states use procedures that do not fit into either major group.

The purpose of this presentation is to depict with a broad sweep the nature and types of foreclosures and the recovery of investments by mortgagees under the provisions of the FHA insurance or VA guaranty programs. Space does not permit a complete and detailed discussion of the various types of foreclosure proceedings nor all the variations that apply when filing a claim with either FHA or VA.

A judicial foreclosure calls for the institution of legal proceedings by the owner of the mortgage in civil court. Legal action usually is carried out in three basic steps: filing a complaint, entry of a decree or judgment, and foreclosure sale by public auction.

In almost every case, the investor is the only bidder at the foreclosure sale. As a result, the investor usually acquires title to the foreclosed property. In some states, the investor gets marketable title at the foreclosure sale. In other states, the mortgagor has a right to redeem his property by repurchasing it within a specified time after the foreclosure sale. Six months and twelve months are the most common redemption periods. In redemption states, the mortgagee does not acquire marketable title until after the redemption period has expired.

With only a few exceptions where foreclosure is identified either as a "strict" foreclosure or as a foreclosure "by entry and possession," foreclosure in most other states is carried out by exercising a power of sale provision incorporated in the mortgage instrument. The power of sale enables the mortgagee to sell the property without court action. In some states, such sale can be held at the courthouse or at the mortgaged premises 30 days after proceedings are started. As in the case of states with judicial proceedings, some states with power of sale provisions have redemption periods while others do not. Foreclosure by exercise of power of sale is ordinarily less expensive and more expeditious than a judicial foreclosure from the point of view of acquiring the property quickly in order to protect the mortgagee's interest.

After completion of the foreclosure sale under either of the proceedings and expiration of the redemption period where applicable, the property belongs to the mortgagee. The mortgagee is then free to do what he wants with the property, presumably either to retain it as an investment or to dispose of it by sale. These are the only choices available to the mortgagee on a conventional loan. In the case of VA and FHA loans, however, the mortgagee has additional alternatives.

Alternatives under FHA Under the FHA program, if a default occurs, the lender, after acquiring title and custody of the property through foreclosure or by means of voluntary conveyance, has a choice either of retaining the property and selling it, in which case he takes any profit or loss resulting from the sale, or of turning both title and custody of the property over to the FHA. If the investor elects to convey the property to FHA and file a claim for FHA insurance benefits, he receives cash or long-term debentures from the FHA (cash was being paid at the time this book was written) for the unpaid balance of the loan plus reimbursement for the mortgagee's advances for taxes, hazard insurance, FHA mortgage insurance premiums, and approximately two-thirds of the cost incurred in connection with foreclosure and acquisition of the property.

Interest on a foreclosed mortgage is not calculated in the normal manner on the unpaid balance of the loan. If debentures are used for payment by FHA, interest is paid by back-dating the debentures to a date one month after the due date of the earliest unpaid installment on the loan. If cash is paid, a similar method is employed and interest is computed at the appropriate debenture rate, which is considerably lower than mortgage interest rates. Where there has been a default under a forbearance agreement entered into pursuant to FHA regulations, interest at the mortgage rate may be paid from the date of the original default to the date of foreclosure.

Alternatives under VA   The Veterans Administration's concept of handling defaulted mortgages differs from that of FHA. VA does not insure the mortgagee against default; it guarantees the lender against loss in excess of 60 percent of the original amount of the loan up to a maximum of $12,500. As the loan is amortized, the dollar amount of the guaranty is reduced while the percentage remains constant. Usually, VA acquires the property from the mortgagee by purchase, paying the mortgagee's claim for the balance of the debt, including foreclosure expenses. Attorney's fees, however, may not exceed VA limitations. Under the VA program, the mortgagee foreclosing a loan actually has three choices. He may retain the property after the foreclosure sale and not file a claim for the guaranty. Or, he may file a claim and simultaneously exercise one of two options: (1) transfer title and custody of the property to VA in exchange for full payment of the indebtedness, or (2) retain the property and file a claim for the difference between the upset price or the successful bid, whichever is greater, and the total indebtedness. Although VA always pays in cash, its right to pay the guaranty and abandon the property to the mortgagee has been exercised in rare instances.

Investors generally prefer to transfer properties to VA. This eliminates the need for an investor making loans on a nationwide basis to maintain real estate sales facilities in every location where it lends money. However, for the mortgagee to be paid in full and for VA to take title and custody of the property, the mortgagee must follow all VA's requirements in connection with the conduct of foreclosure. While FHA does not involve itself in foreclosure proceedings, VA is very much involved in every step of the foreclosure process, even to the point of specifying an amount to be credited to the debt incident to loan termination, which in effect influences the amount of the investor's bid at the foreclosure sale.

Comparison of FHA and VA practices   The significant difference between the payment by FHA and by VA is that VA pays soon after the foreclosure sale, but FHA pays only after the investor has conveyed marketable title to the property to FHA. In states where there is a redemption period following the sale, payment may be delayed for a considerable time.

Although both FHA and VA pay in cash FHA (at the time this book was written), retains the option to pay claims in cash or in long-term debentures. Should FHA return to payment of its claims in debentures, the investor who receives them would have to hold such debentures until they are called or mature, or, because the debentures carry an interest rate considerably lower than those prevailing in the open market at the time the loan was made, sell them at a loss. Debentures may be used by mortgagees to pay mortgage insurance premiums on other home loans; however, the supply of debentures at any one time may exceed the amounts needed for premium payment.

Generally, FHA accepts the property only when it is vacant and undamaged by fire, flood, earthquake, or tornado, which add to the mortgagee's risks. VA does not impose these requirements. In some states, FHA's payment of two-thirds of the foreclosure expenses, including attorneys' fees, is more favorable to the mortgagee than VA's payment for all reasonable expenses, but only $250 for attorneys' fees.

Alternatives to Foreclosure

Before foreclosure action is recommended and approved, consideration must be given once again to the several alternatives available to the mortgagee to avoid foreclosure. The alternatives to foreclosure that should be considered include: special forbearance, modification or extension, assignment of mortgage to FHA and VA, military forbearance under Soldiers and Sailors Relief Act, and voluntary conveyance or deed in lieu of foreclosure.

Special forbearance   Forbearance is granted by a collector every time he agrees to accept a partial payment plan to assist the mortgagor in clearing a substantial default in a reasonable period of time. *Special forbearance*, however, connotes a written agreement of longer duration available primarily for FHA loans and usually only entered into with the mortgagor if the default was caused by death in the family, illness, curtailment of income, or damage to the property against which the mortgagor was either not insured or not adequately insured. The FHA special forbearance agreement provides for a reduction in, or suspension of, regular monthly payments for a fixed period of time not to exceed 18 months, after which regular monthly payments must be resumed. FHA's prior approval is not needed for the mortgagee to enter into such an agreement with the mortgagor unless the period of forbearance is longer than 18 months. If a mortgagor is unable to comply with the terms of such agreement, the local FHA insuring office may approve a request to extend the agreement or to assign the loan to the FHA. The terms of the loan may be modified or foreclosure proceedings may be instituted by the mortgagee. FHA encourages investors to grant special forbearance agreements to deserving borrowers if it produces a way by which foreclosure may be avoided. A special forbearance agreement should never be granted purely to delay foreclosure. By approving special forbearance agreements, FHA agrees, in the event of foreclosure, to include in its settlement all accrued, unpaid mortgage interest from the date of the forbearance agreement to the date on which foreclosure was actually started. In this way, it encourages investors to grant special forbearance agreements.

The VA also permits and encourages unusual forbearance in proper cases. The mortgage holder may agree to accept partial payment or no payments at all for a reasonable period on a VA loan, where the cause of the default is temporary in nature. Although such temporary forbearance does not require VA prior approval, it should be reported to VA on the Notice of Default or subsequent to the notice.

Modification or extension   Modification or extension in a legal sense involves any change in the terms of the mortgage after a loan has already been in force. This might include an extension of the maturity date, a reduction of mortgage payments, or a change in the agreed interest rate. For instance, if the borrower's equity is adequate and the property reflects a pride of ownership, under special circumstances such as a serious illness of the borrower or a member of his family, it may be prudent to extend the maturity date and recast the loan over a longer term, thereby reducing the required monthly payments.

FHA has authorized mortgagees to modify loans by reamortizing the existing principal indebtedness over a longer term, provided that the loans are in default due to circumstances beyond the mortgagor's control. The term of the mortgage may be extended up to 10 years without prior FHA approval, and in unusual circumstances FHA may approve longer extensions. A copy of the modification instrument must accompany any subsequent claim for insurance benefits.

VA permits the investor to extend or reamortize a loan. Any agreement entered into between the investor and the borrower to extend or reamortize the loan should be in writing and signed by the parties involved. Accrued unpaid interest may be included in the loan indebtedness. Likewise, it is permissible to include any deficit in the tax and insurance account in the indebtedness to be extended or reamortized in order to bring the tax and insurance account up to the level where it would have been had the borrower paid the required installments on time. It is not necessary for VA to approve an extension or reamortization agreement in cases in which the loan is in default provided (1) that no obligor is released from personal liability and (2) that at least 80 percent of the balance extended on a VA home loan will be amortized within 30 years. If these two requirements are not met, the investor should submit the facts of the case to VA and obtain its approval of the modification before entering into the agreement. VA does require that it be advised of the terms of the agreement, preferably with a copy of the extension or reamortization agreement.

In all instances, of course, the investor must concur with the modification plan. It may be worthwhile to point out the difference between special forbearance and modification. Under the terms of a special forbearance agreement, the original terms of the mortgage are not changed, as the mortgagor is expected to make up the delinquent payments within a specified time and then make payments as originally scheduled. Under the terms of the modification agreement, the terms of the loan are modified or extended and the amount of the monthly payment is permanently reduced or the period over which the loan must be repaid is extended. Under the terms of a modification or extension agreement on a conventional loan, the monthly payments may be reduced without extending the maturity date also; in this case, at the time when the loan reaches the maturity date a lump sum (balloon) payment becomes due.

FHA also permits the reapplication of prepayments, a device that should also be considered when payment problems arise, provided the mortgagor at one time made principal prepayments. Riding prepayments involves the suspension of principal payments to the extent of prepayments previously made. Monthly payments for mortgage insurance may not be suspended and must be paid in accordance with the amortization schedule. VA regulations also permit, and VA encourages, the reapplication of prepayments to take care of delinquent installments.

Assignment of mortgage to FHA or VA In the event an investor is unwilling to grant further leniency or to consider a special forbearance agreement, the district director of FHA, at his discretion, may accept an assignment of the mortgage to FHA to avoid foreclosure. In this case, FHA first investigates the validity and need of its accepting an assignment and, if approved, settles with the investor on a slightly different basis than if the loan had been foreclosed. FHA then works out its own payment plan with the mortgagor. The mortgagor makes his payments to the FHA and the servicer is relieved of his servicing responsibilities for the loan. While assignment of the mortgage to FHA is rare, it is a possible solution for an extremely complex delinquency when the investor is no longer willing to grant leniency.

VA also has authority to purchase a defaulted loan from an investor for the amount due on the loan to avoid foreclosure. Purchases of defaulted loans by VA are unusual because investors generally are willing to grant reasonable forbearance, or even to extend or reamortize the loan to avoid foreclosure in proper cases.

Military forbearance under Soldiers and Sailors Relief Act The Soldiers and Sailors Relief Act protects those mortgagors who are unable to make regular or monthly payments when called into the service. It does not apply to mortgagors who were in one of the military services when their mortgages were made. Both the VA and FHA have special assistance programs to enable the servicer to work out a suitable payment plan either during the borrower's military service or after its completion. Similarly, investors normally are willing to modify the loan, extend its maturity, or do whatever possible to enable the returning servicemen to safeguard their home-ownership. At the conclusion of military service, however, both FHA and VA expect the mortgagor to resume regular monthly payments and pay off the debt by means of a special forbearance or a modification agreement.

Granting relief during service is not automatic; it must be necessary. Many times entering the service does not create a financial hardship. Moreover, military forbearance does not reduce the debt in any way. In many instances, it is to the mortgagor's advantage—a recommendation that should be made to him—to rent the property and have his wife move to a less expensive accommodation in order to avoid a big build-up of accumulated arrearages that must be paid when he returns to civilian life.

Voluntary conveyance or deed in lieu of foreclosure If the borrower is unable to make satisfactory arrangements to bring his loan current, it is often both fair and economical for both parties, borrower and investor alike, to terminate the mortgage obligation by having the investor accept title to the property in exchange for cancellation of the mortgage debt. Both FHA and VA encourage this practice and are willing to accept a deed if offered to them by the borrower through the mortgagee, and to pay a claim as if the property had been acquired through foreclosure. Acceptance of a voluntary conveyance considerably reduces the amount of work that would be required by foreclosure and the expense that would have to be borne by the borrower, the governmental agency, as well as the investor.

The practice of accepting a deed in lieu of foreclosure is of particular advantage to the lender in states where foreclosure involves lengthy and expensive proceedings, including a long redemption period. The ability to obtain and transfer title to FHA quickly reduces the investor's risk of holding such property in vacant condition or in a condition potentially detrimental to its owner. A deed in lieu of foreclosure also partly eliminates any blot on the mortgagor's record, a fact which may be used to persuade the borrower to relinquish title to the property when foreclosure is imminent.

Before acceptance of a deed in lieu of foreclosure is seriously considered, it is advisable to make a preliminary title search, notwithstanding the assurances of the borrowers who claim no encumbrances. If title is clear, this should be a green light to go ahead, although blots on the title may still appear until the very last minute.

If judgments against the borrower or liens against the property exist, a deed in lieu cannot be accepted. However, if judgments or liens are small, a deed in lieu should still be considered since FHA and, to a more limited extent VA, prefer to permit a small lien to be included in the claim than to pay extensive legal costs and then wait for termination of redemption periods before the property can be acquired. The mortgage banker's collection team should not suggest, solicit, or accept voluntary conveyance if the borrower has substantial equity. If it does, it may be accused of taking advantage of a desperate and possibly uninformed borrower.

Properties owned in the course of conducting a regular real estate or related business cannot be voluntarily conveyed to FHA or VA.

In the case of an FHA loan, it is not necessary to obtain FHA's approval prior to accepting a deed in lieu of foreclosure unless unusual circumstances are involved. FHA Form 2068 must be filed to indicate acceptance of the deed and the appropriate time when the property will be conveyed to FHA. Principally, the following conditions must be met and/or documents executed:

1 The mortgage must be in default at the time the deed is executed and delivered.
2 The mortgage note must be canceled and surrendered to the mortgagor and the mortgage of record must be satisfied as consideration for the conveyance.

3 The borrower must execute an estoppel agreement by which he acknowledges the mortgage note and his default thereon and states that conveyance of title is made by him voluntarily.
4 Mortgagee must transfer good, marketable title to the Secretary of Housing and Urban Development.
5 Property must be vacant and the key must be forwarded to the FHA insuring office with a copy of the appropriate claim form.

In the case of a VA loan, a deed in lieu of foreclosure cannot be considered without VA's prior approval. The submission of a request to the VA for such consideration must be accompanied by a Notice of Default and a Notice of Intention to Foreclose. The Veterans Administration then inspects the property, talks to the mortgagors, and examines the mortgagors' equity position. VA does not consent to the acceptance of a deed in lieu of foreclosure unless it is in the government's interest to do so. If the decision is favorable, a deed in lieu of foreclosure arrangement may be consummated and the VA pays the claim just as if a foreclosure had been consummated. The acceptance of a deed in lieu of foreclosure by an investor without the consent of the VA could result in a denial of the guaranty.

EXECUTION OF FORECLOSURE TASK

The Servicer's Responsibility during Foreclosure

The foreclosure task begins with a review of the collection department's activity on delinquent loans; it includes the responsibility of seeing that the various reports required under FHA and VA regulations are promptly filed, and it ultimately involves the formulation of recommendations to foreclose or accept a deed in lieu of foreclosure. It is now assumed that the servicer has properly evaluated the delinquent account, considered and presumably explored the possibilities of saving the loan from foreclosure by means of one of the alternatives available, and made his recommendations to the investor. The investor now forwards the mortgage documents to the servicer with instructions to foreclose. More often than not, of course, the investor does not attempt to analyze his correspondent's recommendation, but accepts it. In the past the servicer's responsibilities may have ceased at this point, but today they continue even if the attorney handling the foreclosure is employed by the lender.

Most investors prefer to have their correspondents work in collaboration with attorneys in handling all legal details and in fulfilling FHA and VA requirements. The responsibility for overall supervision is usually placed with the servicer. Although both FHA and VA will permit supplemental filings and pay claims for expenses that were not listed originally, frequent supplemental filings and other efforts to recover or write off expenses that could have been included in the claim do not speak well of the servicer's handling of the case. Failure to follow VA's instructions in bidding an upset price, for instance, can cause a loss to the mortgagee or the servicer if the latter is at fault.

Claim forms can either be executed by the servicer as agent for the investor, or may be prepared by the servicer and sent for signature to the investor, who then rechecks all the figures, signs the claims, and sends them directly to FHA or VA.

During foreclosure proceedings, tax or insurance bills may have to be paid and the attorneys handling the case may incur additional title and other expenses. While it may be practical to ask the investor for reimbursement of each expenditure, the cost of handling individual items may be greater than the cost of advancing funds to meet these expenditures as they occur and of requesting reimbursement when the foreclosure is completed.

Once foreclosure is initiated, it is the servicer's responsibility to:

1 *Compile necessary data.* At this time, the supervisor of the collection department should notify all department heads of the pending foreclosure to avoid the automatic payment of bills from reserves without prior approval. A notification alerting the staff of a pending foreclosure is also useful because it encourages the staff to channel information that may come to its attention to the employee who handles the foreclosure.
2 *Notify the appropriate governmental agencies.*
3 *Turn files over to attorney.* Unless a long-standing arrangement exists between a servicer and a foreclosure attorney and each party knows exactly what its respective responsibilities are, a definite understanding must be reached between the servicer and the attorney on their respective responsibilities in the foreclosure process. This is of particular significance in those states where redemption periods are long and the foreclosure attorney's responsibility may extend over periods of 18 months or more before title passes to the mortgagee. When judicial proceedings are involved and where court appearances must be made either by attorney or servicer, or both, a follow-up calendar of various deadlines is usually valuable.

During the course of foreclosure proceedings, regardless of the amount of time it takes and regardless of the type of foreclosure that is involved, occasions will arise when the borrower asks that reinstatement of his loan be considered. If definite evidence is at hand to indicate that reinstatement is imminent and that the borrower has the funds to pay up all arrears and foreclosure expenses and attorney fees to date, it is best to have the servicer handle the reinstatement rather than the attorney. In such matters, business judgment comes first. To clarify the terms used, it must be stated that the *reinstatement* referred to here involves payments of all arrears, plus attorney fees and other expenses, to the mortgagee before the foreclosure sale takes place, and not *redemption* which takes place after a sale in states where there is a redemption period. In the former instance, the borrower is dealing with the servicer and his attorney; in the latter instance, the borrower is usually dealing with the court.

The initial letter of transmittal to the attorney should contain the following information:

1 Brief description of property
2 Unpaid balance of loan and date to which interest has been paid

3 Nature and extent of default and a brief description of any special facts that may have a bearing on the legal handling or outcome of the case

4 Complete information on escrow reserves, advances, and the current status of taxes and insurance

5 Information on whether property is vacant or occupied and, if occupied, the names and status of occupants or tenants

6 Information on whereabouts of owner if not on property

7 Details of history of ownership or assumptions

8 Any changes in FHA or VA regulations affecting the loan which are of recent origin and which may not have to come to the attention of the attorney

9 Copies of Notice of Default and Notice of Intention to Foreclose, if VA is involved, or mailing address of VA office having jurisdiction over the property and the VA case number, if applicable

The transmittal letter should also stipulate the division of responsibility and authority. The attorney should supply to the servicer copies of all procedural papers so that the servicer is in the position to follow the case and provide additional information which may be required by the attorney or the court. Proper liaison between servicer and attorney also facilitates the timely and accurate filing of various reports and, of course, of claim forms when such time arrives. The attorney should not be involved in filing FHA or VA forms and should not prepare the claim forms. This is strictly a mortgage banking function and responsibility.

Conduct of Foreclosure

The conduct of foreclosure varies by state and by type of loan. Each criterion imposes the responsibility for independent and yet coordinated action between the attorney and the servicer. While FHA leaves the conduct of the entire foreclosure proceedings to the mortgagee, VA reserves the right to regulate all phases of the conduct of foreclosure.

FHA leaves the compilation of the bid to the mortgagee or his servicer who normally bids the amount of indebtedness including principal, accrued interest, and advances for taxes and all foreclosure expenses. Since FHA pays a claim for insurance only if marketable title can be conveyed, FHA acquires the property only after sale and after termination of the redemption period. The proper determination of the bid is important, however, since if the property is acquired at the sale by a third party for less than what is due the mortgagee, a loss is sustained which is not paid by FHA.

VA, however, has a number of regulations that bear either directly or indirectly on the mortgagee's bid at the foreclosure sale. If VA's *specified amount* is bid at the foreclosure sale, this is the amount for which VA actually buys the property from the mortgagee. Since the indebtedness is usually greater than the upset price, the balance owing the mortgagee, together with interest and reimbursable expenses, is paid upon filing a claim. VA, however, pays the upset price to the mortgagee when he conveys title and custody of the property to the VA regardless of whether there is a redemption period or not. It also pays the claim shortly thereafter.

In states where there is a redemption period and an FHA loan is involved, the servicer's and attorney's supervision of the case extends over the period of redemption during which a receiver, who is appointed by the court, collects rents from the occupant or tenant. Since FHA wishes to acquire the property in a vacant condition and asks that the key to the property be forwarded with the claim, the removal of the occupant of the property remains the concern of the servicer, attorney, receiver, or court having jurisdiction over the property. However, if the property is occupied by a tenant—i.e., anyone other than the owner against whom foreclosure proceedings were instituted—the FHA may agree to accept the property in occupied condition.

Properties securing loans being foreclosed should be checked frequently for occupancy and protection. If the property is abandoned, a homeowner's type of policy may no longer protect the property. Therefore, it may be advisable to purchase vandalism and malicious mischief protection. If a vacancy endorsement to the insurance policy is necessary to maintain coverage, it should be obtained. In freezing weather, provisions should be made to winterize the property.

COLLECTION PRACTICES—INCOME PROPERTY LOANS

Neither the initial contact, the follow-up approach, nor any of the collection steps to be contemplated or taken on income property loans can at any time be handled in a routine or standardized manner. This difference from collection practices on single-family loans stems from the lender's reliance on the income-producing capabilities of the property and the large size of the loan.

The collection department's difficulties are accentuated by the fact that each loan differs from the next to a much greater degree than one residential single-family loan differs from another. Each income property loan represents a combination of many different components: the property may belong to a sole owner, joint owners, a partnership, a syndicate of several individuals, a corporation, or a trust; the property may be an apartment or office building, a warehouse, manufacturing plant, hospital, church, motel, shopping center, or an individual discount store; the property may have a single tenant, a few tenants, or a large number of tenants; or it may be owner-occupied. These variables make each income property loan problem a special challenge. Handling delinquent FHA-insured income property loans, primarily multifamily, are equally difficult. If they are in default or heading in that direction, corrective steps permitted are more limited and are governed in many respects by FHA regulations. The FHA handbook, "Project Mortgage Insurance," explains most of these limitations and provides instructions for handling default situations.

Initial and Follow-up Contacts

Income property loans must be watched more closely than residential loans, for there is neither place nor time for past due notices. A telephone call must be made within 5 days after the due date to inquire about the payment. The initial call must be made by an experienced person, skilled in collections and familiar with the property, who can ask appropriate questions and establish the source of the problem. Knowing the remedies at the disposal of the mortgage banker in enforcing prompt payment, such a person can then initiate appropriate action.

Care should be exercised that any leniency on the part of the servicer, such as accepting monthly payments between the fifth and tenth without too strong an objection, is not construed by the borrower as a license to pay late at all times and that this unofficial tardiness, which the borrower may try to blame on late-paying tenants, does not turn into a permanent understanding. Nor should the borrower be allowed to assume that payments can always be a week or two late as long as they are made monthly. Prompt payment is essential.

The initial and the follow-up contact must be directed to the owner, whether or not he is the president of a company, and not to an employee or a secretary, or even to the owner's accountant.

Of course, an oversight may occur at an apartment manager's office or at the accounting office of an industrial firm; nevertheless, too frequent use of this excuse may portend future trouble and require investigation. If the owner becomes evasive upon contact, a real problem may be at hand which must be promptly checked out. When this happens, an immediate inspection of the property is usually warranted. "Slipping" tendencies must also be watched; i.e., the payment which has come in regularly on the first or second suddenly arrives on the fourth or fifth, only to come later each month.

Despite their desire for accounting uniformity, some lenders feel it is wise to negotiate payment dates other than the first of the month. Actually, experience with staggered due dates has not been very rewarding. All rent payments are normally received by the tenth of the month and the owner has, therefore, no excuse for not remitting promptly. As an alternate defensive measure, however, owners should be reminded that if tenants are late in making their payments, the prior month's rent should be scheduled for use in current monthly payments.

Of course, income property loans which are managed poorly by uncooperative owners place extra burdens on the collection staff and account for most trouble cases. The enforcement of penalties is a justified and effective deterrent to this type of problem.

It is axiomatic that each problem which is not a case of pure oversight should be brought to the attention of the servicing manager or loan administrator. He may then consult with, or refer the problem to the commercial loan staff and/or legal counsel familiar with the documents prepared for the case.

Whether the first symptoms of trouble are brought to the attention of the lender immediately will depend on the existing understanding between servicer and lender. Servicers who make income property loans should be competent at handling all problems that arise. Instead of running to the lender with the discovery of the problem and asking for instructions, servicers should analyze the situation first, inspect the property, and report their findings and applicable corrective measures. Competent servicers know when to go to their investors with their problems and when to follow the matter on their own. The ability to make this decision, to use discretion and judgment, is only a part of the responsibility of the loan administrator.

If an owner of a multitenancy property is late in paying, the initial questioning should ascertain whether there are excessive vacancies and, if so, why. If an owner of a manufacturing plant is late with his payment, perhaps sales are off or collection of outstanding bills is slow; or the reason may often be one for which there is no acceptable excuse. There may be no serious problem with the property, nor with the adequacy of income. It may just be that the management firm or owner has used the funds for other ventures. Since this is a fairly common practice in this era of financial wizardry, the activities of this type of borrower must be discovered early and attempts to use funds belonging to the mortgagee must be halted promptly.

If the property is leased, or even if there are some tenants-at-will, and if the rent is not first applied toward the mortgage payment by the borrower, the mortgagee should be promptly advised of this diversion of funds. This may be accompanied by a recommendation to exercise assignment of rents or leases, provided that this procedure is sound from both a legal and practical standpoint. This will depend on such matters as the law of the state, the wording of the legal documents, the requirements concerning possession and property operation, and the other liabilities to be assumed. It is not a step to be taken lightly. Under this arrangement, the tenants will be instructed to pay rent to the mortgage banker. Sometimes the mortgage banker (on behalf of the lender) mails funds in excess of required monthly payments back to the owner, especially in a single-tenancy occupancy such as a post office or gas station lease. Delinquent income property loans are occasionally cured permanently by this method. In some states, the mortgagee can simply enter into legal possession upon default, especially if foreclosure and/or acceleration of maturity has been decided upon. But fair and positive warning of intention should be given before disturbing the owner's relationship and prestige with the tenants.

Several investors require by the terms of their commitment that the owner submit an annual financial statement usually 90 days after the end of his fiscal year. It then becomes the duty of the servicing agent to see that these reports are received and sent to the investor. If the owner furnishes a report each year, an examination of these reports may signal future problems such as increasing vacancies or declining profits and suggest preventive steps to be taken. The annual vacancy reports on FHA-insured apartment loans can also alert the collection department to impending problems.

Real problems, of course, develop from those circumstances in which the owner, for one reason or another, does not furnish the servicer with the required statement; the payments are made, but little is known of the borrower's financial situation until payments suddenly slow down or stop entirely. A voluntary annual reinspection program for all large loans is strongly recommended regardless of investors' requirements. These should prevent most surprise situations.

Penalty Charge—Conventional Loans

Penalty provisions for conventional income property loans are identical to those already described for residential loans. Usually, the enforcement of such charges must be more strict than on residential loans because handling problems of slow-paying income property loans creates a considerably greater expense to the servicer than dealing with problems on loans of single-family properties. The lender is deprived of the opportunity to reinvest larger sums, and the penalty is assessed against a business enterprise which presumably can better afford such charges than a delinquent homeowner. Of course, the lender must make sure that there are sharp teeth in the penalty provisions of the note. Great care should be exercised, however, that penalty interest be computed carefully so as not to violate the usury laws of the state in which the property is located.

Late Charge—FHA Project Loans

All regulations pertaining to FHA project loans, except those insured under Title 608 (War Housing) and 803 and 810 (Armed Services Housing) contain the following provision:

> The loan may provide for the collection by the lender of a late charge, not to exceed 2 cents for each dollar of payment to interest or principal more than 15 days in arrears, to cover the expense involved in handling delinquent payments; late charges shall be separately charged to and collected from the borrower and shall not be deducted from any aggregate monthly payment.

Of course, the lender must incorporate the proper language in the mortgage papers before closing.

Legal Remedies

An entire volume could be written by members of the legal profession on the variety of legal remedies lenders may apply against owners of income properties who do not make payments promptly. Each delinquent loan must be treated as a separate and distinct case primarily because the mortgage instruments, types of real estate involved, lease forms where applicable, the manner and form of ownership or leasee interest, and many other fundamentals or incidentals vary widely, and because the laws governing these transactions usually are different in each state where the properties are located.

If a serious delinquency occurs, the income property loan staff and/or the loan administrator must inspect the property and make whatever investigation is necessary to establish the cause of the delinquency and to consider all available remedies short of enforcing legal ones. Simultaneously, the loan file should be turned over to the legal counsel of the mortgage banker or the legal department of the investor, if he has indicated preference for handling these cases. Normally, the legal counsel of servicers and lenders have good working relations and can establish the proper course of action.

At all times, the responsibility for carrying the matter forward, including negotiations with the borrowers or their representatives, should be vested in the loan administrator. He should seek maximum assistance from the income property loan personnel, the legal staff of the mortgage banker, or appropriate persons at the offices of the lender. The competence of the servicer's staff and the relationship between the lender and the servicer help determine who is to perform any of the difficult tasks. The performance of any tasks involving delinquent, to-be-foreclosed, or foreclosed income property loans is normally beyond the capacity of the residential collection department staff.

Default and Claim Procedures—FHA Project (Multifamily) Loans

In view of the complexity of the FHA regulations pertaining to defaulted FHA multifamily loans, only the salient points are presented here and no reference is made to loans insured under specific sections of FHA regulations or to technical solutions. The purpose of this presentation is to highlight some of the fundamental differences between FHA philosophy on reporting defaults and paying claims on project (multifamily) loans and that on FHA residential programs.

The reporting requirements pertaining to defaulted FHA project loans are much stricter than those pertaining to their residential counterparts. Specifically, regulations allow the mortgagee very little discretionary power whether to report a default or not. Upon default, Form 2426 (Exhibit 62) must be filed in triplicate on all types of multifamily housing project loans. The form broadly stipulates that in the event of a default which continues for 30 days, whether it be for nonpayment, failure to perform any covenants of the mortgage, or violation of charter or regulatory agreement, the mortgagee is entitled to the benefits of insurance. If this default is not cured within 30 days, the mortgagee is required to notify FHA in writing of such default within 30 days.

If the default is not corrected, the mortgagee has one of two choices at his disposal. He can either assign the mortgage to the FHA at a 1 percent discount or institute foreclosure proceedings, acquire title, and then tender title to the property. After that, FHA pays the lender for the loan at par, but *without reimbursing* the lender for costs of foreclosure, conveyance stamps, or taxes. In several states, these costs may make the 1-percent discount for assignment the better choice, even without assigning any negative value to the nuisance or publicity of foreclosure. In some instances, the FHA may want an assignment to prevent foreclosure. In such cases, the commissioner has the option of waiving part or all of the discount. In most FHA multifamily loans, payment is made in debentures which, depending on current lending rates, may be worth considerably less than par, except when used to pay mortgage insurance premiums on other multifamily loans. However, in Sections 220 and 221 (loans insured on or after July 7, 1961) and Section 236 settlement is made in cash. Under certain circumstances and with certain precautions observed, FHA accepts a deed in lieu of foreclosure involving a multifamily project.

For specific requirements as to the timing of foreclosure and acquisition of title by mortgagee for loans insured under specific sections of the housing act, the mortgagee must consult the appropriate regulations carefully. Regardless of regulations,

EXHIBIT 62   FHA notice of default status on multi-family housing projects

FHA FORM NO. 2426
Rev. 4 68

U. S. DEPARTMENT OF HOUSING AND URBAN DEVELOPMENT
FEDERAL HOUSING ADMINISTRATION

Form Approved
Budget Bureau No. 63-R876.2.

NOTICE OF DEFAULT STATUS ON MULTIFAMILY HOUSING PROJECTS
(Submit in Triplicate)

INSTRUCTIONS: See reverse side for information on reporting defaults and requesting extension of time limits. If non-payment is for replacement reserve only <u>do not</u> use this form but report by letter.

TO: DEPARTMENT OF HOUSING AND URBAN DEVELOPMENT FEDERAL HOUSING ADMINISTRATION DIRECTOR, INSURING OFFICE	FHA Project No. 071-99999 EC	Date December 2, 1969

Project Location

8888 S. State Street
Chicago, Illinois

Mortgagor *(Name, Address and ZIP Code)* Best National Bank, as Trustee under Trust Agreement dated 12-31-67 and known as Trust 88431--Mailing address: J.H. Schmidt, Pres., Hanson Construction Co., 933 S. Wood Street, Chicago, Illinois 60119.

MORTGAGE INSURED UNDER: *(Check title and Fill-in section)*

☐ Title II, _____   ☐ Title VI, _____

☐ Title VIII, _____   ☐ Title IX, _____

☐ Title X

Servicing Agent *(Name, Address and ZIP Code)*
ABC Mortgage Company
233 Maple Street
Chicago, Illinois 60190

REPORT OF DEFAULT

1. Has previous default notice been submitted:

   (a) On this mortgage? ☒ YES   ☐ NO   (b) On this Default? ☒ YES   ☐ NO

2. The following payments have not been made:

Jan.	Feb.	Mar.	Apr.	May	June	July	Aug.	Sep.	Oct.	Nov.	Dec.	
									X	X	X	Date last payment was received: 10-19-69

3. Default other than non-payment: *(Explain)*

4. Reason for default: *(Explain)*

   Notwithstanding regular and consistent collection efforts by this office, the October, November and December payments have not been paid. The owner is diverting some of the income from this project to a new business venture.

5. ☒ REINSTATEMENT EXPECTED   ☐ REINSTATEMENT DOUBTFUL

REPORT OF REINSTATEMENT

The default as last reported under date of _____ has been cured and the Mortgage reinstated

by payment received on _____ .

NOTE: If default consists of more than one monthly installment, reinstatement must not be reported until all installments are paid. For other than monetary defaults, explain method of reinstatement on an attachment.

Eastern Life Insurance Company
By: ABC Mortgage Company, agent
Mortgagee

RECEIPT ACKNOWLEDGED

By *Samuel Tuttle*
Signature

FEDERAL HOUSING COMMISSIONER

Samuel Tuttle, Vice President & Treasurer
Address 233 Maple Street
Chicago, Illinois 60190

By _____

experience demonstrates that it is advisable to take possession or exercise a rent assignment in an FHA loan. The rigidity of FHA's audit procedures is the reason for avoiding this exposure. In any event, it is best to get a court-appointed receiver.

Extension of time to take the appropriate steps and deferment of payments in case of hardship on urban renewal loans (Section 220), just to mention one instance, may be obtained from the Secretary of Housing and Urban Development. Such requests, however, must always be made in writing by the mortgagee. However, FHA officials are usually very cooperative in discussing things informally and many times can give valuable assistance. In the event of action by local FHA officials which seems unreasonable, appeal can always be made to the appropriate assistant commissioner in Washington.

Upon completion of foreclosure and upon tendering title of the property to the commissioner, the latter can either issue debentures or pay in cash for the property at his option, except that he must pay cash at the mortgagee's election under Sections 220, 221, and 223 (loans insured on or after July 7, 1961) and Section 236. Currently, FHA is not electing the cash route where the choice is theirs. Since results, in terms of return of investment to the mortgagee, differ for loans insured under different sections of the FHA multifamily project loan regulations and according to the debenture rate specified when the loan was insured, the alternate solutions and respective results cannot be presented and summarized here. Therefore, in considering foreclosures or assignments of mortgages, FHA regulations should always be carefully reviewed and the current practices as to methods of payment by the commissioner ascertained beforehand for each alternate legal procedure employed.

For instance, if a mortgagee elects to assign a Section 207 or 232 mortgage to the commissioner, debentures are issued only for 99 percent of the unpaid balance of the loan and the 1 percent deficiency is included in a certificate of claim. The certificate may be of value if FHA ultimately disposes of the property for an amount in excess of the debentures it issued—usually an unlikely occurrence. The certificate of claim also includes a reasonable amount of other expenses not included in the original settlement, such as the foreclosure costs, if the loan is foreclosed and title is conveyed.

Multifamily debentures generally mature in 20 years. Interest on the debentures accrues from the date of default specified by FHA regulations and carries a rate which is fixed by regulations and which is applicable to loans insured by FHA during a certain specific period of time. For instance, debentures issued in connection with defaulted FHA 207 loans insured between July 1, 1961 and January 1, 1962 carry an effective interest rate of 3¾ percent while debentures of similar projects insured between July 1, 1963 and January 1, 1967 carry a rate of 4 percent. Old 608 loans specify rates as low as 2½ percent. Obviously, any of these would be used first to pay insurance premiums, if the lender has any other multifamily loans. When interest rates are high, it is solely through this means that mortgagees can dispose of their holdings of debentures at par unless the commissioner redeems them earlier, which has not happened recently. In times when interest rates are high, debentures can be sold on the open market only at heavy discounts if there is any market for them at all.

The above illustrations are results of applying regulations in effect at time of publication. They may also be oversimplifications of some of the provisions. They serve, however, as illustrations of the types of procedures that may be followed and of some of the available solutions which must be considered by the mortgagee as a means of recovery of its defaulted investment. Obviously, there are a great many variables which tend to influence the decision of a lender when there is a choice between forbearance or taking final action in an FHA multifamily loan.

SUPERVISION AND CONTROL

In the course of close supervision of the entire collection activity, management uses a variety of reports, reviews, and surveys. Most of these focus on the progress and success of handling delinquent loans; a few relate to the overall collection program.

Assembling reports and supervising reviews of these reports reveal the effectiveness of collection practices, the results achieved for investors, and the progress of foreclosures. Handling foreclosure cases, where delays may be unnecessarily costly to investors, is particularly important and should be subject to constant surveillance by management. In the last analysis, investors will hold the management of the company responsible for results.

Monthly Review

Management should insist on monthly reports on delinquent loans, preferably in simple tabulations prepared by the tabulating department or the collection department (see Exhibits 18 and 19). For statistical purposes, the tabulation should highlight the number of delinquent residential loans by type of loan, by investors and by delinquency categories. These tabulations provide the means for management, through the loan administrator, to measure accomplishments on a month-to-month basis, examine seasonal trends, and compare results with other mortgage bankers assembling similar figures. They can also serve as a basis for reports to the Mortgage Bankers Association National Delinquency Survey and subsequently for comparing regional and national averages published by MBA. The tabulations also enable the loan administrator to plan for staff requirements, especially when to commit additional help.

Review of Specific Delinquent Accounts

Review of individual delinquent accounts is more meaningful than analysis of summary tabulations. It enables management to (1) evaluate the borrower's predicament, (2) appraise and review the effectiveness of methods employed to cure the delinquency, and (3) assist a member of the staff in deciding to have a showdown which he would not have wished to initiate by himself.

This review can coordinate collection activities through case-by-case discussion by the loan administrator or the servicing manager, the head of the collection department, and those members of the staff who are handling loans in serious default. Problems of the delinquent borrowers and the recommended solutions should be briefly discussed. The appearance of the same borrower in a different category, first as a 60-day delinquent and then as a 90-day delinquent a month later, or the reappearance of the same borrower in any delinquent category indicates that the financial problems have not been resolved. Furthermore, such review injects new ideas and new ways of looking at the same problems and gives the staff an opportunity to receive suggestions for combating recurrent problems or attacking old delinquents with new ammunition.

These reviews may be repeated weekly or whenever the occasion arises to discuss a seriously delinquent account. As a result the loan administrator will become familiar with the names and problems of the company's delinquent borrowers before he is called upon to consider a recommendation for foreclosure.

Control of Foreclosure Activity

Since most lenders have placed the responsibility for handling foreclosure cases on their servicers and their local counsel, it behooves the loan administrator to supervise carefully, through his collection department, the handling of individual cases and to watch their overall progress. While each attorney to whom a case is assigned knows his legal responsibilities, there are innumerable instances where the servicer's assistance and counsel may prove to be invaluable. Attorneys often are not too well versed in FHA and VA requirements; also often because of the modest pay they receive for services of this type they do not use their best talents or devote as much time to a complicated case as may be demanded.

Then again, the mortgage personnel's intimate acquaintanceship with the borrower prior to foreclosure, his knowledge of real estate values, potential receivership complications, and many other eventualities are necessary ingredients to proper execution of the foreclosure process. Furthermore, at times attorneys do not process the cases as promptly and as speedily as the investors would like.

To provide an effective follow-up tool for the servicer and to record the status of each case, it is helpful to set up a simple special foreclosure follow-up card or a foreclosure check sheet on each case.

The foreclosure check sheet illustrated in Exhibit 63 is designed for FHA cases; a similar one pertaining to the procedural steps for VA cases can, of course, be developed. The card or check sheet, of course, should be established as soon as the case is recommended for foreclosure, and all entries regarding compliance with VA and FHA fulfillment of legal requirements should be noted thereon. The illustration probably shows the required steps in greater detail than applicable to most states in the country. However, the card or check sheet should be designed to incorporate the various steps to be taken in chronological order, within the framework of each type of foreclosure case. The card or check sheet may be attached to files or may be kept in a special card box of file on the collection chief's desk. Collection personnel should then carefully enter the steps that have been taken as the case progresses so

EXHIBIT 63 Foreclosure check sheet — FHA

F O R E C L O S U R E   C H E C K   S H E E T

Name   SMITH, John R. & Lora L.   Loan No.   2 6789

Ppty Address   123 Shady Tree Lane, Treetown, Illinois

1/3/65	F/C RECOMMENDATION TO INVESTOR	FHA Case #131-037695 Sec. 203		
1/3/65	FHA Default Notice			

		60 DAY INSPECTIONS		
2/18/65	PAPERS RECEIVED FROM INVESTOR			
2/23/65	Referred to Attorney	Date	Occupied?	Condition
2/26/65	COMPLAINT FILED	9/25/64	yes	Fair
2/27/65	FHA Default Notice	12/10/64	yes	Fair
4/21/65	Date Set for Judgment	1/8/65	yes	Fair
4/16/65	Stmt. of Indebtedness to Atty	2/10/65	yes	Fair
		3/9/65	yes	Fair
4/22/65	JUDGMENT ENTERED	5/28/65	yes	Fair
5/28/65	Date Set for Sale	7/20/65	yes	Fair
5/18/65	Bidding Instructions to Atty	9/18/65	yes	Fair
		10/20/65	yes	Fair
5/28/65	FORECLOSURE SALE HELD	12/18/65	yes	Fair
		1/18/66	yes	Fair
6/5/65	SALE CONFIRMED	2/20/66	yes	Fair
6/6/65	FHA Default Notice	3/20/66	yes	Fair
4/15/66	Report to Investor Recommend-	4/14/66	yes	Fair
	ing Sale or Conveyance	5/28/66	no	Fair
5/28/66	REDEMPTION PERIOD EXPIRES			
5/28/66	FHA Default Notice			
5/28/66	Property Inspected			
5/28/66	Property vacant			
6/10/66	SHERIFF'S DEED RECEIVED	Receiver Appointed		
6/10/66	Deed to FHA to Investor			
	for Signature	Discharged:		
yes	PROPERTY READY FOR CONVEYANCE TO FHA			
6/10/66	Deed to Title Co. for Recording			
6/18/66	DEED TO FHA FILED	Attorney: William Jones		
6/18/66	Form 1025 to FHA	1111 Brown Bldg., Chicago, Illinois		
6/18/66	Hazard Insurance Canceled			
6/18/66	Tax Schedule (2766) to FHA			
6/18/66	Keys to FHA			
		Remarks:		
7/5/66	FISCAL DATA TO FHA			
7/5/66	Title Evidence to FHA			
7/15/66	No Further Attention Notice			
7/15/66	All Reimbursements Received			
	from Investor			

that at any time there is information on the exact status of the case. Thus it may be ascertained who the receiver is, if any, when foreclosure sale is to be held, and when the redemption period expires.

A register, which is also recommended either as a subsidiary control record or as the only one, has the advantage of being a compilation of all foreclosures rather than individual cards which may be lost or become disattached if affixed to files.

However, in controlling the progress of foreclosure cases, it should be noted that the emphasis is not on the format, size of the check-up or control tool, and the procedures employed for recording information thereon, but on the fact that a record is kept. Often the infrequency of foreclosures requires a more careful recording of deadlines than if there were a great number of foreclosures and the clerk assigned to recording various foreclosure steps were more familiar with the subsequent steps to be initiated or to be taken.

Assessment of Effectiveness of Collection Activity in Relation to Expense

The loan administrator alone or in cooperation with the head of the collection department must evaluate the results achieved by the collection department in the light of the expense incurred. How effective is the use of notices? How much money is spent for the telephone? Of what help is field personnel? Which collection tool or method is the most effective and at the same time economical? These questions must be evaluated.

It must also be kept in mind that there is rarely a mathematical ratio between the number of collectors required to do the job and collection achievements. Although it is undeniable that an increase in the number of employees making calls will tend to reduce delinquencies, that is not necessarily the effective and profitable way to do business. Collection work is a quality job where the results will be achieved not by how many calls are made, but by how effective the calls are, how firm the follow-up is, and, most often, how ingenious the collector is in his contact with the delinquent borrower.

Curiously enough, when the number of delinquent loans climbs, the deterioration in the overall collection picture increases at a much faster pace. In other words, the more time spent following up new delinquents, the less time available for problem cases that require meticulous attention. Of course, if delinquencies increase, the staff should be increased correspondingly, except that it is almost impossible to commit adequately trained collection talent on short notice.

Another peculiarity of collection work must also be noted. Regardless of the level of collection activity in a given company, efforts could always be either doubled or halved without decreasing or increasing delinquencies by 100 percent. What is important, therefore, is to establish a balance between expense and results and to make sure that the head of the collection department assigns the right priorities to assure maximum effectiveness.

Care should be exercised that the number of delinquent accounts does not get out of hand and that each case requiring attention receives appropriate and immediate attention. A neglected account is one of the hardest ones to pull out of the fire, even if the borrower is willing to cooperate.

Guidance for Loan Production or Management

One of the most important by-products of the close supervision of collection activities by management is the ability to detect from recurring collection problems possible flaws in its underwriting procedures. Problems may arise from incomplete credit information, inadequate review of this information, or other procedural weaknesses, or may stem from the overzealousness of certain members of the production staff to make loans. But the review of delinquent loans usually does reveal that a loan should not have been made; in fact, it usually reveals such shortcomings about operations as laxity in credit-checking procedures, carelessness in closing loans, or the absence of strong, early follow-up of late payers.

DELINQUENCY SURVEYS

Delinquency surveys are barometers of prevailing delinquency conditions. While month-to-month tabulations of delinquent loan accounts show the loan administrator the improvement or decline in his own collection results from one month or one quarter to another, the comparisons that may be made by checking this tabulation with those of other mortgage bankers of the same investor or other mortgage bankers in the same area or throughout the nation tell a more complete story. Tabulations, therefore, provide a tool for measuring overall performance. They may be used to determine potential benefits of special techniques and tools employed from time to time. They also serve as indicators of trends, changes in economic conditions, and aids in discovering the impact of new problems that tend to increase or decrease delinquency rates.

Delinquency surveys are maintained by most investors and by the Mortgage Bankers Association of America. The former type is distributed to all the investors' servicers by the investors; the latter to all members of MBA. Both types of reports are based on information forwarded by servicers or members of the association.

It is recommended that the loan administrator use all these reports to compare the company's accomplishments with those of others according to as many criteria as feasible. These reports can serve as accurate means by which the company's delinquency situation can be placed into proper perspective. The reports can also supply the loan administrator with source material for discussing company results and providing impetus to the staff for better collection accomplishments.

1 Delinquency surveys by investors   Investors have found that one of the most effective ways to stimulate a servicer's lagging collection efforts is to provide a comparison of his accomplishments with those of his competitors. Some compilations of delinquent loans are released by substituting names with code numbers, thus hiding the identity of the correspondents; investors who are less bashful feel that a little bit of competition among servicers is a good stimulant and print the names of the participants in the survey.

These reports are usually not sent directly to the loan administrator or to the head of the collection department, but to the head of the company in the hope that adverse showings will stir them into taking appropriate steps to improve collection results. A good loan administrator, of course, does not need such prompting since he is on the top of the delinquency situation and knows how he stands in relation to his past record. However, he does not always know how other servicers are doing.

2 National delinquency survey by MBA The National Delinquency Survey was initiated in 1954 by the Loan Administration Committee of the Mortgage Bankers Association of America and conducted by it for several years. Subsequently, this project became a regular service feature of the association and now serves as a major statistical source of the collection accomplishments of the mortgage banking industry. Following this lead among lenders, the Federal Home Loan Bank Board and various commercial and savings banking groups have also developed similar compilations for their cooperating members.

The method of compilation is fairly simple. Near the end of each quarter, **MBA** mails to each of its reporting members a questionnaire with the request that it be

EXHIBIT 64   Report on current home mortgage status

FHA FORM NO. 2068 S Rev. 3/66   Form Approved Budget Bureau No. 63-R1066.1

DEPARTMENT OF HOUSING AND URBAN DEVELOPMENT
FEDERAL HOUSING ADMINISTRATION

REPORT ON CURRENT HOME MORTGAGE STATUS

If you service 250 or more FHA insured mortgages, either for your own account or for others, as of the first of each month, submit this report in duplicate to the FHA insuring office having jurisdiction over the area in which your office is located. If you operate through branch offices, you may elect to have a separate report prepared by each branch office and submitted to the insuring office having jurisdiction over the area in which the branch office is located. Duplicate reports should be avoided. For the purposes of this report a payment is considered past due and the mortgage in default when the next payment becomes due.

FEDERAL HOUSING ADMINISTRATION 219 South Dearborn Street Chicago, Illinois	Name, Address, ZIP Code and Type of Servicing Institution ABC Mortgage Company 233 Maple Street Chicago, Illinois 22503 8

Fold Here

(Use Mortgagee Stamp when Possible)

NUMBER OF FHA MORTGAGES SERVICED	NUMBER OF MORTGAGES IN DEFAULT STATUS AS OF August 1, 1968					FORECLOSURE COMPLETED OR DEED IN LIEU OF FORECLOSURE			
TOTAL	Total In Default	Number of Payments Due and Foreclosure Not Started			Foreclosure Started But Not Completed	Property Held By Mortgagee		Action Taken During Past Month	
		1	2	3 or More		Pending Expiration of Redemption Period	Pending Withdrawal or Transfer to FHA	Property Transferred To FHA	Property Not to be Transferred FHA Insurance Terminated
	(C+D+E+F)								
(A)	(B)	(C)	(D)	(E)	(F)	(G)	(H)	(I)	(J)
3873	33	20	8	0	5	9	0	3	0

Remarks:

By _____

Title James Clark, Collection Super.   Date 7-31-68

193406-P Rev. 3/66   FHA-Wash., D. C.

promptly returned, indicating on the card the number of loans serviced by type and the number of delinquent loans by type of loan and by number of payments in arrears. It also includes the number of loans in process of foreclosure. From these reports, the National Delinquency Survey is prepared by dividing the reporting members into twelve MBA regions. Comparisons are made with previous quarters and the same quarter of the previous year. The survey enables each mortgage banker and each investor to compare accomplishments against current and past, regional and national delinquency figures. (See Appendix A-10.)

3 Report on current home mortgage status by FHA   The Federal Housing Administration requires each servicer handling more than 250 FHA-insured loans to report (Exhibit 64) on the first day of each month the number of FHA loans serviced, the number in default by one, two, or three payments, and the number of foreclosures started but not completed. The reports from the servicing agents thus provide FHA with an accurate measurement of the delinquency situation and an advance warning of the development of unfavorable trends.

CHAPTER SIXTEEN

Insurance Department

All mortgage bankers owe a responsibility to their lenders to make certain that all properties securing the loans serviced are adequately serviced. Essentially the department's function is twofold: to write insurance (if permitted and if licensed) and to administer insurance matters related to the servicing of loans. Operating methods vary according to state statutes which permit, limit, or explicitly forbid mortgage bankers to compete for insurance business. These statutes determine the choice of structure of the mortgage banker's insurance operation among (1) an internal operating department, (2) an insurance agency separated in location and corporate structure from the mortgage banking company, and (3) an agency located within the same office. In states where mortgage bankers are not permitted to engage in the insurance business, the insurance department performs a servicing function only.

An insurance department may sell insurance on the home, apartment, or plant. It may solicit automobile insurance. And it may write health and accident insurance, mortgage retirement, and all other forms of life insurance. When the mortgage banker's insurance staff develops a relationship of confidence with its clients, the client's insurance business may be retained long after the loan has been paid in full.

Mortgage bankers find that there is no better time to appraise a property for insurance than when the property is appraised for lending purposes. This eliminates duplication of effort and affords the mortgage banker an opportunity to render additional services to the borrower. Despite this obvious economy, mortgage bankers must develop a philosophy of soliciting insurance that is dedicated to service and free from any form of coercion.

It is axiomatic that the mortgage banker does not interfere with the mortgagor's right (1) to place his insurance with an insurance carrier of his choice, both when the loan is made and when the insurance policy is renewed, and (2) to obtain the best policy he can that is consistent with investor standards and at the most advantageous cost. This freedom of choice is not only good business policy, it is prescribed by FHA and VA regulations and is often stipulated in the mortgage banker's servicing contract.

Most adverse legislation affecting the mortgage banker's right to write insurance has been brought about by overzealous lenders, not necessarily and exclusively mortgage bankers, who assumed that the extension of credit gave them the prerogative to write insurance. In spite of actual and threatened restrictive legislation, some lenders have consistently maintained coercive practices. This is most unfortunate since most mortgage bankers have found time and time again that there is no need for tying the sale of insurance to the extension of credit. Insurance can be made an appropriate by-product of mortgage lending if solicitation is conducted with efficiency and dignity. Every mortgage banker should observe the spirit of free competition even if the state in which he operates does not maintain restrictive statutes. This can be accomplished by (1) taking pains to see that no statement of the loan solicitor or loan officer can be construed by the borrower as a requirement that he place his insurance business with the mortgage banker, (2) making certain that the privilege of writing insurance is not made a condition of making a loan, and (3) limiting the solicitation of insurance business to trained insurance personnel rather than loan solicitors.

Alternately, the freedom of choice accorded every borrower can in no way restrict the mortgage banker from rejecting a policy if the insurance carrier does not have sufficient financial strength to protect the investor's security. Lenders typically prefer to avoid accepting many policies from new companies without an appropriate rating by *Best's Insurance Guide*, especially if the properties covered involve a heavy concentration of risk in one area.

Staffing of Department

The task of an insurance department manager is complex, calling for ingenuity, perseverance, imagination, and patience—a difficult set of requirements to meet. On the one hand, he must be fired with the desire to produce insurance business. On the other hand, he must be alert to avoid any practice that smacks of coercion. He must follow the instructions of his investors meticulously. He must supervise salesmen, if they are employed. Most importantly, he must administer the mortgage banker's servicing responsibilities. The manager of the insurance department and those who solicit insurance business must be licensed by the states in which they solicit business as brokers or solicitors.

The department manager must deal with companies which provide the insurance policies and the public which buys them. He must know and understand intimately the coverages available and the various rates and premiums of his own insurance products as well as those of his competitors. Above all, he must be service-minded. Although profit is important, service to the investor and particularly to the insured cannot be relegated to a secondary position.

OPERATIONS AND RESPONSIBILITIES

Responsibility to Mortgagee

From the standpoint of loan administration, the prime responsibility of the insurance department to the mortgagee is to make certain: (1) that the property on which a mortgage loan was made is adequately insured for all insurable hazards required by the terms of the mortgage and required by the lender, and (2) that all losses are properly adjusted, repairs made, bills paid, and applicable FHA and VA regulations complied with. Requirements for insurance are spelled out in the mortgage document, as illustrated below by quotations from an FHA mortgage form and from a conventional mortgage form. The mortgage banker's responsibility for seeing that all the insurance stipulations in the mortgage are adhered to by the mortgagor entails continuous vigilance throughout the life of the loan, in compliance with specifications included in contracts with investors for servicing mortgage loans.

The FHA Mortgage Form 2116M (Rev. 5/66) relative to the mortgagor's obligation reads as follows:

That he [i.e., mortgagor] will keep the improvements now existing or hereafter erected on the mortgaged property, insured as may be required from time to time by the Mortgagee against loss by fire and other hazards, casualties and contingencies in such amounts and for such periods as may be required by the Mortgagee and will pay promptly, when due, any premiums on such insurance provision for payment of which has not been made hereinbefore. All insurance shall be carried in companies approved by the Mortgagee and the policies and renewals thereof shall be held by the Mortgagee and have attached thereto loss payable clauses in favor of and in form acceptable to the Mortgagee. In event of loss Mortgagor will give immediate notice by mail to the Mortgagee, who may make proof of loss if not made promptly by Mortgagor, and each insurance company concerned is hereby authorized and directed to make payment for such loss directly to the Mortgagee instead of to the Mortgagor and the Mortgagee jointly, and the insurance proceeds, or any part thereof, may be applied by the Mortgagee at its option either to the reduction of the indebtedness hereby secured or to the restoration or repair of the property damaged. In event of foreclosure of this mortgage or other transfer of title to the mortgaged property in extinguishment of the indebtedness secured hereby, all right, title and interest of the Mortgagor in and to any insurance policies then in force shall pass to the purchaser or grantee.

In addition to the standard requirements of the FHA mortgage form, a conventional mortgage form applicable to income property loans specifically describes the necessity of furnishing mortgagees with policies no later than 10 days before expiration date.

Insurance: Mortgagor shall keep all buildings and improvements now or hereafter situated on said premises insured against loss or damage by fire and such other hazards as may reasonably be required by Mortgagee, including, without limitation on the generality of the foregoing, war damage insurance whenever in the opinion of Mortgagee such protection is necessary. Mortgagor shall also provide liability insurance with such limits for personal injury and death and property damage as Mortgagee may require. All policies of insurance to be furnished hereunder shall be in forms, companies and amounts satisfactory to Mortgagee, with mortgagee clauses attached to all policies in favor of and in form satisfactory to Mortgagee, including a provision requiring that the coverage evidenced thereby shall not be terminated or materially modified without ten (10) day's prior written notice to the Mortgagee. Mortgagor shall deliver all policies, including additional and renewal policies, to ABC Mortgage Company, or Mortgagee, and, in the case of insurance about to expire, *shall deliver renewal policies not less than ten (10) days prior to their respective dates of expiration.*

These provisions in essence outline the responsibilities of the mortgage banker precisely, since he must see that all stipulations enumerated in the mortgage relative to insurance are adhered to by the mortgagor.

Responsibility to Mortgagor

If the mortgage banker is also engaged in the insurance business and in this capacity obtains an order for the insurance, he automatically assumes the responsibility for the adequate protection of the borrower's equity in the property. In this role, the mortgage banker performs one of his valuable functions since he usually knows better than anyone the insurable value of the property, having previously inspected and appraised it for lending purposes. He can readily make an insurance appraisal and recommend the proper amount of insurance. This is extremely important since underinsuring a property is dangerous and overinsuring it is wasteful. Conversely, if the mortgage banker does not write insurance, but accepts a policy from an agent of a borrower, it is the borrower's agent and not the mortgage banker who is actually responsible for the adequacy of the coverage beyond the lender's interest.

Solicitation Practices

Solicitation practices of mortgage bankers vary throughout the country. To say that one practice is better than another would be to render judgment without examining the evidence. Most mortgage bankers have evolved smooth-functioning solicitation machinery and are employing either:

1 Person-to-person at home contacts
2 Contacts by mail
3 Contacts by telephone only
4 A combination of one or more of these techniques

Curiously enough, each mortgage banker claims, both in terms of efficiency of operation and net commission income, that his is the best technique. This may be so because his procedure fits into the framework of his loan production machinery or his loan-closing procedure, or because the method employed suits the talents and temperament of the insurance staff.

Undoubtedly, a "house call" approach which requires an expensive field force is more costly than phone or mail solicitation. In turn, however, a well-trained and experienced staff of insurance solicitors can create a most profitable insurance operation, especially if the activity involves the solicitation and procurement of life insurance as well as hazard insurance and if the sales efforts are reinforced by mailing of explanatory literature, return envelopes, and other useful solicitation devices. With the growth and complexities of both the mortgage banking business and the insurance field, more emphasis is being given to solicitation by mail since a larger number of borrowers can be contacted more economically by this method than by any other means. A brochure may be used, for example, to explain the mortgage banker's role in the insurance field and emphasize his qualifications for insurance counsel and service. (See Appendix A-11.)

For the purpose of presenting the production of insurance business, first the process of the determination of values for insurance purposes will be described. Then, production of the initial policy, writing the renewal policy, and sale of related insurance will be discussed so the reader may be in a position to judge for himself which of the methods he should choose and for what reason.

Since mortgage banking firms normally produce single-family as well as income property loans, the activities of the insurance department include solicitation of insurance designed for owners of residential properties and for owners of income properties. Since there are a wide variety of income property loans, the business of producing insurance to protect a great variety of structures against ordinary as well as special hazards and to protect the owners from hazards to which they may be exposed in the operation of their businesses calls for a great degree of specialization. Therefore, the description of practices will first cover the single-family and then the income properties. Appropriate methods of solicitation will be presented within these fields.

Determination of Values

To insure a single-family property, an apartment building, or any facility, it is necessary to prepare an insurance appraisal. Inasmuch as it is necessary to appraise a property for lending purposes, the determination of value for insurance purposes is a simple task for every mortgage banker and his insurance staff. Of course, the method used to determine the value of a single-family property is somewhat different from that used to establish the value of an income property. In the same way, determining the value of an existing building for insurance purposes differs from that of a building in the process of construction.

For a new building, the cost of construction and the value of the land determine the total value of a property for lending purposes. If the land value is deducted from this appraisal figure, the cost of reconstructing the building, should it be totally destroyed, may be established. This is called *replacement cost value.*

If the building to be insured is not new, the appraisal of the property must take into consideration the construction cost of the building, but a deduction for wear and tear must be made; this deduction is called *depreciation*. If depreciation is deducted from the replacement cost value, the resulting figure is the *insurable value*.

Properties may be insured for insurable value or replacement cost value. It must be remembered that if an old house is covered for replacement cost, in case of total loss, sufficient funds will be provided by insurance to rebuild it. Replacement cost insurance, because it requires that a higher amount of insurance be carried, will always be more expensive than insurance based on the insurable value only. This is especially true when an old building is involved.

The premium, for instance, for a standard homeowner's policy on an old frame house in an established neighborhood, valued at $50,000 on the replacement cost basis, amounts to $367 for a 3-year term. If, however, the same policy is written on the basis of insurable value, insurance will be written at $25,000 (50 percent depreciation) at a cost of only $163 for the same term.

In today's residential insurance market, the practice is to recommend replacement cost insurance. If insurance is to cover full replacement cost of the building, the property must be insured for an amount equal to at least 80 percent of the replacement cost of the property. To avoid dispute in case of settlement and to provide for an automatic increase in valuation, perhaps through appreciation of improvement in the property, it is advisable to offer insurance at an amount representing 90 or 100 percent of the replacement cost of the building.

Insurance producers may use either the loan application form or an appraisal form. Either form may be placed in the loan file so the necessary data will be readily available for insurance purposes. Alternatively, the insurance department may request the appraisal information from the loan production department.

Production practices described on the following pages are applicable to the solicitation efforts of an insurance department which sells insurance in conjunction with making mortgage loans.

INSURANCE FOR OWNERS OF SINGLE-FAMILY PROPERTIES–INITIAL POLICY

Prime Coverage (Fire and Other Hazards)

Since funds to close a mortgage loan or to start construction cannot be disbursed until the mortgage banker has a permanent insurance policy in his possession, a binder, or a builder's risk policy, it is necessary for the insurance department to solicit insurance in advance of closing or disbursement of construction funds and/or to advise the prospective mortgagor to make the necessary policy available at least 3 days before the funds are to be disbursed. To avoid rejection of the policy and last-minute complications, instructions as to the minimum amount of policy, the required mortgage clause, and other requirements should always be specific. (See Exhibit 65.)

EXHIBIT 65 *Request for mortgage clause*

ABC MORTGAGE COMPANY
233 Maple Street
Chicago, Illinois 60190

September 28, 1970

Mr. and Mrs. Joseph H. Zickert
2026 Evans Avenue
Morgan Park, Illinois

Re: Loan No. G-41310

Dear Mr. and Mrs. Zickert:

In connection with your application for a loan on the property described below, we note that you intend to furnish your own insurance.

We shall appreciate your despositing the original policy together with a paid receipt for the premium due as soon as possible in order that we may examine it prior to the closing.

This policy should be written as follows:

Named Insured:	JOSEPH H. ZICKERT AND BARBARA J. ZICKERT, HIS WIFE
Minimum Amount:	Amount of Mortgage or Replacement Cost, whichever is lower.
Description of Property:	ONE FAMILY FRAME DWELLING LOCATED AT 2026 EVANS AVENUE, MORGAN PARK, ILLINOIS
Mortgage Clause:	XYZ LIFE COMPANY, c/o ABC MORTGAGE COMPANY 233 MAPLE STREET CHICAGO, ILLINOIS 60190

Yours very truly,

Insurance Department

CC: **Loan Closing Department**

Solicitation in person   Solicitation in person offers an excellent opportunity to establish a long-lasting personal relationship and create opportunities for future sales. This holds true even if only a homeowners' policy is sold in conformity with the requirements of the mortgage or if the new homeowner presents a policy of his own.

Some mortgage bankers find it prudent to discuss insurance as soon as the application for a mortgage loan has been completed. The concept of insurance is a most timely subject at that moment. The presentation may be made by the same officer who has taken the application, if he is qualified and licensed or by a staff member of the insurance department. To separate the loan producing activity from the insurance solicitation process, some mortgage bankers prefer to escort the applicants to the insurance department. This also dispels the impression that there is any connection between making the loan and selling insurance.

Personal solicitation may take place when the mortgage papers are signed. Being closer to the actual occupancy of the property, mortgagors can be persuaded at this time to make an immediate decision. If solicitation is delayed until the mortgage documents are signed, the opportunity may be lost to another insurance salesman. By the time the loan is closed, insurance salesmen have acted on their leads gleaned from reports on new home purchases from the real estate salesman or builder contracts. The real estate man himself, if licensed, may sell the policy. Consequently, if personal solicitation is planned, it is advisable to do it when the application is signed.

Solicitation by mail   Solicitation by mail has its advantages and disadvantages, depending on timing and the extent and intensity of competition in the area served by the mortgage banker. Of course, its success hinges greatly on the completeness and clarity of presentation. The most appropriate time for solicitation by mail is when the mortgage documents are to be executed by the mortgagors—when it is imperative that a decision be made. It is advisable, however, to put mortgagors on notice, by means of an advertising folder, when they sign the loan application that a written insurance proposal will be sent to them shortly. This may prevent prospective mortgagors from going elsewhere for their insurance, but it will not entirely forestall their succumbing to good salesmanship by others.

Those who solicit insurance by mail feel that the best psychological impact for a sale is attained when a written insurance presentation accompanies the unsigned mortgage papers. If prospective borrowers are asked to sign the mortgage documents as well as an insurance order, the financial responsibility which comes with home ownership readily establishes the necessity of protecting the home with insurance.

One mortgage banking firm which operates an insurance department entirely by means of mail solicitation uses a four-part form with great success. (See Exhibits 66 and 67.) Only the *insurance recommendation* and the *insurance order forms* are mailed out with the mortgage papers. The second and third parts, which are duplicates of the first, are retained in the insurance department and serve as a binder copy for the risk offered and a file copy. The purpose of the *binder copy* is to bind the risk with one of ьne insurance companies until a firm order or another policy is received from the prospective mortgagor. The binder copy may also be used to order the policy

EXHIBIT 66 *Insurance recommendations*

ABC MORTGAGE COMPANY

233 Maple Street
CHICAGO, ILLINOIS 60190

INSURANCE RECOMMENDATIONS

NAME _____ JOHN SMITH AND MARY SMITH, HIS WIFE AS JOINT TENANTS _____

ADDRESS _____ 1604 KINGSTON LANE, HOMEWOOD, ILLINOIS 60430 _____ LOAN NO. _____ G-48324 _____

It is important that your property be adequately insured. Since you have authorized us to place your insurance, we are recommending a Homeowners policy, which is designed to provide you in one policy—at one premium—and at considerable saving —the different kinds of insurance which you need.

From the information available to us we have estimated the replacement cost of your home at $ _____ and recommend that you carry one of the following Homeowners policies for at least this amount:

	"Special" Homeowners	"Standard" Homeowners
Dwelling	$ 20,000	$ 20,000
Detached Structures	$ 2,000	$ 2,000
Personal Property: On Premises	$ 8,000	$ 8,000
Off Premises	$ 1,000	$ 1,000
Additional Living Expense	$ 4,000	$ 2,000
Comprehensive Personal Liability	$ 50,000	$ 50,000
Medical Payments	$ 500	$ 500
Physical Damage to Property of Others	$ 250	$ 250
3-year Premium in advance	$ 201.00	$ 134.00
Annual Premium on 3-year installment Plan	$ 70.00	$ 47.00

While the amount of coverage differs very little between the forms, the difference in coverage between the above policies is explained on pages 5 to 11 and illustrated on the folded insert in the enclosed booklet opposite page 6. All Homeowners policies written in the State of Illinois are now subject to a $50 deductible clause, the operation of which is explained on page 6 of the enclosed booklet.

We will be pleased to give you further details on our recommendations, or discuss with you the other types of insurance policies now available. If you, for one reason or another, wish to carry more insurance than that recommended we shall be pleased to give you a quotation on the amount desired. We are sure that we can write a policy that will fit your needs and suit your budget in every respect. May we also suggest that you read our insurance booklet. It will explain our services to you.

Will you please indicate your preference by completing the attached Insurance Order and returning it to us with your signed mortgage papers. We will send you a duplicate copy of the policy for your files as soon as the policy is issued.

ABC MORTGAGE COMPANY

INSURANCE DEPARTMENT

Date: January 2, 1969

EXHIBIT 67 *Insurance order*

ABC MORTGAGE COMPANY

233 Maple Street
CHICAGO, ILLINOIS 60190

JOHN SMITH AND MARY SMITH, HIS WIFE AS JOINT TENANTS

1604 KINGSTON LANE, HOMEWOOD, ILLINOIS 60430   G-48324

INSURANCE ORDER

ABC MORTGAGE COMPANY
233 Maple Street
Chicago, Illinois 60190

Gentlemen:

Please write a "Special" Homeowners policy in the amount of...........$ 20,000

☐ 1. For a three year term at...$ 201.00

☐ 2. For a three year term on a budget plan at............................$ 70.00
    for the first installment followed by two annual installments of $ 70.00
    (You save $ 9.00   if you purchase a three year cash policy)

Please write a "Standard" Homeowners policy in the amount of.......$ 20,000

☐ 1. For a three year term at...$ 134.00

☐ 2. For a three year term on a budget plan at............................$ 47.00
    for the first installment followed by two annual installments of $ 47.00
    (You save $ 7.00   if you purchase a three year cash policy)

_____

_____

PLEASE DETACH, SIGN AND RETURN THIS ORDER BLANK WITH YOUR

SIGNED MORTGAGE PAPERS

from the insurance company if the order is received. The forms are self-explanatory and their use ties in with the booklet referred to in Appendix A-11, which describes the process of determining values and recommends policies that are available to home-owners through the company's insurance department.

Of course, if the insurance order is not returned with the signed mortgage papers by the borrowers, a call must be made promptly. If the prospective mortgagor decides to favor his insurance broker with the business, information on the requirements of the policy may then either be given to him on the telephone or supplied by letter.

Solicitation by telephone Some mortgage bankers feel that insurance can be sold by telephone most effectively and with the least amount of expenditure. An insurance salesman who knows his product can easily obtain an order by presenting the prospective borrower with the best and least expensive insurance. On the telephone, he can also answer questions which are not asked if mail solicitation is employed. Furthermore, an insurance salesman can immediately offer other types of insurance if he finds the homeowner receptive.

Solicitation by telephone is based on successful telephone salesmanship which is an art in itself. In contrast to solicitation by mail, this method eliminates the need for preparing forms.

The major point to be made in favor of mail in contrast to personal solicitation is that sale by mail will appear to be an adjunct of the mortgage-making process without the special pressure or hard sell that insurance agents on commission may exert to obtain an order. Under the sale-by-mail arrangement, those soliciting insurance are employees of the agency or the company and not commissioned salesmen. Admittedly, less insurance may be sold by mail than by personal solicitation. However, less friction will be created with competing insurance agents and brokers who may feel that aggressive sale of insurance soon after making the loan constitutes a coercive practice.

From the standpoint of loan administration, the effectiveness and usefulness of one method over the other should not be evaluated solely on the basis of gross premiums produced, but on the basis of net results after deducting solicitation expenses. In each instance, it is necessary, however, to give considerable credit on which no dollar value can be placed for the goodwill and public relations aspect of each type of contact. Although the advantages of each method can be easily justified by the head of the insurance department, the profitability of the operation on a year-to-year basis to the company and to the insurance department staff, in terms of compensation, must be placed into proper perspective and determined on a net profit basis by other than the head of the insurance department.

Allied Coverage

Profitability of the insurance operation can be greatly enhanced by promotion and sale of allied coverages, either at the outset of the loan or, for that matter, any time throughout the life of the loan. Under the term *allied coverage*, only those policies which directly benefit homeowners are considered. Person-to-person solicitation of insurance could not be maintained profitably were it not for the insurance department's opportunity to sell insurance other than of the primary homeowners' variety. Among the insurance coverages offered and sold to homeowners other than property insurance are life insurance of all types including mortgage protection (retirement) coverage, accident and health insurance, and automobile insurance.

Insurance other than that designed to cover the mortgagor's home, automobile, or other possessions such as life and accident and health insurance is usually sold on a group insurance policy basis. The group concept offers the homeowner an advantageous rate and a convenient payment method since the premium may be paid in twelve installments and added to the monthly mortgage payment. The Federal Housing Administration now recognizes that it may be beneficial for a mortgagor to carry life insurance or accident and health protection, or both. Neither FHA nor VA will permit a lender to require a mortgagor to obtain such insurance as a condition to obtaining an insured mortgage. If permission has been obtained from FHA to commingle escrow funds, the mortgage banker may deposit insurance premium payments in the escrow account. Of course, only monies collected for life and disability insurance premiums can be expended for these purposes. If approval to commingle escrow funds has not been obtained, the mortgagee is required to separate the premiums for other-than-hazard insurance from all other elements of the payment and deposit them in a separate escrow account. In either case, the mortgage banker must maintain his records so that each element is separately identifiable.

Some life insurance investors object to their correspondents' activities and efforts in the sale of life, mortgage protection, or accident and health insurance, contending that it is their role to sell insurance and that their correspondents should be content producing and servicing loans only. During this decade, a considerable compromise has, however, been reached between some life insurance investors and their correspondents on this issue, with the sale and handling of accident and health protection by servicers receiving an almost universal acceptance.

Care should be exercised by the loan administrator to see that the sale of allied coverages does not unduly encumber the mortgagor's financial ability to meet monthly mortgage payments. An overzealous and aggressive insurance department can sell insurance to a borrower beyond his capacity to pay the premiums, which may possibly contribute to delinquency in making loan payments. For this reason, it is often advisable to withhold solicitation and sale of allied coverages, such as life insurance, until the loan is seasoned and the mortgagor has paid for all the necessities the acquisition of a home requires.

Life insurance Solicitation and sale of life insurance are discussed under two separate classifications, primarily because the mortgage protection (retirement) insurance, if sold on a group basis, can be considered a mortgage banking function, while the sale of life insurance often presents problems for the mortgage banker because it is not directly related to his functions and responsibilities.

It seems logical to sell a borrower life insurance since the preservation of the homestead, in case of death, often hinges on adequate life insurance. Many mortgage bankers have, therefore, embarked quite profitably in this field.

Many life insurance companies discourage, if not outright forbid, their correspondents from selling life insurance to their mortgagors. Others, a minority, appoint their correspondents as agents for the sale of life insurance because they recognize that a mortgage banker's frequent contact with the borrower through the monthly payments on the mortgage or sale of homeowner's policy brings him closer to the borrower than a salesman representing a life insurance company can ever be. Those life companies which hold that the sale of life insurance to their own mortgagors is their sole privilege request that their correspondents furnish their local agency offices, upon receipt of the loan commitment, with insurance leads containing certain information on the mortgagors. Unfortunately, as many mortgage company personnel can testify, salesmen representing other life companies in the field who watch the arrival of new homeowners, particularly in new subdivisions, approach the new homeowner (and obtain his order) long before the life insurance man who receives his lead through company channels.

Mortgage protection (retirement) insurance　This insurance is life insurance which decreases in protection as the unpaid balance of the mortgage is reduced and will, upon the death of the mortgagor, pay the loan in full. Statistically, it is a worthwhile protection for the family since the chance of a breadwinner's death during the term of his mortgage is considerably greater than the destruction of his home through fire. The sale of this type of policy may be beneficial, especially to young homeowners, since the premium is relatively low. At the same time, it is profitable to the mortgage banker to solicit and sell such insurance since its promotion and sale can easily be related to sale of homeowner's insurance. The advantage to the homeowner of purchasing this policy may be justified since he can pay for this policy with the monthly mortgage payments.

Accident and health insurance　An accident and health policy may be called *Home Security*, *Home Protector*, or *Mortgage Payment Protector* (all of which are trade designations). The policy is designed to provide the homeowner with his monthly mortgage payments should he become disabled as a result of sickness or accident. The borrower who must be gainfully employed to be able to purchase participation does not necessarily have to be in a hospital nor does he have to be bed-confined to qualify for benefits.

There are a great variety of plans in force. In general terms, they are group insurance plans offered by both life and casualty companies to the mortgage banker for for the protection of his mortgagors. Essentially, one plan differs from the other chiefly in the eligibility of a mortgagor to collect benefits: some call for the elimination of protection during the first 14 or 30 days of sickness or disability; others pay retroactively from the first day. Considerable difference also exists in exclusions and in clauses which preclude eligibility of borrowers with case histories of certain diseases or illnesses or bar them from participation for at least 1 year. Age limits of eligible mortgagors also vary and so does the maximum number of years during which benefits will be paid.

In considering the adoption of any of the plans available, the mortgage banker must weigh the benefits that will accrue to his mortgagors, the expense involved in the administration of the plan, and the potential fees or commissions that may be earned. The last consideration, although important, should not be the decisive factor. In addition to liberal payment of benefits, the promptness with which benefits are paid and the administrative ease with which the plan may be handled are most important.

Collateral benefits will accrue to the company in the operations of the collection department, since the benefits will either provide monthly mortgage payments to mortgagors whose wages have been curtailed or eliminated as a result of sickness or accident or, if the mortgagor was able to make his payments, replenish his reserve funds which would have been depleted otherwise.

Because of the extensive use of data processing equipment in the performance of the solicitation task, in billing, and in accounting, the adoption of any of the plans now available is fairly simple. Companies which underwrite this type of risk usually perform the initial solicitation work and much of the promotional activity throughout the term of the contract. Although some companies adjust the claims in their home offices and issue the claim checks, others permit the mortgage banker to handle the claims and issue checks for the monthly benefits, an arrangement that normally speeds up the settlement of claims and the processing of payments or delinquent loan accounts.

Automobile insurance   There is a considerable difference of opinion as to whether the mortgage banker's insurance department should solicit and engage in insuring the mortgagor's automobile. Some contend that the automobile represents the mortgagor's most important means of getting to his job and that the protection of such transportation, therefore, demands the concern and attention of the mortgage banker. Others, while they may or may not subscribe to this theory, believe that as mortgage bankers they are not properly equipped to handle the intricate and often immediate demands that may arise in case of automobile accident and resulting claims. Automobile losses in general call for a 24-hour service most mortgage bankers are not able to provide.

Yet, many mortgage bankers conduct a complete and successful one-stop insurance department and solicit profitable automobile business. Although the commission rate per policy is lower than that on a homeowner's policy, the premium on an affluent mortgagor's car or cars may be considerable. The decision to engage in the solicitation of this type of business depends on the company's willingness to perform a give-it-all type of service, lest inadequate service provided on the automobile would alienate customers from other types of policies.

Other types of insurance   There is a great variety of other policies available for solicitation, covering a great variety of needs. Most of the protection, however, can be incorporated in the homeowner's policy. If not, the policies may be offered separately; they include comprehensive personal liability, personal articles floater (jewelry, furs, coin collections, etc.), pleasure boats (hull), or tenant's package.

INSURANCE FOR OWNERS OF SINGLE-FAMILY PROPERTIES--RENEWALS

The renewal of insurance policies is a highly important function. Depending on the mortgage banker's position as far as the solicitation and sale of insurance is concerned, this is either an income-producing and -servicing function or solely a servicing function. Handling renewal policies when not initially solicited and sold by the mortgage banker will be discussed later under "Continuity of Insurance Coverage." The following discussion is limited to situations where the mortgage banker can solicit and write insurance.

Solicitation of Renewal Policies

It is the practice of some mortgage bankers to notify each borrower, generally about 4 to 6 weeks prior to the expiration date of the policy, that his insurance will expire. and to solicit a renewal policy. Frequently this letter of solicitation or phone call is also used to offer other types of coverage. Often there is an opportunity for the mortgage banker to change a fire policy into a homeowner's policy or to offer the borrower other insurance products. Timing is important, however. Renewal reminders should be furnished early enough to limit competition and yet not so far in advance of renewal to enable the mortgagor to shop around for a better price quotation.

Before solicitation of a renewal, the original computations made for insurance appraisal purposes must be updated. This process is called *retrending*. It involves checking original costs and applying a multiplier for the increase in construction costs for the years elapsed. Of course, improvements and additions must also be taken into consideration. These can be ascertained either by inquiry (Exhibit 68) or by physical inspection. If increased protection is solicited or obtained, the reserves available for the payment of premium must also be checked or ascertained at this time and incorporated in the letter of solicitation (Exhibit 69).

Automatic Renewals

Most mortgage bankers, once they obtain an order for the initial policy, renew the coverage automatically. This is an efficient, effective, and economical practice. To provide adequate up-to-date coverage, it is the current practice of most mortgage bankers to increase the amount of coverage automatically by about 10 to 15 percent at renewal time. The use of this flat percentage increase is a practical method of updating coverage; however, it cannot be continued indefinitely and indiscriminately, but must be related periodically to an examination of actual values. Individual solicitation of renewals may still be made in those cases where the borrower has only a fire policy instead of a homeowner's policy or in situations which warrant special consideration.

Renewal orders must also be prepared if the borrower or his broker who normally furnishes the insurance policy fails to submit a renewal policy before the deadline set by the mortgage banker for the submission of renewal policies--normally 10 days before the expiration date. On the day of policy expiration, it then becomes necessary to place insurance on the property. If, after the expiration date of the

EXHIBIT 68   *Solicitation of renewal of insurance*

ABC MORTGAGE COMPANY
233 Maple Street
Chicago, Illinois 60190

September 28, 1970

Mr. John Smith
1604 Kingston Lane
Homewood, Illinois 60430

Re: Loan No.:	G-48324
Company:	Everyone's Ins. Co.
Policy No.:	12345
Amount:	$18,000
Expiration Date:	11-1-71

Dear Mr. Smith:

In order to determine whether or not you are adequately insured, we have updated the appraisal of your home and find that the replacement cost is now approximately $20,000. If you have made any substantial additions to your home since our original appraisal was made, please let us know when such improvements were completed and the cost at that time so that we may revise our figures accordingly.

We now suggest that you renew your Homeowners Policy for the following amounts:

"Special" Form insurance on your dwelling	$20,000
"Special" Form insurance on any detached structures (The absence of such structure does not reduce the premium)	$ 2,000
"Broad" Form insurance including burglary on personal belongings such as furniture and clothing:	
On Premises	$ 8,000
Off Premises	$ 1,000
Additional Living Expense if your home becomes uninhabitable because of an insured loss	$ 4,000
Comprehensive Personal Liability Coverage	$50,000
Medical Payments (To others who might be injured because of your actions)	$ 500
Property Damage of others	$ 250

Effective January 1, 1970, there is a mandatory deductible of $50.00 in all Homeowners Policies on all insured losses. For more information on the coverage listed above and the workings of the deductible clause, please refer to the enclosed booklet.

The three year premium for this coverage will be $201.00. On the installment plan, the annual premium will be $70.00

Please indicate your renewal instructions on the enclosed duplicate copy of this letter. A self-addressed return envelope is enclosed for your convenience in replying.

Please do not hesitate to call if you have any questions regarding your insurance or our recommendations.

                                  Very truly yours,

                                  Insurance Department

EXHIBIT 69 *Solicitation of renewal of insurance*

ABC MORTGAGE COMPANY
233 Maple Street
Chicago, Illinois 60190

September 27, 1970

Mr. John Smith
1604 Kingston Lane
Homewood, Illinois 60430

Re: Loan No. G-48324
Company: St. Paul Fire Co.
Policy No.: 912345
Amount: $18,000
Expiration Date: 11-1-70

Dear Mr. Smith:

Fire and extended coverage insurance covering the dwelling only at the above location in the amount of $18,000 will expire November 1, 1970. This coverage may be renewed for the same amount, with a premium of $40.00 for one year, or $120.00 for three years. The renewal coverage will be subject to a $50.00 deductible on all losses. The renewal deductible is now mandatory in the State of Illinois.

After receipt of the October, 1970 mortgage payment, you will have $50.00 in your Hazard Insurance Reserve that can be used for the renewal premium.

Because building materials and the cost of labor have increased substantially in the last few years, we recommend that you consider increasing the amount of this coverage to $21,000. The premium for this amount of coverage would be $50.00 for one year, or $150.00 for three years.

Please indicate your renewal instructions on the enclosed duplicate copy of this letter. A self-addressed return envelope is enclosed for your convenience in replying. If we do not hear from you by October 15, 1970, we shall renew the same amount of coverage for one year, with a premium of $40.00.

Yours very truly,

Insurance Department

policy, the borrower's policy does arrive, this policy, which is often accompanied by a letter explaining the reasons for the delay, will have to be accepted. If accepted, the policy ordered by the mortgage banker for the protection of the mortgagee will have to be cancelled. Such cancellation will create a minimum premium charge to the borrower even if the policy was in force only a day or two, and although this short-term charge may create some unpleasantness between mortgage banker, borrower, and his broker, the charge is both necessary and useful in enforcing future compliance with the requirements of depositing a renewal policy before a stipulated deadline. Automatic renewal is most necessary when the loan is delinquent and the borrower is uncommunicative or there is an impending foreclosure.

INSURANCE FOR OWNERS OF INCOME PROPERTY

With the considerable upsurge in income property lending, new fields of insurance opportunities have opened for the enterprising insurance-minded mortgage banker. Paralleling the great increase in apartment and commercial property financing, the insurance industry developed new insurance products and applied the same concept of packaging to underwriting and merchandising of insurance that made insuring single-family residences so economical to the homeowner and the insurance producer.

The determination of adequate coverage on residential properties is reasonably simple in that there is always a definite relationship between the valuation placed on the property by the FHA or VA and the insurable or replacement cost value of the property. In contrast, when the determination of adequate coverage for income properties is involved, the insurance staff must rely on detailed mortgage loan appraisals, depreciation factors, and construction cost figures to perform an accurate insurance underwriting job.

Whichever solicitation practice is employed to procure residential insurance business, the sale of insurance protection covering income properties and the sale of all other applicable and related insurance policies cannot be standardized or handled in a routine manner. Each type of property requires careful appraisal of the premises, an evaluation of risks, and a considerable effort in the placement of the risk once an order is acquired. Although much of the original contact may be made by correspondence or phone calls, the best results may be attained through personal contact, which should be initiated by the manager of the insurance department in the early stages of the negotiation for the mortgage loan. This involvement is particularly significant when the construction of a commercial building, industrial plant, or apartment complex is involved. The value of such business relationship and the premium that may be generated by such relationship, of course, justifies personalized handling.

The most frequently arranged insurance coverage for owners of income properties includes:

The multiperil package policy which may combine almost all the coverages previously purchased separately. The coverage on such buildings as apartments, offices, or industrial plants may be tailored to include not only protection against fire and extended hazards, but protection against vandalism, malicious mischief, sprinkler leakage, and burglary damage to the building. Replacement cost insurance may also be included, provided the amount of coverage is at least 80, 90, or 100 percent of the replacement cost.

All-risk builder's risk, which includes fire, extended coverage, and all-risk perils including collapse during construction. Since the builder's risk policy is considerably less expensive than similar protection on a completed project, it is necessary to convert the builder's risk contract to a permanent multiperil policy before occupancy of the project. If conversion is not affected, the protection becomes void. Prudent insurance agents preclude the possibility of a lapse in protection by arranging in advance for an endorsement for permission to occupy.

If the mortgage banker is involved in construction financing, particularly that of apartment buildings or other large commercial projects, the surety bond business may become a fertile field for the insurance producer. Among the bonds that owners may need for the protection of their business venture and that are often difficult to obtain are

Performance bond which guarantees "to the owner that the contractor (builder) will perform all the terms and conditions of the contract between him and the owner and, in default thereof, to protect the owner against loss up to the bond penalty."

Bid bond guarantees that if a contract is awarded to a builder, he will enter into the contract and furnish a performance bond. If the builder fails to do so, the owner will collect the sum up to the amount of the bond necessary to complete the job with another contractor.

Completion bond generally insures the owner so that the project will be completely free of liens.

License and permit bonds which guarantee, for instance, that tradesmen will comply with statutory regulations.

Maintenance bond which guarantees that workmanship and materials used are not defective. This guarantee may be included in the terms of the performance bond.

Subdivision bond which is usually furnished by a builder or a developer to a city or a county and which guarantees the construction or financing of construction of roads, grading, sewers, or water systems.

Permanent coverages, some of which may be included in a multiperil policy that an alert insurance department may be able to, and should, solicit to merit the business from the owners of income properties, are business interruption, loss of rents, comprehensive crime, elevator liability and collision, plate glass, boiler liability insurance, personal injury, sprinkler leakage, mercantile open stock, and valuable papers insurance.

Although co-insurance is usually not a part of a homeowner's contract, it is a factor in commercial, industrial, and apartment fire and special multiperil insurance. As a matter of fact, in some states co-insurance on commercial properties is mandatory. Since the application of co-insurance provides considerable saving to the insured, providing that the requirements of the co-insurance clause are strictly met, it is necessary that it be understood. The co-insurance clause is accurately explained in a folder presented by The Home Insurance Company, entitled "Let's Take the Mystery Out of Co-Insurance." This pamphlet is reproduced in Exhibit 70.

EXHIBIT 70   Explanation of co-insurance

CO-INSURANCE

Also referred to as the

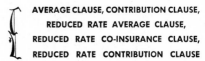

AVERAGE CLAUSE, CONTRIBUTION CLAUSE,
REDUCED RATE AVERAGE CLAUSE,
REDUCED RATE CO-INSURANCE CLAUSE,
REDUCED RATE CONTRIBUTION CLAUSE

WHAT IT IS – AND HOW IT WORKS

The true purpose of the co-insurance clause is to distribute the cost of insurance equitably among property owners and it has been universally adopted by insurance companies. Its fairness is demonstrated by the companies' willingness to grant a reduction in the rate or cost of insurance for the acceptance of this clause. The operation of the clause furnishes an incentive to the owner to insure his property fully and to increase his insurance when there is an appreciation in values. The presence of the co-insurance clause does not prevent an insured from reducing his insurance when values decrease.

The co-insurance clause is not as complicated as it might seem — in fact, it is rather simple when thoroughly understood. In brief, the clause is an agreement between the insured and the company that the insured shall maintain insurance on his property equal to a certain percentage of its value. When the insured carries sufficient insurance to comply with the co-insurance clause he will be entitled to collect the entire actual loss, not to exceed the amount of the policy. If the insured fails to carry sufficient insurance, then in the event of loss, he must bear his share of the loss just as though he were an insurance company. In other words, he may collect only that proportion of the loss which the amount of insurance carried bears to the amount of insurance he should have carried under the terms of the co-insurance clause.

EXAMPLE No. 1:

In This Case the Insured Carried Sufficient Insurance

Actual Cash Value of Property	$100,000
Amount of insurance required to be carried by the 80% co-insurance clause (80% of $100,000)	$ 80,000
Insurance Actually Carried	$ 80,000
Loss Sustained	$ 40,000
Amount Collectible from Insurance Company	$ 40,000

Note that the insured collects his loss in full

EXAMPLE No. 2:

In This Case the Insured *Did Not* Carry Sufficient Insurance

Actual Cash Value of Property	$100,000
Amount of insurance required to be carried by the 80% co-insurance clause (80% of $100,000)	$ 80,000
Insurance Actually Carried	$ 60,000
Loss Sustained	$ 40,000
Amount Collectible from Insurance Company	$ 30,000
Note that the insured must contribute	**$ 10,000**

THE ABOVE EXAMPLES ARE BASED UPON THE FOLLOWING SIMPLE FORMULA:

$$\frac{\text{Amount of Insurance Carried}}{\text{Amount of Insurance Required}} \text{ X Amount of Loss} = \text{Amount Collectible.}$$

INSURANCE SERVICING RESPONSIBILITIES

All insurance policies must be handled, accepted, and serviced by a single set of standards, whether the policy for the borrower was written by the mortgage banker or by another insurance agent. It must be remembered at all times that the customer is being served and that the service must transcend any disagreement between an agent and the servicer. Conflicts which arise between agents and mortgage bankers in the insurance production area are likely to result from uncooperative servicers who, after failure to secure the business, put procedural obstacles in the way of competing agents.

The tasks that must be performed in compliance with the terms of servicing contracts and some of the tools that can be used are discussed in the following groups: (1) examination and acceptance of policies; (2) preparation and maintenance of records; (3) continuity of insurance coverage; (4) safekeeping of policies; (5) certification procedures; (6) administration of loss claims and handling loss drafts; (7) handling insurance assignments; and (8) substitution of policies.

Examination and Acceptance of Policies

All initial policies and their renewals must be carefully examined before they can be accepted, carded, and filed regardless of whether the policies were written by the mortgage banker or furnished by others.

There is less likelihood of error if the mortgage banker, or a company or agency under his direction familiar with investors' requirements, prepares the policy or if the policy received by the insurance department is a renewal of the existing insurance, whatever its source, by the same insurance company which wrote the initial policy. On the matter of accepting a policy, it is recommended as a general procedure that the insurance department deal with the owner of the property only and not with an agent who represents himself as acting for an owner. Dealings with agents or brokers are recommended only if the agent or broker produces a so-called "broker of record" letter signed by the owner.

The first policy must not be examined hastily. Loan proceeds cannot be disbursed or construction loans opened until the insurance department has in its possession an insurance policy—or a builder's risk policy, if new construction is involved—which meets all the preset requirements. If there are difficulties in obtaining a policy, a binder may occasionally be accepted, although this is not a recommended procedure. A binder must be furnished on approved forms and signed by an authorized agent; it provides temporary coverage, usually for 30 days, until a permanent policy can be written.

The examination of each policy must include the following particulars:

Original policy   The policy must be the original copy.

Name of insured   All owners must be shown and each name must conform to the name of owner or owners of the property. If there is a contract purchaser, this fact must also be recorded.

Address of property   It is imperative that the address of the property be properly designated. If it is located on a "street," is should be so stated since there may be an "avenue" in the same town of the same name. Property addresses may also be designated by legal description.

Amount of policy   On residential loans, a policy must be in an amount not less than the outstanding principal balance or in an amount equal to 100 percent of the replacement cost value of the property, whichever is less. In practice, by insuring the property for full replacement, the insurance producer creates a built-in reserve for small additions and for potential appreciation of property values.

Co-insurance   If there is co-insurance, the policy must conform to requirements of the co-insurance clause. Failure to comply might jeopardize the mortgage holder's investment in the event of a serious loss. Co-insurance normally does not apply to residential properties.

Mortgage clause   This is normally a standard form which affirms ownership of the mortgage. Certain investors wisely require that the mortgage clause be issued in the name of the owner of the mortgage (lender), in care of the mortgage banker, with the mortgage banker's address shown. This arrangement assures the lender that loss drafts will be sent directly to the servicer for disposition and not to the lender. To avoid changes in mortgage clauses if the permanent mortgagee is not known when insurance is ordered or requested, the permanent mortgagee's name may be shown in the following manner:

XYZ Insurance Company
and *ABC Mortgage Company*
as their interest may appear

The mortgage clause requires the mortgagee be named in each loss draft unless the mortgagee instructs the insurance company in advance to omit its name from loss checks. Instructions to omit the name of the lender usually apply to checks not exceeding certain amounts, normally, $100. The mortgage clause also provides for 10 days' notice of cancellation to the mortgagee in the event the policy is cancelled for any reason, including nonpayment of premium. Some mortgage clauses also include a provision which obligates the agent to notify the company if change of ownership or occupancy or increased hazard comes to his attention, with penalty of cancellation for such noncompliance. The inclusion of such a paragraph in the mortgage clause constitutes an unusual risk for the mortgage banker because he may not be able to prove that such factors have not come to his attention through the borrower's contacts with numerous employees of the company.

Description of property   It is most important that a property be described properly as to its construction. For example, frame buildings cannot be described and rated as if they had been built from brick and vice versa. Also, if there is a garage, it should be so stated in the policy.

Total concurrent insurance Policies, if more than one is issued, must agree within the contract in every particular such as perils and co-insurance percentage if nonresidential property is involved.

Signature of policy The policy must be signed by an agent for the company.

*　　*　　*　　*　　*　　*　　*　　*　　*　　*　　*　　*　　*

The strength and therefore the acceptability of an insurance policy is most often revealed by the issuing company's rating as shown in *Best's Insurance Guide*. This guide, published annually, gives each company a *policyholder's rating* and a *financial rating*.

The policyholder's rating is Best's opinion on the relative position of the company in comparison with others based on such factors as underwriting, economy of management, adequate service, net resources to meet catastrophic losses, and sound investment of its funds.

The insuring company's financial rating signifies the *size of the company* by *policyholder's surplus,* which normally is the sum of capital and surplus. Most investors instruct their correspondents to use *Best's Insurance Guide* and normally state the minimum qualifications in terms of the letters used to express policyholder's rating and the maximum amount of insurance acceptable from any one company. There are, of course, different sets of requirements for policies on residential and on income property loans.

As an illustration for residential real estate loans, one investor allows its correspondents to accept hazard insurance policies of a company in amounts up to 10 percent if paid-in capital and surplus (financial rating) are $500,000 or more with a maximum of $5,000,000 on any one risk. If the company's paid-in capital and surplus are less than $500,000, policies are allowed only in amounts up to 5 percent of paid-in capital and surplus. Under either qualification, the company must have a policyholder's rating of A. Most mortgagee's minimum requirements normally do not vary from the specifications listed above. The servicer, of course, must use his own judgment to avoid great concentration of risk among weaker companies. Some investors, however, maintain in their manuals a specific list of hazard insurance carriers whose policies servicers are advised to accept or reject. These investors watch the insurance field closely and update their list from time to time.

Similar basic requirements are normally set up in company manuals for the acceptance of insurance policies on income property loans. If the company writing the insurance does not meet minimum qualifications, its policy may still be accepted if that part of the coverage which is in excess of the particular lender's minimum requirement is reinsured by another company.

Acceptance of a policy issued by any company is, of course, a matter of judgment. Since Best's financial rating signifies relative size and not quality of company, policies of smaller but well-managed companies may be accepted provided there is no concentration of risk involved. Policies in companies with less than minimum rating may also be accepted if the policy is reinsured by an acceptable carrier and such reinsurance is evidenced by attachment of the endorsement of assumption of liability.

Preparation and Maintenance of Records

Preparing and maintaining records by its very nature is a business of paperwork and detail. The smooth and successful operation of any insurance department depends largely on the accuracy, completeness, and prompt availability of its records. Because most investors no longer require that they maintain custody of policies or even renewal certificates, the entire responsibility for proper initial and renewal coverage as to location, amount of coverage, and acceptability of company rests solely with the servicing agent. Furthermore, when the mortgage banker writes insurance, his failure to renew because of oversight or inadequate expiration records is costly. In addition to the exposure that may result in a claim under the errors and omissions coverage, the company may lose commission income on a policy that should have been written.

Many mortgage bankers can rely to a great extent for expiration reminders from the source of their insurance policies, but if a mortgage company places its business with several companies or writes its own insurance, or both, *it must rely on its own records.* In any event, the assistance rendered by insurance companies and insurance agencies in providing renewal reminders or expiration records should be considered only as a subsidiary protection against oversight. Preparation of invoices on the servicing agent's letterhead and insurance accounts payable media is often a much-appreciated assistance rendered by insurance agencies and companies to the insurance department. Those who have not availed themselves of this assistance should review their relationships with their insuring companies.

Three systems are now in use for maintaining records of insurance policies, all of which offer reliability and flexibility with a minimum amount of work and expense. They are the two-card system, the billing system, and a system of filing policies by expiration dates.

Two-card system   Pertinent information from each insurance policy is recorded on two cards, each serving a different purpose: a "master card" which records the policy according to the mortgagor's name or property address and an "expiration card" which provides a policy expiration record.

The master card should contain all the information illustrated on Exhibit 71, and should be filed in a drawer or cabinet in alphabetical order according to the borrower's name. In case of a sale of property and after insuring company consented to assignment of policy, it is imperative that the new owner's name be promptly recorded on the master card and that the card be refiled according to the new borrower's name.

The expiration card is the backbone of the insurance department's operation. It should generally contain the same information as the master card and usually is a duplicate copy of the master card. It is filed in a separate drawer or cabinet according to the month and year of expiration and is intended to serve as an expiration reminder to the insurance department.

Both cards can be prepared in one operation if the snap-out type of card record is used. The two cards, separated by a carbon, are identical except for a difference

EXHIBIT 71   *Master card – insurance*

. NAME   BENDER, Sam and Ruth   LOAN NO.F34422

PROPERTY ADDRESS   326 Oakwood Street, Forest, Illinois

· MORTGAGE CLAUSE   XYZ Company

HOLDER'S No.   294037   ded CL & 1&2

Construction: Brick   Form Nos.: Mic-2; H060; OMC-1; with $50

COMPANY	POLICY No.	KIND OF INSURANCE	TERM	%	AMOUNT	RATE	TOTAL PREMIUM	EXPIRES
Atlantic	H8441446	Dwell	3		16,000		108 00	2-8-69
		Priv Str			1,600			
		Pers Ppty			8,000			
		Add Liv Exp			3,200			
		CPL			50,000			
		Med			500			
		Ea Accident			25,000			
		Phys D			250			

DOWN PAYMENT:

BROKER OR AGENCY: W. W. Mosley & Co.   INSTS: __2__ x

in color which identifies the purpose of the cards. The quality of the card is stiff, yet flexible enough to permit easy typing and handling.

Billing system   Four to six differently colored bills are prepared in one typing operation. These are then used as the master and expiration records, invoice, accounts receivable record, and a reminder copy to request the unpaid premium, if necessary. Such a set of bills is frequently furnished by insurance agencies with the policies. The use and method of filing the master and expiration record bills is similar to the two-card system.

Policy system   By keeping all policies in the insurance department and filing them by their expiration dates, the policies properly serve as records of expiration. This arrangement necessitates recording the policy for master card purposes only. An alternate procedure consists of filing policies by names of borrowers in alphabetical order and preparing expiration cards or lists only. The advantage of keeping the policies at hand at all times is that carding errors are reduced.

Evaluation and recommendation   Since the basic purpose of recording policies is to provide a means of controlling renewal coverage, the arrangement established should be one which is best adapted to the company's insurance operations. Of the first two arrangements, the two-card system based on the preparation of two cards in one single operation seems the more economical and effective for establishing basic insurance department records. Although the billing system produces from four to six copies which may be used for a variety of purposes, it has inherent shortcomings in that the quality of the paper is usually poor and the copies designated for master records or expiration records may easily become torn or smudged from continuous handling. A system of maintaining expiration or master records by policies seems most desirable if supported by information prepared each month on data processing equipment which provides a listing of policies either in the alphabetical sequence of names of those insured or by expiration dates of policies.

Continuity of Insurance Coverage

The mortgage banker is responsible for maintaining adequate and continuous insurance coverage on all properties securing the mortgages he services. Whatever procedure is used, it must be foolproof, because a failure to pay premiums when due can result in cancellation of insurance protection and jeopardize the mortgagor's as well as the mortgagee's interest in the property. Even a policy written on a continuous basis remains in effect only when renewal premiums are paid when due.

Continuity of coverage is assured by two separate and yet overlapping procedures: (1) control of expirations and (2) payment of insurance premiums.

Control of expirations The mortgage banker who writes insurance orders renewal policies for his own customers. Others must be supplied with policies by borrowers or by agents authorized to write insurance for them. When borrowers or their agents fail to supply renewal policies on time, the mortgage banker, who does not follow a policy of automatic renewals, must order renewals through his own insurance department or an insurance agency prior to the expiration date. No exception can be permitted to the rule that each renewal policy must be ordered before the date of expiration.

The expiration cards or computer list of expiring policies warn the mortgage banker of pending renewals and provide a checklist against renewal policies received as well as those still outstanding.

Exhibit 72, statement of premium disbursement, is an example of a computer listing of expiring policies by one agent who is responsible for supplying renewal policies. This listing also illustrates the manifold uses of the type of report that data processing equipment is now geared to supply to the insurance department. Policies expiring in any given month may be listed by expiration dates on the same form. If the policies are arranged by investors' code numbers, the same form can be used as documentation for checks issued against investors' custodial accounts to pay insurance premiums.

Payment of insurance premiums Several insurance companies quickly cancel a policy if the premium is not paid, at times without providing adequate notice of cancellation. Accordingly, it is imperative that premium billings be paid when due. Particular care should be exercised in paying renewal premiums on continuous policies.

Premiums are paid from investors' custodial accounts or from a premium trust fund

EXHIBIT 72 *Statement of premium disbursement*

ABC MORTGAGE COMPANY
233 Maple Street
Chicago, Illinois 60190

STATEMENT OF PREMIUM DISBURSEMENT

☑ EXPIRATION
☐ CODING
☐ FINANCE
☐ SELF PAY
☐ INITIAL DISBURSEMENT
☐ FINAL DISBURSEMENT

ACCOUNT NUMBER	NAME	INV.	LOAN NUMBER	TYPE LOAN	AGENT	PRE-FIX	POLICY NUMBER	TRAN CODE	AMOUNT	MO	DAY	INTL YR	EXPR YR	TERM	F N	MONTHLY ACCRUAL	TOTAL PREMIUM

| | | | | | | | | | 1412 95 * | | | | | | | | |
| | | | | | | | | | 1412 95 | | | | | | | | |

H O

377

account. The premium trust fund account is the custodial account for all funds belonging to agents and insurance companies with whom the mortgage banker does business. Maintenance of this type of account is often required by state insurance regulations.

If insurance accruals in custodial accounts are not adequate to pay premiums, the borrowers must be billed for the difference. If the shortage is not received, the premium must still be paid in full by the mortgage banker. Insurance funds on hand should never be paid to an insurance agent with instructions to collect from the borrower, for the mortgage banker would not be assured that the premium would be paid when due. Should the borrower pay the insurance renewal himself, the insurance reserves on hand should be refunded upon presentation of a paid receipt.

Safekeeping of Policies

It is the investor's prerogative to decide who has custody of the insurance policy, the lender or the servicer. All lenders, with few exceptions (usually state-chartered banks and some smaller life insurance companies), require that all insurance policies issued in connection with residential single-family properties be retained by the mortgage banker. Many mortgagees also permit the servicer to retain insurance policies on income property loans, although this arrangement often is contingent on the size of the policy or loan. Some lenders specify loan amounts for income property loans which serve as a bench mark below which servicers are instructed to retain policies and above which policies are to be sent to the investor.

In lieu of the policy, investors may require that the mortgage banker issue a certificate of insurance that an original policy, meeting the investor's specifications, has been received. Often on the delivery of a loan it is necessary to attach the *first* policy to the certification; after the examination of the certificate and the policy by the lender, the policy is returned to the servicer for safekeeping. This procedure is maintained on the assumption that if the first policy is correct and acceptable to the lender, the renewal policy is likely to be correct also. Quite a number of certificates in use stipulate that the mortgagee be promptly notified of any changes in ownership.

The issuance of a certificate in lieu of submission of the actual insurance policy affords great savings to the lender since he has the servicer's assurance that the property or properties are covered. For the servicer, it reduces the expense of mailing bulky policies and eliminates the necessity of recalling policies when changes or substitution occur.

The servicer may then keep the original policies in a separate fire-resistant cabinet located in the insurance department where they are available for corrections, amendments, or even midterm replacements, or may keep them filed with the other mortgage documents and correspondence in the loan file in the file room. The policies must be protected from loss through fire although filing claims for loss is not contingent on presentation of the policy.

All endorsements which change the policy, whether in ownership, coverage, or ownership of the mortgage, must be attached to the policy. This then requires that the insurance clerk either obtain the loan file and attach the endorsement to the policy to finalize any of these changes, or pull the policy itself from the filing cabinet and take similar steps. In the latter instance, the responsibility for refiling the policy rests with the insurance clerk since it is important that the policy be in its proper place for expiration purposes. This requirement does not place an identical burden on the insurance department if the file containing the policy, which now has the endorsement attached, is returned to the loan file by the file clerk.

Space permitting, it is a good practice to retain all expired homeowners' policies until the statute of limitation in a particular state expires. Whenever a loss claim is pending, policies should not be destroyed, even if the term of the policy has already expired.

Certification Procedures

Some lenders do not accept any certifications. Those who do accept certifications normally outline their requirements in their manual or in a letter of instructions on handling insurance policies. While the certification procedure is generally applicable to residential loans, most insurance companies have special requirements for income property loans. These arrangements include complete certification of all risks, certification of risks up to certain loan amounts, the requirement of making the first policy available for inspection, and returning the policy thereafter for certifications. Certificates must also assure the lender that the servicer will not permit reduction of coverage originally stipulated and that coverage will be renewed in the same company or in a company of equal rating approved by the lender.

Types of certificates   Certification may be one of many different types of forms developed and designed by investors. These fall into two basic varieties: the *general type* applying to all loans serviced and the *specific type* applying to individual loans.

  1 General Type

    a Certification as part of the servicing contract   In this instance, certification is written in a clause in the servicing contract whereby the servicing agent agrees to be solely responsible for the borrower's maintaining and renewing adequate coverage. This is a fairly new practice which satisfactorily replaces other types and kinds of certificates.

    b Annual certification   According to this stipulation normally incorporated in the servicing contract, the servicer is obligated to issue a certificate annually signed by an officer which states:

    This is to certify that we have in our custody hazard insurance policies in full force and effect on all mortgages serviced by us for XYZ Insurance Company containing the standard mortgagee clause in favor of XYZ Insurance Company, and in amounts at least equal to the principal balance of the mortgage on each property or the full insurable value of the buildings thereon, whichever is less.

    Annual certifications often include assurance to the lender that there is no undue concentration of risks in one company. Some certificates also state that the borrower had complete freedom in placing his insurance. The annual insurance certifications may be combined with certification by the servicer that real estate taxes and FHA mortgage insurance premiums were paid.

2 Specific Type

  a Loan delivery certificate In this instance, the servicer certifies at the time the loan documents are delivered that:

We hold subject to your order, a fire and extended coverage policy (or Home-owner's or Comprehensive type policy according such coverage) on the above premises, written in accordance with your requirements, with the owner named as insured and with Standard Mortgagee Clause in your favor attached. We further certify that we have done nothing to divest the owner of control over the placement of hazard insurance.

This certificate is part of a form letter transmitting the loan documents to the investor. It applies to the first policy in each loan delivered; thereafter an additional annual certification is required.

  b Permanent individual certificate This certificate is issued in lieu of submission of the policy and is forwarded to the mortgagee at the time of delivery of the loan documents. The reference to co-insurance, Exhibit 73, indicates that the lender requiring this type of certification permits certification of insurance on income property loans.

Evaluation of types and forms of certificates From the foregoing discussion, it is eminently clear that there is no uniformity in the form of certifications required. Each method or type of certification apparently best suits its users or corresponds to the requirements of state or other regulatory bodies. The lack of uniformity in this area of operation does not impose so much of a burden on the servicer as does that still prevailing in handling loss drafts which, in spite of continuous efforts by the mortgage bankers, still needs further simplification and standardization.

There was a time when the servicer considered the retention and safekeeping of policies an inconvenience; this is no longer the case. It is most convenient for the servicer to hold the policy in custody so endorsements may be added to it, its provisions may be checked in case of loss, or it may be canceled if this becomes necessary, without any delays resulting from correspondence with lenders.

The most satisfactory arrangement is to submit a certification to the lender, based on information contained in the initial policy, at the time the loan is delivered. This assures the lender that an initial policy is in force and on hand.

In weighing the advantages and disadvantages of the certification method against that of forwarding policies to the investors, the viewpoints of both the investors and the mortgage companies must be considered. For the investor, the certification offers the following advantages: it eliminates the necessity of maintaining expiration records and filing equipment; it eliminates the work involved in checking policies for term, amount, and endorsement; and it eliminates correspondence on policies.

In contrast to these immediate advantages, the investor must consider the following

EXHIBIT 73 Certificate of insurance

CERTIFICATE OF INSURANCE   **Mtge. No.** 1234

TO

Mortgage Department
XYZ LIFE INSURANCE COMPANY
P.O. Box 7010
New York City, New York

The undersigned hereby certifies that it has effected and holds in its possession, subject to your order, policy or policies for:

Type of Insurance	Amount	Coinsurance	
Fire & Extended Coverage	$300,000	80 %	**If this space is**
	$	%	**used complete**
	$	%	**reverse of this**
	$	%	**form.**

Covering premises at: 540 Longdale Road, Rolling Meadows, Illinois

written in accordance with your requirements in the name of the owner, with standard mortgage clause in your favour, as first mortgagee, attached to each policy.

The undersigned hereby agrees that no changes will be made in the type, or reduction in the amount, of the coverage without the prior written consent of   XYZ Life Insurance Company

ABC MORTGAGE COMPANY
(Correspondent)

January 7, 1970   Per. Phil Jones

front side

reverse side

Where a coinsurance or a similar clause is made a part of the policy or policies please quote the current reproduction value less depreciation on which the amount of the insurance is based.

Current Reproduction Value		$	375,000
Less:			
Depreciation	$ 0		
Exclusions permitted			
by policy	4,000		4,000
Value for Insurance Purposes		$	371,000

disadvantages: the possibility that the servicer, due to negligence, may fail to provide adequate coverage; the possibility that the servicer may not obtain the proper mortgage clause; the possibility that the servicer may not place the insurance with an acceptable company; and the possibility that the servicer may fail to observe the requirements of co-insurance.

Most investors, who have adopted the method of permanent certification, consider as an ordinary business risk any possible failure on the part of the servicer to comply with the terms of the insurance certification or with that portion of the servicing contract which pertains to insurance. They contend that an actual loss would result only through a highly improbable chain of events pertaining to a single loan; i.e., the servicer's overlooking the renewal, the absence of a policy not being discovered at the periodical audit examination, and a loss occurring while the absence is still undetected. The last risk, of course, is covered by an errors and omissions policy.

As far as the servicer is concerned, the advantages of retaining policies include the reduction in mailing expense and the decrease in correspondence and postage involved in sending policies and obtaining policies for corrections or cancellations. The only disadvantage as far as the servicer is concerned is his additional responsibility and that additional filing space is required to house policies. In balance, the advantages of retaining the policies still far outweigh the disadvantages.

Administration of Loss Claims

Handling insurance losses is one of the mortgage banker's most valuable functions in servicing insurance policies. Regardless of who produced the insurance contract, however, the mortgage banker must do a conscientious and impartial job in this complicated role for both or one of his masters. The burden of handling losses varies from mortgage banker to mortgage banker depending in part on his role in the insurance-producing picture. If the mortgage banker is a producer of the insurance contract, he receives the loss reports and reports them to the company; if he does not write the insurance, he only discharges those responsibilities for which he is called upon by the lender, i.e., handling loss drafts; if he is both, he must be prepared to handle loss reports for his clients and dispose of the loss drafts.

It must be borne in mind that notwithstanding his servicing responsibilities to both lender and mortgagor-insurance client, the mortgage banker or, as a matter of fact, the insurance agent or broker does not get directly involved in the adjustment of losses. All adjustments—except those few where the loss does not exceed $50 and the insurance company empowers his agent to settle the claim—must be made between the insurance company adjusters and the insurance clients. Technically, the mortgage banker's job commences only after settlement of loss has been agreed upon by the insurance company and the insured, and a check has been issued for the payment or settlement of repairs.

In handling a loss claim, the servicer protects his investor by: (1) seeing to it that the property is restored to its condition prior to the loss; (2) seeing that the bills incurred are paid by the owner or that the loss draft is used to pay them; and

(3) seeing that the policy continues in full force and effect for the amount in effect prior to the loss.

The service to the borrower, however, consists of the mortgage banker's efforts to make the proceeds of the loss draft available either to pay the bills or to reimburse the owner for the expenditures already incurred. Since no one likes to wait for money as reimbursement for payment he has made on repair bills, the job of handling loss drafts—despite the precautions servicers must take to protect the lender—must be performed as expeditiously as possible.

Although the administration of loss claims appears to be a routine task, it requires judgment and common sense, and most lenders recognize the intricacies of some of the problems. One lender who is most cognizant of the often difficult task that his servicers perform gives them the following instructions: "It will be your responsibility to take such precautions against impairment of the security as may be reasonable, considering the nature and extent of the damage, the type of loan, the margin of security and other pertinent factors."

Each loss differs, not only in amount but also in the nature of the loss, the urgency of repairs, and the financial status of those sustaining the loss. No set of instructions can encompass all the steps that a mortgage banker may have to take within the bounds of common sense in the event of a complicated or extensive disaster loss. For instance, a loss draft may cover losses that have been repaired by several contractors including the owner, so that several parties are to be paid, and yet only one check is available to pay all parties involved. How can the investor be protected, but most importantly how can all repairs be paid without disregarding many of the requirements? Although most lenders establish sets of instructions for all possibilities that may be normally anticipated, there are always cases where the logical solution transcends instructions and mortgage bankers are called upon to take certain responsibilities not covered by such instructions.

As a practical matter, it is best to discuss the actual handling and disposition of losses according to two arbitrary size classifications of small and large losses. Basically, the size of the loss determines the speed with which the loss draft may be processed and the kind of precautionary measures that must be taken by the servicer to protect the lender's interest. The recommended method is for the mortgagee to give the servicer complete discretion in handling losses up to $500. The use of intermediate brackets ranging up to $100, from $100 to $200, then $200 to $500, and so on, may be superfluous, especially when the graduated scale is used to differentiate between procedures for handling the loss draft. Losses which require specific precautionary measures range upwards from $500.

The servicer must always remember that, whatever task he performs in administration of losses and handling of loss drafts, promptness is the most important product. This may not be easily accomplished since those losses which call for the greatest amount of service occur on disaster-type occasions such as a tornado or windstorm when a great number of borrowers expect individualized and prompt service. The mortgagor may quickly forget all the good things about the servicer if his check is bogged down in processing, regardless of where, how, and why the slowdown occurs.

Also, a mortgagor normally does not understand or care to understand the need for including the lender's name in the loss drafts nor many other requirements of the red-tape variety, and he consequently is prone to be annoyed and to complain to his agent or the mortgage banker.

To acquaint each mortgagor and his agent with the requirements of the lender in the event of the loss, it is advisable to inform each mortgagor what to do in that case. A brief description of what the mortgagor has to do and the duties and responsibilities of the servicer appears in the mortgage banker's booklets (Appendix A-5 and A-11). The information needed may be excerpted from the booklet in a letter and forwarded to each mortgagor with the insurance policy or sent at renewal time as a reminder. Bear in mind, however, that this information was prepared by a servicer who also writes insurance.

Another way to improve service or to promote greater understanding by the customer on handling losses is the following letter disseminated periodically by a servicer who has a considerable insurance clientele and deals primarily with policies supplied by others:

> As you are no doubt aware, each hazard insurance policy contains a Mortgagee Clause to protect the lender's investment. Since we service loans for a great number of investors, each with different requirements for handling claims, it is impossible for us to provide one procedure for all our mortgagors to follow. In addition, there are certain requirements which must be met on all FHA and VA loans.
>
> To expedite the clearance of loss drafts on your dwelling/building, you should notify your insurance agent as soon as a loss occurs. After he has investigated the loss, *if the claim is covered*, he should call our Insurance Department *prior* to the repair or replacement of the loss and before the issuance of the loss draft. Upon receiving his call, we will give your agent the procedure to follow to satisfy your particular investor and also FHA/VA if they are involved.
>
> It is suggested that this notice be kept with other important papers concerning your loan.

This type of information not only informs the borrower of the problems that may arise and his responsibilities and those of his agent, but expedites the settlement of losses. Furthermore, precautions of this type reduce the strain on the embattled insurance clerk who, when a storm strikes a subdivision, is besieged by calls from homeowners who do not know where to turn or what to do. To insurance clerks, the problems that arise in the event of a loss are a part of their office experiences or vocation, and they lose sight of the fact that each loss occurrence, or the events that caused it, may be a harrowing experience for the insured and his family.

Handling of loss draft According to generally accepted procedures, when a loss draft is either received in the mail or presented by the owner in person, a letter is dispatched and the following steps are taken and the following documentations are obtained. (See Exhibit 74.)

EXHIBIT 74   *Loss draft letter*

ABC MORTGAGE COMPANY
233 Maple Street
Chicago, Illinois 60190

January 15, 1971

Mr. Richard Smith
3846 Holly Lane
Hometown, Illinois

Re: Loan No. G128973
3846 Holly Lane
Hometown, Illinois

Dear Sir:

Please be informed that a check in the amount of $1200.00,
payable to you, your wife and the holder of your mortgage,
has been issued by the insurance company in settlement of
your claim for damage to your income that occurred on
December 10, 1970. In order to satisfy the requirements of
your mortgage and to enable us to place these funds into
your hands as soon as possible, it will be necessary that you
comply with one or several of the requirements checked below.

(X) Kindly endorse the check (you and your wife) payable to
the order of ABC Mortgage Company and return it to us. A new
check will be sent to you for the same amount.

(X) After repairs have been fully made, the enclosed affidavit
should be completed by you and your wife, notarized, and
returned to us.

(X) Because of the amount of loss involved, an inspector from
our office will have to visit your property to confirm that
repairs, as made, satisfy mortgage requirements.

(X) We enclose two copies of our sworn construction statement.
One of these should be completed in detail by the contractor
handling the repairs and we should be furnished with final
waivers of lien from all other contractors, subcontractors, and
material suppliers listed thereon. If you have any questions
regarding these requirements, please call our construction
department.

( ) If you do not have funds on hand to pay the contractor as
repairs progress, kindly endorse the check (you and your wife)
and return it to us. We shall obtain the endorsement of the
holder of your mortgage, and deposit the check in an escrow
account and pay the contractor for his work upon his presenting
proper waivers of lien to us.

( ) The loss check is not enclosed for your endorsement. We
are holding it in our file until we receive an inspection
report, notarized affidavit signed by you and your wife
certifying to completion of repairs, and proper waivers of
lien and contractors statements. The loss check together
with these documents, will then be sent to
              for endorsement of the check over to you and your
wife and return to us. Upon return of the check, we shall
mail it to you.

ABC MORTGAGE COMPANY

Insurance Department

Determination of loss   Ascertain facts relative to loss; when and where the loss actually occurred and whether repairs have been made; if not made, how and when repairs will be accomplished. Check loan account; since loss proceeds must be handled in cooperation with mortgagors, ascertain whether the loan is current. If the loan is not current, a loss check may not be released to mortgagor to pay bills; they must be paid by the servicer.

Affidavit or letter of completion   If the repairs have been completed, an affidavit composed along the lines shown on Exhibit 75 must be procured from the owner indicating that the restoration of the property is satisfactory and bills have been paid. If the loss is under $200, however, an informal letter from the mortgagor reporting the loss and completion of repairs may be acceptable, providing the

EXHIBIT 75   *Affidavit—completion of repairs*

A F F I D A V I T

STATE OF ILLINOIS)
)SS
COUNTY OF COOK   )

Richard Smith and Dolores Smith _____ , being duly sworn on their oath, deposes and says that they are the owners of the property known as

3846 Holly Lane, Hometown, Illinois _____ and which was damaged by ___fire___

on ___December 10, 1970_____ and that the necessary repairs have been made and all bills paid, and no mechanics liens filed.

                        This affidavit is made for the purpose of procuring from the

XYZ Life Insurance Company _____ their endorsement on Insurance

Company check covering satisfaction of claim in full amount of $ _1200.00_ .

Date repairs completed____1/6/71_____   X_____

                                                                          X_____

Subscribed and sworn to before me this

___17th_____day of _January____ A.D. 19_71_

               X_____
                        Notary Public

mortgagor states the nature of the loss and that the repair bills have been paid. The amount under which the latter simplified arrangement is acceptable is contingent on the nature of the loss and other local circumstances and lien laws. If bills were not paid, the loss draft must be endorsed by the mortgagor to pay bills.

A word of caution about affidavits should be made here. Generally, the reliability of affidavits leaves a lot to be desired in that many people execute and have affidavits notarized even though facts as to completion of repairs, but particularly payment of bills, are not true. Affidavits, therefore, especially in case of larger losses, must be supported by waiver of liens or paid bills and inspection of properties.

Waiver of lien   If the loss exceeds $200 and the repairs are completed by a contractor or a repairman, a waiver of lien as to both work and material must be obtained.

Inspection of losses   In most instances, if the amount of loss exceeds $500 or whatever limit the lender establishes, the property must be inspected. Before such inspection is made, it is advisable to inform the inspector about the nature and specific location of the loss so that he may specifically inspect the repairs. It is also advisable to retain a copy of his written report should it become necessary later—in the event of foreclosure—to prove to FHA or VA that restoration of the property was properly accomplished.

Processing loss drafts   The loss draft may be handled and processed in any of the four ways. Normally, the size of the loss determines the method employed.

1   *Elimination of name of lender from loss draft*   The standard mortgage clause automatically includes the lender's name in each loss draft. Nevertheless, it is a common practice to have the lender's name omitted from the draft if the loss is under $50 or $100. The lender makes a prior request to all insurance companies that his name be omitted from losses up to specified amounts. The check is then turned over to the mortgagor or contractor. If a bill is unpaid and both mortgagor's and contractor's names appear on the draft, it is better to send the check to the contractor for he will surely obtain endorsement of the mortgagor to pay the bill. Of course, the inclusion of a $50 or $100 deductible clause in the insurance coverage has greatly decreased the number of loss drafts and claims as the great majority of losses are under $100.

2   *Endorsement of loss drafts*   In most instances, lenders authorize their correspondents to endorse loss drafts as shown below. After such an endorsement and in compliance with other requirements, the check may be given to the insured.

> Pay to the order of (name of mortgagors)
> without recourse
> *XYZ Insurance Company*
> By *ABC Mortgage Co.,* as Agent
> Name of Servicer
> (Signature)
> Vice President

3 *Depositing loss drafts*   Rather than authorize the correspondent to endorse the lender's name as indicated above, lenders often require the insured to endorse the loss draft and have the loss draft deposited in the custodial account. The servicer then reissues the check (or several checks) to the borrower or persons who have done the work. This task is usually executed by the type of endorsement shown below. This procedure is unpopular since it requires the borrower to handle and endorse a loss draft twice: once when he is asked to do so by the mortgage banker and then again a few days later when the check, having been reissued, is cashed.

> For deposit only for credit of
> (Names of Borrowers)
> _____
> FHA-VA Custodial Account
> *XYZ Insurance Company*
>
> By *ABC Mortgage Co.*, as Agent
> _____
> (Signature)
> _____
> Vice President

4 *Sending loss drafts to lender*   If a loss in excess of $1,000 is involved, the lender does not always delegate the job of handling losses to the servicer. However, on submission of evidence that all prescribed precautionary measures were taken, the lender endorses the draft. Some lenders have a member of their local staff check the completion of repairs. Actually, insurance company regulations do not permit them to authorize endorsement of checks for large sums by their correspondents.

Compliance with FHA or VA requirements   FHA and VA requirements differ but each must be observed.

FHA loans   FHA relies entirely on the mortgagee and his servicer to restore the property to acceptable condition. If the mortgagee wishes to have a letter of assurance on losses over $2,500 that the restoration of the property is satisfactory to FHA, FHA issues such a letter either during the restoration or after its completion. Since different FHA offices have slightly different approaches to this matter, a check with the local FHA office on the issuance of a letter of assurance is advisable.

VA loans   VA does not require that it be notified if a loss occurs. But VA inspects the property before it takes title in the event of a foreclosure, and if it does not find the property in good condition, it may question the maintenance or the manner in which repairs may have been handled if a loss did occur. The only VA requirement a servicer must enforce is that the loss draft be applied to the reduction of debt if the borrower does not wish to make certain repairs. For instance, the borrower may not want to rebuild a detached garage which has burned down. This is acceptable both to the lender and VA if the loss draft is applied to the reduction of the outstanding indebtedness.

Special methods for larger losses or problem cases Handling loss drafts for large losses often tests the ingenuity of the servicer since the problems that arise cannot be anticipated. Some of the following methods may be used if complications arise.

1 *Loss draft covers several payees, and repairs were completed and inspected.* If a loss draft is made out to a lender, mortgagor, and several of the contractors, it is best to obtain first the endorsement of the mortgagor and each of the contractors, with assurances that they will be paid. Then the check should be endorsed by the servicer for the lender and deposited in the custodial account, and separate checks should be issued to the mortgagor and each of the contractors involved.

2 *Loss draft covers several payees, and some of the jobs are completed and some are not.* The above procedure may be used if one of the contractors who completed his job insists that he be paid. Funds for contractors who have not completed repairs may then be held in the custodial account until completion.

3 *Loss draft covers a large repair job, but repairs have not yet been commenced.* If a substantial loss is involved, it may become necessary for the servicer to ask the mortgagor to endorse the draft and, after endorsing for the mortgagee or obtaining his endorsement, to deposit the funds in a special construction account. The servicer can then disburse the proceeds of the draft against waiver of liens and bills to the various contractors as jobs are completed. Rather than deposit the check and disburse it, the check may be held with the mortgagor's endorsement until it may be released. Caution must be taken, however, that the check not be held too long since certain checks may become void after a specified time, normally 90 days.

4 *Loss draft covers unpaid material and supplies and payment of repair work performed by a borrower who is delinquent.* In this instance, the servicer must obtain endorsements of the mortgagors and the supplier, then have the check deposited in the lender's custodial account, and finally issue two checks—one to pay for the material (against receipt of waiver of material lien) and the other to apply loss proceeds due the borrower on the delinquent installments.

5 *Loss draft does not include name of contractor who has not been paid.* If a check includes the name of the lender but not the contractor, the servicer automatically becomes responsible for any unpaid bill if the job is satisfactorily completed. Therefore, after obtaining an endorsement of the check by the borrower and endorsing the check on behalf of the lender, he should mail it to the contractor. If such check is sent to the contractor, a letter should accompany the remittance with a copy of such letter to the mortgagor. Or if the check is to be reissued (after being endorsed by the lender and borrower), the contractor's name should automatically be included as payee (even if it was not included in the original draft) and then sent to the mortgagor. In this manner, the payment of the bill to the contractor is normally assured.

General observations It is worthwhile to emphasize that whatever the amount of the loss or however strong the lender's precautions may be, losses must be administered with loan-to-value ratios in mind. A $500 loss even if it is not properly administered on a 50 percent loan does little to jeopardize the investment of the lender, while a considerably smaller loss, let us say $200, if not properly handled on a no-equity loan, may impair the lender's investment.

The servicer should keep a record on the insurance card, preferably on the master card, of each loss by date and amount. This information may be useful particularly in dealing with loss-prone mortgagors. Information may also be needed during a subsequent foreclosure, if dates and amounts of repairs are needed to justify a claim with FHA or VA.

All FHA multifamily loan commitments stipulate that, in addition to the name of the mortgagee, the mortgage clause include a loss-payable provision to the Secretary of Housing and Urban Development, Washington, D.C. Consequently, each loss draft must be forwarded for endorsement to the Federal Housing Administration field office director having jurisdiction over the area in which the property sustaining the loss is situated. Upon presentation of satisfactory evidence and inspection of repairs by the FHA office, the loss draft is endorsed and returned to the servicer for disposition.

Handling Insurance Assignments

It is a peculiarity of an insurance contract that only the individual who was the owner of record when the loss occurred is insured. It is imperative, therefore, that the insurance policy always show current ownership. It is not sufficient for the records of the insurance agent or the mortgage banker to show the current owner's name. The mortgagee's interest will be impaired if there is a failure by the mortgage banker in reporting change of ownership so the insuring company's records reflect the correct name. To assure acknowledgement of a change of ownership, it is necessary that the insuring company consent to the assignment as soon as possible after title changes hands. If the company for one reason or another does not consent, the coverage must be replaced immediately.

Exhibit 37 is a standard form which the seller of a property is asked to execute in duplicate. A copy of this form must be forwarded to the company insuring the property. This form, when returned acknowledging change of ownership, must be attached to the policy. In most mortgage banking organizations, this form is one of several which are normally sent by the cashier or the individual responsible for the proration or loan assumption statements involving transfer of ownership.

Because of the danger of loss occurring during change of ownership, when the insurance company's records of ownership may not be current—a period that may last from a week to a month—or where the possibility of refusal to consent exists, an assignment of policy under purchase agreement may be used. This assignment stipulates the payment of loss "to the name insured and the vendee, as their respective interests may appear." (See Exhibit 76.) If a delay is expected in consummation of the transaction, it is advisable to use the above type of assignment form.

EXHIBIT 76 Assignment of policy under purchase agreement

ASSIGNMENT OF POLICY UNDER PURCHASE AGREEMENT

A contract of sale covering the premises described in the Policy designated below, having been entered into between the named Insured, as Vendor(s), and................ John Smith and Mary Smith ....,
as Vendee(s), loss, if any under this Policy, shall be payable to the named Insured and said Vendee(s), as their respective interests may appear. Such payment shall not exceed the amount that would have been payable to the named Insured in the event of loss had this endorsement not been executed, nor in any event shall such payment exceed the amount of the Policy designated below.

Upon consummation of said contract of sale, Policy No. .... AH 8516451 ....of the
.... XYZ Insurance Company ....is hereby assigned to
John Smith and Mary Smith
VENDEE(S)

/s/ John Doe

/s/ Mary Smith
NAMED INSURED

Dated........ December 1, ...19 68

CONSENT TO ASSIGNMENT

The above named Insurance Company hereby consents to the above endorsement and to the above assignment of said Policy.

Issued at its........ Chicago, Illinois ....Agency. Dated........ December 1, ...19 68
CITY OR TOWN   STATE ABC Insurance Agency
By: /s/ James Johnson ....Agent.

Upon receipt of executed insurance assignments, it is good practice for the cashier, insurance department, or whoever handles change of ownerships to notify all other departments that the property has changed hands and instruct them to change their servicing records accordingly. Most investors require notification also.

Substitution of Policies

It is the prerogative of every mortgagor to purchase the best insurance coverage available at the lowest possible price. If the mortgagor chooses to purchase a new policy, he must ask the lender to accept the new policy and to return his current policy for cancellation. Without considering the merits of the policies or the savings in premiums to the borrower, the expense that the mortgage banker incurs to return the policy and to check, card, and file a new one must be taken into account. A substitution is especially expensive if it occurs at midterm, when the mortgage banker would not normally be required to take any actions on the old policy. The work involved may be even greater if the policy sent is not in correct form or in the proper amount or does not contain an appropriate mortgage clause.

In certain states where substitutions are not daily occurrences, mortgage bankers usually do not charge a substitution fee; in areas where substitutions are common, however, the mortgage banker does not accept and process the new policy unless a fee ranging from $5 to $15 is sent with the substitution. Exhibit 77 is a form letter

EXHIBIT 77   Transmittal letter – insurance policy

ABC MORTGAGE COMPANY
233 Maple Street
Chicago, Illinois   60190

Re :

Dear Sir:

The policy is enclosed and in order to process it the following checked (X) items are needed:

( ) The Mortgage Clause on the policy must read:

_____

( ) _____

_____

( ) $7.50 Service Fee, payable to ABC Mortgage Company for processing policy substitution in mid-term. Next date at which policy substitution can be made without the Service Fee is _____. Substitution of policies on anniversary date of expiration date must be furnished to this office at least 15 days prior to the due date.

( ) An Invoice was not enclosed. If you have paid the premium now due please forward a paid receipt with the policy. If the premium is not paid, and you wish to utilize the available insurance funds in your escrow account, please forward an invoice for processing. The enclosed Monthly Insurance Deposit letter outlines the procedure relative to the disposition of insurance escrow accruals.

( ) The insurance escrow reserve accrual is insufficient to pay the entire premium due on the enclosed policy. Your check for $_____, payable to ABC Mortgage Company is needed to enable us to pay the premium in full.

It will not be possible to process the policy until it is returned with all of the requested items. Renewal policies must be presented prior to the policy inception date.

Very truly yours,

MANAGER, INSURANCE DEPARTMENT

Enc.

used by a mortgage banker when he receives a policy after its expiration date or which was not acceptable for one of the reasons indicated in the form letter. In the interest of good customer relations, it is advisable to inform mortgagors in advance of the fee. The announcement itself may discourage substitutions.

OTHER MATTERS

Maintenance of Errors and Omissions Coverage

Most servicing agreements require the mortgage banker to maintain errors and omissions coverage. Investors may also require that an endorsement be attached to the policy indicating that the insuring company has agreed to notify the investor, within 10 to 30 days, that the policy was terminated, canceled, or reduced in amount. (See also Chapter 6.)

Use of Cost-saving Forms

To speed up service but keep clerical work at a minimum, it is customary to use work-saving forms. These readily replace form letters that require fill-in typing and appear to be obvious form letters. The most frequent use of these forms is in connection with dissemination of duplicate copies of policies, endorsements to policies, and loss drafts.

Single-interest Insurance Protection

The *single-interest policy*, otherwise called *mortgagee impairment policy*, is a relatively new insurance product. It insures the mortgagee in the event of direct physical loss to the borrower's property if the mortgagor has failed to keep insurance in force as required, the mortgagee elects to foreclose, and the sale of the property is insufficient to satisfy the outstanding mortgage debt. A single-interest policy may be purchased by a mortgagee, such as a life insurance investor or bank, for the loans serviced directly or through its correspondents. It may also be purchased by a mortgage banker for the protection of its servicing portfolio.

When a mortgagee or mortgage banker acquires a single-interest policy, it examines evidence of acceptable insurance only at loan closing, and then reminds the borrower to maintain such insurance in effect over the life of the mortgage loan. Thus, the entire responsibility for maintaining proper and adequate insurance coverage is placed upon the borrower, although some mortgagees send annual reminders to their borrowers of their obligation to maintain insurance under the terms of the mortgage.

Although the single-interest policy appears to be a cost-saver in servicing work, it also raises problems and creates exposures. The disadvantages may outweigh the advantages of eliminating standard clerical insurance tasks such as maintaining expiration records and safekeeping policies.

The adverse factors which must be carefully reviewed and evaluated by all those who consider the purchase of a single-interest policy are:

1 Placing the responsibility for maintenance of insurance solely on the borrower may be an admirable objective for the education of the public. However, it hardly represents a philosophy that most mortgage bankers normally maintain or that coincides with those precepts on which FHA was founded. Single-interest insurance protects the mortgagee, but fails to extend any concern for the borrower other than putting him on notice that he must protect himself against insurable hazards.

2 Since FHA does not permit elimination of monthly insurance reserve deposits, the mortgagee must refund to each borrower annually an amount equivalent to the insurance premium which was deposited, or pay the premiums. Thus, no saving will be attained as far as FHA loans are concerned. Reserve collections for VA and conventional loans may be suspended; however, such a step may adversely affect the benefit that a mortgage banker normally attains by holding such funds in custodial bank accounts.

3 Most importantly, the single-interest policy exposes the mortgagee or the mortgage banker to a far greater risk than it portends to cover since the owner of the policy must recall the policies from borrowers on 90- or 180-days notice and set up insurance records once again if the company writing the single-interest policy no longer wishes, or is unable, to provide the protection, and if the experience gained in writing such policy requires an increase in the premium to an amount greater than the savings anticipated.

4 Furthermore, the existence of a single-interest policy may bring about a relaxation of insurance underwriting efforts in areas where risks are hard to place, allowing the single-interest insurance carrier to pay for losses where actually little or no attempt was made to write or procure insurance in the first place.

On balance, it seems that the adverse factors considerably outweigh the advantages of single-interest insurance, and therefore, all factors involving the purchase of such a policy should be seriously weighed before any company undertakes to discontinue the maintenance of insurance records and of safekeeping policies. In 1965, the Mortgage Bankers Association of America took the position that the single-interest insurance program is not in the best interest of the borrower, lender, or investor.

CHAPTER SEVENTEEN

Tax Department

Failure to pay real estate taxes and assessments can cause the placement of a lien against the property which then impairs the value of the mortgagee's investment. If this lien is not satisfied it may cause the loss of the entire investment through tax sale by the taxing authority. Avoiding this possibility is the responsibility of the mortgage banker and his tax department. He must pay or verify payment of real estate taxes and special assessments on the properties securing the mortgage loans he services. He must also inform his investors that the tax bills have been paid by submitting the receipted bills or a tax certification.

If the mortgage document requires the mortgagor to make monthly deposits to cover tax bills, as is the case for all FHA and VA loans and a large proportion of conventional loans, the mortgage banker pays tax bills out of the mortgagor's custodial reserves. In the absence of such requirements, the mortgagor-owner pays the taxes and the tax department verifies that payment has been made.

Most servicing contracts require the mortgage banker to maintain errors and omissions coverage which, among other matters, protects him, within specified limits, from losses on claims against him for negligent acts that result from failure to pay real estate taxes. This coverage is included in the standard mortgage bankers blanket bond.

ORGANIZATION OF DEPARTMENT

Payment of taxes from escrow reserves may appear to be a fairly routine task, but tax time can be a most harassing 45- to 60-day period for mortgage servicing employees, especially those in the tax department. The staff must complete a heavy volume of work in a brief period of time while maintaining a high degree of accuracy in processing and approving tax bills for payment. The size of the staff of the tax department should vary according to the frequency of tax payment dates, the number of tax bills to be paid and the number of days available for processing them for payment, the methods used to obtain the tax bills, and the internal procedures used in paying them.

Tax work cannot be spread over a 12-month period; in fact, little work can be done before the tax bills are received. Even updating tax escrow information, the only preparatory work necessary, can be completed in a few weeks or months, still leaving considerable free time for other activities for a regular tax staff. Only if the servicing portfolio includes loans in many states with various tax due dates is tax work performed on a round-the-year basis.

In offices which service several hundred loans, the bookkeeper or collector becomes a tax clerk for the few weeks when it is necessary to process and pay the bills. If the volume of loans is large enough to warrant a permanent tax department with one or more tax clerks, temporary help may be hired during peak periods to assure payment of bills before the penalty date. The review of tax escrow accounts for adequacy and the collection of any shortage necessary to pay the tax bills should be made by the collection personnel, either alone or in cooperation with the tax clerk. Unless there are substantial shortages, this job can be performed shortly after tax time.

The preparatory tax work and the processing of tax bills for payment can be simplified by using data processing equipment which can readily be adapted to analyze reserve accounts, bill for shortages, and establish new and revised payment requirements.

ESTABLISHING TAX RECORDS

The tax card is the department's basic operating tool. On this single card, all pertinent information relating to the tax status of the property is recorded and all necessary tax information is maintained. The tax card may be prepared by the tax department. However, the recommended procedure is to prepare the tax card in the department responsible for preparing mortgage documents. This assures the minimum amount of errors in establishing correct legal descriptions, which are consistent with information used in the legal description of the mortgage documents. Some of the data are taken directly from the title policy or the official property records, if accessible. Other information, especially estimates of future tax bills on new nonresidential properties where construction loans are involved, may be supplied to the closing staff by the supervisor of the tax department after he examines the tax records and consults the tax collector.

From an operational standpoint, the tax department begins to function after the loan is closed. The loan-closing staff is generally responsible for preparing mortgage documents, including the tax card and the loan-closing statement. It is also responsible for the following tax matters:

1 Paying all outstanding tax bills and assessments before closing.

2 Prorating the tax bill, if available or if the amount can be ascertained, between the purchaser and seller.

3 Charging the purchaser on the loan disbursement statement with that portion of the future bill which he does not pay monthly, but which must be accrued to pay a tax bill on a certain date. For instance, if the tax bill is due May 1 and the loan is closed in December with the first payment due January 1, eight-twelfths of the bill must be withheld from the loan proceeds and four monthly tax deposits must be paid by the mortgagor to provide the monies needed to pay the bill when due. If the bill is underestimated, of course, there will be a shortage on May 1 which must then be collected from the mortgagor.

4 Transferring to the tax reserve account the amount withheld when the loan is disbursed. These funds together with tax deposits in future months are used to pay the first tax bill due during the term of the loan.

5 Determining the amount of tax deposits to be collected as required under the terms of the mortgage, if applicable, by dividing the anticipated bill by twelve and relaying such information to cashiers and the accounting department. This information will then be included in the "first payment" letter.

It is imperative that tax bills be accurately estimated since there is no recourse to the seller for adjustment of incorrectly prorated tax bills unless a special agreement has been made in advance. Where a construction loan is involved, the estimate of the tax liability and the necessary tax deposits should be based on the value of the property after improvements are completed. It is wiser to risk a subsequent adjustment in the borrower's favor than to establish reserves based on a tax bill on unimproved property for which the borrower must make up a substantial shortage.

Several mortgage bankers have developed arrangements with their builder customers to prorate the tax liability after the first tax bill is issued. For this purpose, tax deposits collected are based on the builder's estimate, with stipulation that an adjustment be made by the mortgage banker once tax bills on the improved property are available. Upon the issuance of tax bills computed on the improved basis, the builder pays the balance of his tax liability or gets a refund from the owner.

On FHA multifamily construction loans, it is, of course, the mortgagee's responsibility to collect taxes on the basis of FHA's tax estimate and to make adjustments in either direction when the tax bill on the improved property is finally issued. As a practical matter, the same procedure should be employed on construction loans on all conventional income property, with the head of the tax department taking the responsibility for determining the estimated assessment and tax.

Also, it is the responsibility of the mortgage banker to watch for intentional underestimation of future tax bills by builders and brokers who, to effect a sale or to help a borrower qualify for a loan, particularly in new subdivisions, are prone to gloss over the anticipated size of the tax bill. Unfortunately, mortgage bankers, willingly or unwillingly, often become a party to this type of deception and permit the establishment of inadequate reserves and inadequate monthly reserve accruals. Such unsound practices, if tolerated as a part of loan production activity, will explode in the tax department after the end of the first year when the true amount of the tax bill is revealed. Mortgagors, billed for tax shortages as well as substantial increases in their monthly payments, will complain. Some may be unable to make an extra payment as well as larger monthly payments. Such unsound loan production practices increase the burden of the tax work and may have serious adverse effects on the borrower's ability to maintain ownership of the property.

Tax Cards

After the loan is closed, the tax card is given to the tax department. The tax card can be of any size, but should be on fairly heavy paper so that it is usable for several years and can be filed time and again in a departmental file cabinet.

The tax card should contain, or provide for, the following information:

1 Name of mortgagor
2 Address of property
3 Name of mortgagee
4 Company and investor loan numbers
5 Detailed legal description
6 Space for entries of each tax bill
7 Space for recording state, city, or other municipal taxes; if the nonpayment of water, sewer, school, or other similar assessments may become liens on the property, space should also be provided for recording payment of such items

Since mortgage bankers make loans which call for tax reserve deposits or require the mortgagor to pay his own tax bill, it is best to have tax cards on two different colored cards to distinguish between the two arrangements. Cards may then be interfiled or filed in separate cabinets according to loan number or borrower's name. If the responsibility for paying the tax bill is identified by the use of cards of different colors, the control over the paid and unpaid bills of both variety can be automatically maintained.

Several companies maintain a tax card library by retaining tax cards on loans which have been paid in full or by preparing extra cards for various types of properties and types of buildings in various localities. These cards are then referred to in preparing any required estimates of taxes on certain areas and certain types of buildings.

Delinquency Control

In localities where all tax bills are due on a specific date or are payable in two or more installments each year, the control of tax delinquency is usually a simple matter. If all tax cards are placed in one drawer of a file cabinet and then removed and placed into another drawer as taxes are paid, the tax cards that remain in the first drawer on a certain date are the properties on which taxes have not yet been paid.

If the company services loans in several municipalities and tax bills or their install-ments become due and payable almost every month, a more elaborate system of delinquency control must be established. Special control records may be prepared in addition to the regular, detailed tax card by any of the following means:

1. Two cards: one is the master tax card which is filed according to loan number or borrower's name and the other is the due date and control card which is filed according to date the tax bill is due. As payments are made on various properties at different intervals, they are entered on the master tax card as well as on the control card. The master card is returned to the cabinet after entry of a payment and is filed by either the borrower's name or loan number; the control card is returned to the group of cards which is filed according to the next due date.
2. A tax payment control book of several types. One type may show the list of loans on which taxes are to be paid to certain municipalities on certain dates. Under this system, the master tax card is marked when a payment is made for a particular installment and a corresponding entry is made in the control book. An entry in the book may consist of stamping "paid" on the line opposite the loan number. Thus, at the end of the month or before penalty date, all unpaid tax bills may easily be discerned.
3. Tax calendar. The establishment and maintenance of a tax calendar are advisable if a great number of different tax bills must be paid to different states and town-ships, if the due dates vary, or if some bills may be paid with a discount for pay-ing ahead or incur a penalty if paid late. A calendar record of these particulars may serve as a useful reference guide.

PAYMENT OF TAXES FROM ESCROW RESERVES

The task of paying the borrower's tax bill from the accumulated escrow reserves in-cludes the following steps: (1) obtaining tax bills from either the borrower or the tax collector; (2) verifying each tax bill by comparing it with the legal description, ap-propriate tax account, or code designation of the applicable mortgaged property; (3) approving payment after determining the adequacy of funds on hand for such purpose; (4) collecting shortages if funds are not adequate to pay the current bill; and (5) establishing tax reserve requirements to provide sufficient funds to pay future bills. Most of these tasks are often performed simultaneously. Since the tax bill must be paid before a specific due date, collecting shortages to pay bills is normally more urgent than setting up adequate reserve requirements to pay future bills.

Obtaining Tax Bills

Tax bills may be obtained by the mortgage company directly from the tax collector's office or from the borrowers to whom the tax collector has mailed them. The first method is the general practice; however, in many states, the law requires that the bills be sent to the property owners. Under some circumstances and servicing methods, obtaining the tax bills from borrowers is practical and economical. Tax bills may also be obtained and paid through companies that render this type of service.

From tax collectors To procure tax bills from the collector's office, it is often advisable for the loan-closing department, at the time the loan is closed, to have the borrower sign a letter authorizing the tax collector to deliver all future bills to the mortgage company. Retaining such an authorization on file or forwarding it to the collector, the mortgage company can:

1 Annually submit a list to the various taxing authorities, which includes the addresses and/or legal descriptions of those properties on which taxes are paid by the company rather than the property owner. Companies using data processing equipment or employing an addressograph machine can easily run off the entire list in one speedy and inexpensive operation.
2 Mail a card or letter of notification to the tax collector at the time the loan is closed requesting that the company be billed for payment until further notice. When the loan is paid in full, the tax collector's office must be notified to discontinue sending tax bills on a particular property.

The choice between submitting a list each year or sending a permanent notification for each loan to the collector depends on the degree of cooperation and accuracy that may be expected from the tax collector's office.

Tax cards may be forwarded to the collector with a request that the applicable tax bills be attached to the respective tax cards and returned to the mortgage company. Although this method eliminates the necessity of preparing a list each year, it is effective only if the tax office returns all cards and bills promptly. Companies operating in smaller towns find this method successful. Unfortunately, this procedure cannot be followed when the number of loans serviced is large or when a great number of different taxing authorities must be contacted for bills.

From borrowers The mortgagor is asked by letter each year to forward the tax bill to the mortgage company upon receiving it from the tax collector's office. If the borrower does not respond to this request, a second request is mailed just before the penalty date. If this fails, a duplicate bill is obtained by the mortgage banker directly from the collector's office and is paid promptly to protect both the mortgagor and mortgagee.

Mailing the request for the tax bill is more practical if it is automated and is made through the use of a self-addressed, postage-paid envelope, which also asks for the difference between the tax bill and the reserves held in the account. A precoded envelope showing the loan number and the code number of the investor facilitates processing the bill for payment. The information appearing on the envelope can be transcribed to the tax bill immediately, reducing the number of mistakes caused by erroneous identification of tax bills.

As a matter of customer relations, in those states where homestead exemptions are granted to property owners or special tax exemptions are granted to disabled veterans, mortgage bankers customarily remind borrowers annually to file for their tax exemptions. This is usually done before the yearly tax work rush.

From a tax service company Bills may also be secured through a company specifically engaged in the business of obtaining and paying tax bills and making tax searches.

Comparison of procedures Basically, each arrangement of obtaining tax bills has merits, provided the entire tax procedure is geared to take advantage of its maximum benefits. The great advantage of obtaining the bills from the tax collector is that if sufficient funds are on hand to pay the bills and if, according to a preestablished custom, it is not necessary to notify the borrowers of the amounts of the bills before payment, bills received can be promptly and automatically paid. Furthermore, if the bills are picked up at the collector's office or are received from him in one mailing, the company is assured that all bills to be paid are in its possession at one time and, therefore, can plan and execute the entire tax work accordingly. If the company wishes, the borrowers can be notified of the amount of their tax bills while the bills are actually being processed for payment or shortly thereafter.

However, companies that wait for borrowers to mail the bills to them have less time to process them and must spend time collating each bill with their tax records. There are conditions, however, under which this system is either mandatory or can be made highly advisable and economical. In some states, e.g., Florida, the mortgage companies have no choice but to get their tax bills from the borrowers since the state law requires that the tax bill be mailed directly to the property owner. In states, counties, or cities where tax burdens are steadily increasing and where tax protests are likely, it is often best to obtain the bills from the borrowers since the company cannot take the chance of paying the bills without the borrower's approval. The main disadvantage of this practice is that the yearly request for tax bills and for authorizations to pay them increases the possibility of questions and protests and consequently retards the payment of taxes.

Obtaining bills from borrowers can be made quite effective, however, by using a return envelope, which incorporates a request for the tax bill and authorization for its payment with a statement of reserves on hand and a request for the payment of any shortage. Furthermore, use of the return envelope can speed up processing considerably and provide a first-class medium for the collection of shortages at the same time. (See Exhibit 78.)

Companies operating in more than one state or city use both systems; i.e., they pick up the tax bills for those loans which are in their own state or town at the collector's office, and for loans in other cities or in states where the law does not permit bills to be mailed to the mortgage company, they ask borrowers to send in their bills.

Data processing equipment enables mortgage bankers to automate the preparation and dissemination of requests for tax bills and subsequent processing. In lieu of a return envelope which is a satisfactory tool when the number does not exceed 10,000, an automated notice is prepared and dispatched, accompanied by a return envelope. (See Exhibit 79.) When the borrower responds and returns the notice with the tax bill

EXHIBIT 78 Tax advice

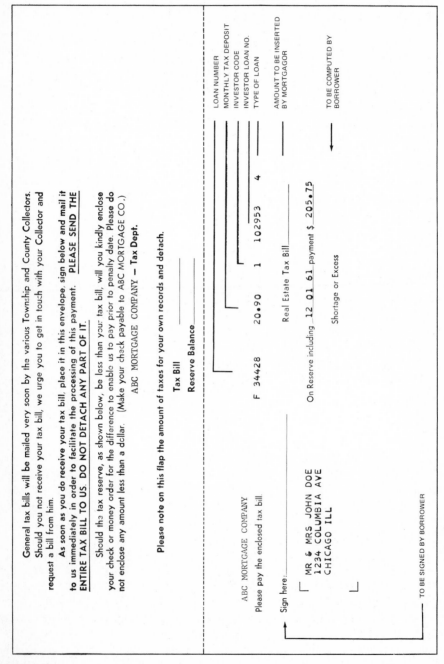

General tax bills will be mailed very soon by the various Township and County Collectors. Should you not receive your tax bill, we urge you to get in touch with your Collector and request a bill from him.

As soon as you do receive your tax bill, place it in this envelope, sign below and mail it to us immediately in order to facilitate the processing of this payment. **PLEASE SEND THE ENTIRE TAX BILL TO US. DO NOT DETACH ANY PART OF IT.**

Should the tax reserve, as shown below, be less than your tax bill, will you kindly enclose your check or money order for the difference to enable us to pay prior to penalty date. Please do not enclose any amount less than a dollar. (Make your check payable to ABC MORTGAGE CO.)

ABC MORTGAGE COMPANY – **Tax Dept.**

Please note on this flap the amount of taxes for your own records and detach.

Tax Bill _____

Reserve Balance _____

LOAN NUMBER
MONTHLY TAX DEPOSIT
INVESTOR CODE
INVESTOR LOAN NO.
TYPE OF LOAN

F 34428   20•90   1   102953   4

AMOUNT TO BE INSERTED
BY MORTGAGOR

Real Estate Tax Bill _____

On Reserve including 12 01 61 payment $ 205•75

TO BE COMPUTED BY
BORROWER

Shortage or Excess

ABC MORTGAGE COMPANY

Please pay the enclosed tax bill

Sign here: _____

MR & MRS JOHN DOE
1234 COLUMBIA AVE
CHICAGO ILL

TO BE SIGNED BY BORROWER

402

EXHIBIT 79 *Tax notices*

General tax bills will be mailed by the various Township and County Collectors. Should you not receive your tax bill, we urge you to get in touch with your Collector and request a bill from him.

ABC MORTGAGE COMPANY
233 MAPLE
CHICAGO, ILLINOIS 60190

As soon as you do receive your tax bill, place it in the enclosed envelope with this notice and mail to us immediately in order to facilitate the payment of this bill to the Collector. PLEASE ENCLOSE BOTH THE FIRST AND SECOND INSTALLMENT PORTIONS OF THE BILL. DO NOT DETACH ANY PART OF IT.

Should the tax reserve, as shown below, be less than your tax bill, will you kindly enclose your check or money order for the difference to enable us to pay prior to penalty date. Please do not enclose any amount less than a dollar. (Make your check payable to   ABC Mortgage Co.

MR & MRS ROBERT NEWBERG

399 PLEASANT ST

ROSELLE ILL

LOAN NO F - 34488   269-007902
PRESENT MONTHLY TAX DEPOSIT $ 35.82

1965 REAL ESTATE BILL   FOR COOK COUNTY
BALANCE IN THE TAX RESERVE ACCOUNT INCLUDING
THE 08/01/66   MONTHLY INSTALLMENT $ 384.39

SHORTAGE OR EXCESS

SECOND NOTICE

General tax bills will be mailed by the various Township and County Collectors. Should you not receive your tax bill, we urge you to get in touch with your Collector and request a bill from him.

ABC MORTGAGE COMPANY
233 MAPLE
CHICAGO, ILLINOIS 60190

As soon as you do receive your tax bill, place it in the enclosed envelope with this notice and mail to us immediately in order to facilitate the payment of this bill to the Collector. PLEASE ENCLOSE BOTH THE FIRST AND SECOND INSTALLMENT PORTIONS OF THE BILL. DO NOT DETACH ANY PART OF IT.

Should the tax reserve, as shown below, be less than your tax bill, will you kindly enclose your check or money order for the difference to enable us to pay prior to penalty date. Please do not enclose any amount less than a dollar. (Make your check payable to   ABC Mortgage Co.

MR & MRS ROBERT NEWBERG

399 PLEASANT ST

ROSELLE ILL

LOAN NO F - 34489   269-007902
PRESENT MONTHLY TAX DEPOSIT $ 35.82

1965 REAL ESTATE BILL   FOR COOK COUNTY
BALANCE IN THE TAX RESERVE ACCOUNT INCLUDING
THE 08/01/66   MONTHLY INSTALLMENT $ 384.39

SHORTAGE OR EXCESS

IF YOU HAVE RECENTLY SENT YOUR TAX BILL
TO US — PLEASE DISREGARD THIS NOTICE

attached, the bill may be processed for payment since the information on the notice is normally what would be obtained only by matching the tax bill with the tax card and by checking reserves; therefore, the notice accomplishes all that the tax clerk would otherwise obtain through laborious processing. The second notice, prepared at the same time the first notice is made out, but held in abeyance, is mailed when no response is received to the first notice, as shown when tax cards are not removed from the filing cabinet.

Notices or envelopes are prepared several months before the tax time. If a non-automated procedure is used, the envelope or notice system may still be employed. The tax clerk types the addresses and other information on the envelope or notice required later for processing the bill, or runs the envelopes or notices through an addressograph machine. The reserves on hand for each account may then be transcribed from the ledger card to the envelopes. All notices or envelopes are placed in the mail a few days before tax collectors send out bills.

The company originating the envelope system and those adopting it have found that the system does more than just speed up processing. Over 75 percent of those borrowers who did not have sufficient funds on hand for the company to pay tax bills promptly remitted the difference between the tax bill and the reserves on hand. For the other 25 percent, the account must be reviewed and the borrower contacted for payment of the shortage. The proper monthly reserve requirements may be established at the same time or later.

Recommendations Since the savings and efficiency of obtaining tax bills through the use of envelopes or notices are considerable in relation to the cost of printing and mailing, these procedures are highly recommended. They specifically accomplish the following: (1) they enable the tax department to identify the tax bill and match it against the tax card since all particulars concerning it are marked either on the envelope in which the bill is returned or on the notice which the borrower is required to return in the self-addressed envelope; (2) the envelope provides space for the borrower to authorize payment of the bill in areas where authorization is necessary (this is important especially in communities from which a large percentage of tax protests may be anticipated and where it is to the advantage of the tax department to know in advance whether or not the borrower intends to protest the bill); and (3) by urging the borrower to compare the tax bill with the amount shown, he is notified that a shortage may exist and that the difference, if any, should be remitted with the tax bill.

Verifying Tax Bills

Before paying a tax bill, the tax clerk must carefully check the legal description or the appropriate identifying account or code numbers that appear on the bill against the tax card. This usually consists of verifying the subdivision, lot, and block numbers (and/or volume and item numbers, whichever may be used for the basic classification of properties in the state or county). This method of checking is generally considered sufficient, provided the name and address on the bill correspond to the name of the mortgagor of record and the address of the property.

Some tax clerks also check the computation of the tax bill by multiplying the rate by the assessed value. This job is not only cumbersome, but usually unnecessary; a simple comparison of the current year's tax bill with the one for the preceding year should suffice to ascertain whether the tax bill is correct. Naturally, in case of a substantial increase or decrease, the tax bill should not be paid until its validity and correctness have been checked at the tax office.

Some companies which receive tax bills directly from the borrowers believe that they are not responsible for the correctness of the legal description and the amount, on the grounds that the borrower has had the opportunity to check both. This notion, however, implies a misconception of the servicing function. It is the mortgage company's duty to see that the tax bill received conforms in every respect to the legal description of the property and that all discrepancies and errors on tax bills are corrected immediately to forestall the payment of incorrect bills and to avoid the accumulation of tax penalties.

Approving and Paying Tax Bills

Once a bill is approved for payment—and adequate funds are on hand for this purpose—it should be turned over to the accounting or escrow reserve department for immediate payment. Such promptness prevents last-minute bottlenecks. Tax bills to be paid out of one investor's custodial bank account should not be paid individually, but by means of statements covering a number of tax bills. The use of a disbursement clearing account has the advantage of simplifying and accelerating payment of bills to one collector from many custodial bank accounts.

If the borrower protests his bill or if the funds on hand are not sufficient to cover the bill, the payment, of course, cannot be made. It is, therefore, important to keep protests to a minimum, to set up reserves properly, and to collect the shortages promptly.

Establishing Tax Reserve Requirements and Collecting Shortages

Regular review and adjustment of tax reserve requirements are necessary to assure that sufficient funds are provided to pay future tax bills and shortages to pay current bills are collected. To perform these tasks with the least amount of adverse public reaction, the mortgagor should be informed, at the time the loan is closed, of how tax reserves are computed. A clear understanding of this arrangement makes many explanations unnecessary when a shortage arises. It is also a good policy to convince the borrower of the advantages of setting up tax reserves, even if the investor's commitment does not provide for such provision. On a construction loan, as stated earlier, it is wise to establish reserve requirements on the basis of an improved property tax bill, even if the bill may or will be issued on an unimproved basis in the first or even the second year. This procedure is advisable; first, because it is easier to refund an excess accumulation of reserves than to collect a shortage in the first year; and second, because it is better to set the mortgage payments at the figure that will represent permanent tax reserve requirements than to increase the payment substantially several months after the first payment. Any excess collections may be refunded or retained as a cushion for future tax increases.

If it is possible, tax reserves on all properties should be established to accumulate sufficient funds one or two months before the tax bill is due. Then, if collections are underestimated or the loan is delinquent, the funds on hand will still be sufficient to pay the entire tax bill.

Both FHA and VA regulations permit collection of tax funds on a calendar year basis, even if the tax bills are not payable until May and September of the following year, as is the case in Cook County, Illinois. Excess funds thus accumulated can absorb increases in the tax bill, make the immediate payment of the entire bill possible, and provide ample time for the company to adjust the collection or reserves to the actual tax bill. Such reserves, furthermore, provide an opportunity for the tax department to make a single annual tax payment instead of several, an arrangement which undoubtedly reduces tax work for companies operating in states where the tax bill may be paid in two or more installments. If reserves are accumulated in excess of the requirements, the monthly collection should be lowered or a refund of excesses of more than $25 should be considered.

The collection of tax shortages should be well organized and begun as soon as possible after receipt of the tax bills. Shortages create an especially perplexing problem in those communities where the taxes have been raised considerably over the previous year's rate and where the borrower has not been willing to make increased monthly deposits in anticipation of a tax increase or does not have the ready cash to pay the shortage.

The collection or tax personnel should concentrate their efforts, first, on the immediate collection of substantial shortages. To avoid penalties, they can use the hazard and FHA insurance reserves at this time to pay the tax bill if necessary. If the shortage does not exceed $10, it may be advisable not to ask the borrower for this shortage, especially at tax time, providing of course that there are funds for other purposes in the account.

Collection policy involving tax shortages must be flexible. The tax department must first concentrate on those shortages which prevent the payment of even the first installment of the bill due. As a practical matter, small shortages may be collected after tax time or may even be allowed to stand until the following year, at which time a more substantial shortage will warrant a request for funds and an increase in the monthly collections.

Many of the problems that arise during tax time can be avoided or minimized by a consistent yearly review of the tax reserve accounts and subsequent adjustments in reserve requirements. The shortages may be eliminated by (1) asking the borrower for a lump sum to cover the shortage, a method recommended in instances where there is a large discrepancy between the tax bill and the escrow reserve funds on hand; (2) increasing the monthly payments for a specified period so the borrower can replenish the reserve account; and (3) combining the two methods—i.e., by asking for an additional lump payment sufficient to cover an overdraft and by increasing the monthly payment for a number of months.

Several methods are now used to examine the borrower's account and to inform the mortgagor of the status of his account. The borrower can be notified by letter or by mailing the escrow analysis worksheet with a cover letter. Of course, the analysis of tax reserve accounts may also be performed by most data processing installations or by a service bureau.[1] A machine-prepared form which combines the analysis of the reserve account with the notification of a new monthly payment is illustrated in Exhibit 80.

---

[1] Escrow Department—Procedures and Responsibilities, Exhibits 19 and 24 (Appendix A-6).

EXHIBIT 80   Analysis of escrow reserve account and payment change notice

ABC MORTGAGE COMPANY
233 Maple Street
Chicago, Illinois 60190

ANALYSIS of ESCROW RESERVE ACCOUNT
and PAYMENT CHANGE NOTICE

THIS ANALYSIS OF ESTIMATED ESCROW REQUIREMENTS IS BASED ON LAST KNOWN TAX AND INSURANCE BILLS. THE MONTHLY DEPOSIT TO THE ESCROW RESERVE ACCOUNT IS SUBJECT TO ADJUSTMENT TO MEET CHANGES IN SUCH BILLS

**FOR OFFICE
USE ONLY**
MORTGAGE NO
AND CODE

)0910011940L00577190

Loan No	F042082
Analysis Date	06/70

120 507371

Please read reverse
side for explanations

Item	MOST RECENT BILL			Monthly Requirement	No. of Mos Required	Escrow Reserve Required To Be On Deposit
	Term In Mos.	Accrual Date	Amount			
FHA PREMIUM	12	01/70	95.04	7.92	6	47.52
HAZARD INS.	12	01/70	52.00	4.33	6	25.98
R.E. TAXES	12	12/69	543.98	45.33	6	271.98

Your monthly payment	OLD	NEW
Principal and interest	123.96	123.96
Escrow reserve deposit	54.04	57.64
Home security insurance	8.40	8.40
Mortgage life insurance	0.00-	0.00-
Total monthly payment	186.40	190.00
New payment effective date		06/01/70

Your total escrow balance
should be   345.48
Your escrow balance including
your 06/70   payment is   269.06
Your escrow account
is SHORT   76.42-

Please remit   76.42   with
your next monthly payment

**EXHIBIT 80   Analysis of escrow reserve account and payment change notice
(reverse side)**

EXPLANATIONS

1. The monthly requirement for FHA insurance is calculated by dividing the most recent FHA insurance bill by 12.

2. The monthly requirement for hazard insurance is calculated by dividing the most recent insurance payment by the number of months the payment covers.

3. The monthly requirement for real estate taxes is calculated by dividing the last annual tax bill by 12.

4. The new monthly payment is rounded to the nearest whole dollar by adjusting the escrow reserve deposit.

5. An asterisk (*) next to number of months required indicates that only one installment of the real estate tax bill has been paid.

6. We recommend that an excess of less than $25 be retained in your escrow reserve account to cover possible increases in insurance premiums and real estate tax bills.

Handling Tax Protests

A tax protest, because of the tax rate or the assessed valuation, is a quasi-legal matter to be settled between the taxpayer and the taxing authority. Basically, handling and processing a protest are a job for an attorney and not for an employee of a mortgage company. Although the company should recognize the wishes of the borrower if he intends to file a protest, its tax department should avoid handling a tax protest or giving advice on technical matters connected with tax protests. In localities where a tax rate protest may be filed by paying the tax bill "under protest," the mortgage company should assist the borrower by paying the bill under protest. Many companies follow this practice automatically, though some pay bills under protest only if the bills are high enough to involve a sizable refund.

PAYMENT OF TAXES BY MORTGAGORS

When the terms of the mortgage do not require a tax deposit, handling tax payments poses no problems to the tax clerk at the time the tax bills are released to the public. He must make sure later, however, that the taxes have actually been paid by the mortgagors. The company can perform the job of checking soon after the due date either by requiring that mortgagors exhibit the receipted tax bills or by inspecting the tax records at the collector's office. The former procedure is recommended because records are traditionally not up to date, especially immediately after the due dates of bills. This requirement eliminates frequent and premature visits to the tax office. After a lapse of time, of course, it is best to check the records. When verified, each payment should be noted on a tax card. This card should be filed along with cards for those loans on which reserves are collected and should be of a different color to indicate that it was the borrower who made the payment. Tax payments by mortgagors may also be confirmed by a company specializing in tax searches. In many municipalities, the tax office itself renders such tax search service for a small fee for each item involved.

TAX CERTIFICATIONS

Mortgage companies must certify to their mortgagees annually that all tax bills have been paid. The certificate covers bills that have been paid by the mortgage banker as well as bills that have been paid by the mortgagor, which in turn was verified by the tax clerk. As an added precaution against changes in tax descriptions or misapplication of payments by the taxing authorities, the tax clerk should search the tax records before issuing a certification. The certificate also lists all unpaid items as exceptions and the reason for their nonpayment.

Although the majority of investors accept tax certifications, some insist that the receipted tax bills be submitted each year. Other investors accept tax certifications on their residential loan portfolio, but require the submission of receipted tax bills in connection with loans made on large projects and commercial or industrial buildings.

Mortgagees often supplement their tax records, or substitute their tax certification requirements, by asking their correspondents to make entries on their own records which they forward to their correspondents periodically. As part of the audit procedure, many investors inspect receipted tax bills, a practice which usually assures compliance with tax certification requirements on the part of the mortgage companies.

Each year after investors' requirements for certifying payment of taxes are satisfied, the mortgage company should send the paid tax receipts only to those borrowers who asked for them. When receipted bills are not requested, they should be placed in the loan file and returned to the borrower when the loan is paid in full. Alternatively, a growing number of mortgage bankers automatically send copies of paid tax bills to mortgagors.

Appendices

APPENDIX A

Pamphlets can be obtained by writing the Mortgage Bankers Association of America, 1125 Fifteenth Street, N.W., Washington, D.C. 20005.

1 "What is Mortgage Banking"—An Operations Guide
2 MBA's Record Retention Schedule
3 Employment Manual
4 MBA's Suggested Chart of Accounts and Financial Statements for Mortgage Banking Companies
5 "What You Should Know About Your Mortgage Loan"
6 Escrow Department—Procedures and Responsibilities
7 MBA Standard Aggregate Accounting and Reporting System
8 Punched Card Data Processing for Mortgage Bankers
9 FHA-VA Foreclosure and Claim Procedures
10 MBA Quarterly Delinquency Survey
11 "What Every Home Owner Should Know About His Insurance Protection"

APPENDIX B-1   FHA AND VA SERVICING AGREEMENT

THIS AGREEMENT made and entered into this 17th day of May 1968, by and between ABC Mortgage Company, an Illinois corporation, of Chicago, Illinois, hereinafter called Servicer, and XYZ, a Wisconsin corporation of Milwaukee, Wisconsin, hereinafter called Investor.

WITNESSETH;

WHEREAS, Servicer desires to close for Investor or to assign to it certain FHA insured or VA guaranteed loans acceptable to Investor and to retain the servicing thereon;

NOW, THEREFORE, in consideration of the sum of One (1) Dollar in lawful money of the United States to each of the parties hereto in hand paid by the other, receipt of which is hereby respectively acknowledged, and in consideration of the performance by the parties of their respective undertakings herein, it is mutually agreed as follows:

Servicing. Servicer covenants and agrees:

1. It will maintain accounting records and follow accounting procedures satisfactory to Investor, will collect on the several maturity dates whenever reasonably possible the interest, principal, and escrow requirements on said loans, and, as collected, will remit such principal and interest (less retention as provided herein under "Compensation") to Investor each week; provided, however, that Servicer shall not be liable to Investor for any such items not collected or received by Servicer, and provided further that Servicer shall not be obligated to commence or prosecute any legal proceedings to make such collections.

2. As to FHA loans, it will deposit all collections, including the escrow for ground rents, taxes, assessments and hazard insurance and FHA mutual mortgage insurance premiums in a Federal Insured Depository in an account used exclusively for FHA loans being serviced for Investor, and will pay as they severally become due from said escrow deposits all ground rents, taxes, assessments, and premiums for hazard insurance and FHA mutual mortgage insurance, and will notify FHA and Investor promptly in the event of default and, in general, do all things on behalf of Investor required by the National Housing Act and Rules and Regulations of the FHA to keep the mutual mortgage insurance in full force and effect. In case the mutual mortgage insurance shall lapse due to the failure of the Servicer, the Servicer at the request of Investor shall repurchase the mortgage loan at its then balance of principal, plus accrued interest and plus advancements made by Investor.

3. As to VA loans, it will deposit all collections, including the escrow for ground rents, taxes, assessments and hazard insurance premiums, in a Federal Income Depository in an account used exclusively for VA loans being serviced for Investor, and will pay as they severally become due from said escrow deposits all ground rents, taxes, assessments and premiums for hazard insurance, and will notify VA and Investor promptly in the event of default and, in general, do all things on behalf of Investor required by the Servicemen's Readjustment Act of 1944, as amended, and Rules and Regulations of the Veterans Administration. In case the guaranty shall become invalid due to the failure of the Servicer, the Servicer at the request of Investor shall

repurchase the mortgage loan at its then balance of principal, plus accrued interest and plus advancements made by Investor.

4. It will see that hazard insurance policies are kept in force or renewed (any shortage in escrow funds to pay necessary premiums to be made up by Investor) and will forward all policies to Investor with proper mortgage loss clauses attached. It will assist in the collection of any insurance loss proceeds and supervise any repairs made necessary by fire or other casualty.

5. In the event of delinquency in the payment of any installment, it will make a full investigation of the mortgagor and reasons for the default and report the same to Investor within 25 days thereafter, and during the continuance of any default will make a further investigation when requested by Investor and give recommendations as to foreclosure.

6. At Investor's request, it will cooperate in the foreclosure or other settlement of a delinquent loan; cash outlays by the Servicer under this sub-paragraph to be reimbursed to it by Investor.

Compensation. As full compensation for its services hereunder, Servicer shall deduct from its remittance to Investor and shall retain that portion of the interest collected which is stipulated in the action of Investor's Finance Committee approving the individual loan. It shall also retain any late charges collected by it.

Termination.

1. This agreement shall terminate immediately and without notice should there be appointed for the Servicer a receiver, conservator, or trustee, or should Servicer become otherwise incapacitated by operation of law or fact for the faithful performance of its duties hereunder.

2. This agreement may be terminated by Investor by written notice delivered to Servicer either personally or by registered mail in the event of a violation or material breach by Servicer of its obligations under this agreement, or in the event Servicer shall be suspended (either temporarily or permanently) by FHA or VA.

3. This agreement may be terminated by Servicer at its option upon 30 days' written notice delivered to the Home Office of Investor by registered mail.

4. This agreement may be terminated by Investor at its option upon 30 days' written notice delivered to Servicer by registered mail; provided, however, that in event of termination under this sub-paragraph, Investor shall pay Servicer as a termination fee one year's servicing in advance, computed on each loan on which there is no delinquency exceeding 45 days at the date of termination.

5. Upon Termination of this agreement in any manner Servicer shall forthwith deliver to Investor a statement showing the payments collected and all moneys held by it for the payment of ground rents, taxes, insurance and other charges, and shall immediately pay over to Investor all moneys so collected and held. Servicer shall further turn over to Investor all books, papers and records, or transcripts thereof, pertaining to the loans covered by this agreement.

Effective Date. As of the first of the month following the date hereof this agreement shall supersede, replace and terminate all existing servicing agreements between the parties hereto covering FHA or VA loans, except those pertaining to Section 608 FHA loans.

IN WITNESS WHEREOF, the parties hereto have caused these presents to be signed in duplicate in their respective names (and where a corporation, by their duly authorized officers and have affixed their corporate seals) the day and year first above written.

ABC Mortgage Co.   **XYZ Insurance Company**

By _____   By _____
                          President   Vice President

᛫ Attest:_____   Attest: _____
                          Secretary   Assistant Secretary

APPENDIX B-2   MODEL SALE AND SERVICING AGREEMENT

(Between Mortgage Bankers and Investors Other Than Savings and Loan Associations)

   I.   THIS AGREEMENT is made in the State of _____
        between _____
        herein called "Seller-servicer," and _____
        (investor) _____, herein called "Buyer," for mutual con-
        siderations herein evidenced.
  II.   This agreement, under which from time to time the Seller-servicer may offer to
        sell and the Buyer may agree to buy from Seller-servicer first mortgage loans on
        real estate, hereinafter called collectively "mortgages" and individually "the
        mortgage," shall govern the sale and transfer of such mortgages by Seller-servicer
        to Buyer, and the servicing and other incidents thereof, and each such mortgage
        shall be subject to the warranties, representations and agreements herein.
 III.   Seller-servicer represents and warrants as to each such mortgage offered for sale
        under this Agreement that:
        A. The mortgage has been duly executed by the mortgagor, acknowledged
            and recorded, is valid, and is a first lien on the real property held in fee
            simple.
        B. The Seller-servicer is the sole owner of the mortgage and has authority to
            sell, transfer, and assign the same on the terms herein set forth; and there has
            been no assignment, sale, or hypothecation thereof by Seller-servicer, except
            the usual past hypothecation of the papers in connection with Seller-servicer's
            normal banking transactions in the conduct of its business; and that the sale
            is free and clear of claims or encumbrances of any type.
        C. The full principal amount of the mortgage has been advanced to the mort-
            gagor, either by payment direct to him or by payment made on his request
            or approval; the unpaid principal balance is as stated; all costs, fees and ex-
            penses incurred in making, closing, and recording the mortgage have been
            paid; no part of the mortgage property has been released from the lien of the
            mortgage; the terms of the mortgage have in no way been changed or modi-
            fied, and the mortgage is current and not in default.
        D. Each mortgage which the Seller-servicer represents to be insured by the Fed-
            eral Housing Administration or by a private mortgage insurance company, or
            to be guaranteed by the United States of America under the Servicemen's
            Readjustment Act of 1944, as amended, is so insured or guaranteed.
        E. The mortgage was originated and has been serviced since the date of its
            origination by the Seller-servicer.
        F. The real property security is located in the United States.
        G. All applicable Federal rules and regulations have been complied with, and all
            conditions within the control of the Seller-servicer as to the validity of the
            insurance or guaranty as required by the National Housing Act of 1934, as
            amended, and the rules and regulations thereunder, or as required by the
            Servicemen's Readjustment Act of 1944, as amended, and the rules and regu-
            lations thereunder, or by the mortgage insurance companies, have been prop-
            erly satisfied, and said insurance or guaranty is valid and enforceable.
        H. There is in force a paid-up title insurance policy on the mortgage issued by

an accredited title company in an amount at least equal to the outstanding balance of the mortgage.

I.   There is in force for each such loan hazard insurance policies meeting the specifications of Clause IX.

J.   The assignment, if any, of the mortgage from the Seller-servicer to the Buyer is valid and sufficient.

K.   All documents submitted are genuine, and all other representations as to each such mortgage are true and correct and meet the requirements and specifications of all parts of this Agreement.

IV. The Seller-servicer agrees to perform all acts necessary to perfect title to the mortgages in the Buyer, and shall sell, assign and deliver to the Buyer with respect to the purchase of each such mortgage the following supporting documents where applicable, all subject to the approval of the Buyer and its legal counsel as to the proper form and execution:

A.   Mortgage note properly endorsed by the Seller-servicer without recourse, and if an FHA or a mortgage insurance company insured mortgage, duly endorsed by Federal Housing Commissioner or the mortgage insurance company, and if a VA mortgage accompanied by the Loan Guaranty Certification.

B.   Mortgage, accompanied by those documents and instruments necessary to record and perfect ownership thereof in the Buyer.

C.   Appraisal report of an appraiser whose qualifications are acceptable to the Buyer.

D.   Mortgagee title insurance policy, with any exceptions therein subject to approval of Buyer's legal counsel, and proper assignment thereof if required in event a mortgage assignment is being placed of record.

E.   Survey of premises identifying property by address and legal description, this being required only if title policy contains an exception as to boundary and building line restrictions.

F.   If an FHA mortgage, application, commitment, amortization schedule, notice of transfer and all required documents of a similar nature; if a VA mortgage, all such required documents of a similar nature.

G.   Hazard insurance policies meeting the specifications of Clause VIII.

H.   Statement showing unpaid principal balance on mortgage, amount of periodic installments and date to which interest is paid.

I.   Certified copy of resolution of Seller-servicer authorizing sale of the mortgage.

V.   The Seller-servicer shall comply with, and shall use its best efforts to cause each mortgagor to comply with all applicable state and federal rules and regulations or requirements of the mortgage insurance companies, including those requiring the giving of notices. Where applicable, the Seller-servicer shall comply with the National Housing Act of 1934, as from time to time amended, or with the Servicemen's Readjustment Act of 1944, as amended, and with all rules and regulations issued under either, and with the requirements of mortgage insurance companies, including the giving of all notices and submitting of all claims required to be given or submitted to the Federal Housing Administration, the Veterans Administration, or to the mortgage insurance companies to the end that the full benefit of either the Federal Housing Administration insurance, the guaranty of the United States of America, or the mortgage insurance will inure to the Buyer. The Seller-servicer will forward copies of all such notices or claims to the Buyer.

VI. On request of the Buyer, Seller-servicer shall arrange for appropriate registration and payment of any fee which might be required under the laws of the state where mortgage security property is located in connection with doing business by the Buyer in such state, the Seller-servicer's costs to be reimbursed by the Buyer promptly upon submission of a statement.

VII. The Seller-servicer agrees to repurchase any mortgage covered by this agreement within one year after date of the Buyer's remittance if any misstatement of material fact is disclosed by actual inspection by the Buyer or its representative, or otherwise, for an amount equal to its then unpaid principal based on the same percentage rate at which it originally was purchased, plus accrued interest and costs incurred by the Buyer for action taken, but this provision shall not apply to FHA insured, VA guaranteed, or mortgage insurance company insured mortgages. In the case of insured or guaranteed mortgages, if the FHA insurance, the VA guaranty, or the insurance of a mortgage insurance company with respect to any of the mortgages lapses as a result of the Seller-servicer's act or omission, the Seller-servicer upon the Buyer's request shall repurchase such mortgage for an amount equal to its then unpaid principal based on the same percentage rate at which it originally was purchased, plus accrued interest and costs incurred by the Buyer for action taken, and remit the aggregate of said amounts to the Buyer.

VIII. The Seller-servicer shall see that the improvements on the premises securing each mortgage are kept insured by hazard insurance policies issued by a company acceptable to the Buyer in an amount at least equal to the outstanding principal of the mortgage or the full insurable value of the improvements, whichever is less, and of a type at least as protective as fire and extended coverage, containing a mortgagee clause to the Buyer substantially in the form of the standard New York mortgagee clause, and containing suitable provisions for payment on all present and future mortgages on such premises in order of precedence. If directed by the Buyer, Seller-servicer shall hold for the Buyer's account such policies and renewals thereof.

IX. The Seller-servicer, at its expense, shall maintain at all times, while this agreement is in force, policies of fidelity, fire, and extended coverage, theft, forgery, and errors and omissions insurance. Such policies shall be in reasonable amounts satisfactory from time to time to buyer.

X. Upon Buyer's request, the Seller-servicer shall furnish a detailed statement of its financial condition, and give the Buyer or its authorized representative opportunity at any time during business hours to examine the Seller-servicer's books and records. The Seller-servicer shall cause a certified public accountant employed by it to provide the Buyer, not later than ninety days after the close of the Seller-servicer's fiscal year, with a certified statement of the Seller-servicer's financial condition as of the close of its fiscal year. The Seller-servicer agrees to keep records satisfactory to the Buyer pertaining to each mortgage, and such records shall be the property of the Buyer and upon termination of this Agreement shall be delivered to the Buyer.

XI. Until the principal and interest of each such mortgage is paid in full, the Seller-servicer shall:

A. Proceed diligently to collect all payments due under the terms of each mortgage as they become due.

B. Keep a complete and accurate account of and properly apply all sums collected by it from the mortgagor on account of each such mortgage for principal and interest, taxes, assessments and other public charges, hazard insurance premiums and FHA insurance or mortgage insurance premiums, and to furnish Buyer with evidence acceptable to the Buyer of all expenditures for taxes, assessments and other public charges, hazard insurance premiums and FHA insurance or mortgage insurance premiums. In the event any mortgagor fails to make a payment to said Seller-servicer required to be made under the terms of said mortgage, Seller-servicer agrees to notify the Buyer of such fact within thirty days after the same shall have become due and payable.

C. Deposit all funds received in behalf of such mortgage, subject to withdrawal on demand, in a segregated trust or custodial account in a state or national bank, the deposits of which are insured by the Federal Deposit Insurance Corporation. Such account shall be held by Seller-servicer as trustee or custodian and the holder shall maintain detailed records to show the respective interests of each individual mortgagor in the account. Each such account shall be established and maintained in a manner which complies with the applicable rules and regulations of the Federal Deposit Insurance Corporation.

D. From the funds so deposited (1) pay promptly to the proper parties when and if due FHA insurance premiums, mortgage insurance premiums, taxes, special assessments, ground rents, and premiums on hazard insurance, and (2) on or before the twentieth of each month, pay to the Buyer all amounts of principal and interest due to it under the mortgage, retaining as full compensation for all services performed hereunder the earned portion of the servicing fee per annum agreed to in the commitment for each specific loan or block of loans, plus "late charges" if any collected from the mortgagor pursuant to the terms of the mortgage.

E. Submit to the Buyer at least annually an audit of the balances in each such trust account, together with a certificate that all disbursements were made for proper purposes, and that all payments required to be made hereunder have been made, with exceptions, if any.

F. The Seller-servicer shall perform such other customary duties, furnish such other reports and execute such other documents in connection with its duties hereunder as the Buyer from time to time reasonably may require.

XII. The Seller-servicer shall use due diligence to ascertain, and shall forthwith notify the Buyer of the failure of any mortgagor to perform any obligations under the mortgage, and also of any of the following which might come to the attention of the Seller-servicer.

A. The vacating of or any change in the occupancy of any premises securing a mortgage.

B. The sale or transfer of any such premises.

C. The death, bankruptcy or insolvency of a mortgagor.

D. Any loss or damage to any such premises, in which event, in addition to notifying the Buyer, the Seller-servicer shall also promptly notify the insurance companies concerned.

E. Any lack of repair or any other deterioration or waste suffered or committed in respect of the premises covered by the mortgage.

It is understood, however, that the Seller-servicer shall not be obligated to give notice to the Buyer of any facts other than those of which the Seller-servicer shall have actual notice, and those of which it would, except for its negligence, have had notice.

XIII. The Seller-servicer shall not accept any prepayment of mortgage principal except as permitted by the terms of the mortgage, nor waive, modify, release or consent to postponement on the part of the mortgagor of any term or provision of the mortgage without the written consent of the Buyer.

XIV. The Seller-servicer shall be required to reinspect only those properties on which the mortgage becomes sixty or more days delinquent.

XV. The Seller-servicer shall upon the request and under the direction of the Buyer assist in the foreclosure or other acquisition of the property securing any mortgage, the transfer of such property to the FHA or VA and the collection of any applicable mortgage insurance, and pending completion of these steps, protect such property from waste and strip. At the option of the Buyer, Buyer may assign such mortgage to the Seller-servicer which shall then conduct all such proceedings in its own name, promptly thereafter assigning or conveying to the Buyer any title, equity, or other property or right acquired by such proceedings. Seller-servicer will take title to the property in the name designated by the Buyer. Buyer agrees to reimburse the Seller-servicer for its reasonable out-of-pocket expenses so incurred, including attorney's fees mutually agreed upon in advance.

XVI. In the event the Buyer shall assign its interest under the terms of this contract and in the mortgages to a third party, the assignee shall accede to all of the rights and obligations hereunder of the Buyer and this Agreement shall remain in full force and effect, and the Seller-servicer shall remit all principal and interest installments payable under the mortgages so assigned directly to such third party after deduction of the service fee as herein provided. The obligation to make direct remittances to such third party shall arise upon thirty days' written notice of such assignment given by the Buyer to the Seller-servicer.

XVII. Compensation of the Seller-servicer shall be as agreed at the time each mortgage is accepted and as evidenced by each commitment to purchase made by the Buyer. Such compensation shall be earned, computed and payable as of the time interest on each individual mortgage is paid to Buyer, except that the compensation represented by late charges, if any, shall be retained as paid by the mortgagor. Compensation shall be earned and computed only upon mortgages on which payment of interest actually occurs. No additional compensation shall be payable to the Seller-servicer in the event of termination of this Agreement, except as provided in Clause XVIII.

XVIII. The Buyer may, by notice to the Seller-servicer, terminate this Agreement as to mortgages being serviced if:

A. The Seller-servicer becomes insolvent or bankrupt or is placed under conservatorship or receivership.

B. The Seller-servicer assigns or attempts to assign its rights and obligations hereunder, or there is a transfer of a controlling interest in Seller-servicer, without written consent of the Buyer.

C. The Seller-servicer fails to take positive action to correct any deficiency in the performance of its obligations hereunder within sixty days after the Buyer has given Seller-Servicer written notice of such deficiency.

D. In any event, and without cause, upon sixty days' written notice and payment to the Seller-servicer of a sum equal to _____ percent of the aggregate principal amounts then outstanding of all of the mortgages subject to this agreement.

XIX. This Agreement may be terminated as to the future acceptance of mortgages by either party at any time upon giving thirty days' written notice of termination to the other party, but such termination shall not in any respect change or modify the obligation of the Seller-servicer to service mortgages then already accepted, and the Seller-servicer shall continue to service such mortgages unless the Buyer shall act pursuant to Clause XVIII hereof.

XX. Upon any termination of this Agreement under Clause XVIII the Seller-servicer shall account for and turn over to the Buyer all funds collected under each mortgage, less only the compensation then due the Seller-servicer, and deliver to the Buyer all records and documents relating to each such mortgage described in Clauses IV and VIII that it may have in its possession.

XXI. The words "mortgage" and "mortgages" as used herein shall include mortgages, security deeds, trust deeds, and deeds of trust, and the words "mortgagor" and "mortgagors" shall be deemed to mean mortgagors, trustors, of trust deeds and deeds of trust, and the grantors of any security deeds, it being agreed that the appointment of any trustees under any trust deeds or deeds of trust shall be subject to the approval of the Buyer. This document contains the entire agreement between the parties hereto and cannot be modified in any respect except by an amendment in writing signed by both parties. The invalidity of any portion of this Agreement shall in no way affect the balance thereof. This Agreement shall remain in effect until the Buyer's interests in all of the mortgages referred to, including the underlying security, are liquidated completely.

IN WITNESS WHEREOF, each party has caused its corporate seal to be affixed hereto and this instrument to be signed in its corporate name on its behalf by its proper officials duly authorized.

This _____ day of _____, 19 _____

_____ Seller

By _____
PRESIDENT

_____
SECRETARY

_____ Buyer

By _____
PRESIDENT

By _____
SECRETARY

APPENDIX B-3 PURCHASE AND SERVICING AGREEMENT

AGREEMENT dated, November 18, 1965 between Eastern Investor (EI), a New York corporation and ABC Mortgage Company ("Contractor"), an Illinois corporation.

WHEREAS, Contractor may offer bonds, notes or other obligations secured by mortgages, deeds of trust or other liens on real property (the "mortgages") for sale to EI and EI may purchase certain of said mortgages; and

WHEREAS, it is anticipated that Contractor will service mortgages owned by EI on the terms set forth below:

EI AND CONTRACTOR, INTENDING TO BE LEGALLY BOUND HEREUNDER, AGREE AS FOLLOWS:

1. *Scope*
   This Agreement shall be applicable to all mortgages (i) presently serviced for EI by Contractor, (ii) which EI may purchase from Contractor after the date of this Agreement, unless EI shall in writing except such mortgage from the operation of this Agreement, or (iii) which EI may hereafter refer to Contractor for servicing and which Contractor shall accept hereunder, except that Section 2 to 5 hereof, inclusive, shall apply only to mortgages purchased by EI after the date of this Agreement. In performing its duties hereunder Contractor is not, and shall not represent itself to be, the agent of EI, and EI shall neither direct nor have a right to direct, the method or means by which Contractor, fulfills its obligations under this Agreement.

2. *Offers and Delivery of Mortgages*
   All offers to sell mortgages shall be made to EI at its office at 123 Main Street, New York, United States. Mortgages acceptable to EI will be committed for purchase by EI at such office by issuance of its commitment for such purchase, subject to Contractor's obligation to deliver to that office all loan documents, assignments, title policies and supporting papers which EI may require (the "Documents") in form, substance and recordation satisfactory to EI, which shall pay the purchase price at its office after delivery and approval of the Documents. If the commitment contains an expiration date, payment may be made at any time prior to that date or any extension thereof.

3. *Warranties by Contractor*
   Contractor makes the following representations and warranties (the "warranties") with respect to each mortgage sold by it to EI, effective on the date of the disbursement of the purchase price by EI (the "purchase"):

   (a) The mortgage is a good and valid instrument and has been duly recorded.

   (b) Contractor is a corporation duly organized and existing under the laws of the state of its incorporation, duly qualified and licensed to do business in the state in which the property secured by the mortgage is located.

   (c) Contractor has full power to act as mortgagee and to sell the mortgage to EI. and is accepted without qualification by FHA and VA as an approved mortgagee.

   (d) The full principal amount of the mortgage has been advanced to the mortgagor, the principal amount remaining unpaid is as stated to EI, and there are no defaults existing under any of the mortgage covenants.

   (e) As to FHA-insured mortgages, all mortgage insurance premiums have been paid, the bond or note has been validly insured by FHA, and nothing has been done or omitted which would invalidate the contract of insurance or adversely affect any benefit which otherwise would be available thereunder.

(f) As to VA-guaranteed mortgages, the obligation has been validly guaranteed by VA to the extent stated in the Guarantee Certificate, and nothing has been done or omitted which would invalidate the guarantee or adversely affect any benefit which otherwise would be available thereunder.

(g) There is in effect a valid policy of title insurance which inures to the benefit of EI insuring the lien of the mortgage on the mortgaged premises (the "property"), issued in forms and by a company approved by EI.

(h) Contractor has good title to the mortgage and the assignment of the mortgage to EI is good and valid.

4. *Substitution of Mortgages*

If any mortgage purchased at par or at a premium is paid off within one year after the time of purchase, Contractor shall, upon request, promptly offer to sell to EI pursuant to all terms of this Agreement a substitute mortgage of like principal amount, interest rate, kind and quality. If EI shall accept Contractor's offer, the substitute mortgage shall be sold to it at par without any charge, commission or cost of any kind whatsoever to EI.

5. *Repurchase by Contractor*

(a) If within 180 days after the time of purchase of any mortgage EI shall notify Contractor that any warranty has not been substantiated to its satisfaction and Contractor within 30 days after such failure tender to Contractor at New York all Documents delivered to EI in connection with the sale of the mortgage and Contractor shall repurchase the mortgage at New York promptly at the price indicated in sub-paragraph (c).

(b) EI may, at its option, pay for any mortgage offered by Contractor for purchase by EI prior to the receipt of all Documents or upon the receipt of the Documents and before examining the same. EI shall examine any mortgage so purchased within 180 days from the time of purchase, and within that period shall notify Contractor of any matters (including missing Documents) which EI finds unacceptable in accordance with its normal standards. If Contractor within 30 days after such notice fails to correct all matters raised therein, EI may within an additional 60 days after such failure tender to Contractor at New York all Documents that were delivered by Contractor to EI, and Contractor shall repurchase the mortgage at New York promptly at the price indicated in sub-paragraph (c).

(c) All mortgages repurchased by Contractor under this paragraph 5 shall be repurchased at a price equal to the unpaid principal amount of the mortgage, plus accrued interest, plus the premium, or less the discount, if any, upon a percentage basis, paid or allowed by or to EI, together with the aggregate amount of any advances made by EI pursuant to the mortgage.

(d) The right of EI to require repurchase by Contractor shall not reduce or affect any right or remedy otherwise available to it.

6. *Servicing Duties*

Contractor shall maintain adequate facilities and personnel to perform, and shall perform, the following duties:

(a) Contractor shall promptly comply with and discharge all obligations of the mortgagee (and shall use its best efforts to cause each mortgagor to comply with its obligations) under (i) the mortgage, (ii) the National Housing Act and the Veterans' Benefits Act as now or hereafter amended and all regulations issued thereunder, (iii) any FHA or VA contract of insurance or guarantee, and (iv) all other State or Federal statutes, regulations or requirements applicable to EI with respect to the mortgages serviced (all of which obligations are hereinafter called the "Legal Requirements").

(b) Contractor shall not without the consent of EI waive or vary the terms of any mortgage or grant any indulgence to the mortgagor or take any other action which would adversely affect the terms of the mortgage or the lien thereof.

(c) Contractor shall use its best efforts to collect all sums payable under each mortgage. All amounts collected shall be deposited in trust accounts insured by F.D.I.C. in banks selected by Contractor and approved by EI, which accounts shall be carried in such name and form as EI may designate. Contractor's records shall clearly reflect the interest of EI and each mortgagor in all such accounts.

(d) All amounts paid by the mortgagor pursuant to the mortgage for any purpose except payments of principal, interest or late charges shall promptly be applied by Contractor to discharge when due the taxes, assessments, liens, insurance costs and other charges and expenses for which those funds were intended. Contractor shall retain in its possession receipts for the payment of all such charges and shall furnish EI annually with a certification that all such charges have been paid. Contractor shall analyze each loan at least once a year for the purpose of determining whether sufficient amounts are being collected to meet the required charges as they accrue.

(e) Contractor shall remit to EI at the direction of EI, but at least once each month, all payments applicable to interest and principal not previously remitted, less the servicing fee set forth in Section 7 below. Any amounts collected in full payment or substantial partial payment of a mortgage, including all prepayment fees, shall be remitted immediately to EI as a special remittance. Late charges paid by the mortgagor on all mortgages or one to four family dwellings may be retained by Contractor; late charges on all other mortgages shall be remitted to EI.

(f) Contractor shall maintain at all times during the existence of the mortgage at its own expense (i) Blanket Fidelity Insurance, and (ii) Fire and Extended Coverage Errors and Omissions Insurance. All such policies shall be in amounts and with coverage and in insurance companies satisfactory to EI. A certificate of each such policy shall be furnished to EI, together with the insurer by Registered Mail of 15 days' notice of termination.

(g) Contractor shall take all necessary action to cause the mortgagor to keep all of the buildings and improvements upon the property insured at all times under standard policies, with appropriate mortgagee clauses in favor of EI, against loss or damage by fire and such other hazards as EI may require. Such policies shall be for an amount equal to the full insurable value of such buildings and improvements but not less than the unpaid principal of the mortgage. All such policies of insurance shall be written by insurance companies satisfactory to EI and in compliance with any applicable Legal Requirements. At the option of EI, Contractor shall retain and service all such insurance policies, in which case Contractor shall deliver to EI certificates in a form prescribed by EI evidencing compliance with the requirements of this paragraph. Contractor shall promptly notify EI of any loss or damage to a property by fire or other cause. Contractor shall take all steps necessary to make sure that all insurance coverage is continued despite any change in occupancy or ownership of the property or the occurence of any other event which might jeopardize the insurance.

(h) With respect to each mortgage, Contractor shall keep detailed records which shall be available for examination or audit by EI at any time during normal business hours, and shall furnish to EI from time to time such records and reports as EI may request.

(i) Contractor shall promptly notify EI if any property becomes damaged or vacant, or if the ownership or occupancy is changed, and shall recommend to EI such action as Contractor deems desirable to protect EI.

(j) At periodic intervals specified by EI, Contractor shall inspect each property and report to EI concerning the conditions and/or the appraised value of the property.

(k) In the event that any default occurs under the mortgage and is not corrected within a period of 45 days, Contractor shall comply promptly with all applicable Legal Requirements and shall notify EI of the default, and recommend action to protect EI. At the request of EI, Contractor shall initiate and complete promptly all action necessary to enforce the mortgage and to obtain the full benefits of any FHA insurance or VA guarantee. If the property is conveyed to FHA or VA, Contractor shall attend to the settlement and the filing of all necessary forms and claims needed to complete the conveyance and to obtain the full insurance or guaranteed benefits. EI shall reimburse Contractor for its necessary out-of-pocket costs and expenses in connection with any foreclosure or conveyance.

(l) In the event that action is taken to foreclose or to obtain a deed in lieu of foreclosure, Contractor from the date such action is initiated until the disposition of the property shall manage and protect the property, including but not limited to (i) the renting of the property and the collection of rents, if requested by EI, (ii) the initiation, management and supervision of necessary repairs and maintenance of the property, and (iii) the placing of insurance covering vandalism and malicious mischief with respect to any vacant property. In connection with such property management, Contractor shall render such reports as EI may require, and shall hold for EI until paid over to it, with appropriate segregation of funds, all rentals or other moneys in respect of the property which may come into its hands.

7. *Servicing Fee*

Contractor shall receive with respect to each mortgage serviced hereunder an amount, payable only from the interest portion of each payment actually received from the mortgagor, at the rate of one-half of one percent per annum (or such other percentage as may be specified in the purchase commitment), computed on the same principal amount and for the same period as the interest payment.

8. *Duration of Agreement*

Unless sooner terminated by EI as herein provided, this Agreement shall continue from the date hereof until the principal and interest of all mortgages now or hereafter serviced hereunder are paid in full and remitted to EI.

9. *Termination for Cause*

EI may at its option terminate this Agreement immediately and without prior notice upon the occurrence of any of the following events:

(a) The failure of Contractor to properly perform its duties hereunder, or the violation by Contractor of any provision of this Agreement.

(b) Any change in the ownership or control of Contractor whether by (i) sale of assets, (ii) merger, (iii) consolidation, (iv) sale of stock interests in Contractor, or (v) any other circumstances where the effect is to pass control of Contractor from the persons now exercising control to others.

(c) Any substantial impairment of the capacity or ability of Contractor to perform its duties under this Agreement.

(d) The filing with respect to Contractor of any petition for bankruptcy, voluntary or involuntary, the effecting of any assignment by Contractor for the benefit of creditors, or the commission by Contractor of any act of insolvency, however expressed or indicated.

A determination of the existence of any grounds for termination listed above made by EI in good faith shall be conclusive upon the parties.

10. *Termination or Withdrawal of Mortgages Without Cause*

EI may without cause terminate this Agreement or withdraw any mortgage from the application of this Agreement upon thirty (30) days' notice to Contractor. If the right to terminate or to withdraw any mortgage without cause is exercised by EI, it shall pay to Contractor one percent (1%) of the unpaid principal amount of the mortgages affected by the termination or withdrawal.

11. *Contractor's Duty Upon Termination or Withdrawal*

Upon termination of this Agreement or the withdrawal of any mortgage, Contractor shall forthwith deliver to EI or its designee all Documents in its possession relating to the mortgages affected by the termination or withdrawal, including all ledger or other cards, tax bills, accrual records, insurance policies, and other records needed to prove the debt and security or to enable EI to comply with all Legal Requirements. Contractor also shall furnish to EI a statement showing the monthly payments collected by Contractor and all funds held in trust by it with respect to the mortgages, and shall immediately pay over to EI or its designee all funds held by Contractor. Upon termination or withdrawal, all obligations of the parties relating to the mortgages affected thereby shall cease hereunder, except that the following obligations and liabilities of Contractor shall survive termination:

(i)   The duties established by this Section;

(ii) All liabilities of Contractor arising out of events which antedate the termination;

(iii) Contractor's obligations and liabilities under the warranties set forth in Section 3.

(a) EI may sell any mortgage covered by this Agreement without the consent of Contractor, and in connection with that sale may assign the obligations of Contractor under this Agreement. Upon giving notice of such Assignment, EI shall be released from all obligations hereunder as to such assigned mortgage.

(b) EI shall, before assigning any mortgage serviced by Contractor hereunder, allow Contractor a period of fifteen days in which to buy or find a buyer for any such mortgage upon the same terms and conditions as the sale proposed by EI, unless the proposed sale constitutes warehousing of the mortgage or EI exercises its option to withdraw such assigned mortgages pursuant to Section 10.

(c) Contractor may not assign its interest under this Agreement or delegate any of its duties hereunder except with the written consent of EI. Any attempt to assign or delegate without such consent shall be a breach of this Agreement.

12. *Assignment*

(a) EI may sell any mortgage covered by this Agreement without the consent of Contractor, and in connection with that sale may assign the obligations of Contractor under this Agreement. Upon giving notice of such Assignment, EI shall be released from all obligations hereunder as to such assigned mortgage.

(b) EI shall, before assigning any mortgage serviced by Contractor hereunder, allow Contractor a period of fifteen days in which to buy or find a buyer for any such mortgage upon the same terms and conditions as the sale proposed by EI, unless the proposed sale constitutes werehousing of the mortgage or EI exercises its option to withdraw such assigned mortgages pursuant to Section 10.

(c) Contractor may not assign its interest under this Agreement or delegate any of its duties hereunder except with the written consent of EI. Any attempt to assign or delegate without such consent shall be a breach of this Agreement.

13. *Prior Servicing Agreement*

All prior servicing agreements between the parties are hereby cancelled by mutual consent, and all obligations of the parties thereunder are hereby terminated, except liabilities of Contractor arising (i) out of events which antedate such cancellation and/or (ii) under any warranties set forth in such prior agreements. Any purchase commitment outstanding between the parties shall be treated as though such commitment had been made while this Agreement was in effect.

14. *Miscellaneous Provisions*

(a) Within 60 days after the end of each of its fiscal years, Contractor shall furnish to EI a balance sheet as of the end of such fiscal year and a profit and loss statement showing Contractor's income for such fiscal year, both certified by a certified public accountant. Contractor also shall furnish EI such other information relating to Contractor's financial status as EI may reasonably request from time to time.

(b) This Agreement shall be deemed a separate agreement with respect to each mortgage.

(c) The interpretation, construction and effect of this Agreement and any assignment or conveyance pursuant hereto and the existence of any right of termination shall be governed by the laws of New York.

(d) The term "mortgagor" shall include (i) any person who subsequently assumes the mortgage, and (ii) any owner of the property.

(e) Any notice permitted or required by the provisions of this Agreement shall be deemed given when deposited in the United States mails, postage prepaid, addressed to the address indicated below, or to such other address as either party may from time to time designate by written notice to the other.

EASTERN INVESTOR

ABC Mortgage Company
_____
                                                                 Contractor

233 Maple Street, Chicago, Ill.
_____
                                                                    Address

IN WITNESS THEREOF, the parties have executed this Agreement as of the day and year aforesaid.

EASTERN INVESTOR

Attest:

_____   By _____
                    Assistant Secretary   Vice President

(Seal)   ABC Mortgage Company
                                                     _____

Attest:

_____   By _____
                                 Secretary   President

Glossary

Acceleration Clause. A clause in a note, bond, or mortgage which provides that in the event of a default by the debtor the entire balance outstanding shall become due and payable.

Accrued Interest. Interest that has been earned, but not yet collected for the period that has elapsed since the last interest date.

Agent, Insurance. Any person or firm who or which solicits or negotiates insurance policies on behalf of any company.

Amortization. Loan repayment by equal periodic payments calculated to retire the principal at the end of a fixed period and to pay accrued interest on the outstanding balance.

Assessment. A valuation of property for tax purposes; also refers to a levy against property for a special purpose, as a sewer assessment.

Assignment of Leases. Additional security often taken in connection with mortgages of commercial properties.

Assignment of Mortgage. A document which evidences a transfer of ownership of a mortgage from one mortgagee to another.

Assignment of Rents. A written agreement executed by an owner of a property whereby possession of the property but not ownership is transferred to another, usually the mortgagee or other creditor, with the right to collect rents and otherwise manage the property, applying the net income toward payment of arrears.

Assumption Agreement. An agreement by one party to pay an obligation originally incurred by another.

Audit. The official examination and verification of bookkeeping accounts for the purpose of proving the accuracy of the figures and adequacy of controls. An audit may be done by a firm of public accountants hired for the purpose or by a company's own employees. In the latter case the audit would be called an *internal audit.*

427

Binder. A written evidence of temporary coverage which must be replaced by a permanent policy—and which runs only for a limited time, usually 30 or 60 days.

Broker, Insurance. Any person or firm who or which acts or aids in the solicitation or negotiation of insurance policies for or on behalf of the assured, with or without compensation.

Builder's Risk Insurance. Insurance coverage of a building during the course of construction. This type of insurance must be replaced by permanent insurance once the property becomes occupied.

Bureau Rate (Standard Rate). A standard rate established by a rating bureau for all companies writing insurance business in one specific area.

Call. To accelerate a loan; to declare the entire balance due.

Claim. (VA & FHA) The amount due the mortgagee as benefits under the VA guaranty or FHA insurance.

Collateral. Any property pledged as security for a debt, e.g., the real estate pledged as security for a mortgage.

Complaint. The initial petition or pleading filed with the court in a lawsuit or civil action outlining the plaintiff's cause of action against the defendant and the relief or remedies sought by the plaintiff.

Constant Payment. A periodic payment of a fixed amount which includes interest and principal. As the loan amount reduces, the portion applied to interest decreases and the portion applied to principal increases.

Construction Loan. Funds expended on the security of real estate for the purpose of constructing improvements on the property and usually advanced during the period of construction.

Continuous Policy. A policy without expiration date. It is in force continuously upon payment of required premium on anniversary date.

Conventional Mortgage. Any mortgage not insured or guaranteed by a governmental agency.

Correspondent. An abbreviated term meaning *mortgage loan correspondent.* A mortgage banker who services mortgage loans as agent for the owner of the mortgage or investor. Also applied to the mortgage banker in his role as originator of mortgage loans for the investor.

Custodial Accounts. Bank accounts used for deposit of funds belonging to others. (See *escrow account.*)

Custody. Responsibility for the property, as when the mortgagee turns "custody" of a foreclosed property over to VA. This is a specialized VA term that may, but does not necessarily, include the legal right to physical possession of the property.

Decree of Foreclosure and Sale. In a judicial foreclosure, the court decree or judgment that establishes the amount of the mortgage debt and orders the property sold to satisfy the debt.

Default. A failure to do or perform a required act, usually the failure to make a payment called for by the note and mortgage.

Deficiency. The difference between the amount of the mortgage indebtedness and any lesser amount recovered by the mortgagee from the foreclosure sale.

Deficiency Judgment. A personal judgment created by court decree for the amount of the deficiency against any person liable for the mortgage debt.

Delinquency Ratio. Ratio of number of delinquent loans to total loans—usually computed on a 30-, 60- and 90-day delinquent basis.

Deviated Rate. A rate which is established by means of reduction from bureau (or standard) rate. It may be 10 or 15 percent off bureau rate. (See *bureau rate.*)

Direct Writer. A term applicable to that insurance agent who is an employee rather than an agent of a company for which he solicits insurance. The term is also applicable to a company which employs agents to procure insurance contracts for the company only.

Discount. A reduction in loan proceeds expressed in percentage of par value. Discounts are applied to government-insured or -guaranteed loans bearing fixed interest rates to adjust the fixed or contract rate to conventional market yield. For example, a $10,000 loan closed at 96 percent of par or a 4 percent discount would indicate proceeds to the borrower of $9,600. Since the borrower would repay the full $10,000, the effective yield to an investor would be higher than the interest rate specified in the note.

Escrow Account. An account in which the borrowers' monthly deposits for taxes, hazard insurance, and FHA mortgage insurance are placed and held in trust by the lender.

Escrow Analysis. The periodic examination of escrow accounts to determine if monthly deposits will provide sufficient funds to pay tax and insurance bills when due.

Escrow Overage or Shortage. The difference, determined by escrow analysis, between escrow funds on deposit and escrow funds required.

Exercise of Power of Sale. A type of foreclosure proceeding used in some states in which the mortgagee has the power to conduct a foreclosure sale without court action.

Extended Coverage Endorsement. An endorsement which may be attached to fire insurance policies and which generally includes coverage against the perils of windstorm, hail, explosion, riot, civil commotion, damage by aircraft or vehicles, and smoke.

FDIC. Federal Deposit Insurance Corporation.

Federal Housing Administration (FHA). A federal agency, created by the National Housing Act of 1934, for the purpose of expanding and strengthening home ownership by making private mortgage financing possible on a long-term, low-down payment basis. The vehicle is a mortgage insurance program, with premiums paid by the homeowner, to protect lenders against loss on these higher-risk loans. Since 1965, FHA has been part of the newly created Department of Housing and Urban Development.

FHA Case Number. An identifying number assigned to each loan by FHA. This number appears on all correspondence from FHA and must be included when writing to FHA. For example: 01-123456-XX. The prefix identifies the state in which the property is located. The suffix or absence of a suffix indicates the section of the National Housing Act under which the loan was insured. If a suffix is used, it may be 1, 2, or 3 characters and they may be alphabetic or numeric.

FHA Debentures. Interest-bearing, negotiable securities issued by FHA to the mortgagee in repayment of the principal balance and allowable expenses incurred through foreclosure or deed in lieu of foreclosure.

FHA Insurance. An undertaking by FHA to insure the lender against loss arising from a default by the borrower. (See *mutual mortgage insurance.*)

Fiduciary. Person in a position of trust with respect to money or property who is charged with the strict duty of management and investment expressed by the prudent man rule or its derivatives.

Forbearance. The act of refraining from taking legal action despite the fact that a mortgage is in arrears—usually granted only when a mortgagor makes a satisfactory arrangement by which the arrears will be paid at a future date.

Foreclosure. The legal process by which a borrower in default under a mortgage is deprived of his interest in the mortgaged property. The usual method is a forced sale of the property at public auction with proceeds of the sale going to satisfy the debt.

Independent Agent. A term normally applicable to that insurance agent who represents many companies usually for several types of insurance.

Insurable Value. Value of property without cost of land and after deductions for depreciation and allowable exclusions.

Interim Loan. Short-term construction loan made to finance improvements on real property.

Investor. Any mortgage lender, e.g., mutual savings bank, life insurance company, pension or other trust fund, commercial bank, or savings and loan association, that invests its own funds in mortgages. Also, the holder of the mortgage, the permanent lender for whom the mortgage banker services the loan.

Judicial Foreclosure. A type of foreclosure proceeding used in some states that is handled as a civil lawsuit and conducted entirely under auspices of a court.

Late Charge. An additional charge which a borrower is required to pay as a penalty for failing to pay a regular installment when due.

Lease. A written document by which the possession of land and/or a building, or specific space in a building, is given by the owner (landlord) to another person (tenant) for a stated period and for a stated consideration (rent).

Lien. A claim against a particular piece of property which may be enforced by a legal action to have the property sold; an encumbrance. Taxes, special assessments, and judgments, as well as mortgages, are liens. In addition, there are mechanic's and materialmen's liens for furnishing labor or materials.

MIP. Abbreviation for Mortgage Insurance Premium required for all FHA-insured mortgages and for some conventional mortgages insured by a private agency.

Maturity. The date on which an agreement expires.

Mechanic's Lien. A lien given by law to insure payment for their labor to workmen who have been employed in the construction of a building. The lien becomes effective upon nonpayment of wages earned.

Mortgage. A formal document executed by an owner of property, pledging that property as security for a debt. The security instrument.

Mortgage Bankers Association of America (MBA). A national trade association of mortgage bankers and other organizations engaged in the business of mortgage financing.

Mortgage Clause (Mortgagee Clause) Standard. A clause which expresses the interest of someone in the property, other than owner, usually lender. Mortgage clause causes company providing hazard insurance coverage to include name of the lender in all loss drafts (unless instructed to the contrary, with provisions for notice in event of cancellation).

Mortgage Portfolio. The aggregate of mortgage loans or obligations held by a bank as assets.

Mortgagee. The lender in a mortgage transaction.

Mortgagor. The borrower or owner who pledges his property as security for a debt.

Mutual Mortgage Insurance. A descriptive term referring to the concept of mutuality incorporated in the FHA insurance program. If FHA's overall losses have been low, FHA borrowers may receive a partial refund of insurance premiums paid. Refunds, if any, come after an individual loan is paid in full.

Net Rate. The rate of interest remitted to an investor by the correspondent after it has deducted its servicing fee from the gross rate.

Note. A written paper acknowledging a debt and promising payment.

Owner's Title Insurance Policy. A policy issued by a title insurance company insuring the owner against loss due to any defect in his title to real property existing prior to the issuance of the policy.

Partial Payments. Parts of payments which are collected and usually held until the total collections amount to a full payment.

Performance Bond. A bond to guarantee performance of certain specified acts, such as the completion of a property or off-site improvements.

Power of Attorney. An instrument authorizing one to act as the attorney or the agent of the person granting it.

Prepayment Privilege. A provision in a note or bond that gives the borrower the right to make payments in excess of the required payments.

Proof of Loss. An affidavit signed by the insured and submitted to the hazard insurance company or companies as a claim for the loss sustained. Proofs of loss are usually prepared by the insurance broker and contain full particulars of the policies under which the claims are being made, as well as a detailed statement of the property destroyed or damaged.

Receiver. An appointee of a court to collect rents and manage properties which are in the process of being foreclosed.

Reinstatement. The curing of all defaults by a borrower; the restoration of a loan to current status through payment of arrearages.

Reinstatement Program. A program or schedule of partial payments leading to reinstatement of the loan to a current status.

Reinsurance Agreement. An agreement by which all or a certain part of an insured risk is reinsured by another company. Reinsurer pays company which it insured.

Release of Record. The act of recording a release deed or satisfaction of mortgage to release or eliminate the lien of the mortgage on the public records.

Replacement Cost Value. Value of property without cost of land, based on the cost of reconstructing it in case of total loss.

Return Premium. The refund of unearned advance premium resulting from cancellation of a hazard insurance policy prior to its expiration date or date to which the premium has been paid. (See *short rate.*)

Right of Redemption. A legally enforcible right provided by law in some states permitting the mortgagor or owner to reclaim foreclosed property by making full payment of the mortgage debt or the foreclosure sales price, as applicable. The right of redemption exists for a specified period of time known as the "redemption period."

Satisfaction of Mortgage. The recordable instrument given by the lender to evidence payment in full of the mortgage debt. Sometimes known as "release deed "

Security. Collateral; property pledged to secure repayment of a debt, as the real estate security.

Security Instrument. The mortgage or trust deed evidencing the pledge of the real estate security (as distinguished from the note or other credit instrument).

Self-Insurer. A company or organization that chooses not to buy insurance for certain risks but provides for losses either by absorbing them as they occur or by establishing a fund from which they can be paid. Self-insurance is usually undertaken as a cost-saving device where the risks are well diversified. FHA and VA are self-insurers with respect to fire and similar hazards on properties they own.

Short Rate. A method of calculating the premium refund on a hazard insurance policy cancelled between anniversary dates. To reimburse the insurance company for the additional administrative work involved in midterm cancellation, a short-rate refund is less than it would be on a prorated basis.

Soldiers & Sailors Civil Relief Act. A federal law restricting the enforcement of civilian debts against military personnel whose ability to pay has been severely hampered by entry into military service after the debt was incurred.

Solicitor, Insurance. Any person who acts in the solicitation of insurance policies for any licensed agent or broker.

Specified Amount. A dollar amount determined by the VA that must be credited against the veteran's indebtedness at completion of foreclosure. Used as the amount to be bid by the lender at the foreclosure sale and also used in calculation of the lender's claim under the VA guaranty.

Strict Foreclosure. A type of foreclosure proceeding used in some states in which title is invested directly in the mortgagee by court decree without holding a foreclosure sale.

Subrogation. The substitution of one person in the place of another with reference to a lawful claim or right.

Trust Deed. A security investment used in some states in place of a mortgage. In wording, a trust deed transfers title to the real estate to a third party as trustee to be held as collateral security for the debt with the condition that the trustees shall reconvey the property upon full payment of the debt, and with power of the trustee to sell the property and pay the debt in the event of a default by the debtor.

Upset Price. See *specified amount*.

VA Guaranty. An undertaking by the federal government to guarantee the lender, subject to limitation, against loss arising from a default by the borrower.

Veterans Administration (VA). An independent agency of the federal government created by the Servicemen's Readjustment Act of 1944 to administer a variety of benefit programs designed to facilitate the adjustment of returning veterans to civilian life. Among the benefit programs is the home loan guaranty program designed to encourage mortgage lenders to offer long-term, low-down payment financing to eligible veterans by guaranteeing the lender against loss.

Voluntary Conveyance. A voluntary transfer of title to the real estate security on a defaulted mortgage by deed from the borrower to the lender as an alternative to foreclosure. By agreement between the parties, the lender saves the expense of foreclosure and the borrower receives credit for payment of the debt in full.

Waiver of Lien. A written evidence, in many states from contractor (or supplier of material), surrendering his right of lien to enforce collection of debt against property.

Warranty Deed. A deed in which the grantor or seller warrants or guarantees that he is conveying good title, as opposed to a quit-claim deed which contains no representation or warranty as to the quality of title being conveyed.

Waste. Damage to property caused by willful neglect, abuse, misuse, etc.

Yield. Effective return on a mortgage based upon the face rate of interest and the price paid for the mortgage.

Index

Acceleration (of maturity):
  inevitability of, 323, 324
  recommendation for, 325–326
  threat of, 317
Accountant (*see* Accounting officer)
Accounting machines (equipment):
  conversion to, 117–119
  cost of, 118
  information on, 151
  use of, 118–119, 253–256
Accounting officer, duties of, 80–81
Accounting services, 132
Accounting systems, establishment of, 81
Accounts (*see* Escrow reserve accounts)
Accounts payable, 180–181
Accounts receivable, 181
Acquisitions, 122–130
  projections for, 128
  purchaser's viewpoint of, 123–125
  reasons for, 122–123
  seller's viewpoint of, 125–126
Activity report, 258
Administration (*see* Loan administration)
Administrative expense, 150, 153, 156, 158
  allocation of, 150
    to personnel, 156
  reallocation of, 158
Advertising expense, cost accounting of, 157

Affidavit of completion, re
  insurance, 386
Aggregate accounting, 282
Agreement to pledge, 94
Amortization of purchase price, 124
Amortization schedule, use of: in accounting
  department, 255
  in cashier department, 233
Annual statement, 204, 283–285
Assessments, special, 395
  deductibility of, 286
Assets, protection of, 106
Assignment and disclaimer form, 238, 242
Assignment of mortgage:
  to FHA, 332
  to VA, 332
Assignment of policy (*see* Insurance,
  assignment)
Assumptions (*see* Loan assumption)
Attorney, collection letter by, 317
Auditor, 184–188
  employment of, 107
  relationship with, 184
    independent, 184–187
    investors', 187–188
  review by, 82
Automation, 80
  resistance to, 121

Balance sheet, 102, 149
   pro forma, 127
Bank account, 96–98
   clearing, 98, 229–230
   construction, 97
   construction reserve, 97
   corporate, 96, 97
   custodial, 96, 98
   custodial disbursement, 98
   deposit, 97
   disbursement clearing, use of, 267
   establishment of, 81, 94, 96
   general, 96
   inactive, internal control of, 180
   investors', reconciliation of, 183
   loan disbursement, 97
   opening of, 99
   payroll, 97
   premium trust, 98, 376
   real estate, 97
   reconciliation, 181
   segregated, 96–98
   trust, 96
Bank credit (*see* Line of credit)
Bank line (*see* Line of credit)
Bank transfer of funds, arrangements for, 262,
      263
Billing:
   quarterly payments, 246–247
   semi-annual payments, 246–247
Block accounting (*see* Single debit)
Bond:
   bid, 369
   completion, 369
   fidelity, 111
      required amount of, 113–114
   license, 369
   maintenance, 369
   Mortgage Bankers Blanket, 112–113
   performance, 369
   subdivision, 369
Bonus (*see* Compensation, bonus)
Bookkeeping machines (*see* Accounting
      machines)
Bookkeeping operations, 256
   manual, 117–119
   mechanical, 117–119
Borrower:
   delinquent, classification
      of, 306–311
   ledger card, 82–84
   relationship: with lender, 289
      with servicer, 14
service to, 10

Borrower's ledger card (*see* Ledger, card)
Borrowers' records, 218–223
Borrowing:
   activity, 94–95
   authority for, 93–94
   cost of, 93
   of funds, 91–95
Branch office, operation of, 130
Breakeven point, 164–167
   in loan production, 164–166
   in servicing, 166–167

Calculated risk, 106
   theory of, 31
Card index (*see* Index cards)
Cashier:
   card, 58, 223–229
      prescheduled, 223
      use of, 223–228
   duties of, 211–212
   function of, 212
   qualifications of, 212
   records, 223–229
Certificate of insurance (*see* Insurance,
      certificate)
Certified public accountant (CPA), 33
   employment of, 107
   single audit by, 109
Change of ownership, 238–245, 390–391
   handling of, 216
      charge for, 25
   notification of, to insurance
      company, 216
Chart:
   of accounts, 102
      pamphlet on, 80
   organization, 41–45, 46
      components of, 41
      preparation of, 41
      types of, 41
Check for nonsufficient funds:
   handling of, 248–249
   replacement of, 23, 26
      charge for, 26
Check-signing authority, establishment of,
      81, 100, 101
Clearing account, 229–230
   checks drawn on, 262
   disbursement, use of, 267
   transfer from, 263–265
   use of, 229, 230, 262
      evaluation of, 230

Co-insurance, 369–370
  explanation of, 370
  requirements of, 370, 372
Collateral, pledging of, 180
Collection:
  of escrow shortages, 405–407
  follow up (*see* Delinquency)
  of late charges, 298–299
  letter by attorney, 317
  records (*see* Record, follow up)
  techniques (*see* Collection practices)
  telegram
    use of, 315
Collection practices:
  FHA multifamily loans, 340, 341–344
  income property loans, 337–341
  single-family loans, 297–337
    preventive, 294–297
    routine, 294, 297–302
    selective, 294
    specialized, 302–324
Commingling (*see* Escrow reserve
    accounts, commingling of)
Commission:
  compensation (*see* Compensation)
  insurance, 155
  loan (*see* Fee)
  unearned, 102
Commitment, 14, 15
Communication:
  coordination, through, 189–199
  function of, 11
  role of, 192
Company story, 195–196
Compensation, 68–71
  adequacy of, 68
  bonus, 68–69
  car, use of, 70
  commission, 68–69
  fringe benefits, 68, 70–71
  hospitalization, 70
  life insurance, 70
  lunchroom use of, 70
  methods of, 68
  pension plan, 70
  profit-sharing plan, 70
  salary, 68–69
  survey of, 68*n*
  types of, 68–70
  vacation, 70
Complaints, handling of, 202
Compliments, acceptance of, 206

Coordination, 189–199
  benefits of: to borrower, 191
    to company, 190–191
    to investor, 191–192
  through communication,
    189–190
  by consultation: on delinquent loans,
    196–197
    on preforeclosure cases, 196–197
    on reinspection of properties, 197
  function of, 11
  by meetings, 197–199
    general purpose, 198
    special purpose, 198–199
  through reports, 193
    intra-office memo, 194
    company story, 195–196
Constants, in single debit, use of, 269
Contract (*see* Servicing, contract)
Control (*see* Internal control)
Controller (*see* Accounting officer)
Conversion, 81, 116–122
  to data processing equipment, 120–122
  from manual operation, 117–119
  to use of service bureau, 119–120
Corporate accounts (*see* Bank account)
Corporate resolution, 99
Correspondent (*see* Servicer)
Cost accounting, 145–169
  classification, 149–151
    of data, 149
  illustration of, 148–162
  methods: analytical, 147–148
    systematic, 147
  records, preparation of,
    146
  reports: extent of, 146
    frequency of, 146
  survey by Mortgage Bankers
    Association of
    America, 145
Cost analysis (*see* Cost
    accounting)
Coupon:
  cards, 219–221, 222
    prepunched, use of, 221
    advantage of, 228
  paper, 219–220
    booklets, use of, 219–220
    advantage of, 228
Courtesy reminder,
  mailing of, 300

Credit information:
  personal, 238
    form of, 243
  release of, 286–287
Custodial accounts (*see* Escrow
    reserve accounts)
Customer relations, 200–208
  building of, 201–205
  preservation of, 205–208
Customer service operations, 283–287

Data processing equipment, 256
  conversion to, 49, 116, 120–122
  sharing of, 116, 122
  use of, 121, 152
    in mortgage loan accounting, 251
Debentures, FHA, 330, 343
  rates of, 329
Deed of conveyance, 241
Deed in lieu of foreclosure, use of, 333
  approval of FHA for, 333–334
  approval of VA for, 333–334
Default, 297
Default Notice, VA (*see* Notice of
    Default)
Delinquency:
  analysis of, 306–311
  report: preparation of,
      141–144
    in single debit, 278, 280, 282
  survey, 344, 348–350
    by FHA, 349, 350
    by investors, 348
    by MBA, 349–350
  (*See also* Collection)
Delinquent accounts:
  determination of, 299–300
Delinquent borrower, 303–304, 308–311
  classification of, 303
    chronic, 309–311
    temporary, 308–309
Delinquent loan:
  reinstatement of, 335
  letter re, 205
Delinquent payments, definition of, 297–299
Depositing, 229–231
Depreciation, use of, in insurance, 356
Destruction of records, 55–64
  schedule for, 58–59
Disbursement clearing account
    (*see* Clearing account)

Discount:
  allocation of, 154
  handling of, 87, 90
    unearned, 103
  internal control of, 177–178
Diversification, 115, 131–132
  assistance in, 5

Earnest money deposit, 84, 89
Earnings statement (*see* Statement,
    of earnings)
Education, of personnel, 74–75
Electronic data processing (EDP) (*see* Data
    processing equipment)
Employee:
  benefits, 70, 71
  education of, 74, 75
  introduction of, 73
  relations
    maintenance of, 206
  suggestion system, 77, 78
  training of, 207
Employment, 71–74
  application for, 72
  manual, 76, 77
  of personnel, 71–74
Equipment:
  data processing (*see* Data processing
      equipment)
  purchase of, 54
  protection of, by insurance, 106
  rental of, 156
Errors and Omissions, 81, 111–114,
      393, 395
  coverage: required, 111
    recommended, 111
      for agents, 112
      for brokers, 112
  definition of, 111
Escrow reserve accounts,
      265–267
  analysis of, 406–407
  commingling of, 99–100
  establishment of, 88, 89
  for FHA mortgage insurance,
      265, 266
  for hazard insurance, 265, 267, 376–378
  inactive accounts, internal control
      of, 184
  issuance of checks on, 265, 266
  reconciliation of, 282, 283

Escrow reserve accounts: for replacement
 (FHA project multifamily loans):
 collection of, 98
 investment of, 267
 for taxes, 266, 267, 396
 trial balance, 282, 283
 use of, 265
Exception accounting (*see* Single debit)
Expense(s):
 accounts, internal control of, 181
 allocation of: administrative,
  150, 158
 advertising, 157
 entertainment, 157
 general, 150, 158
 overhead, 150
 travel, 157
Extension of maturity
 (*see* Modification)

Factors (*See* Servicing, fees)
Fair Credit Reporting Act, 287
FDIC (*see* Federal Deposit Insurance
 Corporation)
Feasibility report (*see* Report, feasibility)
Federal Deposit Insurance Corporation:
 compliance with regulation of, 252
 coverage by, 100
  interpretation of, 100
 insurance protection by, 229
 overdrafts, ruling on, 283
Federal Housing Administration:
 accounts, commingling of, 99, 100
 ceilings established by, 87, 89
 charges established by, 86, 87, 89
 clearing accounts, approval of,
  219
 directive re financial statements,
  100
 insurance by, 7, 16
 regulations: compliance with, 293
  for collection, 291
  for late charge, 234
  for prepayment charges, 234
  for release fee, 25
  for release of seller, 245
  ₊or termination of loan, 234
  observance of, 16
 reimbursement by, for foreclosure
  expense, 294
 requirements of: accounting, 252
  insurance, 362

Federal Housing Administration: requirements of: notice of default, 234
 reporting on delinquents,
  141, 318–320
Federal National Mortgage Association:
 loans owned by: interest charges
  on, 234
 permission to sell servicing of, 125
 servicing contract with, 17
Federal Reserve Board, 93
Fee:
 for assumption, 25
 determination of, 24
 for handling NSF checks. 26
 legal, allocation of, 157–158
 mortgage, 25
 for mortgage changes, 25, 26
 origination, 23, 86
  cost accounting of, 154
  internal control of, 177, 178
 professional, allocation of, 157–158
 for release and assumption, 155
 service, 241
 servicing, 23, 24
  computation of, 24, 258, 260–261
 special, 23–25
 substitution: of insurance policies,
  26, 391
  of mortgagors, 25
 transfer, 23, 25, 155, 241
FHA (*see* Federal Housing Administration)
FHA debentures (*see* Debentures, FHA)
FHA mortgage insurance premium
 computation of, 235, 266
 deductibility of, on income tax
  return, 286
 payment of, 266
 refund of, 266
 reimbursement for, by FHA, 328
FHA project (multifamily) loans:
 default and claim procedure, 341–344
 FHA premium on, 235
  computation of, 235
 late charges on, 340
 loss payable provision, 390
 notice of default, 342
 replacement reserves (*see* Escrow reserve
  accounts)
 reporting requirements for, 341–343
 statistical reports on, 136
 termination notice, 235, 237
Fidelity bond:
 approved schedule, 113–114
 required amount, 113–114

File clerk, 51, 61
File room, 56, 61
Financial statement, 102-106
First payment date:
  requirements: by FHA, 297-298
  by VA, 297-298
  setting of, 295
First payment letter, 14, 31,
  84, 217
  illustrations of, 217, 244
  mailing of, 14
  on assumption, 244
  use of, 216-217, 295
FNMA (*see* Federal National Mortgage
  Association)
Follow-up record (*see* Record, follow-up)
Forbearance:
  application for, 313
  arrangements for, 314
  military, 332-333
  special (*see* Special forbearance)
Foreclosure, 324-337
  activity, control of, 345-347
  alternatives to, 328-334
    under FHA, 328-329
    under VA, 329-330
  check sheet, 345-346
  comparison of practices: under FHA,
    330
    under VA, 330
  conduct of, 336-337
  inevitability of, 323, 324
  nature of, 326-330
  recommendation for, 307, 324-326, 327
  responsibility of servicer during, 334-336
  task of, execution of, 334-336
  threat of, 317
  types of, 328
Forms (*see* Supplies)
Fringe benefits (*see* Compensation, fringe
  benefits)
Fund requirements, projection of, 95, 136

General expense (*see* Expense, general
  allocation of)
Goodwill, 126
Guaranty by VA (*see* Veterans
  Administration, guaranty by)
Guide, procedure, 41

Hazard insurance (*see* Insurance, home-
  owners)
Hillman, James T., article by, in *Mortgage
  Banker*, 168
Historical loan record (*see* Activity report)
Home improvement: article on, 132*n*.
  lending, 132
Home Mortgage Default Notice (Form 2068),
  318-320
Homeowners policy (*see* Insurance, home-
  owners)
Home Protector, 363
Home Security, 363
Homestead exemption, 400
House organ, 196

Identification card for loan numbers, 218
Income: account, deferred, 86
  allocation of, 152-155
Income stream, 124
  purchase of, 126
Index cards:
  changing of, 247
  maintenance of, 247
  preparation of, 56, 57
  use of, 59, 218
Inspection of loss, 387
Insufficient fund check (*see* Check for
  nonsufficient funds)
Insurable value, determination of, 356
Insurance:
  accident and health, 363-364
  assignment, 216, 238-241, 390-391
    consent to, 374
  automobile, 362, 364
  Best's Insurance Guide, 352
    ratings by, 373
  binder, 358
  card: expiration, 374-376
    master, 374-376
  certificate, 379-382
  commissions
    (*see* Commission)
  corporate, 110-114
    recommended, 109-114
      Errors and Omissions, 111
      fidelity, 111
  expiration, control of, 376
  FHA (*see* FHA mortgage insurance)

Insurance: fire (*see* Insurance, homeowners)
hazard (*see* Insurance, homeowners)
homeowners, 359–360, 362
premium charge for, 88
life, 362–363
loss draft: deposit of,
388
endorsement of, 387
handling of, 384–390
letters re, 385
processing of, 387
losses, 382–390
mortgage protection, 363
multiperil package, 368–369
order, 361
other types, 364
all-risk builder's risk, 369
builder's risk, 356, 371
comprehensive personal liability, 364
floater, 364
premium (hazard), payment **of**, 376
responsibility of, department, 351
solicitation of: by mail,
358
in person, 358
renewal, 365–368
by telephone, 361
Insurance policy:
endorsement of, by attachment, 379
initial, 356–364
for owners of income property,
368–370
for owners of residential property, 356–368
renewal, 365–368
safekeeping of, 378
Interest:
allocation of, 154–155
charging of: by banks,
179–180
to borrowers, 178–179
computation of, 154–155
expense, 154–155
handling of, 89
income, 154–155
internal control of, 178, 179
payment of, by investors, 90
penalty (*see* **Late** charge FHA, VA,
and conventional loans)
rate, net, 23
Interim financing, 92

Internal control, 107, 109, 170–188
activity, 176–184
corporate, 176–181
servicing, 181–184
of bookkeeping department, 183–184
of collections, 182–183
elements of, 171–173
means of, 173–176
through personnel, 173–174
through safeguards, 174–176
nature of: accounting,
172
administrative, 172
of pay-off statement, 238
responsibility for, 171–172
safeguards, 174–176
direct control, 174–176
through personnel, 173
Internal Revenue Service:
amortization: permitted by,
124
inquiries referred to, 285
Interview:
collection, 312, 316
exit, 74
practices, 72
by psychologist, 73
techniques of, 67, 71
Inventory (*see* Loan inventory)
Investor:
relationship with servicer, 14
improvement of, 21–23
service to, 10

Jensen, Raymond A., article by, in
Mortgage Banker, 132*n*.
Job description, 45, 47
how to prepare, 45
purpose and use of, 45
Journal sheets, 257–261

Late charge (FHA, VA, and conventional loans):
assessment of, 23
collection of, 298–299
internal control of, 180
conventional loans, 339–340
enforcement of, 301–302

Late charge (FHA, VA and conventional loans):
  FHA project loans, 340
  waiving of, 302
Late payer, follow up of, 296
Ledger:
  card: accounting, 85–91
    borrower's, 58,
      82–84
    design of, 257
    establishment of, 82
      borrower's, 82
      disbursement, 82
    inventory, 82, 84, 85, 89–90
    preparation of, 257–261
  record: establishment of,
    253
    maintenance of, 253–256
    posting to, 253–256
Legal fees (see Fee, legal)
Legal remedies on income property loans,
  340–341
Level payment plan, 261
Line of credit:
  availability of, 95, 96
  establishment of, 93
Loan:
  completion letter, 205
  construction, 87
    fees on, 87
  delinquency (see Delinquency)
  file: creation of, 56
    destruction, 58, 61
    numbering of, 57
  inventory, 82, 85, 86, 135
  ledger card (see Ledger, card)
  marketing, 164, 167–169
  origination (see Loan, production)
  production: income,
    154
    report on: income property,
      135–136
    single-family, 134–135
  purchase of, 15
  register, 56, 58, 60
    establishment of, 57, 58
    maintenance of, 57, 58
  seller of, 15
Loan administration
  Committee (see Mortgage Bankers Associa-
    tion of America, Loan Administration
    Committee of):
  development of, 7–10
  functions of, 4–6
  goals, 6–7
  history, 7–10

Loan administration:
  income of, 152
  manager of, 8
  records, establishment of, 82
Loan administrator, 21, 27–35, 40, 81
  availability of, for consultation, 30
  contribution of, 115
  coordinating efforts of, 189
  duties of, 28
  education of, 8, 33
  fiscal and fiduciary responsibilities of, 81, 84
  managerial talent of, 33
  personal traits of, 33
  in personnel management, responsibility
    for, 65
  responsibility of, 8, 27, 28, 30, 31
  role of, 27
  special problem of, 32
Loan assumption
  fee for, 25
  handling of, 296
  with release of seller, 25, 245–246
  statement for, 238–246
  straight, 25, 238–245
Loan closing:
  dissemination of information at, 203
  staff, responsibility of, at closing (re taxes),
    396
  statement, 89
  transaction, recording of, 84
Loan servicing (see Servicing)
Lock box arrangement:
  cost of, 231
  use of, 230–231
Loss inspection (see Inspection)
Loss draft (see Insurance loss draft)

Management:
  contract, 18
  office, 39–64
    tools of, 41–48
  personnel, 65–78
    philosophy of, 66
      re compensation, 68
    policies of, 67
    responsibility of, 66
    review of, 74
    scope of, 66
  senior, responsibility of, 4, 34, 35
Manager:
  responsibilities of: insurance depart-
    ment, 352
    office, 49–54

Manager:
  responsibilities of: personnel, 71, 72
    servicing, 7, 21, 28
Manual (*see* Servicing, manual; Employment,
  manual; or Procedure manual)
Manual operation (*see* Bookkeeping opera-
  tions, manual)
Manual of operations (*see* Operations guide)
MBA (*see* Mortgage Bankers Association
  of America)
Mechanical operations (*see* Bookkeeping
  operations, mechanical)
Merger, 81
Messengers, 51
Microfilming, 62
Military forbearance (*see* Soldiers and
  Sailors Relief Act of 1942, military
    forbearance under)
Modification:
  charge for, 25, 26
  use of, 331–332
Modified single debit (*see* Aggregate
  accounting)
Monthly billing, 218, 221–223
  advantage of, 228–229
  copy of, 226
  disadvantage of, 228–229
Monthly Payment
  handling of (*see* Cashier)
  information re, 84
  rounding of, 216
Monthly statement, 102
Mortgage, merchantable, 82
Mortgage Bankers Association of
    America (MBA):
  chart of accounts, recommended by, 102
  delinquency survey by, 349, 350
  Insurance Committee of, on fidelity
    bond, 113
  Loan Administration Committee, recom-
    mendation regarding foreclosure, 326
  Model sale and servicing agreement, 16
  Mortgage Servicing Committee of, 7, 8,
    programs of, 8
  position of, regarding single-interest
    insurance, 394
  practices endorsed by, 81
  record retention schedule recommended
    by, 61
  Research Committee of, 7, 68
    cost survey of, 145
    report of, 120
    survey of management compensation, 68*n*.
  School of Mortgage Banking, 76
  single audit program of, 108, 109

Mortgage Bankers Blanket Bond, 112–113
Mortgage(e) clause:
  form of, 372, 390
  for multifamily loan, 390
  request for, 357
Mortgage insurance (*see* FHA Mortgage
  Insurance)
Mortgage loan administration (*see* Loan
  administration)
Mortgage record change, 245
Multifamily loans (*see* FHA project (multi-
  family) loans)
Multiperil package policy (*see* Insurance,
  multiperil package)

National Association of Mutual Savings Banks,
  108, 113
  insurance committee, recommendation by,
    113–114
National Record Maintenance Council, 55
Newsletter:
  dissemination of, 204
  property tax information, 204
Notice:
  billing, 32
  final, 301
  past due, 300–301
    internal control of, 182–183
    mailing of, 300
    worth of, 304
  payment change, 407
  written requirements for, 233
Notice of Default, filing of, 319, 321, 323,
  326, 336
Notice of Intention to Foreclose, filing of,
  319, 322, 323, 326, 336
NSF checks (*see* Check for nonsufficient
  funds)

Occupancy, 156
Office guide (*see* Operations guide)
Office layout, 52–54
Operating report (*see* Report, operating)
Operations guide, 41, 48, 75
  use of, 75
  value of, 48
Organization chart (*see* Chart,
  organization)
Origination fee (*see* Fee origination)
Overdrafts, handling of, 283

Overhead expense (*see* Expense, allocation of overhead)
Ownership change (*see* Change of ownership)

Paid-up loan, 61
Pamphlets (company):
 on insurance, 203–204
 on mortgage loan, 203
Participation (*see* Servicing; Fees)
Past due (*see* Delinquent)
Past due notice (*see* Notice, past due)
Payment:
 card: prepunched, 227
  use of, 226, 228
 envelope: use of, 218–219
 receiving of, 214–229
Payment change notice, 406–407
Payoff statement:
 notification of investor, 233
 preparation of, 232–246
 responsibility for, 212
  internal control over, 238
Payroll (*see* Compensation)
Penalty charge (*see* Late charge)
Pension plan (*see* Compensation, pension plan)
Personnel:
 in cost accounting, 155
 development of, 29
 dismissal of, 74
 employment of, 71
 expense, 155
 handling of, 33, 34
 promotion of, 29
 quality control of, 107
 records, 73
 review of, 74
 training of, 29
Personnel manager, 71, 72
Petty cash, internal control of, 183
Premium (insurance):
 allocation of, in cost accounting, 154
 disbursement of, 376–378
 payment of, 267
 trust account, 88, 98
Prepayment:
 charge (penalty): collection of, 234–235
  deductibility of, 286

Prepayment, principal:
 handling of, 247–248
 internal control of, 183
Principal prepayment (*see* Prepayment, principal)
Procedure manual, 41, 48
Professional fees (*see* Fee, professional)
Profit-sharing plan (*see* Compensation, profit-sharing plan)
Project loans (*see* FHA project (multifamily) loans)
Property management, 132
Proration statement (*see* Loan assumption, statement for)

Quality control, of staff, 107

Receipt:
 issuance of: for cash payments, 216
  for payment, 223
  for payment of taxes, 408
Receptionist, 51
Record:
 accounting: corporate, 82–91
  mortgage loan accounting, 253–256
 borrower's, 218–223
 cashier, 223–227
 cost accounting (*see* Cost accounting)
 destruction of, 55–64
  schedule, 58–59
 establishment of, 13, 55–64
 follow-up, use of, 317–318
 insurance, 374–375
 personnel, 73
 retention of, 55–64
  schedule, 63
 tax, 398–399
Reinspection of properties, coordination of, 197
Reinstatement of delinquent loan, 335
Release:
 charge for, 25
 of seller: by FHA, 245–246
  by VA, 245–246
Remuneration (*see* Compensation)
Replacement cost value, determination of, 355–356

Replacement reserve (*see* Escrow reserve accounts for replacement)
Report:
  delinquency (*see* Delinquency)
  feasibility, 120-121
  inspection (also reinspection), 197
  loan inventory, 135
  loan production, 134-136
  on mortgage status, 349
  operating, 133-137
  remittance, 257-262
    frequency of, 258
    use of, 258, 262
  statistical, 133, 137-144
  warehousing, 135
Repurchase, requirement, 18
Requisition form:
  for checks, 265
  for supplies, 54
Research Committee (*see* Mortgage Bankers Association of America)
Reserves (*see* Escrow reserve accounts)
Retrending (insurance) of policies, 365
Rose, Irving, article by, in *Mortgage Banker*, 127

Salary (*see* Compensation, salary)
Sale of property, statement on, 238-244
  fee for, 25
School of Mortgage Banking (*see* Mortgage Bankers Association of America)
Service bureau, 116, 119-120
Service charge (*see* Fee, service)
Servicer:
  relationship with borrower, 14
  relationship with investor, 14
    improvement of, 21-23
Servicing:
  agreement (*see* Servicing, contract)
  contract, 15-18
    description of, 15-18
    evaluation of, 18
    study of, 14
    termination of, 17
    types of, 15-16
    value of, 125-126
  duties, unwritten, 21-25
  fees: computation of, 258-261
    retention of, 260
      under level payment plan, 261
  functions of, 13
  fundamentals of, 13

Servicing:
  income, 23
  manager, 7, 21, 28
    qualifications of, 8
    (*See also* Loan administrator)
  manual, 18-20
  portfolio: acquisition of, 124
    pricing of, 126-129
  responsibilities, 21-23
  staff requirements, 50-51
  tasks, 13
Single audit, 108, 109
Single debit, 268-282
  delinquency reports, as part of, 278
  fundamentals of, 269-270
  mechanics of, 270-282
  use of constants, 269
  for use of statistical reports, 137
Single-interest policy, 393-394
  position of MBA regarding, 394
Soldiers and Sailors Relief Act of 1942, 304
  military forbearance under, 332-333
Special delivery letter, use of, in collection, 316
Special assessments (*see* Assessments, special)
Special forbearance, 326, 330, 331
Specified amount, 334, 336
Staff requirements (*see* Servicing staff requirements)
Statement:
  of account (*see* Payoff statement)
  of assumption (*see* Loan assumption)
  of earnings, 105
  for substitution of mortgagors (*see* Loan assumption)
Statistical reports (*see* Report, statistical)
Storage room, 61
Straight assumption (*see* Loan assumption, straight)
Substitution:
  fee (*see* Fee)
  of mortgagors (*see* Loan assumption)
  of policies, 391-393
    fee for, 26, 391
Succession, training for, 29
Suggestion system (*see* Employee, suggestion system)
Supervisor(s), authority of, 74
Supplies:
  cost accounting of, 157
  purchase of, 54
  work order for, 54
Switchboard operator, 51

Table of organization (*see* Chart, organization)
Tax:
  bill: obtaining of,
      399–404
    payment of, 399–405
    verification of, 404–405
  card, 398–399
  certification, 408
  deductibility of, information on, 284–285
  exemption, letter regarding, 205
  notice, 403
  protest, handling of, 408
  records: delinquency control,
      398–399
    establishment of, 396–398
  reserves: establishment of,
      405–407
    responsibility for, 12
  service, 401
Telegram, use of in collections, 315
Telephone, use of:
  in collections, 305–306
  training for, 207
Teller (*see* Cashier)
Termination:
  clause, 16, 17
  of loan: through foreclosure
      (*see* Foreclosure)
    by payment in full, 233–238
  statement (*see* Payoff statement)
Test:
  aptitude, 73
  intelligence, 73
Training of personnel, 74, 75
Transfer:
  fee (*see* Fee)
  of property (*see* Loan assumption)
Treasurer, responsibilities of, 80, 81

Unearned discount (*see* Discount,
    handling of, unearned)
Upset price (*see* Specified amount)

VA (*see* Veterans Administration)
Veterans Administration:
  accounts, commingling of, 99, 100
  ceilings established by, 87, 89
  charges established by, 86, 87, 89
  clearing account, approval of, by, 219
  guaranty by, 86
    processing for, 89
  regulations, compliance
      with, 293
    for collections, 292
    for foreclosures, 292
    for late charges, 234
    for loss drafts, 381
    for notice on payoffs, 237
    for notice requirements, 234
    for release by seller, 245
    for reporting of delinquencies, 319,
      321–323
Voluntary conveyance (*see* Deed in lieu of
    foreclosure)

Waiver of lien, 387
Warehousing, 91
  report on, 135
Welcome letter, 205